THE
FELLOWSHIP

THE
FELLOWSHIP

The Literary Lives of the Inklings:

J.R.R. TOLKIEN, C. S. LEWIS,

OWEN BARFIELD, CHARLES WILLIAMS

PHILIP ZALESKI AND CAROL ZALESKI

FARRAR, STRAUS AND GIROUX   NEW YORK

Farrar, Straus and Giroux
18 West 18th Street, New York 10011

Owing to limitations of space, all acknowledgments for permission to reprint
previously published material can be found on pages 641–644.

Library of Congress Cataloging-in-Publication Data
Zaleski, Philip.
    The fellowship : the literary lives of the Inklings: J.R.R. Tolkien, C. S. Lewis,
Owen Barfield, Charles Williams / Philip Zaleski, Carol Zaleski.
        pages   cm
    Includes bibliographical references and index.
    ISBN 978-0-374-15409-7 (hardback) — ISBN 978-0-374-71379-9 (e-book)
    1. Inklings (Group of writers)   2. Tolkien, J. R. R. (John Ronald Reuel),
1892–1973.   3. Lewis, C. S. (Clive Staples), 1898–1963.   4. Barfield, Owen,
1898–1997.   5. Williams, Charles, 1886–1945.   6. Literature and society—
England—History—20th century.   7. Oxford (England)—Intellectual life—20th
century—Biography.   I. Zaleski, Carol.   II. Title.
PR478.I54 Z35 2015
820.9'00912—dc23
[B]
                                                                                    2014040390

Designed by Jonathan D. Lippincott

Farrar, Straus and Giroux books may be purchased for educational, business, or
promotional use. For information on bulk purchases, please contact the Macmillan
Corporate and Premium Sales Department at 1-800-221-7945, extension 5442,
or write to specialmarkets@macmillan.com.

www.fsgbooks.com
www.twitter.com/fsgbooks • www.facebook.com/fsgbooks

5   7   9   10   8   6   4

To Léonie Caldecott and the memory of Stratford Caldecott (1953–2014)

nemo nisi per amicitiam cognoscitur

CONTENTS

THE
FELLOWSHIP

PROLOGUE:
DABBLERS IN INK

D uring the hectic middle decades of the twentieth century, from the end of the Great Depression through World War II and into the 1950s, a small circle of intellectuals gathered on a weekly basis in and around Oxford University to drink, smoke, quip, cavil, read aloud their works in progress, and endure or enjoy with as much grace as they could muster the sometimes blistering critiques that followed. This erudite club included writers and painters, philologists and physicians, historians and theologians, soldiers and actors. They called themselves, with typical self-effacing humor, the Inklings.

The novelist John Wain, a member of the group who achieved notoriety in midcentury as one of England's "angry young men," remembers the Inklings as "a circle of instigators, almost of incendiaries, meeting to urge one another on in the task of redirecting the whole current of contemporary art and life." Yet the name Inklings, as J.R.R. Tolkien recalled it, was little more than "a pleasantly ingenious pun . . . suggesting people with vague or half-formed intimations and ideas plus those who dabble in ink." The donnish dreaminess thus hinted at tells us something important about this curious band: its members saw themselves as no more than a loose association of rumpled intellectuals, and this modest self-image is a large part of their charm. But history would record, however modest their pretensions, that their ideas did not remain half-formed nor their inkblots mere dabblings. Their polyvalent talents—amounting to genius in some cases—won out. By the time the last Inkling passed away on the eve of the twenty-first century, the group had altered, in large or small measure, the course of imaginative literature (fantasy, allegory, mythopoeic tales), Christian theology and philosophy, comparative mythology, and the scholarly study of the *Beowulf* author, of Dante, Spenser, Milton, courtly love, fairy tale, and epic; and drawing as much from their scholarship as from their experience of a catastrophic century, they had fashioned a new narrative of hope amid the ruins of war, industrialization, cultural disintegration, skepticism, and anomie. They listened to the last enchantments of the Middle Ages, heard the horns of Elfland, and made designs on the culture that our own age is only beginning fully to appreciate. They were philologists and philomyths: lovers of *logos* (the ordering power of words) and *mythos* (the regenerative power of story), with a nostalgia for things medieval and archaic and a distrust of technological innovation that never decayed into the merely antiquarian. Out of the texts they studied and the tales they read, they forged new ways to convey old themes—sin and salvation, despair and hope, friendship and loss, fate and free will—in a time of war, environmental degradation, and social change.

Some among the Inklings and their circle attained a worldwide fame that continues to grow, notably the literary historian, novelist, poet, critic, satirist, and popular Christian philosopher C. S. Lewis (1898–1963), the mythographer and Old English scholar J.R.R. Tolkien (1892–1973), the historian of language, Anthroposophist, and solicitor (Arthur) Owen Barfield (1898–1997), and the publisher and author of "supernatural shockers," Charles Walter Stansby Williams (1886–1945). Others, like the Chaucer scholar and theatrical producer Nevill Henry Kendal Aylmer Coghill (1899–1980), the biographer and man of letters Lord David Cecil (1902–86), the poet and Magdalen divine Adam Fox (1883–1977), the classicist Colin Hardie (1906–98), the medievalist J.A.W. Bennett (1911–81), Lewis's older brother Warren ("Warnie," 1895–1973), and the sharp-tongued don Henry Victor Dyson Dyson ("Hugo," 1896–1975), achieved lesser but still considerable eminence. Tolkien's youngest son, Christopher (1924–), who would become the chief editor and interpreter of his father's mythological project, began attending Inklings meetings after he returned from RAF duty in World War II. Additional members, guests, and relatives drifted in and out of the fellowship, while friends who were not strictly Inklings, such as the mystery novelist, playwright, and

Dante translator Dorothy L. Sayers (1893–1957), nonetheless found ways to draw from and enrich the stream.

The Inklings met typically in Lewis's rooms at Magdalen College on Thursday evenings, when most of the reading and criticism unfolded; they also could be seen regularly on Tuesday mornings, gathered for food and conversation in a side nook of a smoky pub at 49 St. Giles', known to passersby as the Eagle and Child but to habitués as the Bird and Baby. A wit might say that the Inklings' aim was to turn the bird into a dragon and the baby into a king, for their sympathies were mythological, medieval, and monarchical, and their great hope was to restore Western culture to its religious roots, to unleash the powers of the imagination, to reenchant the world through Christian faith and pagan beauty. How they realized or miscarried these great (or grandiose) hopes constitutes a large part of our tale.

Oxford

The story of the Inklings unfolds mostly in Oxford, a city in the English Midlands, originally a medieval market town set down higgledy-piggledy in the wetlands where Saxons once forded the Rivers Cherwell and Thames with horses, thanes, and oxen (hence Oxenford) to dig themselves in against the invading Danes; where the Normans built bridges and circled the settlement in stone; where mendicant friars and secular masters built their schools of theology and liberal arts under the watchful eyes of God, pope, and king; where town-gown rivalry erupted into periodic brawls. Thanks to its natural watercourses, its stagecoach inns, its eighteenth-century canals and nineteenth-century rails, this city of monks and dons has also been a congenial setting for factories, from Frank Cooper's Oxford Marmalade to Morris Motors, humming and spewing alongside the printing presses for the city's intellectual industries: the *Oxford English Dictionary* (*OED*) and Oxford University Press (OUP).

Oxford in the Inklings' day was not so different in look and smell from the Oxford of today. Then, as now, one felt the irony that from this tangle of traffic-clogged streets, the cloisters of learning lift up to heaven their dreaming (if not always worshipping) spires; that the black-gowned, bicycle-pedaling undergraduates maintain their scholarly idyll at the price of damaging their lungs and risking their lives. Then, as now, one was tempted to fantasize one's surroundings as a Camelot of intellectual knight-errantry or an Eden of serene contemplation. Then, as now, there was bound to be disappointment.

Matthew Arnold idealized Oxford as "whispering from her towers the last enchantments of the Middle Ages," as summoning her votaries "to the true goal of all of us, to the ideal, to perfection,—to beauty, in a word, which is only truth seen from another side . . ." Yet for all its whispering, Oxford could not possibly deliver the full draught of the Middle Ages— of holiness, wisdom, and beauty—for which its inhabitants longed. When Max Beerbohm came to Oxford as a freshman in the fall of 1890, his boyish hopes were dashed:

> Did I ride, one sunset, through fens on a palfrey, watching the gold reflections on Magdalen Tower? Did I ride over Magdalen Bridge and hear the consonance of evening-bells and cries from the river below? Did I rein in to wonder at the raised gates of Queen's, the twisted pillars of St. Mary's, the little shops, lighted with tapers? Did bull-pups snarl at me, or dons, with bent backs, acknowledge my salute? Any one who knows the place as it is, must see that such questions are purely rhetorical. To him I need not explain the dis-appointment that beset me when, after being whirled in a cab from the station to a big hotel, I wandered out into the streets. *On aurait dit* a bit of Manchester through which Apollo had once passed; for here, among the hideous trams and the brand-new bricks—here, glared at by the electric-lights that hung from poles, screamed at by boys with the *Echo* and the *Star*—here, in a riot of vulgarity, were remnants of beauty, as I discerned. There were only remnants.

The Inklings knew intimately what Beerbohm meant. To live and work in such a rarefied intellectual ambience, with chapel, scriptorium, and Faërie woodland close at hand, among gifted companions who could share a pint and spin off a limerick or clerihew at will, was a rapture that never quite realized itself. For one had also to contend with troublesome families, threadbare pockets, cantankerous colleagues, dim students, urban con-gestion, and—twice in the Inklings' lifespan—war. The unavoidable harshness of life surprised none of them, for they were Christians one and all, believing that they inhabited a fallen world, albeit one filled with God's grace. Yet it would be a mistake to label them, as did one early biographer, "the Oxford Christians," and to presume that this sufficed. This would be tantamount, as Warnie Lewis complained the moment the term arose, to saying that the Inklings were no more than "an organized group for the propagation of Christianity." Nonetheless, the Inklings were unmistakably Christians in Oxford, and this plays no small part in their cultural significance.

Christianity on the Banks of the Isis

Oxford is, as Jan Morris puts it, "as organically Christian as Bangkok is Buddhist." Before a university appeared in Oxford, the town was a jumble of hermitages, holy wells, monasteries, and churches. The colleges of medieval Catholic Oxford began as quasi monasteries designed to provide the Church with learned clergy and to offer Masses for deceased patrons to speed their souls through purgatory. The colleges of post-Reformation Anglican Oxford renounced purgatory and all other "popish" devices, insisting that its members subscribe to the Thirty-nine Articles of Religion, thus excluding every Jew and Catholic in England as well as dissenters and atheists. The gowns of an Oxford don were patterned after religious habits, and until the 1880s the man beneath the gown was required, with few exceptions, to be celibate. Bachelorhood remained the ideal and family life a concession to prosaic mediocrity well into the early twentieth century.

As the doctrinal center of English Christianity, Oxford historically has cherished orthodoxy; as the intellectual center of English Christianity, Oxford has often put orthodoxy to the test. Here followers of Duns Scotus and William Ockham debated the semantics of divine being and the modalities of Christ's presence in the Eucharist, Wyclif produced the first English Bible, and Bishops Ridley, Latimer, and Cranmer, denying transubstantiation, were martyred in 1555 for the Protestant cause. When Protestantism won out, it was here that Edmund Campion, brilliant orator and favorite of Queen Elizabeth I, shocked his admirers by changing course for the Catholic Church, thus taking the first steps that would lead him to martyrdom at London's Tyburn Gallows.

Whether high or low church, Evangelical, Broad Church, or Catholic, Oxford was in love with the idea of Christian perfection. It was here in 1729 that Charles and John Wesley founded their "Holy Club" and from here that George Whitefield went forth to evangelize America. It was from Oxford in the 1830s that the Tractarian movement set out to re-Catholicize the national church, and it was in Oxford that the saintly John Henry Newman made his submission to Rome. Here John Ruskin, who had a love-hate relationship with the city and with his own Evangelical roots, sought to awaken the nation's sleeping conscience to his vision of Christian socialism, medieval artisanship, and educational reform; and it was here, in the cathedral-like University Museum that Ruskin helped to design, that the ornithologist and bishop of Oxford, Samuel Wilberforce, took on T. H. Huxley in the celebrated 1860 debate on the validity of Darwinian evolution. The Victorian crisis of faith took place here, but so did what the historian Timothy Larsen has called "the Victorian crisis of doubt." From Ruskin's time until the days of the Inklings, a pattern of religious rebellion and rediscovery would repeat itself; one could be a militant skeptic like Huxley relishing the escape from Victorian restraints, or a militant believer like Ronald Knox relishing the escape from modern liberalism, or an initiate in any of the manifold schools of occultism, theosophy, and spiritualism that flourished in Oxford as well. All the spiritual alternatives were on offer, all could be sampled, but there was little room for indifference—certainly not for a generation that lived through the Great War.

Oxford at War and After

We must picture Oxford, during World War I, not as the neomedieval paradise it would like to be, but as the military compound it was obliged to become. The colleges of Oxford turned nearly overnight into hospitals and officer training camps, strangely quiet and emptied of students, "like monasteries where all the monks have died," as Victor Gollancz remembered it. The Oxford University Roll of Service records that of 14,561 students who served in the war, 2,708—nearly 20 percent— perished. In a society known for its masculine "clubbability," yet haunted by the memory of so many friendships severed, so many men cut down in their prime, it scarcely surprises that the surviving remnant would seek out every opportunity for male companionship. The Inklings were, to a man—and they were all men—comrades who had been touched by war, who viewed life through the lens of war, yet who looked for hope and found it, in fellowship, where so many other modern writers and intellectuals saw only broken narratives, disfigurement, and despair.

If Virginia Woolf was right that "on or about December 1910 human character changed" in the direction of modernism and daring social experiments, the Great War intensified that change; according to standard histories of this period, the rising generation of British writers reacted to the catastrophe by severing ties to tradition and embracing an aesthetic of dissonance, fragmentation, and estrangement. Yet the Great War also instilled in many a longing to reclaim the goodness, beauty, and cultural continuity that had been so violently disrupted. The Inklings came together because they shared that longing; and it was the Inklings, rather than the heirs of the Bloomsbury Group—the other great, if ill-defined, English literary circle of the twentieth century—who gave that longing its most enduring artistic form and substance. Far from breaking with tradition, they understood the Great War and its aftermath in the light of tradition, believing, as did their literary and spiritual ancestors, that ours is a fallen world yet not a forsaken one. It was a belief that set them at odds with many of their contemporaries, but kept them in the broad currents of the English literary heritage. They shared much with Bloomsbury, including love of beauty, companionship, and conversation, but they differed from their older London counterpart in their religious ardor, their social conservatism, and their embrace of fantasy, myth, and (mostly) conventional literary techniques instead of those dazzling experiments with time, character, narrative, and language that mark the modernist aesthetic.

No doubt Bloomsbury has exerted more influence over what Anthony Burgess once called "higher literary aspirations," those giddy and often glorious assaults upon convention that have found a secure place in the twentieth century's literary canon. And yet the Inklings have made serious inroads into that canon. The literary status of both Tolkien and Lewis and, to a lesser extent, Williams, Barfield, and other Inklings, is undergoing rapid ascent as academic courses and mature literary criticism focused upon their work blossom around the world, and—unlike Bloomsbury, which now seems part of history, a brilliant stream of art and thought that one admires over one's shoulder—the Inklings continue to shape significant aspects of modern religion and worldwide culture.

Tolkien and Lewis wield most of this posthumous influence. That *The Lord of the Rings* was voted "Book of the Century" in a massive 1997 poll conducted by Waterstones, a British bookseller, may be dismissed as a transient phenomenon; but if we consider its sales figures (estimates of worldwide sales run from one hundred and fifty to two hundred million), it's clear that Tolkien has a secure place in the pantheon of popular culture. Far more important, though, *The Lord of the Rings* and the vast mythology that surrounds and pervades it possess an intrinsic grandeur, breadth, and profound originality—it is simply the case that nothing like this has ever been done before—that make them, we believe, landmarks in the history of English literature. To be sure, the fan fiction, derivative fantasy novels, and sword-and-sorcery illustrations inspired by Tolkien can be artless at best; but no unprejudiced critic can deny the bracing effect of Tolkien's rich mythopoeic imagination upon generations of readers and writers disillusioned with modernist themes and techniques, and longing for reenchantment.

Lewis has made a comparable mark. Arguably the bestselling Christian writer since John Bunyan, he is also credited with the conversion or reversion to the faith of a considerable number of twenty-first-century intellectuals and the consolation and instruction of millions more. Yet none of this would have been possible had Lewis not shared with Tolkien the sense of mission and the narrative skill to reclaim traditional storytelling values, not only through fantasy fiction but also through scholarly recovery of the literary past. These achievements have earned Lewis—to the catcalls of some, overwhelmed by the applause of many—a permanent memorial stone in Westminster Abbey's Poets' Corner, close by the remains of Chaucer, Spenser, Addison, and Dryden.

An Oxford Fantasia

Everyone knows this about the Inklings: that they expressed their longing for tradition and reenchantment through the literature of fantasy. The Inklings' penchant for the fantastic is quintessentially English; folktale, fairy-tale, and fantasy motifs permeate English literature from

Beowulf through *The Faerie Queene* and *The Tempest*, to the poetry of Byron, Shelley, and Coleridge. In the middle of the nineteenth century, this national love for the fantastic gave rise to the modern fantasy novel. Immediately Oxford moved into the foreground, as John Ruskin, in his neo-Grimm fable *The King of the Golden River* (1841, written at Leamington Spa while he was an Oxford undergraduate), and Lewis Carroll, in *Alice's Adventures in Wonderland* (1864, the quintessential Oxford classic), laid the groundwork for a genre brought to early perfection by the Scotsman George MacDonald, their mutual friend, in his three children's classics (*At the Back of the North Wind* [1871], *The Princess and the Goblin* [1872], and *The Princess and Curdie* [1883]) and his two fantasies (*Phantastes* [1858] and *Lilith* [1895]). MacDonald suffused almost all his works—which also include sermons, poems, literary criticism, translations, and more than two dozen verbose and sentimental novels—with a gentle Christian sensibility that would lead Lewis to call him "my master." A few years later, William Morris, Edward Burne-Jones (both Oxford alumni), and other members of the Pre-Raphaelite Brotherhood produced novels, poetry, and paintings with fantastic themes, bathed with a lovely, romantic, neomedieval light that would deeply influence the artistic maturation of both Lewis and Tolkien.

Fantasy, then, was in Oxford's blood, and it is no wonder that the major Inklings experimented in so many fantastic subgenres (myth, science fiction, fable, epic fantasy, children's fantasy, supernatural thriller, and more). They chose to be fantasists for a variety of reasons—or, rather, fantasy seemed to choose them, each one falling in love with the genre in youth (Lewis in Ireland, Tolkien in Birmingham, Williams and Barfield in London) many years before coming to Oxford. Their passion arose, in part, from the sheer excitement of the genre, the intoxication of entering the unknown and fleeing the everyday. For all of the leading Inklings, however, the rapture of the unknown pointed also to something more profound; it was a numinous event, an intimation of a different, higher, purer world or state of being. Fantasy literature was, for the Inklings, a pathway to this higher world and a way of describing, through myth and symbol, its felt presence. Fantasy became the voice of faith. And it made for a cracking good story.

Interest in the Inklings often first dawns in the minds of readers who have fallen in love with Tolkien and Lewis, and wish to enter more deeply into their spiritual and imaginative cosmos. But there are others who, though immune to the evangelizing power of Faërie, are curious to know more about a movement that arose not long ago in the colleges and pubs of Oxford and continues to cast a spell upon our culture. We have written with both kinds of readers in mind.

Our book focuses primarily upon four Inklings: Lewis, Tolkien, Barfield, and Williams. Why these four and not that graceful flower Lord David Cecil, or the lovable, ogreish Hugo Dyson? Why not Lewis's sidekick, his admirable alcoholic brother Warnie? Lewis, Tolkien, Barfield, and Williams are the best-known of the group, but that is only one reason for our choice. They are also the most original, as writers and as thinkers, and thus most likely to be read and studied by future generations. They make a perfect compass rose of faith: Tolkien the Catholic, Lewis the "mere Christian," Williams the Anglican (and magus), Barfield the esotericist. In their beliefs, habits, marital arrangements, and private obsessions, they differed strikingly. From certain angles, it may appear that they had very little in common, apart from being Christian writers who lived in Oxford during the twentieth century. Yet somehow they found one another and together created one of the great literary sagas of the ages: the story of the Inklings.

I

"A STAR SHINES ON THE HOUR OF OUR MEETING"

T he story of the Inklings might begin with any of the company: Charles Williams, the first to be born, the first to publish, the first to die; Clive Staples Lewis, the most celebrated and execrated; Owen Barfield, the least known but, some say, the most profound; or any of the other brilliant figures who joined, reveled in, and (sometimes) quit the fellowship. We start, however, with John Ronald Reuel Tolkien, for with Tolkien the Inklings constellation began its ascent into the English literary firmament; he was the first to create work that bears the group's special stamp of Christian faith blended with pagan beauty, of fantastic stories grounded in moral realism. And we start our portrait of Tolkien with his mother—a welcome surprise in this tale of a group that rigorously excluded women—because Mabel Tolkien set in motion her son's madly spinning top of a mind, from which epic poems, children's stories, fantasy novels, invented languages, literary essays, philological studies, songs, watercolors, and pen-and-ink sketches would take flight for the next eighty years.

Mabel

Mabel Tolkien was born an English Suffield, a family with roots in the West Midlands, an urbanized county flecked with green about one hundred miles northwest of London. Her father, John Suffield, an exuberant merchant with a luxuriant beard, looking rather like his grandson's future portraits of Father Christmas, enthralled Mabel with his many skills, which included jesting, punning, and inking the Lord's Prayer within a circle the size of a sixpence. He and his wife, the improbably named Emily Sparrow, had seven children. The family ran a drapery shop in downtown Birmingham. More distant ancestors had sold books and stationery; Tolkien would carry in his blood a love of paper and the words it bore.

From this cozy mercantile background emerged a woman with a taste for adventure, a streak of independence, and an iron will. Mabel's strong personality has given rise to many colorful legends; one, repeated in several biographies of her son, asserts that she and her sisters traveled as missionaries to Zanzibar, where they proselytized the sultan's wives and concubines. This makes a good tale but has no basis in truth. Mabel's brick-and-mortar life was, however, dramatic enough. She accepted, at eighteen, the ardent attentions of Arthur Tolkien, a thirty-one-year-old banker; their romance, conducted largely sub rosa, via clandestine correspondence and the occasional family gathering, survived a two-year parting begun in 1889, when Arthur quit England for southern Africa. He went to seek his fortune, a common enough event in this era of Victorian enterprise that produced a British empire that spanned the globe. Mabel followed him in 1891, sailing, with typical intrepidness, alone from Southampton on the *Roslin Castle.* The reunited couple married in Cape Town's Anglican cathedral and set out for Bloemfontein, the dusty, dreary capital of the Orange Free State, a Boer republic where Arthur, having mastered Dutch, had become the assistant manager of the local branch of the Bank of Africa. Two children came in rapid succession: John Ronald Reuel on January 3, 1892, and Hilary Arthur Reuel on February 17, 1894 (the reason for the curious third name "Reuel"—"friend of God," drawn from Exodus 2, where it is assigned to Moses' father-in-law—remains obscure; Tolkien believed it to be the surname of an old family friend and passed it on to his own children as well).

John Ronald Reuel had, from the start, something fey about him, a whiff of pixie, which Mabel relayed to Arthur's parents in a letter dated March 4, 1893. Addressing her in-laws with nineteenth-century formality as "My dear Mr. & Mrs. Tolkien," she reports on the challenges of life in this very un-English land ("the next door pet monkeys had been over & eaten 3 of Ronald's pinafores"; "the weather is still intensely hot & trying") and enthuses over her fifteen-month-old boy. Her baby, she reports in terms whose allusive prescience sends shivers of bliss down the spines of Tolkien aficionados, resembles "a fairy when he's *very* much dressed up in white frills & white shoes," but "when he's very much *un*dressed I think he looks more of an elf still." The letter, suggesting a strong mental correspondence between mother and child, touches on many of Tolkien's favorite future motifs: voyages to strange lands, nostalgia for home, imaginary beings. We may even read, in Mabel's ornate calligraphy, with its curlicues and runic slashes, a hint of her son's eventual love of elaborate and invented scripts, alphabets, and languages. And while the adult Tolkien didn't resemble a fairy, he did approximate, with his long thin face and owlish eyes, one of his own fantastic inventions, a beardless Gandalf, perhaps. This is true of all the Inklings; they came to look like embodiments of their work. Lewis, with his red face, rotund figure, and bright bald pate, was the perfect model of the robust, full-bore (if not wholly muscular) Christian; Williams looked, so everyone said, like a monkey, with the wizened features of someone who has pored over too many magical tomes; Barfield was slender, soft-spoken, and ethereal, as if more at home in the rarefied atmosphere of the astral plane than the heavy miasma of the material world.

If we would picture Mabel, however, only one published photograph is available, taken November 16, 1892, in the garden of the house in Bloemfontein. It shows her at the center of a conventional Victorian family portrait, seated in a wicker chair, surrounded by a corona of relatives and servants. Arthur stands to her right, slouching with studied nonchalance in a white summer suit, the hard brim of his straw hat echoing the soft curve of his handlebar mustache. A trio of uniformed servants cluster in the background; one holds Ronald (as he was called), ten months old, looking like a plaster doll with his frilly petticoat, button eyes, and bright red mouth. Everyone seems at ease under the blazing African sun, pleased to pose in their Sunday finest. Everyone, that is, except Mabel. Something is amiss in her expression. She is dressed like the rest, in formal tropical wear: flowered hat, puff-shouldered blouse, long patterned skirt. But she sits erect, tense, her long fingers gripping the arms of her chair, her lean face turned to one side, her hawklike eyes looking quizzically

toward the camera, as if watching some unwelcome thing loom up behind the photographer. Perhaps she glimpses the future, the catastrophe
to come. For within a dozen years, everything in this photograph—father,
mother, the Bloemfontein household, the great African adventure, the
dreams of idyllic family life—would vanish, erased by exile, illness, and
death, proving as ephemeral as Arthur's boater or Mabel's leg-of-mutton
sleeves.

The dismantling of Mabel's life commenced immediately upon her
arrival in Africa. From the start, she had felt out of place in this dry, merciless land, with its racism, its stifling weather, its un-British ways, its marauding animals. Monkeys, snakes, and locusts invaded the garden and
a large spider, perhaps a tarantula, bit baby Ronald. Tolkien would later
deny any connection between this childhood spider bite and the spider-
monsters of his fiction; yet it is tempting to imagine that this horrific
creature nestled in his subconscious until it reemerged, swollen to gigantic size, as the spiders of Mirkwood in *The Hobbit*, the insatiable Shelob in
The Lord of the Rings, and Shelob's mother, Ungoliant, in *The Silmarillion*, the primary collection of Tolkien's mythopoeic tales.

Above all, it was the intense heat that proved intolerable; as one blast-
furnace day followed another, Mabel began to fear for her older boy's life.
By 1895 she had had enough and retreated to England with both children in tow. She moved in with her parents, pledging to return to Arthur
as soon as possible. It was not to be. Mired in Bloemfontein, he fell ill with
rheumatic fever, and by the following February he hovered on the brink
of death. News of his illness arrived via telegram on the same day that
Ronald, barely four years old, was preparing to post his first letter—his
first literary production of any sort—a rapturous note to his father anticipating their reunion. Arthur, only thirty-nine, died of a hemorrhage the
next day. The poignancy of hope denied is acute, as is the circumstantial
intertwining of literature and tragedy, touchstones of much of Tolkien's
later work.

Mabel, fighting fate, resettled with her children in a two-story semidetached house in Sarehole, a rural community near Birmingham. This
was an inspired choice. Memories of the benign hamlet, with its old mill,
bogs, forests, swan ponds, and sandpits, loomed large in her elder son's
imaginative universe and would become, in time, the landscape of the
Shire, the idyllic homeland of the Hobbits. Here Ronald encountered the

dialects that so fascinated him as a mature philologist, local variations on the King's English, including *gamgee*, a regional term for cotton wool, from a surgical dressing devised by the Birmingham physician Joseph Sampson Gamgee (a name that would descend by a complicated philological route to Tolkien's hobbit hero, Sam Gamgee, as we shall see in chapter 17).

Mabel gave Ronald more than a lovely world in which to grow up; she gave him an array of fascinating tools to explore and interpret it. We know little of her own education, but she clearly valued learning and vigorously set about transmitting what she knew to Ronald. She instructed him in Latin, French, German, and the rudiments of linguistics, awakening in him a lifelong thirst for languages, alphabets, and etymologies. She taught him to draw and to paint, arts in which he would develop his own unmistakable style, primitive and compelling, Rousseau with a dash of Roerich. She passed on to him her peculiar calligraphy; he would later master traditional forms and invent his own. She tried to teach him piano, although that proved a failure. And she introduced him to children's literature, including *Alice's Adventures in Wonderland, The Princess and the Goblin, The Princess and Curdie*, and Andrew Lang's collections of fairy tales. In George MacDonald he encountered goblins and, although he did not realize it at the time, Christian mythopoesis; in Lang's retelling of bits of the Old Norse Völsunga saga he met Fáfnir the dragon, a creature that excited his imagination like no other, and the prototype of Smaug of *The Hobbit*: "The dragon had the trade-mark *Of Faërie* written plain upon him . . . I desired dragons with a profound desire." It was his first baptism into the enchantments of Faërie, an otherworldly realm just touching the fringes of ordinary life and leading, in its farthest reaches, to the outskirts of the supernatural.

Bequeathing interests and skills to offspring is a means of ensuring continuity in the face of death, and we can read in Mabel's intense tutoring of her children a response to her husband's early demise. She may have sensed, too, that her own life would not last long. But Mabel wished to give her children more than the metaphorical immortality of transmitted gifts; she wished to give them true eternity. This she accomplished in 1900, by bringing herself and her two boys into the Roman Catholic Church.

It is difficult for us, surveying the past from our comfortably pluralistic aerie, to grasp what Mabel's conversion signified in England at the end of the nineteenth century. Anti-Catholicism ruled the land, the legacy of Henry VIII's lusts, Elizabeth I's ambitions, Pope Pius V's machinations, and Guy Fawkes's treason, mixing with misplaced nationalism and fear of Irish immigration. To be Catholic was, in the lurid popular understanding, to be blatantly un-English and probably a fifth columnist for the Roman pope, himself possibly the Antichrist. During the height of anti-Catholic paranoia, first in the "Catholic emancipation" debates of the late eighteenth and early nineteenth centuries, and then in the "Papal Aggression" of 1850, when the Catholic hierarchy returned to England, political cartoonists such as James Gillray and John Tenniel fanned the flames of civic alarm, and one regularly heard advice of the sort proffered by Charlotte Brontë in 1842, that anyone favorable to the Catholic Church should "attend mass regularly for a time to note well the mummeries thereof also the idiotic, mercenary, aspect of *all* the priests and *then* if they are still disposed to consider Papistry in any other light than a most feeble child- ish piece of humbug let them turn papists at once that's all."

Yet against this general backdrop of patriotic bigotry, we have to envision the counterfascination exerted by the Roman Catholic tradition among a small but influential group of British intellectuals, for whom it offered an alternative England that remained united to the broad central current of Christianity flowing from Rome. Nineteenth-century British Roman Cath- olics, whether of recusant families or converts, included a dazzling array of names such as John Henry Newman, Henry Edward Manning, Nich- olas Wiseman, Coventry Patmore, and Augustus Pugin—to be followed, in the years after Mabel's entry into the Church, by G. K. Chesterton, Ron- ald Knox, Evelyn Waugh, Siegfried Sassoon, Graham Greene, Christo- pher Dawson, Eric Gill, Muriel Spark, Elizabeth Anscombe, and a host of others. This brilliant Catholic stream fascinated the unchurched as well; Virginia Woolf has one of her characters wonder "why, if people must have a religion, they didn't all become Roman Catholics."

We have no record of why Mabel decided to join the Roman church; some will read in it a longing for hierarchy or authority, perhaps a replace- ment for a missing husband; others will see it as a genuine conversion of mind and soul. Whatever the motive, the act was not taken lightly. She had begun as an ardent high church Anglican but soon felt herself drawn from that confession's aesthetic splendor to the liturgy of the modest Roman Catholic church of St. Anne's on Alcester Street, in the impoverished Digbeth district. St. Anne's was in all respects a convert's church, having been transformed by John Henry Newman in 1849 from a gin distillery into the first chapel and residence for his fledgling congregation. Joined by her sister May Incledon, Mabel was received into the Roman Catholic Church there in June 1900.

A further unraveling of her life instantly ensued. This time, she must have anticipated it: the Baptist Tolkiens and the Unitarian and Methodist Suffields united in furious denunciation of the conversions. Only one or two family members supported the sisters. May's staunchly Anglican husband commanded her to renounce her new faith (she turned, instead, to Spiritualism) and severed the small allowance he had been sending Mabel. The next few years proved bitterly hard for Mabel, as she and her children moved into a succession of dreary residences, struggling to survive on the paltry remains of Arthur's estate, the result of his amateur investments in South African mining ventures.

There were, during these dark days, a few solaces. The first was King Edward's School, founded in 1552, a day school, one of the best in the nation, where Tolkien began his formal education, the costs underwritten initially by the handful of relatives who remained friendly to Mabel and later by academic scholarships. Another was the Birmingham Oratory, founded by Newman in 1848. Among the many benevolent Oratorians who befriended the beleaguered family, Fr. Francis Xavier Morgan (1867–1935) stands out. This bespectacled, pipe-smoking, dog-loving priest descended like a fairy godfather upon Mabel and the boys, filling their straitened lives with hope and joy. He paid regular visits to their home, vacationed with them, offered financial help and paternal counsel, and generally brightened their days with his unrestrained bearlike warmth and goodwill. In later life, Ronald would credit Father Francis with teaching him the meaning of charity and forgiveness, and in his honor he named his first child John Francis Reuel. But not even Oratorian love could stave off the doom hovering over the family, and in 1904 Mabel fell desperately ill from diabetes. There was no effective treatment—insulin would not be available for medical use until the 1920s—and on November 14, 1904, in the presence of Father Francis and May Incledon, she died.

☙

Leon Edel, speaking of one of Tolkien's contemporaries, Leonard Woolf, who lost his father when he was eleven, commented that "there is no hurt among all the human hurts deeper and less understandable than the loss of a parent when one is not yet an adolescent." Tolkien was twelve when Mabel died. In a 1941 letter to his son Michael, he remembered her as a "gifted lady of great beauty and wit, greatly stricken by God with grief and suffering, who died in youth (at 34) of a disease hastened by persecution of her faith." These notes of admiration and bitterness accompanied his memories of his mother all his life. At age seventy-three, he reiterated the theme, describing, again to Michael, her death "worn out with persecution" in "rented rooms in a postman's cottage at Rednal." In Tolkien's mind, the cruel shunning that Mabel suffered after her conversion led inexorably to her fatal disease, and she thus became for him not just a beloved mother but a Job figure, a saint, and a martyr, even a type of Christ, a selfless victim whose death gave life to those whom she loved and who loved her. Mabel appears in his fiction in countless sacrificial figures, a gallery of quasi Christs: Galadriel the Elven queen, who willingly surrenders her power for the good of Middle-earth; Gandalf the wizard, who submits to death to save his companions; Aragorn the king, who puts his rightful rule and very life to the ultimate test; Arwen (and her ancestor Lúthien Tinuviel), who gives up her immortality for love; and the hobbits Frodo and Sam, companions in sacrifice. The bitterness of death, the sweetness of faith, the ransom to be paid in blood; thanks in large measure to Mabel's indelible presence in his consciousness, these would become keynotes of Tolkien's imaginative world.

Perhaps the greatest of Mabel's legacies to Tolkien, however, was love of the Catholic Church. He became a lifelong believer, and in later years he recalled with shame those times when other pursuits—clubs, romance, art—tempted him away from prayer and Mass. He had a passionate love for the Eucharist and counseled his children to memorize important devotional prayers such as the Magnificat and the Litany of Loreto. "If you have these by heart you never need for words of joy." In later life, he translated Catholic prayers—the Pater Noster, Ave Maria, Gloria Patri, Sub Tuum Praesidium, and the Litany of Loreto—into Quenya, the High Elvish tongue of his devising. He was, as one friend summed it up, "a devout and strict old-fashioned Catholic" with a special regard for Mary and her motherly ministrations; she became for him a kind of muse, the source, he believed, of all goodness and beauty in his work. The Tolkien biographer Humphrey Carpenter argues that after Mabel's death, the Church became Tolkien's new mother. Carpenter means this in the ordinary psychological sense, that the Church filled in for a missing parent, but it is true also in a deeper sense. There is nothing idiosyncratic about embracing the Church as mother; as early as the third century, St. Cyprian declared that "no one can have God as Father who does not have the Church as Mother," a saying appended, in the 1994 Vatican-sponsored *Catechism of the Catholic Church*, to the declaration, "The Church is the mother of all believers." Throughout his life, Tolkien would draw comfort, courage, and artistic inspiration from this second mother, who, unlike Mabel, would never die ("Upon this rock I will build my church, and the gates of hell shall not prevail against it").

Ruginwaldus Dwalakōneis

Mabel's death transformed Tolkien's life. She had responded to the loss of her husband, to poverty, to disease, and to family cruelty with boldness and ingenuity, by opening herself to others, especially to her children and to her Church, pouring into these precious vessels her knowledge, hope, and devotion. Ronald responded to the same afflictions—plus the additional discovery that he and Hilary must now live with Beatrice Suffield, Mabel's widowed sister-in-law, an insensitive woman who had no affection to spare for her young, bereft, and brooding Catholic charges—by closing in upon himself, by inventing private languages, landscapes, creatures, and worlds, eventually composing a personal mythology of exceptional richness and depth. Accompanying this inward movement, however, was an intense increase in knowledge and perception of the outer world. Inventing languages required learning the genetic code that governs all language; inventing fantastic landscapes meant learning the real landscapes of his boyhood: the Birmingham streets, the waters of Lyme Regis, the stones of Whitby Abbey.

When young, Tolkien excelled in nature studies: drawings of a flower, a starfish, and what look like oak leaves fill a juvenile notebook. The subject matter turns somber as his mother's illness progresses; a sketch from 1904, drawn while Mabel was in the hospital and Ronald had taken refuge in the house of Edwin Neave—an insurance clerk who would soon marry his aunt Jane—carries the heartrending title *What Is Home Without a Mother (or a Wife)*. It depicts Ronald and Edwin sitting before the fire, mending clothes—rarely a man's pursuit back then. The drawing, with its close observation of Victorian furnishings and its symmetrical composition, shows considerable raw talent. Another early work, a watercolor depicting two boys, presumably Ronald and Hilary, on the beach, sustains this interest in symmetry: the boys mirror each other, with one, in red shirt and blue-black pants, facing the viewer, while the other, in blue-black shirt and yellow pants, turns away; two islands neatly divide the seascape. Throughout these early sketches, such symmetries of line and color, shape and movement, rule Tolkien's images, a visual analogue to the contrapuntal harmonics of Catholic scholasticism, and one might surmise, a deeply felt aesthetic response to the chaos of disaster and death that had ripped apart his childhood. This obsession with balance would recede in many of his subsequent sketches, such as one of Lyme Regis (where he stayed with Hilary and Father Francis in the summer of 1906), awhirl with swirling clouds, choppy seas, and moored boats, but would return in full force in his mature paintings for *The Hobbit* and *The Lord of the Rings*—books that contain a longing for peace and stability in the face of cosmic disorder and that speak, as we shall see, a distinctively Catholic idiom.

Language, however, held pride of place from the start in Tolkien's imagination. In Bloemfontein, he must have heard Afrikaans and perhaps Zulu, Xhosa, Sotho, and other native tongues, and soon after his return from South Africa, as noted above, his mother began to tutor him in European languages. French left him cold—indeed, he disliked throughout his life all things French, including haute cuisine and, later, existentialism. But he warmed to Latin, and came to delight in the shapes and sounds of its vocabulary, syntax, and grammar. In part this may be explained by his love of the Mass, celebrated in the ancient tongue until he was in his seventies; his grandson Simon recalls attending a Bournemouth Mass with his grandfather after the sea change of Vatican II and watching the old man make "all the responses very loudly in Latin while the rest of the congregation answered in English." Tolkien also felt the lure of Welsh, whose strange spellings he spied on the side of passing coal trucks. But it was German and Germanic languages that won his heart; he garnered prizes for German proficiency at King Edward's and began to study Anglo-Saxon (now commonly called Old English) and Gothic. The latter, a tongue that had flourished during the late Roman Empire and died out by the ninth century, he discovered through a secondhand copy of Joseph Wright's *Primer of the Gothic Language*. It utterly captivated him, "the first [language] to take me by storm, to move my heart . . . a sensation at least as full of delight as first looking into Chapman's *Homer*." Immediately, he peppered his other books with Gothic inscriptions and inscribed them with his Gothicized name, Ruginwaldus Dwalakōneis.

Joseph Wright (1855–1930) would play a significant role in the growth of Ronald's intellect, not only through his celebrated Gothic grammar but as Ronald's instructor, friend, and mentor at Oxford, where he took the budding philologist under his wing, guiding his studies and inviting him to Sunday afternoon teas. Wright's is one of the great Cinderella stories in the annals of English philology. Born in Yorkshire, the son of a charwoman and a miner who drank himself to death, he went to work in Blake's dark Satanic mills at the age of seven, changing bobbins on spinning frames and, in his spare time, selling horse manure. A lifetime of illiteracy and drudgery beckoned, but—like Mabel Tolkien—Wright resisted fate, in his case successfully. When he was fifteen, a fellow mill worker taught him to read and write, using the Bible and *The Pilgrim's Progress* for texts. Wright followed up by teaching himself Latin, French, and German through grammars purchased from his paltry income. Then he added Welsh, Greek, Lithuanian, Anglo-Saxon, Old Saxon, Old Bulgarian, and Old High German to his repertoire, acquiring a doctorate in the process at Heidelberg University. At thirty-three, he published his *Middle High German Primer* and later edited the six-volume *English Dialect Dictionary*. He became, upon the death of Max Müller, England's leading philologist, and was named professor of comparative philology at Oxford. In his breathtaking ability to master new languages, "Old Joe," as Tolkien referred to him, served as an inspiring professional model; in his moral goodness, fortitude, and kindness, combined with his rough Yorkshire ways, he was a prototype for Tolkien's Hobbits. When Wright died, Tolkien declared that "it was your works, that came into my hands by chance as a schoolboy, that first revealed to me the philology I love."

What was this discipline that so entranced the young Tolkien? Philology, defined by C. S. Lewis as "the love and knowledge of words," may also be usefully described as the zone where history, linguistics, and literature meet. The field began to take its modern form in 1786, when William Jones, a.k.a. "Asiatic" Jones, "Oriental" Jones, and "Persian" Jones, an Anglo-Welsh judge in the supreme court of Bengal and a linguistic prodigy of the first order—he mastered more than two dozen languages during his brief life—announced to the Asiatic Society of Bengal and to the world his discovery that Sanskrit, Greek, and Latin share a common ancestry. Further progress came through two significant, far-ranging nineteenth-century enterprises: the application of linguistic analysis to Biblical studies and the ongoing decipherment of ancient tongues, including Assyrian and Egyptian. Behind these practical studies lay powerful, intertwined, and potentially contradictory beliefs: that language provides a key to the rational, scientific understanding of the world and that language is more than human speech, that it claims a divine origin and is the means by which God created the cosmos and Adam named the beasts. As we will see, both ideas strongly influenced the Inklings, whose leading members wrote many words about the nature of words. For Owen Barfield, language is the fossil record of the history and evolution of human consciousness; for C. S. Lewis, it is a mundane tool that "exists to communicate whatever it can communicate" but also, as in *That Hideous Strength*, an essential part of our metaphysical makeup for good or ill; for Charles Williams, language is power, a field of force for the magician, a vehicle of prayer for the believing Christian; for Tolkien, language is a fallen human instrument and a precious divine gift (*"O felix peccatum Babel!"* he exclaimed in his essay "English and Welsh"), a supreme art, and, as "Word," a name for God.

Tolkien experienced words as a maddening liquor, a phonic ambrosia, tastes of an exquisite, rapturous, higher world. The sound of words affected him as colors or music do others; he complained to his aunt Jane, in later life, of adults who fail to hear the music of words but only grasp their meaning, and he recommended that when encountering a new word—for example, *argent*—one should first approach it as a "sound only . . . in a poetic context" before thinking about its meaning. In "English and Welsh," he writes of the phrase "cellar door" (long celebrated as a striking word combination) that "most English-speaking people . . . will admit that *cellar door* is 'beautiful,' especially if dissociated from its sense (and from its spelling). More beautiful than, say, *sky*, and far more beautiful than *beautiful*." He then adds that "in Welsh for me *cellar doors* are extraordinarily frequent." Tolkien made similar declarations about Finnish, which he first encountered at Oxford, likening it to a wine cellar filled with bewitching new vintages. As these various cellar images suggest, languages became for Tolkien vaults of beauty and seeds for his fiction. He came to see language in mystical terms, claiming that each of us possesses a "native language" that is not our first tongue but rather our "inherent linguistic predilections," something deep in the soul, or perhaps the genes. And language for Tolkien was also the soil from which his literary garden grew, as he explains in a 1966 interview, referring again to "cellar door": "Supposing you say some quite ordinary words to me—'cellar door,' say. From that, I might think of a name, 'Selador,' and from that a character, a situation begins to grow."

Tolkien's rapturous romance with words produced numerous offspring: his mythological fiction, of course, but before that, his invented languages. The first hint of things to come appeared in 1904, in an illustrated letter to Father Francis that uses the rebus principle, in which each syllable is indicated by a picture that suggests, without spelling out, its pronunciation (thus a map of France and a hissing snake add up to "Francis"). From now on, Tolkien would never approach words simply as dead lumps of information. At about the same time, he learned Animalic, a rudimentary language invented by his cousins, Mary and Marjorie Incledon, in which the names of birds, fish, and animals replace standard English words. These early tastes of what he later termed his "secret vice" soon led to the invention of Nevbosh (i.e., "New Nonsense"), which he pieced together with Mary, and which included coinages like *woc* for "cow" and *maino* for "my." The vice grew more entrenched at King Edward's, where in 1907 he concocted Naffarin, a tongue heavily salted with Latin and Spanish and with, possibly, its own rudimentary grammar; it is difficult to assess, as only a snippet remains. A few years later he devised his first private alphabet, a mishmash of English letters, runic slashes, and "monographs" (i.e., ideographs), and inscribed its rules in a sixteen-page notebook written in English and Esperanto entitled "The Book of the Foxrook." But all this was prelude to the sophisticated language-creation, complete with invented grammar and syntax, of his later Elvish tongues, and to the mythos that grew up alongside it. In a largely autobiographical paper Tolkien wrote in 1931 for the Oxford Esperanto Society

("A Hobby for the Home," later entitled "A Secret Vice"), he would maintain that the making of a language necessitates the making of a mythology
in which that language is spoken, that the two processes are intertwined,
each giving rise to the other. People thought Tolkien was joking when he
later said that he wrote *The Lord of the Rings* to bring into being a world
that might contain the Elvish greeting, so pleasing to his sense of linguistic beauty, *Elen síla lúmenn' omentielmo* ("A star shines on the hour of
our meeting"). The remark is witty—but also deadly serious.

"Friendship to the Nth Power"

The grammar of Tolkien's outer life was evolving as well. He had lost both
father and mother and needed, in loco parentis, more than art and wordplay. Father Francis helped to fill the void, counseling and consoling,
entertaining in his gruff, exuberant way, taking the boys kite flying and
catechizing them in the faith. But a middle-aged man cannot sate a teenager's hunger for companionship, and Tolkien soon turned to his fellow
students at King Edward's, forming with three of them—Rob Gilson,
Geoffrey Smith, and Christopher Wiseman—a club known as the Tea
Club and Barrovian Society (TCBS for short), named after the shop
(Barrow's Stores) in which they met and the beverage that they drank while
debating, as most sensitive young people do, religion, art, and moral behavior. All four were bright, idealistic, and a tad prudish; perfectly fitted to
each other, they remained a tight-knit band until the Great War unraveled
the fellowship. Within the TCBS, Tolkien came into his own, reciting from
Beowulf, Pearl, and *Sir Gawain and the Green Knight,* urging his friends
on to great artistic and moral heights, finding his voice in the loud, exuberant, sometimes boorish thrust-and-parry of male camaraderie—the
milieu in which he and all the future Inklings achieved much of their
work. "Friendship to the Nth power," Tolkien called it.

There was nothing odd in this; exclusively or primarily male clubs—
from the local lepidopterist circle to the gentleman clubs of London to
the Royal Society—had dominated English social and intellectual life for
centuries. Often these associations devoted themselves to pastimes such
as gambling, drinking, or hunting, but nobler pursuits, literature in particular, inspired more than one celebrated private club. Early models for
the TCBS (and for the Inklings), at least some of which Tolkien and his

friends may have been aware of, include the seventeenth-century Friday Street Club at the Mermaid Tavern in Cheapside, with its boisterous Elizabethan roster of Ben Jonson, John Donne, and Francis Beaumont, a paradise of male society immortalized two centuries later by John Keats in his "Lines on the Mermaid Tavern" ("Souls of poets dead and gone, / What Elysium have ye known, / Happy field or mossy cavern, / Choicer than the Mermaid Tavern?"); the early eighteenth-century Scriblerus Club, a Tory group led by Alexander Pope, Jonathan Swift, John Arbuthnot, and others, which Colin Hardie, himself an Inkling, identified as a prototype of the Oxford group; and, later in the eighteenth century, Samuel Johnson's dinner-and-discussion circle, generically entitled "The Club," with Joshua Reynolds, Oliver Goldsmith, Edmund Burke, and "Asiatic" Jones among its members, which convened every Monday at Turk's Head Tavern in Soho and was designed, according to Bishop Thomas Percy, to "consist of Such men, as that if only Two of them chanced to meet, they should be able to entertain each other without wanting the addition of more company to pass the Evening agreeably"—a fair description, too, of the TCBS and the Inklings at their best. As Keats's poem and Bishop Percy's remarks suggest, these clubs offered grand things: escape from domesticity, a base for intellectual exploration, an arena for clashing wits, an outlet for enthusiasms, a socially acceptable replacement for the thrills and dangers of war, and, in the aftermath of World War I, a surviving remnant to mourn and honor fallen friends. Tolkien and his fellow Inklings made much of these opportunities, and clubs and fellowships loomed large in their lives and in their fiction.

But male company, however convivial and stimulating, could not meet all needs. Tolkien, sometimes accused of ignoring women in his fiction, sought them out in life, in their manifold roles as mother, lover, companion, guide: first Mabel, then the Blessed Virgin, then a young pianist with smoldering eyes by the name of Edith Bratt, who stole his heart. She was nineteen, he sixteen, when they met amid the drab hunting prints and overstuffed furniture of a middle-class boardinghouse. That she was older than he troubled them not at all; they shared an orphan's independent spirit and longing for love. Edith, born in Gloucester in 1889, the illegitimate child of a paper dealer and a governess, lost her mother at the age of fourteen; after some years at school, where she took to music with considerable skill, she moved to lodgings in Edgbaston, close

by the Birmingham Oratory. At about this time, in one of those serendipitous acts that makes or breaks a life, Father Francis, casting about for
a home for the boys more congenial than that offered by their unwelcom-
ing aunt Beatrice, moved them into the very Edgbaston rooming house in
which Edith Bratt resided.

It took Tolkien and Edith less than a year to fall in love. One wonders
why it took a week. A photograph of Edith shows a young woman with
dark, intense eyes looking directly at the camera, a mass of thick black
hair framing her soft, full face; to someone as unfamiliar with young
women as Tolkien, her beauty must have come as a shock and a revelation. In addition, she was lithe and musical, a singer and dancer. He, by
contrast, was thin, average in height, athletic (he played rugby at King
Edward's, coming away with a broken nose and a lacerated tongue, the
source of his mumbling diction), a careful dresser, a tidy, attractive, but
not handsome package; but what he lacked in physical presence, he made
up for in kindness, intelligence, and romantic disposition. It was a good
match and an early marriage might have been anticipated. There was,
however, one insurmountable obstacle. Father Francis sniffed out the relationship and, concerned for Tolkien's studies and doubtful of any underage
passion, separated the couple, forbidding them to meet again until Tolkien
turned twenty-one. Despite some minor breaches, the wall Father Francis
erected held firm. Edith moved to Cheltenham and Tolkien prepared for
Oxford. Romance was in suspension, but the seeds of Tolkien's future
had been sown: a Catholic faith, a love of words, a creative, artistic mind,
the promise of connubial bliss.

2
HEAVEN IN A BISCUIT TIN

What a pity there are no color photographs of Clive Staples Lewis. To see just once in all its splendor that balding pate, that bright red face, those sagging pouches beneath the shrewd brown eyes—trademarks of a heavy daily intake, sustained for decades, of tobacco, beef, and beer! Almost every account of Lewis's appearance mentions his ruddy complexion. Even death could not snatch it away: J. B. Phillips, Anglican clergyman and Bible translator, reports that while watching television in late November 1963, the recently deceased Lewis "'appeared' sitting in a chair within a few feet of me . . . ruddier in complexion than ever, grinning all over his face and . . . positively glowing with health." *Time* magazine's September 8, 1947, cover drawing by Boris Artzybasheff interprets the florid countenance; Lewis's head turns slightly to the right, exposing the left side of his face, stained from forehead to chin by a mottled brown-and-red flush. His left cheek is dark, reflecting the gloomy presence of an irate steel-gray demon hovering over his left shoulder—Lewis is being portrayed here as author of *The Screwtape Letters*, instructional epistles from a senior devil to his apprentice—but the right side of his face, lightened to pale peach and white by the presence of an angel (we glimpse only one wing and a corner of the nimbus) is calm, alert, intent.

Lewis resembled, many said, the neighborhood butcher. Add the ubiquitous tweed jacket and flannel slacks, and he comes up in the world, but only as far as a midlevel accountant. He dressed like an ordinary man. Some of his friends and colleagues took this at face value: Luke Rigby, a pupil of Lewis's at Oxford during World War II and later a Benedictine abbot, writes that his teacher wore clothes "verging on the shabby" that "reflected the warmth and geniality of the man . . . a straight-forward and down-to-earth condemnation of the 'pseudo'—the shoddy and the insincere." But this is to underestimate Lewis's canny sense of person. He cultivated an image, that of the ordinary chap, endowed perhaps—one can do nothing about these things—with extraordinary brains, who lived an ordinary life of plain talk, plain food, and plain faith. He called himself Jack, a plain handshake of a name, a far cry from the Clive Staples he had been christened, and to be Jack was the hard work of a lifetime. Lewis longed to be ordinary: as a child, to talk like the other children in school-boy slang instead of the learned vocabulary that was all he knew; as a youth, to be one of the lads accepted by the Bloods, the school elite, in-stead of sticking out for his lack of athletic skill and oversized brains; as an adult, to be a "mere Christian," the next-door neighbor to millions of BBC Radio listeners. As a scholar, he made sure never to be mistaken for an aesthete. What is life's greatest pleasure? he asked his doctoral student, the future Renaissance scholar Alastair Fowler. Lewis ticked off the possibilities—Fowler remembers them as great art, mystical ecstasy, simultaneous orgasm—rejecting them one by one. "I'll tell you," Lewis said. "It's the pleasure, after walking for hours, of coming to a pub and relieving yourself."

But this sensuous side of Lewis's nature was a late development. Though Lewis the Oxford don would delight in bathing nude in the se-cluded "Parson's Pleasure" section of the River Cherwell or in a flooded clay pit near his Headington home, Lewis as a youth was extraordinarily uncomfortable in his body. Dances were a torment, sports a nightmare. This is hardly unusual among the young of either sex. Lewis, however, made much of it, more than do most people reminiscing about their youth; for he was aware not only of his body, but of the image he projected to others. He describes himself as having been an outsized, awkward lout. His face betrayed him, broadcasting arrogance or anger in just those moments when he was feeling particularly meek or contrite. In an early autobiographical scrap he speaks contemptuously of the "thick lips" he shared with his father. Above all, he singles out his hands, indicting them as the source of his early pessimism, his sense that the inanimate world and he did not conform. Each thumb had only one joint, a defect that led, when shaving, tying laces, or attempting other normal manipulations, to fury and tears. He inhabited his young body as if it were a suit of armor; and if his face was doomed to miscommunicate his true feelings, he would have to learn to play the parts assigned to him, until, as an adult, he could assume his chosen part as Everyman.

Ulster-Born

Everyman or not, Lewis was Anglo-Irish by birth, born in Belfast on November 29, 1898. As a young child he lived in a Belfast suburb surrounded by glens and meadows, permeated by the salt tang of the Irish Sea, with the Antrim mountains dissolving into mist in the distance. He fell in love with Northern Ireland's basalt slopes and steep granite tors—"I have seen landscapes . . . which, under a particular light, made me feel that at any moment a giant might raise his head over the next ridge"—and the Belfast Lough, teeming with ships and shipbuilding. Distances of sight or sound enchanted him. He thrilled to the call of a far-off steamer's horn at night. Through the nursery windows he could gaze at the green Castlereagh Hills: "They were not very far off but they were to children, quite unattainable. They taught me longing . . . made me for good or ill, and before I was six years old, a votary of the Blue Flower."

Filled with romantic urgings, he identified in his youth with the Celtic Revival, proclaiming Yeats "an author exactly after my own heart," and confessing to his friend Arthur Greeves, "I am often surprised to find how utterly ignored Yeats is among the men I have met: perhaps his appeal is purely Irish—if so, then thank the gods that I am Irish." Yet this ardor for things Irish, like much else in his makeup, was tinged with irony. The leading lights of the Celtic Revival—not only Yeats but Lady Gregory, "AE" (George William Russell), and J. M. Synge—had been, like Lewis, Anglo-Irish and Protestant by birth and upbringing, Gaelic by aspiration and choice. Lewis found himself at the crossroads Yeats and AE also faced: one could choose to cultivate a poetic and political Irishness or "go native" as a self-conscious Englishman; an uncomplicated identity was not an option for the Ulster-born.

Lewis experienced these ambiguities from an early age. Thanks to being half reared by an Irish nursemaid named Lizzie Endicott, "in whom even the exacting memory of childhood can discover no flaw—nothing but kindness, gaiety, and good sense," he began life furnished with a fine store of Irish folktales and fairy traditions, a promising beginning for a future storyteller and mythologist. "Through Lizzie we struck our roots into the peasantry of County Down," he wrote, and inspired by Lizzie's peasant wisdom, he and his older brother Warnie tracked the end of a rainbow to their own front garden and dug deep, but in vain, for the crock of gold. On returning home from work that night, their father fell in the hole, scattering his legal papers and roughing up his fine suit. Nothing could convince him that his sons had not been deliberately plotting against him. It was not the last time that the boys' intentions would be misconstrued; as a lesson in the futility of nursery room Faërie, the incident speaks volumes. Lewis longed to inhabit a world of myth, but he was prepared from an early age to be disappointed.

He would have liked to believe that the gods and fairies were returning at last; he acknowledged, with Yeats and AE, that compared to the Celtic world, England was lacking in a native mythology. "I see the great tree of English literature arising out of roast beef and watered with much rum and beer," AE had said. But Lewis loved roast beef and beer, and his craving for Anglo-Saxon steadiness and common sense (as the stereotype has it) trumped his craving for Celtic enchantment. If Irishness opened a door to visions of the Other World, of magical springs, holy mountains, and fantastic sea voyages, Englishness grounded him. He warned a friend not to be overly attached to the Irish mystique: "Remember that the great minds, Milton, Scott, Mozart and so on, are always sane before all and keep in the broad highway of thought and feel what can be felt by all men, not only by a few." Once he overcame his initial antipathy to English manners and the English landscape ("The flatness! The interminableness!"), he gradually acquired the spoken accent that to his young ears had "seemed like the voices of demons" and immersing himself as scholar, soldier, philosopher, and literary historian in the central currents of English culture.

Yet it would be wrong to view Lewis's Englishness as a rejection of his roots. The Ireland of Lewis's birth and boyhood was wholly if not wholeheartedly British. The counties that made up the Ulster region in the north were predominantly Protestant, home to Church of Ireland Anglicans and Presbyterian Ulster Scots, groups not always in harmony with each other but ready to close ranks against their Catholic neighbors. Belfast, in particular, depended on its close ties to England to sustain the prosperity of its linen mills and dockyards; the bond was economic as well as spiritual. Considering, too, that Lewis's Welsh, Scottish, and Anglo-Norman ancestors had settled in Ireland at different times and under different political auspices, it's understandable that he never decided precisely how Irish God had made him.

He valued, too, the Welsh within him. "I'm more Welsh than anything," he told George Sayer, "and for more than anything else in my ancestry I'm grateful that on my father's side I'm descended from a practical Welsh farmer. To that link with the soil I owe whatever measure of physical energy and stability I have. Without it I should have turned into a hopeless neurotic." The connection to the soil was remote, however; not since his great-great-grandfather Richard had the Lewises been farmers. Great-grandfather Joseph gave up tilling the soil to harvest souls for Christ as a Methodist minister. Grandfather Richard rose from a menial occupation as dockworker at the Mersey shipyard to master boilermaker in Cork and eventually to partnership in a Belfast shipbuilding firm. Welsh farmer practicality notwithstanding, Lewis felt that his paternal lineage revealed its Welsh character by being "sentimental, passionate, and rhetorical, easily moved both to anger and to tenderness; men who laughed and cried a great deal and who had not much of the talent for happiness." Grandfather Richard's extreme mood swings and religious brooding made life a trial for his family, but he raised his sons with high expectations, providing Albert, Lewis's father, with the schooling needed to achieve a respectable professional post as police-court solicitor, to hold his own in the political and cultural life of Belfast, and to marry significantly above his class.

Lewis's mother, Florence ("Flora") Augusta Lewis (1862–1908), was the daughter of the Reverend Thomas R. Hamilton (1826–1905), a prominent Church of Ireland clergyman and former chaplain to the Royal Navy. Hamilton was the first rector of St. Mark's, Dundela, Belfast, an imposing parish church designed by the English architect William Butterfield in a Tractarian Gothic style similar to that of his masterpiece, Keble College, Oxford. The Lewis family worshiped here, Albert married Flora here, and the boys were baptized here by their distinguished grandfather. On the door to the old rectory, where the Reverend Thomas Hamilton resided, is a circular brass handle depicting the head of a majestic lion, emblem of St. Mark; eager pilgrims to this landmark at the starting point of the Belfast "C. S. Lewis Trail" believe they are face-to-face with the prototype of Aslan, the lion-god, Lewis's most celebrated literary invention.

"The Hamiltons were a cooler race," Lewis would observe in his 1955 autobiography, *Surprised by Joy*. But there was nothing cool about Grandfather Thomas's robustious oratory, whether in the pulpit or the pub; he was fond of good company and good argument and loved to hold forth on his favorite prejudice: the superstition and perfidy of the Church of Rome. Lewis's grandmother, Mary Warren Hamilton, matched her husband in strong opinions. But Mary was a liberal who favored Home Rule, staffed her household with southern Irish servants, and neglected the housekeeping to indulge her political interests. All this shocked her Belfast neighbors and relations, most of whom, like the Lewises, strongly supported the Unionist (pro-British) cause, convinced that Ireland under Home Rule would be Ireland under "Rome Rule," with the Protestant minority marginalized and abused. Over dinner and at family gatherings, conversation would turn inevitably to the ever-present threat of Irish nationalism; at age ten, Lewis was writing essays on "the Irish problem," though for a while he declared himself a Home Ruler. Ultimately, he wearied of the debate; from the unedifying spectacle of grown-ups carrying on "an endless and one-sided torrent of grumble and vituperation" (as Warnie described it), he acquired a loathing of politics, newspapers, and sectarian partisanship of all kinds. This led him to temper his inherited anti-Catholicism as well; his deepest wish as an adult convert was to be all things to all men, to unite in himself the warring factions and reclaim for English-speaking Christendom a unified literary and spiritual past.

Flora passes through her children's memoirs without leaving a detailed portrait. She appears in photographs as small and squat, with a likable but forgettable elfin face. As a child of twelve, she witnessed a "miracle" in a Catholic church in Rome, as the preserved body of a young female saint encased in glass "slowly lifted her eyelids and looked at me." When her mother scoffed at the miracle, Flora refused to retract what she had seen but only reconsidered how the effect had been produced: it must have been "all done by cords." The episode suggests an imaginative disposition as well as a capacity for analytical reasoning. She was not easily persuaded to doubt the evidence of her senses (one thinks of Lucy in *The Lion, the Witch, and the Wardrobe*). She knew her own mind, as Albert would discover when, emboldened by long-standing close relations between the Lewis and Hamilton families, he proposed marriage to her in 1886. "I always thought you knew that I had nothing but friendship to give you," Flora said. When she finally accepted him, it was more as a companion than as a lover. She explained that the Hamiltons dislike effusion; no swooning should be expected. While Albert's letters to Flora ardently praise her virtues, Flora's to Albert remain calm and analytical: "I wonder do I love you? I am not quite sure. I know that at least I am very fond of you, and that I should never think of loving anyone else." The marriage, if not an idyll, was happy and stable.

Nonetheless, Flora possessed a romantic streak, which found its outlet in amateur literary production. She wrote many stories, one of which, "The Princess Rosetta," appeared in *The Household Journal* but has since vanished along with all her youthful literary attempts. Her love of novels, according to Lewis, was responsible for most of the fiction in the family library. She was also a gifted mathematician, having passed her examinations in geometry, algebra, and logic at the Royal University (now Queen's University) in Belfast with first-class honours. She tutored the boys in French and Latin, and she took them on seaside holidays—the highlight of every year, according to Warnie—without Albert, who could not bear to have his daily routines disrupted and joined them on occasional weekends, only to pace the beach in a blue funk.

These few facts suggest that it was from Flora, if not solely from his own idiosyncratic genius, that Lewis derived his peculiar blend of intellect and imagination, his skill with words, his philosophical dexterity, his willingness to trust his own impressions. The transfer of talents from gifted mother to gifted son was soon truncated, however, when Flora fell ill with what proved to be abdominal cancer. In his autobiography, Lewis re-creates in poignant detail the "strange smells and midnight noises and sinister whispered conversations" of the sickroom and the terror of waking at night "ill and crying both with headache and toothache and distressed because my mother did not come to me." When Flora died seven months later at the age of forty-six—Warnie was then thirteen and Lewis nine (three years younger than Tolkien had been when Mabel died)—"all settled happiness, all that was tranquil and reliable, disappeared from my life. There was to be much fun, many pleasures, many stabs of Joy; but no more of the old security. It was sea and islands now; the great continent had sunk like Atlantis." Lewis woke at night in terror, imagining that his father and brother had left for America, in the wake of financial ruin, abandoning him alone and friendless in the great house.

The Pudaita Bird

To some degree, Lewis's mother plays the same role as Tolkien's father—longer on the stage but notable, like Arthur Tolkien, above all for her passing. There is, however, no counterpart in Tolkien's biography for Lewis's father, Albert Lewis (1863–1929), surely one of the more peculiar men to sire a famous author. Albert looms large in both Jack's and Warnie's memoirs. He worked all his life as a solicitor, an occupation conventionally considered dry and uninspiring, and yet he was a man of volatile feelings, a spellbinding orator and storyteller, a gifted mime. He loved his wife and two sons dearly, and his sons loved him, too; but the tensions that would lead to their estrangement were evident early on. From his "low Irish" way of saying "pudaita" for "potato," the boys took to calling him "Pudaitabird" or "P'daytabird"—"P" for short—and later, as young men, collected his aphorisms and anecdotes ("wheezes") in *The Pudaita Pie: An Anthology*. Albert exhibited two pronounced traits that drove his children to distraction and then to escape (one of the reasons that both settled in England was to avoid his presence): he meddled and he muddled. The meddling, born from misplaced desire to compensate his boys for the loss of their mother, meant that whenever Jack or Warnie sought solitude, Albert would insert himself and make it a duo, and whenever a friend came to visit, Albert would be sure to make it a crowd. Monday, when he returned to work and could no longer intrude, became for his children "the brightest jewel in the week."

The muddling sprang from a short circuit in Albert's mental processes, leading him to rethink every important choice he faced ad nauseam, until his response was "infallibly and invincibly wrong." One result, wrote Lewis, was that he "had more capacity for being cheated than any man I have ever known." Another was that he consistently misinterpreted his sons' intentions ("It was axiomatic to my father . . . that nothing was said or done from an obvious motive") and, more generally, whatever was said to him:

> Tell him that a boy called Churchwood had caught a field mouse and kept it as a pet, and a year, or ten years later, he would ask you, "Did you ever hear what became of poor Chickweed who was so afraid of the rats?" For his own version, once adopted, was indelible, and attempts to correct it only produced an incredulous "Hm! Well, that's not the story you *used* to tell."

He excelled, too, at non sequiturs—sins against sense of the sort that precocious adolescents find hilarious and rarely have the patience to forgive:

> "Did Shakespeare spell his name with an e at the end?" asked my brother. "I believe," said I—but my father interrupted: "I very much doubt if he used the Italian calligraphy *at all*."

He possessed, wrote Lewis, "more power of confusing an issue or taking up a fact wrongly than any man I have ever known." Moreover, Albert's mood swings—the moments of bonhomie and companionable fun, at which he excelled, could give way without notice to storms of reproach and wounded pride—made emotional displays of any kind seem "uncomfortable and embarrassing and even dangerous." When the boys committed some small infraction, Albert deployed all his Ciceronian skills as a public speaker and police-court prosecutor—skills Lewis inherited along with a zest for argument—to bring the miscreants to justice. A moment later all was forgiven.

This brilliant, passionate, capricious domestic god was at the same time uncannily regular in his habits. To the question "What time would you like lunch?" there could only be one answer: 2:00 or 2:30 p.m., a meal of boiled or roasted meat in a dining room facing south. Years later, when Lewis was hospitalized in England for war wounds, Albert, at home in Belfast, refused to disrupt his schedule long enough to visit. In Warnie's judgment, their father suffered from a crippling obsession ("I never met a man more wedded to a dull routine, or less capable of extracting enjoyment

from life") and became, in his final years, an "inquisitor and tyrant." Both
boys lived in chains while Albert walked the earth.

"I would not commit the sin of Ham," Lewis said; yet the portrait of his
father in *Surprised by Joy* is, as A. N. Wilson points out, "devastatingly
cruel." It is less cruel than it might have been, given that Lewis waited
until long after his father's death before skewering him in print. But that
he could produce, in his fifties, a send-up so damning, so funny, and so
finely wrought, suggests that he never fully escaped his father's influence.
If his mother's death was the sinking of Atlantis, his struggles with his
father wounded him, if anything, more deeply still, perhaps because the
relationship suppurated for so many years. The one good thing to come
from this slow-motion debacle was the deep, lifelong companionship he
would enjoy with Warnie: "the unfortunate man, had he but known it, was
really losing his sons as well as his wife. We were coming, my brother
and I, to rely more and more exclusively on each other for all that made
life bearable; to have confidence only in each other"—and, although
Lewis does not mention it in this passage, in the magic worlds they built.

Boxen

From their earliest years, the Lewis brothers realized that other worlds,
entrancing imaginary creations lying beyond or nestled within the ordinary scheme of things, brought into being by art, will, love, and hard work,
could offer incomparable joy and consolation. In an episode that now
belongs to the Lewis legend, one day Warnie "brought into the nursery
the lid of a biscuit tin which he had covered with moss and garnished
with twigs and flowers so as to make it a toy garden or a toy forest." In
Lewis's memory, the biscuit garden became a simulacrum of Eden, a
foretaste of paradise, "the first beauty I ever knew."

The house the boys and their father inhabited was another magical
realm—or at least the vestibule to one. The family moved into "Little
Lea" when Lewis was seven. A rambling, three-story brick building ("to a
child it seemed less like a house than a city") in the suburbs of Belfast, it
was drafty, roomy, with defective chimneys and noisy plumbing; delightful,
Warnie remembered, precisely because it was "atrociously uneconomical"
and full of unused crawl spaces. In *Surprised by Joy*, Lewis would recast it
as the foothills of Parnassus, the place where he first tasted his destiny:

"I am a product of long corridors, empty sunlit rooms, upstairs indoor silences, attics explored in solitude, distant noises of gurgling cisterns and pipes, and the noise of wind under the tiles." The house groaned with books, jammed into bedrooms, attics, landings, closets, books for children and for adults, books for the naïve and for the sophisticated. "I had always the same certainty of finding a book that was new to me as a man who walks into a field has of finding a new blade of grass."

It was at Little Lea that Lewis acquired his passion, not only for reading, but for writing. In one of the empty attics, safe from grown-up interference, he set up an "office" in which he composed reams of juvenilia, including essays, novels, journals, histories, and above all, the chronicles of Animal-Land, a medieval kingdom featuring knights and "dressed animals." By 1906 (age seven) he had written *The King's Ring*, a three-act play set in 1327 during the reign of King Bunny I, involving the theft of the king's ring by a mouse named Hit and its recovery by Mr. Big the Frog (later Lord Big) and Sir Goose. The dialogue is what one expects from a seven-year-old who had been steeped in Beatrix Potter's rabbit worlds, Conan Doyle's *Sir Nigel*, and his brother's copy of *The Three Musketeers*:

KING BUNNY: This wine is good.
BAR-MAN: I shall drink a stiff goblet to the health of King Bunny.
KING BUNNY: For this good toast much thanks.
SIR PETER: Draws near the dinner hour so pleas your Magasty.

Meanwhile, Warnie was devising his own imaginary country, a bustling, modern, industrialized "India" whose "ships and trains and battles" he delighted to draw. Soon the boys fused their two disparate creations into a fantastic über-realm they called Boxen. Lewis furnished this new land with an elaborate if choppy history from medieval to modern times, composed with relentless attention to detail. He proved to be a "systematizer" akin to Trollope; Boxen was his Barsetshire, and he filled it with citizens and statesmen like the frog Lord John Big (a father figure, according to *Surprised by Joy*, and "a prophetic portrait of Sir Winston Churchill"); Big's nemesis, the navy lieutenant and bear James Barr (who was, Lewis would later say, remarkably like the poet John Betjeman, who would be his most challenging pupil at Oxford); Orring the lizard MP; and assorted Chessmen of low birth, all drawn with an ungainly realism as mirrors of the adult society Lewis knew best, preoccupied with questions of money, politics, and power.

There was little enchanting about Boxen itself. Its magic resided in the bond it forged between two brothers, beginning in the idyllic years before their mother's death. As different as Animal-Land was from India, as different as Jack was from Warnie, they succeeded in creating a common imaginary world that they would share until Lewis's death. "Neither of us ever made any attempt to keep that vanished world alive," Warnie recalled, "but we found that its language had become a common heritage of which we could not rid ourselves. Almost up to the end, 'Boxonian' remained for Jack a treasured tongue in which he could communicate with me, and with me only. The Harley street specialist of that world had been a small china salmon, by name Dr. Arrabudda; and Jack, during the closing weeks of his life, on the days when his specialist was due to visit him, would say to me with a smile, 'I'll be seeing that fellow Arrabudda this morning.'"

Unlike Tolkien, Lewis didn't turn to writing to escape from family tragedy. His motive was far more ordinary: writing was the most ready-to-hand amusement for a child confined to the house whenever the weather threatened. He began to write in the limpid dawn of an idyllic childhood, before his mother's death, when he was little "Jacksie" to his beloved brother "Badgie," and their parents confided in each other as "Doli" to "dearest old Bear." He set down, in his first diary, the picture of a household that was settled and secure, though not without its irritants: "Papy of course is the master of the house, and a man in whom you can see strong Lewis features, bad temper, very sensible, nice wen not in a temper. Mamy is like most middle-aged ladys, stout, brown hair, spectaciles, kniting her chief industry, etc., etc. I am generaly wearing a jersy . . ."

Lewis enjoyed the constant companionship of his brother, and when Warnie went to school in 1905, the two kept up a correspondence. Lewis also wrote about Warnie in his diary: "Hoora!! Warnie comes home this morning. I am lying in bed waiting for him and thinking of him, before I know where I am I hear his boots pounding on the stairs, he comes into the room, we shake hands and begin to talk . . . Well I was glad to have him but of course we had our rows afterwards . . ."

This loving companionship would prosper, despite separations and occasional rows, for the rest of Lewis's life. Three years older than his brother, heavier, and more earthbound in his hobbies and interests, Warnie comes across in letters and diaries—his own as well as his brother's—as a gentle man forever devoted to Lewis (though sometimes exasperated by him), with a character more gracious to others and less assertive of his own interests than his famous sibling possessed. John Wain, not the most tender-minded of Inklings, described Warnie as "the most courteous [man] I have ever met—and not with mere politeness, but with a genial, self-forgetful considerateness that was as instinctive to him as breathing." Warnie would become an active Inkling in his own right, the author of several books on seventeenth- and eighteenth-century French history, a dedicated diarist, a career military officer, and a chronic alcoholic. For now, it is enough to think of him as Lewis's closest companion, and his first collaborator in literary pursuits.

～

Lewis's boyhood reading early coalesced around fantasy literature, with its fabulous lands, mutations of time and space, and metaphysical conceits, along with a secondary concentration in sentimental historical fiction. By the age of twelve, he had scouted Edith Nesbit, Arthur Conan Doyle, Mark Twain, F. Anstey, H. Rider Haggard, and H. G. Wells, along with Henryk Sienkiewicz and Lewis Wallace; but he also swallowed large doses of poetry, especially by Longfellow and Milton. Intensive, at times compulsive, reading became for him a lifelong habit. By his late teens he was extraordinarily well versed in classical literature and English, so much so that one of his teachers, William T. Kirkpatrick, indicated that "he has read more classics in the time than any boy I ever had, and that too, very carefully and exactly." Lewis was already acquiring the skill and taste to claim, one day, the mantle of twentieth-century heir to Samuel Johnson, the most widely read man in eighteenth-century England. To generations of students, astonished by his prodigious literary memory, he would give this simple counsel: "The great thing is to be always reading but never to get bored—treat it not like work, more as a vice!"

Lewis's early reading delivered more than excitement, knowledge, or even deepening analytic and imaginative skills. On rare occasions, an image, a tone, a rhythm, an unexpected juxtaposition, would lift him clean out of himself, out of Little Lea, Belfast, and Boxen, translating him to the threshold of a new state of being. He called this state "Joy" and identified it with the German *Sehnsucht*: the infinitely desirable, sweetly wounding, ungraspable and unforgettable, the apotheosis of longing itself: "an unsatisfied desire which is itself more desirable than any other satisfaction." Joy would become for Lewis a siren, a mirage, a lodestone, a signpost, and finally, a way to God. It came in the form of a series of shocks or epiphanies, fleeting in duration but marking Lewis forever. He first experienced it on a spring day when, standing by a flowering currant bush, he was swept up in "a memory of a memory" of Warnie carrying his miniature garden in a biscuit tin into the nursery. The recollection flooded him with a sensation he could only compare to "Milton's 'enormous bliss of Eden.'"

Beatrix Potter's *The Tale of Squirrel Nutkin* administered the next shock: "It troubled me with what I can only describe as the Idea of Autumn." Was it a sense of things passing, even passing away, of waning sunlight, cooling air, leaves erupting in color before crumpling to the ground? Lewis doesn't say; but it is noteworthy that the minimal plot involves Squirrel Nutkin challenging Old Owl with a series of riddles, all left unsolved, evoking the mystery of existence, felt most keenly as dark and cold usurp sun and light.

The third shock came while thumbing through a volume of Longfellow, when Lewis stumbled upon the opening lines of "Tegnér's Drapa": "I heard a voice that cried, / Balder the Beautiful / Is dead, is dead!" and immediately found himself immersed in "Northernness," a sensation "cold, spacious, severe, pale, and remote"—spring had given way to Nutkin's autumn, and autumn to winter as the season of epiphany. Balder is, of course, a dying-and-rising god (an idea Lewis encountered in Frazer's *The Golden Bough*), a mythic anticipation of Christ. To have his child's heart stirred by Balder's death may be, then, an anticipation of his later Christian faith; in any event, it shows Lewis's critical perspicacity at a precocious age, selecting deeply evocative lines from a sometimes thumpingly overblown Norse-inspired cycle of poems ("The Saga of King Olaf," which initially attracted Lewis to Longfellow, begins "I am the God Thor, / I am the War God, / I am the Thunderer! / Here in my Northland, / My fastness and fortress, / Reign I forever!").

Like the Romantic poets, Lewis sensed the numinous in words that pointed to a realm beyond, to empty sky, open landscapes, things passing, things beyond reach, dim foreshadowings of a God who is wholly Other. That the young Lewis would be so stirred by fall and winter, by the advent of cold and dark; by the death of beauty, by death itself, speaks to his essential Romanticism. Each of the epiphanies he experienced contained within it, as part of its evanescent loveliness, a memento mori: the death of Balder; the near death of Squirrel Nutkin, whom Old Owl captures and almost skins alive; and, most poignantly, the death of the happy early childhood of Warnie and himself, builder and beholder of the miniature Eden. Underlying all was the one great death: that of his mother.

The Banks of the Styx

Tolkien, after the death of his mother, found love and a home through the help of Father Francis. Lewis suffered the opposite fate. After his mother's death, he was exiled from home, sent abroad by his father to the first of a succession of boarding schools, each disastrous in its own incomparable way. This may strike the modern reader as needlessly cruel; but at the time, for families like the Lewises and Hamiltons, boarding school seemed like the normal, obvious, and essential route to adult achievement for an Anglo-Irish boy whose prospects at home were far from secure. So off Lewis went, trussed in an Eton collar, knickerbockers, boots, and bowler, via four-wheeler and ship on September 18, 1908—less than four weeks after his mother's death—his brother alongside, to Watford, Hertfordshire, in England, to enroll in Wynyard School, where Warnie was already a pupil.

England, at first glance, looked like "the banks of Styx," an apt introduction to the regions of hell Lewis would soon traverse. His account of his two years there, and his subsequent stay at three other schools, occupies a large, perhaps disproportionate, chunk of his autobiography, about half of the whole, and proves a formidable obstacle to readers, especially those from foreign lands, not as entranced as British males of Lewis's generation by the minutiae of public school existence. Nonetheless, his vivid description of the Grand Guignol he witnessed, which ranged from cruelty to sexual exploitation to outright madness, offers both literary and sensationalistic compensation and constitutes a fierce indictment of a pedagogical system that has now largely vanished.

Each school offered its own variety of moral or mental disarray. Wynyard, called Belsen (after the concentration camp) in *Surprised by Joy*, harbored a headmaster, Robert Capron ("Oldie"), who beat his charges mercilessly. A High Court action for abuse, taken by one of the boy's parents, precipitated the school's decline; by the time Jack arrived, Capron had been declared insane, but the school continued to operate. "I think I shall like this place," Jack wrote to his father, "Misis Capron and the Miss Caprons are very nice and I think I will be able to get on with Mr. Capron though to tell the truth he is rather eccentric." Ten days later he wrote, "My dear Papy . . . Please may we not leave on Saturday? We simply *cannot* wait in this hole till the end of term." Albert's answer was not encouraging: "All schools—whether for boys or the larger school of life for men—press hardly and sorely at times. Otherwise they would not be schools. But I am sure you will face the good and the bad like a brave Christian boy, for dear, dear, Mammy's sake."

Little in the way of real education went on at Wynyard: for the most part it was endless sums and arbitrary floggings. Capron did know how to teach geometry, thus giving Jack his first systematic introduction to critical thinking and in so doing creating an association between success in logical argument and belligerence in rhetorical style. Lewis would have to learn, by painful self-correction, how to temper his zeal for good argument with humor and charity.

It was also at Wynyard that Lewis first took Christianity seriously. The school's Anglo-Catholic style deeply offended his Ulster Protestant sensibilities; perhaps otherwise it would not have caught his attention. "I do not like church here at all because it is so frightfully high church that it might as well be Roman Catholic," he told his father in October 1908. Some months later, he recorded in his diary, "In this abominable place of Romish hypocrites and English liars, the people cross themselves, bow to the Lord's Table (which they have the vanity to call an altar), and pray to the Virgin." Eventually, though, he overcame his distaste enough to appreciate hearing "the doctrines of Christianity (as distinct from general 'uplift') taught by men who obviously believed them." He began to think about hell, examine his conscience, pray earnestly, and study the Bible.

Here, too, Lewis developed his taste for the works of Rider Haggard and Wells, opening vistas both mythopoeic and extraterrestrial. These two authors, he emphasized later on, offered him "coarser" pleasures than those he associated with Joy. His hunger for their works was "ravenous, like a lust." There was in it nothing spiritual; it was, he came to believe, an expression of deep-seated psychological forces, and he saw his adult science fantasies as an "exorcism" rather than a maturing of this passion. Nevertheless, he acknowledged Haggard's influence and called his talent "the text-book case of the mythopoeic gift pure and simple." He and Warnie also made plans to create a book club, fed by subscriptions to *Pearson's Magazine*, *The Strand*, and *The Captain*, which would mean an unending stream of boys' adventures stories, including those of Kipling, Chesterton, and Conan Doyle.

Conditions at Wynyard grew worse by fits and starts. By September 29, 1908, Warnie wrote to his father, "You have never refused me anything Papy and I know you won't refuse me this—that I may leave Wynyard. Jack wants to too." But on November 22, Lewis wrote, "I find school very nice but it is frightfully monotenis," and a week later: "as to what you say about leaving I cannot know quite what to say, Warnie does not particularly want to, he says it look like being beaten in the fight"; and "in spite of all that has happened I like Mr. Capron very much indeed." No doubt there is an element of bravado in these statements. In February 1909, Lewis reported that he had been shut out of a secret society headed by a certain "Squivy," but that Squivy's throne was tottering, and Capron's pupils were fleeing one by one. Warnie abandoned ship in April, morally spent and under an indictment for incorrigible laziness, leaving Lewis to hang on with the handful of remaining pupils. In June 1910, Wynyard finally collapsed under its headmaster's lunacies and was closed by High Court order. After a brief clerical career, cut short when he persisted in flogging the choirboys and church wardens, Capron was committed to an asylum in Kent, where he died of pneumonia in 1911.

Lewis passed the summer of 1910 with Albert and Warnie (by now a student at Malvern College, England). He then enrolled at Campbell College, a boarding school in Belfast. While there he became a devotee of Matthew Arnold's "grave melancholy," savoring his *Sohrab and Rustum*, an epic poem derived from the Persian *Shanameh*, in which the legendary

hero Rustum inadvertently kills his son Sohrab in single combat. Looking back, Lewis prized this literary discovery as a foretaste of the *Iliad*;
others will note that *Sohrab and Rustum* is the tale of a powerful father's
tragic misunderstanding of his chivalrous son.

Having developed a bad cough while at Campbell, Lewis crossed the
Irish Sea again in January 1911, this time to attend Cherbourg Prepara-
tory School ("Chartres" of *Surprised by Joy*) near Warnie's college in Malvern, Worcestershire, a health resort with curative waters. Cherbourg
proved momentous. Here he advanced in Latin and in English literature,
here he came to love the miniature beauties of the English countryside—
and here he abandoned Christianity. He himself evinced many causes
for his loss of faith. One was the influence of that gentle Cherbourg
House matron, the beloved G. E. Cowie ("Miss C." in *Surprised by Joy*),
who had a taste for occultism of the Theosophical/Rosicrucian stripe and
awakened a like hunger in Lewis. But was the culprit really Miss Cowie?
The real tempter, Lewis suggests in his autobiography, was the Devil, who
made use of Miss Cowie's innocent guile. Let us note in passing that this
is one of the difficulties and pleasures of studying the Inklings; Christians all, they offer, along with expected twentieth-century psychosocial
explanations for behavior, unexpected spiritual ones: as the biographer
can neither peer into his subject's unconscious nor interview the Enemy
(as Lewis terms him), both forms of explanation must be taken, at least
provisionally, on faith—or, at a minimum, faithfully recorded.

Lewis cites other reasons, too, for his newborn skepticism. One was
the onslaught of scruples, a problem well attested in the spiritual life,
especially among the young, where religious observances must be done
perfectly and achieve a certain result. However the Enemy may turn them
to his advantage, scruples can be understood psychologically as a temporary obsessive-compulsive disorder triggered by the turmoil of adolescent
sexual development. In Lewis's case, during the period of his religious
awakening at Wynyard, he had come to demand of his nightly prayers a
"realization," "a certain vividness of the imagination and the affections"—a
sure recipe for sleeplessness and misery, and, as Lewis says, the road to
madness. Loss of faith came as blessed relief.

Another source for Lewis's religious doubt was his conviction that
"the universe was, in the main, a rather regrettable institution." He now
harbored an inveterate pessimism born of his mother's death, his father's

many dire announcements of impending financial ruin, his own physical clumsiness, and also, he later speculated, reading Wells's tales of cosmic coldness and menace. Could there be anything more terrifying to an insect-phobic adolescent (as a child Lewis had been terrified by a stag beetle in a pop-up picture book) than the inexorable invasion of insectoid Martians in *War of the Worlds*, anything more bitter than the final desolation of the earth seen on a far-future beach in *The Time Machine*? Some of his skepticism may have been no more than an expression of adolescent angst; a sense of universal meaninglessness is not only common among adolescents and young adults today, but has been always a characteristic of that stage of life, at least in literate cultures, as one may glean from *Al-munqidh min al-dalāl* (*The Deliverer from Error*), al-Ghazālī's medieval predecessor to *Surprised by Joy*.

Lewis's breach with Christianity was, by his own telling, the greatest but not the only disaster that befell him at Cherbourg. He became not only an apostate but a "fop, a cad, and a snob." The influence of a glamorous young master (Percy Gerald Kelsall Harris, nicknamed "Pogo") played a part; but Lewis, characteristically, later blamed not the master but the "withdrawal of myself from Divine protection." The Devil had his due, and Lewis felt, for the first time in his recorded memories, lust (for the school's dancing mistress) and surrendered to an unspecified "sexual temptation," probably masturbation. Yet this fall from innocence was counterweighed, in the balance of the soul, by the rediscovery of Joy. It came about in a schoolroom at Cherbourg, while leafing through a periodical: he came across the words *"Siegfried and the Twilight of the Gods"* and, beneath it, an Arthur Rackham illustration from the volume of that name. "Pure 'Northernness' engulfed me," and with it the memory, "almost like heartbreak," of Joy. It was a spiritual earthquake; he was a dying man brought back to life. Insatiable thirst for Wagner's music, for Wagnerian landscapes, for books about Norse mythology consumed him. Asgard, the Aesir, the Edda became his gods, with a quasi-religious adoration. His life split in two. On one track he studied, ate, enjoyed erotic fantasies and did what was expected of him; on the other, he sought for Joy. This was his "secret, imaginative" life; this was the life that won his heart, until he lost it to Christ. The quotidian and the joyous. These two lives, he wrote later, had "nothing to do with each other: oil and vinegar, a river running beside a canal, Jekyll and Hyde."

Cherbourg was followed by a year at Malvern College (Wyvern of *Surprised by Joy*), a school Lewis despised for its odious hierarchy of Masters, Bloods (the ruling class), Tarts (catamites for the ruling class), Punts (outsiders), and proletariat, and for the way in which the incessant demands of this system—which involved "fagging," that curious English custom, faintly echoed in American fraternity life, in which young boys must do the bidding, no matter how reckless, of elder pupils or suffer brutal retaliation—sapped his energies and will. He told his father that "all the prefects detest me and lose no opportunity of venting their spite. Today, for not being able to find a cap which one gentleman wanted, I have been sentenced to clean his boots every day after breakfast for a week . . . When I asked if I might clean them in the evening . . . I received a refusal, strengthened by being kicked downstairs." He had some insight, at least in retrospect, into what made him so unpopular a New Boy: "I was big for my age, a great lout of a boy . . . I was also useless at games. Worst of all, there was my face. I am the kind of person who gets told, 'And take that look off your face too.'"

After attending a House Supper with Jack at Malvern, Warnie's chief impression was his brother's "gloom and boredom." It was a great disappointment to Warnie, who loved Malvern and had left the school for a military career reluctantly, after an embarrassing incident in which he was caught smoking: "I had an idea that Malvern would weave its influence round Jacks as it did around me, and give him four happy years and memories and friendships which he would carry with him to the grave." On reading *Surprised by Joy*, Warnie could only say that "I find it very difficult to believe in the Malvern that he portrays. In July 1913 I had been on more or less close terms with all the brutes of prefects whom he describes, and I found them (with one exception) very pleasant fellows." To be just, there were happy times for Lewis at Malvern, too; but mostly he escaped into his intellect, looking down upon the vulgar Bloods with withering scorn (unspoken; he was a clever lad), and at the same time climbing the ladder of literature, savoring Horace, Virgil, and Euripides under the aegis of the sublimely courteous classics master Harry Wakelyn Smith ("Smugy," pronounced "Smewgy"), from whom he learned to study a poem with a scholar's accuracy and recite it with a lover's zeal. He cherished blissful interludes with Milton and Yeats in the sanctuary of the school library (where boys were "unfaggable"), discovered Celtic mythology, and wrote a tragedy, "Norse in subject and Greek in form," called *Loki Bound*, in which the title character, a stand-in for himself, opposes both Odin, creator of a meaningless world, and Thor, who rules, like the Bloods, through tradition and violence. "Why should creatures have the burden of existence forced on them without their consent?" Lewis/Loki demanded to know of God, while with adolescent indignation he shook his fist at God— for not existing.

Wynyard, Cherbourg, Malvern: three circles of Hell. Where next? The future must have looked black to Lewis, now fifteen, an age when life blackens for so many. Nightly toothaches and a daily grind of school work, arbitrary errands, and obligatory clubs had brought him to the end of his rope, "dog-tired, cab-horse tired, tired (almost) like a child in a factory." "Please take me out of this as soon as possible," he wrote to his father. He even threatened to shoot himself. Happily, this time his father listened. Instead of descending into the seventh circle of suicides or blasphemers, Lewis found himself rescued by two very different but complementary figures: his "First Friend" and his greatest teacher. It was the annus mirabilis of 1914—the liberation of Jack—even while the troubles were escalating in Ireland, and Britain was on the verge of its most horrific war.

The First Friend

The friend was Arthur Greeves (1895–1966), who lived just across the road from Little Lea. Arthur was the youngest of five children. His father, Joseph Malcomson Greeves, was the patriarch of one of the great linen industry families of Belfast. Quaker by birth, Joseph had joined the Plymouth Brethren and ruled his household with an iron hand. His Brooklyn-born wife, Mary, was, at least in the opinion of the Lewis brothers, a silly goose who doted on her youngest; after an early misdiagnosis of heart trouble, Arthur lived as a semi-invalid, cosseted by the mother and preached at by the father.

The Greeves and Lewis families met often, and Arthur made several overtures of friendship to Lewis and Warnie. Each time, he had been rebuffed. But now, at the end of the Easter holidays leading up to his last term at Malvern, upon learning that Arthur was ill and requesting a visit, Lewis decided to stop by. The patient was propped up in bed, with a copy of *Myths of the Norsemen* nearby. A letter of introduction from Siegfried himself couldn't have been more effective. Instantly, lifelong friendship blossomed, as the two boys discovered that each loved Norse myth ("'Do *you* like that?' said I. 'Do *you* like that?' said he") and, yet more important, that each had encountered in it the same haunting, bittersweet frisson of Joy. Lewis, spreading his thanks over years, made Greeves the recipient of his first splendid cascade of letter writing: a letter a week for years, each epistle abloom with ideas, abristle with opinions, alight with portraits of people, places, and things that caught his eye.

Until Albert died, the friendship resided as much in letters as in visits. When Lewis was at home, he felt obliged to spend time with his father rather than indulge his preference to be with Arthur at Bernagh (the Greeveses' home) or Glenmachan (his cousins' home), and he could not think of inviting Arthur to Little Lea: "You know how I would love if I could have you any time I liked up in my little room with the gramophone and a fire of our own, to be merry and foolish to our hearts content: or even if I could always readily accept your invitations without feeling a rotter for leaving him alone." Despite this impediment, merriment spiced with foolishness flourished, as the pals planned an operatic treatment of *Loki Bound*—Arthur, who was a painter, pianist, and composer, was to supply the music and illustrations, Lewis the plot and text—and though it never came to fruition, that did nothing to mute the delicious sense of conspiracy: "neither of us had any other outlet: we still thought that we were the only two people in the world who were interested in the right kind of things in the right kind of way." Arthur was a willing confidant who could be counted on to keep his friend's secrets. Hence it is from the letters that Lewis wrote to Arthur (Arthur's letters to Lewis are not extant) that we learn of Lewis's infatuation with a Belgian refugee girl (there is some evidence that Lewis may have made this up, perhaps to impress Arthur), his first experience of getting drunk ("The story that you have a headache after being drunk is apparently quite a lie <(like the other one about going mad from THAT)>"), and his opinions on such subjects as the difference between love and friendship and the mysteries of "Terreauty" (terror and beauty combined), expressed with unstudied and unabashed immediacy.

Arthur was both inspirer and sounding board, Lewis's vast future readership in miniature, and a model for his conception of the ideal reader.

That Arthur could be dull and lacking in original ideas meant nothing; he knew Joy, and he kept intact the love of "homely" things and the spirit of humility. On their rare walks together during the holidays, Lewis began to see things about the world around him that he had never noticed or valued before: not just the wild and distant sublime, but the small, local, and humdrum could delight. What was wonderful was the contrast; to look out at the landscapes of County Down, as Lewis now learned to do, was, in effect, as he later wrote, to see "Niflheim and Asgard, Britain and Logres, Handramit and Harandra, air and ether, the low world and the high." Under Arthur's influence even the factories and trams and shipyards of Belfast, even the "crowing cocks and gaggling ducks," the "barefoot old women, the drunken men stumbling in and out of the 'spirit grocers'" became lovable and claimed attention. "I learned charity from him and failed, for all my efforts, to teach him arrogance in return."

Arthur was homosexual, though his sexual life, at least at this stage, was probably limited to onanistic fantasy: "My dear Galahad," Lewis addressed him in tribute to his purity; otherwise, "Cher Ami," "My dear Arthur," "Dear little Archie," "*mon vieux*." A few writers speculate that the intimacy of the friendship points to a homosexual inclination in Lewis as well, however successful he may have been at hiding this fact from himself. But this is doubtful; even if one does not accept that Lewis had a years-long affair with Mrs. Moore (see chapter 4) or take seriously the ardor of his middle-age marriage, he was unmistakably heterosexual, with a penchant for sadism, in the fantasies he revealed to Arthur.

Yet in all these confiding letters, the greatest passion was reserved for the world of art, for literary battles fought and literary enthusiasms shared. They compared notes about the delights of book shopping ("Do you ever wake up in the morning and suddenly wonder why you have not bought such-and-such a book long ago, and then decided that life without it will be quite unbearable? I do frequently: the last attack was this morning à propos of Malory's 'Morte D'Arthur' . . ."), the bindings of books ("With the Chaucer I am most awfully bucked: it is in the very best Everyman style—lovely paper, strong boards, and—aren't you envious—not one but two bits of tissue paper"), and the latest recordings ("I feel my fame as a 'Man-about-the-Gramaphone' greatly put out by

your remarks à propos of Lohengrin Prelude Act III, as, I must confess, I
never heard of it on Columbia"). Arthur sometimes complained that their
talk was too much of books and music, not enough of inner struggles;
but Lewis made light of Arthur's sentimentality, arguing that "feelings
ought to be kept for literature and art, where they are delightful and not
intruded into life where they are merely a nuiscance." He conceded (half-
mockingly), however, that it was Arthur who stood, in this case, for the
deeper truths of the heart: "I am a coarse-grained creature who never could
follow the feelings of refined—might I say super-refined?—natures like my
Galahad's."

Though they did not share the same sexual orientation ("<You are interested in a brand of *That* which doesn't appeal to me, and I in one that
doesn't appeal to you>"), there does seem to be something akin to the
first blush of love in this first friendship, exclusive as it was and seasoned
with occasional quarrels. Moreover, they shared a common history of a
psychosexual development complicated by early experiences: Lewis had
internalized as eros the boarding school culture of flogging and fagging,
while his housebound friend Arthur was the stereotyped picture of the
mother-engulfed homosexual youth. Lewis saw these patterns and began
to worry about them; as their correspondence progressed, while he encouraged Arthur to be true to his real inclinations, he begged for restraint: "Let us talk of these things when we want, but always keep
them on the side that tends to beauty, and avoid everything that tends to
sordid-ness <and beastly police court sort of scandal out of grim real life
(like the O. Wilde story).> Cher ami, please, please don't think this is
preaching . . ." For the rest of his life, Lewis would adopt a nonjudgmen-
tal attitude: same-sex attraction wasn't something he struggled with;
better to direct his moralizing to the host of temptations that did assail
him, most of which were exaggerated forms of his characteristic virtues.
The cruelty and sycophancy he witnessed at Malvern were far more soul-
destroying, he felt, than the pederasty which "however great an evil in
itself, was, in that time and place, the only foothold or cranny left for
certain good things . . . the only chink left through which something
spontaneous and uncalculating could creep in." He saw more moral danger
for himself in the thirst to be part of the "inner ring" of the elite and in
the intellectual arrogance with which he compensated himself for daily
humiliations, than in any of the carnal temptations.

A Purely Logical Entity

Not long after Lewis encountered his First Friend, he met his master teacher: William Thompson Kirkpatrick (1848–1921), a.k.a. "Kirk," a.k.a. "The Great Knock." Kirkpatrick has risen to the status of an archetypal hero among Lewisians, who know him both as Lewis's tutor and, fictionalized, as the skeptical MacPhee (or McPhee) in *Perelandra, That Hideous Strength,* and *The Dark Tower,* and as Professor Kirke of the Narnian Chronicles. Kirkpatrick was an Ulster Scot, originally from Boardmills, County Down, who grew up in Belfast, attended Queen's College, and achieved a licentiate in theology in preparation for the Presbyterian ministry, but did not pursue ordination, instead directing his course toward education and working his way to the position of headmaster at Lurgan College, the public grammar school attended by Albert Lewis. A revered mentor to many (including Albert) at Lurgan, Kirkpatrick stayed in touch with his former pupil and occasionally retained his services as solicitor.

By 1914, Kirkpatrick was living, semiretired, with his wife in Great Bookham, Surrey. He had recently helped Warnie surmount an undistinguished academic record to achieve a prize cadetship at the Royal Military Academy at Sandhurst. Now it was time for Lewis to come under his wing, as a way of delivering him from Malvern. Even Albert, slow to grasp the facts about his children, though genuinely moved when their miseries came to his attention, acknowledged to Warnie that Lewis was "simply out of his proper environment, and would possibly wither and decay rather than grow if kept in such surroundings." Why not send him to Kirkpatrick, Warnie proposed, adding rather acridly that "there would be no one there except Mr and Mrs K for him to talk to, and he could amuse himself by detonating his little stock of cheap intellectual fireworks under old K's nose." After some dithering and negotiating, the question was settled, and Kirkpatrick agreed to take on Lewis come September.

On June 7, 1914, Lewis was freed, under gas, from the two "hopelessly rotten" teeth that had tormented him all year. By August he was set free from Malvern, too, and on a memorable Saturday, September 19, he was on the train to Great Bookham anticipating, based on wholly misleading reports from his father, a cataract of sentimentality from the famous teacher. When the train pulled into the station, Lewis found himself before a tall, lean, muscular man with graying mustache and side whiskers, dressed like a laborer; a man whose body, as it proved, reflected his mind. Lewis essayed some small talk, to the effect that the local scenery was wilder than he had anticipated. "Stop!" said Kirkpatrick. "What do you mean by wildness and what grounds had you for not expecting it?" This peremptory challenge set the tone for an intellectual apprenticeship, in which Lewis learned how to think in the same rigorously logical, combative mode, demanding precedent, statistical or experiential evidence, a "ruthless dialectic" leading to the final verdict, "Do you not see, then, that you had no right to have any opinion whatever on the subject?" Lewis adored this style and made it his own; when, later, some of his tutees accused him of intellectual bullying, it was this take-no-prisoners rational assault that they had in mind. It slaked one half of his mind's thirst for meaning, as Joy filled the other half.

Kirkpatrick proved an exemplary instructor. Following a rigorous daily program, he instilled in his pupil the fugal glories of high dialectic while unveiling to him the literary splendors of Homer, Euripides, Sophocles, Aeschylus (until Lewis found himself thinking in Greek, "the great Rubicon" of language learning, as he puts it); of Lucretius, Catullus, Tacitus, Herodotus; and of the divine Dante. Lewis added to this his own enthusiasms, soaking up Milton, Malory, Sidney, and William Morris. This was the life of the mind, perfected in the English countryside. These were the best years of Lewis's life, when "I suppose I reached as much happiness as is ever to be reached on earth."

All this glory Lewis laid at Kirkpatrick's feet. And what a character he describes for us in his autobiography! His teacher's nickname, the Great Knock, refers presumably to his debating style or to his ability to knock nonsense out of and sound thinking into his pupil. It might also describe his approach to the cosmos at large: he battered it down, hammering away at irrational beliefs and sentimental fancies, turning, in the course of his adult life, from a ministerial candidate into a fierce atheist, a devotee of Schopenhauer and *The Golden Bough*. Although he had renounced religion, his regular habits, such as wearing his Sabbath best when he gardened on Sundays, suggested a Puritan scrupulosity, and his skepticism and logical rigor savored of a Puritan's zeal for testing the spirits to see whether they are of God. "If ever a man came near to being a purely logical entity," Lewis wrote, "that man was Kirk." The phrase gives one pause. "A purely logical entity" is, of course, a fiction—a character in fiction, like MacPhee in *That Hideous Strength*, declaiming, "I have repeatedly explained to you the distinction between a personal feeling of confidence and a logical satisfaction of the claims of evidence."

There is, unfortunately, little independent corroboration of Lewis's portrait in *Surprised by Joy* of the Great Knock. One pupil, who remembered Kirkpatrick as a young man in his twenties, when he was teaching at the Royal Belfast Academical Institution, describes him as "a man of unusual mental power and grasp, of an overmastering influence on the mind, and of an intellectual honesty and vigour before which pretence and make-believe were dissipated like smoke before a strong wind." The same source adds that "he became an almost incomparable teacher, and under him the boys swept on to victory over their work and to mastery of their subjects and of themselves. His pistol never missed fire; but he gave you the impression that, if it did, as Goldsmith said of Johnson, you would be knocked down by the butt-end." This hints at Kirkpatrick /MacPhee, but it is a thin charcoal sketch, while Lewis offers us a portrait soaked in color and animated by his own inner life. For Lewis, Kirkpatrick personified noble, sane, cultured, manly, skeptical, liberating Reason. When Kirkpatrick died in March 1921, Lewis fancied him accosting God with Voltairean irony: *"Je soupçonne entre nous que vous n'existez pas."*

Eager to occupy the same higher plane as his great teacher and reveling in the *otium liberale* that prevailed at Gastons, the Kirkpatrick home, Lewis hoped he could avoid having to return to Belfast for his confirmation in December 1914. As he put it to Arthur, "firstly, I am very happy at Bookham, and secondly, a week at home, if it is to be spent in pulling long faces in Church & getting confirmed, is no great pleasure—a statement, I need hardly say, for yourself alone." To his father he sent an officious letter pointing out the inconvenience and cost: "It seems a great pity this confirmation should occur when it does, thus cutting out a week of valuable time. Although fully sensible that it is of course of more importance than the work, yet if it could possibly be managed at some more convenient date in the near future, I should think it an advantage." It was a craven exercise, he felt, looking back on it later. He went through with the confirmation, already an unbeliever but unwilling to court interminable wrangling with his father by pressing the point.

By the time he was ready to leave his tutor's home, Lewis was at once a poet—creator of vaguely spiritual, excruciatingly earnest lyric poems about dream gardens and mist-clad peaks, mostly written during the holidays—and a philosopher, eager to display his newly won freedom from what he considered Christian dogma and cant:

> You ask me my religious views: you know, I think, that I beleive [*sic*] in no religion. There is absolutely no proof for any of them, and from a philosophical standpoint Christianity is not even the best. All religions, that is, all mythologies to give them their proper name are merely man's own invention—Christ as much as Loki. Primitive man found himself surrounded by all sorts of terrible things he didn't understand—thunder, pestilence, snakes etc.: what more natural than to suppose that these were animated by evil spirits trying to torture him. These he kept off by cringing to them, singing songs and making sacrifices etc. Gradually from being mere nature-spirits these supposed being[s] were elevated into more elaborate ideas, such as the old gods: and when man became more refined he pretended that these spirits were good as well as powerful.

Armed with his new skills in debating and analyzing, and immunized from what he now deemed a childish, secondhand credulity, Lewis moved on from the Stoic Porch that was Great Bookham and headed for Oxford. There he would meet his future, and the war, and Owen Barfield, his Second Friend.

3

ADVENT LYRICS

Tolkien entered Oxford University in October 1911, arriving by automobile with another King Edward's student, L. K. Sands, who would be cut down four years later by a German machine gun on the Western Front. On this particularly hot autumn day, however, Archduke Franz Ferdinand was still romancing his Duchess Sophie at the Austrian court, and the future, with its promise of great trials and greater triumphs, beckoned fairly to a young man about to enter the most celebrated university in the world.

Oxford University had been in existence for more than seven centuries. In the year that Tolkien became a resident, it was as breathtakingly beautiful as it is today, medieval and neomedieval structures piercing the sky like lances declaring the triumph of the mind, a bastion of elitism, the nation's intellectual epicenter. Tolkien enrolled at Exeter, one of the oldest colleges (founded in 1314), famed for its cozy common rooms and its Pre-Raphaelite alumni, including Edward Burne-Jones (also a King Edward's alumnus) and William Morris, whose tapestries, murals, paintings, and tales of other worlds would influence Tolkien's own productions. His rooms looked over Turl Street, an ancient shunt between the main arteries of Broad Street and the High Street; Exeter shares this passage with two other colleges, Jesus and Lincoln, leading to the following jest, which reflects the lighthearted spirit and burgeoning religious skepticism of this prewar era: "In what way is the Church of England like the Turl? It runs from the High to the Broad and goes straight past Jesus."

Tolkien never passed by Jesus, but during his first year at Oxford, he seemed to have difficulty choosing between high-minded studies and broad-minded antics, and he came dangerously close to fulfilling the popular image of the brilliant, languid, unfocused undergraduate. He joined every undergraduate circle that caught his eye, signing up for the Stapledon Debating Society, the Dialectical Society, the Essay Club, and others. The King Edward's School *Chronicle* reported that "Tolkien, if we are to be guided by the countless notices on his mantelpiece, has joined all the Exeter Societies which are in existence." He also established two clubs of his own, first the Apolausticks (Aristotle's term in the *Nicomachean Ethics* for vulgar masses who devote their lives to pleasure), then the Chequers Clubbe, both specializing in whimsical lectures and elaborate dinners. In addition, he took to collecting Japanese furniture and wearing expensive clothes, making liberal use of his allowance from Father Francis. He had many friends, but few close ones apart from Colin Cullis, a handsome boy who would die a few years later in the great flu epidemic.

Amid all these diversions, Tolkien's studies suffered. His chosen field was classics, in which he read widely but spottily, and in 1913 he made a poor showing in Honour Moderations, the first exam hurdle for those who specialized in "Greats" or Literae Humaniores, the study of Greek and Latin classics in the original tongues along with allied subjects. This draconian rite of passage consisted of twelve written exams, each three hours long, spread over a week; students were required to translate Homer and Virgil, explain the principles of Greek and Latin grammar and composition, and display a knowledge of antiquities. Tolkien earned a second-class degree, not a dreadful showing but poor for a student of limited means eager to justify his scholarship. Bacchus had taken his toll.

Hail, Éarendel!

Humphrey Carpenter suggests that after the death of his mother, Tolkien became "two people": one "cheerful, almost irrepressible," the other "capable of bouts of profound despair." With this in mind, Tolkien's undergraduate taste for glittering dinner parties and dandyish dress may be read as the behavior of an ebullient boy chasing every passing fancy—or that of a wounded boy running as fast as he could from the abyss of loss opened by his mother's death. It may be, however, that he was simply biding his time, feeling his way, giving everything a try, uncertain where to pour his energies. All changed in November or December 1911—the same late autumn in which Lewis encountered Balder and Northernness— when he made two discoveries, one in his studies, one in his art, that set his course for years to come.

On November 25, 1911, he checked out, from the Exeter Reading Room, C.N.E. Eliot's *A Finnish Grammar*. This small maroon volume became for Tolkien the gateway to a new and magical world. Part of its attraction, to a dreamy undergraduate surfeited with the exactitude of Greek and Latin declensions and conjugations, may have been the in- definiteness of the language it presented. Eliot contends in his preface that "the Finnish language is still in so unsettled and fluid a condition, as regards both forms and style, that it is often hard to say what is correct and what not," a description that must have appealed to Tolkien's sense of whimsy, just as Finnish's many difficulties (according to Eliot, it "de- serves its undesirable reputation of being the most difficult language spo- ken in Europe, except perhaps Basque") must have appealed to his sense of challenge. To W. H. Auden, forty-four years later, Tolkien likened his encounter with Finnish to the discovery of a wine cellar stocked with an exquisite new vintage that "quite intoxicated me." In this state of philo- logical inebriation, he began to flesh out his own invented languages with Finnish elements, leading in time to the formulation of Qenya (later "Quenya"), the most exalted of his Elvish tongues and a catalyst for his mythological inventions.

In or around the same *mensis mirabilis*, Tolkien found a second wine cellar stocked with unsuspected, heady possibilities—in this instance not those of words but of pencil, ink, and watercolor. Since learning to draw under his mother's direction, his subjects had been mostly landscapes and seascapes, many sketched or painted while on vacation in Lyme Regis or Whitby, displaying a good if stiff sense of design (his drawings never en- tirely escaped this architectural rigidity, reminiscent of the formal symme- tries of Art Nouveau; traces exist even in his best paintings of Middle-earth). In December 1911, however, he broke lose from naturalism, beginning a series of abstract or "visionary" sketches. Wayne G. Hammond and Chris- tina Scull, preeminent Tolkienists who have written about Tolkien's art with great sensitivity, frequently use the latter term. Tolkien, however, was a visionary only in a very restricted sense. With one or two exceptions, most notably his 1944 vision of God's light in Sts. Gregory & Augustine Church (see chapter 12), he did not enjoy—or suffer from—waking visions, unlike many famous Christian mystics and that earlier English mythologist, writer, and watercolorist, William Blake. Tolkien's "visions" usually arrived in dreams, notably the recurring image of a towering wave that threatened to engulf him, from which he would awaken "gasping out of deep water," and which he translated into fiction in the Atlantis-like drowning of the island of Númenor. Other visions came to him in the same way that melody comes to a composer or metaphor to a poet, as the fruit of that mysterious artistic process we call, obscurely, inspiration.

Tolkien's new art shared with dream imagery a remoteness from the scenes of ordinary life. Many of his pictures depict no scenery at all. They bear sometimes playful abstract titles like *Before*, *Afterwards*, *Thought*, *Grownupishness*, and *Undertenishness*, the suffixes of the last two titles lending their name to the entire group, which Tolkien called "Ishnesses." In these images, one spies hints of the great creations to come. *Wickedness*, drawn in black and red pencil, suggests Melkor (later Morgoth, the prince of evil in Tolkien's mythology), with its skull surmounted by innumerable eyes behind a cauldron spewing flames. *Before*, too, has the cyclopean architecture and flaming braziers of a primordial temple dedicated to death. *End of the World* is, by contrast, whimsical, with an impossibly long-legged man striding off a cliff into a swirl of sea beneath a starry sky topped by a looming sun. *Thought* discloses a third mood, neither nightmarish nor comical but monumental, with a robed figure seated outdoors on a chair or throne, head lowered, deep in meditation. Light, emanating from the head, fans across the sky. This drawing resembles Blake's depictions of Los, archetypal poet and prophet, embodiment of the imagination—an appropriate antecedent image for a young man on the verge of unleashing his own creative daemon. One senses, in these early pictures, no organized artistic or intellectual program, no deliberate project to explore the possibilities of abstraction, simply a young mind expanding beyond the confines of realism, energetically sending out root and branch into black soil and bright sunlight.

Tolkien needed to make the same bold leap in his academic studies. Learning new languages and cultivating his own invented ones brought frissons of joy but failed to assuage his disappointed tutors or his own conviction that he could (and must) do better. Flubbing the Honour Mods had been a severe blow; the saving grace was the splendid "pure alpha" that he had earned for his exam in comparative philology. With this in hand, he successfully petitioned, with the support of his tutors and the classicist Lewis Richard Farnell, rector of Exeter, to switch into the English Honours School, with a concentration in language.

It was a brilliant move, flinging open the gates to his scholarly career. Now he could study Old English, Middle English, and Old Norse "lang. and lit." along with the more standard fare of Chaucer and Shakespeare. He came under the influence of Rhodes Scholar Kenneth Sisam, a New Zealander who would become his tutor in Old and Middle English. Sisam was not an easygoing man, and Tolkien and he would butt heads on many occasions in subsequent decades, competing in 1925 for the Professorship in Anglo-Saxon and disputing in the 1960s over aspects of the Beowulf epic. But Sisam was a splendid scholar and Tolkien, as an undergraduate, benefited greatly from his ideas.

In the spring of 1914, Tolkien won Exeter College's Skeat Prize for excellence in English. He spent the five-pound prize on a Welsh grammar and three books by William Morris: a translation of the Völsunga saga and two narrative poems, *The Life and Death of Jason* and *The House of the Wolfings*. Purchasing the Morris volumes proved to be another watershed, profoundly affecting Tolkien's understanding of what literature could do. Most likely, he had been aware of Morris while still at King Edward's School, where in 1909 the Literary Society sponsored a talk on his work, or perhaps even earlier, for Morris's Arts and Crafts movement and its neomedieval sensibility were much discussed in late Victorian and early Edwardian society and it is likely that both Tolkien and Edith, with their shared interest in calligraphy and other decorative arts, came under its spell. In Oxford, at any event, the great Pre-Raphaelite's presence was unavoidable. Along with Burne-Jones and Dante Gabriel Rossetti, Morris had painted the tempera murals, now fading like old ghosts, that adorn the Oxford Union library, and his magnificent tapestry, the *Adoration of the Magi*, with its Catholic theme, elflike angel, and haunting forest backdrop, hung in the chapel of Exeter College.

Tolkien was thrilled by his purchases, in particular by *The House of the Wolfings*, with its blend of prose and poetry recounting an epic war between Goths (a Germanic people) and Romans. From it he drew nomenclature that will be familiar to his readers—in Morris's tale, the Goths inhabit the Mark, in Mirkwood—and, more significantly, the over-arching structure of a bitter clash between a bucolic, peaceful people and an imperialist military power, which would become the framework for *The Lord of the Rings*. Catholicism had already nudged him toward a be-lief in lost Edens and an associated love of nature as the imperfect mirror of God; Sarehole had given him faith in the moral integrity of simple agrarian folk. Morris now taught him how these values could be expressed in hauntingly beautiful, elaborately constructed fantasy fiction. Unfortu-nately, Morris also taught Tolkien a deliberately archaic style, filled with inverted syntax and outmoded expressions. This "heigh stile" (the expres-sion comes from Chaucer) permeates both *The House of the Wolfings* and, to the chagrin of many of Tolkien's readers, large portions of *The Silmarillion* and more than a few passages in *The Lord of the Rings* ("Name him not!" says Gandalf, describing his battle with the Balrog in *The Lord of the Rings*; "Long time I fell . . . Thither I came at last, to the uttermost foundations of stone . . . Ever he clutched me, and ever I hewed him . . ."). Tolkien considered the neomedieval affectations of "heigh stile" essential to the atmosphere of ancient myth and legend he wished to convey. Many critics disagree, but it is worth noting that C. S. Lewis defended Morris's archaisms, calling this approach "incomparably easier and clearer than any 'natural' style could be." This defense appears in his 1939 essay collection, *Rehabilitations*; as the title suggests, Morris's repu-tation was sinking at the time. But then, Lewis always enjoyed a good fight against received opinions.

Tolkien's ability to absorb Morris's experiments in decorative arts proved far more successful. Many of Tolkien's sketches, especially those that Hammond and Scull term "patterns and devices"—doodles and designs on letters, envelopes, napkins, newspapers, and the borders of paintings—show the influence of the Pre-Raphaelite's exuberant orna-mentation, and Tolkien's 1960 drawing of a Númenorean carpet, with red, yellow, and blue geometric symmetries, could pass for a Morris tapestry seen through a kaleidoscope.

Tolkien immediately set to work applying the lessons he had learned at Morris's feet. In a letter to Edith in late 1914, he announced, while speaking of the tales in the Finnish epic the *Kalevala*, that "I am trying to turn one of the stories—which is really a very great story and most tragic—into a short story somewhat on the lines of Morris' romances with chunks of poetry in between." His interest was not idle, but an attempt to supply a sorely felt need: to restore to England some remnant of its scattered and ruined mythological tradition. To a meeting of Corpus Christi College's Sundial Society on November 22, 1914, he declared his admiration for "that very primitive undergrowth that the literature of Europe has on the whole been steadily cutting and reducing for many centuries," and added, "I would that we had more of it left." Many years later, he would tell Auden that his legendarium (as he liked to call it, borrowing a Latinism found in medieval collections of saints' lives) began in "an attempt to reorganize some of the Kalevala, especially the tale of Kullervo the hapless, into a form of my own." Kullervo's story, a seething stew of mass murder, revenge, involuntary servitude, incestuous seduction, and talking swords, eventually would become the tale of Túrin Turambar, a key part of the *Silmarillion* mythos.

The retelling of the Kullervo tale began in October 1914. Just a few weeks before, Tolkien had had another literary epiphany with an even more momentous result. In late September, he, Hilary, and their aunt Jane had visited a farm owned by family friends in Gedling, Nottinghamshire. While there he had made a pencil-and-ink sketch of the slate-roofed, three-story farmhouse. It is a lovely but unremarkable building, yet it looms large in Tolkien's life, for within it he wrote the first lines of what would become the seed of his mythology of Middle-earth; it was here, in a register yet dimly understood, that his imaginary cosmos first found voice. Tolkien had been reading—without much interest—the Anglo-Saxon poem *Crist* (formerly attributed to the poet Cynewulf) from the tenth-century Exeter Book, when his attention was caught by the following line, which evoked in him "a curious thrill, as if something had stirred in me, half wakened from sleep":

éala éarendel, engla beorhtast,
ofer middangeard monnum sended

Hail Éarendel, brightest of angels
Sent unto men upon Middle-earth

The poem itself is based upon the fifth of the Latin "O" Antiphons sung at Vespers during the season of Advent, and familiar to modern church-goers from John Mason Neale's nineteenth-century rendition in "O Come, O Come Emmanuel." But who is *Éarendel*? This mysterious Old English word looks like a proper name; Albert Cook, in his 1900 edition of *Crist*, which Tolkien would have known, translates it as "rising sun," which would seem to point to Christ. Yet in the tenth-century Blickling Homilies, as Tolkien would note later, *eorendel* (as it is spelled there) refers to John the Baptist in his role as herald of Christ, the rising sun. The image has bibli-cal roots (Luke 1:68–79); John the Baptist is "brightest of angels" by virtue of being the messenger (in Greek, *angelos*) of Christ, and he is the morning star—namely, Venus—by virtue of being forerunner of the dawn. Tolkien thought he could see, in these associations, the baptized version of an astral myth.

With hints like these in the back of his mind—though without con-scious Christian intent, since it was mainly the sound of the words that enchanted him—Tolkien composed a poem, "The Voyage of Éarendel the Evening Star," in which Éarendel steers his ship of burning light across the sky in pursuit of the sun, in endless round, until cold and age end his quest. The poem's creation seems to have been a matter of seren-dipity, or inspiration, without much conscious design on Tolkien's part, for when his TCBS pal G. B. Smith asked him what the poem meant, he confessed that he didn't know but intended to find out. It took him decades to do so. Eventually "The Voyage of Éarendel the Evening Star," the spear-head of the entire legendarium, became part of *The Silmarillion*, telling of Eärendil the Mariner, half Elf, half human, who pleads with the Valar—Tolkien's immortal godlike beings—to show mercy upon both Elves and Men, and who rides his ship Vingilot through the sky, bringing hope to all of Middle-earth. Eärendil is, as the pioneering Tolkien au-thority and Old English scholar Tom Shippey points out, "not a Re-deemer, but an Intercessor," thus akin to a third New Testament figure, Mary, to whom Tolkien had throughout his life a fierce devotion. The keen-eyed reader will also note, in the original lines from *Crist* that gave rise to Tolkien's poem, the word *middangeard*, cognate with the Old

Norse *Miðgarðr* (Midgard), the middle "yard" where humans dwell, linked by its similar sound to the Old English *eorðe*, "earth": hence Middle-earth, which Tolkien would adopt for his mythology.

La Vita Nuova

During these years of discovery, Tolkien's love life blossomed apace. Edith was now openly his fiancée. At the stroke of midnight on his twenty-first birthday, January 3, 1913, the ban put in place by Father Francis officially ended, and immediately Tolkien wrote to Edith, still living in Cheltenham with family friends, to proclaim his undiminished, undying love. He emerges here as a young man in command, with the integrity to wait until the midnight hour and the alacrity to wait not one second more before reclaiming his heart's desire. When Edith replied with the potentially stupefying news that during Tolkien's enforced silence she had become engaged to someone else, he rushed to Cheltenham and won her back. He then demanded—further evidence of his newfound imperiousness—that Edith convert to Catholicism. This was not strictly necessary, according to canon law, but the Church (and Tolkien) preferred an all-Catholic wedding, and it ensured that the couple's children would be raised in the fold. Edith agreed. At the time, she was a practicing Anglican, faithful but without fervor; according to at least one family friend, she agreed to switch altars largely in order to marry the man she loved.

While wooing and winning Edith, Tolkien also cultivated his relationship with the members of the TCBS. He stayed in close touch with Wiseman and Gilson, both at Cambridge, and became fast friends with G. B. Smith, who entered Oxford in 1913. Tolkien and Wiseman corresponded regularly, often discussing religion, which Tolkien affirmed as "the moving force and at the same time the foundation of both of us." The TCBS fellowship culminated in the "Council of London," held on December 13–14, 1914, at Wiseman's family home, where the four friends, gathered around a gas fire, smoked pipes and hashed out their philosophies of life. Gilson later wrote of the "bliss" of this gathering, declaring that "I *never* spent happier hours."

They were productive hours, too, for at this and later meetings the TCBS proclaimed themselves a force against corruption and a bastion of goodness, especially in the realm of art. The group's aim, wrote Smith, was "to drive from life, letters, the stage and society that dabbling in and hankering after the unpleasant sides and incidents in life and nature which have captured the larger and worser tastes in Oxford, London and the world" and "to reestablish sanity, cleanliness, and the love of real and true beauty in everybody's breast." Despite its artlessness and prissiness, this declaration seems, in its moral and aesthetic program, an authentic forerunner of the Inklings. Tolkien shared in the general excitement, declaring a few years later, after learning of Gilson's death in battle, that the TCBS "had been granted some spark of fire . . . that was destined to kindle a new light, or what is the same thing, rekindle an old light in the world." It was not to be; he was, half-knowingly, describing what soon would become a solo mission.

Meanwhile, he plunged into the TCBS program with gusto, expanding the legend of Éarendel, deepening his knowledge of Qenya by preparing a lexicon, the *Qenyaqetsa*, and producing *The Land of Pohja*, a painting, based on a tale from the *Kalevala*, that in its intricately repeating borders and elongated trees, its tints of purple, blue, and yellow, and its atmosphere of otherworldly mystery and magic, powerfully foreshadows his mature canvases. Soon the creative flow became a flood: paintings such as *Water, Wind, and Sand*; *Tanaqui*; and *The Shores of Faery*; poems, including "Kor: In a City Lost and Dead" and "The Shores of Faery," in which appear some of the names and places that would later fill *The Silmarillion*. One poem, "Goblin Feet," appeared in *Oxford Poetry 1915*. It was his first published piece of writing. The editor was his friend T. W. Earp, whose name may have been the origin of "twerp"— coining words from names was an Oxford passion at the time, but the attribution remains uncertain. A poem by G. B. Smith also made it into the volume, along with work by Aldous Huxley (writing as A. L. Huxley) and Dorothy L. Sayers, whose poem "Lay" is distinctly better than Tolkien's. This is the first time Sayers's path crossed that of the Inklings; it would not be the last. Tolkien's contribution, drenched in Victorian fairy lore, describes a walk along a fairy path, lit by fairy lanterns, to the tune of fairy horns and the hum of fairy wings, rising to a crescendo of fairy-instilled ecstasy. That Tolkien calls the fairies in his poem goblins, leprechauns, and gnomes does nothing to disguise their conventional character, first cousin to the precious flower-fairies of Victorian lore. Later he would abandon this view of fairy folk—epitomized forever in the fraudulent 1917–1920 Cottingley photographs of tiny winged nymphettes prancing in the fields that caused a sensation in post–World War I England—for his far more formidable Elves, Goblins, and Orcs.

In June 1915, Tolkien took the examination for the Honours School in English Language and Literature. He earned a First, vindicating his move into the study of philology and Anglo-Saxon. Academic triumph, poems, paintings, first forays into private mythology, discovery of Finnish, heightened cultivation of his own imagined tongues—all came at breakneck speed. Everyone around him shared the same sense of urgency; the world was falling to pieces, and time was running out. War had erupted in 1914 and Oxford was now chockablock with soldiers. Tolkien, who as an undergraduate received military training in the King Edward's Horse, a cavalry regiment (and earlier as a schoolboy in the King Edward's School Cadet Corps), knew that sooner or later he would find himself on the front, where rumor placed the life expectancy of newly arrived soldiers at less than two weeks. Unlike many of his friends, he did not break off his studies to enlist, for he dreaded the dreariness and brutality of military life. But with examinations over, he applied to join the Lancashire Fusiliers, passed his physical, and received a commission as a temporary second lieutenant. He learned to signal in code, utilizing devices ranging from heliographs to carrier pigeons, an appropriate military role for a man more suited to language invention than the dispatching of enemy combatants. Even this congenial activity didn't reconcile him to army life, however, and he lamented "those grey days wasted in wearily going over, over and over again, the dreary topics, the dull backwaters of the art of killing." In March 1916, he graduated from Oxford—the ceremony had been delayed due to the war—and on March 22, he and Edith married at St. Mary Immaculate in Warwick, spending part of their honeymoon rehearsing versions of her new married name: "Edith Mary Tolkien, Mrs. Tolkien, Edith Tolkien, E.T., Mrs. J.R.R. Tolkien." Even in the midst of training for battle, he had writing and painting on his mind, and he submitted a sheaf of poems, *The Trumpets of Faërie*, to the publishing firm of Sidgwick & Jackson. The manuscript was rejected on March 31. It appeared that his fate—or doom—was closing in. On June 6, he sailed to Calais and joined the British Expeditionary Force in France. A poem he composed about this time is entitled "The Lonely

Isle" and dedicated "For England." The last words, "O lonely, sparkling isle, farewell!" constitute Tolkien's wistful adieu to his adopted land, his new wife, and perhaps his life.

Tolkien at War

Tolkien's stay in France lasted five months. His experience differed little from that of other soldiers in what Robert Graves called the "soul-deadening" trenches: a nauseating diet of mud, cold, rain, lice, fleas, spoiled food, collapsing walls, soaked clothes, festering wounds, rotting corpses, packs of rats who fed on the corpses and grew large as cats, and now and then a dollop of fear or dash of pure terror. The trenches themselves were like elongated graves, ditches deep enough to hide a body, alive or dead, long and narrow, zigzagging to confound enemy shells. Paul Fussell estimates that the two opposing sides dug twenty thousand miles of trenches, nearly enough to circle the globe. "Theoretically," he writes, "it would have been possible to walk from Belgium to Switzerland entirely below ground."

Tolkien arrived at the front less than four weeks before the beginning of the Battle of the Somme, an Allied offensive designed to repel German troops along the Somme River in northern France. It turned into the bloodiest conflict of the war, a prolonged tug-of-war in which clashing armies moved millimeters on the map over the course of months. The first day of the clash, July 1, 1916, was a debacle for Allied troops. Fussell calls the outcome "one of the most interesting in the whole long history of human disillusion." Wave upon wave of British soldiers rose from the trenches to be mowed down by German machine gun fire, like hay before the scythe, with shouts and screams in the air, blood on the ground, hope evaporating in the heart. Henry Williamson, author of *Tarka the Otter*, was there:

> I see men arising and walking forward; and I go forward with them, in a glassy delirium wherein some seem to pause, with bowed heads, and sink carefully to their knees, and roll slowly over, and lie still. Other roll and roll, and scream and grip my legs in uttermost fear, and I have to struggle to break away . . . And I go on with aching feet, up and down across ground like a huge ruined honeycomb,

and my wave melts away, and the second wave comes up, and also melts away, and then the third wave merges into the ruins of the first and second . . .

At day's end, twenty thousand Allied forces had died, including Rob Gilson, the first but not the last of the TCBS to be killed in the war. Thirty-five thousand more lay wounded. As the battle progressed through summer and autumn, the Allied position improved, but only incrementally. The reason for the slow advance lay, at least in part, in stout German defense, inadequate Allied artillery, and bungled Allied intelligence. Exemplifying the last, alas, is a trench map now housed in the Bodleian Library, beautifully drawn on the battlefield by Tolkien in red and black ink, and containing incorrect information on German barbed-wire placements. He wasn't at fault—he based his map upon false descriptions supplied by German prisoners of war—but rather a victim of the iron rule that truth is the first casualty in war.

How did Tolkien survive this unfolding nightmare? In large measure, as he had survived the deaths of his father and mother: through the love of others. There was Edith, of course, praying for him back home in England and tracking his shifting position, which he provided against army regulations by tattooing his letters to her with dots in a code that he and she had devised before his departure. And there was the TCBS—Smith in France, Wiseman aboard a ship in the North Sea—corresponding whenever the conflict allowed, reminding one another of their shared aspirations to greatness, of their shared love, of their very existence.

Then came the delayed news of Gilson's death, and the realization that the German war machine had ripped apart the TCBS fellowship. Tolkien wrote to Smith on August 12 that he was "hungry and lonely," that "something has gone crack," that he felt "a mere individual at present." Four months later his isolation deepened, when the hounds of war turned their teeth upon Smith, dead of gangrene poisoning from a shrapnel wound.

Cut off from his friends, from Edith, from England, Tolkien found solace in his faith, that inexhaustible well of hope that lay unperturbed beneath everything that happened, good or bad. He also made use of another means of renewal, mentioned in his August 12 letter to Smith when he refers to the "spark of fire" granted the TCBS; for Tolkien, this

spark meant "finding a voice for all kinds of pent up things and a tremendous opening up of everything," a voice that would "testify for God and
Truth" through poetry, art, and language.

The war, to borrow a phrase from Samuel Johnson, had concentrated
that voice wonderfully. It did the same for many young writers, whose
art quickened under gunfire: Rupert Brooke dreaming of an English
heaven, Wilfred Owen recording "the monstrous anger of the guns," Isaac
Rosenberg describing the "shrieking iron and flame / Hurled through still
heavens." Why this literary flowering during World War I? World War II
produced only a handful of significant English writers, and subsequent
conflicts have given rise to fewer yet. It may be that what Fussell calls
the ironies of this particular conflict played a role: the most horrific of
wars after the most halcyon of days, the reversion to barbarism after the
heyday of the myth of progress. The war may have opened a gap between
expectation and fulfillment that literature was uniquely prepared to occupy
and investigate. Or it may be that the poetry of World War I, at least in
its lyrical mode, was itself the last flowering of the Age of Innocence
that preceded the war, that the horrors of the trenches sparked this final
blossoming, as friction gives rise to fire; that the daily nightmare unfolding
before the soldiers sharpened their sense of beauty, prophecy, and mission.
If this is so, one may regard the traditionalism of the Inklings, not as a
return to the past, but as the past still alive in the present, as the spirit
of World War I poetry, the last articulation of ordered innocence, finding
new voice amidst the nearly incessant wars of flesh, mind, and spirit that
marked the twentieth century.

One cannot underestimate boredom, too, as an incentive to write. Men
on the march or sighting along a gun barrel are unable to hold pen and pad;
but the trenches meant long, desperate hours of waiting: time enough to
pour out one's heart and soul. Sometimes "you might scribble something
on the back of an envelope and shove it in your back pocket but that's
all," while on other occasions, more was possible. Tolkien pressed forward with the legendarium "in grimy canteens, at lectures in cold fogs, in
huts full of blasphemy and smut, or by candle light in bell-tents, even
some down in dugouts under shell fire."

And there was yet another motive for his obsessive attention just now
to his private mythos. Tolkien longed to *escape*. He had no desire to shirk
his job as a soldier—his sense of duty was far too strong for that—but he

wished, whenever the ebb and flow of battle allowed, to flee in his imagination the sorrow, pain, and ugliness of the trenches. "It is plain," he would
say years later, "that I do not accept the tone of scorn and pity with which
'Escape' is now so often used . . . Why should a man be scorned if, finding
himself in prison, he tries to get out and go home? Or if he cannot do so, he
thinks and talks about other topics than jailers and prison-walls?" Another
Great War writer, Siegfried Sassoon, knew the same impulse; he remembers
"being huddled up in a little dog-kennel of a dug-out, reading *Tess of the
D'Urbervilles* and trying to forget about the shells which were hurrying
and hurrooshing overhead." Tolkien, lucky man, had a protected realm of
his own invention to which he could flee. Robert Graves, embittered by
battle, writes in his poem "Babylon": "The child alone a poet is: Spring and
Fairyland are his . . . Wisdom made him old and wary / Banishing the
Lords of Faery." It was not this way for Tolkien. As a child and as an adult,
he escaped into Faërie and found there, if not safe harbor, at least fair
dreams.

In October 1916, Tolkien contracted trench fever, a virulent lice-borne
illness. He was back in England by November 10, his days as a combatant over. During his convalescence, which lasted for the remainder of the
war, he helped to edit and wrote the introduction to a posthumous—and
undistinguished—collection of poems by G. B. Smith, *Spring Harvest*.
Tolkien's introduction is curiously businesslike, even cold, as if he knew
the poems were bad and, while giving them a formal salute, wished to turn
his attention to the future. And why not? New languages, new images,
new legends, and new mythologies crowded his mind; World War I had
stirred the waters and the return to England would open the floodgates.

4

HARD KNOCKS AND
DREAMING SPIRES

As Tolkien looked to the future, Lewis rummaged in the past. A
letter Lewis wrote on November 22, 1916—forty-six years to
the day before his death—reveals an eighteen-year-old with the
energy of a schoolboy and the tastes of an octogenarian. His lust for culture, preferably nineteenth-century or earlier, was prodigious. He chats
about *Aïda* and *The Magic Flute*, enthuses over *House of the Seven Gables*,
knocks *Guy Mannering*. He confesses his mad love for a radiant woman—
in this case, Dorothy Osborne, a celebrated epistolarian who died in 1695.
We get an early sample of his wit, as he announces that "I am desperately
in love with her and have accordingly made arrangements to commit suicide from 10 till 4 to-morrow precisely." At the same time, he senses the
dangers of making the past an idol. Earlier in the year he had composed
The Quest of Bleheris, a sixty-four-page romance in Morrisian mock-
medieval prose; now he declares his new work, a fantasy, will be in
modern English, which he hopes "will be an improvement."

It's evident from this tilt toward modern idiom that, though he has
been seriously misunderstood in this regard, Lewis was not an antiquarian. He had no use for modernism, a dismissal that would lead to
clashes later on with writers and critics, yet he turned away from the
artificial medievalism of Morris and the intricate sentences of Morris's
Victorian peers in favor of a simple, direct manner—verging on condescension in his nonfiction works—that suited perfectly the minds and

ears of his twentieth- (and twenty-first-)century readers. He disliked aestheticism and pedantry, shunning both his father's rhetorical extravagance and his own childish precocity. Most of all, he wanted to break the mold.

He was, at least on the surface, a brilliant, energetic, and likable young man. Kirkpatrick had sent Albert glowing reports about his pupil's literary and linguistic prowess ("He hardly realizes—how could he at his age—with what a liberal hand nature has bestowed her bounties on him . . . He has read more classics than any boy I ever had—or indeed I might add than any I ever heard of, unless it be an Addison or Landor or Macaulay"; moreover, "He is always cheerful, pleasant and obliging to the highest degree.") But signs of trouble peeped out from beneath the gaiety. The letters to Arthur Greeves that speak of suicide—always worrisome in an adolescent, even if mentioned in jest—give one pause. So, too, does Lewis's increasing fixation during this period upon sadomasochism. Four of his letters to Arthur he signs Philomastix ("whip lover"), sometimes in Greek characters to thwart snoopy readers (Lewis's father snatched up and read his correspondence whenever possible, and Lewis may have feared that the same reign of terror prevailed in Greeves's household). He daydreams in these letters about lashing young ladies of his acquaintance; he even wonders, baselessly, whether William Morris was also entranced by "the rod," on the strength of a stray sentence in *The Well at the World's End*. Sadomasochism may be the English vice, but Lewis's jaunty tone, his eagerness to describe his imagined victims and their stripes, suggest a mind knocked more than usually askew by the fierce energies of teenage sexuality.

He also stepped up his assault on Arthur's piety, utilizing as his weapon "the recognized scientific account of the growth of religions." It dismayed Lewis that Arthur still required instruction in these basic facts. If only his friend could be made to realize what he himself now understood with perfect clarity: that setting aside naïve belief liberates the imagination as well as the senses, making all mythic and literary universes available for unalloyed enjoyment. He could imagine himself, when reading *Beowulf*, "as an old Saxon thane sitting in my hall of a winter's night, with the wolves & storm outside and the old fellow singing his story." He could enjoy Malory as the closest thing to an English national epic and Valdemar Adolph Thisted's lumbering afterlife fantasy, *Letters from Hell*,

without agonies of pious fear; above all, the glorious Milton, if one overlooked the overt Christian content of *Paradise Lost*, could be savored for
his "Leopard witches" and the like: "He is as voluptuous as Keats, as romantic as Morris, as grand as Wagner, as wierd as Poe, and a better lover
of nature than even the Brontës." With this essentially Romantic, post-
Christian conception of the rewards of literary experience, Lewis was
primed to embrace all that Oxford University life had to offer.

"Absolutely Topping"

How different, compared to Lewis's first schoolboy glimpse of England,
was the impression Oxford made on him when he arrived in December
1916 to sit for his scholarship examination. The city was hauntingly lovely;
without dissembling, he could send an enthusiastic report to his father—
"the place has surpassed my wildest dreams: I never saw anything so
beautiful, especially on these frosty moonlight nights"—only complaining
that the poor heating system at Oriel College made it necessary to write
his examination papers with gloves on. To his brother in France he wrote,
"Oxford is absolutely topping, I am awfully bucked with it and longing
to go up . . ." Though he had harbored doubts about his exam performance, University College offered him a Scholarship, with the added
financial support of an Exhibition. The offer was complicated, however,
by the expectation that, once an Oxford man, he would present himself
for military service; and there was still the hurdle of Responsions, the
university entrance exam, which Lewis would have to pass before he could
go up to Oxford for good.

He returned to Kirkpatrick to continue "cramming" for the upcoming
test, adding Italian, German, and Spanish to his studies so that, if all
else failed, he would be eligible for the foreign service. Nonetheless, there
was time to write to Arthur Greeves about "That" (and to worry that "in
a way we have spoiled our paradise" by dwelling too much on sexual
fancies), to work on "Dymer" (a prose precursor to the narrative poem
he would labor over sporadically until the mid-1920s) and a poem about
"Medea's Childhood," and to read as eclectically as ever, devouring Apuleius, Wilkie Collins, Victor Hugo, Maurice Maeterlinck, Anstey's *The
Talking Horse*, Macaulay's *History of England*, Lamb, Morris, Shelley,
Rousseau, and so on.

The Latin and Greek portions of Responsions presented no problem, but Lewis failed the section on mathematics. He had a terrible head for numbers and was unable to handle even the simplest arithmetical problems—counting change was a daily ordeal—much less algebra, a prominent part of the exam. Algebra is defined by the *OED* as "a calculus of symbols," and Lewis's failure to master it is worth bearing in mind, in light of his later controversial forays into the application of logic to metaphysics and theology. Nonetheless, he was accepted into University College and returned to Oxford on April 26, 1917, enrolling as an undergraduate on April 29.

The university had changed dramatically since Tolkien's entry six years earlier. Now it swarmed with troops. Stripped down by the war, University College retained less than a dozen undergraduates when Lewis arrived, and many of them were anxious to head for the front. Although as an Irishman he was for the time being exempt from conscription, eventual military service seemed nearly inevitable. He signed up for the Officer's Training Corps (better to work toward a commission, the thinking went, than to be conscripted into the lower ranks should things change) and began to gaze across the Channel to France, where Warnie, commissioned as a second lieutenant in the Royal Army Service Corps after a short course of training at Sandhurst, had already been serving, as a supply officer rather than an active combatant, since the end of 1914. Perhaps Lewis felt drawn to follow his big brother, for whom the transition from Malvern to military life, by way of Kirkpatrick, had been a wholly satisfying one; Kirkpatrick restored Warnie's self-confidence, while Sandhurst and the Service Corps gave him a career in which he could succeed (war was one of the three realms—French history and drinking being the others—in which Warnie would outshine Jack). In any case, it was the temper of the times: unless one was too old, too young, too infirm, or—God forbid—a pacifist, one entered the service.

Outside the scheduled hours of military training, ordinary undergraduate pursuits filled Lewis's day. He read classics, bathed in and punted on the Cherwell, browsed the books in the Oxford Union, and peered up with admiration at the fading remnants of the Arthurian frescoes painted on the Union ceiling by Morris, Rossetti, and Burne-Jones. He also enjoyed the company of a second cousin, a young woman with the delightful name of Cherry Robbins, a volunteer at a military

hospital in Oxford and an enthusiast for Wagner, Rackham, and northern mythology, who was "a really ripping kind of person—an awfully
good sort."

Meanwhile, little cracks appeared in his carapace of pessimism and
materialism. One or two had surfaced earlier, under Kirkpatrick's tutelage, for even materialism was vulnerable to the Kirkian challenge. "Do
you not see, then, that you had no right to have any opinion whatever on
the subject?" Having delivered a ponderous lecture to Arthur in an October 1916 letter on the mythological origins of the "Yeshua" cult, he had
gone on to admit, "Of course, mind you, I am not laying down as a certainty that there is nothing outside the material world . . . Anything MAY
exist: but until we know that it does, we can't make any assumptions.
The universe is an absolute mystery: man has made many guesses at it,
but the answer is yet to seek. Whenever any new light can be got as to
such matters, I will be glad to welcome it. In the meantime I am not
going to go back to the bondage of believing in any old (& already decaying)
superstition."

Now that he was at Oxford, his intellectual horizons inevitably expanded. The vestiges that remained of Oxford's fin de siècle aestheticism
and the first shoots of its postwar religious revival made a deep impression, suggesting to Lewis, though he remained as argumentative an unbeliever as ever, that there existed attractive alternatives to the antireligious
positivism of Kirkpatrick. His new friend Theobald Butler, an Irish nationalist with whom Lewis enjoyed "brekker," bicycling, nude bathing in
Parson's Pleasure, and comparing notes on the dullness of Anglo-Saxons,
turned out when drunk to be quite devout in his own way, falling pros-
trate on Lewis's floor and calling upon the Holy Ghost, Venus Aphrodite,
and the Holy Mother of God. Butler, a man of catholic literary tastes,
suggested also that Lewis might like reading the Marquis de Sade. John
Robert Edwards, an "ardent Newmanite" recently converted from atheism, provided additional mental challenge: "He came into my rooms last
night, and sat till about 12. We had a long talk about religion, Buddhism,
poetry and everything else. How I like talking!" So far, though, it was all
talk; Lewis felt no impetus to insert John Henry Newman—or John Keble
or Edward Bouverie Pusey—into the week's diet of reading Walter Scott,
Ernest Renan, and Andrew Lang, and gazing at Albrecht Dürer prints; it
was exciting enough just to absorb all the conflicting impressions. In

early June, before moving to Keble College to join his battalion, he mentioned to Arthur that he had been enjoying a book on psychical research, adding that the observed phenomena "do not actually prove the agency of real spirits—yet." That "yet," with its anticipation of future revelations, makes all the difference. Like MacPhee in *That Hideous Strength*, he was open to the preternatural, but remained deaf to supernatural claims. This could not have been a comfortable position. Those who delight in mythology and fantasy already have one foot in a spiritual cosmos; now the other foot was beginning to slide.

Five days later, Lewis switched quarters to Keble. He passed the next four months rehearsing for war, bivouacking, and digging trenches in the nearby hills. There was still time to read, though, and he delved into the works of Bishop Berkeley, pronouncing him "one of our few philosophers and a very interesting fellow" and absorbing, though not yet embracing, Berkeley's subjective idealism and belief in an omnipresent, omniscient creative Mind. That he was already beginning to toy with some form of theism is evident from a July 22 letter to his father expressing a longing to read H. G. Wells's new book *God the Invisible King*; this was Wells in his wartime religious phase, proposing an experimental nonsectarian utopian creed, rooted in conscience but sans dogma, miracles, priestcraft, or dreams of afterlife.

There was also time, during these curious, unreal months preceding the plunge into the trenches, to get "royally drunk" at a party hosted by his new friend Butler and by E. R. Dodds, an Anglo-Irish classicist and later a celebrated scholar. Neither served in the war, out of sympathy for the Irish nationalist cause; the party celebrated their achievement of first-class degrees, Butler in law and Dodds in Literae Humaniores. During the same period, Lewis also befriended Laurence Bertrand Johnson, a second lieutenant in the Somerset Light Infantry who, like Lewis, held a scholarship to an Oxford college and, unlike Lewis, lived in unwavering obedience to his principles. This came as a revelation: for the first time, Lewis saw that an intellectual interest in aesthetics, metaphysics, and literature might coincide with a daily struggle to be chaste, honest, loyal, and all the rest of the conventional virtues. Johnson was a budding theist as well as a vigorous defender of traditional ideas of beauty and goodness; he would have been an excellent prospect for the Inklings if he had survived the war. He did not.

But of the many friends and acquaintances Lewis made during that period who would die on the French or Palestinian front, there was one who by his death would forever change Lewis's life.

Sons and Mothers

Edward "Paddy" Moore, by himself, counts little in Lewis's story. The two were billeted at the same time at Keble and assigned as roommates only because their names fell next to one another on an alphabetical list. Paddy was a handsome Anglo-Irishman, raised near Dublin and in Bristol, unintellectual but friendly. Lewis describes him in letters as a "good fellow" and "very decent." He would be shipped off to France in October as a rifleman. What mattered, in the long run, was not Paddy but his mother: Janie King (Askins) Moore (1872–1951), known to history as "Mrs. Moore."

Perhaps fittingly, or at least a piquant irony, for a man who epitomized for decades the inveterate bachelor and whose fictional women reveal, to some readers, an equally inveterate misogyny, the two great mysteries of Lewis's life revolve around women. We will meet Joy Davidman, his future wife, later. The current problem—and it is one that has bedeviled hordes of Lewis scholars, fans, and despisers—is Mrs. Moore.

She looks, in the rare extant photo, as bland as her name: a mop of light hair crowning plain features. Born in County Tyrone, Northern Ireland, the daughter (like Lewis's mother) of a Church of Ireland clergyman, she became a surrogate parent to her four younger siblings after her mother died in 1890. In 1897 she married Courtenay Edward Moore, a civil engineer in Dublin whose father also had been a clergyman. The marriage fell apart in 1907 (although the couple never divorced), and Mrs. Moore moved with her two children, eight-year-old Paddy and one-year-old Maureen, across the Irish Sea to Bristol, to be near one of her brothers, a physician, and to secure the chance of English schooling for her son; Paddy would receive a public school education at Clifton College.

When Lewis first cast eyes on Mrs. Moore, a few months after meeting Paddy, she was forty-five years old. He took to her immediately, writing to his father in August that he liked her "immensely." When did liking turn into love? Was it love, or some other uncategorized blend of sexual fascination, longing for a lost mother, and misplaced filial duty? We know that by September 1917, during a month's leave from his battalion, Lewis chose to forego a long visit with his father to spend two weeks with the Moores in Bristol; he then dashed home to Ireland for six days before heading for South Devon to join his regiment. In a letter to his father, he had telegraphed his plans in a curt sentence or two, as if realizing the enormity of his slight; and indeed his father was deeply wounded by his son's choice. We know, too, thanks to Paddy's sister Maureen, that during Lewis's visit with the Moores, he and Paddy pledged that if one of them died in combat, the other would look after the deceased's parent.

When—or whether—Lewis commenced an affair with Mrs. Moore remains unclear. At the end of October, he wrote to Arthur, warning him that all discussion of his relationship with her was henceforth forbidden. That Lewis banned any mention of this subject with his closest friend, who hitherto had received all his sexual confidences, suggests strongly that the romance, if that is the right word, had begun during his September sojourn, if not earlier (he also had visited the Moores for a weekend in August). In any event, one immediate effect of Lewis's entanglement with Mrs. Moore was to damage further his already rickety relationship with his father. Ordered to the front in early November, Lewis spent his last forty-eight-hour leave in Bristol with her and telegraphed his father to come see him there. Albert, surely livid, replied, "Don't understand telegram. Please write. P." Lewis did shoot off an apology of sorts, but the die was cast. All that remained of Albert's relationship with Lewis crumbled, while Mrs. Moore became, for the rest of her life, Lewis's companion and (as he himself described her) "mother."

"Men . . . Like Half-Crushed Beetles"

On November 17, 1917, Lewis arrived in France. By November 29, his nineteenth birthday, he was sloshing through the trenches at the front near the village of Monchy-le-Preux. His experience of war was typical in its boredom, its miseries, its culminating wounds. In *Surprised by Joy*, he recalls "the frights, the cold, the smell of H.E., the horribly smashed men still moving like half-crushed beetles, the sitting or standing corpses, the landscape of sheer earth without a blade of grass . . ." and the relentless marching: "I have gone to sleep marching and woken again and found myself marching still. One walked in the trenches in thigh gum

boots with water above the knee; one remembers the icy stream welling
up inside the boot when you punctured it on concealed barbed wire."
The sight of so many dead bodies reminded him of what it was like, as a
child, to see his dead mother and realize that she was absolutely *not
there*.

He read, lounging in mud, rain, and filth, *Lavengro* (George Borrow's
tale of philology and intrigue among gypsies and priests in the English
countryside), Honoré de Balzac's *Le Père Goriot*, Benvenuto Cellini, Al-
gernon Blackwood, Boswell, and most of George Eliot; wrote letters to
his father and Arthur; suffered from trench fever; took part in a curious
episode in which he inadvertently captured some sixty German soldiers;
and in the Battle of Arras, on April 15, 1918, was felled by friendly fire,
receiving shrapnel wounds in his chest, left wrist, and left leg. The metal
fragments in his chest, deemed harmless to lungs and heart, remained
inside him until an operation in July 1944. Lewis's friend Johnson was
killed by the same errant shell, and so was "dear Sergeant Ayres," who
filled his subordinate rank with captivating grace and "turned this ridiculous and painful relation into something beautiful, became to me almost
like a father." "Guns and Good Company" would be the title of his chapter about the war in *Surprised by Joy*, and it was in this good company of
"west country farmers . . . barristers, and university men" that Lewis had
his first experience of fellowship across class lines and of service under a
hierarchy that deserved his submission. The tragedy was that, like Tolkien,
he lost this fellowship almost as soon as he had tasted it. Of the friends
he made while billeted at Keble College, four were dead by the end of
March 1918, among them Paddy Moore, reported missing on March 24
and buried in the field south of Péronne.

Superficially, it seems that Lewis, unlike Tolkien, did not reel under
the war's steady blows; or that if he did, it remained one of his many
secrets. Certainly, the Battle of Arras did not radicalize him, as it did
Siegfried Sassoon. The whole period, he later reported, "shows rarely and
faintly in memory. It is too cut off from the rest of my experience and often seems to have happened to someone else," a response far removed
from the eruptive psychoses that threatened many other ex-soldiers.
Perhaps it was difficult to assimilate such experiences to the story he
would tell, in *Surprised by Joy*, of his journey from pessimism toward
faith. Moreover, he sensed that for those who have never lived through

such things, what he endured at the front and in its aftermath was nontransferable.

Nonetheless, the war left its permanent mark. Even before joining his battalion, Lewis had brooded over the prospect of battle. When Warnie came home from leave in July 1915, his description of conditions at the front ("a boy lay asleep on a bank and the mess by his head was his brains") gave Lewis "ghastly dreams." Recurring nightmares afflicted him after the war as well. He says nothing of this in *Surprised by Joy*. Only in his imaginative writings—in poetry, science fiction, and fantasy—did Lewis give war its due. Though he will never be classed with the greatest of the Great War poets, the immature verse he produced during this time shows that he had looked upon the same horrors:

> Long leagues on either hand the trenches spread
> And all is still; now even this gross line
> Drinks in the frosty silences divine
> The pale, green moon is riding overhead.
>
> The jaws of a sacked village, stark and grim,
> Out on the ridge have swallowed up the sun,
> And in one angry streak his blood has run
> To left and right along the horizon dim.
>
> There comes a buzzing plane: and now, it seems
> Flies straight into the moon. Lo! where he steers
> Across the pallid globe and surely nears
> In that white land some harbour of dear dreams!
>
> False mocking fancy! Once I too could dream,
> Who now can only see with vulgar eye
> That he's no nearer to the moon than I
> And she's a stone that catches the sun's beam.

It was, as we have seen, an exceptionally literary war, at least for those upper-class and middle-class officers who had been beneficiaries of British higher education; a war, as Paul Fussell describes it, presided over by *The Oxford Book of English Verse*, the Greek and Roman classics, the whole English literary canon. Lewis was fortunate enough to have the spare time, huddled in his trench bunk or convalescing in military hospitals, not only to read but to call up, as aids to reflection, his most powerful literary memories. Upon hearing for the first time the distant whine of a bullet, he remarked to himself, "This is War. This is what Homer wrote about." Only thus could he make sense of it all—not by political analysis, not by counting casualties, not by replaying scenes of dismemberment, disease, and death, but by relating what he witnessed to the *Iliad*, the greatest of all war tales. He lived in books, even while men were dying all around him, not because he was unaware of the catastrophe but because he saw it more clearly in this way; even when his own breath was stopped by an exploding shell, Lewis's thoughts were calmly analytical: "Here is a man dying."

In a famous 1915 lecture ("Thoughts for the Times on War and Death"), Freud points out that this detached third-person viewpoint, that of spectator rather than participant, is a common response to the threat of imminent death. By this mechanism, Freud believed, the unconscious reinforces its denial of death. Lewis read Freud's *Introductory Lectures on Psychoanalysis* with interest after the war; but for Lewis, the experience of detachment was better understood philosophically than psychoanalytically, as a taste of the transcendental ego who sees all, knows all, and is immune to death. Later on, when he studied Kant, this experience enabled him to make sense of the "noumenal" self; for he knew by experience what Kant thought could only be known through philosophical inquiry, "that there was a fully conscious 'I' whose connections with the 'me' of introspection were loose and transitory."

The Second War

Meanwhile, another war raged throughout the war years and well into the 1920s, a war of ideas, as rival worldviews contended for dominance over Lewis's mind and heart. His pessimism and materialism were about to give way to a succession of philosophical pictures, each claiming to be complete, none holding its commanding position for very long.

By May 1918, convalescing from his war wounds in Endsleigh Palace Hospital in London, Lewis was able—when not staring out the window at the green hill of Hampstead and the red sunset beyond—to send Arthur an assessment of his current Weltanschauung. He begins with some Berkeleyan speculation, explaining that when we find a tree beautiful, we are not experiencing the tree in itself, which is a medley of atoms devoid of color and shape; instead, the beauty we enjoy is "something purely spiritual, arising mysteriously out of the relation between me & the tree"—and perhaps out of a relation with the dryad or "indwelling spirit" of the tree. Thus is Warnie's evocative biscuit-tin garden come home with a vengeance! He then drops the example and states his philosophy baldly: Spirit (which he capitalizes in the neo-Hegelian manner) exists; it is at war with matter; and beauty is its way of calling to the kindred spirit that abides within each of us.

How did this change of mind come about? By what stages did as belligerent a skeptic as Lewis come to accept the existence of Spirit? *Surprised by Joy* traces the progression with an immediacy that no one can overlook, although perhaps it is too neat. As we saw earlier, Lewis believed that the seed of transformation first sprouted in Warnie's miniature garden, in the discovery of that sickening, intense longing for *something other*, which he called Joy. Pursuing this elusive quarry, Lewis soon lost his way; the search for Joy became a scholarly study of the images and words—largely at this time found in the Eddas—that gave rise to it. Realizing this, he sought desperately to rediscover the original experience by recapturing the same "thrill" or "state of mind" (his words) that he had known when gazing at Warnie's garden, when reading Longfellow on the death of Balder, when discovering the Idea of Autumn in *The Tale of Squirrel Nutkin*. This proved a dreadful mistake, to which Lewis believes Wordsworth succumbed also, with his lifelong nostalgia for the lost glory of heaven: the mistake of looking for the transcendent in an experience and particularly in the duplication of a previous experience. This leads, Lewis argues, to the spiritual counterpart of autoeroticism, making of religion "a self-caressing luxury." Rather—and here Lewis makes a claim of delicious subtlety—the longing for Joy is itself Joy; more concretely, that when he recalled with longing a place and time ("a particular hill walk on a morning of white mist") when he had experienced Joy, he was, in that recollection, experiencing Joy anew, though he knew it not. Joy was not a state; it was an arrow pointing to something beyond all states, something objective yet unobtainable—at least during our earthly existence.

So went Lewis's reasoning as an adolescent; and in this reasoning or questioning, in this incessant worrying over and gradual penetration into the mystery of Joy, Lewis avoided any self-crystallization into adamantine atheism. Moreover, his catalyst for this process of circumnavigating, possessing, and losing Joy was almost always a work of the imagination with spiritual overtones—an opera by Wagner, a drawing by Rackham, a novel by Morris. No wonder the possibility of the reality of spirit never wholly died within him, even when it retreated underground. For years, as he describes it in *Surprised by Joy*, he lived a double life: "to care for almost nothing but the gods and heroes, the garden of the Hesperides, Launcelot and the Grail, and to believe in nothing but atoms and evolution and military service."

Upon this soil of nascent spirituality fell other seeds, some of which bore fruit. Under Kirkpatrick he had learned Greek, to the extent, he tells us, of learning to think in it and absorb its metaphysical tendencies. More important, he made a couple of literary discoveries that forever changed his outlook. One was Yeats—the magical and esoteric Yeats of *Rosa Alchemica* and *Per Amica Silentia Lunae*. Lewis had encountered what he calls "the passion for the Occult" before, at Cherbourg House, under the influence of Miss Cowie, the devotee of Higher Thought. Miss Cowie played a paradoxical role in Lewis's life: through her he discovered the possibility of worldviews beyond the Christian creed; through that discovery his faith in the creed loosened, then slipped altogether; and yet the taste for occultism that she instilled in him would boomerang in time and help lead the way back to faith. For through Yeats and then Maeterlinck, Lewis discovered—living in reverse his experiences with Miss Cowie—the possibility of worldviews beyond strict materialism; and through that discovery and others, his faith in skepticism loosened, then slipped altogether. The chance remained, at least for a while, that he might become a dedicated magician, a modern Simon Magus or Cornelius Agrippa—he had the imagination and brains to pull this off—but soon he realized that the lure of magic had little to do with the search for Joy; it was another form of autoeroticism, bent toward power rather than pleasure, and skirting the edge of madness.

Altogether more wholesome was the unexpected discovery of conscience. As is the case with many adolescents, Lewis's increased command over the things of the world brought with it a corresponding atrophy of the moral sense. He lived for his own pleasure, which took the form of intellectual pursuits and a few close friendships. He believed in being kind to companions, even lending them money if called for; for the rest of it, morality was no more than a fascinating mental study; reading Latin or Greek classics on ethical matters was all well and good, even bracing, but it had nothing to do with one's own behavior. Then came a flurry of events that turned his values upside down. The first, by Lewis's own reckoning, was the discovery of George MacDonald, whose fiction had earlier deepened Tolkien's understanding of fantasy motifs.

The great breakthrough came on March 4, 1916, when Lewis purchased, from a train bookstall in Leatherhead, through what amounted (as he saw it in retrospect) to "a superabundance of mercy," a worn Everyman's copy of MacDonald's 1858 novel, *Phantastes*. This picaresque tale of the adventures of Anodos (a Platonic term for the ascent to truth) in Fairyland, offers a slew of fantastic characters, including a fairy grandmother, a knight in armor, tree spirits, and a malevolent presence that is the hero's own shadow, along with an atmosphere that Lewis describes in *Surprised by Joy* as a "bright shadow," "something too near to see, too plain to be understood," something that "seemed to have been always with me." Lewis defines this mysterious something that *Phantastes* possesses as "Holiness" (the capital letter is his).

At least in Lewis's case, the holiness of *Phantastes* was not confined to the book; when he closed its covers, rather than finding ordinary things dull by comparison, he discovered that its enchantment had spilled into the real world, "transforming all common things." Lewis's imagination, he tells us, was forevermore "baptized." What this means is not precisely clear: at most, it suggests that Lewis believed his imagination was in some way marked by supernatural grace; at least, it means that he glimpsed the possibility of goodness and purity in the everyday world, that Joy was no longer confused with magic, eroticism, or power but was something that he could seek among ordinary people and things. In either case, it meant that his imagination—both his way of perceiving reality and his artistic accounting of that reality—became a means of self-transformation, self-purification, possibly even salvation. After reading *Phantastes*, Lewis became more open to traditional moral influences, although he still believed in absolute autonomy and was capable of behaving—at least in his relations with his father—with little regard for the feelings of others.

Another stage in Lewis's moral ascent arrived a year and a half later—in November 1917, on the verge of heading to the front—and again via a book. This time it was Arthur Clutton-Brock's *The Ultimate Belief*, a slim volume that had a tremendous circulation during the war. In it, Clutton-Brock celebrates lovers, saints, scientists, and artists—a motley crew, one would think—for their common allegiance to the "human spirit," which inspires mystery and awe and which manifests itself, above all, through beauty, be it the beauty of holiness, of cosmic order, or of romance. Beauty is its own reward, for it not only expresses but magnifies the spirit. This may be true, but is rather insipid; as T. S. Eliot observed of Clutton-Brock's work, "its thought is not daring, but its commonsense is sound."

Lewis, however, was thunderstruck. Before reading Clutton-Brock, he had seen but two ways of understanding morality: as either "god-imposed laws" (and he did not believe in God) or "rules for convenience" with no higher authority. Clutton-Brock offered a third alternative, that morality was a mode of art, "an object to be pursued for its own beauty." Art, Lewis already held dear to his heart, as a portal to Joy; now it appeared that art was, in some mysterious way, allied to morality as well. It seemed as if Clutton-Brock had sought his own form of Joy. Curiously, Sir William Rothenstein's portrait of Clutton-Brock in the National Gallery shows a face uncannily like Lewis's—longer, more ascetical, but with the same clean-shaven, forthright, pleasantly pugilistic expression. Nor does the resemblance end there; a glance at *The Ultimate Belief* or any of Clutton-Brock's works, with their sturdy, simple titles—*Essays on Art, Essays on Books, Essays on Religion, What Is the Kingdom of Heaven?*—brings to mind the popular philosophical and religious books Lewis would produce after his conversion. This is how the first chapter of *The Ultimate Belief* begins:

Most people in England think of a philosopher as one who talks in a difficult language about matters which are of interest only to philosophers. But Philosophy is concerned with what must interest every human being, with the nature of man and the nature of the universe. Every man is born a philosopher, but often the philosopher is suppressed in him by the hand-to-mouth thinking needed for the struggle for life. So boys are often more philosophical than men, pupils than their teachers; and what they miss in their lessons, without knowing it, is philosophy.

In its relaxed, down-to-earth tone, one chap talking to another without pretense or fuss; in its appeal to common sense and ordinary life; in its short, declarative sentences, with their simple syntax and rolling rhythms, this is pure Lewis, or at least a very close relation. Above all, this is the Lewis of the World War II BBC Radio talks and of *Mere Christianity*. The voice is radically different from that of Morris or MacDonald or Chesterton; it sounds far more like the mature Lewis than do any of his other early literary enthusiasms. Did Lewis consciously adopt Clutton-Brock's prose as a model for his own? He never acknowledged this, but he did read *The Ultimate Belief* at the age of nineteen, when the wet clay of a young person's literary style is ready to be molded and fired.

Other books read during this time also shaped his future thought. While in the hospital recovering from trench fever, he read a collection of Chesterton's ebullient apologetic essays (Chesterton was an Anglican during the war years, though edging ever closer to the Catholic Church); Lewis admired his brilliance, his humor, and his essential goodness, and listened with pleasure, if not approbation, to his arguments for faith. He had been aware of Chesterton for many years, as one of the literary celebrities always referred to by their initials (G.K.C.) by the highbrows at school, and whom Lewis had lumped together with other contemporary writers who were all the rage at Oxford ("I have often sat in amazed silence amid glib talk of Rupert Brooke, Masefield, Chesterton, Bottomley, etc"). However, he was not prepared for and had no ready defense against the "immediate conquest" made of him, so soon after encountering Mac-Donald, by the mirthful earnestness and scintillating paradoxes of this second Christian author. "A young man who wishes to remain a sound Atheist cannot be too careful of his reading" would be his tongue-in-cheek assessment in *Surprised by Joy*. The force of his remark is lessened by the gratingly coy remark that follows—"God is, if I may say it, very unscrupulous"—but the point remains that MacDonald and Chesterton proved so enchanting, so bracingly convincing to this young atheist that, as Chesterton said of Samuel Johnson, and as Maisie Ward in turn said of Chesterton, they managed to "walk into the heart without knocking."

But though they did take up residence in Lewis's heart, his head remained for the time unconverted.

He was turned, rather than converted, by another creed encountered
during convalescence, that of Henri Bergson, whose elegantly expressed
philosophy, affirming that the moral subject transcends space and time
and therefore is genuinely free, defending immediate intuition as a valid
mode of knowledge, and celebrating the life force (*élan vital*), Lewis found
profoundly exhilarating. From Bergson he learned "to relish energy, fertility,
and urgency; the resource, the triumphs and even the insolence, of things
that grow." The best thing was that one could be a Bergsonian without
making any irrevocable religious decisions. With Bergson's help, Lewis
fashioned what he would later call his "New Look," neither pessimist nor
optimist, neither materialist nor spiritualist. He resolved, like Margaret
Fuller, to accept the universe—without a Carlyle to retort, "Gad, he'd
better." His decision amounted to more than a lull in the search, however;
the universe still had business to discuss with him.

Was Lewis, then, no longer a materialist by 1919? This is not a simple
question. Pure materialism, of the reductive or eliminative kind, the doctrine that matter accounts for all that exists including our mental life, that
we are nothing but specks of dust in a cold, purposeless cosmos, is far rarer
in the history of thought than many realize, though one finds such rhetoric
in the writings of popular controversialists like Joseph McCabe (1867–
1955), a Franciscan priest turned antireligious crusader to whom Chesterton devoted a teasing chapter in his 1908 book *Heretics*. By Lewis's time,
however, this soapbox materialism was already fading. After peaking in the
seventeenth and eighteenth centuries it now lived on past glories, with
most materialists flirting with the *élan vital* or similar modifications, content to exempt their own free choices from the determinist implications of
their creed. The great mathematical logician and passionate agnostic
Bertrand Russell, whose "A Free Man's Worship" (1903) celebrated Stoical
virtue in a universe of blind chance ("Brief and powerless is man's life. On
him and all his race the slow doom falls pitiless and dark . . ."), was now at
work on a philosophical system, "neutral monism," that would enable one to
be a materialist and a mystic at the same time; and to many, the findings
of modern physics were making the old materialism look dogmatic and out
of date, though it would be periodically revived (witness, in the early
twenty-first century, the writings of Richard Dawkins).

It remained for Lewis to sort out the entangled strands of materialism and spiritualism, Romanticism and realism in his own worldview. He was barely out of his teens, after all, and had yet to tackle the peculiar form of idealism, expounded by T. H. Green, F. H. Bradley, and Bernard Bosanquet, that, though in decline, still had its staunch defenders at Oxford; nor had he mastered the philosophical realism that was vigorously overtaking it. Under the circumstances, Lewis was wise to carry his intellectual schemas lightly and withhold decision until he could see things more clearly.

Return to Oxford

By January 1919, Lewis was back at Oxford, elated that "the Junior Common Room is no longer swathed in dust sheets" and enjoying meals in the great hall with a skeleton crew of twenty-seven fellow University College students. In April he moved into new rooms, which soon reflected the studied ordinariness he had admired in Clutton-Brock's prose: the walls a drab grayish-blue adorned with Dürer prints and a single piece of good furniture—predictably, a bookcase. Writing to Arthur, he singled out for praise the ceiling beam, the deep windows, and the old tree outside, all of which reminded him of *Phantastes* and *Wuthering Heights*, and expressed regret (perhaps out of politeness) at having left behind the pictures Arthur had given him. To live in reasonable comfort with one's "household gods" close by was enough for Lewis; not for him the aestheticism of Tolkien's Exeter College rooms, with their Japanese prints and fine furniture. For Lewis this was a conscious and enduring choice; he wore baggy flannels until his death and, once converted, espoused a "mere Christianity" as gloriously ordinary as his imagination could devise.

Like Tolkien, though, Lewis plunged into the extracurricular debate and lecture scene, honing the dialectic skills that would bring him both happiness and misery in later years. He joined the Martlets, a University College literary society and in some ways a prototype—albeit in formal dress—of the Inklings, with organized lectures (four per term), a membership limited to twelve, and regular minutes. Lewis read papers to the Martlets on Spenser, Morris, Boswell, and other favorite authors, and first formulated in a public forum his ideas on literary criticism and on the nature of stories. Writing to his father, he reported that he had been elected secretary of the Martlets and that in consequence, even if history forgot him, his handwriting would remain for posterity—a sarcastic aside that simultaneously veils and reveals his youthful hunger for fame.

January 1919 brought Mrs. Moore and her daughter, Maureen, to rented lodgings in Oxford, in order to be close to him. In letters to Albert and Warnie, Lewis pretended that the Moores were still in Bristol, but for Arthur he painted a different picture: "After breakfast I work (in the library or a lecture-room which are both warm) or attend lectures until 1 o'clock when I bycycle out to Mrs. Moore's. They are installed in our 'own hired house' (like St Paul only not daily preaching and teaching). The owner of the house has not yet cleared out & we pay a little less than the whole for her still having a room." Note the "we"; evidently Lewis's peculiar relationship with Mrs. Moore—whom he now called "Minto" after Nuttall's Mintoes, a popular sweet compounded of treacle, butter, sugar, and mint flavoring—had thickened. From then on, Lewis would shuttle between academic and domestic worlds; there would be no hope of an ivory tower existence nor of a serene home life (in a July 4, 1923, diary entry, Lewis recalls nine different lodgings shared with Mrs. Moore beginning in 1919—"most of them vile"). Yet from the complications and strain in his life would come many of Lewis's best insights into the psychology of virtue and vice. By May 1919, Albert was seriously worried by what he termed "Jack's affair" (he recognized the likelihood of a sexual element), disturbed by Mrs. Moore's age, marital status, and lack of money. "She is old enough to be his mother," he wrote to Warnie, suggesting, perhaps, a fear that she was replacing both mother and father in Jack's affections. In June, Warnie wrote back to say, "I am greatly relieved . . . to hear that Mrs Moore HAS a husband: I understood she was a widow; but as there is a Mr Moore, the whole complexion of the business is altered. We now get the following very unsatisfactory findings. (1) Mrs Moore can't marry Jacks. (2) Mr Moore can't blackmail him because 'IT' hasn't enough to make it a paying risk. (3) You can't be blackmailed because you wouldn't listen to the proposition for one moment."

Lewis tried raising the matter of Mrs. Moore with his brother but was harshly cut off, for Warnie, like Albert, felt somewhat elbowed aside in his brother's affections. "The daily letter business *does* annoy me," Warnie told their father, "especially as I have heard from Jacks *once* since January of this year." It became increasingly clear to both brother and father that for Lewis, whatever the nature of her hold might be, Mrs. Moore came first.

The summer of 1919 brought visits to Lewis in Oxford from Arthur and Warnie; the two brothers then paid a sentimental call on the Kirkpatricks at Great Bookham, followed by a belated, obligatory, and thoroughly disastrous stay with their father in Ireland. Lewis had delayed the return to Little Lea as long as he could, claiming that he still had work to do after the end of term. Albert had been depressed, drinking heavily, and suffering excruciating pains from an undisclosed ailment; as a result, he was "fast becoming unbearable," Lewis told Warnie. Political tensions in Ireland—which did not interest Lewis—were spreading gloom among its citizens as well. The appalling postscript with which he ended a June letter to Arthur—"Haven't heard from my esteemed parent for some time; has he committed suicide yet?"—may not have been far off the mark.

When the brothers finally arrived in Little Lea, an explosion seemed inevitable. A bit of snooping on Albert's part revealed that Lewis had lied about the state of his finances, claiming to be five pounds in the black when he was twelve pounds overdrawn (the difference having gone to help support Mrs. Moore and her daughter); when the truth came out, so did all of Lewis's stored-up resentments, and he unleashed against his father a litany of ancient grievances. Albert poured out his grief in his diary: "On 6 August he deceived me and said terrible, insulting, and despising things to me. God help me! That all my love and devotion and self-sacrifice should have come to this—that 'he doesn't respect me. That he doesn't trust me, and cares for me in a way' . . . The loss of Jacks' affection, if it be permanent, is irreparable and leaves me very miserable and heart sore." It was, for Lewis, a considerable relief to return in August to Oxford and help the Moores move house once again. He wrote to his father, although less frequently than before, attempting to justify his harsh words in the name of sincerity and to reduce their painful effects by means of chattiness and expedient deceptions; he signed his letters, as always, "your loving son, Jack." In retrospect, he would call this period "the blackest chapter of my life."

In November 1919, Lewis forged a friendship that further challenged his skepticism—and one that has proved invaluable for those who seek to understand him, for many decades later this friend provided, in a retrospective essay, our earliest glimpse of Lewis by someone outside the family circle. Leo Kingsley Baker (1898–1986) was in some ways Lewis's double: both were twenty-one, veterans wounded on the French battlefield, Oxford scholars, and aspiring poets; Baker, however, would enjoy a very different destiny, working as an actor, a weaver, and an Anthroposophical priest before winding up as a teacher at a drama college in South East London. Baker learned of Lewis from another University College student, Rodney Marshall Sabine Pasley, who spoke of "a strange fellow who seemed to live an almost secret life and took no part in the social life of the college"—an understandable impression, since Lewis was spending much of his free time with Mrs. Moore—and yet who was, as a scholar and poet, "right up our tree."

After an introduction in Pasley's rooms, Baker and Lewis began exchanging poems and taking long afternoon walks together. Lewis wrote Arthur that his new friend was the product of a progressive school "where everyone seems to have written, painted and composed" and that he had a propensity for the spiritual and the outré: "He is so clairvoyant that in childhood 'he was afraid to look round the room for fear of what he might see.' He got a decoration in France for doing some work in an aeroplane over the lines under very deadly fire: but he maintains that he did nothing, for he was 'out of his body' and could see his own machine with 'someone' in it, 'roaring with laughter.'" On the whole, Lewis said, "I like and admire him very much, though at times I have doubts on his sanity."

Lewis was fascinated by, yet distrusted, Baker's spiritual side. Tongue in cheek, he offered to be Baker's "amateur disciple in mysticism," but received a fright on one occasion when he looked into Baker's eyes: "presently I could hardly see anything else: and everything he said was real—incredibly real. When I came away, I moved my eyes off his, with a jerk, so to speak, and suddenly found that I had a splitting headache and was tired and nervous and pulled to pieces. I fancy I was a bit hypnotised. At any rate I had such a fit of superstitious terror as I have never known since childhood and have consequently conceived, for the present, a violent distaste for mysteries and all that kind of business." A few months later, however, he was describing Baker, in a May 1920 letter to Arthur, as "in every way the best person I have met in Oxford." The friends talked incessantly about their literary enthusiasms and hatreds (a resounding yea to *The Mabinogion* and *The Crock of Gold*, nay to free verse and the Sitwells), and analyzed the nature of inspiration. They joined forces with

Pasley to produce an anthology whose title, "The Way's the Way," came from *The Pilgrim's Progess*, as a "counterblast" to the "Vorticist" poetry—vers libre in form, modernist in philosophy, world-weary in spirit—that was all the rage. Eventually, Lewis drew close enough to Baker to introduce him to Mrs. Moore and invite him to her house.

Yet always Baker sensed a deeply rooted impediment to a deeper or freer friendship. That obstacle, according to Baker, was Lewis himself. He found Lewis's prejudices odd and his sympathies constrained: "I was interested in contemporary events, social conditions, the arts, marriage, and even politics. Lewis was not. He crossed them all out, except insofar as they bumped into him." To Baker, Lewis was a caged beast, a dogmatic rationalist who "lived in an enclosed world with rigid walls built by his logic and intelligence, and trespassers would be prosecuted. Within these walls were his ambition and single-minded determination to get the highest class in the examinations, which in his case meant the classics and philosophy . . ."

Like a caged beast, Lewis liked to pace and he liked to roar, astonishing Baker—who had never met a self-proclaimed atheist—by one day shouting over tea, "You take too many things for granted. You can't start with God. *I don't accept God!*" Had Lewis been more settled in his atheism, he might have been calmer in his denunciation; but he was already coming to suspect, as he told Baker in September 1920, that "some sort of God" (presumably an H. G. Wells or Clutton-Brock sort of God) had to be postulated; merely postulated, that is, not submitted to in faith. "Were you much frightened in France?" Baker asked Lewis. "All the time, but I never sank so low as to pray."

Shouting over tea was the least of Lewis's flare-ups. Once, Baker tells us, Lewis lashed out at him for no apparent reason "with deep and uncontrollable hatred." A second explosion, coming via letter, led to an estrangement that lasted until 1935, when Lewis, informed that Baker was seriously ill, wrote to him "to try and pick up some of the old links. That they were ever dropped was, I imagine, chiefly my fault—at least even self-love on my part cannot find any substantial respect in which it could have been yours. Will you forgive me?"

Baker ascribes Lewis's black moods to the three great trials of his early years: the death of his mother, the troubled relationship with his father, and the miserable years at school; the result, in Baker's view, was a young man who rarely laughed, who worshipped only mind, and who encased his heart in lead. This seems too one-sided; Baker profoundly unsettled Lewis, and as conversation strayed into the mystical regions that alarmed him so, Lewis behaved his worst. Still, Lewis was surely unhappy. At times he exuded an aura of deeply settled sorrow, nowhere more evident than in his first book, the lyric cycle begun in 1917 and published in 1919 under a title that again recalls the caged beast: *Spirits in Bondage*.

Lewis's original title, actually, was *Spirits in Prison*, alluding to the belief (based on 1 Peter 3:18–20) that Christ preached the Gospel to the spirits in Hades. He changed it after his father pointed out its similarity to the title of a 1908 novel, Robert Hichens's *A Spirit in Prison*. The title also nearly duplicates *The Spirits in Prison*, an 1884 book on the Harrowing of Hell by the celebrated dean of Wells Cathedral and former University College scholar, Edward Hayes Plumptre. We don't know if Lewis read this work by one of his college's alumni, but in any event, he had a more radical project in mind, for *Spirits in Bondage* inverts the Gospel story: in Lewis's telling, the spirits have been imprisoned by an oppressive God, and it is the Romantic rebel-poet, Lewis himself, an inspired adversary rather than a dutiful only-begotten son, who sings of their release.

Spirits in Bondage

We forgive Tolkien his "Goblin Feet," for in its whimsical conceits and singsong rhymes we discern the outlines of later, far greater work. Lewis's early publications deserve the same indulgence. Walter Hooper, who served as Lewis's secretary during the final months of his life and then as literary executor, editor, and custodian of Lewis's entire intellectual legacy, begins his preface to the 1984 edition of *Spirits in Bondage* by remarking that "we are all young once." This is just the right defense, for Lewis's immaturity radiates from every page. He published the book under the pseudonym of "Clive Hamilton," wedding his disliked first name to his mother's maiden name, as he explained to Albert, in order to avoid sarcastic asides from his fellow soldiers about "our b——y lyrical poet." Albert may have noticed, however, that the armistice was signed and Lewis demobilized and secure in Oxford's ivory towers before the book appeared on March 20, 1919. A more painful explanation may have occurred to him, that his son's pseudonym was a declaration of filial independence. The name carries, too, implications of an identity adrift. "I was at this time living," Lewis recalls in *Surprised by Joy,* "in a whirl of contradictions." He did not believe in God; he blamed God for not existing; he blamed God for making the world. From this intellectual chaos he had evolved, as we have seen, a somewhat Gnostic perspective, admitting to his picture of the cosmos, if not God, at least something he called "Spirit," which calls to us through Beauty and is locked in battle with matter.

This is the ideology that permeates the poetry of *Spirits in Bondage.* Happily, Lewis did not let it infect his aesthetic choices. Spirit may be, as he wrote to Arthur, "matter's great enemy," and yet as a poet he depicted the gossamer realm of spirit with lush, earthy imagery drawn from the material world. Typical is "Death in Battle," the last poem in the collection but the very first of his works to be professionally published, appearing in John Galsworthy's magazine *Reveille* two months before *Spirits in Bondage* came out. Here the poet, on the battlefield, "driven and hurt beyond bearing," petitions for admission to a higher, purer world. Lewis paints this spiritual abode in a series of vivid (if not always original) images, as "the peaceful castle, rosy in the West," "the sweet dim Isle of Apples," "flowery valleys," "dewy upland places," the "garden of God," a "Country of Dreams!" The poem is lovely, taut, unsentimental, suffused with nostalgia for paradise. Similar is "Ballade Mystique," identified by Warnie as expressing his brother's "considered opinion of his own youth," in which the poet proclaims his wretchedness among his friends and moons over a land "Beyond the western ocean's glow / Whither the faerie galleys steer."

These are among the best of the matter-vs.-spirit poems. Elsewhere in the book, Lewis shows his age. In "Satan Speaks," oddly suggestive of a later era's heavy-metal album lyrics, the devil celebrates his own dark majesty, his seductive disguises ("I am the flower and the dewdrop fresh / I am the lust in your itching flesh") and his cruelty ("I am the spider making her net / I am the beast with jaws blood-wet"). "De Profundis" curses God artlessly ("Come let us curse our Master ere we die, / for all our hopes in endless ruin lie. / The good is dead. Let us curse God most High"), in a vein reminiscent of A. E. Housman. Not until much later would Lewis see the justice of Chesterton's observation that "the curse against God is 'Exercise I' in the primer of minor poetry."

Often—too often—Lewis laments the weight of life, the ravages of time, the falsity of hope ("But lo!, I am grown wiser, knowing that our own hearts / Have made a phantom called the Good . . ."). How weary to bear the world's weight upon one's shoulders! Has any twenty-year-old been as old as Lewis? Yet alongside the precocious spiritual and moral exhaustion, one spies glints and flashes of something more—not only the longing for Joy that emerges in so many images of fairies and western islands and gardens of delight, hinting at the Perelandrian and Narnian fantasies to come, but also, here and there, an appreciation of the stolid, beefy England that both Tolkien and Lewis would later defend in their writings. "In Praise of Solid People" declares

> Thank God that there are solid folk
> Who water flowers and roll the lawn,
> And sit and sew and talk and smoke,
> And snore all through the summer dawn.

Even better is the astonishing "The Ass," in which the poet, wandering in the heather, encounters a sleepy brown ass and wonders

> Can it be true, as the wise men tell,
> That you are a mask of God as well,
> And, as in us, so in you no less
> Speaks the eternal Loveliness.

In its pastoral serenity, its humor ("O big, brown brother out of the waste, / How do thistles for breakfast taste?"), its Franciscan love of lowly creatureliness, this is a poem one might expect from Lewis at fifty years of age; it is a happy harbinger of things to come.

Spirits in Bondage slipped into print with few reviews and those lukewarm at best. *The Scotsman* noticed the "emotional glooming" but declared the text "never unhealthy, trifling, or affected." *The Times Literary Supplement*, more realistically, remarked that "the thought, when closed with, is found rather often not to rise above the commonplace." A sharper knife thrust, from a different angle, came from Warnie, who lamented in a letter to Albert the book's "purely academic" atheism and how it might affect Lewis's future career. Albert, showing unusual balance, replied,

"He is young and he will learn in time that a man has not absolutely solved the riddle of the heavens above and the earth beneath and the waters under the earth at twenty."

Nor could Lewis at twenty solve the riddle of reconciling his family to his "family." Whenever Lewis visited Belfast he was reduced to exchanging his daily letters with Mrs. Moore on the sly, Arthur acting as intermediary. By 1921, Lewis was a permanent member of the Moore household, though he continued to hide the truth from his college and from his father. When Albert, much to everyone's surprise, announced a plan to visit his son in Oxford in July, Lewis wrote back, "I have been moved out of College and you will probably find me sharing with a man who is up to his eyes in work. This means we can't spend much time on my own hearth." For the next thirty years Lewis would live with—or, as Warnie saw it, under—Mrs. Moore, moving from one dismal rented home to another, until they settled in the Kilns.

Warnie met Mrs. Moore and her daughter, Maureen, for the first time in August 1922, while visiting Oxford during a leave from his West African tour of duty. He thoroughly enjoyed himself, writing in his diary, "I am glad to have met Mrs. M and Maureen, not only intrinsically but because it gives me a larger share in J's real life: happy though I think we can be together at Leeborough, there cannot in the nature of things be any return to the old days, nor indeed is it to be desired." By 1933, Warnie's attitude toward Mrs. Moore would harden; he came to consider her "notably domineering and possessive by temperament" and thought her relationship with his brother a flagrant abuse. In particular, he was outraged to see Lewis carrying out mundane household chores. Too often, he felt, the pen played second fiddle to the broom, mop, and dish towel; what right had this thoroughly unintellectual older woman to demand such sacrifices from a young man of Lewis's great promise? Warnie's heart sank when he heard Mrs. Moore tell visitors that "he is as good as an extra maid in the house." He could not see what his brother saw, that Mrs. Moore could be loving and supportive, and that during the early years of their life together the couple shared many moments of fun and gestures of tenderness and mutual encouragement.

Thus conflicted both in his personal arrangements and his intellectual outlook, Lewis might have retreated into his fortress of argumentative unbelief and built so high those walls of restricted sympathies and dogmatic rationalism of which Baker speaks that no one could clamber over them, but for the advent of one man: "the Second Friend," "the man who disagrees with you about everything," who "has read all the right books but has got the wrong thing out of every one," the great comrade with whom you engage in perpetual argument that concludes with victory—a greater access to truth—on each side. Baker introduced Lewis to his Second Friend sometime near the end of 1919, when Owen Barfield had just gone up to Wadham College as a classical scholar.

5

"WORDS HAVE A SOUL"

The good are befriended even by weakness and defect," observed Emerson. "Our strength grows out of our weakness." As a young child, Owen Barfield, future philologist, novelist, poet, essayist, playwright, solicitor, a man who would devote his life to the secret life of words—and an assiduous student of Emerson, who knew that "every word was once a poem. Every new relation is a new word"—had no particular strength when it came to language. It was music that captured his heart. He was six or seven years old, not yet attending school, when workers delivered a grand piano to the family home in the northern London suburbs and his mother, Elizabeth, sat down to play a romantic melody, an impromptu or nocturne by Schubert or Chopin. "I remember that awfully well," he said as a very old man, just as he remembered and cherished everything to do with music and dance. His father, Arthur Barfield, a solicitor, was also musical. Father and mother would play piano duets, and while still a very young boy, Owen absorbed a good portion of the classical piano canon. He was, he said, "always surrounded with music."

Years later, he realized that in his childhood home, music had taken the place of religion, a subject in which his parents had no interest. He knew, as a child, nothing about prayer, or any sacred words, and he felt acute embarrassment when his nurse looked astonished at his failure to kneel before bedtime. It was hardly his fault; music alone occupied the household lararium, and Owen gladly shared in its worship. This early devotion, but not the accompanying dismissal of religion, stayed with him always. When he grew up to be a philosopher and wordsmith, he came at words as a musician might, searching out the rhythm and melody in poetry, and the secret songs that language sings as it matures over centuries, songs that reveal, or so he believed, the secret history of consciousness. As an old man, he confessed that if he were forced to choose between music and poetry, music would win out.

Owen began his formal education at seven or eight years of age, entering Highgate School, a public (nongovernmental) school for the upper middle class, founded in 1585. There he began to open to the power of words, studying Latin and Greek, reading voraciously, and discovering, in a most unexpected way, that words carry their own peculiar force. "I chalked on the wall in large letters, 'Mr. Kelly is a fool' . . . I was terrified of what I had done. I cried I think; and either my mother or my father, brother, or uncle advised me to go and wash it off very early in the morning." He did so, but the memory proved indelible. So did that of a more significant episode, around the age of twelve, that taught him that words possess beauty as well as frightening power. He was seated in a Highgate School Latin class, pondering the line "*Cato, octoginta annos natus, excessit e vita*" (conservatively translated as "Cato, eighty years of age, left this life"), when the boy sitting beside him declared, "Cato, at the age of 80, *walked out of life* [the italics are Barfield's]—that's rather nice!" Barfield returned throughout his life to this episode, "the actual moment when [I] was first made aware that it was possible to enjoy language *as such*—the very nature of language," and when he first realized the beauty and power of metaphor. The moment becomes more piquant when one learns that the schoolboy sitting next to him was Alfred Cecil Harwood, destined to become his lifelong friend and eventually C. S. Lewis's as well.

Owen's burgeoning interest in classical studies and in the power of words might have presaged a career as an orator or rhetorician—his mother, a feminist, attended women's gatherings at Hyde Park, which may have demonstrated to him how well-wrought words mold minds— but a formidable problem with language itself soon undercut all ambition in this direction. He developed a stutter. It proved a devastating affliction— not an occasional disruption in the flow of words but an intense, pervasive disability that he called "a great shadow in my life." For a time, he found that he "couldn't say anything."

Psychologists and medical researchers remain uncertain about the cause of stuttering; both genes and environment seem to play a part. There is no known cure. In Owen's case, it is not difficult to see this speech defect as an expression of his struggle, common among adolescents but accentuated in the case of a sensitive, musical soul, to find a proper relationship between inner and outer world. He tried a number of therapies, all to no avail. Hope fled and one night—he was fifteen or sixteen years old—he wondered whether it might not be better to fall asleep and never awake. These somber musings had an unexpected effect: they resulted, not in an attempt on his own life, but in his first stab at poetry. "Sleep has a brother . . ." reads one of the lines. The brother, of course, is death; but for Owen, poetry became the means to reclaim his life. He didn't write much at this age, but he found that while reciting poems, whether his own or others, and also when singing (what is song but musical poetry?), his stutter eased, sometimes dramatically. Poetry, then, was the hitherto unknown link between his two great loves, words and music. Naked words eluded him, but words clothed in music, rhyme, or rhythm rang forth without impediment.

At about the same time, he made a related discovery: that the body possessed its own melody and rhythm. He became an expert gymnast, swooping, spinning, flying, and springing on the parallel bars, the horse, and the other vaguely menacing implements of this mysterious new art. Soon he was Highgate's senior gymnast. "I was rather well developed, had rather a good figure and held myself well." Away from the gym, he continued to recite poems, particularly lyric verse. Soon he realized that poetry not only stilled his stutter but instilled hope and joy. He came to believe that it contained uncanny power; that the joy he felt was more than pleasure at a poem's wit, beauty, or insight. It sprang from the power of poetic metaphor—that power he had first glimpsed while listening to Harwood translate—to bring new meaning into the world. "Poetry," he now realized, "had the power to change one's consciousness a little." This insight would have profound implications for his later life.

World War I interrupted these breakneck youthful discoveries. For Barfield, unlike Tolkien and Lewis, the war proved a placid, even boring, affair. He entered the Officers Training Corps and then the Royal

Engineers, learning Morse code and wireless telegraphy while safe on British soil. His unit, comically, set sail for the continental battlegrounds only after the armistice; once arrived in Belgium, he whiled away six months polishing his French. Then the army decided that its idle soldiers needed a useful occupation. Why not go in for education? Barfield was detailed to Oxford University for three weeks, to learn how to teach English literature to the troops. During this brief idyll he discovered Georgian poetry, including the writings of Rupert Brooke, Robert Graves, John Masefield, Walter de la Mare, and Siegfried Sassoon. He grew to love the simple lyric beauty, tinged with melancholy, that marked their work, a poetic style that would be swept away in the avant-garde floodwaters of modernism loosed by Eliot and Pound. He turned to writing verse, but his early efforts, with simple rhymes and little depth, failed to match the work of those Georgians he most admired. His first published poem, "Air Castles," appeared anonymously in *Punch* on February 14, 1917; a comic soufflé, it is as insubstantial as its subject:

> When I grow up to be a man and wear and wear
>   Whate'er I please,
> Black-cloth and serge and Harris-tweed,
>   —I shall have none of these;
>   For shaggy men wear Harris-tweed . . .

Nonetheless, Georgian poetry had won his heart, and when he entered Wadham College, Oxford, some months later, he abandoned his plan to concentrate on Latin and Greek and chose to read English language and literature. In time, philology—in particular, what the history of words reveals about the history of mind—would become his ruling intellectual passion. But he was still very young, with an athlete's physique and love of movement, and while he was at university and for some years beyond, he addressed the world as much through his body as through his mind. He studied the English classics, but in every spare moment, "the sort of thing my mind was full of—it wasn't literature, it was . . . dancing and so forth."

Dance became his new mistress, an advance upon gymnastics, for it added to that sport's power and grace the incomparable spiritual beauty of music. Joining the English Folk Dance Society, he learned Morris dancing and other ancient forms, kinetic counterparts to the lyric traditionalism of Georgian poetry. Morris dancing was a revelation. A vigorous folk dance, traditionally reserved for men, that involves rhythmic arm and leg movements, foot stomps, handkerchief waving, and stick clapping, it opened to him a new realm of quasi-mystical inner experience, in which music served as his daemon or psychopomp. One day in particular, he enjoyed "a vivid experience," a near ecstasy "at the end of one of the movements," when, his hands caught by one rhythm and his feet by another, he "had a very strong experience of the music flowing through [him]"; he was the vessel, the music a supernormal force. "It was very strong."

Sophianic Revelations

Music brought strength, rapture, intimations of a higher world, but something remained amiss. While still at Oxford, Barfield received an invitation to travel to Cornwall for the summer, joining a small troupe of musicians and dancers led by two young sisters named Radford. The group planned to go from village to village, making music and dancing galliards, pavanes, bourrées, and other preclassical forms. "It was a kind of new world" for Barfield, one that he found "delightful." He reveled in the work and in boat journeys around the stunning Cornish coast. But as all Romantics know, beautiful landscapes and sunny days often harbor, like arsenic in paint, the taint of corruption. Like so many young people before him, Barfield fell prey, in the midst of joy and splendor, to Weltschmerz. The immediate catalyst was a young woman, a cousin of the Radfords, who rebuffed his timid advances; but, as he himself realized, he was not in love with her but with "the idea of love." He was "in despair," "very much oppressed," with "no confidence . . . that life had any meaning." No doubt growing pains triggered many of the tears; but there was something more at work. Many years later, Barfield surmised that "what was really at the root of the misery" was "being caged in the materialism of the age." His doubts about existence forced him into a miserable solipsism. On August 20, 1920, he wrote a despairing note to a close Oxford friend, Leo Baker—the same Baker who would later introduce him to C. S. Lewis—describing his sense of cosmic solitude:

> I have been seeing practically no-one with whom I can talk naturally of the things I want to talk about, and the result is that I am

being forced in on myself like an ingrowing toe-nail. It has come to such a pass that I seem to be living in a land of dream. My self is the only thing that exists, and I wear the external world about me like a suit of clothes—my own body included. It—the world—seems to have about as much objective importance as a suit of clothes, and quite often I have a suspicion that I am really naked after all. When I am alone at night, I sometimes feel frightened of the silence ringing in my ears. Something inside me seems to be so intensely and burningly alive, and everything round me so starkly dead . . .

The anguish was nearly unbearable, as he found himself "pondering the problem of existence at most hours of the day & some hours of the night"—and this not for a few days or weeks, but for "years." He later termed it a case of "acute depression."

Trapped in this slough of despond, Barfield visited Switzerland. There, without warning, at the very end of his vacation, he enjoyed an instantaneous and utter remission of his world-weariness, a metanoia that he came to call his "Sophia experience," as an unbidden transformative wisdom (sophia=Greek for wisdom) flooded his mind. The volte-face came "suddenly one evening, one fine evening . . . the clouds sort of lifted—I know this sounds very dramatic, but it is rather essential—all the misery that I had felt, all this lifted with it."

What scattered the clouds? To any skeptic—say, to Lewis at the same age (and he was almost exactly the same age, born only twenty days after Barfield)—the depression would be traceable to Barfield's failed love affair, with adolescent angst a predictable emotional variation on the theme, and its alleviation just as obvious; for at just this time, Barfield met a new love interest: Matilda "Maud" Douie (1885–1980), who would become his wife. Maud, a friend of the Radfords, was thirteen years older than Barfield, but the age gap meant nothing to either of them. She entranced him with her choreography and her Scottish ballads, and they married in 1923.

Barfield, however, understood his epochal "Sophia experience" not as a rebound from lovesickness, but as a spiritual epiphany that cured a spiritual illness. Although he remained circumspect about what occurred, the broad outlines of the event are apparent. It seems to have been an episode of nature mysticism, akin to those described by Richard Maurice Bucke in *Cosmic Consciousness* (1901) and by William James with more sophistication in *The Varieties of Religious Experience* (1902): an overwhelming sense of unity with the cosmos, accompanied by certitude and bliss. By the time Barfield had his own Sophia experience in the early 1920s, the doctrine of "cosmic consciousness" had penetrated the Weltanschauung of the age and may have helped to shape what he underwent. An apprehension of beauty was also an important component, for Barfield realized, in his ecstasy, that he "would be able to find all the beauty I had fallen for in this woman [the Radfords' cousin] in the whole world of nature."

This sounds banal in the telling, and perhaps it is, but Barfield's Sophia experience brought with it a profound discovery: that the heightened perception that he had tasted previously only through poetic metaphor, especially that of Keats, Shelley, Shakespeare, and the Georgians, could be experienced directly, in life as well as in art, a transforming event available to anyone at any moment. Later, he would argue in book after book that this experience had been commonplace among the ancients and that in the future it would become so again, albeit in a more self-aware, sophisticated form. The Sophia event changed his life. It "led into the whole shape and development of my literary and philosophical work," by pointing him toward the monumental idea that would become the focus of his life's work: the nature and evolution of human consciousness.

The Evolution of Consciousness

For over seventy years, the question of how human perception has changed (and continues to change) over the course of centuries would remain at the center of Barfield's thought, so much so that he once observed that while there is an early C. S. Lewis and a later C. S. Lewis, there is only one Barfield from beginning to end: a man devoted to a single idea, the evolution of consciousness, and how language reveals this evolution by serving as a fossil record of human consciousness as it existed in the past and as a harbinger, with the aid of spiritual insight, of its possible future state.

Barfield's first step in examining the question, in the wake of the Sophia experience, came in August 1920, when a little essay, "Form in

Poetry"—his first published prose work—appeared in the *New Statesman*. The essay offers a vigorous response to the Bloomsbury critic Clive Bell's *Art* (1914), a widely read work that argues that one arrives at the meaning, value, and significance of a work of art by looking at its "significant form"— in the case of a painting, the play of line, shape, and color. Subject matter counts for nothing. Bell's disciples applied the same principles to poetry, contending that a poem's art lies in its sound, stress, and cadence, and that its content—for example, the ideas and events it may present—is irrelevant. To this Barfield tartly answers that it follows that "Hey-diddle-diddle ranks as an idyll." Instead, he proposes that the form of a poem unfolds in the reader's consciousness and is different for each reader, that every word in a poem is "the final objective record for each person of the whole series of thoughts or sense-impressions received by him every time he has spoken or heard that word," and that the art of poetry consists in the juxtaposition of these thoughts or sense-impressions. That is to say, "the poet's material . . . is memory." Contra Bell and his disciples, a poem does not mean only how it says; it means what each reader reads in it when he brings his full experience to bear upon it. This leads ineluctably to the unstated but implicit conclusion that words transmit more than sound, even more than lexical meaning—more, that is, than the sort of information one might find in a dictionary; words are catch-basins of experience, fingerprints and footprints of the past that the literary detective may scrutinize in order to sleuth out the history of human consciousness.

The radical idea that words carry such hidden cargo is elaborated in a second essay that Barfield published two years later in the *London Mercury* for December 1922. He begins his piece, "Ruin," by quoting with approval Maupassant's declaration that *les mots ont une âme* ("words have a soul"). Making industrious use of the *OED*, he then bares the soul of the English word "ruin" by exploring its etymology (here one may note that Emerson declared in "The Poet" that "language is the archives of history," and in "In Praise of Books" that dictionaries are "the raw material of possible poems and histories," and one wonders about the extent of his influence on Barfield, largely unacknowledged apart from scattered references in the latter's 1931 *Poetic Diction* and a few essays). Barfield finds in the Latin origin of "ruin," *ruo*, "a large sense of swift, disastrous movement." This sense would not last. "Ruin" changes—or evolves— through the writings of Chaucer, Gower, Spenser, Shakespeare (in the latter's writings it becomes "a warm and living thing"), Milton, Pope, Dryden, and others, each contributing to its shifting meaning, to the import of the word's "four magical black squiggles, wherein the past is bottled, like an Arabian Genii, in the dark." By the late eighteenth century with its Enlightenment, neoclassical, and satirical sensibilities, "ruin" had been bled of its original power, speed, and terror, becoming "all tumble-down walls and mossy masonry." The case is exemplary; "ruin" is but one of ten thousand "ancestral words embalming the souls of many poets dead and gone and the souls of many common men." It is also, Barfield proclaims in an ending burning with eschatological fever, a word with a bright future. For all words, all language, invented so that people can relate to one another, are "striving still towards that end and consolation." As language "grows subtler and subtler, burying in its vaults more and more associations, more and more mind, it becomes to those same spirits a more and more perfect medium of companionship. In the beginning was the Word, and the Word was with God, and the Word was God."

Barfield's task from now on would be to illuminate these dark vaults, this past, this future; in so doing, he would uncover an understanding of history scarcely guessed at by the vast majority of his contemporaries. Words contain the "souls" or minds of people in the past; as such, they tell the story of consciousness. And by scrutinizing the record of how words change and of how we coin new words with new meanings, Barfield is beginning to grope toward his great discoveries: that consciousness is not the same now as it was in the past or will be in the future; that in the deep past, human consciousness "participated" directly in nature, it was alive, vigorous, and resplendent, but not fully aware of itself; that our modern consciousness is utterly different, aware of itself and able to analyze and reflect upon itself, while at the same time enervated, depressed, wallowing in materialism, atheism, and despair; and that the future offers hope of a new golden age, in which we will recapture our primordial vigor while retaining our modern self-awareness.

The Coming of Rudolf Steiner

At this stage in his life—he was in his twenties—Barfield had worked these ideas out in haphazard, inchoate form. A new perspective was needed in order to place them in a reliable or at least internally coherent historical, scientific, and philosophical framework. It came from an un-expected quarter: Anthroposophy, the teachings of the Austrian spiritual seer Rudolf Steiner (1861–1925). Barfield discovered Steiner during a summer in Cornwall spent in the company not only of the Radford sisters but of his old classmate Harwood and Harwood's future wife, Daphne Olivier. After hearing Steiner lecture in Stuttgart, Olivier had become an enthusiast, and before long she and Harwood were attending talks at the headquarters of the Anthroposophical Society in Gloucester Place, London. When Barfield heard about Steiner, his initial skepticism quickly melted. He came to realize that "Steiner had obviously forgotten volumes more than I had ever dreamed," embraced his occult teachings, joined the society, and made much of his membership card (number 15), signed by Steiner himself. Admiration soon gave way to adulation; Steiner became for Barfield a philosopher with a "stature . . . almost too excessive to be borne," "a key figure—perhaps on the human level, *the* key figure" in the evolution of consciousness, a man in whom "we observe, actually beginning to occur, the transition from *homo sapiens* to *homo imaginans et amans.*"

To describe Rudolf Steiner is to bottle a tornado. A thin, frail man with dark hair and deep-set eyes, he was, like many European esotericists—Bruno, Swedenborg, Gurdjieff—a polymath, producing, in forty years of work, over three hundred volumes of lectures and other writings, along with paintings, sculpture, architectural designs, a new system of dance, and revolutionary theories of education, medicine, and agriculture. The titles of his books range from the reassuringly earthbound—*The Philosophy of Freedom, The Education of the Child*—to the extravagantly outré—*Occult Significance of Blood, The Mission of Gautama Buddha on Mars*. He commenced his prodigious labors in the 1880s, as editor of a scholarly edition of Goethe's scientific works; by 1904 he had become the leader of the German branch of Madame Blavatsky's Theosophical Society; in 1913 he broke away to form his own Anthroposophical Society, dedicated to expounding "Spiritual Science"—a method of occult insight that offered, he claimed, reliable, verifiable, clairvoyant exploration of the spiritual realm.

Armed with the discoveries of this new cognitive tool, Steiner rewrote the history of the world, describing lost ages and unknown civilizations like Lemuria and Atlantis, whose inhabitants possessed multiple psychic powers, most notably telepathy. He filled in this historical framework with teachings about reincarnation, karma, the astral planes, the Akashic Record, and other familiar elements in the European occultist's kit. A new version of Christianity emerged, in which Christ becomes the pivot of cosmic and human evolution. Steiner spent his last decade crisscrossing Europe like a modern St. Paul, lecturing, writing, planting his legacy— Barfield heard him speak in London on August 24, 1924—before passing away in 1925, worn to a thread by his intense labors and by worry over the threat of National Socialism (as early as 1921, Hitler had ranted about Steiner being too close to the Jews). The Anthroposophical Society flourished after its founder's death, establishing schools, farms, special-needs communities, banks, and churches on many continents; as the years passed it found its place, for most observers outside the fold, as a colorful and fruitful chapter in the story of Western esotericism and as a curious footnote in the history of Western thought.

What attracted Barfield to this remarkable man, who has drawn his share of illustrious followers—Saul Bellow and Andrei Tarkovsky among them—but who strikes most people as a thinker inhabiting the fringe between reality and fantasy? The initial appeal lay, for Barfield, not in Steiner's more bizarre theories—although in time Barfield would embrace most of them—but rather in an extraordinary convergence of views. He soon realized, while attending lectures in Gloucester Place and reading the Anthroposophical literature, in particular Steiner's *The Philosophy of Freedom*, that his own etymological researches and Steiner's spiritual explorations had revealed the same astonishing truth. Barfield later described it this way: "The essence of Steiner's teachings . . . is the evolution of human consciousness . . . I, in a way, came to the same conclusion on my own before I heard of Steiner . . . He began where I left off. All I had done was to establish, in a hostile intellectual atmosphere, that there *was* such a thing as the evolution of consciousness from a more pictorial, more living, if you like, form or quality to our own. He assumes that, to start with, and builds on that this terrific edifice."

From this time on, Barfield harbored no doubts. Steiner was a second Aristotle, bestowing upon the world a philosophico-scientific system of breathtaking intricacy and truth that offered the key to humanity's purpose and destiny. He was, quite simply, "*il maestro di color che sanno*—master of those who know" (Dante's encomium to Aristotle in *Inferno* IV: 131).

The "Great War"

Several of Barfield's friends scoffed at this assessment. Among them was C. S. Lewis, for whom, as we shall see, Steiner was not a man of destiny but a Pied Piper leading his disciples away from common sense as well as sound spiritual philosophy. Lewis and Barfield had met during the fall of 1919, as Oxford undergraduates and near neighbors, their residences a half mile apart. The encounter seems inevitable, for the two had a great deal in common, including love of philosophy, literature, talking, and walking. Leo Baker engineered the rendezvous. Soon a nucleus of bright young men, including Baker, Lewis, Barfield, Harwood, and W. Eric Beckett—later a celebrated lawyer knighted for work in the British Foreign Office—began assembling regularly to share poems and essays and to debate religion, philosophy, and literature. Their tastes were conservative and refined. They adored mythology, traditional art, and the Romantics, and despised all bohemian movements. They disagreed, intensely, about the existence of God, the nature of Christ, the meaning of history. These gatherings, in some ways foreshadowing Inklings meetings, cemented the bond between Lewis and Barfield. Then and always, comradely disputation lay at the heart of their relationship; in *Surprised by Joy*, Lewis calls Barfield not only his "Second Friend" but his "anti-self."

The meetings of this proto-Inklings circle continued through much of the 1920s; so, too, did private exchanges between Barfield and Lewis. Often their discussions became full-scale battles. "We went at our talk like a dogfight," remembered Lewis, while Barfield confessed to having "a reputation among my own friends of being argumentative." Lewis, he was glad to say, enjoyed the pugilism: "Most people—here, especially, Lewis was different—are apt to flinch at the verbal aggression, taking it as a kind of personal attack or even as a kind of contempt . . . nobody but Jack could argue so freely, hitting so hard, but knowing it won't hurt." For a time, Barfield shared with Harwood a thatched cottage near Beckley, a few miles outside Oxford; Lewis would often cycle over to carry on the argument. The three companions formed a perfect debating circle, a study in types: Barfield, slender, elegant, gently but insistently advancing esoteric doctrines; Lewis, boisterous and belligerent, his face turning bright red as he bellowed objections and *distinguos*; Harwood, quiet and observant, the go-between—"a summoned voice rather than a vociferous one"

Barfield described him. These jousts enhanced the idyllic nature of the relationship: young men, in the peak of youth and intellectual fervor, joyfully clashing ideological swords. Recalling one such happy day, Lewis wrote in his diary: "We got into conversation on fancy and imagination: Barfield cd. not be made to allow any essential difference between Christina dreams [wish-fulfilling fantasies] and the material of art . . . At supper I drank Cowslip Wine for the first time. It is a real wine, green in colour, bittersweet . . . After supper we went out for a walk, into the woods on the edge of Otmoor. [The] black and white cat, Pierrot, accompanied us like a dog all the time. Barfield danced round it in a field—with sublime lack of selfconsciousness and wonderful vigour—for our amusement and that of three horses." Lucky horses, blessed young men!

Barfield, in love with Maud, vibrant with life, on the track of cosmic secrets, was not only dancing, he was writing at top speed: poems, reviews, literary criticism, philological analyses. In 1925 he published his first novel, *The Silver Trumpet*. It is an anomaly in his work, a witty fairy tale for children, free of philology or theorizing about the nature of consciousness. The plot reads like a burlesque of Hans Christian Andersen, with a wicked princess plotting her good sister's death, turning people into toads, driving a kingdom to ruin, only to see her machinations thwarted by a pure-hearted prince, a good-natured dwarf, and a benevolent witch. What to make of it? One critic has seen in the tale a prophecy of the rise of fascism, but this seems a stretch; what depth it possesses lies in the central image of the silver trumpet, whose glorious peal, sounded at key moments throughout the tale, invariably jolts the characters into a higher, purer, more noble mode of perception and understanding. The Barfield scholar Simon Blaxland–de Lange points out that the trumpet signals the same "felt change of consciousness" that Barfield believed was wrought in the imagination by poetry. He may well have had this analogy in mind while composing his tale; he likely also had in mind the passages from the Book of Numbers in which God commands Moses:

> "Make two silver trumpets; of hammered work you shall make them; and you shall use them for summoning the congregation, and for breaking camp . . . on the day of your gladness also, and at your appointed feasts, and at the beginnings of your months, you shall blow the trumpets over your burnt offerings and over

the sacrifices of your peace offerings; they shall serve you for re-
membrance before your God: I am the Lord your God." (Numbers
10:1–2, 10)

In Barfield's tale, the silver trumpet serves a sacramental role, bridging
through its music—the music that Barfield so loved, that he valued more
than poetry—heaven and earth, instilling in all who hear it conscience,
repentance, and renewal. It works miracles, too, for through its pure notes
a decrepit king is brought back to his senses and a dead princess back to
life. With the advantage of hindsight, we can see that *The Silver Trumpet*
trumpets a new literary movement, for it marks the first publication of
fantasy fiction by an Inkling-to-be, a harbinger of all the golden works to
come. Lewis rejoiced at its call, "in which with prodigality [Barfield]
squirts out the most suggestive ideas, the loveliest pictures, and the raci-
est new coined words in wonderful succession. Nothing in its kind can
be imagined better." So he wrote in his private diary, far from his friend's
eyes and therefore most likely his honest assessment of the book's virtues. *The Times Literary Supplement* concurred, calling it "one of the best
new fairy stories this year." Thirteen years later, the Tolkien family added
its applause, as Lewis relayed to Barfield: "I lent the *Silver Trumpet* to
Tolkien and hear that it is the greatest success among his children that
they have ever known. His own fairy-tales, which are excellent, have now
no market; and its first reading—children are so practical!—led to a universal wail 'You're *not* going to give it back to Mr. Lewis, are you?' . . . In
fine, you have scored a direct hit." The bull's-eye was not to be repeated.
Barfield's future fiction output, apart from philosophical works in the
form of imagined symposia, would consist of unremarkable short stories
and plays and a realistic, unpublishable novel. He opened the vein of
mythopoeic gold for his fellow Inklings but failed to mine it successfully
himself; the loss is palpable.

While Barfield worked on *The Silver Trumpet*, his debates with Lewis
mounted in intensity. The turning point came when he and Harwood
confessed their enthusiasm for Rudolf Steiner. Lewis was aghast, exclaiming in his diary (July 7, 1923) that "Steiner seems to be a sort of panpsychist, with a vein of posing superstition, and I was very much disappointed
to hear that both Harwood and Barfield were impressed by him." Many
years later, in *Surprised by Joy*, he would provide more details about his

reaction: "I was hideously shocked," he writes, for "here . . . were all the abominations . . . gods spirits, after-life and pre-existence, initiates, oc-cult knowledge, meditation. 'Why—damn it—it's *medieval*,' I exclaimed." His revulsion may seem extreme but should not surprise, for during the early 1920s he was still a self-proclaimed pagan, a proponent of *élan vital*, in love with energy, growth, and truth—all of which, he was con-vinced, perished the instant supernatural considerations entered the conversation. Barfield and Harwood had gone over to the enemy. Lewis would win them back if possible; in any event, he would fight them tooth and nail. So opened his first great analytical campaign, which he de-scribed as "an almost incessant disputation . . . which lasted for years" to de-anthroposophize Barfield, in large measure by denying any value to the imagination, upon whose wings Steiner had soared into the higher world of supersensible realities, as a vehicle for the discovery of truth. Lewis called this prolonged debate the "Great War," a nod to its dura-tion, ferocity, and high stakes, the intellectual counterpart to that other Great War both disputants had experienced firsthand.

The Barfield-Lewis "Great War" lasted from 1923 or 1924 until 1931. It was waged via letters, treatises, and poems, and in one-on-one and group debates, at home and on walking tours. This last venue deserves special notice, for philosophical rambles in woods and fields, from pub to pub, lasting from an afternoon to several days, would become a favorite activ-ity of the Inklings. Barfield was the first to suggest the practice. Lewis, Baker, and Harwood readily agreed, other friends joined in, and soon these latter-day Peripatetics tramped the countryside while tussling over God, literature, art, and a thousand other subjects. Many of the partici-pants wrote about these walking tours; almost all accounts place Lewis at the center. Thus the future Inkling Nevill Coghill: "we used to fore-gather in our rooms or go off for country walks together in endless but excited talk about what we had been reading the week before . . . we walked almost as fast as we talked—disputing and quoting, as we looked for the dark dingles and the tree-topped hills of Matthew Arnold . . . Lewis, with the gusto of a Chesterton or a Belloc, would suddenly roar out a passage of poetry that he had newly discovered and memorized . . . we had, of course, thunderous disagreements and agreements . . ."

How one longs for a recording of this thunder! At least we have some of the written documents, and while they may not capture the youthful joy and abandon that must have imbued these country walks, they possess their own, more polished, charm. The title of one of the principal texts, Lewis's *Clivi Hamiltonis Summae Metaphysices contra Anthroposophos*, modeled upon Aquinas's *Summa contra Gentiles*, suggests the schoolboy vigor and jocularity—and the sophisticated attacks—that characterized the "Great War." Barfield countered with *Replicit Anthroposophus Barfieldus*; later broadsides include Lewis's *De Bono et Malo*, Barfield's *De Toto et Parte*, and Lewis's rejoinder, *Commentarium in Tractatum De Toto et Parte*. Twice in later life, Barfield tried unsuccessfully to get the major documents into print, but the publishers he approached ruled, perhaps correctly, that the "Great War" documents, in their prolixity and their recondite obscurities, would hold little interest for the public, even a public ravenous for Lewisiana.

Yet the "Great War" circled around a vital subject—the nature of the imagination—and is well worth revisiting. Barfield believed that the imagination was a legitimate tool for acquiring objective truth. It was a delicate instrument, often abused, but if properly employed—as he believed it to be in the case of Steiner's Spiritual Science—it provided access to knowledge unavailable to ordinary perception. Lewis, on the other hand, argued that the imagination pointed toward truth but could not disclose it directly. Truth, he believed at this time, was always somewhat elusive. "We must be content to feel the highest truths 'in our bones': if we try to make them explicit, we really make them untruths," he said to Harwood. In a letter to Barfield, he drew three sketches that characterized his views. The first shows Lewis tied to a post and looking into a mirror to catch a glimpse of whatever reality is revealed by reason (the primary instrument for investigation into truth claims) and controlled imagination; the second shows "a gentleman" (Barfield) also tied to a post, attacking the mirror with a hammer and chisel to get at the esoteric reality that lies behind it; the third shows the same Barfieldian gentleman assaulted by a phantom (the embodiment of occultism) unleashed by his irrational hammerings.

Needless to say, Barfield rejected these caricatures. To grasp the intensity of his conviction, however, and to understand how and why he came by his conclusions regarding the nature of truth, consciousness, and their interplay, it will help to turn to two books that he wrote while the "Great War" raged, books that advance his case with all guns blazing.

History in English Words

In 1926, Barfield published *History in English Words*, his first full-length philosophico-philological treatise. Note the preposition in the title. Barfield's aim is not to recount the history of English. He is attempting something far rarer: to see how words capture history, how "words may be made to disgorge the past that is bottled up inside them, as coal and wine, when we kindle or drink them, yield up their bottled sunshine." In many ways, then, the book is an expansion of his essay on the word "ruin," but encompassing a much vaster set of examples, the fruit of countless hours of meditation upon the *Oxford English Dictionary* and its semantic and etymological treasures. *History in English Words* may also be considered the opening chapter of Barfield's one and only book, which took him a lifetime to write.

On one level, *History in English Words* is a compendium of entertaining facts. The author tells us, for example, that in the sixteenth century "Sir John Cheke began a translation of the New Testament in which none but native words were to be used; and we find in his *Matthew moond* for *lunatic, hundreder* for *centurion, frosent* (from-sent) for *apostle, crossed* for *crucified, freshman* for *proselyte*, and many other equally odd-sounding concoctions." In a provocative passage about the evolution of words, he reports that "for the Romans themselves the old goddesses called the Fata, or *Fates*, turned quickly into an abstracted notion of destiny. But contact with the dreamy Celts breathed new life into their nostrils, and 'Fata' in late Latin became spiritual once more. The sharp sounds were softened and abraded until they slipped imperceptibly into Old French 'fée' (Modern English *fay*), and so *fa-ery* and *fairy*. *Demon* is the result of a similar metamorphosis."

This erudition is enjoyable but little more than a jeu d'esprit. Happily, Barfield employs these philological bonbons as a foundation for substantial fare, arguing that words make possible, and the study of words reveals, new avenues of knowledge. For example—this is the first instance in the book—scientists coined the phrase "high tension" in order to signify the relationship between two bodies carrying an electric charge ("I was anxious . . . to obtain some idea of the conducting power of ice and solid salts by electricity of high tension"—Michael Faraday, *The Philosophical Transactions of the Royal Society*, 1833). But in less than a century,

the phrase had become a metaphor for emotional stress between two people ("Eugene, strung to the highest tension, does not move a muscle"—
George Bernard Shaw, *Candida*, 1898). "The scientists who discovered
the forces of electricity," Barfield contends, "actually made it possible for
the human beings who came after them to have a slightly different idea,
a slightly fuller consciousness of their relationship with one another."
Similarly, while scrutinizing "absolute," "actual," "attribute," and a score
of other words that pertain to the relation between matter and spirit, he
observes that medieval thinkers not only drew these words (or their Latin
equivalents) from the pagan Greeks but modified them to carry richer
and more subtle meanings. "No one who understands the amount of
pain and energy which go to the creation of new instruments of thought
can feel anything but respect for the philosophy of the Middle Ages."

Using language in this way, as a device for discovering how people, in
any era, thought and felt about the world around them and within them,
leads Barfield to remarkable conclusions. The Middle English word "love-
longing," for example, signals a "new element . . . [in] human relationships, for which perhaps the best name that can be found is 'tenderness.'"
He hastens to add that this statement may oversimplify the situation, as
evidence of tenderness can be found as far back as ancient Egypt. And
yet "love-longing" and other newly coined terms tell us that during the
Middle Ages humanity made a great leap in self-understanding. "Perhaps,"
he suggests, laying all his cards on the table, "it can best be expressed as
a new consciousness of the individual human soul." His argument is now
in the open: the Middle Ages marks a new epoch in human consciousness;
in effect, a new way of being human. Elsewhere he presents in clear
stages the unfolding of this evolutionary scheme. At first, "when our
earliest ancestors looked up to the blue vault they felt that they saw not
merely a place, whether heavenly or earthly, but the bodily vesture, as it
were, of a living Being." In the "Dark Ages" (by which he seems to mean
the early Middle Ages), "there came for the first time into the consciousness of man the possibility of seeing himself purely as a solid object situated
among solid objects." Change followed upon change, leading to the most
astonishing transformation of all, for "self-consciousness, as we know it,
seems to have first dawned faintly on Europe at about the time of the
Reformation."

Claims like these, the reader soon realizes, deliver far more than Barfield's title promises. This is not only history in English words, but the secret history of human nature. In this book, Barfield draws a line between his own thought and that of all the other future Inklings, between himself and almost all his contemporaries, indeed between himself and the self-understanding of Western civilization. For he asserts that through the evolution of consciousness, there has been "a change not only in the ideas people have formed about the world, but a change in the very world they experience."

A half century earlier, James George Frazer and Edward Burnett Tylor had advanced evolutionary accounts, akin in some ways to Barfield's, that describe how humankind had progressed from magical to scientific thinking, and Jacob Burckhardt had identified, in *The Civilization of the Renaissance in Italy*, the precise moment (*Augenblick*) in human history when the human being achieved self-awareness of his own individual personhood (*eine auf sich selbst gestellte Persönlichkeit*). But Burckhardt, Frazer, and Tylor retail no more than cultural history, not ontological change; they recount how certain ideas and social institutions begin, grow, clash, and give birth to new ideas and institutions within a human consciousness that has remained fundamentally unchanged over millennia. They do not contend that the very nature of consciousness—and therefore of the world with which consciousness interacts and, to some extent, creates—evolves over time, sometimes changing dramatically in the course of a few decades. Barfield would spend the rest of his life attempting to place this revolutionary claim on a solid philosophical, historical, literary, and scientific foundation; and all without reference to Hegel, the master architect of evolutionary schemes, whom Barfield did not read extensively until late in life.

Lewis wrote Barfield a cheerful letter upon receiving a copy of *History in English Words*, assuring the author that although the book lacked "perfect clearness," it was "completely and certainly *readable*," a work that sets "windows opening in all directions." His praise was not widely echoed, however, as the book received little attention upon publication, although it was reviewed favorably in *The Observer* (January 17, 1926). *The Times* (London) didn't get around to noticing it for twenty-eight years, when Cyril Connolly, assessing a revised edition in the Sunday paper of

January 24, 1954, pronounced it "learned, imaginative, moving and fe-
licitously factual."

Salvation by Poetry

Barfield's next work, *Poetic Diction* (1928), expands and deepens the argument formulated in *History in English Words*. Moving beyond etymology, he scours the history of poetry to bolster his claims about the evolution
of language and consciousness, proposing "not merely a theory of poetic
diction, but a theory of poetry: and not merely a theory of poetry, but a
theory of knowledge." This grand undertaking began in humble fashion,
as a thesis to fulfill the requirements for an Oxford B.Litt. degree, written at a time when Barfield's main interests lay elsewhere. He and Maud
had started a children's theater, performing skits based on nursery rhymes
("The frog he would a-wooing go" featured Owen as frog, Maud as mouse);
he was dancing in Oxford and Cornwall; he was absorbing Steiner's doctrines with accelerating admiration; and he was warring with Lewis.
Still, he squeezed in enough time to propose a thesis on poetic diction
(that is, on the way a poet arranges words for artistic effect), only to discover that his examiners couldn't find an appropriate supervisor. "They
decided it wasn't at all what they were used to," he remembered; they
preferred "the very scholarly sort of question," such as "whether Coleridge
had an unusual number of toenails." Finally, however, the examiners
agreed to let him write his thesis unsupervised.

By now, Barfield's evolutionary argument had advanced in complexity
and detail. He believed that very early human beings had experienced a
profound intimacy with the world, in which thoughts, feelings, and the
objects of perception lay in healthy and proper relationship to one another (Barfield would later call this state "original participation"); that
over centuries human beings had developed an acute self-awareness in
which this primordial unity disappeared, resulting in the philosophical
skepticism that afflicts modern times; and that the future (which Barfield
had tasted during his Sophia moment) promises a return to our original
experience of unity, while retaining the discernment and ability to think
abstractly that we have acquired during our evolutionary odyssey. *Poetic
Diction* focuses upon the place of language in this scheme. Primordial
man, Barfield contends, possessed a poetic language drenched in mean-

ing. He quotes with approval Shelley's famous line from "In Defence of Poetry": "in the infancy of society every author is necessarily a poet, because language itself is poetry." As consciousness evolved, this poetic language, and the poetic experience of reality that it made possible, faded away. This is the crisis in which we find ourselves today.

Barfield's most impressive elaboration of his theory comes in his discussion of the Greek word *pneuma* (Latin *spiritus*). To Max Müller, the celebrated Victorian philologist—and a principal target of Barfield's argument—*pneuma* originally meant "wind"; when the Greeks required an abstract word for the life principle, they simply appropriated the word *pneuma* and altered its meaning. Not so, counters Barfield; *pneuma* and the words from which it derived "meant neither *breath*, nor *wind*, nor *spirit*, nor yet all three of these things, but . . . simply had *their own old peculiar meaning*, which has since, in the world of the evolution of consciousness, crystallized into the three meanings specified—and no doubt into others also." The history of language is, then, a history of "crystallization," of rigor mortis, of death and decay.

Or so it appears at first glance. But this is illusory; for there exists in the history of language, and thus in the life of human beings, all of whom employ language to apprehend the world, a second, life-giving force. This salvific force is poetry. The world can and will be saved by poets. The lost meaning of primordial language reappears, under the conscious art of the poet, as metaphor, "a re-creating, registering as *thought*, one of those eternal facts which may already have been experienced in perception." Poetry induces a "felt change of consciousness" (the "felt" was added at the suggestion of Lewis, who read the work in manuscript). This change is in effect a return, partial though it may be, to the poetic richness of our primordial consciousness, but now in a state of full self-awareness. Metaphor is the catalyst for this felt change of consciousness. Every effective metaphor brings with it a more complete perception of the world and its interrelationships. It reveals more truth, it brightens, expands, clarifies—in effect, it helps to create—our understanding of the world. Through metaphor we receive "in addition to the moment or moments of aesthetic pleasure in appreciation . . . a more permanent boon. It is as though my own consciousness had actually been expanded." As Barfield promised, his book offers a theory of knowledge. Poetry and its metaphors are means of cognition:

Now my normal everyday experience, as human being, of the
world around me depends entirely upon what I bring to the sense-
datum from within; and the absorption of this metaphor into my
imagination has enabled me to bring more than I could before. It
has created something in me, a faculty or a part of a faculty, enabling me to observe what I could not hitherto observe. This ability to recognize significant resemblances and analogies, considered
as in action, I shall call *knowledge*; considered as a *state*, and apart
from the effort by which it is imparted and acquired, I shall call it
wisdom.

Lewis admired *Poetic Diction*. Although he never embraced fully Barfield's
view of the imagination as the royal road to truth, he learned to appreciate the power of metaphor, going so far, in his 1939 essay "Bluspels and
Flalansferes," as to assert that a metaphor may be a means, and even the
only means, by which we arrive at new ideas and new understandings.
Other friends of Lewis also absorbed some of the book's arguments with
pleasure. His pupil Alan Griffiths (the future monk Bede Griffiths) declared that it "had a permanent effect upon my life." Tolkien, too, felt its
impact. "Your conception of the ancient semantic unity ha[s] modified
his whole outlook," Lewis informed Barfield in 1928. It seems likely,
as the Tolkien scholar Verlyn Flieger has proposed, that Barfield's theories
influenced Tolkien's views on the nature and evolution of language and
played a hand in the shaping of his own invented tongues; in *The Hobbit*,
for example, Tolkien writes of Bilbo spying the dragon's treasure that
"there are no words left to express his staggerment, since Men changed
the language that they learned of elves in the days when all the world was
wonderful," a very Barfieldian observation. Still, Tolkien's and Barfield's
views on language diverged in many ways. For Tolkien, "ancient semantic
unity" describes the state of language in Eden, before the metaphysical
catastrophe of the Fall and its aftermath, expressed mythically in the
story of Babel; for Barfield, the same term describes the state of language
at the dawn of the evolution of consciousness, which will conclude in the
reacquisition by language of its primordial unity and purity. Tolkien, an
orthodox Christian, believed that this second golden age will arrive only
when time itself vanishes in the "new heaven and new earth" (Revelation
21:1); it is not a part of human history but an aspect of eternity.

Outside the circle of future Inklings and their friends, critical reaction to *Poetic Diction* was lukewarm. This irked Lewis, who wrote to Barfield blasting the *Times Literary Supplement* review of May 17, 1928, as "marvelously absurd" and its anonymous author as "obviously unable to make anything" of the book's main argument. In fact, the author of the unsigned piece, Edmund Blunden, winner of the Hawthornden Prize and future professor of poetry at Oxford, understood Barfield's argument well—without, however, perceiving its Anthroposophical underpinnings— and praised his "careful and sensitive critical talent" while objecting to his colorless academic prose and his misuse of the term "minor poet." As for the rest of the literary and academic world, the book, like its predecessor, was largely ignored, although possible traces of its argument can be discerned in widely scattered works such as Arthur Waley's masterful study of Taoism, *The Way and Its Power* (1934), in which the author argues, "I see no other way of studying the history of thought except by first studying the history of words, and such a study would seem to me equally necessary if I were dealing with the Greeks, the Romans, the Egyptians, the Hebrews, or any other people. For example, in reading the Bible, whether for edification or literary pleasure, we do not trouble . . . to ask what the different words rendered by 'soul,' 'spirit,' and so on really meant to the people who used them. But anyone studying the history of Hebrew thought would be bound to ask himself these questions, and I cannot think it is superfluous to ask them with regard to Chinese." But Waley remains the exception. Perhaps in reaction to the work's long cold-shouldering by intellectuals and the academy, its scattered fans lean toward hyperbolic praise; thus the poet Howard Nemerov, who tells us that "among the few poets and teachers of my acquaintance who know *Poetic Diction* it has been valued not only as a secret book, but nearly as a sacred one." This assessment, which appeared in Nemerov's introduction to the 1964 edition of *Poetic Diction*, may have troubled Barfield, for whom sacred books meant the Bible and, in a weaker sense, the writings of Rudolf Steiner.

Who won the "Great War"? Both combatants, one is tempted to reply. Lewis said that it had changed him more than his rival. Barfield's "Great War" arguments, along with *History in English Words* and *Poetic Diction*, revealed to Lewis the fallacy of "chronological snobbery," the assumption, as common now as then, that the present owns more of the truth than the past, that ideas no longer in vogue are most likely false. The "Great War" shook his confidence in materialism and undermined his belief that truth is discoverable exclusively through the senses. At the same time, it did nothing to dent his dislike of Anthroposophy. In *The Pilgrim's Regress* (1933), as Cecil Harwood points out, Lewis places the land of *Anthroposophia* next to that of *Occultia*, and later he would trivialize Steiner's teachings by seeing in them "a reassuring Germanic dullness." Anthroposophy, with its astral planes, its Buddha on Mars, and its Spiritual Science, remained always beyond the pale. As for Barfield, he credited the "Great War" with teaching him how to "think responsibly and logically." Lewis, he believed, was the more agile thinker, the more brilliant debater; what a pity, then, that Lewis's materialism had led him to reject the higher insights of Anthroposophy and the great secret of the evolution of consciousness.

6

A MYTHOLOGY
FOR ENGLAND

H e is improving but requires hardening." So declared the Hull
military medical board upon examining Tolkien on May 1,
1917, six months after his return from England. He was overjoyed to be back in "dear old Blighty" (a trench soldier's affectionate term
for Britain, derived, via the Raj, from the Hindi *bilayati*, "foreigner"), but
the health that young men take for granted, and that he hoped soon
would be his—trench fever usually runs its course in a couple of months—
proved, despite the military board's guarded optimism, elusive. He sickened, improved, and relapsed with agonizing regularity, each advance
derailed by attacks of fever, headache, weakness, loss of appetite, or joint
pain. The military issued him repeated reprieves from active duty, and he
spent much of 1917 shuttling between his army unit, hospital, and brief
but blissful visits with Edith, now pregnant with their first child.

Love ripened between the parents-to-be. Tolkien wrote, read, and
drew, while Edith enchanted him with her piano playing and, one day in
a "small woodland glade filled with hemlocks at Roos in Yorkshire," with
her dancing, offering to his exhausted eyes a vision of beauty and grace,
a glimpse of paradise. "In those days," he wrote, "her hair was raven, her
skin clear, her eyes brighter than you have seen them, and she could
sing—and *dance*." The forest interlude inspired him to write "Of Beren
and Lúthien," to his mind the narrative heart of *The Silmarillion*. A quasi-
autobiographical tale, it recounts the love of Beren, a man, and Lúthien,
an Elven princess he spies dancing in the woods, and their terrible trials

in search of a magical jewel, culminating in Lúthien's fateful decision to become mortal in order to remain with her beloved. Their sufferings, as many critics have noticed, echo the multiple ordeals, including separation, war, and religious hostility, faced by Tolkien and Edith during their youth.

On November 16, 1917, Edith gave birth in a Cheltenham nursing home to John Francis Reuel, after a painful and dangerous labor. Tolkien, who had been confined to an officers' hospital in Hull since mid-August, was unable to visit until nearly a week after the birth. John's baptism, with Father Francis in attendance, offered a few hours of normalcy, but the respite was illusory. During the next nine months, Tolkien fell prey to recurrent fevers, influenza, and gastritis, dropping nearly thirty pounds by mid-August. Compounding his trials, in late July the War Office erroneously ordered the emaciated young officer back to France. Five tense days later the directive was canceled, and in early September a medical board pronounced him completely disabled and dispatched him to a convalescent institution in Blackpool. This was to be his last prolonged hospital stay; by midautumn, he had returned to Oxford and civilian life, although his official discharge did not arrive for another six months, shortly after the signing of the Treaty of Versailles. Tolkien left the army with the rank of temporary lieutenant, a fitting title, for he was never, at heart, a warrior; he had done his duty and helped to save England, but his greatest contribution to the war effort would come decades later, when *The Lord of the Rings* apotheosized, in its account of hobbits battling ultimate evil in a landscape of fantastic redoubts and talking trees, the achievements of ordinary Tommies and Doughboys among the barbed wire, rats, mud, and machine gun fusillades of rural France.

Opening a New World

Tolkien's convalescence, despite the prolonged suffering it entailed, proved to be a blessing in disguise, for his recurrent illness prevented return to the front lines and gave him the leisure to assess, refine, and expand his mythology. His friends urged him on. A month after his return to England, he received a letter from Wiseman, apart from Tolkien all that remained of the TCBS, declaring that "if you do come out in print you will startle our generation as no one has yet." As prophecy, this was hyperbolic, two generations off, and yet not entirely askew, for Tolkien startled his children's and grandchildren's generations as much as any author; it was, in any case, a welcome spur.

Tolkien aimed higher, however, than startlement; his ambitions soared to dizzying heights. He intended to bestow upon England a priceless gift: its own literary dowry, the mythology, fairy tales, and heroic legends it deserved but had never possessed. Olympian ambitions simmered in many young authors of this generation; it was just a few years earlier, in 1909, that James Joyce, as dissimilar to Tolkien in narrative strategy as any writer could be (although the two shared a Catholic upbringing and Catholic imagery) confessed to Nora Barnacle his aim to "become indeed the poet of my race." As Tolkien recalled it years later, "I was from early days grieved by the poverty of my own beloved country: it has no stories of its own (bound up with its tongue and soil), not of the quality that I sought, and found (as an ingredient) in legends of other lands . . . Do not laugh! But once upon a time . . . I had a mind to make a body of more or less connected legend, ranging from the large and cosmogonic, to the level of romantic fairy-story . . . which I could dedicate simply to: to England; to my country."

Iceland boasted the Norse sagas, Finland the *Kalevala*, Germany the rich subsoil of folklore and legend unearthed by the Grimm brothers. Britain, however, had no native tales to offer, its mythological and folkloric potential snuffed out by the Norman invasion and the subsequent Latinization of the culture. Arthurian mythology, despite its inherent nobility and beauty, had in Tolkien's eyes at least three fatal flaws. It owed too much to French poets like Chrétien de Troyes, and Tolkien disliked all things French—its fussy food, its language teeming with "polysyllabic barbarities," and now its battlefields, on which two of his closest friends had fallen. Stylistically, the Arthurian cycle was "too lavish, and fantastical, incoherent and repetitive." And it was openly Christian. Tolkien believed that while myth and fairy tale must reflect religious truth, they must do so subtly, never depicting religion as it appears in "the known form of the primary 'real' world." The Arthur cycle failed the test. Nothing else would do: if Tolkien's beloved land were to possess a mythology, it would be up to him to create it.

What inspired this wildly high dream? Other English writers—
Langland, Bunyan, Shakespeare, Milton, Coleridge, Peacock, and Shelley among them—had elaborated extant myths or invented their own;
Blake had gone further by imagining a primordial Britain (Albion) swirling with spiritual beings. But Tolkien's plan to create a full-fledged mythological story-cycle in poetry and prose is unmatched in English literature.
The idea may have come to him first while reading, at King Edward's, the
Kalevala. To encounter the Finnish national epic was, he said, to open "a
new world," to "revel in an amazing new excitement. You feel like Columbus
on a new Continent, or Thorfinn in Vinland the Good." Perhaps Tolkien
saw himself as another Elias Lönnrot, the physician and philologist who
had created the *Kalevala*, scouring the Finnish countryside for traditional
songs which he then wove, along with material collected by other eth-
nologists, into an epic tale stretching from the creation of the cosmos to
the coming of Christ. The atmosphere is bleak, tragic, and violent, like
much of Tolkien's legendarium.

Tolkien first encountered the *Kalevala* in the Everyman's edition, fea-
turing a translation by William Forsell Kirby, an entomologist and popular author of works like *Familiar Butterflies and Moths* and *Marvels of Ant
Life* who studied languages as a hobby (one can't help noticing how many
philologists, including the Grimm Brothers, Müller, Schlegel, Joseph
Wright, Kirby, and Tolkien himself, were prodigies, polymaths, or both).
Kirby's rendition of the opening lines might have been written by
Tolkien himself, so perfectly do they capture the young mythmaker's
aspirations:

> I am driven by my longing,
> And my understanding urges
> That I should commence my singing,
> And begin my recitation.
> I will sing the people's legends,
> And the ballads of the nation.

This singing, as Tolkien conceived it, was to be "cool and clear," distinctly
northern, evoking Nordic snows rather than Grecian sands, but leavened
by that "fair elusive beauty that some call Celtic, although it is rarely found

in genuine ancient Celtic things." The literary voice was to be archaic, medieval, in the "heigh stile," but modified for prose in the manner of William Morris's romances.

With these qualifications in place, Tolkien's stories flowed, often arising in his mind unbidden, "as 'given' things . . . always I had the sense of recording what was already 'there,' somewhere: not of 'inventing.'" This is a well-attested experience, as old as Plato's *Meno* and much celebrated among the Romantics; thus Blake's claim in a famous 1803 letter to be no more than a "Secretary" transcribing poems by "Authors [who] are in Eternity," and Coleridge's cognate image of the poet as "The Eolian Harp" (1795) sounded by divine winds to produce "such a soft floating witchery of sound / As twilight Elfins make, when they at eve / Voyage on gentle gales from Fairy-Land." There are parallels, too, with an Old English poem well known to Tolkien, that of Cædmon, the seventh-century cowherd who had a dream or vision in which a mysterious man orders him to tell (as St. Bede describes it in his *History of the English Church and People*) "the beginning of created things." Inspired by grace, Cædmon sings a nine-line hymn of praise to God, which includes the first appearance in English poetry of *middangeard*, or Middle-earth, that portion of creation reserved for human beings, the land in which Tolkien's legendarium would unfold:

Nu we sculon herigean heofonrices weard,
Meotodes meahte ond his modgeþance,
Weorc wuldorfæder, swa he wundra gehwæs,
Ece drihten, or onstealde.
He ærest sceop eorðan bearnum
heofon to hrofe, halig scyppend;
Þa middangeard moncynnes weard,
ece drihten, æfter teode
firum foldan, frea ælmihtig.

Now must we praise the guardian of heaven-kingdom,
the might of the measurer and his mind's aim,
the work of the glory-father, as each of the wonders
the eternal lord set forth in the beginning.

First he shaped for the sons of men
heaven as a roof, the holy maker made.
Then middle-earth the guardian of mankind,
the eternal lord, afterwards established
to be a solid ground for men, almighty is the lord.

Cædmon's hymn is the oldest-known Old English poem and stands, as such, at or near the origins of English literature; Tolkien could not have found a more perfect seed from which to grow his imaginary world. In keeping with the hymn, he always insisted that Middle-earth was neither supernatural nor fantastic—akin neither to heaven nor to Wonderland—but was simply the "objectively real world."

Among Tolkien's first tales in his newborn mythology is "The Cottage of Lost Play," composed in late 1916 or early 1917, the fair copy being inscribed by Edith on February 12, 1917, from Tolkien's pencil original into a "High School Exercise Book." Set in the distant past, long before the Angles, Saxons, and Jutes entered Britain, "The Cottage of Lost Play" serves as a frame (a device ubiquitous in popular fiction of the era) for most of the early tales. A wandering sailor named Eriol ("One who dreams alone," suggesting a Tolkien alter ego) arrives at the Lonely Isle of Tor Eressëa, enters the enchanted Cottage of Lost Play in the town of Koromas, and there encounters kindly gnomes who recount the history of Middle-earth. Tolkien's notes indicate that Tor Eressëa, with its hills and hamlets and "broad and woody plain," is primordial England, Koromas is Warwick (where Tolkien and Edith married), and Eriol is the father of Hengest and Horsa, the legendary brothers described in Bede's *Ecclesiastical History* and the *Anglo-Saxon Chronicle*, who sailed from Jutland to England in the fifth century to fight the Picts. Middle-earth, then, includes England, but the England of an exceptionally generous imagination, a land inhabited not only by humans and fairies, but also by goblinlike Orcs (whose name Tolkien took from an Anglo-Saxon word for demon), Balrogs (cruel fiery monsters who wield whips or swords), Ainur or Valar (angels, godlike demiurges), Maiar (lesser Ainur), Melkor (the rebel angel, also known as Melko and Morgoth), and Eru Ilúvatar (the one God, creator of all things, modeled upon the biblical archetype). Tolkien details the interactions of these sublime or monstrous beings, in archaic England

and in the divine enclave of Valinor, in a series of stories written, for the most part, between 1917 and 1920. The titles—"The Coming of the Valar," "The Chaining of Melko," "The Flight of the Noldoli," "The Tale of Tunúviel," "The Fall of Gondolin," and so on—nicely adumbrate the tumultuous heroic-fantastic content, a vast sweeping history encompassing the creation of the world and the rise, triumph, and fall of his vast ensemble of human and imaginary beings.

The most impressive of Tolkien's early narratives is surely his creation myth, "The Music of the Ainur," which tells how Ilúvatar creates all that is, ex nihilo. He sings "into being" the Ainur, builds them "dwellings in the void," teaches them music, implants in them "the Secret Fire that giveth Life and Reality," and, in what seems like a Neoplatonic variant on the Genesis account, presents them with musical themes to elaborate through their own heavenly instruments in "mighty melodies changing and interchanging, mingling and dissolving amid the thunder of harmonies greater than the roar of the great seas." The Ainur's celestial symphony, at first perfect in beauty and power, is soon marred by the jarring notes of the Satan-like Melko, who fashions his own discordant music, a cry of pride, cruelty, gloom, and decay. This act of musical high treason proves to be the prelude to a yet more astonishing work of creation, as Ilúvatar displays his omnipotence as sole creator by bringing into existence all that had been prefigured in the music of the Ainur: the earth, with its waters, winds, and light, and, in time, Elves and Men. For all the arresting strangeness, the implicit doctrine of creation is wholly compatible with Christian orthodoxy.

But the tales do not make easy reading. Tolkien's decision to cast these first stories of ancient days in the pseudoancient heigh stile, with its ceremonious utterances, convoluted syntax, and nightmarish glossary of names (for which Ilúvatar, Ainur, and Melko/Melkor/Morgoth are fair examples), resulted, as noted in chapter 3, in a false archaism that bears no relation to any stage in the history of the English language and strains the patience of many—a decidedly odd contribution from a trained philologist and literary historian. Nonetheless, in these early tales we see the promise of a new mythopoeic cosmos, if sometimes little more than biblical mythology aslant, that would blossom into the vast canvas of *The Silmarillion* and *The Lord of the Rings*.

Waggle to Walrus . . . To Leeds

Tolkien had found his voice and vocation. But with an exhausted wife and bawling baby to support and unpublished manuscripts piled high on his desk, he desperately needed a job. In October 1918, he traveled to Oxford, hoping to land a university position but meeting one rebuff after another. Salvation came in the form of William Alexander Craigie, professor of Anglo-Saxon, who had tutored Tolkien in Old Norse before the war. Craigie was himself a proto-Tolkien of sorts, a small, wiry, energetic, and clever man, a philologist, a lover of northern tongues, folklore, and Faërie, and the anonymous translator of many of the Nordic tales in Andrew Lang's fairy books. It has been said of him that "facts seemed to run round and rattle in his head like dried peas, and then suddenly to form a convincing pattern . . . to have made one's first steps in the study of an Anglo-Saxon or an Old Norse text under Craigie, was to acquire almost imperceptibly the ambition to become a keen and exact puzzle-solver." In addition to his academic post, Craigie was deeply immersed in what can fairly be described as the greatest philological puzzle-solving enterprise of all time: the construction of the *Oxford English Dictionary*. The brainchild of Victorian intellectuals like Herbert Coleridge, grandson of the great poet, and Richard Chenivix Trench, an Anglican archbishop, this prodigious project, which had been in progress for more than half a century by the time Tolkien knocked on Craigie's door, aimed at nothing less than a comprehensive account of the definitions, etymology, pronunciations, and literary uses of every word in the English language, excluding only those that had died out before or during the first years of the Norman conquest.

Craigie had been at the *OED* since 1897 and had served, since 1901, as one of its three principal editors, and was thus in the perfect position to help his old pupil. He welcomed Tolkien with open arms and a tantalizing offer. How would Tolkien like to join the *OED* staff as a lexicographer, helping out Henry Bradley's team on the letter *w*, coming up with Middle English and Anglo-Saxon derivations for words? Tolkien leaped at the chance. The position would provide a steady income, a return to Oxford, pleasant scholarship rummaging amidst the roots of language, and the chance to work closely with Bradley, whom Tolkien knew as the author of a celebrated history of the Goths and of a philological classic, *The Making of English*.

Tolkien commenced work in January 1919, strolling each morning from the family's new residence on St. John Street, past the monument to the Reformation heroes Cranmer, Latimer, and Ridley with its anti-Catholic slogan, to the dictionary's offices in the Old Ashmolean brownstone building on Broad Street. His task, as one of four assistants to Bradley, was to prepare "dictionary slips," each a six-by-four-inch bit of paper with definitions, variant spellings, and pronunciations for a single word, along with its etymology and one or more literary quotations demonstrating its use. Tolkien's first assignment, pleasing to his puckish sense of humor, was to prepare slips for words from "waggle" to "waggly." He came up with an acceptable definition for "waggle" ("to move [anything held or fixed at one end] to and fro with short quick motions, or with a rapid undulation") but his etymology proved inadequate, requiring Bradley's intervention. He soon got the hang of things, however, and successfully tackled "wait-a-bit," "wake-robin," "walnut," "want," "warlock," and "wold." Curiously, "walrus"—its etymology deriving from Old Norse *rosmhvalr*—vexed him mightily, occasioning six or seven draft slips and a packet of additional notes assembled after leaving the *OED*. But he savored the challenges and declared that he had "learned more" during his stint at the dictionary "than in any other equal period of my life." Always he had loved the internal workings of language; now etymological fever raged within him, and when not occupied with *OED* slips, he toiled on Qenya, devising hosts of new words. He also invented a cursive script, written both horizontally and vertically, which he called the Alphabet of Rúmil. He used this to inscribe Qenya and to keep a diary; the alphabet evolved so rapidly that in time he found it difficult to read his earlier entries.

In June 1919, Kenneth Sisam, Tolkien's former tutor, invited him to provide a glossary of Middle English for Sisam's forthcoming volume, *Fourteenth Century Verse & Prose*. Tolkien gladly assented, admiring the scholarship and bibliographical expertise of the man who had taught him "not only to read texts but to study second-hand book catalogues." Unfortunately, this relatively simple project would set a baleful precedent for almost all of Tolkien's academic writings, ballooning, as a result of his perfectionism, to monstrous proportions with labyrinthine complications, expressed in interminable doubts, procrastinations, and rewritings. Tolkien was well aware of the problem, calling himself a "natural niggler" and an inveterate "beginner . . . and non-finisher," and admitting that "I compose only with great difficulty and endless rewriting." The degree of his fastidiousness, often indistinguishable from fussiness, may be gleaned from his conviction that the Middle English glossary must cover "the ordinary machinery of expression," including idiomatic phrases and "the uses of such innocent-looking little words as the prepositions *of* and *for*," considerations that demanded "exceptionally full treatment to what may rightly be called the backbone of the language." The result, as he admitted, was "a mole-hill glossary (grown into a mountain . . .)," although he preferred to ascribe the delay to "accumulated domestic distractions," by which he meant, above all, the birth in October 1920 of a second son, Michael, with all its attendant disruptions.

Needless to say, he missed the deadline. Sisam's book was published, bereft of its glossary, in October 1921. The following May, Tolkien's glossary appeared on its own as *A Middle English Vocabulary*; four weeks later, the two works came out in a single volume as originally intended. Tolkien's snail-like pace, he confessed to Elizabeth Wright, Joseph's wife, had brought "curses on my head." Thus began his widespread academic reputation as a time waster and dreamer, a man who would rather write a fairy tale than a scholarly study of Faërie. To the reading public this may be a badge of honor, but to many of Tolkien's Oxford colleagues, who lacked the ability to write fiction and any sympathy for the effort, it was a badge of shame. Some accused Tolkien of indolence; this charge is unwarranted. He worked indefatigably, often toiling long past midnight on his projects (including scholarship, about which he could be, sporadically, passionate). He dithered but never dallied. His priorities, however, remained firm: art trumped academia. He was a poet and storyteller by nature, a scholar by profession.

A Middle English Vocabulary soon became a minor classic. As the first comprehensive Middle English glossary, with more than 4,700 entries, it ably filled a void, and *The Year's Work in English Studies 1920–1921* commended it as "a piece of work which can hardly be praised too highly," lauding in particular its "exhaustive textual references." The praise cost Tolkien dearly, however, for the project had consumed months that might have been devoted to his legendarium, and he had shelved *The Book of Lost Tales* in order to complete it. The loss of creative opportunity was "terrible to recall."

On March 10, 1920, in the midst of his labors on the *Vocabulary*, Tolkien crossed a personal Rubicon, for the first time exposing his private mythology to public view by reading portions of "The Fall of Gondolin" to the Exeter College Essay Club. The talk, he told his audience, came from a "complete cycle of events in an Elfinesse of my own imagining" that "has for some time grown up (rather than been constructed) in my mind." The presentation was a roaring success, despite Tolkien's rapid, often incomprehensible delivery, with the Club minutes applauding his tale as "very graphically and astonishingly told . . . with a wealth of attendance to detail interesting in extreme." In the audience were Henry Dyson and Nevill Coghill, two future Inklings; Coghill later remembered losing several days at the Bodleian fruitlessly trying to pin down "what Gondolin was."

Tolkien must have been delighted by this successful unveiling, but he held no illusions about making a living by his pen. He still longed for and needed a secure academic post, one with greater earning potential than the *OED* could offer. In 1920 he found it, landing the Readership in English Language at the University of Leeds, a position paying six hundred pounds per annum. His professional future was now, if not assured, at least well launched. In September, he moved to Leeds for the autumn term. Edith, again pregnant, remained in Oxford until the birth. The baby arrived on October 22 and was christened with the usual garland of family names as Michael Hilary Reuel Tolkien. The family separation, a painful trial for everyone concerned, continued for several months more; not until March did Tolkien find suitable lodgings and Edith sufficient strength to permit relocation of mother and children to Leeds. As a result, this year's Christmas reunion took on heightened importance, marked by one of Tolkien's merriest concoctions. John, now an inquisitive three-year-old, had been quizzing his father about Father Christmas and his North Pole hideaway, and Tolkien responded by handing him an envelope, addressed in a wobbly hand to "Mrs. Tolkien & Master John Francis Reuel Tolkien" and postmarked "North Pole, 22 Dec. 1920." The envelope contained, in the same shaky hand, a letter from Father Christmas announcing that he was setting off for Oxford with his bag of toys and enclosing pictures of himself and his house. The self-portrait shows a surprisingly slender Santa toting a large sack bulging with gifts, his long white beard blown nearly horizontal by the snow-flecked wind; another drawing depicts his igloolike polar redoubt, surrounded by mysterious snow towers and—a botanical anomaly—high firs. The Father Christmas letter would become an annual tradition, delighting the Tolkien children for the next twenty-three years.

In the spring, Edith and the boys joined Tolkien in Leeds, moving into a house owned by a niece of John Henry Newman. They soon relocated to new lodgings closer to the university, but these did not suit, either: the polluted air of Leeds "rotted the curtains" and required Tolkien to "change his collar three times a day"—an annoying problem for a natty dresser. He could not afford much in the way of new clothing, however; his salary was low, and he began to spend his summers grading exams to supplement the family funds, further eroding his precious writing time.

Happily, the School of English at Leeds proved a congenial place to work. Tolkien fell under the spell of its head, George Stuart Gordon, Professor of English Language and Literature, a brilliant scholar who had broad literary tastes, from Greek classics to Shakespeare, and, like Tolkien, a scrupulous diligence often mistaken for procrastination. Gordon, beloved by students and fellow teachers for his kindness and wit—Lewis, who also knew him, called him "more like a man and less like a don than any I have known"—went out of his way to befriend Tolkien and make him a key player in his campaign to enlarge and strengthen English studies at Leeds. "It is not often in 'universities,'" wrote Tolkien, "that a Professor bothers with the domestic difficulties of a new junior in his twenties; but G. did. He found me rooms himself, and let me share his private room at the University . . . I do not think that my experience was peculiar. *He was the very master of men.*"

Tolkien shouldered, while at Leeds, a heavy teaching load. Over several semesters, he taught the history of English, Old and Middle English philology, Germanic philology, Gothic, Old Icelandic, Medieval Welsh, and more. To his relief, the department expanded by adding a second bright light, the Canadian scholar E. V. (Eric Valentine) Gordon ("his name is a disadvantage," wryly observed George Stuart Gordon, who was unrelated to his new hire). E. V. was a former Rhodes scholar, a dashing fellow with a mop of dark hair and a goatee. Tolkien, who had tutored him at Oxford, knew him as an "industrious little devil"; at Leeds he soon became "my devoted friend and pal." E. V. held Tolkien in equally high regard. Together they founded the Viking Club, dedicated to the study of Old Norse and Anglo-Saxon letters and manners, a goal that entailed many nights of beer swilling and singing. Tolkien composed poems and songs for the revels, including an Anglo-Saxon lyric, "Syx Mynet," to be sung to the tune of "I Love Sixpence," while Gordon contributed "When I'm Dead Don't Bury Me at All, Just Pickle My Bones in Alcohol" in Old English, Gothic, and Scottish dialect. Soon the entire English faculty began to sing as one. To the delighted George Stuart Gordon, his cohorts made up "not so much a staff as a Club!" while to Tolkien, the faculty was a "team fired not only with a departmental esprit de corps, determined to put 'English' at the head of the Arts departments, but inspired also with a missionary zeal." After two years of hard labor, Gordon's "Club" had so enlarged its enrollment that an ebullient Tolkien could write to Elizabeth Wright that "the proportion of 'language' students is very high, and there is no trace of the press-gang!" Philology was a major beneficiary. At the time Tolkien arrived in Leeds, one student in twelve studied philology; by 1925, the ratio had changed to nearly one in three.

In addition to teaching, Tolkien toiled away at his legendarium and began an alliterative translation of *Beowulf* (finally published in 2014, long after Tolkien's death). He and E. V. Gordon collaborated on an edition of *Sir Gawain and the Green Knight*, Tolkien handling the text, Gordon the notes. United in their distaste for pedantry, both editors hoped the volume would "provide the student with a text which, treating the unique manuscript with all due respect, is yet pleasant for the modern reader to look at, and is free (as are few Middle English texts) from a litter of italics, asterisks, and brackets, the trail of the passing editor." They succeeded admirably. *The Modern Language Review* praised the book, in unconscious echo of the poem's alliteration, for its "clearness, conciseness, scholarship, and commonsense," although the reviewer went on to indulge in the sort of scholarly nitpicking that Tolkien and Gordon despised, raising nearly a hundred quibbles over seven pages.

The happy team assembled by George Stuart Gordon did not last. Its dismantling was not due, as is so often the case in academia, to internal dissent, but rather to external allurements. In the late summer of 1922, George Stuart Gordon left for Oxford to become the Merton Professor of

English Literature, one of the more prestigious academic positions in England. Tolkien applied for his vacated professorship, but the position went to Lascelles Abercrombie, one of the Georgian poets. As a result of this and other blows, Tolkien soon felt ready to depart himself. The city of Leeds, with its belching factories and ungainly architecture, held little appeal. In his brief tenure there, the family had suffered from more than its share of illnesses: Edith and the boys had contracted measles, Michael appendicitis, and Tolkien himself pneumonia, a severe bout that brought him close to death. He remembered his grandfather John Suffield, who visited at the height of Tolkien's fever, "standing by my bedside, a tall thin black-clad figure, and looking at me and speaking to me with contempt—to the effect that I and my generation were degenerate weaklings." Some months after Tolkien's recovery, the house was burglarized—an inside job that involved the maid—and Edith's coat and engagement ring were stolen. But there were compensatory domestic joys, above all the birth of a third boy, Christopher Reuel, named for Christopher Wiseman, on November 21, 1924 (a fourth child, Priscilla, would arrive in 1929), and public accomplishments, especially Tolkien's appointment to the newly created position of Professor of English Language. He had managed to publish some undistinguished poems, too, mostly in local venues, such as *Yorkshire Poetry* and the university's own magazine, *The Gryphon*. Yet he longed for greater things. Edith, although fond of the university's casual atmosphere, was willing to move as well.

In 1925, Tolkien's opportunity arrived, when he learned that William Craigie, his old benefactor, planned to vacate the Rawlinson and Bosworth Professorship of Anglo-Saxon at Oxford. Tolkien had already looked into other teaching venues, applying for posts in Manchester and at Cape Town; he won the latter but turned it down, fearing that the requisite travel and African climate would prove too exhausting for Edith and the children. But to teach at Oxford—that would be a dream fulfilled! The Anglo-Saxon chair was a choice position with a venerable history, bequeathed in 1755 by Richard Rawlinson, bishop and bibliophile, first occupied in 1795, and filled throughout the nineteenth century by a series of first-rate scholars, not least Joseph Bosworth, author of the pioneering *Elements of Anglo-Saxon Grammar* (1823), whose name was added to the professorship in 1916. Tolkien prepared an outstanding application, including a twelve-page pamphlet containing his own summary of his qualifications, along with warm endorsements by leading Anglo-Saxonists and other scholars. The enthusiasm for his candidacy can be gauged by the testimony of Lascelles Abercrombie, who wrote that "I have never consulted him without gaining an illumination that can penetrate as well as expatiate. But I must not omit to mention that I have gained at least as much from the keen artistic sensibility as from the science of his scholarship." George Stuart Gordon went even further, declaring that "there is no philological (or literary) scholar of his generation from whom I have learned so much, with whom I have worked more happily, or from whom, in my opinion, greater things may be expected." Henry Bradley and Joseph Wright also wrote in his favor. Notably absent among his endorsers was Kenneth Sisam. But then Sisam, by now assistant secretary—an exalted post, despite the name—at Oxford University Press, was his chief rival for the position. The board of electors split the vote evenly; Tolkien triumphed when the university vice-chancellor, either impressed by Tolkien's youthful zeal (he was only thirty-three at the time) or put off by Sisam's reputation as a martinet, cast the deciding vote for Tolkien. The victory sat poorly with Sisam's supporters, who interpreted it as an upstart displacing his better; after all, it wasn't long ago that Tolkien had sat at Sisam's feet in Oxford lecture halls. The resentment simmered for decades; nearly a half century later, the Arthurian scholar Eugène Vinaver would declare that "for many years I have felt strongly that much less than justice had been done to Sisam the scholar and the model of scholarship. Everyone knows what a terrible mistake Oxford made when they by-passed him for the Chair of Anglo-Saxon." Despite the kerfuffle, however, Tolkien's friendship with Sisam remained more or less intact, albeit strained, as it had been during Tolkien's tardiness while completing his Anglo-Saxon glossary. Whatever his faults, Sisam—unlike his supporters in the battle against Tolkien—was capable of dropping a grudge.

Benedictus Qui Venit in Nomine Domini

The move to Oxford was a strain. Contractually obliged to remain at Leeds University until the end of 1925, Tolkien spent many autumn weekends shuttling between Leeds and Oxford's Pembroke College, where he delivered his first set of lectures. This exhausting regimen ended in January 1926, when the family moved to a new brick house at 22 Northmoor

Road, in a neighborhood thickly populated by dons and their families. The Tolkiens enjoyed the location and remained on Northmoor Road until 1947, ensuring their children the stable, secure, two-parent childhood that both of them had lacked. Tolkien's enlarged income—he was now earning a thousand pounds a year—permitted extravagances: John and Michael attended the Dragon School, a prestigious prep school founded to educate children of university faculty, and an Icelandic au pair girl was brought in to supervise them when at home.

Not all was well, however. Tolkien had begun, while in Leeds, to slacken his religious observances, and this lassitude continued at 22 Northmoor Road. He ascribed his failure to "wickedness and sloth," a stinging self-indictment that must be taken seriously. We don't know what caused this falling-off, although a heavy workload, added to the stress of two moves in six years, likely played a part; Tolkien may also have been distracted by the pomp and prestige of his professorships. The memory rankled, even forty years later; in 1963 he would tell Michael that "I regret those days bitterly (and suffer for them with such patience as I can be given); most of all because I failed as a father. Now I pray for you all, unceasingly, that the Healer (the *Hælend* as the Saviour was usually called in Old English) shall heal my defects, and that none of you shall ever cease to cry *Benedictus qui venit in nomine Domini* ['Blessed is he who comes in the name of the Lord']." In any event, he overcame the trial, spiritual fervor returned, and he began to attend Mass daily, often accompanied by the boys—Edith would join in on Sundays—walking on the Woodstock Road to St. Aloysius, a Jesuit church with a Victorian Gothic exterior and a rich Italianate interior, including a relic chapel, an imposing black marble altar, and flocks of brightly painted angels and saints crowding the reredos, elements that suited well his heigh-stile aesthetic and traditional Catholic bent.

He spent much time at home—an anomaly among Oxford professors, many of whom, during this era, lived in bachelor quarters at college— and enjoyed playing with his boys in the garden or thrilling them with tales of fantastic beings, including Tom Bombadil, a merry creature who represented "the spirit of the (vanishing) Oxford and Berkshire countryside." Tolkien was well-placed to watch the countryside shrink, as new houses filled up North Oxford and his beloved local trees—poplar, quince, apple, hawthorn—fell right and left, a denudation that cut him to the bone. In 1930, the family moved next door to 20 Northmoor Road, a large eight-bedroom house vacated by the bookseller Basil Blackwell; Tolkien took advantage of his new grounds to plant trees and transform the tennis court into a vegetable garden, while Edith erected an aviary filled with canaries and parakeets, bringing some of the spirit of the countryside back into the encroaching city.

Even as a youth, trees had captured Tolkien's heart. In his writings they represent the Platonic virtues of beauty, truth, and goodness; as early as 1916, he had imagined Kortirion, the fairy city on the enchanted Lonely Isle, as girdled by "a thousand whispering trees." In "The Coming of the Valar," two trees, Laurelin and Silpion (later Telperion) shed golden and silver light over the land of the immortals, and when a foul beast destroys them, their fruit and flower give rise to the sun and moon. His ardor for trees was intense, even eccentric; he despised the wanton destruction of any tree and did not hesitate to label normal horticultural practices like pruning and felling as "torture" and "murder." In the late 1930s, he would be especially fond of "a great-limbed poplar tree that I could see even lying in bed. It was suddenly lopped and mutilated by its owner, I do not know why. It is cut down now, a less barbarous punishment for any crimes it may have been accused of, such as being large and alive. I do not think it had any friends, or any mourners, except myself and a pair of owls."

In 1926, however, Tolkien was too busy to mourn for long any arboreal amputations. The new position at Oxford severely taxed his time and energy. Sometimes he managed to spend mornings after Mass sequestered in his book-lined office. A photo shows him, in tweed jacket and tie, poring over a pile of manuscripts, notes, and examination papers that nearly overwhelm his tobacco jar and pipe-filled Toby jug (a pottery jug in human shape). His children remember, too, "a row of coloured Quink and Stevenson inks, and sets of sealing-wax in different shades to match his large supply of stationery . . . [and] wonderful boxes of Koh-i-Noor coloured pencils, and tubes of paint with magical names like Burnt Sienna, Gamboge and Crimson Lake." He was still drawing and painting at this time, although his tight schedule drastically limited his output.

On other days, however, he would dash off after Mass on his high-seated bicycle to the university, his academic gown trailing in the wind. The typical professorial contract of the time required at least thirty-six lectures a year, but Tolkien soon exceeded this number. Students flocked to his *Beowulf* talks, though few stayed the course. He talked rapidly, slurring and swallowing his words, and his speech was often incomprehensible, especially to students not seated in the front row. By the third or fourth class, his voice and his erudition had frightened away all but a small coterie of devotees. The circle that remained included W. H. Auden, who said of one lecture that "I do not remember a single word he said but at a certain point he recited, and magnificently, a long passage of *Beowulf*. I was spellbound." Another student, J.I.M. Stewart, who would become a mystery novelist under the name of Michael Innes, remembered that Tolkien "could turn a lecture room into a mead hall in which he was the bard and we were the feasting, listening guests." Barfield's stutter vanished when singing or reciting poetry; so, too, did speaking in Anglo-Saxon turn Tolkien's leaden tongue to gold.

In addition to lecturing, Tolkien oversaw postgraduate work and graded School Certificate exam papers (administered to all British students at the age of sixteen). The latter was torture, but he kept it up for years despite the trickle of money it produced; he once estimated that earning one hundred pounds by grading exams consumed the same energy as writing a novel. At this time, he also began serious work on an edition of the *Ancrene Wisse* (or *Ancrene Riwle*), a Middle English rule for West Midland anchorites that he had started to study while at Leeds. But as always, his heart lay in telling stories, and he devoted every spare moment to his craft. In 1925, while on vacation at Filey, an old-fashioned beach resort in North Yorkshire, his son Michael lost a little leaden toy dog on the sand; Tolkien dried the boy's sobs with a tale about the dog come to life, and a sand-magician named Psamathos Psamathides (modeled closely upon Edith Nesbit's Psammead, or sand-fairy, who first appears in her 1902 novel, *The Five Children and It*). In 1927, Tolkien turned his tale into a written narrative entitled *Roverandom*, which would remain unpublished until 1988. *Roverandom* shows the influence not only of Nesbit but of Lewis Carroll, Howard Pyle, Norse and Welsh mythology, and late Victorian and Edwardian whimsical fairy lore. Although not a very original or cohesive tale—it reads like a series of set pieces—it does offer two exciting voyages, to the moon and to the depths of the sea, with fantastic characters (a wizard, the Man in the Moon, a Great White Dragon, merfolk), lyric prose ("the great indiarubber trunks of the trees bent and swayed like grasses, and the shadow of their endless branches was thronged with goldfish, and silverfish, and redfish, and bluefish, and phosphorescent fish like birds. But the fishes did not sing . . ."), labored humor, and a hint or two of the legendarium, as Roverandom espies "the Mountains of Elvenhome and the light of Faery upon the waves." The best part of the production may be Tolkien's illustrations, especially his watercolor of *The Gardens of the Merking's Palace*, a rich fantasia of underwater life, in which a white whale, a writhing octopus, a jellyfish, and other sea beasts swim through a dazzling pink, green, and blue seascape of weed, fronds, and domed palaces. Tolkien's art at this time outstripped his stories in beauty and elegance.

A few years later, Tolkien wrote another children's tale, *Mr. Bliss*, based on other playthings—a toy car and three teddy bears—belonging to his children. It is a minor effort, notable only for a cameo appearance by Gaffer Gamgee, father of Sam Gamgee, the hobbit sidekick of *The Lord of the Rings*. Again, Tolkien's paintings from the time, especially those inspired by his legendarium, are far more impressive. These include images of pouncing or coiled dragons, towering peaks, undulating hills, and trees. "The Tree of Amalion," in colored pencils, depicts a sinuous brown trunk with curvilinear branches bearing bright multicolored flowers that represent, Tolkien said, "poems and major legends"; Christina Scull and Wayne G. Hammond call it "Tolkien's ultimate tree" and see in it the "Tree of Tales," a symbol of the world of story later mentioned by Tolkien in his 1939 essay "On Fairy-Stories."

Despite his triumphal public reading at the Exeter Club, Tolkien continued to fear exposure and its terrifying sequel, ridicule, especially in relation to his legendarium ("I have exposed my heart to be shot at," he would write years later, when *The Lord of the Rings* appeared). Mythology had become the very air in which he thought, taught, painted, and wrote, yet he kept his own mythological inventions almost entirely to himself. Setting aside the principal creation of his years at Leeds, a bleak, two-thousand-line alliterative poem entitled "Lay of the Children of Húrin," he labored during this period on another version of the tale of Beren and Lúthien and—a conceptual breakthrough—a summary to date of the overall legendarium. In *Sketch of the Mythology*, a document of approximately ten thousand words, composed in 1926 and revised periodically until 1930, we can see for the first time the stupendous sweep of Tolkien's vision. The *Sketch* represents, according to Christopher Tolkien, "a new starting-point in the history of 'The Silmarillion.'" But it is far more than this; it marks, one can argue, a new starting point in the long European tradition of fantastic fiction. Tolkien moves, in this remarkable summary, beyond the mystical fables of Novalis, the fairy fables of George MacDonald, and the northern fables of William Morris—not to mention earlier fantastic tales from Aesop to Perrault—constructing for the first time, albeit in outline, a dense, interlocked imaginary narrative, encompassing the rise and fall of worlds, gods, and lesser beings and comprising, as he had long dreamed, a mythology for England. As fictional history on a cosmic scale, the only work that bears comparison is Blake's. But Tolkien's art, with its dense prose narratives, its playful extension into maps and languages, its love and admiration for ordinary people, and its pervasive Catholic sensibilities, has little in common with the inventions of the gnostic Blake, with his strange waking visions of angels and ghosts, his fascination with Swedenborg, his attacks upon conventional morality, his converse with his dead brother and other spirits, and above all, his basso profundo of Romantic rebellion.

Tolkien wrote the *Sketch* at white heat, without reference to his other texts (according to Christopher Tolkien), as a summary and guide for R. W. Reynolds, a former master at King Edward's School to whom he had been sending, since the war, his writings for critical comment. He sent it off to Reynolds in early 1926, along with portions of *The Children of Húrin* and *The Lay of Leithian*, for which it provided the mythological context. Reynolds's response is unknown, apart from a comment in Tolkien's diary that "*Tinúviel* meets with qualified approval, it is too prolix . . ." In any event, it is the *Sketch* itself that matters. Upon its choppy outline, the bulk of Tolkien's future creative writings would rest. Although omitting the creation of the cosmos, it encompasses in truncated form much of the legendarium, from the uprising of the Satanic figure Morgoth through the retreat of the Valar to the "uttermost west," the birth of the Elves and the rise of Elvish civilization, tales of the magical jewels known as Silmarils, and the emergence of Men and Gnomes (Dwarves), to the conquest of Morgoth and the fading of the Elves. In the *Sketch*, Tolkien mapped out his future course. The vein of gold had been struck, now the minting could begin in earnest.

7

WANTED:
AN INTELLIGIBLE ABSOLUTE

D uring the early 1920s, as we have seen, Lewis's life was in disarray, both intellectually and in his family relations. There were, too, other sources of disappointment and sorrow. Not least was his encounter with William Butler Yeats, who had moved into a house across the street from Balliol College. Lewis called on him twice, a young poet visiting the old master for the "purpose of worshipping devoutly." On his first visit, March 14, 1921, he and a fellow guest—the Jesuit writer C. C. Martindale, a "little twinkling man like a bird"—sat on hard chairs while the famous poet, fat and gray-haired, discoursed on dreams, ghosts, and magic lore. Yeats was at this time hard at work with his wife, who lounged on a nearby divan throughout the visit, on that strange, convoluted, nearly unreadable masterpiece of occult lore, *A Vision*. What a shame, Lewis wrote to his father, that a man who had met William Morris, Rabindranath Tagore, and Arthur William Symons should pander to the "sham romance of flame coloured curtains and mumbo-jumbo." Describing the visit to Arthur, he said, "I have seldom felt less at my ease before anyone than I did before him: I understand the Dr Johnson atmosphere for the first time—it was just like that, you know, we all sitting round, putting in judicious questions while the great man played with some old seals on his watch chain and talked. The subjects of his talk, of course, were the very reverse of Johnsonian: it was all of magic and apparitions. That room and that voice would make you believe anything." The man was a "Kod" ("humbug," in Ulster slang), he told his father.

Later, under the influence of Charles Williams and a concomitant re-awakening of adolescent enthusiasms, Lewis's views on Yeats would mellow, and he apologized, in the 1950 edition of *Dymer*, for having used the poet as the model for his portrait in this work of a deranged magician: "if he were now alive I would ask his pardon with shame for having repaid his hospitality by such freedom."

A few weeks later, on March 28, the Great Knock died. "Poor old Kirk! . . . I at least owe to him in the intellectual sphere as much as one human being can owe another," Lewis wrote his father upon hearing the news. William T. Kirkpatrick had been Yeats's opposite, a skeptic rather than a spiritualist, a hero rather than a shattered idol, delivering hard truths in place of soft imaginings—or so Lewis saw it at the time. Curiously, though, his death made Lewis warm to an idea that Yeats held but Kirkpatrick abhorred: the immortality of the soul. Kirkpatrick "is so indelibly stamped on one's mind once known, so often present in thought," wrote Lewis, "that he makes his own acceptance of annihilation the more unthinkable. I have seen death fairly often and never yet been able to find it anything but extraordinary and rather incredible. The real person is so very real, so obviously living and different from what is left that one cannot believe something has turned into nothing. It is not faith, it is not reason—just a 'feeling.' 'Feelings' are in the long run a pretty good match for what we call our beliefs."

To reconcile the mysticism of Yeats and the rationalism of Kirkpatrick would be a task for the decade to come; for now, there were too many light distractions and heavy concerns. Living far from Warnie (and not enjoying his company, when together, as in the past), deceiving his father about Mrs. Moore, bound to her by a strange contract of desire and filial obligation, anxious about present needs and future prospects, Lewis understandably fell prey to vagaries of temper and mood, which he recorded, along with the details of daily life with the Moores, in a diary he kept from April 1922 until the beginning of 1927.

As the diary—published posthumously in abridged form by Walter Hooper from Warnie's typescript as *All My Road Before Me*—opens, Lewis and the Moores have moved into a semidetached house at 28 Warneford Road, walking distance from the center of Oxford. Lewis is preparing for his June 1922 Greats examination and working on his poetry; Maureen is attending Headington Day School; Mrs. Moore is exhausting herself by putting the house in order; money is desperately short. "I wish life and death were not the only alternatives," Lewis writes one morning, "for I don't like either." Yet there are other times when, thanks to a small victory at home or a brief stint out of doors, he catches a "whiff of what I used to call 'the real joy.'"

Throughout the diary, Lewis refers to Mrs. Moore by the Greek letter Δ (delta), transliterated to D in the published edition. Δ has a long history as an erotic symbol, and in particular it may be that Lewis was thinking of Diotima of Mantinea, priestess of eros in Plato's *Symposium* and a Romantic icon ever since Friedrich Hölderlin gave the name "Diotima" to the married woman who was his paramour and muse. The Diotima of Lewis's diary is a domestic rather than a romantic priestess, however; a figure ever-present in the log of dishes washed, guests tolerated, lawn games played, colds nursed, books read, chores done. If Lewis wrote passages that pay homage to Δ as an object of passionate love, they have not survived in the typescript.

From the diary we learn that while Lewis was preparing for Greats, the Moore household was rarely without visitors. After exams, the pace of entertaining quickened, with frequent, extended visits from friends and relations, including Barfield, Greeves, Baker, Lewis's aunt Lily (a voluble champion of women's suffrage, birth control, and animal rights), the landlady, and Mrs. Moore's brother, "Doc" Askins. Neighbors crowded in, too, along with the obligatory P.G. (paying guest) to help make ends meet. Of one P.G., Lewis writes, "A greater bore I have never met: passions and sympathies I fancy she has never known. Worst of all, she has given up her habit of going to bed immediately after supper." Notable among the regular visitors was Vida Mary Wiblin, the admirable but chubby and plain "Smudge," who came to give Maureen music lessons. Wiblin worked as a music teacher by day and read for her Greek and Latin exams by night. Lewis coached her for these exams and she conceived an unrequited love for him, which caused her to prolong her visits and to suffer nervous attacks and fainting spells; she never married, and eventually became musical director at the Magdalen College School.

This household commotion meant that, whatever their degree of intimacy may have been, Lewis and Mrs. Moore had little chance of privacy (except on Sunday mornings, Maureen recalled later, when they would send her off to church by herself). Lewis grumbled about the constant visitors in his diary, but Mrs. Moore showed no inclination to curtail their hospitality; she even encouraged him to be indulgent to poor Smudge: "In the midst of all this confusion Smudge flitted from room to room saying she thought she'd better go home tonight. A thousand times I felt tempted to reply 'Well then GO!', but of course she always yielded to D's pressure . . . there was endless delay in getting to bed and of course, as the last straw to a perfect day, I was left alone with Smudge. To bed at last, and I had a few moments alone with D, who stands this bad time wonderfully."

Lewis read the diary aloud to Mrs. Moore, and she must have been pleased at incidents that place her in a favorable light: D transforming an army blanket into a heraldic drawing room curtain, winning the hearts of a friend's housemaids, holding the hand of a distraught prisoner's wife ("very characteristically," says Lewis) while waiting in a courthouse for jury duty. There is shared pathos—and perhaps a touch of shared pathology—in the descriptions of D suffering, in syncopation with Lewis, headaches and sore throats, shabby surroundings, gossipy neighbors, and overdrawn bank accounts. Together they anguished over the negligence of Mrs. Moore's husband ("the Beast") and the difficulty of surviving on Albert's allowance. As a zealous housekeeper, Mrs. Moore would drive herself to the point of collapse, and though she encouraged Lewis in his career ambitions, she also expected him to pitch in. Lewis, who had a boyish disregard for household niceties, chafed under the necessity of handling her moods and meeting her standards, as well as coping with the "stupidity" at lessons and incipient feminism of Maureen, a teenager at the time. Occasionally, as in this entry from June 1923, he came close to the breaking point:

Found D and Dorothy [Dorothy Broad, the maid] polishing in D's room. Had hardly left them when I heard an awful crash and rushed back thoroughly frightened and half believing that the wardrobe had fallen on D. I found however that it was only she herself who had fallen and hurt her elbow: she was badly shaken. All attempts to get her to stop polishing and rest on her laurels were treated in the usual way. After tea she went on again and said I could not help: finally she came down quite breathless and exhausted.

This put me into such a rage against poverty and fear and all the infernal net I seemed to be in that I went out and mowed the lawn and cursed all the gods for half an hour. After that (and it was about as far down as I have got yet) I had to help with rolling linoleums and by the time we got to supper a little before ten, I was tired and sane again.

When Lewis and Mrs. Moore did find time apart from others, a favorite way of relieving stress was to compare notes on their grievances, the follies of their friends and relations, and the hostility of their neighbors; thus, after supper on a late November evening, "we sat in judgement on Headington and its people (whom God reject) and perhaps felt the better for it." The mocking subjunctive "whom God reject" recurs in his letters and diaries of the early 1920s; it was merely a way to let off steam, but it was hardly charitable. On the other hand, Mrs. Moore forced Lewis to be magnanimous toward various unfortunates in whom she took an interest—a young would-be dancer named Maisie ("Moppie") Hawes, for example, whom they sheltered at the risk of legal complications from her domineering father and his wife, identified by Lewis as "that foul hag" or simply "the Bitch." Much later, Lewis told George Sayer that Mrs. Moore "was generous and taught me to be generous, too . . . If it were not for her, I should know little or nothing about ordinary domestic life as lived by most people."

What a paradox, then, was Lewis's existence during the 1920s! Why would a young man who cherished autonomy, resented interference, preferred the company of males, and regarded marriage as a lamentable lapse ("that fatal tomb of all lively and interesting men") enter into a relationship akin to marriage—and one fracturing from within—with a woman who, whatever her virtues, excelled at quarrels and giving orders? Lewis's solemn pledge to Paddy Moore that he would look after his mother had something to do with it, of course; even while an atheist, he held some things sacred. Most likely, sexual attraction for Mrs. Moore played also a part. The war entered in as well, or rather its aftermath, when a generation sought to redefine itself by at once salvaging the past (thus Tolkien's intensified search for England's mythology) and beginning anew. Had Lewis been a bit younger, he might have been one of the Bright Young Things worshipping Oscar Wilde while throwing off conventional restraint; but the world lay too heavily upon Lewis and his generation of returning soldiers for ironic hedonism to present itself as a solution. And for Lewis in particular, the weight of the world meant, in large measure, his father. In Mrs. Moore he found the counterweight that would give, however painfully, a new sense of balance and the promise of a second chance. It was just that: a chance to create a world of his own away from his father and a chance to re-create the domestic paradise despoiled by his mother's death. By surrendering to Mrs. Moore, Lewis kept his promise to Paddy, escaped his father, reclaimed his past, and built a new future, albeit in the oddest way possible: by surrendering the freedom of college life for the dictatorial matriarchy he called "ordinary domestic life."

Lewis's domestic arrangements also served—in retrospect this would seem providential—as a cure for self-absorption. As he put it in *Surprised by Joy*, his "hostility to the emotions was very fully and variously avenged." In later years, Lewis liked to quote George MacDonald's maxim "the one principle of hell is—'I am my own.'" Life with Mrs. Moore ensured that Lewis could not call his soul his own, could not shield himself, as he had done with his father, from interference and irrational demands. So it was a purgatory, but not a hell. Lewis may have suffered under her roof, but he certainly didn't stagnate: his diary records many lively conversations with intellectual friends, conversations in which Mrs. Moore sometimes took part; and he continued to read omnivorously from Greek and Roman classics to Shelley, Freud, Jung, William James, and Walter de la Mare. Best of all, an exciting new friendship was dawning. In 1923 he befriended Nevill Coghill, an admirer of Tolkien and a future Inkling.

Coghill, five months Lewis's junior, had grown up a few hundred miles south of him, in an Irish Protestant family among the lush green hills and nationalist ardors of County Cork. He, too, had fought in World War I, on the Macedonian front, enrolled in Oxford right after the war, distinguished himself as a fiddler and boatman, and, like Lewis, won his First in English literature and language in a single year rather than the usual three. He had a rough-and-tumble, earthy air about him, which attracted Lewis right away. John Wain later painted a memorable portrait of him: "[Coghill] was a big man built on generous lines . . . He smiled easily, revealing somewhat battered teeth, and indeed his whole face had a slightly rough, knocked-about quality, like a chipped statue. But it was a noble statue, generous in expression and bearing. His voice was deep and strong, his speech soft and gentle, and this contrast was carried through everything. He was totally courteous, a gentleman by instinct as well as by tradition . . ." W. H. Auden—inspired by his tutorial sessions with Coghill to change course from engineering to English—would pay tribute to Coghill's courtesy in a poem on the occasion of Coghill's retirement, reminding him that "you countenanced all species" yet "never looked cross or sleepy" even "when our essays were / more about us than Chaucer." Auden also dedicated his celebrated collection of essays, *The Dyer's Hand*, to Coghill as "a tutor in whom one could confide."

Lewis first noticed Coghill in a class taught by George Stuart Gordon, by now Merton Professor of English Literature. During Hilary term each year, Gordon held a weekly discussion class for Honours candidates in English. It was on February 2, 1923, in this happy setting, ideal for the formation of intellectual friendships, that Coghill read a paper on "Realism from *Gorboduc* to *Lear*." Lewis's diary entry for the day speaks of him almost in a schoolgirl's smitten voice, as "a good looking fellow . . . an enthusiastic sensible man, without nonsense, and a gentleman, much more attractive than the majority." Two days later, Lewis met Coghill again, at a tea held by the formidable tutor of Old English at St. Hugh's College, Edith Elizabeth Wardale, who remained in the background as the two students volleyed merrily over literary likes and dislikes. Coghill said he couldn't share Lewis's love of Morris and Langland (strangely, since Coghill would one day be a renowned interpreter of Langland as well as Chaucer). They agreed that Blake was as inspired as Joan of Arc had been, but differed about the source of that inspiration, Lewis bristling at Coghill's accusation that he (Lewis) was a materialist.

The following week, Lewis read his paper on *The Faerie Queene* to Gordon's class. As class stenographer, Coghill had the usual task of preparing the minutes in verse. He wrote in a mock-Chaucerian vein, prefacing a long description of his new acquaintance's argument with a courteous exordium that begins "In Oxenford some clerkés of degree / Were gadréd in a goodlye companye" and goes on to praise "*Sir Lewis . . .* a good philosopher," noting in particular "Well couthe he speken in the Greeké tongue." Later Coghill would recall how dazzled he had been by Lewis's "combative pleasure" while delivering his paper, which "was certainly the best the class had heard." *The Faerie Queene*, he wrote, was a world he could inhabit and believe in . . . its knights, dwarfs, and ladies were real to him, and became real even to me while he discussed them: he rejoiced as much in the ugliness of the giants and in the beauty of the ladies as in their spiritual significances, but most of all in the ambience of the faerie forest and plain that, he said, were carpeted with a grass greener than the common stuff of ordinary glades; this was the *reality* of grass, only to be apprehended in poetry: the world of the imagination was nearer to the truth than the world of the senses . . .

We may detect here the early influence of Barfield's viewpoint. Even the gods, Coghill noticed, were real to Lewis, as long as they remained in the world of imagination and did not challenge his atheism directly.

Within a few days the friendship blossomed. Their mutual love of literature and of conversational fencing—Coghill's deep and mellow voice a perfect match for Lewis's deep, more strident one—glued them one to the other. They spent the year, under the shared tutelage of F. P. Wilson, exploring English literature for eight or ten hours a day. Their minds caught fire. "It was," Coghill wrote, "a continuous intoxication of discovery: to almost every week came its amazement." With the war behind them, a life of art and scholarship ahead, "we were uninhibitedly happy in our work and felt supported by an endless energy."

Coghill knew nothing at this time of Lewis's problems with his father or of his relationship with Mrs. Moore. He did know that Lewis was at his best out of doors, preferably at a distance from home and college. The two friends met regularly for country rambles, bounding from one hill and one idea to another as they talked for hours on end. They agreed—rapturously—about Milton, Matthew Arnold, and so much more; they disagreed—violently—about Congreve, Restoration comedy, and the value of theater; but above all, they disagreed about Christianity. For Coghill, Lewis was astonished to discover, was a Christian.

Here was something new: a bright, creative, voracious mind who was a "supernaturalist" and, what's more, an orthodox one with a love of ecclesiastical and liturgical tradition. Coghill was a devout Anglican, deeply committed to the English Catholic revival of the 1920s; he would be one of the few laymen invited to address the 1927 Anglo-Catholic Congress on the Holy Eucharist (his speech echoes Lewis's skepticism about finding evidence for God in nature; but in Coghill's view, the failure of the classical argument from design is all the more reason to believe in and adore the Real Presence of Christ in the Eucharist, undetectable to the senses).

The ground was rolling and cracking under Lewis's feet, as he recounts in *Surprised by Joy*: so many of his favorite writers, MacDonald, Chesterton, Johnson, Spenser, Milton—and now friends like Coghill— all Christians. How could this be? And, compounding his distress, why was he still unable to find a job? In 1924, Coghill landed a fellowship in English at Exeter, while Lewis found every door shut. One solace remained, putting pen to paper. Long letters and longer diary entries poured out, recounting his reading, his passions, his hopes. At the same time, he toiled away on what would become his longest and perhaps best narrative poem, *Dymer*.

Dymer

The idea had come to him when he was seventeen; Lewis said he did not consciously invent it. It was, on the surface at least, a horrific tale: a man fathers a monster; the monster slays his father and becomes a god.

Lewis began to write the story in prose during Christmas 1916 at Little Lea; in December 1918, while convalescing in a military hospital, he attempted a verse version, "The Redemption of Ask," soon abandoned. Finally, on April 2, 1922, sitting by the sunny window in his bedroom while Mrs. Moore cut up oranges for marmalade, he had his breakthrough: he saw how he could re-create *Dymer* as a narrative poem in rhyme royal. So he began:

> You stranger, long before your glance can light
> Upon these words, time will have washed away
> The moment when I first took pen to write,
> With all my road before me . . .

For the next three years, Lewis labored to draw forth from his initial inspiration a story of mythic proportions and a prosody noble enough to go with it.

Lewis told Arthur that the main theme was "development by self-destruction"; to Coghill he called it "redemption by parricide." The poem seethes with anger against totalitarianism and war and coruscates with insatiable longings. It begins as a broad social satire, with Dymer's birth in a Perfect City—a modern Plato's Republic with a planned economy and all-embracing bureaucracy from which no misfit can hide:

At Dymer's birth no comets scared the nation,
The public crêche engulfed him with the rest,
And twenty separate Boards of Education
Closed round him. He passed through every test,
Was vaccinated, numbered, washed and dressed,
Proctored, inspected, whipt, examined weekly,
And for some nineteen years he bore it meekly.

When the life force (Lewis had been reading Bergson) invades the stifling classroom in the form of an April breeze, young Dymer breaks into a wild mirth, kills his teacher, and flees to the open field. So far he would seem to be a rebel after the pattern of Blake's Los, championing the cause of imagination, energy, sensuality, and freedom; but Dymer's rebellion, which sets off a bloody revolution, propels him into desperate adventures. He wanders naked into a castle, where he spies his body in a mirror, triggering a narcissistic trance. He dreams he is a great hero, then a great tyrant, and then he enjoys passionate sex with a girl who appears in the dark of night and slips into his arms.

In the morning his lover is gone—he never even saw her face. Maddened by loss, he sets out after her, confronting an old matriarch and a succession of gruesome figures. A magician (based on Yeats) offers Dymer an occult potion that will empower him to retrieve his beloved and recapture his lost ecstasy; Dymer drinks but by now he has begun to repent, and the potion fails to overpower his will. The magician goes mad and shoots him. In agony from the wound, Dymer at last meets his mysterious bride, only to discover that she is none other than his own desire for transcendence, misconstrued as lust. In the final canto, he confronts the monstrous son born from their union, kills him, and dies declaiming heroic platitudes. Out of all this death—and, readers might ruefully note, out of all this furious convolution of plot—good comes: spring returns and all revives, "that country clothed with dancing flowers / Where flower had never grown," the monster-son becomes a god, and Dymer, though dead, is redeemed.

Dymer succeeds, as Lewis acknowledged, in at least one of its purposes: to write the poem had been a necessary catharsis. He, like Dymer, had been obsessed with recapturing the ecstasies of the past. "To 'get it again,'" he would write in *Surprised by Joy*, "became my constant endeavor; while reading every poem, hearing every piece of music, going for every walk, I stood anxious sentinel at my own mind to watch whether the blessed moment was beginning and to endeavor to retain it if it did." He found it couldn't be done. Like Dymer, his initial reaction to this failure was angry rejection; and with the "new psychology" whispering to him that his romantic longings were really sublimated lust, he set out to "unmask and defeat" the stratagems of wish-fulfilling fantasy. Like Dymer, Lewis succumbed for a time to pessimism and, like Dymer, he was tempted by magic; but in the end he came to his senses, rejecting both despair and empty promises. He grew up.

Among the wish-fulfilling fantasies that died with Dymer was Lewis's image of himself as a major poet. The first blow was a peremptory rejection from Heinemann, publisher of *Spirits in Bondage*. This stung Lewis so bitterly that he sat down and wrote himself a long letter minutely analyzing his desire to see *Dymer* succeed:

My desire then contains two elements. (a) The desire for some proof to myself that I am a poet. (b) The desire that my poet-hood should be acknowledged even if no one knows that it is mine . . . As far as I can see both these are manifestations of the single desire for what may be called mental or spiritual rank. I have flattered myself with the idea of being among my own people when I was reading the poets and it is unpleasing to have to stand down and take my place in the crowd. Such a desire is contrary to my own settled principles: the very principles which I expressed in Dymer.

Dymer finally did make its mark—it was published by Dent, Lewis's friends were encouraging, and there were a number of highly positive reviews. AE (under the pseudonym "V.O.") had kind things to say about it in *The Irish Statesman*. The detective novelist Rupert Croft-Cooke called it a "great poem" in *G.K.'s Weekly*. The most favorable notice, by the poet and critic Hugh l'Anson Fausset in *The Times Literary Supplement*, called the poem "notable because it is in the epic tradition and yet is modern in idiom and reflects a profoundly personal intuition" in which the hero's adventure takes place "not on the high seas but in the swamps and arid places of his own soul-making." But the triumph was fleeting; the book did not sell, and the more enthusiastic reviews struck Lewis as "silly."

The problem was this: the poem, taken stanza by stanza, gleams like gold, but it is partly fool's gold. At least that is how *The Poetry Review* saw it in November 1926: "One is little impressed by the allegory that is hard to understand, amazed at the alternate flashes of brilliance and dullness in the style of writing, and wholly delighted by the lyrical quality of many of the lines." A friend of Barfield's judged that "the metrical level is good, the vocabulary is large: but Poetry—not a line." Coghill, whose appreciation for the spiritual themes had been an encouragement to Lewis, admitted later that he was never quite sure what the poem meant; he just knew that it felt mysteriously significant, and though he didn't say this to Lewis, he judged that its "Pre-Raphaelite stained glass imagery" and its "toe-hold in Wardour Street" (a reference to its pseudo-archaic language, the same problem that afflicted Tolkien) would prevent it from having lasting power. Coghill was convinced that Lewis was better at prose than poetry, and more than one reviewer agreed: the stories would be captivating, if only the verse didn't get in the way.

Lewis was crushed. There was no way to deflect a verdict shared so widely by critics he respected (in a letter to Harwood he quoted John Henry Newman quoting Augustine: *Securus judicat orbis terrarum*—the world is a sure judge). Later he told Arthur, who was suffering similar agonies about his painting, that "from the age of sixteen onwards I had one single ambition, from which I never wavered, in the prosecution of which I spent every ounce I could, on wh. I really & deliberately staked my whole contentment: and I recognise myself as having unmistakably failed in it." He had worshipped at poetry's altar and monitored himself, as well as his friends, for any sign of flagging devotion to the art. A decade earlier or a few decades later he might have fared better, but he had the misfortune to publish just as the critical tide turned against narrative poetry, against formal rhyme and meter, against pastoral landscapes, heroic quests, and archaisms of all kinds. His middling talent could not buck the modernist surge, and his dream collapsed. Even after he abandoned hope of poetic greatness, however, his love for poetry never ceased. He continued to turn out short lyric verse, and he labored for two decades (1918–1938) on a narrative poem transposing the Hippolytus myth to fairyland, reciting it, under the title "The Queen of Drum," at a 1938 "Oxford Summer Diversion." It remained unpublished during his lifetime.

Realism . . .

Finishing *Dymer* coincided with another sea change in Lewis's life. As an adolescent he had learned to view the universe as "a meaningless dance of atoms" and had assumed a Romantic posture in defiance of this harsh truth. By the time he had completed *Dymer*, however, Lewis had taken his first steps in the direction of a Romanticism without defiance, a Romanticism wedded to sanity and reason.

To accomplish this, he needed to decouple poetry and magic. He'd had enough of the hankering for mystical secrets that had made a tawdry spectacle of the great poet Yeats, turned the benign Leo Baker into an alarming enigma, and sent more than a few of his contemporaries into sectarian coteries or worse. He'd had enough of second-rate revelations from the spirit world and psychical researchers whose proof of an afterlife was always just around the corner. There was "Cranny," the Reverend Frederick Walker MacRan, an Anglo-Irish priest and friend of Mrs. Moore who had entered Holy Orders without believing in Christ and had ended up—as Lewis describes him in *Surprised by Joy*—"an old, dirty, gabbling, tragic, Irish parson" and an unwelcome weekend guest, obsessed with finding evidence for survival of death. His fellow student, Pasley, had become a spiritualist and was, Lewis thought, much the worse for it. "The whole question of immortality became rather disgusting to me," Lewis writes in *Surprised by Joy*; it was encouraging to find that Barfield, though desperate to find an alternative to pessimistic materialism, shared his friend's contempt for pie-in-the-sky consolations.

Most disturbing of all was the descent into madness of Mrs. Moore's brother, John "Doc" Askins, who was now living nearby with his family. Lewis enjoyed his company, and when Askins held forth on his favorite metaphysical subjects, whether Atlantis or the afterlife, Lewis was a willing sounding board. On one such occasion, however, Askins bared his soul; he was haunted by evil thoughts, terrified of Hell, convinced of his own sinfulness. Lewis was unsure whether the pathology stemmed from actual misdeeds or subconscious impulses, from untreated syphilis or war neurosis. Things soon came to a crisis, and Mrs. Moore insisted they shelter her brother as he writhed on the floor, tortured by fiendish blasphemies and thoughts of imminent damnation, while his wife (a consummate witch in Lewis's opinion) was having fits of her own upstairs. A doctor was sent for, and later a policeman. Lewis needed all his strength to hold Doc down while they chloroformed him. He was hospitalized, only to die three weeks later when his exhausted heart gave out.

The worst part of this experience for Lewis, who had been suffering nightmares of his own, was the feeling of being drawn into a maelstrom—"a sort of horrible sympathy with the Doc's yellings and grovellings—a cursed feeling that I could quite easily do it myself." It seemed to him, moreover, that Askins had opened himself to spiritual invasion by dabbling in the arcana of theosophy, yoga, and psychoanalysis. An ardent spiritualist friend, the wife of Lewis's history tutor, hardly helped matters with her suggestion that Askins's troubles would end as soon as he crossed over to the etheric plane. Yeats, Cranny, dear Miss Cowie, and now Doc Askins—the message could not be more clear: "it was to this, this raving on the floor, that all romantic longings and unearthly speculations led a man in the end." Lewis resolved to be normal: "Safety first, thought I: the beaten track, the approved road, the center of the road, the lights on." He wrote to warn Arthur: "Keep clear of introspection, of brooding, of spiritualism, of everything eccentric. Keep to work and sanity and open air—to the cheerful & the matter of fact side of things. We hold our mental health by a thread: & nothing is worth risking it for."

This commitment to commonsense, stoical realism "satisfied an emotional need," he tells us in *Surprised by Joy*. "I wanted Nature to be quite independent of our observation; something other, indifferent, self-existing." He would accept the universe as it is: "No more Avalon, no more Hesperides. I had . . . 'seen through' them. And I was never going to be taken in again." His spiritual longings could be safely reclassified as aesthetic longings and enjoyed as such; for as his philosophy tutor E. F. Carritt (fellow in philosophy at University College and a disciple of Benedetto Croce) assured him, art was a sphere of its own in which even the most hardheaded realist could take moral holidays.

. . . And Idealism

But Lewis was not consistent. *Surprised by Joy* depicts a steady progression from materialism to idealism to pantheism to Christianity, but Lewis's letters and diary entries—often at odds with the chronology in his memoir—show that he was trying out various philosophical positions throughout the 1920s. This is what intellectual development is really like; as Lewis liked to point out, only the stodgiest of thinkers advances from one worldview to the next in an orderly fashion, as if traveling by train from station to station. And Lewis was certainly not stodgy; his mind was in constant motion. He was fully aware that the commonsense realism (the position he calls, in *Surprised by Joy*, "the New Look") that he had adopted as a defense against eccentricity and brooding could not satisfy all of his intellectual and spiritual needs. Barfield had shown him the contradictions in his position; he was trying to have it both ways—to accept "as rock-bottom reality the universe revealed by the senses" but also to shield his logical, moral, and aesthetic judgments from scientific explanations that would empty them of truth-value. He wanted—needed—to overcome the antinomies in his thought, but it would mean hard philosophical work; he would have to formulate a philosophy of mind and matter coherent enough to withstand critical scrutiny.

If realism failed, the obvious place to turn to was idealism. Idealism had been the dominant philosophical school in Britain from the mid-to-late nineteenth century and still had significant influence. For the classically educated, idealism of one sort or another was a natural tendency; everyone at least knew Plato. Broad sympathy for the school, accompanied by the patriotic thought that, although derived from Plato, Kant, and Hegel, it had now assumed a distinctively British form, created a climate favorable for the Oxford idealism associated with Thomas Hill Green (1836–82), F. H. Bradley (1846–1924), and Bernard Bosanquet (1848–1923).

Oxford idealism was a complex brew—a system of metaphysics adapted from Kant and Hegel, and their Scottish exegetes McTaggart and Caird, and linked (though by tenuous threads) to a program of moral uplift and social reform. Distilled, it amounted to asserting the existence of a purely mental or spiritual Absolute and acknowledging the existence of things and individuals only as aspects of that Absolute. The real universe, the Oxford idealists maintained, is a single unified whole, a perfect Idea, however manifold and conflicted it may appear. Thus Bradley wrote, in a famous passage in *The Principles of Logic*, "That the glory of this world in the end is appearance leaves the world more glorious, if we feel it is a show of some fuller splendour; but the sensuous curtain is a deception and a cheat, if it hides some colourless movement of atoms . . ." Even though perceived through a sensuous curtain, reality is intrinsically intelligible; to awakened reason, the universe is already perfect and eternally at peace. It was an immensely consoling doctrine to one caught in a dreary materialist world; Lewis was particularly delighted by a remark he found in Bosanquet's *Some Suggestions in Ethics* about the possibility of friendship with the lower animals: befriend an animal, Bosanquet said, and you will feel "as if the Absolute came to eat out of your hand."

To be sure, this was not Lewis's first encounter with idealism; he had been thoroughly steeped in Plato from his days reading classics with Kirkpatrick, loving everything in the Greek philosopher except the utopian despotism of the *Republic*. Lewis's letters to Arthur Greeves on poetry and art read like Platonic rhapsodies on the transcendent reality of the beautiful. He even flirted with a dualism more Gnostic and Romantic than Platonic in tone, in which beauty, as pure spirit, was perennially at war with matter. From his bed in the military hospital at Étaples, Lewis wrote to Arthur, "out here, where I see spirit continually dodging matter (shells, bullets, animal fears, animal pains) I have formulated my equation Matter=Nature=Satan. And on the other side Beauty, the only spiritual & not-natural thing that I have yet found."

When, in 1923, Lewis decided to immerse himself in the idealism of Green, Bradley, and Bosanquet, he was a trifle embarrassed to be deserting his hard-won realism in order to follow what he thought was the dominant philosophical fashion. But he soon found out that idealism was already tottering on its high throne. G. E. Moore had published his "Refutation of Idealism" at Cambridge in 1903, and the analytical approach was poised to take Cambridge philosophy by storm, while in Oxford, the commonsense "direct realism" of Cook Wilson (which in turn gave rise to "ordinary language philosophy") was in the ascendant. In 1901 the humanist F.C.S. Schiller (Oxford's counterpart to the American pragmatist William James) published *Mind!*—a wicked and occasionally hilarious parody of the prestigious journal *Mind*—mocking his philosophical ancestors and elders (among them "F.H. Badly") and interpreting Lewis Carroll's *The Hunting of the Snark* as a Bradleian allegory for the pursuit of the Absolute (whose portrait, a blank sheet of pink translucent vellum paper, forms the frontispiece).

Lewis thus found himself caught between two philosophical worlds—he was one of the small band of returned soldiers (the Great War, in cutting a disproportionate swath through Oxbridge scholars, also decimated a whole generation of future philosophers) who found themselves outnumbered both by their seniors and by the rising generation who had been too young to serve in the war. The old guard were mainly idealists of one sort or another, while the newcomers were determined, with the help of recently honed logical and linguistic tools, to cut through the tangles left by their predecessors. Lewis's generation would play a mediating role, not blazing new trails but seeing to it that the newcomers learned to understand their seniors before they consigned the old philosophy, with its soaring abstractions, to the dustbin.

Philosophical "isms" rise and fall like hemlines; real philosophers—and Lewis had the makings of one, even if his path led elsewhere—ignore fashions and steer clear of party politics. Thus, in his materialist period Lewis could sympathize with idealists, and in his idealist period he could appreciate the telling criticisms made by rival schools. It was useful to have idealism as a standpoint from which to teach (a classified ad from a desperate instructor in the back pages of *Mind!* read "WANTED IMMEDIATELY, for Teaching Purposes, an INTELLIGIBLE ABSOLUTE. Money no object. Apply to 'Tutor' c/o Ed., MIND!"), but Lewis soon found, when he had to face actual students, that "the Absolute cannot be made clear" and that British idealism, at least in its post-Berkeleyan form, consisted largely of "mystifications."

Once Lewis became a Christian, he would look back on his absolute idealism as a "quasi-religion" that "cost nothing," mainly because there was no way to trace the lines of connection between the Absolute and the empirical individual self. "We could talk religiously about the Absolute: but there was no danger of Its doing anything about us." Idealism was a system of ideas and aspirations that "cannot be lived"—and a philosophy that cannot be lived is no philosophy at all. In *Surprised by Joy*, Lewis heightens the drama of his conversion account by depicting Barfield and Griffiths as rebuking him on this point (philosophy "wasn't a *subject* to Plato . . . it was a way"); but according to Barfield the story is "pure applesauce"—Lewis, he said, was "constitutionally incapable of treating philosophy as a merely academic exercise."

Whatever its defects as a *way*, however, Lewis never regretted his idyll with idealism. When he had shed his materialist skin and was feeling painfully naked, idealism provided a way to cloak that nakedness for a time. He saw, with its help, that if one trusts one's own judgment, one's ability to discern truth—as he did, as all thinking people inevitably do—then one must embrace the idea that "mind was no late-come epiphenomenon; that the whole universe was, in the last resort, mental; that our logic was participation in a cosmic *Logos*" (the influence of Barfield is palpable). Lewis found in idealism a more satisfactory account than materialism could supply of the sacrifices of his comrades in war, the moral seriousness of his friends, and the demands of his own conscience. When his instinct for adoration seemed thwarted at every turn, idealism offered a higher reality to adore intellectually, purely for its own sake, without a hell to fear or a heaven to hope for. Idealism was a rational and ethical mysticism, full of Spirit and free of spirits. It made no occult—or Anthroposophical—claims about intercourse with beings from other worlds. It was sane and wholesome, noble and disinterested. It cleared away obstacles, overcame intellectual inhibitions, and upheld the sense of a universal moral standard (the Tao, as he would call it in *The Abolition of Man*). "And so the great Angler played His fish and I never dreamed that the hook was in my tongue."

The hook was in the tongue, but of more importance to Lewis at the time, his tongue had finally found an audience. In the spring of 1924, he expanded his philosophical studies, reading with great zest the biography and ethical writings of the Cambridge Platonist Henry More with a view to a D.Phil. dissertation, and lecturing to the Oxford Philosophical Society on "The Promethean Fallacy in Ethics"—a talk that one professor of moral philosophy, William Ross David of Oriel College, found "very attractive." E. F. Carritt tipped him off about a philosophy fellowship at Trinity College. The prospect dazzled Lewis, who reported in his diary that while heading home in the icy wind, he found himself "in a strange state of excitement—and all on the mere hundredth chance of getting it." He didn't get it, but entry into the promised land was delayed, not withdrawn: on May 5, University College asked him if he would like to tutor philosophy in place of Carritt, who was on his way to America for a year. Lewis gladly accepted; his desert wanderings had ended.

Contemplation and Enjoyment in the Lecture Hall

Lewis spent the next academic year (1924–25) tutoring, grading examination papers, and lecturing—a twice-weekly series beginning in October (Michaelmas term) on "The Good, Its Position among Values" and a similar series during Hilary term. A year later, he landed a position as fellow and tutor in English at Magdalen College, with additional responsibility to tutor in philosophy. *The Times* heralded the five-year renewable appointment; Lewis would keep the post for twenty-nine years. He made no note of the pivotal day—May 20, 1925, two months before Tolkien would land his professorship in Anglo-Saxon at Oxford—in his diary, which he had suspended writing for several months. Fortunately, his father kept up his own journal, recording that when he, well aware of his son's poverty, heard the news via telegram, "I went up to [Jack's] room and burst into tears of joy. I knelt down and thanked God with a full heart. My prayers have been heard and answered." Lewis himself was at the moment applying poultices to his right thumb, bitten deeply on this joyous day by a cat, as he rushed to stop it from lacerating a dog; as he was coming to realize, kindness and pain, joy and suffering are twins in this fallen world.

This truth applies also to the microworld of academia. The Oxford system, in which attendance at lectures was optional, made it difficult for a rank newcomer to fill a classroom. By the end of his term as a substitute lecturer on philosophy, Lewis wrote in his diary, "my audience had dwindled to two—Hawker [Gerald Wynne Hawker, an undergraduate] and the old parson. As they professed a wish to continue the course, I had them to my room. I said we could now be informal and I hoped they would interrupt whenever they wanted. The old parson availed himself of this so liberally that I could hardly get a word in." Lewis was determined to do better in his new incarnation as a lecturer in English and accordingly trained himself to talk from notes rather than read from a prepared script.

From one perspective, the change from philosophy to English was a step down. English studies still had a lingering reputation for being the "soft option" in the Arts, suitable for women and second-rate scholars destined to become schoolmasters or civil servants; during his undergraduate days, Lewis had found the atmosphere of the English School (as the Faculty of English was known) "amateurish" compared to Philosophy. But he made the best of it, telling his father, "I have come to think if I had the mind, I have not the brain and nerves for a life of pure philosophy. A continued search among the abstract roots of things, a perpetual questioning of all that plain men take for granted, a chewing the cud for fifty years over inevitable ignorance and a constant frontier watch on the little tidy lighted conventional world of science and daily life—is this the best life for temperaments such as ours? Is it the way of health or even of sanity?" Philosophy was too solitary and esoteric a discipline for the healthy person he dearly wished to be; nonetheless, he valued the ammunition it (and Barfield) gave him against the naïve positivisms of the day: "It will be a comfort to me all my life to know that the scientist and the materialist have not the last word: that Darwin and Spencer undermining ancestral beliefs stand themselves on a foundation of sand; of gigantic assumptions and irreconcilable contradictions an inch below the surface. It leaves the whole thing rich in possibilities: and if it dashes the shallow optimisms it does the same for the shallow pessimisms."

He was also, according to his diary, rereading the *Hippolytus* of Euripides in March 1924, an event that, according to *Surprised by Joy*, "annihilated the last remains of the New Look." We can only guess at what it was about the *Hippolytus* that affected him so deeply; certainly there was little to incite devotion in the capricious gods and ill-fated heroes that Euripides describes. But whatever applications Lewis may have found to his own life in this story, the main outcome of reading it was to reawaken the longing for Joy. "I was off once more into the land of longing, my heart at once broken and exalted as it had never been since the old days at Bookham. There was nothing whatever to do about it; no question of returning to the desert. I had been simply ordered—or, rather, compelled—to 'take that look off my face.'" In retrospect he would see this as the "first Move" God made toward an impending checkmate. The second Move came the following week, when he read Samuel Alexander's 1920 book (based on his Gifford Lectures), *Space, Time, and Deity*. Largely forgotten today, Alexander was a pivotal figure in debates between realists and idealists, an influence on Alfred North Whitehead and a forerunner of process philosophy. He developed an emergent model of mental life, in which conscious experience, and with it the sense of self and all the moral and aesthetic intuitions, arises out of neural structures as a genuine *novum*, dependent upon yet irreducible to its material elements. At the end of May, Lewis heard Alexander in person, a classically eccentric don, now "bearded and deaf and very venerable," deliver to the Oxford Philosophical Society a paper on artistic creation—a "satisfying attack on all Croce's nonsense," culminating in a grand (though to Lewis hard to follow) vision of "cosmic creation."

What Lewis found most helpful in *Space, Time, and Deity* was the distinction Alexander made between enjoyment and contemplation, a phenomenological analysis of experience that did much, Lewis thought, to overcome the mind-body split, by showing that in every experience there are two aspects: an act of perceiving and an object of perception. One enjoys the act of perceiving and one contemplates the thing perceived. He tried explaining this idea to his philosophy students while a strike was raging outside. "My class was completely unruffled by the strike and still very interested in Berkeley. Miss Thring read a paper. The discussion turned on the self. I told them about Alexander's distinction of contemplation and enjoyment and they all (I think) got it quite clear. Miss Colborne was specially good, saying to Miss Grant (who wanted to 'know' the self) 'It is as if, not content with seeing with your eyes, you wanted to take them out and look at them—and then they wouldn't be eyes.'"

Alexander pointed out that the error of the materialist is to count as real the thing seen and discount as mere epiphenomenon the act of seeing. But there is an opposite error, at once moral and epistemological, which Lewis thought he could see in himself: that of the subjectivist who overvalues his experience and undervalues its object. "I saw that all my waitings and watchings for Joy, all my vain hopes to find some mental content on which I could, so to speak, lay my finger and say, 'This is it,' had been a futile attempt to contemplate the enjoyed." It was a liberating discovery. The "quiver in the diaphragm" wasn't what he was searching for; that was the path of the spiritual voluptuary. Now he had discovered the "inherent dialectic of desire," realizing that "all images and sensations, if idolatrously mistaken for Joy itself, soon honestly confessed themselves inadequate. All said, in the last resort, 'It is not I. I am only a reminder. Look! Look! What do I remind you of?'" However Alexander may have helped in the process of discovery, Lewis's account of the dialectic of desire is far closer in spirit and rhetoric to the *Confessions* of the great convert-saint Augustine of Hippo:

> I asked the earth and it answered, "I am not He"; and all things that are in the earth made the same confession. I asked the sea and the deeps and the creeping things, and they answered, "We are not your God; seek higher." I asked the winds that blow, and the whole air with all that is in it answered, "Anaximenes was wrong; I am not God." I asked the heavens, the sun, the moon, the stars, and they answered, "Neither are we God whom you seek." And I said to all the things that throng about the gateways of the senses: "Tell me of my God, since you are not He. Tell me something of Him." And they cried out in a great voice: "He made us." My question was my gazing upon them, and their answer was their beauty.

Lewis was approaching the "region of awe," convinced that the call of Joy was drawing him out of himself toward a reunion with that mysterious Other (he stopped short of saying "God") that held the secret of his identity.

But there was much else on his mind just now. At the beginning of Michaelmas term 1925, he relocated his academic home to rooms in Magdalen College's eighteenth-century "New Building," overlooking the Deer Park, in surroundings "beautiful beyond expectation and beyond hope," as he told his father; and once inducted there as a fellow (the ceremony of admission was, embarrassingly, "a kneeling affair" involving Latin declarations for which no one had prepared him), his horizons instantly broadened. Since there were not enough students reading English to fill up his requisite tutorial hours, he began to tutor in philosophy and political science as well. Magdalen was the wealthiest of the Oxford colleges, but undeveloped in some areas—particularly the new PPE (Philosophy, Politics, and Economics) program, the modern alternative to Greats. It also had the reputation of being the foppish and reactionary aristocrats' favorite among Oxford colleges, a place for Etonians and Harrovians to win boat races, make the right connections, and academically squeak by (it was, after all, Bertie Wooster's college). All this would soon change, however, thanks to maverick dons like the Philosophy tutor T. D. (Harry) Weldon, of whom Lewis said, "Contempt is his ruling passion: courage his chief virtue"; and though Lewis's sympathies were with the old-guard dons, who were, in the main, churchgoing humanists, medievalists, and defenders of philosophical idealism, he would support efforts to raise the admission standards and make Magdalen as distinguished academically as it had been for "rowing, drinking, motoring and fornication."

From the beginning, his lectures—on "Some Eighteenth-Century Precursors of the Romantic Movement," followed the next year by "Some English Thinkers of the Renaissance"—were gratifyingly well attended, "a pleasant change," he told his father, "from talking to empty rooms in Greats." It was not long before he began to make a powerful impression both as lecturer and tutor. His most famous lectures—"The Romance of the Rose and its Successors" beginning in Michaelmas term 1928, the "Prolegomena to Medieval Poetry" lectures beginning in Hilary term 1932, and the "Prolegomena to Medieval and Renaissance Studies" lectures throughout the 1930s, in which the previous two series were combined—soon would make him a genuine celebrity in Oxford and beyond.

Reminiscences by those who attended these talks tell of the red face and booming voice, the rich, detailed presentations, and the rapt, enthusiastic crowds. Lewis had developed a trademark style, slow enough for note taking, loud enough to rouse the dullest listener, straightforward, abundantly furnished with quotations, and lavish in wit. He supported his prodigious memory by keeping two notebooks at the podium, one with a detailed outline on the left and illustrative matter on the right, the other a "Thickening" notebook furnished with additional anecdotes and examples. Paul Johnson remembers Magdalen Hall filled with "girls squatting or lying at his feet, displaying their stocky legs." Harry Blamires, in a note he sent to Warnie Lewis, recalls that "as a lecturer he was the biggest 'draw' the English School had in the nineteen-thirties. He could fill the largest lecture rooms. He was popular because his lectures were meaty. He purveyed what was wanted in a palatable form. Proportion and direction were always preserved, but without forcing. Points were clearly enumerated; arguments beautifully articulated; illustrations richly chosen." The poet and medievalist Sister Mary Madeleva Wolff, C.S.C., who during a sabbatical year in 1934 attended the "Prolegomena to Medieval Poetry" lectures (as well as lectures by Tolkien), before returning to America to become president of St. Mary's College in Indiana, wrote to her Mother Superior to say that they were the best lectures she had ever heard. Alastair Fowler, who attended the "Prolegomena" lectures in the 1950s, recalls being impressed by Lewis's "avuncular informality":

> At times, 'Uncle Lewis' seemed hardly to be performing but rather exploring a thought for the first time. And, so far was he from standing on ceremony or authority or superior learning that he started his lecture as he came through the door and finished it as he walked out. He was a popular and (not at all the same thing) *good* lecturer—lecturing sometimes to an audience of three hundred or more. He towered above his colleagues in the English faculty—at a time, admittedly, when lecturing standards were not high. His resonant voice suited the rostrum; he was always easily audible (something that could not be said of Tolkien).

Duties and Pleasures

Lewis also tutored, in his private digs, a select group of students not always of his own choosing. Some were women, as he reported to Albert in June 1926: "I have been bothered into the last job I ever expected to do this term: taking a class of girls once a week at one of the women's Colleges. However, I am not engaged to be married yet, and there are always seven of them there together, and the pretty ones are stupid and the interesting ones are ugly, so it is alright." Reminiscences from several "ladies of St. Hugh's" whom he would tutor during World War II—including Rosamund (Rieu) Cowan, daughter of the Homer translator E. V. Rieu—agree that, after overcoming their trepidation about approaching this red-faced "man's man" who disliked tutoring women and brooked no nonsense, they found him courteous and even kindly, demanding only that they speak their own minds clearly. Given that women outnumbered men in the English School, it was hardly possible for Lewis to avoid them.

Some of his charges drove him half-mad; for instance, John Betjeman, future poet laureate, whose aestheticism and frivolousness—including hauling around a teddy bear named Archibald Ormsby-Gore (inspiration for Sebastian Flyte's Aloysius in *Brideshead Revisited*) and prostrating himself on Lewis's floor declaring that he had no choice, given his poor performance as a student, but to enter Holy Orders—clashed badly with Lewis's heartiness. The two did have points of connection, however, for Betjeman was no modernist, and they plotted together to submit parodies of T. S. Eliot poems to *The Dial* and *The Criterion* (the latter journal being edited by Eliot). Lewis also enjoyed a gathering of "super-undergraduates" in Betjeman's rooms, including an "absolutely silent and astonishingly ugly person" from the Belfast region—the poet Louis MacNeice, Betjeman's schoolmate.

Betjeman represented the new breed, the Bright Young Things who came up between the world wars, for whom university life was champagne, plovers' eggs, silk dressing gowns, sexual experimentation, and "luncheons, luncheons all the way." He surprised Lewis with occasionally "creditable" papers, but the grammatical paradigms of Old English held absolutely no interest for him, and making excuses for work undone was an art form ("he hasn't been able to read the O.E., as he was suspected for measles and forbidden to look at a book. Probably a lie, but what can one do?"). After Betjeman, notwithstanding his high church leanings, failed "Divvers" (a very basic exam in theology required of all undergraduates) for the second time, Lewis suggested he settle for a pass degree, without honors. Betjeman (who did in fact succeed at Divvers on the third try) blamed Lewis for his poor showing. He made the rift between them public, paying mock tribute in his 1933 poetry collection, *In Ghastly Good Taste*, to "Mr C. S. Lewis . . . whose jolly personality and encouragement to the author in his youth have remained an unfading memory for the author's declining years," prefacing his 1937 poetry volume, *Continual Dew*, with an acknowledgement to Mr. C. S. Lewis "for the fact on p. 256" (the book is forty-five pages long), and broadcasting his grievance with these lines in "A Hike on the Downs":

Objectively, our Common Room
Is like a small Athenian State—
Except for Lewis: he's all right
But do you think he's *quite* first rate?

The novelist Henry Green—known at Oxford by his birth name, Henry
Yorke—also went in for dissipated undergraduate parties and struggled
with Lewis as a tutor, calling him "rude and incompetent." Unlike Betjeman, however, Green liked Anglo-Saxon and shared this interest with
Nevill Coghill, who became for a while a close friend; his jaundiced view
of Lewis may have arisen from differing literary inclinations, for Green,
as Maurice Bowra wrote, "thought nothing of Lewis' gods, Sidney and
Spenser," while Lewis knew nothing of Green's beloved nineteenth-
century Russian novelists—a clash of tastes exacerbated, as the Green
biographer Jeremy Treglown suggests, by the volatile mix of "Lewis's abrasiveness [and] Henry's passivity."

    With most of his tutorial charges, Lewis maintained a portcullis of
reserve. When John Lawlor (later professor of English at the University
of Keele) knocked one day on Lewis's door to apologize for missing a
scheduled session, "He cut short my apologies: 'I'm not your schoolmaster, you know.' It was coldly said, and coldly meant . . . I mustn't think of
our relationship as a personal one." Yet sometimes the tutor-tutee relationship blossomed into friendship. Many pupils, including Lawlor, have
recorded fond memories of their tutorial sessions with Lewis, the don
perched in his tatty armchair in a swirl of tobacco smoke, dressed in
shabby tweeds ("He looked more like an angler than a don"), doodling
on a pad, always ready to challenge students on every possible intellectual
front. Alan (Bede) Griffiths and Derek Brewer found him a sympathetic,
incisive, challenging, inspiring guide. Martin Lings (who would become
an influential Muslim thinker, discussed below) was grateful above all
for his tutor's "implacable criticism." Alan Rook (who would become a
successful war poet and vintner) said that tutorials with Lewis and occasional nightlong Madeira-and-dialectics sessions in Lewis's Magdalen
rooms left him feeling "happy but incompetent." The literary critic
W. W. Robson, though he disagreed profoundly with Lewis on questions
of literary judgment, rejected the picture of him as a bully: "Lewis did not

want to bully anyone . . . Nor—though his controversial manner sometimes lends colour to this belief—was he a brow-beater. His fault as an
examiner was quite contrary to what undergraduates feared; he was too
kind, being apt extravagantly to over-mark the papers of a candidate whose
views he disliked." Tutoring stole time from more important pursuits—it
was the intellectual counterpart to all the domestic chores that awaited
him at home—but it was, after all, what he was paid to do, and Lewis
believed strongly in doing one's duty.

Duty left room for pleasure, though. For Lewis, pleasure took three
intense forms. One was solitary walks; he knew all the footpaths in Oxford and tramped them regularly. Another was solitary reading. Helen
Gardner, the formidable critic whose admiration for Lewis was matched
by her disagreements with him on many points—she wrote two admiring
books on T. S. Eliot, one of Lewis's bêtes noires, and clashed with him over
changes in the English syllabus—marveled at his capacity and generosity
as a reader. A. N. Wilson attributes to the poet and critic William Empson (Lewis's sometime adversary) the opinion that Lewis was "the best
read man of his generation, one who read everything and remembered
everything he read"—and many biographers have repeated the statement,
though the source for it remains elusive. It is a plausible enough remark,
though, for it is difficult to posit an alternative; Eliot, an obvious contender,
was too busy with his banking job to challenge for the title.

A favorite place to read was Duke Humfrey's Library, a fifteenth-
century reading room at the Bodleian, with vaulted ceiling, hidden study-
nooks, mullioned windows, and unlimited provisions of books and
incunabula close to hand. "If only you could smoke and if only there were
upholstered chairs, the Bodleian would be one of the most delightful
places in the world," Lewis wrote. He was thankful that talking was
allowed, for he found the hum of conversation soothing rather than
distracting. Like all great readers, he could create for himself a "wall of
stillness," as Helen Gardner put it. "To sit opposite him in Duke Humphrey," Gardner recalled, "when he was moving steadily through some
huge double-columned folio . . . was to have an object lesson in what
concentration meant."

The third recreation, balancing the other two, was hobnobbing. His
latest discovery in this line was the Wee Teas (named after the "Wee
Frees," a minority sect of the Free Church of Scotland), a regular gath-

ering of six junior lecturers convened over a three-course dinner, at a more convenient hour than the "Philosophers' Teas" held in the afternoon by their seniors. Here Lewis locked philosophical horns with Gilbert Ryle (a realist and ordinary language philosopher in the tradition of Cook Wilson, adept at exposing the pitfalls of mind-body dualism), Harry Weldon, Frank Hardie (brother of future Inkling Colin Hardie), H. H. Price, and John Mabbott. Sometimes, intellectual games lightened the proceedings; Mabbott recalls hearing Frank Hardie quote John Alexander Smith's Latin lines about Noah's Ark:

> *Cum bove bos, grue grus, sue sus, cum tigride tigris,*
> *Rhinoceros tum cum rhinocerote venit*

> With cow bull, with female crane male crane, with sow pig, with
>   tigress tiger,
> Then came bull rhinoceros with cow rhinoceros

At which, according to Mabbott, Lewis and Frank Hardie instantly added four more lines (though there is reason to think the four lines were composed beforehand by Barfield and Lewis):

> *Necnon ridicula cum mure it ridiculus mus,*
> *Tum tom felis cum fele leone leo;*
> *Et pterodactylium par nobile, parque draconum*
> *Et dinos saurus dinaque saura sua*

> Likewise the silly mouse goes with his silly doe mouse,
> Then tom-cat with molly-cat, lion with lioness;
> And a noble pair of pterodactyls, and a pair of dragons,
> And the terrible lizard with his terrible lizardess

Still, Lewis's participation in the Wee Teas was limited. He relished intellectual scrapes but needed deeper comradeship. To date, Greeves, Barfield, and to some extent Coghill had filled that want. But Greeves was far away and a lesser intellect, and Barfield, although always exciting ("To Clive Hamilton: Opposition Is True Friendship" reads the dedication of *Poetic Diction*), insisted on cloaking his scintillating mind in

Anthroposophical clouds. On May 11, 1926, however, at another tea—
the late afternoon Merton College "English Tea" of the Oxford English
School—he met a man who would become a close friend and profoundly affect his thought and work, a "smooth, pale fluent little chap"
by the name of J.R.R. Tolkien.

8

A MEETING OF MINDS

L ewis's impressions of his first meeting with Tolkien appear in his diary in telegraphed fashion: "can't read Spenser because of the forms—thinks the language is the real thing in the school—thinks all literature is written for the amusement of *men* between thirty and forty—we ought to vote ourselves out of existence if we were honest— still the sound-changes and the gobbets are great fun for the dons." Lewis records Tolkien's academic conservatism, noting that "his pet abomination is the idea of 'liberal' studies. Technical hobbies are more in his line" (presumably this would include calligraphy, painting, and invented languages) and ascribing to him a degree of male exclusivity that sounds just a bit too much like Lewis's own view of the matter. Beyond that, he clearly has no idea of what he has encountered, remarking flippantly that there was "no harm in him: only needs a smack or so." But it was Tolkien who would supply the smack, jolting Lewis—with the help of other friends and Lewis's own desperate yearning—into Christian faith.

The first contact between the two was, however, professional. When Lewis remarked that Tolkien "thinks the language is the real thing in the school," he was referring to a controversy over the proper balance between philological and literary study in the English syllabus—a controversy resolved in 1931, only to erupt more violently in the "lang. and lit." debates of the 1950s and '60s.

English has now become, for better or worse, the quintessential humanities subject. At this time, however, it was a relatively new field of study, established as an Honours subject in 1894 against much opposition. As the younger and scruffier cousin to Classics, which had long been the preeminent subject for Honours candidates in the Arts, the Faculty of English could not hope to achieve a similar dignity if it appeared simply to cater to a taste for Shakespeare's plays, let alone modern novels. It needed rigor, and that rigor could be supplied by the demand that students master the ancient and medieval roots of their literary heritage, its Germanic antecedents, its Norman and Celtic influences, and its most recondite texts. But this posed a serious problem. From the earliest days of the English School, most candidates for instruction cared nothing for these subjects. An unsigned 1890s pamphlet, "A Perilous Protest Against Certain Lewd Fellows of the Baser Sort, banding Themselves together under the name of 'Philologists,'" reads like a precursor of Betjeman's tirades:

> The school of English Lang. and Litt.
> In our opinion should be split,
> For he who has the sort of wit
> To score a bit on English Litt.,
> Is not, egad, the kind of man
> To babble Lithuanian.

The crux of the issue, as Tolkien saw it, was twofold: the "lit." track lacked necessary grounding in the philology and sources of English literary tradition, while the "lang." track shortchanged the study of medieval texts qua literature. He despised the very term "lang. and lit.," suggesting that its "banishment is probably the first need of reform in the Oxford School," and argued for "A" and "B" instead. He did not think language the primary subject and literature an appendix, as some charged; in his view, they had equal merit and should be partners rather than rivals. In an essay, "The Oxford English School," that appeared in May 1930 in *The Oxford Magazine* amid ads for a recital by the harpsichordist Wanda Landowska and "Hayes and Son, the Oldest Established Bookbinders in Oxford"—traditionalism was in the ascendant in Oxford just then— Tolkien advanced his agenda. To many modern eyes, it will appear to be traditionalism run rampant. He urged educators on the lit. side to cut back the study of "the thousand years at the modern end" of literature, including the elimination of nineteenth-century studies, to be replaced by "worthy Anglo-Saxon and Middle English texts." The lang. track needed similar reform; the syllabus should stop at A.D. 1400—even though this would mean sacrificing Shakespeare's transformation of the English tongue—to make room for the study of cognate languages like Old Icelandic, with its rich literary tradition, and Gothic, "a main source of the poetic inspiration of ancient England and the North."

Lewis, although far more sympathetic to postmedieval English literature, came to share Tolkien's vision for the reform of the syllabus and joined in the campaign, which lasted from their first acquaintance in 1926 until victory in 1931. Lewis read a paper ("Our English Syllabus") to the English Society at Oxford, lambasting the study of modern literature as "an intrinsic absurdity," declaring that "the student who wants a tutor's assistance in reading the works of his own contemporaries might as well ask for a nurse's assistance in blowing his own nose." The analogy says, inter alia, much about Lewis's view of modern literature. In "The Idea of an 'English School'" (a paper he delivered to a joint meeting of the Classical and English Associations), while proudly proclaiming his literary conservatism ("if any question of the value of classical studies were before us, you would find me on the extreme right"), Lewis argues that the origins of modern English literature, and therefore the necessary study of those who would understand this literature, lie not, as is commonly supposed, in Greek and Roman classics, which brought to English neither form nor spirit but only "matter" (i.e., subject matter), but in Anglo-Saxon. In the tongue of Beowulf he discerns "a sense of language . . . native to us all."

By the early 1930s, those members of the English School who shared the same viewpoint established, along with Tolkien and Lewis, a club known as "the Cave" to advance their interests. They took their name from the biblical Cave of Adullam (1 Samuel 22:2), in which "every one that was discontented" assembled around David, awaiting their return to power—by then "Cave of Adullam" was a familiar way to lampoon any group of political malcontents (such as the Jacobites in Sir Walter Scott's historical novel *Waverly*) that retreats in the hope of better days ahead. The Cave lasted until World War II, becoming, once its core agenda had been achieved, a distant cousin of the Inklings. In addition to Lewis and Tolkien, Cave members who would double as Inklings included Nevill Coghill, the Anglo-Saxonist C. L. (Charles Leslie) Wrenn, who collaborated with Tolkien on the curriculum and in *Beowulf* studies (he would succeed Tolkien, in 1946, as the Rawlinson and Bosworth Professor), and Henry Dyson, a World War I veteran with an Oxford degree in English (Exeter College), then a lecturer in English, a passionate teacher and boisterous advocate for traditional humane learning at the University of Reading (he would return in glory to Oxford in 1945 as a Merton College fellow and tutor); activities included readings, dinners, and chat, but differed from those of the more celebrated circle by, among other things, inviting women to participate.

By October 1931, Lewis was crowing to Warnie that "next year is the first exam held under the syllabus which my party and I have forced upon the junto after much hard fighting: so that if I get a good colleague we shall be able to some extent to mould the new tradition. In fact, in English School politics, the anti-junto is in the ascendant—perhaps, from a prejudiced point of view, might be said to have become the junto." Lewis was too much the moralist, however, and too recent the convert, to forget that any junto, however correct its views, may turn into an "inner ring": "How long will it take us to become corrupt in our turn?" he asked. As it happened, the views of Tolkien and Lewis, with some compromises and modifications, prevailed at Oxford for many years, with the study of English literature beginning with *Beowulf* and ending just shy of the Victorians. Old English, the heart and soul of the old regime, ceased to be a required course only as of 2002.

"The Fire Was Bright and the Talk Good"

The Cave was not the only proto-Inklings group at Oxford during this era. In 1926, Tolkien founded the Kolbítars (coal-biters; that is, men who huddled around the fire against the Icelandic cold) devoted to intensive study of Old Norse literature. The club lasted for seven years, meeting, when possible, every other Monday morning. It counted among its members Lewis, Coghill, George Stuart Gordon (soon to become president of Magdalen College), and the lexicographer C. T. (Charles Talbut) Onions (1873–1965), fourth editor of the *OED* and a tutor and fellow of Magdalen. Tolkien dominated the meetings with fluent translations of extensive blocks of texts, while the novices, notably Lewis and Coghill, followed along as best they could or tackled, with considerably less success, much briefer passages. Lewis reveled in the study, poring over his Icelandic dictionary to catch sight of the names of gods or giants that would send him into "a wild dream of northern skies and Valkyrie music." He liked the group's philological tilt, but he loved its focus on myth and the opportunity it afforded to mingle with others who shared this love. His enthusiasm was unbounded; he records, in a letter to Arthur, that one evening he stayed up until 2:30 a.m., talking with Tolkien about "the gods & giants & Asgard for three hours, then departing in the wind & rain—who cd. turn him out, for the fire was bright and the talk good?"

The friendship with Tolkien blossomed. In a letter to Arthur, Lewis describes his colleague as a friend "of the 2 class," along with Dyson—just a notch below Greeves and Barfield. The feeling was warmly reciprocated; Tolkien, if he had thought in these categories, may have even considered Lewis a friend of the first class, for he removed his concealing armor and read out loud to him, in the intimate privacy of 22 Northmoor Road, substantial portions of the legendarium. At the end of 1929, he sent Lewis his long poem about Beren and Lúthien; Lewis read it and wrote back immediately, applauding the work's "sense of reality," mythic power, and freedom from contrived allegory: "I sat up late last night . . . I can quite honestly say that it is ages since I have had an evening of such delight: and the personal interest of reading a friend's work had very little to do with it." This must have been honey in Tolkien's ear. Lewis followed this initial report, a month or two later, with a fourteen-page analysis that parodied assorted literary and theological styles while lauding and pinpointing problems in Tolkien's work. Basking in the glow of Lewis's initial praise and open to suggestion, Tolkien accepted most of his friend's recommendations.

Despite Lewis's enthusiasm, however, Tolkien continued to withhold his legendarium from publishers. Only some minor poems, an essay on the *Ancrene Wisse,* and a few other bits of scholarship made it into print at this time. In 1931 he further lifted the veil on his private creations, delivering to an Oxford philological gathering a talk he called "A Hobby for the Home" (later retitled "A Secret Vice"). In this essay, Tolkien reveals his passion for inventing artificial languages, recounting his explorations in Animalic, Nevbosh, Naffarin, Quenya, Noldorin, and the like. He also makes the following observation, detailing what might be called the Tolkien Law of Language Creation: "For perfect construction of an art-language it is found necessary to construct at least in outline a mythology . . . the making of language and mythology are related functions; to give your language an individual flavour, it must have woven into it the threads of an individual mythology . . . The converse indeed is true, your language construction will *breed* a mythology." To bring this to fruition, and to present his most closely held secret vice to the world, would be the great work of the next two decades.

Allegories of Love

It has been observed that a man becomes a man, in the fullness of being, only when his father dies; this seems to be true in the case of C. S. Lewis. The relationship between father and son had improved; in his diary, Albert described a visit from Lewis and Warnie to Belfast over the 1926–27 Christmas holiday as "Roses all the way." For Lewis the roses bristled with briars, but this was a distinct improvement over previous years. Several more visits ensued over the next few years. In May 1928, Albert resigned with a pension from his post, held for nearly forty years, as county solicitor. He had little more than a year to enjoy retirement, for in August 1929 he fell seriously ill. Lewis rushed to his bedside; an operation disclosed cancer; Albert died on September 25, 1929. Lewis sent a telegram to Warnie, stationed in Shanghai, informing him of their father's death. It took the two brothers, with Lewis shouldering most of the burden, nine months to dispose of Little Lea and its contents. Warnie returned from Shanghai in April 1930, and the climactic moment in the process came when he and Lewis together retrieved their childhood toys, stored in an attic trunk, and buried them in the vegetable garden. "We will resolve them into their elements," wrote Lewis to his brother, "as nature will do to us." This nine-month obsequies, eerily like an inverted pregnancy, produced an unexpected birth. For two weeks after the sale of Little Lea, the two brothers, along with Mrs. Moore and her daughter, looking for a house in which they could all reside, discovered, far from the Oxford bustle, near a small pond bordered by moss and harboring coots and ducks—where, legend had it, Shelley once passed a day brooding atheistically—a property called the Kilns. "J and I went out and saw the place on Sunday morning, and I instantly caught the infection," wrote Warnie in his diary (July 7, 1930), adding that the garden was "such stuff as dreams are made on." The brothers moved in during October 1930 and would stay there until their death.

But a greater birth impended, for Lewis was about to move into new spiritual quarters as well. Of his conversion to Christianity, we will say more below; first there is a scholarly transformation to record. The long hours in Duke Humfrey's Library poring over manuscripts, incunabula, and recondite editions of medieval and Renaissance poetry were beginning to bear fruit in his first and most important book of literary scholarship, to be published in 1936 as *The Allegory of Love*. He dedicated the book "TO OWEN BARFIELD WISEST AND BEST OF MY UNOFFICIAL TEACHERS."

Lewis had originally contemplated writing a book about Erasmus, but found that Renaissance studies sent him back to the Middle Ages, and the Middle Ages to classical antiquity. Now he decided that his subject was simply "Old Europe." Reaching from late antiquity to the cusp of early modernity, Old Europe was the perennial spring from which the modern wasteland could be reirrigated; the "Renaissance," on the other hand, was a fiction concocted to devalue the "Middle Ages." Nevill Coghill recalled running into Lewis on Addison's Walk, just as this realization was dawning:

> . . . I saw him coming slowly towards me, his round, rubicund face beaming with pleasure to itself. When we came within speaking distance, I said, "Hullo, Jack! You look very pleased with yourself; what is it?"
>
> "I believe," he answered, with a modest smile of triumph, "I *believe* I have proved that the Renaissance never happened in England. *Alternatively*"—he held up his hand to prevent my astonished exclamation—"that if it did, *it had no importance!*"

In May 1928, he told Barfield his plan: he was starting a book on *The Romance of the Rose* "and its school." "I have actually begun the first chapter," he told his father in July 1928, of a study that would look at "mediaeval love poetry and the mediaeval idea of love which is a very paradoxical business indeed when you go into it: for on the one hand it is extremely super-sensual and refined and on the other it is an absolute point of honour that the lady should be some one else's wife . . ." The seven years the book took to complete coincided with Lewis's "Great War" with Owen Barfield, his journey from atheism to the threshold of Christianity ("I . . . wrote nearly the whole of the *Allegory* book while I was still an agnostic," he told the critic George Watson), his first meetings with Tolkien, and his belated efforts to forge an adult relationship with his father.

Lewis's aim in *The Allegory of Love* was "rehabilitation." He sought to recover "that long-lost state of mind for which the allegorical love poem was a natural mode of expression." Unearthing its classical and early medieval antecedents, he traced the form to its high-water mark in *The Faerie Queene* of Edmund Spenser, the sixteenth-century poet Lewis called "the greatest among the founders of that romantic conception of marriage which is the basis of all our love literature from Shakespeare to Meredith." His canvas was vast, encompassing the structure of medieval narrative poetry, the dream-vision genre, the origins of romantic love, the ethos of chivalry, the moral psychology embodied in medieval lists of the virtues and vices—virtually, the whole late-antique and medieval cosmos. His interest in these matters was neither nostalgic (Lewis condemned "that itch for 'revival'") nor merely antiquarian. "Humanity does not pass through phases as a train passes through stations: being alive, it has the privilege of always moving yet never leaving anything behind. Whatever we have been, in some sort we are still." Lewis was studying literary history with the present and future in mind: the history of a period (medieval), a rhetorical practice (allegory), and an ethos (courtly love), which had something important to contribute to modern culture if only they could be better understood.

It would be difficult to overstate the significance of his achievement. Not alone, but with decisive impact, he opened a new era in the study of medieval literature and culture. Reading medieval and Renaissance poetry with generous sympathy, he was able to see—and convincingly show—that it expressed a philosophical worldview, with pagan as well as Christian roots, as profound and viable as anything ancient or modern civilization had to offer. He did indeed, and lastingly, "rehabilitate" Spenser, making *The Faerie Queene* morally meaningful to readers who had hitherto viewed it as an intriguing political period-piece. He also offered groundbreaking if not unassailable insights into the origin of romantic love.

We moderns, Lewis points out in *The Allegory of Love*, are conditioned to believe that romantic love—"the love interest"—is essential to literature, drama, and film; we take it for granted, even as formal courtesy erodes and sexual liberties expand, that romantic love has the power to ennoble and inspire. What we don't recognize, Lewis maintains, is that we owe our exalted vision of love to a small group of medieval poets whose transformation of both pagan and early Christian eros opened a new spiritual epoch:

> French poets, in the eleventh century, discovered or invented, or were the first to express, that romantic species of passion which English poets were still writing about in the nineteenth. They effected a change which has left no corner of our ethics, our imagination, or our daily life untouched, and they erected impassable barriers between us and the classical past or the oriental present. Compared with this revolution the Renaissance is a mere ripple on the surface of literature.

Yet it was not romantic love as we conceive of it today that the troubadours and poets of the high Middle Ages celebrated. Rather, Lewis points out, it was *fin' amor* (pure love), a highly specialized form of passion, ascetical in the extremes of self-abasement and disciplined courtesy it demanded, cultlike in its ardent devotion, and, since medieval marriage was, according to Lewis, an affair of property and inheritance, not of the heart, strictly confined to adulterous love.

The object of *fin' amor*, then, is essentially unlawful and unattainable, even if fleetingly enjoyed. *Fin' amor*, one can't help notice, approaches everything Lewis meant by Joy: that delicious sharp pang of pure desiring, desiring what cannot be possessed, that leads beyond the narrow confines of the self. Did Lewis, too, think that joy could not be found in married life? It would be reasonable to suspect so, given his domestic situation; yet the whole point of *The Allegory of Love* is to show how *fin' amor* came at last, in Spenser, to be translated to the sphere of married life. The revolution that began in adultery ended in Christian domesticity.

Courtly love was, according to Lewis, a genuine *novum*, irreducible to historical or sociological terms. The sudden increase of landless knights attached to the isolated castle where a powerful lady and her damsels held sway was a favorable condition for this development, not an adequate cause. The medieval cult of the Blessed Virgin was more likely a beneficiary than a source of the new religion of love. Classical love poetry contributed material but not did shape the essential vision of courtly love; and early Christianity did not foresee it. Thus in *The Allegory of Love*, Lewis rejected the determinism of history, much as in later apologetic books like *Miracles* he would reject the determinism of scientific naturalism. New things can happen, Lewis insists; there can be miracles of literary as of moral history. One reads him as a literary scholar, only to be brought up short by the realization that he is making a philosophical as well as a historical argument.

Readers of *The Allegory of Love* have sometimes questioned whether Lewis underestimated the rhetorical character of courtly love literature. Was "courtly love" (the expression was coined by Gaston Paris, a nineteenth-century scholar of Arthurian romances) actually felt and practiced by knights and ladies? Or was it merely a stylish literary invention, decked out in allegorical finery? Lewis was inclined to grant the justice of both views: yes, it was a literary phenomenon, but one that afforded a real window into medieval souls. Why could it not be both at once?

The modern reader is predisposed to regard allegorical language as artificial, arbitrary, and insufficiently introspective to provide real insight into the experience of medieval lovers. The personification of abstract qualities, mother's milk to medieval writers, came to seem alien and repugnant to modern thought. But Lewis loved nothing more than the chance to defend ways of thinking that moderns find alien and repugnant. Hence, with a degree of exaggeration, he insists that allegory belongs to "the very nature of thought and language." It is a fragment of the perennial language, signaling immaterial feelings by material images that remain constant across the ages and around the world: heaven images the highest good, dark caverns image evil, life is a journey, reason the unconquered sun, conscience a voice. "To ask how these married pairs of sensibles and insensibles first came together would be great folly; the real question, is how they ever came apart."

Owen Barfield had given Lewis a way of answering this question: rejection of allegory is a symptom of estrangement from the poetic roots of our own everyday language. The irony is that allegory is inescapable: the modern Freudian psychodrama of ego, superego, and id is as artificial an allegory as one can find in any medieval mystery play. Moreover, the allegorical personification of abstract qualities and ideals reflected a moral psychology that, in Lewis's opinion, was more robust, demanding, objective, and exhilarating than the shapeless and chronically unfinished self-project of modern psychologies. Allegory did become artificial, Lewis concedes, after Spenser, and it is the debased, contrived form of allegory that for so long gave it a bad name. But allegory before Spenser, and allegory in the hands of Spenser, is another matter altogether. Spenser is the true hero of *The Allegory of Love*: the Christian poet who celebrated "life's golden tree" so vividly "that it is difficult not to fancy that our bodily, no less than our mental, health is refreshed by reading him"; the love poet who transfigured *fin' amor* into a communion to which married couples could aspire; the Renaissance poet who perfected medieval allegory before its decline into a "literary toy."

Allegory, then, is something disenchanted moderns need to know better, but it is not, Lewis intimates, quite as revelatory as symbol or myth. "There is nothing 'mystical' or mysterious about medieval allegory; the poets know quite clearly what they are about and are well aware that the figures which they present to us are fictions. Symbolism is a mode of thought, but allegory is a mode of expression." Allegory is a lower form in that "the allegorist leaves the given—his own passions—to talk of that which is confessedly less real, which is a fiction. The symbolist leaves the given to find that which is more real." The distinction, reminiscent of Coleridge, was rather forced, however; in a 1940 letter, Lewis said it was one of the parts of *The Allegory of Love* with which he felt dissatisfied. While Tolkien would insist to his last breath on the strict separation of the allegorical from the mythopoeic imagination, Lewis was willing to accept that these genres can be difficult to define with precision and often come mixed.

The Allegory of Love is a brilliant literary double helix: it tells the history of courtly love and the history of allegory by turns, revolving around a shared axis. Either history would have been a tour de force on its own; entwined together, the book irritated some as much as it impressed other scholarly reviewers. In an early review (April 1937) in *Speculum*, the American medieval studies journal, Howard Patch, a medievalist teaching at Smith College, acknowledged that the book "affords excellent reading," but could not endorse it: "If his work lacks permanent importance it is because his light touch has at times led him into extravagant statement." The same month, the University of Manchester philologist

G. L. Brook, writing in The *Modern Language Review*, called *The Allegory of Love* "undoubtedly one of the best books on mediaeval literature ever published in this country," and a few months later, Kathleen Tillotson, a scholar of Victorian literature, told readers of *The Review of English Studies* that "it is rarely that we meet with a work of literary criticism of such manifest and general importance as this. No one could read it without seeing all literature a little differently for ever after." She concluded that "Mr. Lewis is a critic alive at all points and wearing his learning like a plumed hat. His book, in addition to its other virtues, celebrates the marriage of *Philologia* and Mercury, too long divided"—by which she meant the marriage of the warring disciplines of philology and literary interpretation, or lang. and lit.

The intense labors of this seven-year period also appeared later in the 1944 Clark Lectures and the *OHEL* volume (discussed below), as well as in the posthumously published *Studies in Medieval and Renaissance Literature* and *The Discarded Image*. Taking these works together, one sees the lineaments of Lewis's entire scholarly project—which was nothing less than to give an account, at once historical and spiritual, of Europe's Christian literary imagination, from its Latin beginnings to its vernacular allegories and romances and its secular spin-offs, and to defend, against modernist prejudices, its enduring significance; to unlearn what we thought we knew about medieval poetry, morality, and science; to overcome the intellectual inhibitions that prevent us from enjoying literature both ancient and modern, on its own terms and for its own sake; to celebrate old books as a means of recovering the roots of Western culture; to savor, within those old books, those elements least congenial to modern prejudices, overcoming even a justified dislike of rhetorical artifice, "for surely to be indulgent to mere fashion in other periods, and merciless to it in our own, is the first step we can make out of the prison of the Zeitgeist?" If Spenser was, as Lewis suggests, "something between the last of the medieval poets and the first of the romantic medievalists," then Lewis, with *The Allegory of Love*, was emerging as the last of the romantic medievalists. He was convinced that it needed only the effort of looking through medieval eyes for us to see a meaningful, humanly habitable, ordered universe—a universe that is truly a cosmos rather than a chaos or a trackless waste; he was convinced that poetry and imaginative literature were a means of keeping alive, by transposing to a new key, the aesthetic and moral sensibilities endangered by a crude scientific positivism.

Checkmate

If Lewis was an agnostic while writing *The Allegory of Love*, by the time it was published he was a Christian and an allegorist in his own right. It was almost inevitable. Not only the poetry that made the subject of the "Prolegomena" lectures and *The Allegory of Love*, but almost all his leisure reading—from George Herbert's rapturous poems to G. K. Chesterton's exuberant history, *The Everlasting Man*—conspired to give him a mental landscape bedecked with symbols and images, even doctrines, of the faith. The balance of Western thought, he was beginning to realize, tilted heavily toward Christianity. His own history followed the same ineluctable curve. The movement along this arc had taken several years, as he moved from Joy as an end in itself, to Joy as a sign of something beyond, to the idealism of Bradley with its impersonal Absolute. But no one with Lewis's romantic yearnings rests content for long with the impersonal Absolute, even under the pseudonym of Spirit. A metaphysical solution that precludes all devotion, all worship—who can lose his heart to such a heartless answer? All the writers he most admired, Lewis notes (Plato, the medieval romancers, Johnson, Milton), and all the friends he most admired (Barfield, Tolkien, Coghill) believed in a personal God. He tells us, in *Surprised by Joy*, that the turning point came in 1929 during a bus ride up Headington Hill, when he realized that he had to choose: "I became aware that I was holding something at bay, or shutting something out." He let that something—which soon proved to be a Someone— in, knowing as he did so that he was turning his back, or kicking apart, the great atheist/agnostic edifice, built of theorizing and prejudices, proofs and hatreds, fear and ambition, that he had constructed over so many years:

> I was to be allowed to play at philosophy no longer. It might, as I
> say, still be true that my "Spirit" differed in some way from "the
> God of popular religion." My Adversary waived the point. It sank
> into utter unimportance. He would not argue about it. He only
> said, "I am the Lord"; "I am that I am"; "I am" . . . You must picture

me alone in that room in Magdalen, night after night, feeling, whenever my mind lifted even for a second from my work, the steady, unrelenting approach of him whom I so earnestly desired not to meet. That which I greatly feared had at last come upon me. In the Trinity Term of 1929 I gave in, and admitted that God was God, and knelt and prayed; perhaps, that night, the most dejected and reluctant convert in all England.

This passage has been taken by most biographers as the gospel truth about Lewis's journey toward the Gospel; it has achieved the status of a classic conversion testimony. But it should be noted that the conversion Lewis describing is to "theism," not yet to full-blown Christianity. And there is a problem about dates; for in the February following the Trinity (i.e., spring) term of 1929, Lewis wrote Barfield that "terrible things are happening to me. The 'Spirit' or 'Real I' is showing an alarming tendency to become much more personal and is taking the offensive, and behaving just like God. You'd better come on Monday at the latest or I may have entered a monastery." On this evidence, it would appear that Lewis was still on the fence. A revised dating suggested by Alister McGrath would place Lewis's conversion to theism in the Trinity term of 1930.

Then, too, God as the "Adversary" who makes "moves" and achieves "checkmate" reminds one much, perhaps a bit too much, of Francis Thompson's "Hound of Heaven" ("I fled Him, down the nights and down the days / I fled Him, down the arches of the years"). Thompson's descriptions of himself—"of all man's clotted clay the dingiest clot" and a "strange piteous futile thing"—are first cousins to Lewis's self-accounting on the eve of his conversion, as "a zoo of lusts, a bedlam of ambitions, a nursery of fears, a harem of fondled hatreds." Self-deprecation is the appropriate response of any new convert, as he matches his stained soul against the purity of God; but Lewis was a well-read man. There is no direct evidence that he knew Thompson's poem, but it appeared in *The Oxford Book of English Mystical Verse* (1917); Tolkien, as early as 1914, had lauded Thompson and his work during a talk to the Exeter College Essay Club, and it is certainly possible that he and Lewis discussed the poem.

The metaphorical language in Lewis's account of his conversion may signal that in at least some instances poetic considerations trump strict historical accuracy: "And so the great Angler played His fish and I never dreamed that the hook was in my mouth." On the other hand, it scarcely surprises that there are discrepancies in chronology. The shift from acknowledging Spirit (abstract noun) to adoring Spirit (personal noun), though tremendous in its implications, may well be a gradual transformation too subtle to date. In any event, if the artistic play of imagery, the conscious shaping of the tale, is everywhere evident, so, too, is the power and the glory of it. As a reviewer in *The Times Literary Supplement* noted, "the tension of these final chapters holds the interest like the close of a thriller."

A Walk at Night

Lewis was now half-ready—and perhaps more than half-willing, perhaps even eager—to know the embrace of a personal God. He couldn't be sure, at first, about what demands God would make—the surrender of Joy might be, he surmised, one of the first. Nonetheless, God's will be done; for God, being God, the fullness of goodness, power, beauty, and truth, deserves obedience; or as Lewis puts it, "To know God is to know that our obedience is due to Him." He discovered one immediate blessing: his relentless introspection, which had plagued him since childhood, abated. He ended his diary. Instead, he learned to pray and read the Bible, attended church, and corresponded with Griffiths, by this time a convinced Christian. He ascribes these acts to his "sense of honor"; now a theist, he thought he should behave like one, even if it meant enduring "the fussy, time-wasting botheration of it all! the bells, the crowds, the umbrellas, the notices, the bustle, the perpetual arranging and organizing," and, worst of all, the hymns and organ music.

All this suggests a deliberate catechumenate, as if Lewis already knew, at least subliminally—as most future converts know, long before the decision dawns in consciousness—where he would wind up. "'Where has religion reached its true maturity? Where, if anywhere, have the hints of all Paganism been fulfilled?'" he began to ask himself, according to *Surprised by Joy*. "Paganism had been only the childhood of religion, or only a prophetic dream. Where was the thing full grown? or where was the awakening?" Chesterton had helped to convince him that there were only two conceivable answers: Christianity and Hinduism (the latter, would, decades later, help to lure Griffiths away from European monasticism into an intermonastic—some would say syncretistic—Christian ashram). But he must have guessed the answer even as he posed the question. For Hinduism, all of Lewis's reading and thinking and desiring proclaimed, was too ahistorical and too redolent of humanity's pagan childhood to win the day, while Christianity offered Christ, in all His incarnate numinosity, the culmination of all myth, the perfection of all paganism, the Joy within Joy. As a result, Lewis told Arthur, he felt he had found a genuine way to rekindle his Romanticism and keep it permanently aflame.

Lewis's brother and friends knew where he belonged. On May 9, 1931, Warnie became a Christian, writing in his diary that "I started to say my prayers again after having discontinued doing so for more years than I care to remember" and adding that his conversion was not an irrational impulse but the conclusion of a long process, resting upon materialism's failure to explain the origins of life and "the inherent improbability of the whole of existence being fortuitous." Lewis makes no mention of Warnie's conversion as an influence upon his own. The two brothers liked, admired, and took counsel from each other, however, so we may assume with some confidence that Jack was swayed, perhaps at a level more fundamental than rational analysis, by Warnie's action.

A few months later, Lewis's friends joined the argument. On September 19, 1931, an event unfolded that has acquired its own mythic numinosity in the minds of Inklings lovers: the Night of Addison's Walk. Lewis, Tolkien, and their mutual friend, Hugo Dyson, strolled for hours along Addison's Walk—a tree-lined path within Magdalen College circling a meadow bordered by the River Cherwell—discussing the nature of myth and its relation to Christianity. Lewis insisted that myths are essentially lies; Tolkien countered that myths are essentially true, for they reflect and transmit, in secondary form, the primary and primordial creative power of God. Tolkien later reworked the conversations of that night in "Mythopoeia," a soliloquy in heroic couplets addressed by Philomythus (myth-lover=Tolkien) to Misomythus (myth-hater=Lewis) and dedicated "To one who said that myths were lies and therefore worthless, even though 'breathed through silver.'"

Moreover, Tolkien argued—and this was the crux of the matter— that in the life, death, and resurrection of Jesus we discover a myth that has entered history. Here God tells—indeed, enacts—a tale with all the beauty and wonder and symbolic power of myth, and yet a tale that is actually true. It was a strange thought, but it reminded Lewis of an off-hand remark he had heard five years before from the atheist Harry Weldon. "Rum thing," Weldon had said, "all that stuff of Frazer's about the Dying God. Rum thing. It almost looks as if it had really happened once." It looked as if it had really happened once—and yet it lost none of its mythic power for having become fact.

Tolkien's exposition hit home; as he talked, a strong wind rustled the overhanging leaves, and all three noted, as Lewis put it, "the ecstasy of such a thing"—almost like the passing-by of a god, or of God. At 3:00 a.m., Tolkien headed home, but Dyson sustained the offensive, delineating the blessings that come from a Christian life, as he and Lewis walked in the cloister garden of New Building. They went to bed at 4:00 a.m.

This night of Lewis's passion—intellectual, as it must surely be—bore fruit on a sunny morning a week or so later. The key moment came, as in Lewis's conversion to theism, while he rode a vehicle, this time not a bus ascending Headington Hill but the sidecar of Warnie's motorcycle as the brothers motored toward Whipsnade Zoo, a new animal park thirty miles north of London. "When we set out I did not believe that Jesus Christ is the Son of God, and when we reached the zoo I did." Henceforth, Joy "lost nearly all interest" for him. He had found, and would henceforth worship and defend with all his might, the very reason for Joy, the Almighty Maker of Joy. On October 1, Lewis wrote to Greeves, "I have just passed on from believing in God to definitely believing in Christ—in Christianity . . . My long night talk with Dyson and Tolkien had a good deal to do with it."

The Pilgrim's Regress

Aside from brief mention in his letters, the first record of Lewis's conversion to Christianity was the allegorical novel *The Pilgrim's Regress*, written in a white heat in August 1932, while Lewis was staying with Greeves in Northern Ireland, and published the following May (Lewis, who rarely wrote second drafts, excelled in lightning-fast production of this sort). Modeled on Bunyan's *The Pilgrim's Progress*, *The Pilgrim's Regress* tells of a boy named John who flees the stern Landlord of Puritania in search of a far-off Island that awakens in him "a sweetness and a pang," an indescribable yearning. The island, of course, is Joy, and John's odyssey is Lewis's own. John's quest takes him past the "barren, aching rocks" of the north ("rigid systems, whether sceptical or dogmatic") and the "foetid swamps" of the south ("the smudging of all frontiers, the relaxation of all resistances") before he learns, with the help of Reason and Mother Kirk, to steer a middle course that brings him, after numerous adventures, to the Island—which he discovers, in the sort of narrative loop beloved by artistic young authors (and deployed by Chesterton, from whom Lewis may have learned the trick), to be nothing other than an outcropping of his homeland, Puritania. The book offers giants, dragons, virgins; a landscape whose features signify spiritual states; characters named Mr. Angular, Vertue, Mr. Sensible. In these rich inventions and in the happy, hard-won culmination of John's quest, Lewis produces a clever homage and, in part, a worthy sequel to Bunyan's masterpiece.

But there is something amiss. Lewis himself admits as much in his preface to the third edition; the tale suffers from "needless obscurity, and an uncharitable temper." The first fault, relatively minor, Lewis ascribes to his naïve understanding of Romanticism and his equally naïve assumption that John is truly Everyman, that his (and Lewis's) path to Christianity is that of every pilgrim; the difficulties of writing allegory, especially one that suits the modern temperament, also played a part. It is the second fault that grates. The tale abounds in straw men, set up to be knocked down. John is faced, not with a series of personified virtues and vices such as Bunyan's Christian faces, but with a catalog of Lewis's bêtes noires, with Theosophists, high Anglicans, scholastics, modernists, materialists, rationalists, Freudians, Hegelians, pantheists, and exponents of "Oriental pessimism and self-torture." Satire overwhelms wit; vulgarity ensues, epitomized by Lewis's depiction of an avant-garde party in which all the women look like men and all the men like women, and one of the "Clevers" sings to the crowd, in crude parody of the poetry of Eliot and other modernists, "Globol obol ookle ogle globol gloogle gloo." The book, for all its good intentions and brilliant passages, lacks what Lewis himself lacked at the time: the gentleness of charity. Like many young converts, he makes too strong a case. He would spend the following decades learning how to cut his venom with honey.

It's noteworthy that Lewis wrote *The Pilgrim's Regress* while completing *The Allegory of Love*. He was also experimenting with allegory in an alliterative poem, "The Planets," written because "the character of the planets, as conceived by medieval astrology, seem to me to have a permanent value as spiritual symbols—to provide a Phänomenologie des Geistes which is specially worth while in our own generation." For the poets of classical antiquity, Lewis observed, allegory was the sleeping chamber of the fading gods; for Christians the planetary gods could live on, in this poetically diminished form, as conduits and symbols of the moral life: "the twilight of the gods is the mid-morning of the personifications." The idea was attractive to Lewis, the lover of myth, for why, he reasoned, should dullness be the price for monotheistic conversion? Why shouldn't the planetary intelligences continue their dance under the all-ruling Sun, just as they did in the Christian Middle Ages? The Lewis scholar Michael Ward has suggested in his deeply insightful *Planet Narnia: The Seven Heavens in the Imagination of C. S. Lewis*, that planetary symbolism is the key to much else in Lewis's work, *The Chronicles of Narnia* above all. At the very least, Lewis never abandoned the medieval model of the cosmos, even though the lukewarm outcome of *The Pilgrim's Regress* taught him to wear his allegory lightly.

"Something Was Broken"

Meanwhile, Barfield, uncertain about his career, had relocated to London. His passion for dancing and theater remained, but passion does not translate easily into a good income. He had enjoyed some success placing poems and essays but longed to tackle a more significant work; perhaps, he thought, he could make a go of it as a literary man. In 1929, while on holiday with Maud in Germany, he began work on a long novel of manners, *English People*. The book recounts the interactions of young people as they discourse on Christianity, psychoanalysis, art, literature, occultism, and other concerns of the day. It features a German seer named Karl Brockmann, obviously modeled upon Steiner, some bright prose (Lewis, in a letter to Arthur, praises Barfield's account of falling asleep), and numerous occult ruminations. It never found a publisher. Barfield, devastated by this failure, turned his back upon a writing career. What next? With a family to support—he and Maud had adopted a child, Alexander (b. 1928), in 1929—earning money had become imperative. He found a viable if not happy solution around 1930 by joining his father's London law firm, a small company that specialized in probate and real estate law and the like. He learned the ropes, passed the solicitor's exam, and practiced law for the next thirty years.

His friendship with Lewis was changing, too. At the end of 1929, Lewis had visited him and Maud for four days, and the two friends had a splendid time talking and poring over Aristotle's *Ethics* and Dante's *Paradiso* in "an uninterrupted feast." But all the while, Lewis was harboring doubts about the relationship. He mentions in a letter to Arthur, while recounting staying awake with Barfield until dawn to hear the cock crow, that "Barfield doesn't really taste a thing like that as keenly as you and I." Barfield felt the estrangement keenly, certainly more keenly than Lewis, and "had the feeling that something was broken" between the two. The friendship was entering a new phase, still warm but more remote. In September 1931, Barfield attempted to reopen the "Great War," but Lewis rejected the overture. "I don't think I ever heard him speak with such emotion," recalled Barfield. "He simply refused to talk at that sort of depth at all. I remember his saying, and again with more emotion than I ever heard him express: I can't bear it!"

Why should he bear it? Lewis, a newly minted Christian, had a new religious cosmos to explore and new opponents to challenge. Barfield, rooted in his old beliefs, felt hurt and half-abandoned. In the 1940s, the bitterness he experienced over the situation would erupt in satire— written in Greek and parodying the prologue of the Gospel according to John—squarely directed at his friend (whom he calls the "philosopher"). "Biographia Theologica" remains, in its portrait of Lewis as an arrogant, spiritually blind philosopher-prophet, the harshest—perhaps the only truly harsh—thing that Barfield wrote. The English translation runs:

> Lo, there was a certain philosopher, and the philosopher knew himself, that he was one. And the Word that came about in the philosopher was the one God. And the Word was the light of his philosophy. And the light shines in the philosophy, and the philosopher knew it not. It was in the philosopher, and the philosophy came about through it, and the philosopher knew it not. And indeed, the philosopher denied that anyone is ever able in any way to behold the light. But when he beheld the light, the philosopher said that its name was "Lord." And the philosophy bore testimony

to the light, that it is the Word and the life of men [*anthropōn*], and to the philosopher, that he was born not of blood, nor of the will of flesh, nor of the will of man [*andros*], nor through a command of a lord, but of God. But the philosopher did not comprehend the testimony.

In a 1969 addendum, Barfield would note that "I don't think I ever showed it to him, although I felt a strong impulse to do so. If I did, then he paid scant attention to it; if I didn't, it was because I was afraid of his paying scant attention to it."

9

ÍNKLÍNGS ASSEMBLE

During 1932, a precocious Oxford undergraduate by the name of Edward Tangye Lean published two novels, *Of Unsound Mind* and *Storm in Oxford: A Fantasy*, that attracted scant attention and small sales. Lean subsequently enjoyed a career as a journalist and broadcaster with the BBC, but he is remembered today for other, more adventitious accomplishments: secondarily as the younger brother of the film director David Lean; primarily as the founder, while an undergraduate, of a small literary society of students and dons that he called the Inklings. The name, which rides the seesaw between cuteness and cloying, pays homage to those who express themselves through ink as well as those who discover, through their inky labors, inklings of a higher world. Many readers will have noticed the aptness and even prescience of Lean's book titles, the first diagnosing the modern world in very Inklings-like fashion, the second foreseeing the Inklings' preferred literary method for effecting a cure.

Lean's group met in his suite at University College, and Tolkien and Lewis soon joined. In a 1967 letter, Tolkien remembered Lean as wishing to buck the general trend of clubs that come and go by producing one that would "prove more lasting." He succeeded beyond all measure, thanks to the course the Inklings would take after his departure from the university in 1933. Lean's original design for the group did much to ensure its longevity. Each meeting, as Tolkien recalled it, consisted of members reading aloud "unpublished compositions"—Tolkien read his poem

"Errantry" at one gathering, and it seems likely that Lean read portions of his unpublished fiction—followed by "immediate criticism" from others. This method differed from that of other Oxford literary circles of the day. The Martlets, for example, in which Lewis was active, also featured readings of unpublished compositions, but these were polished papers, like his "Is Literature an Art?" or Ronald Knox's "Detective-Stories." The Cave offered English School schmoozing and congenial literary chitchat (erotic doggerel dominated one meeting, Lewis told Warnie), but this sort of thing could be found almost anywhere. Lean's innovative emphasis upon work in progress was a brilliant advance that sowed the seeds of its own success; as long as members continued to refine existing works or turn out new ones—and in Lewis, Tolkien, and Lean, among the early members, the will to write was very strong indeed—the group would have momentum. Each meeting led to the next as naturally as one sentence follows another. When Lean graduated from Oxford, the group, or at least its name, fell with seeming inevitability into Lewis's lap. After a brief hiatus, he adopted it for his own "undetermined and unelected" (Tolkien's description) circle of friends, and the assembly that we know today as the Inklings was born.

Thus runs one account—one creation myth, one is tempted to say—of the origin of the Inklings. There are others. Barfield always insisted that the Inklings began, de facto if not de jure, in the late 1920s, long before the group received its formal appellation, in the walking tours and other gatherings of the early principals. If this is so, we might situate the first stirrings in the three-way debates between Lewis, Barfield, and Harwood at Harwood's cottage outside Beckley during the Lewis-Barfield "Great War." During Easter 1927, these three, along with the Anthroposophist Walter O. "Wof" Field, spent their days walking the beautiful Berkshire Downs and their evenings in "philosophical discussion." By 1928, regular meetings between Lewis and Tolkien were in full swing and made for "one of the pleasantest spots of the week," as Lewis wrote to his brother. "Sometimes we talk English school politics, sometimes we criticise one another's poems; other days we drift into theology or 'the state of the nation': rarely we fly no higher than bawdy and 'puns.'" Meanwhile, other embryonic proto-Inkling gatherings took place. In 1927, Barfield met Tolkien for the first time, at a meal sponsored by Lewis at the Eastgate Hotel; Tolkien was in a prickly mood, "ridiculously combative,"

according to Barfield, who, nonetheless, hungry for intellectual companionship, enjoyed himself immensely.

Soon a core group, consisting of Barfield, Tolkien, and Lewis, with
Coghill and one or two others tossed in on occasion, began meeting
regularly for long discussions in Lewis's Magdalen quarters. Conversation was crucial to each session; if the stated purpose of the Inklings
was to read and critique one another's writings, the implicit but universally acknowledged aim was to revel in one another's talk. Often gatherings had no readings at all, only loud, boisterous back-and-forth on
a vast range of topics. Among the Inklings, pen and tongue held equal
sway.

What was discussed? Our knowledge is woefully incomplete. This is a
strange circumstance, at first glance, given the loquaciousness and eventual fame of so many of the members, but it is not entirely strange when
one remembers that at the time, these young men had little or no idea
that their gatherings would pass into literary legend. No minutes were
kept, no recordings made. In later years the Inklings' pens, so ready to
flow on other subjects, remained lamentably dry when it came to early
Inklingsiana. Desire for privacy was the principal reason; the members
liked and protected one another, especially from unwarranted public
scrutiny, even after the group had dissolved. Warnie's lament is seconded
by many: "Had I known that I was to have outlived Jack I would have
played Boswell on those Thursday evenings, but as it is, I am afraid that
my diary contains only the scantiest material for reconstructing an Inklings." Warnie's diary was not without its revealing incidents, however;
as a representative sample, he records an evening in February when conversation ran to "red-brick universities . . . torture, Tertullian, bores, the
contractual theory of medieval kingship, and odd place-names." Humphrey Carpenter's vivid account of a meeting, the centerpiece of his entertaining 1978 study *The Inklings*, is, alas, not what many readers take it
to be, a report of an actual gathering, but rather a patchwork, assembled
from numerous published and unpublished memoirs and letters. Barfield
considered the reconstruction "surprisingly successful," but Havard, reflecting on his Inkling days in an interview with Lyle W. Dorsett, found
it to be "quite unreal." It may be that Tolkien came closest to capturing
the flavor of these Thursday events, which went on for nearly twenty

years, in his little-read, unfinished 1945 novel, *The Notion Club Papers*—
"notion" being, of course, a synonym for "inkling," in the sense of an idea
not yet fully realized.

The Notion Club Papers presents itself as minutes, discovered in
2012 in a waste container in the basement of the Oxford University examination rooms, of a number of meetings of a literary/philosophical circle
clearly modeled upon the Inklings. The recorded conversations focus on
dreams, space travel, language, and related topics, before turning into a
meandering and confusing account of the legend of Númenor, an island
in the Great Sea west of Middle-earth based loosely on Atlantis. Many
find *The Notion Club Papers* difficult to read, but it contains splendid
composite portraits of several of the Inklings. The club's leading personality is Michael George Ramer, professor of Finno-Ugric philology "but
better known as a writer of romances" (Tolkien originally entitled the first
part of the novel "The Ramblings of Michael Ramer: *Out of the Talkative
Planet*"). Others include Rupert Dolbear, a chemist with red hair and
beard; Alwin Arundel Lowdham (originally Loudham), a lecturer in English "chiefly interested in Anglo-Saxon, Icelandic, and Comparative Philology"; and Philip Frankley (originally Franks), "a poet . . . intolerant of
all things Northern or Germanic." Tolkien appended a sheet of paper to
an early manuscript of the book, listing correspondences between these
invented characters and the Inklings. He identified Ramer as "Self," then
changed his mind and wrote "CSL" before crossing that out also. Lowdham is revealed as "HVD" (Henry Victor Dyson) and Dolbear as "Havard"
(i.e., Dr. Robert Havard, Lewis's doctor, who joined the group in 1935).
Later, Tolkien abandoned these strict equivalences, warning his readers—
presumably the Inklings—"not to look for their own faces in my mirror.
For the mirror is cracked . . ." Yet resemblances peek through. Lowdham's irascibility and penchant for cutting jokes, embodied in his original
name of Loudham, perfectly captures Dyson, while Dolbear's red hair
points to Havard. What *The Notion Club Papers* most richly conveys, however, is the rough humor, argument, wordplay, literary passions, and free-
wheeling philosophical and philological speculation of the imagined
club's real-life counterpart.

The Inklings' reticence to describe their gatherings began early in
their history. Lewis's first written reference appears in a letter to Charles

Williams dated March 11, 1936, years after meetings got under way. Tolkien remained silent on the subject, at least in his published correspondence, until February 18, 1938, when he informed his publisher, Stanley Unwin, that Lewis's space thriller, *Out of the Silent Planet*, had been "read aloud to our local club (which goes in for reading things short and long aloud)," adding that the novel "was highly approved. But of course we are all rather like-minded." Like-minded indeed, and that by design. Lewis's letter to Williams characterizes the Inklings as a group of Christians who like to write. That might do as a description of the genus. But *Inkling authenticus*, the actual species, shared more precise characteristics, including intellectual vivacity, love of myth, conservative politics, memories of war, and a passion for beef, beer, and verbal battle. The Inkling David Cecil adds to this "a feeling for literature, which united, in an unusual way, scholarship and imagination." And one had to be male. An apocryphal tale, making the rounds of Oxford to this day, tells that Dorothy L. Sayers, fed up with the group's veto on female membership, hammered one day on the entrance of the Bird and Baby while a meeting of the boys was in session. An owlish Inkling peered out, recoiled, and slammed the door in her face. The tale is an invention—pub doors are not barred against visitors and, in any event, Sayers was far too subtle to confront her friends in this manner—but it does underscore the Inklings' policy, which was hardly unique in Oxford at the time. From first meeting to last, the group remained completely, inviolately male; Lewis spoke for almost every member when he said, "There's no sound I like better than adult male laughter."

Nonetheless, the Inklings were anything but monolithic. Even in the early years, the club embraced a variety of professions, including don, doctor, lawyer, and soldier; the popular image of the Inklings as sequestered academics is clearly inadequate. The members' shared Christianity also included a wide spectrum of views. Tolkien was Catholic; Barfield, Anthroposophist; Lewis, a "mere Christian"; Charles Williams, Anglican with a dash of ritual magic. Differences notwithstanding, the members were glued together by shared adherence to the Nicene Creed (with Barfield a possible exception until the late 1940s) and a shared set of enemies, including atheists, totalitarians, modernists, and anyone with a shallow imagination. Above all, they were friends, encouraging, provoking, enlightening, and correcting one another. They enjoyed themselves immensely, and "adult male laughter" rang through every meeting. A circle of friends, as Lewis observed in 1960, enlarges each participant, making each entirely himself:

> In each of my friends there is something that only some other friend can fully bring out. By myself I am not large enough to call the whole man into activity; I want other lights than my own to show all his facets . . . Of course the scarcity of kindred souls— not to mention practical considerations about the size of rooms and the audibility of voices—set limits to the enlargement of the circle; but within those limits we possess each friend not less but more as the number of those with whom we share him increases.

The Inklings flourished. Voices remained audible, Lewis's plummy baritone and Dyson's shouts the most pronounced; Tolkien continued to mumble, however, reciting at top speed from his works in progress. The room—usually Lewis's sitting room, overlooking the Magdalen College Deer Park—was capacious but shabby, with a bachelor's interior of battered furniture and carpet pockmarked by cigarette burns. Despite these limitations, if such they were, the circle enlarged apace. Lewis, Warnie, Tolkien, Coghill, and Dyson attended most meetings, and Barfield came up from London when possible. Soon after, Dr. Robert Emlyn Havard joined the group. Ill with flu, Lewis had visited Havard's offices, discovered a mutual interest in Thomas Aquinas (Havard was a Catholic convert), chattered on about the Angelic Doctor for twenty-five minutes, and soon after invited Havard to enter the circle. He was a popular and active member, although Warnie, vexed one day by his failure to appear, dubbed him "the Useless Quack," a nickname that stuck, often abbreviated to "U.Q." In 1936, Colin Hardie, a classicist and former director of the British School in Rome, enlisted. He was followed by Lord David Cecil, literary historian and fellow of New College, and by Charles L. Wrenn, a close friend, along with his wife, Agnes, of the Tolkiens. Wrenn, like Tolkien, was a philologist and a scholar of Anglo-Saxon, but he lacked the creative imagination to write fiction. Nearly blind, he nonetheless dazzled students with his teaching: "Occasionally he would hold a note about half an inch away from his eyes; but for the most part he ad-libbed with eccentrically abstracted ease and authority. Linguistic mutations, contractions, assimilations, corruptions, covering anything from Old Icelandic to Anglo-Saxon, Old French to Danish, Scandinavian to Oriental, came from him as readily as the twice-times table." Cecil, too, possessed his eccentricities; a friend describes him as "elegant yet at the same time spontaneously gauche, continually in motion from the twirling thumbs to the enthusiastic forward lurch." Cecil's stuttering, superheated conversation bestowed praise, kindness, and good humor upon all about him. He was brilliant, religiously devout, and universally loved; Virginia Woolf took his measure when she described his wedding in her diary: "David and Rachel, arm-in-arm, sleep-walking down the aisle, preceded by a cross which ushered them into a car and so into a happy, long life, I make no doubt." Adam Fox, a Plato enthusiast, professor of poetry at Oxford and dean of divinity at Magdalen, also joined for four or five years, until appointed canon of Westminster Abbey in 1942. He, too, was an Inkling to the bone, his inaugural lecture as poetry professor declaring that "the pleasure of poetry is like the pleasure of good conversation. If so, it may well be a very intense pleasure, for conversation is a pleasure almost as intense and primitive as eating or making love, to both of which it is a proper adjunct."

In sum, the Inklings resembled an intellectual orchestra, a gathering of sparkling talents in common cause, each participant the master of his own chosen instrument, be it literature, theology, philosophy, history, or medicine. Who was the conductor? Many would say Lewis: the group usually met in his rooms and almost never met without him, although now and then other Inklings might gather in twos or threes for food or chat. Yet this view needs amendment. Tolkien, who had dominated the Kolbítars, a club that included many nascent Inklings, also wielded his baton at the Magdalen meetings, doing much to set the tone with his wit, his reading—including prolonged excerpts from The Lord of the Rings—and his friendly critiques; Havard particularly admired Tolkien's way of correcting his friends, noticing that his remarks "were always made by the way, and not [with a] knock you down, take them or leave them attitude," the latter a dig at the pugilistic Lewis. The truth is that Lewis and Tolkien served as twin pillars, elevating the Inklings to greatness; the humble, welcoming, always genial Warnie was the necessary third support, providing balance and stability.

By Warnie's account, each meeting began in the same way:

The ritual of an Inklings was unvarying. When half a dozen or so had arrived, tea would be produced, and then when pipes were well alight Jack would say, "well, has nobody got anything to read us?" Out would come a manuscript, and we would settle down to sit in judgement upon it—real unbiased judgement, too, since we were no mutual admiration society: praise for good work was unstinted, but censure for bad work—or even not-so-good work—was often brutally frank. To read to the Inklings was a formidable ordeal.

Modest as usual, Warnie neglects to mention his own role as de facto host, greeting new arrivals, taking hats and coats, serving drinks. His report underscores, however, that first and foremost the Inklings was a literary club, with discussion frequently addressing the sort of technical problems any writer runs into, along with the intellectual merits or demerits of the work under analysis.

Apart from the ritual beginning, the Inklings had "no rules, officers, agendas, or formal elections . . . Proceedings neither began nor terminated at any fixed hour, although there was a tacit agreement that ten-thirty was as late as one could decently arrive." As Lewis recalled, "the talk might turn in almost any direction, and certainly skipped 'from grave to gay, from lively to severe'" while always featuring "the cut and parry of prolonged, fierce, masculine argument and 'the rigour of the game.'" Everyone had his quirk. Dyson would interrupt at will. Coghill excelled at puns; put off by H. G. Wells's didacticism, he declared that Wells had "sold his birthright for a pot of message." Lewis quoted long passages effortlessly, utilizing almost the entire canon of Western literature to hammer home his points. Tolkien danced from one idea to the next, nimble as a bird. "His whole manner was elusive rather than direct," said Havard. "The word 'flighty' crosses my mind in connection with Tolkien. It's misleading, because I don't mean it in the ordinary sense at all. But he would hop from subject to subject, in an elusive sort of way." Lewis summed up the meetings in this way: "We smoked, talked, argued, and drank together."

His list omits one key activity. The Inklings, as recounted above, also read works in progress to one another. A partial listing of writings read aloud, in whole or in part, would include Lewis's *Perelandra*, *That Hideous*

Strength, *The Great Divorce*, *The Problem of Pain*, *Miracles*, and *The Screwtape Letters*, Tolkien's *The Lord of the Rings*, Charles Williams's *All Hallows' Eve*, Warnie's *The Splendid Century*, medical papers by Havard, and Owen Barfield's verse drama *Medea*.

And there is one more book that the Inklings may have heard early in their history (clear evidence is lacking either way): Tolkien's first full-length novel, *The Hobbit, or There and Back Again*.

The Hobbit

On February 4, 1933, Lewis wrote to Arthur Greeves:

> Since term began I have had a delightful time reading a children's story which Tolkien has just written . . . Reading his fairy tale has been uncanny—it is so exactly like what we wd. both have longed to write (or read) in 1916: so that one feels he is not making it up but merely describing the same world into which all three of us have the entry. Whether it is really *good* (I think it is until the end) is of course another question: still more, whether it will succeed with modern children.

The "children's story" to which Lewis refers is, unmistakably, *The Hobbit*, Tolkien's classic children's fantasy and the prelude to *The Lord of the Rings*.

The Hobbit belonged, at the outset, to the endless stream of tales Tolkien invented to beguile his restless boys, stories like *Roverandom* and *Mr. Bliss* or the purely silly adventures of "Bill Stickers" and "Major Road Ahead." Invented on the spot and crafted in the writing, these stories were intended at first solely for the family's enjoyment, much like the annual Father Christmas letters. Composing for his own children proved to be a valuable exercise, a sine qua non for *The Hobbit* and for the high fantasy of *The Lord of the Rings*. It freed Tolkien to experiment with world making without worrying about what the public might think and without having, for the time being, to meet the high standards of consistency he demanded of himself where his serious mythology was concerned.

Favorite books by other authors also helped to prepare the way for *The Hobbit*, among them George MacDonald's Curdie books with their mountain strongholds and perfectly realized goblins, and Edward A. Wyke-Smith's 1927 *The Marvellous Land of Snergs*, whose faintly preposterous, surprisingly resilient, perpetually feasting heroes, "only slightly taller than the average table but broad in the shoulders and of great strength," lead their young human friends on a series of perilous adventures.

No one really knows—or at least scholars cannot agree—when Tolkien first began to write down *The Hobbit*. The most that can be affirmed with confidence is that he commenced no later than the summer of 1930, possibly as early as the summer of 1926, and that he worked at it on and off for as long as six and a half years, in whatever hours he could carve out from lecturing, tutoring, advising, grading, agitating for the reform of the English syllabus, and other creative and scholarly work. Beyond that, though a raft of Tolkien experts have combed all the evidence, it is impossible to reconcile the varying accounts. John and Michael remembered sitting in their father's study at 22 Northmoor Road and hearing him tell the story during long Christmas evenings beginning in 1926 or 1927, and Christopher wrote a letter to Father Christmas in December 1937, saying of *The Hobbit* that his father "wrote it ages ago, and read it to John, Michael, and me in our winter 'reads' after tea in the evening . . ." Tolkien believed that he first told his sons the story after they moved, in January 1930, to the large house at 20 Northmoor Road. It was there, on a summer day that year, as Tolkien later recalled, that he found himself scribbling "In a hole in the ground there lived a hobbit" on a blank page of a School Certificate paper he was grading. That precious piece of paper has not survived. Whether or not Tolkien's memory is reliable in this instance, his recollection illustrates his sense of being the discoverer rather than the manufacturer of his secondary world. Like Lewis, who said that Narnia came to him by way of a mental picture of a faun with an umbrella, Tolkien was convinced that genuine creative work originated somewhere beyond the individual creator's conscious mind. At first he had no idea what a hobbit was or where it would lead him, but he was more than willing to be led. He had, as we have seen, a Romantic conception of artistic inspiration as sheerly *other* at its source, and he would build upon that conception, as many fantasy writers before and after him had done and would do, by casting himself as the mere editor or compiler of inherited texts and tales. Bilbo's memoir, *There and Back Again, A Hobbit's*

Holiday, was the real source of *The Hobbit*, we are told; eventually Tolkien would extend this conceit into an increasingly complex scheme of serendipitously discovered, imperfectly compiled and edited, vast yet tantalizingly incomplete chronicles and florilegia of worlds and times and works long past.

As to the word "hobbit," it's not unreasonable to suppose, as Tolkien believed, that it did indeed just pop into his mind. Tolkien scholars have suggested a host of possible influences, from the rhyming but rather unlikely "Babbitt" (the bourgeois antihero of Sinclair Lewis's 1922 novel by that name), "habit" (as in "creature of"), and "rabbit" (an association Tolkien disliked), to an assortment of goblins and sprites, including "hobs," "hobthrusts," "hobyahs," "hobbity-hoy," "hobgoblin," "hobyah," "hubbit," and the like. In 1977, a single instance of "hobbit" was discovered, buried deep in a long list of preternatural beings native to northern England, in a two-volume collection of folklore studies published in 1895. But hobbits are not preternatural beings—they are a branch of the human family, bearing no relation, Tolkien insisted, to spirits or to "fairy rabbits." The existence of "hobbit" on a nineteenth-century folklorist's word list demonstrates at most that Tolkien had an unconscious fully stocked with the shapes and sounds of early Germanic nomenclature; as Tom Shippey points out, it tells us very little about Tolkien's creative process. Tolkien "had been inside language," as Lewis put it, and could intuit where others could only laboriously reconstruct. So it was right, when "hobbit" made it into the *Oxford English Dictionary*, Second Supplement, that it should arrive naked, sans real-world etymology, as an artifact of Tolkien's imagination.

Several scholars have labored mightily to reconstruct the stages by which Tolkien created *The Hobbit*. We now know that in its earliest form, which survives as a six-page handwritten fragment and a twelve-page typescript/manuscript in the Tolkien papers at Marquette University, *The Hobbit* is a comic children's fairy tale centering on the adventures of Mr. Bilbo Baggins, a hobbit who lives in comfortable lodgings at Bag End, Hobbiton Hill (a.k.a. "the Hill"), overlooking the village of Hobbiton in the imaginary land of the Shire. Like all hobbits, Mr. Baggins is a good-natured fellow. Somewhat smaller than a dwarf, beardless, round in the middle and hairy on the feet, he favors bright clothing, good company, cozy surroundings, and frequent meals, and is thoroughly ordinary and unmagical. Mr. Baggins is well-off and respected by his neighbors except for a touch of queerness he inherited from his mother's side of the family, the notorious Tooks, who claim fairy folk among their ancestry and exhibit a certain adventurous streak.

The Tookish element in Bilbo's nature lies dormant until a wandering wizard (known as Gandalf in later versions), a friend of the elder Tooks and master of fireworks, invites thirteen dwarves to a tea party under Mr. Baggins's roof. There Bilbo is persuaded, through a combination of flattery and scorn, to help the dwarves avenge the destruction by a dragon of their treasure trove and ancestral homeland under the Lonely Mountain. This leads to a series of disconnected adventures, in which he encounters Elves (notably the wise Elrond of Rivendell), trolls (who speak with Cockney accents), goblins and wolflike Wargs, a were-bear named Beorn, the wretched Gollum skulking in deep caverns, giant spiders, human beings from a mercantile town of faded splendor, and a crafty, treasure-hoarding dragon.

Tolkien borrowed the names for the dwarves from the *Dvergatal* (dwarf list), a section of the Old Norse Eddic poem *Völuspá*, which mentions Durin, Dvalin, Dain, Bifur, Bofur, Bombur, Nori, Thrain, Thorin, Fili, Kili, Eikinskjaldi (Oakenshield)—and Gandalf. In the earliest version of *The Hobbit*, Gandalf is the chief dwarf, while the wizard bears the unpleasant name of Bladorthin (drawn from Sindarin, Tolkien's invented language for the Grey Elves). The dragon carries the vaguely Welsh name of Pryftan, revised in later versions to Smaug, from the Old English *smúgan*, to squeeze through a hole or "worm" one's way in ("a low philological jest," according to Tolkien, who extended the jest with his fanciful etymology for "hobbit," from *hol-bytla*, "hole-dweller"). Bilbo Baggins is, from the very beginning, the inveterately bourgeois hobbit and reluctant burglar who by luck and ingenuity survives a series of unlooked-for adventures and, with nerves steeled by the possession of an invisibility ring, learns to live up to his burglar's calling. Tolkien's first plan—until he thought better of it—was to have Bilbo be the dragon-slayer, plunging his little sword into the sleeping beast's chest, just as Sigurd does to Fáfnir, the very Smaug-like dragon of the Norse Sigurd lays. In the scuttling of this plan, the Bilbo we know fully emerges: Tookish enough to engage in a battle of wits with a loquacious dragon, humble enough to stand aside while a human king strikes the death blow; seeking, in the end, not glory or riches but general well-being and a chance to retire safely to his armchair with his fourteenth share of the profits in hand.

Tolkien's evolving conception of Bilbo was a watershed in his approach to storytelling. The glorious, solemn, violent, single-handed exploits of ancient Germanic heroes had weighed on his mind throughout the six or seven years during which he composed and revised his tale. Like the *Beowulf* poet, he wished to honor that heroic past, celebrating its memory while subtly Christianizing it. But Tolkien went a step further than his predecessor. While Beowulf is the Germanic hero transposed to a Christian key, preserving the pagan glory-seeking ethos with less swagger and self-absorption than his predecessors, Bilbo initiates a new kind of a hero altogether, exalted because first humbled, yet never exalted too far above his fellows. Tolkien came to realize that hobbits had given him a way to portray heroes "more praiseworthy than the professionals," ordinary beings whose ennoblement epitomized, as he would explain in a letter to W. H. Auden, the *exaltavit humiles* theme ("He lifted up the lowly," a reference to the Magnificat, Mary's song of praise in the Gospel according to Luke). Beowulf was a figure of sacrificial nobility overshadowed by fate, Bilbo a creature of ordinary decency who would sacrifice his homely pleasures when necessary yet return to them—"there and back again"—rejoicing in the kettle on the hearth and the tobacco jar by the hand, embracing a life, though forever touched by a certain queerness, in which he could reasonably expect to remain perfectly content.

As Lewis was among the first to note, and as Tolkien himself acknowledged, the atmosphere of *The Hobbit* changed in midstream "from fairy-tale to the noble and high" just as Tolkien changed, in midcourse, his conception of how one ought to write for children. The earlier chapters are peppered with silly props and pratfalls, as well as chatty parenthetical asides by the narrator ("And what would you do, if an uninvited dwarf came and hung his things up in your hall without a word of explanation?"), that Tolkien regretted but never managed entirely to remove in the process of revision. Nor was he able to give the secondary world of *The Hobbit* the consistency that he felt a work of mythic stature ought to possess. The earliest drafts mention lands as distant as the Gobi Desert and objects as improbable as popguns, train whistles, and tomatoes; even in revision, anachronisms remain.

Yet the anachronisms are not without value. The hobbits are meant to seem parochially modern in their customs and outlook. One easily pictures Bilbo ensconced in the Bird and Baby, exchanging war stories over a pint, or reading drafts of his memoir, *There and Back Again, A Hobbit's Holiday,* in the frayed comfort of Lewis's Magdalen digs. It is an essential effect of Tolkien's art that one should feel the strangeness of being pulled back from the familiar modern world into the archaic North, with its Mirkwood (Old Norse Myrkviðr) and Misty Mountains. It is this anachronism, this bridging of worlds—ours with the archaic past—that gives the story its power to enchant and to disturb.

Undigested elements from *The Silmarillion,* which are especially numerous in the earliest drafts, suggest that *The Hobbit* was, from the beginning, linked, though by no means integrated, with that never-ending, interlocking chain of myths. Tolkien was of two minds about how far to press and how openly to acknowledge these links. Now and then he dropped hints that *The Hobbit* was based on *The Silmarillion,* but more often he was at pains to insist that *The Hobbit* began as a children's story unrelated to *The Silmarillion,* that as time went on it was drawn into his mythology—or, rather, invaded by it—and that it was only under the pressure of creating a sequel that he labored to bridge the gap.

He sent the manuscript around to friends and sympathetic colleagues, often with a self-deprecating note about how the book came to be written and accepted by Allen & Unwin for publication. To R. W. Chambers, professor of English at University College London, he said that the whole thing was an accident; he had written the story for his children, and an employee of his publisher happened to discover it "lying about in a nunnery" (of the Holy Child Sisters at Cherwell Edge). The first official reader's report came from Stanley Unwin's ten-year-old son Rayner, a precocious critic:

> Bilbo Baggins was a hobbit who lived in his hobbit-hole and *never* went for adventures, at last Gandalf the wizard and his dwarves perswaded him to go. He had a very exiting time fighting goblins and wargs at last they got to the lonley mountain; Smaug, the dragon who gawreds it is killed and after a terrific battle with the goblins he returned home—rich!

> This book, with the help of maps, does not need any illustra-
> tions it is good and should appeal to all children between the ages
> of 5 and 9.

Surely it was not lost on Tolkien that a ten-year-old reader saw the book as suitable for five-to-nine-year-olds. Better to downplay the *Silmarillion* elements and characterize *The Hobbit* as a don's folly, lightly tossed off, than to expose his whole mythopoeic project to misunderstanding or ridicule. If *The Hobbit* failed, at least it need not take *The Silmarillion* down with it.

The Hobbit was published in September 1937, lavishly furnished with Tolkien's illustrations, to healthy sales and immediate (if not universal) critical acclaim. R. W. Chambers provided an ecstatically positive blurb. The novelist Richard Hughes, in a glowing review for the *New Statesman and Nation*, observed that Tolkien's "wholly original story of adventure among goblins, elves, and dragons, instead of being a *tour-de-force*, a separate creation of his own, gives rather the impression of a well-informed glimpse into the life of a wide other-world; a world wholly real, and with a quite matter-of-fact, supernatural natural-history of its own." Lewis, now that he had heard and read the finished work, with a more fully realized "there and back again" plot than the first version he had seen, was convinced that indeed it *was* really good and said so in an unsigned review in *The Times Literary Supplement* on October 2:

> The publishers claim that "The Hobbit," though very unlike "Alice," resembles it in being the work of a professor at play. A more important truth is that both belong to a very small class of books which have nothing in common save that each admits us to a world of its own—a world that seems to have been going on before we stumbled into it but which, once found by the right reader, becomes indispensable to him. Its place is with "Alice," "Flatland," "Phantastes," "The Wind in the Willows."

Lewis was also the author of the unsigned review in the London *Times* of October 8, declaring that

> the truth is that in this book a number of good things, never before united, have come together; a fund of humour, an understanding

of children, and a happy fusion of the scholar's with the poet's grasp of mythology. On the edge of a valley one of Professor Tolkien's characters can pause and say: "It smells like elves." It may be years before we produce another author with such a nose for an elf. The Professor has the air of inventing nothing. He has studied trolls and dragons at first hand and describes them with that fidelity which is worth oceans of glib "originality."

Tolkien was clearly delighted, telling Unwin that he had divined the authorship of the two anonymous reviews and that "I must respect his opinion, as I believed him to be the best living critic until he turned his attention to me." Typically, though, he focuses attention in this high-spirited letter on something his best reviewers failed to notice: that *The Hobbit* contains the incorrect plural for "dwarf"—Tolkien's "private bad grammar" preferred "dwarves" to "dwarfs"—along with the puckish observation that the "real" plural is "dwarrows," which "I rather wish I had used."

The Extraordinary Ordinary

Tolkien worked intensely on other projects before and during his plunge into hobbitry. He added to his legendarium, crafted his Elvish languages, and each year expanded, in complexity and size, the family's portfolio of Father Christmas letters. The letter for 1931 features polar mountains in thick bold lines reminiscent of Rockwell Kent, purportedly drawn by "North Polar Bear"; 1932's letter depicts Father Christmas in his sleigh swooping down on nighttime Oxford, along with a whimsical yet remark-ably convincing mimicry of cave painting, probably modeled (as Wayne G. Hammond and Christina Scull have discovered) on Gerard Baldwin Brown's *Art of the Cave Dweller* (1928), with woolly mammoths, woolly rhinoceroses, and goblins riding an imaginary, elongated horselike beast called a *drasil* (from *drasill*, Icelandic for "horse"). "Some" of these cave paintings, drily notes Father Christmas, "are very good (mostly of animals), and some are queer and some bad; and there are many strange marks, signs and scribbles, some of which have a nasty look . . ." The Father Christmas letters faded with the decade, as Priscilla, the youngest child, outgrew them.

The enormous outlay of time and artistic energy that Tolkien ex-
pended upon this family project, which went on for more than twenty
years, highlights an aspect of his character that set him apart from many
other Inklings. As we have seen, he was to a great extent a conventional
family man, a lover of home and hearth. His life during the 1930s was
typical in this regard. His domestic routine was admirable in its regularity and its devotion to others: whenever possible, he ate breakfast, lunch,
and dinner with wife and children, encouraged their hobbies—Edith's
aviary, his sons' model railroading—told fairy tales to put the children to
sleep, shopped for food at Oxford's Covered Market, and enjoyed two-
week family holidays at the shore, where he, Edith, and the kids would
lounge on the beach, swim, shop, and collect shells. Even the occasional
antic—such as in the summer of 1932, when he and C. L. Wrenn lit their
pipes, donned their hats, and stepped into the waters of Cornwall's Lam-
orna Cove for a swimming contest—was the joyous activity of a stable
father and husband acting silly within prescribed and approved limits.
He never gambled, womanized, drank to excess, or took drugs.

In many ways, he excelled as a parent. Late in life he would berate
himself for failures ("I brought you all up ill and talked to you too little,"
he told Michael in 1963), but many would be inclined to judge him more
kindly. Certainly he entertained, encouraged, and enlivened his children, as a group and individually. "He would like to take us out for walks
by ourselves separately," Michael recalled, "because he felt each one of
us had different needs and different kinds of interests . . . they were most
wonderful experiences . . . he tried to make home for us somewhere
where we wanted to go." In 1937, while Christopher recovered from an
appendicitis operation, Tolkien nursed him devotedly, and when Christopher was sent home from the Oratory School in 1938 with heart trouble
and spent nearly a year in bed, his father bought him a telescope to idle
away evening hours peering at the heavens. These acts typified Tolkien's
fatherly ministrations. He grew especially fond of Christopher, noting in
his diary that his youngest son was "a nervy, irritable, cross-grained, self-
tormenting, cheeky person. Yet there is something intensely loveable
about him, to me at any rate, from the very similarity between us." He
stayed attentive to the needs of each child with a love that never flagged,
even in his old age.

Edith's problems proved more complex and difficult to solve. She was lonely and frustrated, too timid to forge many friendships within Oxford's academic community (Agnes Wrenn, the wife of C. L.Wrenn, being one of the few exceptions). As a result, she passed many long days alone. She had no career, no passions apart from family and piano; she displayed exceptional skill at the keyboard and might have been a professional musician, but marriage and motherhood had put an end to that. Never an ardent Catholic, she resented her husband's incessant churchgoing. Her frustrations mounted, sometimes erupting in heated argument.

Tolkien did what he could to assuage the situation, skipping lectures and Inklings gatherings to be at home and help with chores. His love for Edith ran deep, as did her love for him. He was, no doubt, hamstrung by views on marriage that offend many modern conventions. He believed that women are monogamous and men polygamous, and that fidelity in marriage requires, of the man, self-will and self-denial; that men require a career, women children; that men are aggressive, women "receptive"; and that, when differences arise—on "the glass of beer, the pipe, the non writing of letters, the other friend, etc. etc."—the man must hold his ground, the woman must yield. And yet he knew, as his many sacrifices demonstrate, that sometimes the man must yield. It should be noted also that at times his views on marriage possess a startling originality, as when he asserts—this was not a popular view in England at the time—that "nearly all marriages, even happy ones, are mistakes," as a better partner might easily have been found, but that, nonetheless, one's spouse is one's "real soul-mate," chosen by God through seemingly haphazard events. Edith, despite her lack of intellectual depth, her religious recalcitrance, and her fading beauty, was his real soul mate, and to her he pledged his body, his energies, his life.

Why did Tolkien choose such a middle-class, conventional, well-regulated existence? Largely because he believed it was the right way to live. He had a deep admiration for ordinary people—butchers, police officers, mail carriers, gardeners—and a knack for befriending them. He valued their courage, common sense, and decency, all of which he had had ample opportunity to observe in the trenches. Love for the man and woman next door ran deep in Tolkien; it pervades his fiction and explains why he wrote tales of ordinary people in extraordinary circumstances.

Ordinariness carried, also, cultural implications that were important to him and many of the Inklings. The group wore their hair short, their pants baggy, and their Englishness on their sleeve (Tolkien added a fine waistcoat as a touch of elegance but avoided all signs of foppishness). As Humphrey Carpenter points out, this was a rebellion against the dandyism of Oxford aesthetes and a vote for traditional, middle-of-the-road cultural values. But there was more to it than this. A man in Rome may do as Romans do in order to savor the Roman experience or to make a statement about his admiration for Roman ways—or he may do it to disguise his non-Roman status. Ordinariness may be a uniform, or it may be camouflage. In his imaginative life, a vitally important part of the whole man, Tolkien was anything but ordinary. Elves, hobbits, goblins, giant spiders, dragons, wizards: these were the neighbors with whom he trafficked almost every day. Tolkien resembles closely, in this regard, other early twentieth-century fantasists, like David Lindsay or H. P. Lovecraft, who produced their best work around the same time Tolkien was dreaming up hobbits, and who similarly led conventional lives and held conservative views. Tolkien, like Lindsay and Lovecraft, kept his genie bottled in ordinary brown glass, letting it escape and take extravagant shape only in his art.

Was he happy, leading this sort of life? On the whole, yes. Some critics have suggested that his was a divided personality, that he inhabited a black-and-white world and veered wildly from despair to joy. Humphrey Carpenter speculates that the death of Tolkien's mother "made him a pessimist," that as a result of this devastating loss "he was never moderate" and became "a man of extreme contrasts." The truth is that he was often depressed about his own work and the world about him, but he was also in many ways a profoundly contented man. He loved his family, his friends, his writing, his painting; he knew their flaws, but they neither surprised nor embittered him. His domesticity instilled a quiet stability that enabled him to navigate through life without the dramatic conversions and intellectual combativeness so characteristic of Lewis. He found at home a refuge that rarely failed him.

Catholicism continued to be another refuge, indefectible and invincible, the single most important element in Tolkien's mental makeup. His faith shaped his domestic arrangements, his professional work, his art, his way of being. Having passed successfully through the spiritual doldrums of the 1920s, he remained an ardent Catholic for the rest of his life. He attended Mass daily at 7:30 a.m. He confessed regularly. He raised his children Catholic, befriended priests and nuns, and was president of the Oxford branch of the Catenian Association, an international fraternal order of Catholic professionals. Tolkien's pessimism—if that is the right word to use—may be the shadow of his mother's early death, but it came to fruition through his mature belief in the Fall, his conviction that man, left to his own devices, is prone to corrupt all that he touches, including his person, his culture, and his environment. Thus his strong distrust of mechanization and technology, and his passionate admiration and defense of the natural world, of plants and animals who are, by their nature, exempt from moral decay.

Yet underlying his pessimism about humanity was an indomitable hope, born, as surely as his pessimism, from his Catholic faith. Belief in the ultimate triumph of good over evil, light over darkness, logos over chaos, bestowed upon all the oppositions in his life—scholarship and art, male friendship and marriage, high spirits and despair—a final and satisfying unity, a deep and abiding joy. When Tolkien said of himself that "I am in fact a *Hobbit* (in all but size)," he spoke the truth, not only about his material likes (trees, farms, tobacco, mushrooms, plain English food) and dislikes (cars, French cooking, early rising) but also about the disposition of his soul. He, like a hobbit, was at home in his shire; he, like a hobbit, trusted the cosmos—but not necessarily the powers that held sway on earth.

Hermits, Monsters, and Critics

Tolkien's Catholicism also informed his professional research. He was naturally drawn toward the life of the church, especially of the English Catholic Church in its pre-Reformation state, as expressed in Old and Middle English texts. As early as his years in Leeds, he had begun intensive study of a Corpus Christi College, Cambridge, manuscript copy (MS402) of the *Ancrene Wisse*, a thirteenth-century rule for anchoresses (female hermits), who typically inhabited cells (anchorholds) attached to churches and devoted their lives to solitary contemplation. Tolkien was captivated by the language of the text, which he recognized as an important West Midland dialect, "in its day and to its users a natural, easy, and cultivated speech, familiar with the courtesy of letters, able to combine colloquial liveliness with a reverence for the already long tradition of English writing." The manuscript appealed to him spiritually as well, for its account of the earthly struggles and heavenly rewards of the anchoress underwrote his own belief in the transformation, through grace, of suffering into joy, as this passage from part six of the *Ancrene Wisse* well expresses:

> *Vilitas et asperitas*—abjectness and hardship, these two, shame and suffering, as St. Bernard says, are the two ladder-uprights which are set up to heaven, and between these uprights are the rungs of all virtues fixed, by which one climbs to the joy of heaven . . . In these two things, in which is all penance, rejoice and be glad, for in return for these, twofold blisses are prepared: in return for shame, honour; in return for suffering, delight and rest without end.

In 1935, the Early English Text Society invited Tolkien to produce for publication a critical edition of the *Ancrene Wisse*. Tolkien accepted the commission, the first step in a long trail of starts, stumbles, and stops that typified his dilatoriness in academic labors. Family and medical problems, disputes over editorial matters, and the press of other academic work took their toll, but the real reason for delay was that his heart lay elsewhere, in the development of the legendarium and its offspring, including *The Hobbit* and what would become *The Lord of the Rings*. On July 31, 1960, he wrote to Rayner Unwin confessing his many "crimes of omission," most notably his failure to complete work on the *Ancrene Wisse*: "My edition of the prime MS. should have been completed *many years* ago!" The book finally appeared in December 1962, twenty-seven years after inception, surely one of the longer runs from conception to publication in the annals of modern academic publishing.

But whatever crimes of omission Tolkien committed as a scholar in the 1930s, he more than atoned for in a single stroke on November 25, 1936, when he delivered to the British Academy in London the annual Sir Israel Gollancz Memorial Lecture, "*Beowulf*: The Monsters and the Critics."

Of Jabberwocks and Monsters

Beowulf, the most celebrated of all Old English poems, dating from between the eighth and tenth centuries, recounts, in 3,182 lines of highly alliterative verse, the great battles between the titular hero of the Geats (a Germanic people) and a trio of marauding monsters. Tolkien probably encountered the poem long before entering Oxford. It appealed to him from the start, not only for the nobility of its characters and the romance of its bleak northern setting, but for the splendid monstrosities that Beowulf confronts, first the manlike but grotesque Grendel and his mother, descendents of Cain, and then an especially terrifying dragon. During the early 1930s, Tolkien wrote university lectures on the poem under the title of "The Historical and Legendary Tradition in *Beowulf* and other Old English Poems." W. H. Auden, who was present at their delivery, declared them "an unforgettable experience," no doubt in part because of the lecturer's dramatic entrance, striding into the lecture hall and exclaiming in his most stentorian Anglo-Saxon voice the poem's first line, *Hwaet, we Gar-Dena!* ("Hear, We the Spear-Danes"); Tolkien had a flair for theatrics, which would be revealed to the general public many years later in his audio recordings of excerpts from *The Hobbit* and *The Lord of the Rings*.

Tolkien began his Memorial Lecture with a similar flourish, attacking without mercy the old guard of *Beowulf* studies. "It is of their nature that the jabberwocks of historical and antiquarian research burble in the tulgy wood of conjecture, flitting from one tum-tum tree to another." *Beowulf* criticism, he contended, for centuries has been philistine, irrelevant, misdirected, insensitive to the poem's true greatness. The critics have read *Beowulf* as a storehouse of philology, history, allegory, archaeology, "a history of Sweden, a manual of Germanic antiquities, or a Nordic *Summa Theologica*," anything but a great work of art, and yet above all *Beowulf* is a poem, noble and beautiful. Tolkien expressed his contempt by relating a now-celebrated allegory: A man builds a tower with the scattered stones of an ancient building; other men (critics) come along, see the antiquity of the stones, and fell the tower in their craven lust for the "carvings and inscriptions" they believe to be sequestered beneath it. Finding nothing, they turn away, declaring of the tower, "What a muddle it is in!" The tower-builder's relatives join in the chorus, proclaiming "He is such an odd fellow! Imagine him using these old stones just to build a nonsensical tower!" "But," Tolkien wryly pointed out, "from the top of that tower the man had been able to look out upon the sea."

It is this newly revealed sea, this ocean of myth teeming with symbol, meaning, and loveliness, that Tolkien held dear. Past critics, indifferent to myth, blind to its beauty and force, complained that the *Beowulf* author had wasted his genius on a poem about trivialities like monsters and dragons, "as if Milton had recounted the story of Jack and the Beanstalk in noble verse." To Tolkien, however, monsters are not a secondary and unfortunate element in the poem but lie at its heart. *Beowulf* tells of men combating fundamental evils, "the hostile world and the offspring of the dark," and the presence of monsters—Grendel, Grendel's mother, and the dragon—as embodiments of chaos bestows upon the poem "its lofty tone and high seriousness." These fantastic beasts transform an adventure story into early England's finest example of poetry that "glimpses the cosmic"; in *Beowulf* "we look down as if from a visionary height upon the house of man in the valley of the world." *Beowulf* is also a fundamentally Christian myth, revealing the truth that "a Christian was (and is) still like his forefathers a mortal hemmed in a hostile world."

Tolkien's argument changed forever the landscape of *Beowulf* scholarship. He said what everyone wanted to hear but no one had mustered the courage to say: that *Beowulf* was a great poem, a joy to read, a masterpiece of mythopoeic art. And more: that the *Beowulf* author *liked* dragons, and so did Tolkien, and, as almost all Old English critics confessed to themselves then and since, *so did they*. A typically enthusiastic response came from R. W. Chambers, a *Beowulf* expert, who read the work in manuscript and wrote to Tolkien: "You must not delete a single word or line from your lecture. I have read it through twice over with the greatest enjoyment."

The talk does have flaws. Tolkien's structural analysis, in which he argues that the presentation of each line, divided into two balanced halves, echoes the design of the poem as a whole, has not convinced some scholars. Nor do all second his jejeune complaint that criticism can never grasp the mythic imagination, for "myth is alive at once and in all its parts, and dies before it can be dissected," a claim that his own brilliant discussion of myth contradicts. Nonetheless, Tolkien forever reclaimed

Beowulf from its naysayers and returned it to those who love it. In the process, he produced the first of his two important manifestos upon the possibilities of mythic art (the second and greater would come in 1947 in the essay "On Fairy-Stories"). Few who have read *"Beowulf*: The Monsters and the Critics" and absorbed its arguments will agree with those who find *The Silmarillion* and *The Lord of the Rings*, with their wizards and dragons and magic rings, suitable only for children.

Barfield in Eclipse

As Tolkien expanded his literary powers, Barfield reined his in. Legal matters, for which he had little love or aptitude, occupied most of the day. Never the most important figure in the firm—when his father died, another lawyer by the name of Reynolds became the new senior partner—Barfield toiled in the background, mired in the drudgery of mortgages, transfers of property, and other real estate transactions. Sometimes shafts of sunlight broke the dreariness: he and Maud took pleasure in their young son, Alexander, and, a few years later, in a daughter, Lucy (b. 1935), also adopted, who would become Lewis's godchild, "a very lively and happy child—apt for instance to be seen turning somersault-wheels in the garden immediately after a meal."

Badly burned by his experience with *English People*, Barfield had given up writing long novels but mentioned to Lewis that he would like to attempt a play. "Why not take one of the myths and simply do your best with it—Orpheus for instance," was his friend's reply. *Orpheus*, the drama that resulted, displays an impressive array of poetic forms—Lewis spotted alliterative lines, trochaics, couplets, blank verse, and lyrics—and a exultant vision of Steinerian final participation in which the human race "shall ascend Parnassus awake and find his soul." The Anthroposophical elements elevate the dialogue but weaken the dramatic flow; Lewis found act 2 "simply superb," but other parts left him cold. Barfield also managed, during this largely fallow period, to write a handful of poems; he placed the melancholy "The Village Dance" in the *London Mercury* (June 1931), and "Habeas Corpus" in *G.K.'s Weekly* (February 27, 1932). In 1933 he coauthored, with Lewis, a comic soufflé, "Abecedarium Philosophicum" for *The Oxford Magazine*, skewering famous philosophers through rhymed couplets in alphabetical order ("H is for Hume, who awoke Kant from nappin' / He said: 'There's no causes for things, they just happen'"). But as the Lewis scholar Don W. King points out, this conceit is borrowed—without improvement, one might add—from Lewis Carroll's "Examination Statute," a send-up of Oxford dignitaries ("A is for [Acland], who'd physic the masses / B is for [Brodie], who swears by the gases"). Barfield's creative energies, so spirited in *The Silver Trumpet* and *Poetic Diction*, had fallen asleep. He was, in his own words, "under eclipse."

It is the nature of a solar eclipse that the moon occults the sun. During these years, Barfield's interests turned, more forcefully than ever, to the fringe, esoteric, and occult. He joined the executive council of the English Anthroposophical Society and churned out essays and reviews for Anthroposophical journals, and helped to translate texts like Hermann Poppelbaum's *Man and Animal: Their Essential Difference* (1931) and, in 1936, Steiner's own *World-Economy: The Formation of a Science of World Economics*. He became intrigued by C. H. Douglas's controversial Social Credit movement, which favored a "national dividend" to supplement regular wages. The idea generated support among intellectuals and artists, including Ezra Pound, Aldous Huxley, and A. R. Orage, but failed to sway most economists and government leaders and soon faded from view. Douglas's anti-Semitism—he began to point a finger at an international Jewish financial conspiracy—didn't help matters. In the heat of his Social Credit enthusiasm, Barfield enrolled in a degree program in economics at London University but left early, after failing in geography. Things seemed to be falling apart everywhere. Steiner's followers were splintering into factions; Hitler was on the move; Barfield was trapped in a stuffy law office in the Strand and his pen was running dry. His time had not yet come.

Life at the Kilns

It was good to have Warnie at hand, thought Lewis. The two brothers worked in Lewis's Magdalen digs on weekdays, heading to the Kilns every afternoon and on weekends. Once home, they gardened, housecleaned, walked the dogs, and undertook maintenance and improvement projects such as laying gravel-and-sand footpaths through the woods. Barfield and Tolkien came for visits. Warnie edited the family papers and began to study the reign of Louis XIV, a project that would bear fruit in seven acclaimed volumes of French social and political history. He also struck up a friendship with Mrs. Moore's daughter, Maureen. She was teaching music now, first at Monmouth School for Girls and then at Oxford High School, and she gladly began to teach Warnie how to play piano. He regaled her in turn with recordings on his new gramophone. Every so often the brothers traveled afield, visiting relatives in Scotland and going on walking tours in Herefordshire, Wales, the Chilterns, and Derbyshire. Warnie proved to have an eye for landscape: "In the afternoon J and I and the dogs did the Railway walk under conditions which were sheer delight. Everything was still, and a faint blue haze, the merest suggestion of a fog, softened all the colours to a compatible shabbiness—the sort of day when the country seems more intimate, more in undress, than at any other time."

The fly in the ointment was Mrs. Moore. She groused, her complaints often targeting Lewis's new Christian faith (the Eucharist, for example, she considered no more than a "blood feast") "in much the same way," remarked Warnie, "that P [Pudaitabird] used to nag me in his latter years about my boyish fondness for dress, and with apparently just the same inability to grasp the fact that the development of the mind does not necessarily stop with that of the body." Warnie developed for her a fierce dislike, which he kept under wraps as best he could until after Lewis's death. As soon as fear of offending his brother was no longer a consideration, he published a memoir blasting Mrs. Moore as "a woman of very limited mind . . . In twenty years I never saw a book in her hands; her conversation was chiefly about herself, and was otherwise a matter of ill-informed dogmatism." She treated Lewis, he fumed, like a hired servant. Others spoke up in her defense, however, notably Barfield, who condemned Warnie's "false picture" of her as a "baneful stepmother and inexorable taskmistress" and said that to his knowledge the Kilns harbored "a normal and reasonably happy family life."

Some light may be shed on this vexing, almost indecipherable relationship, by Lewis's 1948 essay, "The Trouble with 'X' . . . ," which seems to contain a veiled—if possibly exaggerated for pedagogical effect—description of Mrs. Moore (as "X") and may suggest why the relationship lasted until her death:

> An outside friend asks us why we are looking so glum, and the truth comes out.

On such occasions the outside friend usually says, "But why don't you tell them? Why don't you go to your wife (or husband, or father, or daughter, or boss, or landlady, or lodger) and have it all out? People are usually reasonable . . ." And we, whatever we say outwardly, think sadly to ourselves, "He doesn't know 'X.'" We do. We know how utterly hopeless it is to make "X" see reason . . . You know, in fact, that any attempt to talk things over with "X" will shipwreck on the old, fatal flaw in "X"'s character. And you see, looking back, how all the plans you have ever made always have shipwrecked on that fatal flaw—on "X"'s incurable jealousy, or laziness, or touchiness, or muddle-headedness, or bossiness, or ill temper, or changeableness. Up to a certain age you have perhaps had the illusion that some external stroke of good fortune—an improvement in health, a rise of salary, the end of the war—would solve your difficulty. But you know better now . . .

A Christian's duty, Lewis believed, is not simply to tolerate "X" but to make life with "X" an occasion to work on one's own character flaws. This was the arduous task he assigned himself, and through intense self-discipline, he largely succeeded. His newfound Christianity fit him perfectly, providing him with a sturdy and subtle guide for daily living. In addition, it gave him what he had always needed, a rock-solid platform from which to declaim his philosophy and hone his art. He was now ready to convert the world.

10

ROMANTIC THEOLOGY

C harles Williams was not like other Inklings. Lewis and Tolkien were solid, jocular, beef-and-potatoes men, and even Barfield, for all his dancing and esoteric flights, was practical and predictable, at home, if not fulfilled, in law and real estate. Williams was a will-o'-the-wisp, a figure glimpsed in a fever dream. To attempt his portrait is to paint on air: "Williams! How many people have tried to describe this extraordinary man, and how his essence escapes them." Thus John Wain, who knew him well. Or Lewis, an intimate friend: "No man whom I have known was at the same time less affected and more flamboyant in his manners. The thing is very difficult to describe." Or T. S. Eliot: "I think he was a man of unusual genius, and I regard his work as important. But it has an importance of a kind not easy to describe." Three of the more articulate men of the century, tongue-tied—when it comes to Williams.

How can this be? A few answers come to mind. Above all, Williams was a swirling mass of contradictions. He wrote shockers that failed to shock. He worshipped women but "liked to beat them with a ruler." He was a faithful husband with a harem of besotted acolytes. He was orthodox but heretical, a devout Anglican who practiced magic. He had a face at once hideous and beautiful (Lewis: "His face we thought ugly: I am not sure that the word 'monkey' has not been murmured in this context. But the moment he spoke it became, as was also said, like the face of an angel."). "This double-sidedness," Lewis believed, "was the most strongly developed character of his mind. He might have appropriated Kipling's thanks

> to Allah who gave me two
> separate sides to my head,

except that he would have had to omit the word *separate* . . . In Williams the two sides lived in a perpetual dance or lovers' quarrel of mutual mockery."

In addition, Williams liked—or felt compelled—to construct imaginary personae for himself and those around him. He called himself Taliesin, after the sixth-century Welsh bard; his wife, Florence, he renamed Michal, after King Saul's daughter and King David's first wife; among his female admirers and platonic lovers, he transformed Phyllis Jones into Phillida and Celia, Lois Lang-Sims into Lalage; and he referred to his distinguished superior at Oxford University Press, Sir Humphrey Milford, as Caesar. Indeed, once he joined OUP, it wasn't long before he had turned that booming international firm into a province of his own imperial imagination. Away from work, his friends were more than friends; they and he formed a mystical community, the "Companions of the Co-inherence" (a key Williamsian idea, co-inherence is the mutual relatedness of all beings; we exist, not as isolated monads, but in and through one another). For Williams, who adored Shakespeare, the world was indeed a stage, an occasion for role-playing, for theater, and for the highest form of theater, which is religious ritual. "He was nothing if not a ritualist," said Lewis. He would make sacred signs, such as the Sign of the Cross, over his followers as they rode the London Underground; he had a taste for sadomasochistic rituals as well. Ordinary life—the dull daily routines of marriage, of office work, of an evening's amusement— all this bored him, even filled him with horror. Everyone and everything, with Williams, needed to be raised to its highest level—the teacher must become a mage, the husband a knight errant, the laborer a hero in a sacred drama—intensified, reified, baptized in the turbulent waters of his restlessness, curiosity, and ardor.

At his best, he could almost raise the dead; Dylan Thomas once said to him, "Why, you come into the room and talk about Keats and Blake as if they were *alive*." This impression he gave of electric animation, of a bundle of raw nerves in a business suit, spewing ideas, images, observations in all directions, appears in many accounts of Williams. Typical is that of Theodore Maynard, a poetry reviewer for the *North American Review*, who visited him in London in 1919 and discovered a man "trembling with nervousness" and chattering away with "staccato eagerness." Eliot, who knew Williams and admired him, watched him lecture and saw the same thing: "He was never still; he writhed and swayed; he jingled coins in his pocket; he sat on the edge of the table swinging his leg; in a torrent of speech he appeared to be saying whatever came into his head from one moment to the next." He smoked heavily, walked quickly, zigzagged from one friendship to another; he was monkey, elf, jackdaw rolled into one.

This wondrously strange man came into the world on September 20, 1886, in the pedestrian community of Holloway, a lower-middle-class suburb just north of central London. The family resided at 3 Spencer Road, a nondescript lane of narrow brick homes overshadowed by a huge iron railroad bridge. Williams's father, Walter (Richard Walter Stansby Williams), a foreign business correspondent who worked in the city, never earned enough to make ends meet and poured out his sorrows in mournful poetry that appeared now and then in local journals ("I go to my daily work again / With a feeling of longing akin to pain / The heart beats high in this wearisome life"). His mother, Mary, was resourceful and quiet, seemingly content to be a mother and housewife.

This bland environment, which offered little beyond lounging in front of the coal fire and watching the soot darken the windows, thrust Williams, at an early age, inside himself. He turned to books as bright companions, avenues of escape; like Lewis and Tolkien, he read avidly in romance and adventure, with a liking for Jules Verne and *The Pilgrim's Progress*. As the taste for Bunyan might suggest, his other outlet was the church. His parents, devout Anglicans, recited evening prayers on a daily basis and attended services on Sunday at St. Anne's, a cavernous Victorian-era red-brick church with a high vaulted roof. "He used to march into church as if he owned the place," reported his mother; the church, in turn, marched into his heart. Williams never abandoned Anglicanism; he pushed at its borders, cut occult symbols in its altar cloths, called upon powers that would have amazed the seventeenth-century divines, but remained within the fold. How could he not? He adored the music, the adornments, all aspects of the liturgy; it provided the color and sparkle, and, as he grew a bit older, the meaning and direction that suburban routine lacked. He had tantrums when the family stayed home from services.

When Williams was five, he contracted measles and his eyesight deteriorated; distant objects became a blur. He liked to check the time on a certain public clock; now the clock itself disappeared into the myopic fog. Three years later, his father's sight fell victim to a similar problem; Williams considered it the family malady and called it "the asps of blindness." Compounding the crisis, Walter's company went bankrupt. The family was at a loss, until Mary's ingenuity and courage sprang to life. She withdrew her savings and, with her son, her young daughter, Edith (b. 1889), and her half-blind husband in tow, fled to St. Albans, a tranquil village in Hertfordshire, in the hope that clean country air would restore her husband's vision or at least prevent further decay. She secured lodgings, set up a household, and opened, in the center of town, a stationery and art shop that she called the Art Depot. This was the new world in which Williams would come to maturity.

St. Albans had much to offer: clean streets, friendly neighbors, nearby woods, bits of Roman ruins, and, a godsend to Charles, a medieval abbey with a cathedral church, the second longest in England, with Norman and Gothic arches, a crossing tower, and the tombs of abbots and saints. Here Williams's religious and romantic longings flowered. His reading expanded to include the adventures of Anthony Hope and Alexandre Dumas and books on knights and chivalry, along with more sobering work like *The Scarlet Letter.* He attended Matins and Evensong on Sundays and, after being confirmed at fifteen, frequently received the Eucharist, although never at a Tolkienesque pace. His imagination, however, attained a Lewisian pitch, but instead of the animal fantasies of Boxen, he and a friend by the name of George Robinson spun elaborate theatrics, "a sort of running drama" inspired by *The Prisoner of Zenda.* He and George attended St. Albans Grammar School, adjacent to the Abbey, a venerable public school founded in 948 that counted among its alumni the only English pope, Adrian IV (c. 1100–59). Here, heightening his growing interest in history, Williams performed in class pageants based upon St. Albans's medieval past. "Most of the boys tolerated the whole affair, some loathed it but Charles . . . loved it," remembered George. One gets the sense of an antiquarian in the making: nearsighted, devouring tales of derring-do, seeking exultation in distant times and places. Like other boys who live in the past or in their minds, he abhorred sports. He had, in addition to bad eyesight, a second disability: his hands shook, often uncontrollably, a lifelong affliction brought on by childhood measles or family tensions—the shop never brought in quite enough money—or by the storms that rage in every adolescent and that, in Williams, found no outlet; the tremors left him unable to take up a musical instrument, or shoot or fish, or indulge in other boyish hobbies. Instead, he passed his spare time dreaming, reading, and writing poetry. He might have ended up a narrow-minded scholar or a timid dreamer, in retreat from life, but for the influence of his nearly blind father. For Walter, largely unfit for work, began to take his boy on long country rambles, sometimes twenty miles at a time, while discoursing about poetry, language, art, and faith, imparting, as Williams put it in a poem, "all the good I knew." The father was able finally to be the father, and the son soaked in his lessons, including a love of walking that never left him.

His childhood over, Williams walked, myopically, into adulthood. Lacking clear ambitions, he enrolled in University College London, commuting daily between St. Albans and St. Pancras, taking courses in French, Latin, mathematics, and literature. After two years the family coffers emptied, and he left to attempt the civil service exam. Through lack of caring or lack of preparation—certainly not lack of intelligence—he failed. Boxed into a corner, he took a job as a packer at the Methodist Bookroom, a dead-end position, but at the same time showed the good sense to enroll in the Working Men's College. Here he befriended Fred Page, editor at the London offices of Oxford University Press, who was preparing for publication a seventeen-volume edition of Thackeray. Page knew thwarted intelligence when he saw it, recognized that his new friend was wasted as a packer, and offered him a job. On June 9, 1908, Williams went to work in the "Paper, Printing, and Proof-Reading" department of OUP at Amen Corner—later Amen House—in Paternoster Row.

Williams took immediately to his new environs; his tiny office, shared with Fred Page, overlooked central London, and he thought that he was now in the center of the world. He was, at least, in one of the centers of the publishing world. Oxford University Press, founded in 1478, was by the early twentieth century the largest of all university presses, with headquarters in London and Oxford and branch offices in place or soon to be established in Africa, Asia, and the Americas. A few years after

Williams arrived, the energetic, creative, and ambitious Humphrey Sumner Milford (1877–1952) became publisher. This proved a godsend for Williams, for Milford had a knack for taking successful risks not only with literary projects (for example, publishing Gerard Manley Hopkins when many critics considered his poems unintelligible) but with his editorial staff. He kept Williams on a very loose leash, expanded his responsibilities, and hired a handful of other eccentric, imaginative figures, including Hopkins's nephew, a brilliant translator also named, confusingly, Gerard Hopkins. The younger Hopkins later wrote that "[Williams's] affection for the Oxford University Press was, to no small extent, the moving force of his life. It shared, it symbolized, the fervent religious faith and the happy domestic love which rounded his existence. The City of God in which he never ceased to dwell, contained Amen House as its noblest human monument, and all who lived and worked in it were citizens with him."

Florence . . . or Michal

Williams had found his lifelong employment; he stayed at OUP until his death in 1945. He also found, in that same wonderful year of 1908, his lifelong companion, Florence Conway, daughter of a St. Albans ironmonger. The two met at a Christmas gala. "For the first five minutes," said Florence, "I thought him the most silent, withdrawn young man I had ever met. For the next five minutes I thought him the nicest young man I had ever met. For the rest of the evening I thought him the most talkative young man I had ever met, and still the nicest . . ." Silent and talkative, withdrawn and nice: the oppositions warring in Williams were no secret to Florence. She understood abnormal psychology, for, according to those who knew her later in life, she possessed one herself. The novelist and memoirist Lois Lang-Sims, who met Florence only after Charles's death, wrote that "I used to say that, with one exception, Charles was the strangest human being I had ever met in my life: the one exception was Michal [Charles's private name for Florence]. Michal, in different moods, could display the passions of a maenad and the cool detachment of a sphinx . . . One could be her dearest friend one day, and twenty four hours later find oneself being scathed by her contempt." To the poet and critic Glen Cavaliero, who knew her from 1954 until 1970, Florence's "attitude to her husband could vary almost painfully"; sometimes she described Charles as "shining and lovely in his morning time," while at other times, Cavaliero reports, she wrote of having "married a cross."

This, of course, is Florence after Williams's death. It may be that she was simpler, less fractured by life—and by life with Williams—during her youth. Certainly he loved her dearly. She was for him confidante and critic and, for a time, his Beatrice, muse and model of perfection. The subsequent courtship, touch-and-go at first, intensified a few years after their first encounter, when Williams handed her, in the winter of 1913, a copy of his first book, a collection of eighty-two sonnets entitled *The Silver Stair*, telling her it was about renunciation and asking her opinion. She assumed this meant that the romance would lead nowhere, that he was about to join a monastery, until she arrived home, read the poems by candlelight, and said to herself, "Why, I believe they are about me!"

Well, not quite. Some of the verses do refer to Florence. Williams, a voracious reader, had just discovered Dante, who would be a lifelong inspiration, and Sonnet X, in which he describes glimpses of Florence on the streets of St. Albans, echoes blatantly the Master's glimpses of his beloved Beatrice on the streets of Florence:

How else so long have I gone up and down
Dull and in ignorance? in so small town,
So long have lighted not upon her ways?
But now each street is a path venturous,
Each cross of roads a passage perilous
With loveliness which is this city's praise.

But Florence is but one instance of a universal principle, the Feminine Ideal, and most of the sonnets celebrate, with a young man's ardor and sentiment, the miracle of women:

Fair women are the crown of loveliness
Which hath of Life been throned and set on high;
Unto a sweet and radiant sanctity
Their coming is a marvellous access.
They are the lifted hand of Time to bless,—

His delicate word; soft vanities and shy
Look from their eyes; their voices, passing by,
The very creed of Beauty do profess.

Here and there, among these passionate, purple lines, can be found intimations of an idea that would become the key to Williams's work and life:
that the ascent to God can be achieved in and through created things
and especially in and through heterosexual romantic love. He came to
call this ascent the "Way of Affirmation" or the "Way of Affirmation of
Images," and he saw it as an alternative to the mystic's way of asceticism
and apophaticism (describing and coming to know God by what he is
not). The titles of these early sonnets state the case: "That the Love of a
Woman Is the Vice-Gerent of God"; "That for Every Man a Woman Holds
the Secret of Salvation." In Sonnet LXVII, he for the first time advances,
gingerly and obscurely, his argument:

All lives of lovers are His song of love,
Now low and soft and holy as a kiss,
Now high and clear and holy as a star.

Slave in Man's house, yet builder-up thereof,
The silver and the golden stairs are His,
The altar His—yea, His the lupanar.

God, who is love (1 John 4:16), sings through the life of every lover; to
Him belong the silver and golden stairs, obscure symbols representing,
perhaps, the two ways—denying and affirming—that lead to God. So
far, so uncontroversial; there is plenty of precedent for this, for example,
in the Song of Songs. But the final line is a provocation. Williams means
to shock, declaring that the things of God include not only the altar but
also the lupanar, the celebrated ten-chambered brothel of Pompeii.
This improbable juxtaposition of the spiritual and fleshly would lead
Williams down many a curious path in the years to come, through the
highlands of Arthurian romance and Dantean vision to the swamps of
ritual magic and sadomasochism, as he made his way to God.

For now, however, he was that most glorious of beings, a poet. Sir
Walter Alexander Raleigh, professor of poetry at Oxford, declared *The*

Silver Stair to be "real poetry." Chesterton showed more restraint and, it may be, better judgment; when Williams sent a copy to him, he failed to respond. No matter; neither neglect nor rejection could stop Williams's pen. His brain was teeming with new poems; he published two more volumes, *Poems of Conformity* and *Divorce*, in the next eight years, not a bad rate of production, considering the catastrophic interruption of World War I. His poor eyesight and hand tremors excluded him from active service, but while Tolkien and Lewis trudged through the French mud, Williams did much the same on British soil, joining the St. Albans Volunteers and cutting trenches and building earthworks in London's Hyde Park against the invasion that never came. In 1917, after nine years of dithering—war and financial worries had slowed the pace of romance—he and Florence married, taking a flat in north-central London. Now he must put into practice all his fine poetic thoughts about romantic love, and to all accounts, he did so successfully, at least for a time.

But while his entry into the mysteries of marriage unfolded, a second, more arcane initiation was under way. In 1915, after reading Arthur Edward Waite's *The Hidden Church of the Holy Graal*, Charles sent an copy of *The Silver Stair* to the author. Waite responded "very kindly, asking me to go and see him, and saying pleasant things generally." This agreeable exchange soon gave rise to a friendship that would transform Williams's life.

The Fellowship of the Rosy Cross

Arthur Waite (1857–1942), born in Brooklyn, New York, but raised in England, was by 1915 a world-famous Christian occultist, the author of numerous studies on kabbalah, alchemy, and Freemasonry and codesigner of the enormously popular Rider-Waite Tarot deck. A gentle, learned, handsome man, with a drooping moustache and a lively pen, Waite despised the sloppy scholarship and extravagant claims of many other occultists of the day, including Madame Blavatsky and S. L. MacGregor Mathers, and attempted to steer a purer, nobler, more respectable course into the Christian mysteries. In 1881 he joined the Hermetic Order of the Golden Dawn, an English magical order under the direction of the Freemason William Wynn Westcott. The Order's pseudotraditional vestments and secret rites, stitched together from Catholic, Egyptian, and Rosicrucian threads, attracted a number of writers and intellectuals hungry for spiritual experience but disinclined toward orthodoxy, including William Butler Yeats, Arthur Machen, and Aleister Crowley. Waite remained active in the order for many years. Eventually, however, he had enough of its intemperate magical claims, if not its ceremonial posturing, and he quit in 1914. Almost immediately he established an alternative group, the Fellowship of the Rosy Cross, named after the principal symbol of Rosicrucianism, a cross with a white rose, symbolizing the way of Jesus Christ with occult wisdom at its center. Waite dedicated the group to the study and practice of esoteric Christian mysticism—or, in the pompous language of its "Constitution & Bylaws," "a path of symbolism communicated in Ritual after the manner of the chief Instituted Mysteries."

Williams was vastly impressed by Waite and his teachings. He joined the Fellowship of the Rosy Cross (and not, as many books about him assert, the Hermetic Order of the Golden Dawn) on the autumn equinox of 1917. He remained a member until 1928, enthusiastically participating in this Christian counterpart to Westcott's more generic magical ceremonies. Like almost all esoteric organizations, the Fellowship was small in number (membership peaked at a little more than two hundred), ingrown, obsessed with secrecy ("all copies of Rituals . . . shall be kept in a locked case or box"), and aglow with the sense of its own importance, often indicated by a fondness for capitalized nouns; thus the Fellowship offered "the quest and attainment of the human soul on its return to the Divine Centre" and "true light of understanding on the Path of Union."

None of this bothered Williams. He purchased, from clothiers Spencer & Co., the Fellowship's standard robe for beginners, black with white silk collar, and he memorized the words and movements of the complex rites. Adopting the esoteric name of Frater Qui Sitit Veniat (The Brother Who Thirsts, Let Him Come), he rose in quick succession through the sacramental grades from "Adeptus Minor" to "Adeptus Exemptus" to the "Portal of the Fourth Order," and finally to the "Ceremony of Consecration on the Threshold of Sacred Mystery." During this last rite, which entailed a high priest "seated on his throne in the East between the pillars of the Temple" and a priestess "whose wand is crowned with Lilies," acolytes were exhorted to "be ye transmuted therefore from dead stones into Living Philosophical stones, shining on everlasting hills, radiant on the mount of GOD." During his esoteric ascent, Williams claimed several important positions in the Fellowship, including two six-month terms in its highest post, as Honourable Frater Philosophicus, or Master of the Temple, during which time he donned a red silk collar and a green robe, hung around his neck a large pendant bearing the Hebrew letter *yod*, and wielded a wand with a cross at its head.

Williams's magical career is consistently underplayed by fans, followers, and a surprising number of Inklings scholars. To some extent this can be ascribed to lack of information, as details of twentieth-century British occult movements are not always easy to obtain. It is also, in many cases, wishful thinking—i.e., "Williams may have been a bit odd, but certainly not *that* odd"—and may be, in a few instances, deliberate avoidance. Alice Hadfield, his first biographer, who was also a close friend, insisted that Williams was "not . . . much affected" by Waite's ideas; yet there is ample evidence, in the themes and plot devices of his novels and poems (Tarot cards, hermetic rituals, magi, magical jewels), in his letters, in the ceremonial sword that he kept in his desk, and in his personal behavior, that Williams's occult experience affected him long after he quit the group. Eventually, he established his own version of a magical organization, his Companions of the Co-inherence, in terms that bring to mind both the Golden Dawn and the Rosy Cross. Tolkien would declare himself "wholly unsympathetic to Williams' mind," in part because he intensely disliked Williams's fiction but also, one senses, because as a Catholic he distrusted Williams's fascination with the occult. Lois Lang-Sims, for a time one of his most committed disciples, believed that Williams's obsession with magic never left him and led to his early death.

And yet it would be wrong to call Williams a fully dedicated magician. He remained ambivalent about magic to the end of his life. He distrusted occult power, for it threatened to usurp the power proper to God. What appealed to him—what thrilled him—apart from the ceremonies, which he entered into with gusto, was the promise of real, immediate, spiritual transformation, the Christian metanoia so seemingly unattainable in the mundane world but held out so tantalizingly in the esoteric subworld. Williams sought in Christian magic the same radical transformation that he tried to achieve by changing the names of his friends, lovers, and coworkers, but on a higher plane; instead of symbolically converting the everyday Florence into the biblical Michal or Sir Humphrey Milford into the imperial Caesar, he could transform the everyday Charles Williams, through magical means, into a genuine Christian bard and psychopomp.

The Theology of Romance

All the while he immersed himself in magic, Williams was a communicating Anglican. This unusual dual practice set his mind afire. He drew energy from the cross-pollination of church services and Rosy Cross rituals, and his mind soon bubbled with new ideas for poetry, literary criticism, and theological exploration. By 1924, he was hard at work on *Outlines of Romantic Theology*, a book that he believed would "probably affect profoundly the whole thought of the Universal Church." There is self-deprecating sarcasm in this remark—Williams was thinking of the critical indifference to *The Silver Stair*—but also seriousness. He intended to present in all its splendor his great new discovery, the Way of Affirmation, to show how Christianity sanctifies romantic love, and particularly married love, as a path to God.

The main line of Williams's argument can be simply put: sexual love, especially when sealed by Christian marriage, "is capable of being assumed into sacramental and transcendental heights." As an incarnational faith, Christianity necessarily glorifies the body, and thus marriage came to be counted a sacrament. But for various historical reasons—Williams mentions the Church's emphasis upon asceticism and otherworldliness, as well as residual Manicheanism—theology has paid scant attention to marriage's sacramental nature; the deepest meaning of marriage, as a Way to God, has been lost or obscured. It is not difficult to see, in this thesis, Williams the magician plumbing unknown or forgotten secrets in order to transform the world.

Williams bases his views of marriage, curiously, upon the celibate life of Christ. He presents Christ as the embodiment of love, the stages of Christ's life as akin to those of a marriage, married men and women as akin to the disciples and to "the whole company of the faithful." In support, he enlists Dante, the *Morte d'Arthur*, Donne, the theology of the Mass, and the consummate Victorian poet of marriage, Coventry Patmore.

Not all his arguments convince: the parallels he draws between Christ's life and married life are forced, as he himself realizes, writing that "until this study has been developed further by the Mind of the Church, some of these identifications must be tentative." Nonetheless, *Outlines of Romantic Theology* impresses with its polemical and visionary force, which crests when Williams declares that his understanding of marriage will usher in an Age of Romantic Theology. This exalted claim may lift eyebrows, but at least Williams attempts to give his forecast a practical footing by describing a method for spiritual transformation, the first stage being meditation upon the presence of God in moments of married bliss, the second strict adherence during marriage to the ordinary rites of the Christian faith.

An ambitious project! Alas, such things have a way of bumping up against reality. Williams was unable to find a publisher; Milford turned down *Outlines of Romantic Theology*, saying that "I fear this is not for us. It may be for all time and I may be like the poor Indian, but I am afraid of it and of you." At the same time, Williams's marriage was proving less glorious than romantic theology admitted. He noted that his horoscope urged celibacy as the best course; but he believed that if he had followed this advice, his life's work might have foundered at the outset—for romantic love can lead not only to God but, as Dante shows, to artistic excellence. In 1922, Florence gave birth to their first and only child, Michael. She adored the baby. Williams loved him with reservations, complaining that "a child is a guest of a somewhat insistent temperament, rather difficult to get rid of, almost pushing; a poor relation of a rather pleasant kind. His little voice pulls at my ears; my heartstrings are unplucked." The boy failed to relight the hearth; he annoyed his father, who was obliged to write in the early morning hours, after everyone had fallen asleep, and his mother also grew more testy, perhaps from lack of sleep, for now Williams regularly awoke her in the darkest hours of the night to fix him tea. The marriage had received a boost, but only briefly. Something was missing, at least in Williams's view.

Enter Phyllis or Phillida or Celia

Always restless, Williams negotiated with the London City Council to deliver evening lectures to the public, a plan that would fulfill his desire to pass on his ideas and also keep him away from the baby during some of its crankiest hours. The future was bright, and it brightened still more when, out of the blue, the missing Something appeared. It came in a most unexpected form, not as the foreordained next step in marriage's silver stairs to God, but in the alluring person of the new, comely librarian at OUP, Phyllis Jones. She had fair hair, blue eyes, a pointed nose, and intelligent eyes; Williams spotted her, tumbled for her, and anointed her Phillida ("greenery") and Celia ("heavenly"). He composed for her one hundred poems, which he called "A Century of Poems for Celia"; in them he declares his adoration, he longs for embraces, he apotheosizes her as holy wisdom, immaculate perfection, "Christhood" incarnate.

Phyllis attended his lectures, marveled at his energy and intellect, and fell entirely under his spell. He became the Teacher, she the Disciple. Their ardor intensified; the very air danced; an acquaintance spotted the two walking together and saw around them "a radiance rising . . . almost a golden mist." They sent passionate letters back and forth; he called her "my saint, my hero, my beauty." For Williams, this was his portal into the joy that his master Dante had known, a taste of romantic love at its most splendid and pure. In his introduction to *The New Book of English Verse* (1935), he would coin the term "Celian moment" to signify instances of spiritual or artistic illumination, "the moment which contains, almost equally, the actual and the potential; it is perfect within its own limitations of subject or method, and its perfection relates it to greater things. It is the moment of passion . . ." It was, indeed, the moment of passion, but of a passion never to be consummated. Williams remained true to his marriage vows, and he and Phyllis never advanced beyond embraces. The final gift of himself he reserved, throughout his life and without hesitation, for Florence.

For a while, though, he knew bliss supreme. His happiness with OUP and with Phyllis brimmed over in the late 1920s into three lighthearted masques, composed for performance at Amen House in front of Milford and the assembled staff. In these pieces—plays with music and dance, designed to be performed once only—Williams blended Christian, Greek, and Arthurian motifs in his continuing aspiration to elevate a publishing house, its occupants, and its labors to mythic proportions. In *The Masque of the Manuscript*, performed on Milford's birthday in 1927, the story of how an obscure book on Syrian nouns makes its way from initial appraisal to final publication becomes a tale of ritualized death and rebirth. Alice Hadfield thought that "the effect of the Masque on C.W.'s position in the Press and with Sir Humphrey was incalculable. The atmosphere was changed from that of an office to a court, with Caesar on the throne and C.W. among the paladins." Williams had worked magic, merging myth and reality, revealing to all the staff their higher selves, sending them into "an extraordinary state of delight and exaltation."

The inspiration for the success, he had no doubt, was Phyllis. At first this may seem another instance of "a man and his muse," as in the case of Williams's contemporary, Robert Graves, who required a succession of women to stimulate his indwelling genius. But for Williams, schooled in Dante, a woman, be she platonic lover or spouse, was a manifestation of God's glory and, more important, a guiding light on the way to God, and her role as muse unfolded within this larger objective. For a few happy years, Phyllis/Phillida/Celia filled her role to perfection. Williams's ideal woman was never Calliope, but always, sublimely, Beatrice.

The bliss faded, as it usually does. Phyllis was too young and curious to tie herself to a man in his early forties. She fell in love with Gerard Hopkins, and then with an employee of an oil company, whom she married and accompanied to Java. Williams suffered terribly during this drawn-out separation, but he soon found comfort elsewhere. Other young women fell under his spell; he didn't love them or sleep with them, but he enjoyed their devotion, confessing to one of them that all his young women students fell in love with him. This bevy of admirers, many of whom popped into OUP at all hours to seek his counsel or just to enjoy his jittery, dazzling company, came to be known to his office mates as "C.W.'s young women."

C.W.'s platonic harem was for him, however, but a minor distraction. His love, deflected by Phyllis, now poured into writing. From 1930 to 1936, those years in which he suffered most acutely from her rejection, he published fourteen books, ranging across poetry, anthologies, literary criticism, biographies, and fiction. *Poetry at Present* (1930) stands out among the critical studies. It examines the work of eighteen contemporary poets with forthrightness and wit (of T. S. Eliot, Williams begins, "In some former existence, among the myths of Greece, Mr. Eliot was probably a

gadfly"), and concludes each essay with a poem of Williams's own com-
position inspired by the poet he has just been discussing. *The English Poetic Mind* (1932), a more ambitious but less interesting volume, based on a course he had taught at the London Day Training College in 1931, investigates the poetic genius of Shakespeare, Milton, and Wordsworth, concluding, à la Barfield, that great poetry not only depicts an experience but also awakens in us a capacity to live that experience: "We are told of a thing; we are made to feel as if that thing were possible to us; and we are so made to feel it . . . that our knowledge is an intense satisfaction to us." During this period, Williams also wrote lives of Bacon, James I, Rochester, and Queen Elizabeth. They are uninspired, competent, and no longer read. Eliot, who apparently took no umbrage at being called a gadfly, correctly dismissed some of Williams's books as potboilers, add-ing, however, that "he always boiled an honest pot."

On a different level entirely are the five novels Williams produced during this fecund span. They deliver that rarest of treats, intelligent Christian fantasy. Almost always, the plots involve the eruption into ordi-nary reality of a supernatural power or substance. These tales are, then, first cousins to the science fiction romances of H. G. Wells, especially *The Invisible Man* and *The War of the Worlds*, with miraculous events replacing scientifically plausible, if improbable, ones. In *War in Heaven* (1930), the second of Williams's novels to be written but the first to be published, the Holy Grail appears in the pokey English village of Fardles; *Many Dimensions* (1931) replaces the Grail with the Stone of Suleiman, a chunk of primordial matter that confers upon its owner the power of granting wishes, teleportation, and the like. In *The Greater Trumps* (1932), the fantastic element is a magical Tarot deck; in *Shadows of Ecstasy* (1933), the weakest of the novels, begun in 1925 and rewritten in 1932, it is a preternaturally long-lived magician who fosters an African uprising against Europe.

But surely the most intriguing of Williams's novels, in its ingenuity of conception and the gossamer beauty of its unfolding, is *The Place of the Lion* (1931), in which the Platonic Forms descend to earth in the guise of enormous animals—lion, butterfly, snake, eagle, phoenix, unicorn, horse—and begin to reabsorb their material counterparts. Thus a huge butterfly, the Form of Beauty, appears in an English garden, "two feet or more across from wing-tip to wing-tip . . . tinted and coloured with every conceivable brightness . . . lovely and self-sufficient," and draws to itself all ordinary butterflies:

> Away across the fields they came, here in thick masses, there in thinner lines, white and yellow, green and red, purple and blue and dusky black . . . he turned his head, and saw a cloud of them hanging high above the butterfly of the garden, which rushed up towards them, and then, carrying a whirl of lesser iridescent fragilities with it, precipitated itself down its steep descent; and as it swept, and hovered, and again mounted, silent and unresting, it was alone.

The giant butterfly does not content itself with absorbing its simulacra; it also enchants a human being too obsessed with beauty—"'O glory, glory,' Mr. Tighe said, 'O glory everlasting!'"—who falls into a contemplative trance and then into death. The Forms quicken or destroy a number of people before the central character, Anthony Durrant, who has the intellectual purity and moral power to understand what is happening and how to respond, sends the Forms back to their archetypal world through a magical invocation,

> a sound as of a single word, but not English, nor Latin, nor Greek. Hebrew it might have been or something older than Hebrew, some incantation whereby the prediluvian magicians had controlled contentions among spirits or the language in which our father Adam named the beasts of the garden . . . He called and he commanded . . . By the names that were the Ideas he called them, and the Ideas who are the Principles of everlasting creation heard him . . . They were returning, summoned by the authority of man from their incursion into the world of man.

Anthony's invocation reached as far as the halls of Magdalen College, and there, too, its summons was heard. Nevill Coghill had urged Lewis to read *The Place of the Lion*, and on February 26, 1936, Lewis wrote to Arthur Greeves, "I have just read what I think a really great book . . . It is not only a most exciting fantasy, but a deeply religious and (unobtrusively) a profoundly learned book. The reading of it has been a good preparation for Lent as far as I am concerned: for it shows me (through the heroine) the special sin of abuse of intellect to which all my profession are liable, more clearly than I ever saw it before. I have learned more than I ever knew yet about humility. In fact it has been a big experience."

On March 11, Lewis wrote to Williams out of the blue, declaring "I never know about writing to an author . . . But I feel I must risk it," and went on to say that *The Place of the Lion* was "one of the major literary events of my life—comparable to my first discovery of George MacDonald, G.K. Chesterton, or Wm. Morris." He then took a bold and fateful step: he described to Williams the Inklings, an "informal club . . . the qualifications (as they have informally evolved) are a tendency to write, and Christianity," and invited him to attend a meeting. Williams responded instantly, praising *The Allegory of Love*, which he had been reading in proofs for Amen House, and declaring it the first book since Dante to fathom the relation between love and religion: "If you had delayed writing another 24 hours, our letters would have crossed. It has never before happened to me to be admiring an author of a book while he at the same time was admiring me."

Mutual admiration had rarely commenced at such a high pitch; the Inklings would never be the same.

II

SECONDARY WORLDS

While Lewis and Williams swapped compliments, Tolkien enjoyed his own share of praise and laurels. The British Library Association nominated *The Hobbit* for the Carnegie Medal for 1937, and in 1938 it won the Children's Spring Book Festival prize from the *New York Herald Tribune*. Friends and strangers continued to congratulate him and say how much they enjoyed the book. The accolade that most thrilled him, however, came from the children's writer Arthur Ransome, adored by all the Tolkien offspring for his Swallows and Amazons tales (*Pigeon Post*, sixth in the series, had won the first Carnegie Medal). Ransome, in a nursing home after an operation for umbilical hernia, wrote to Tolkien on December 13, 1937, describing himself as "a humble hobbit-fancier." He also ventured a small criticism, suggesting that Gandalf had misused the word "man" when speaking of Bilbo (who is, of course, a hobbit). Tolkien responded immediately, expressing his pleasure at the letter, welcoming the correction—"man" became "fellow" in the second edition—and asking after Ransome's health. In reply, Ransome piled on the praise, assuring Tolkien that his book "has done a great deal to turn these weeks [of convalescence] into a pleasure," lauding his "delicate skill," and assuring him that his book would see "dozens" of editions. Such honeyed words from a famous author meant much to Tolkien, who lacked Lewis's red-cheeked self-confidence and would have seconded Conrad's celebrated (but possibly apocryphal) cry, "I don't want criticism, I want praise!"

"Man, Sub-Creator"

Despite Ransome's encouragement and that of others, however, Tolkien had difficulty moving on to another full-length tale. Instead, he refined his Elvish languages and worked on a novella, *Farmer Giles of Ham*, that had seen first light as a bedtime story for his kids; it would remain unpublished until 1949. One day in 1936 or 1937, Lewis said to him, "Tollers, there is too little of what we really like in stories. I am afraid we shall have to try and write some ourselves." The two agreed on the spot that each would produce an "excursionary 'Thriller,'" Lewis taking on space travel—resulting in the 1937 novel *Out of the Silent Planet*—while Tolkien tried his hand at time travel. He set about writing *The Lost Road*, the tale of a family that time-slips through dreams, an adventure culminating in the inundation of the great island of Númenor. For many years now, as noted in chapter 3, Tolkien had suffered from nightmares of a great, deadly wave; perhaps *The Lost Road* would destroy the power of this terrifying oneiric image by transforming it into art. But the tale never gelled; the exasperated reader at Allen & Unwin, to whom he sent it as a possible sequel to *The Hobbit*, declared it "a hopeless proposition."

Almost simultaneously, a heavier blow descended. Tolkien had added, to the package that contained *The Lost Road*, large chunks of *The Silmarillion*, including *The Lay of Leithian*, "The Fall of Númenor," and the prose *Quenta Silmarillion*, the last a vastly expanded version of portions of *Sketch of the Mythology* and its immediate successor, the *Quenta Noldorinwa*. Tolkien's publisher rejected the entire collection, explaining that the firm would much prefer a hobbit sequel. *The Lay of Leithian*, wrote an outside reader, was "of a very thin, if not always downright bad, quality." Thankfully, the official report to Tolkien blunted the criticism, and he was able to write back that "my chief joy comes from learning that the Silmarillion is not rejected with scorn. I have suffered a sense of fear and bereavement, quite ridiculous, since I let this private and beloved nonsense out; and I think if it had seemed to you to be nonsense I should have felt really crushed." He was feeling low, in any case, from a bout with the flu, and when an acquaintance wrote to point out inconsistencies in *The Hobbit*, he responded, with a note of exasperation, that "I don't much approve of *The Hobbit* myself, preferring my own mythology (which is just touched on) with its consistent nomenclature . . . and organized history, to this rabble of Eddaic-named dwarves out of Völuspá, newfangled hobbits and gollums (invented in an idle hour) and Anglo-Saxon runes." In the event, Unwin's magnanimity in sending a cushioned report proved providential, for Tolkien agreed that a direct sequel to *The Hobbit* did indeed make sense.

What sort of sequel, though? He told Stanley Unwin in October 1937 that his fount of hobbit ideas had run dry. "Goodness knows what will happen," he continued on December 16. ". . . What more can hobbits do? They can be comic, but their comedy is suburban unless it is set against things more elemental. But the real fun about orcs and dragons (to my mind) was before their time." He cast about for a new story line, wondering if "Tom Bombadil, the spirit of the (vanishing) Oxford and Berkshire countryside, could be made into the hero of a story?" He was riddled with doubts and hesitations, yet soon his marvelously fecund brain brimmed with new ideas, and on December 19 he informed C. A. Furth, a production staffer at Allen & Unwin, that he had completed the first chapter of the sequel, "A long expected party."

This celebrated opening to *The Lord of the Rings*, describing Bilbo Baggins's eleventy-first birthday bash, would go through multiple rewrites before Tolkien was satisfied. Unlike Lewis, who composed with consummate ease, Tolkien scribbled and erased, cut and rewrote, and reworked again. The first version of "A Long Expected Party" has Bilbo celebrating his seventieth birthday; the second brings in Gandalf; in the third, Bilbo's son Bingo organizes the party; in the fourth, a cousin, Bingo Bolger-Baggins, undertakes the task. In the months to come, the project advanced in imaginative leaps. Tolkien realized that the magic ring from *The Hobbit* would dominate the sequel, that a terrifying Necromancer would threaten global doom, that the new *Hobbit* would be painted in altogether darker pigments than the original. It would not be a book solely for children; perhaps it would not be for children at all.

He typed up the first chapter, sent it along to Furth, and shared the manuscript with his son Christopher and with Lewis. He was eager to press on, but academic obligations kept interfering—lectures, work on Old Norse and Old and Middle English texts—and for many months there was no additional progress. Frustrated, he complained to Furth in February 1938 that all his ideas had been "squandered" on *The Hobbit*. By July, blocked and disgusted, he declared that the sequel had "lost my favour" and that all work with hobbits would be set aside until *The Silmarillion* was complete. Thus was *The Lord of the Rings* nearly aborted—a crisis that would repeat itself more than once. Happily the muses and a few days of rest from academic labors worked their charms, and in late August he reported to Furth that the project was "flowing along, and getting quite out of hand." By October, he began to grow seriously concerned that his new approach would prove too frightening for children—he was, after all, known as a children's author; perhaps, he worried, the prewar gloom now permeating England had affected the tone. But he forged ahead at a steady pace and by the following February had produced over three hundred manuscript pages. His heart lifted; he might even be finished by June 1939! His estimate would prove to be off by nearly ten years.

"Story-Making in Its Primary and Most Potent Mode"

During 1938, when not engaged on the *Hobbit* sequel, Tolkien made progress on several projects, including his edition of the *Ancrenne Wisse* and one of the *Pearl*, a fourteenth-century Middle English poem by the anonymous author of *Sir Gawain and the Green Knight*. Tolkien's theatrical skills, honed by reading during Inklings meetings, entranced a wide audience when, in response to a request from John Masefield and Nevill Coghill, he appeared in the Summer Diversions at the Oxford Playhouse. Robed in green, with a turban and false beard, he recited, without benefit of notes, almost all of Chaucer's "Nun's Priest Tale." A reporter from the *Oxford Mail*, beside himself with admiration, reported that "Prof. Tolkien spoke his lines magnificently" and that "one can only stand amazed at his bravery." These accomplishments pale, however, beside a far more important event: Tolkien's delivery, on March 8, 1939, while the shadows of war pressed ever closer, of the annual Andrew Lang Lecture at the University of St. Andrews in Scotland. He called his talk "On Fairy-Stories."

Andrew Lang, as George Stuart Gordon had pointed out when inaugurating the lecture series ten years earlier, was the great modern champion of folklore. His collections of folktales, published in a rainbow array—*The Blue Fairy Book*, *The Red Fairy Book*, *The Green Fairy Book*, and so on, twelve in all—had taken Victorian and Edwardian England by storm. Tolkien and thousands of others devoured them while children, and adults enjoyed them, too. Not only did Lang make fairy tales popular, he made them academically respectable. His scholarship sharply rebutted the contention of Max Müller—whom Barfield had pilloried in *Poetic Diction*—that mythology is a "disease of language" (caused, Müller believed, by the personification of natural phenomena as gods and goddesses), and that folklore is its attenuated aftereffect. For Lang, folklore is not debased mythology but mythology's very basis; fairy tales are the building blocks of the mythic imagination. Tolkien, staking his literary life on the intrinsic value of folktale and myth, was strongly sympathetic toward Lang's view. However, he rejected Lang's insistence, inspired by Edward Burnett Tylor and anticipating James George Frazer, that myth and folktale belonged to a primitive stage of human culture, now superseded by our more enlightened scientific epoch. When the University of St. Andrews extended its invitation, he seized the opportunity to counter Lang, Tylor, and Frazer by presenting a theory of folklore grounded, not in an account of cultural evolution, but in Christian theology and the religious underpinnings of literary art.

Tolkien commenced his address in high spirits, quipping that as an Englishman lecturing on fairies in Scotland, he felt like a conjuror before an Elvish court. He then plunged boldly in—good magicians excel at courage as well as sleight-of-hand—examining definitions of fairies, fairy stories, and the like, in the process puncturing several popular beliefs. Most fairies are not miniature (he laid this slur at the feet of William Shakespeare and Michael Drayton); nor is a fairy story identical to a beast fable (such as *Reynard the Fox*), a traveler's tale (*Gulliver's Travels*), or a dream tale (*Alice's Adventures in Wonderland*); nor do fairy stories reject reason (rational understanding of the difference between frogs and princes is necessary for the enjoyment of a tale in which a prince becomes a frog).

What, then, is a fairy story, and what is its use? A fairy story tells of Faërie, "the realm or state in which fairies have their being"; Faërie is the world itself—our world, but only "when we are enchanted." A fairy tale's essence is enchantment or magic: not the mechanical magic of the conjuror or the power-seeking magic of the magus, but the magic of Elvish enchantment that bares the mystery and beauty of creation. In a fairy story, enchantment is the result of applying adjectives in new and startling ways—in effect, rearranging the constitutive elements of the world—so that we have flying broomsticks or green suns or walking woods.

This process has two stages. First, the writer (or painter) employs imagination to produce images "not actually present"; then he or she turns to art to channel, tame, and refine these images. Through this process—and here we encounter the heart of Tolkien's religio-aesthetic theory—the artist becomes a *subcreator*, echoing on a human scale God's great work of creation. The power to subcreate lies within our grasp because we are stamped with the image of God: "we make in our measure and in our derivative mode, because we are made: and not only made, but made in the image and likeness of a Maker." We do not make miraculously, ex nihilo, as God does, but we have been given the power to subcreate, to bring into being secondary worlds, by means of the imaginative arts.

The theory of subcreation did not originate solely with Tolkien. Shakespeare famously celebrated, in *A Midsummer Night's Dream*, the tandem work of imagination and poet to conjure images "not actually present": "as imagination / bodies forth / The forms of things unknown, the poet's pen / Turns them to shapes, and gives to airy nothing / A local habitation and a name." In *Characteristics of Men, Manners, Opinions, Times* (1711), the third Earl of Shaftesbury described the poet as "a second *Maker*, a just Prometheus under Jove": this definition would circulate widely among the Romantics. Coleridge advanced the metaphor by positing a primary and secondary imagination—a terminology that surely influenced Tolkien's account. The primary imagination, argued Coleridge, is the power of the mind to perceive, regulate, and give form to the inchoate raw data of perception, just as God brings order out of chaos: "the living Power and prime Agent of all human Perception . . . a repetition in the finite mind of the eternal act of creation in the infinite I AM"; the secondary imagination takes the world perceived and shaped by the primary imagination, scatters it, and reassembles it as art: "The secondary Imagination I consider as an echo of the former, co-existing with the conscious will . . . it dissolves, diffuses, dissipates, in order to re-create."

Tolkien was a realist who would not have been interested in the Kantian idealism implicit in Coleridge's notion of the primary imagination. It was the secondary imagination—the desire to subcreate—that interested him, and it was fantasy, he believed, that best fulfilled this desire. In "The Rime of the Ancient Mariner," "Kubla Khan," and other poems, Coleridge disclosed a taste for the fantastic, but he never granted it the privileged position that Tolkien did. Fantasy for Tolkien was "not a lower but a higher form of Art, indeed the most nearly pure form, and so (when achieved) the most potent." Such an achievement, he readily admitted, is an "elvish craft," for fantasy entails creation of a different world from the one that we inhabit, and yet, to succeed as art, this newly minted world must offer the "inner consistency of reality." We must believe in the green sun, the flying horse, the diminutive hobbit. This takes surpassing skill, but when a writer succeeds in crafting a believable fantasy, he has achieved "story-making in its primary and most potent mode."

It is precisely story making in this mode that Tolkien sought to achieve in the *Hobbit* sequel, begun fifteen months before delivering "On Fairy-Stories." To accomplish this, he needed a fundamental change in his approach to narrative. The Lang lecture would point the way. Tolkien already knew that fairy tales appeal to adults; his own taste had settled that. Now it dawned on him that the tastes of children, while less informed than those of adults, may not be, should not be, satisfied by watered-down representations of Faërie. He had erred, he realized, by writing *The Hobbit* as he did, modifying his tone to appease a young and naïve readership. In *The Lord of the Rings*—a book for children and adults, for all who gather beneath the Tree of Tales (a tree whose seeds, Tolkien archly comments, may sprout even in England's unpromising soil)—he would develop to its fullest every element of the fantasist's art.

In his Lang lecture, Tolkien analyzes the most important of these elements: *Recovery, Escape,* and *Consolation* (the capitals and italics are his). Recovery is regaining the ability to see things with clarity, "freed from the drab blur of triteness or familiarity—from possessiveness." Escape is flight from the horrors of the modern world (factories, pollution, bombs, and technology ranked high on Tolkien's list); it is not a sign of weakness, but of strength and sanity. Does not a man in prison do well to escape? To escape means also to overcome the embargo imposed by our natural limitations; in fantasy, we may fly through the clouds, talk with bees, or reach the ocean floor. Consolation is the satisfaction of desires, which include our deep-seated longing for a world, if only a secondary one, of wonder and enchantment. One desire surpasses all others, by joining Consolation to Escape: the "Escape from Death"—a theme that abounds in fairy stories around the world. Escape from death is itself the supreme instance of the greatest of all Consolations: the "Happy Ending."

For Tolkien, the Happy Ending lies at the heart of fantasy and fairy story; it is so essential to the genre that when he revised his talk for publication in *Essays Presented to Charles Williams,* he coined the word "eucatastrophe" from *eu* (Greek for good) and *catastrophe* (Greek for overturning) to describe those glorious volte-faces in which evil, on the verge of triumph, gives way to good, corruption to innocence, grief to rejoicing, certain death to yet more certain life. It is "a sudden and miraculous grace . . . a fleeting glimpse of Joy, Joy beyond the walls of the world, poignant as grief." There are echoes here of Lewis's idea of Joy, that painful, delicious longing that only God can fulfill. It may be that Lewis drew inspiration for his carefully constructed account of Joy in his autobiography from Tolkien's earlier presentation. In any event, eucatastrophe is for Tolkien the crucial event in fairy tale, the hinge upon which the greatest stories turn, imparting "a catch of the breath, a beat and lifting of the heart, near to (or indeed accompanied by) tears, as keen as that given by any form of literary art, and having a peculiar quality." There is a peculiar reason for this "peculiar quality": the joy that floods us as eucatastrophe unfolds is not limited to the fairy story in which it originates; here art oversteps its bounds, and joy breaks into the primary world. Eucatastrophe leads us out of literature and into faith. Through it we glimpse "a far-off gleam or echo of *evangelium* in the real world." Fairy tale, then, is a door opening upon divine truth. Recovery, Consolation, Escape, in their highest modes of Escape from Death and eucatastrophe, would play a crucial role in *The Lord of the Rings.*

The Deepening Eclipse

It's not easy to be a missionary, even with the key to the cosmos in your hand. By 1930, Barfield knew that when he mentioned Rudolf Steiner's ideas to persons outside the Anthroposophical fold, the response would fall somewhere between polite disbelief and outright scorn. His friends' reaction proved the point; even Lewis, "who would never, for instance, express an opinion even on a minor but all too prolix poet of the sixteenth century without first having read the great bulk of what the man himself had actually written . . . on more than one occasion, broke his rule in the case of Steiner."

Barfield was "shocked and puzzled" by the pervasive rejection of Steiner's self-evident genius. How to get around this infuriating boycott? He hit upon the plan of presenting the seer's teachings indirectly, by exploring their affinities to Romanticism, and he began to turn out essays (later published in *Romanticism Comes of Age*, 1944), arguing that Steiner, like the Romantics, grasped the cognitive value of imagination but that he had gone further by seeing that "Imagination" must blend with what Barfield termed "Inspiration" in order to attain "Intuition" (the capitals are Barfield's): that is, objective knowledge of supersensible and supernatural realities. Imagination by itself offers mystical and aesthetic insights, but only Steiner's Spiritual Science, the end of a "long, sober process" of which Imagination is but the first step, produces "exact results." Anthroposophy, Barfield concluded, "was nothing less than Romanticism grown up."

At about the same time that he initiated this campaign, he began to step away from regular participation in the Inklings. The difficulty of traveling from London to Oxford played a part, but so, too, one suspects, did dismay and embarrassment over his literary disappointments. He viewed the situation with bitter humor tinged with resignation, noting that by entering a law firm, he had "lost the inestimable privilege of leisure and as a result was able, as far as the lettered world was concerned, to advance cautiously from inaudibility to silence." His Oxford jaunts dwindled to one or two per academic term; during these brief but happy interludes he would attend an Inklings meeting, to the great pleasure of the assembly, who enjoyed his soft-spoken contributions and the skill that he alone possessed to temper Lewis's more heated outbursts; he would then pass the weekend with Lewis at the Kilns, reading together in Virgil, Homer, and Dante. Each time Lewis welcomed him warmly, but the two friends never regained their earlier intimacy: the termination of the "Great War" and Lewis's conversion had put an end to that.

Barfield's marriage was under strain as well. There was no mystery about the reason: Maud distrusted Anthroposophy and disliked her husband's involvement in it. On September 27, 1928, she had written him a furious letter, describing a text by Steiner as "nauseating" and "petty," accusing Barfield of being obsessed with his own spiritual path without "any desire to find out what my mind was like or on what high quest I was traveling" and of failing to acknowledge her prayers on his behalf.

The Barfield scholar Simon Blaxland–de Lange speculates that this letter, "a private outpouring of grief and anger," was never sent. In any event, the couple remained together. Maud continued to loathe Anthroposophy and all its trappings, while her husband nursed the wound inflicted by this "sword through the marriage knot."

Frustrated in art, in proselytizing, in friendship, in marriage, Barfield burrowed yet more deeply into Anthroposophy. But there, too, he found discord and, soon enough, internecine warfare. Following the Master's death in 1925, his followers had split into two rival camps: those who believed that his writings constituted a definitive and changeless canon, and those who thought that his teachings could be developed further by mature disciples. Barfield, Cecil Harwood, and others in the English Anthroposophical Society held the latter view. Unfortunately, Steiner's widow, the formidable Marie Steiner, did not. When Barfield and Harwood traveled to Dornach in the mid-1930s for a general convention, they entered a minefield. At a "very fiery meeting" filled with "strong antagonism," Barfield spoke his mind—silenced in mainstream literary journals, he would at least have his say in this most important of arenas—arguing for a liberal interpretation of Steiner's legacy. His courageous (or rash) act "rather flung the stone in the middle of the discussion" and disaster ensued. Frau Steiner's allies established a new English Anthroposophical group, with its own headquarters and journal, that held copyright over Steiner's publications in England. Suddenly Barfield found it difficult to get permission to publish his Steiner translations, and the Dornach hierarchy and its English branch made harsh demands upon him and his companions, including the dismissal from the movement of several liberal members. Even in the cozy world of Anthroposophy, there was no escape from the terrible friction inherent in the evolution of consciousness.

The Happiness of the Cross

Lewis, by contrast, brimmed with happiness; everything was falling into place. Since becoming a Christian, his teaching, reading, writing, and scholarship had all acquired zest and purpose. He had found his vocation: to fight the Lord's battles in the academy and the world at large, armed with wit, dialectic, and invincible faith. True, his living arrangements remained eccentric, what with the regular commute between Magdalen and the Kilns, but he felt at home in both locales. True, Mrs. Moore continued to order him about as if he were her private manservant, but he had settled into the role. Like other intellectuals, he welcomed the mindless drudgery as a refreshing change of pace, and her irrational demands gave him a chance to practice humility, one of the Christian virtues he feared he most lacked.

To crown his pleasures, he was surrounded by friends. "Friendship is the greatest of worldly goods. Certainly to me it is the chief happiness of life," he wrote to Arthur. The Inklings were flourishing under his orchestration and Warnie's kind ministrations, assembling on Thursday evenings at Magdalen and Tuesday mornings at the Bird and Baby, drinking, laughing, cajoling, and disputing; even Williams turned up now and then, grabbing the train from London, although, like Barfield, he found Oxford too distant for regular participation and sustained his friendship with Lewis largely through letters. Lewis's correspondence with Arthur continued, but in a subdued key, Lewis sounding at times like an elder brother instructing a less-educated younger sibling, patiently tolerating Arthur's spiritual experiments with Unitarianism, Baha'i, and the Quaker tradition of his ancestors. He continued to count Barfield a peer—this high regard never wavered—but refused to argue with him, and the letters they exchanged lacked fire. As always, though, Lewis itched for combat, and during the mid and late 1930s he found his match in Alan Griffiths (1906–93).

The friendship between Lewis and Griffiths has drawn little attention from literary historians, largely because Griffiths never joined the Inklings. Surely he would have been invited to join if he had remained in Oxford after earning his degree, but within a few years he had become a contemplative Benedictine monk, taking the name of Bede, and later settled in India as a Catholic *sannyasin* (renunciant), embracing a land and lifestyle alien to the Inklings' intransigently Western outlook. Nonetheless, he meant a great deal to Lewis; *Surprised by Joy* is dedicated to Griffiths, and we learn in its pages that during the months prior to Lewis's conversion, "my chief companion . . . was Griffiths, with whom I kept up a copious correspondence." Griffiths seconds this memory, writing that during this time "I was probably nearer to Lewis than anyone else."

Their relationship had begun in 1927, when Lewis became Griffiths's English tutor. The two met weekly, and their talks ran late into the night.

After Griffiths left Oxford, they almost never saw one another—although Griffiths joined Barfield and Lewis on a walking tour in 1932—but their correspondence blossomed. The teacher-student relationship evaporated, replaced by a rich and lively exchange of equals. "I think that it was through him," said Griffiths, "that I really discovered the meaning of friendship." At first the two shared literary views, but before long they turned to intense discussions on philosophy, metaphysics, the Bible, Christology, and so on, forging an intellectual and spiritual companionship that Griffiths held forever dear.

The friendship ran aground, however, when Griffiths became a Catholic and a monk. The two ceased to see eye to eye and tempers flared over Thomism, ecclesiology, poetry, mysticism, prayer, life after death, and more. By 1934, Lewis advised Griffiths "once and for all" that he would no longer discuss "any of the questions at issue between our respective churches." This declaration closely parallels, as readers will note, Lewis's recent and abrupt cessation of debate with Barfield. Luckily for us—for Lewis is always most splendid when on the attack—in this case he failed to follow his own edict and his subsequent letters to Griffiths bristle with poisoned darts ("I think your specifically Catholic beliefs a mass of comparatively harmless human tradition which may be fatal to certain souls under special conditions") along with perceptive observations on Christian discipline:

> [Obedience] appears to me more and more the whole business of life, the only road to love and peace—the cross and the crown in one . . . What indeed can we imagine Heaven to be but unimpeded obedience. I think this is one of the causes of our love of inanimate nature, that in it we see things which unswervingly carry out the will of their Creator, and are therefore wholly beautiful: and though their *kind* of obedience is infinitely lower than ours, yet the degree is so much more perfect that a Christian can see the reason that the Romantics had in feeling a certain holiness in the wood and water.

Griffiths, however, like Barfield before him, was deeply wounded by Lewis's ban on religious debate. To him it "was a great embarrassment. It meant that I could never really touch on much that meant more to me than anything else, and there was always a certain reserve therefore afterward in our relationship." Eventually their friendship would have faded in any event, for in 1955 Griffiths relocated to India, and by the time of Lewis's death in 1963, he had begun to absorb elements of Hinduism into Christian worship. Lewis disliked Eastern thought. When he learned that another former pupil, Martin Lings, had been nosing about Hinduism and wished to encourage Lewis in this direction, he shot off a letter to Griffiths slithery with condescension, in which he calls Lings "my wretched man," laments his "confusion," and allows that since Lings "was up till this a person of exclusively literary interests, I daresay even Hindooism [sic] is a step upwards." Lings would later become a prominent Muslim and the author of an acclaimed English-language biography of the Prophet Muhammad based upon traditional sources.

Lewis's problems with Griffiths and Lings scarcely surprise; although he retained all his life a love of pagan mythology, no orthodox religion sat well with him other than what he would call "mere" Christianity. Tolkien was convinced that Lewis never wholly uprooted the anti-Catholic bias of his Ulster upbringing (his "Ulsterior motive"). According to Humphrey Carpenter, who takes Tolkien's view of the matter, Lewis at times labeled Irish Catholics "bog-rats" or "bog-trotters"; Carpenter adds that on one occasion, when Tolkien mentioned to Lewis his devotion to St. John— John being, let us remember, Tolkien's first name and the name of his oldest son—Lewis barked a scornful retort. It is also true that the term "papist" peppers Lewis's letters: of Mauriac's *Vie de Jesus*, "it is papist, of course, and contains what English and Protestant taste" (that is to say, Lewis's taste) "would call lapses, but it is very good in spite of them"; of the publishing house of Sheed & Ward, "I don't much like having a book of mine, and specially a religious book, brought out by a Papist publisher." But we are more inclined to view this way of speaking as a passing vulgarism of the sort that Lewis would permit himself among friends. Lewis certainly felt discomfort with some Catholic practices—but essentially it was a discomfort he would struggle to overcome, rather than a deep-seated antipathy.

Warnie shared in this discomfort with Catholicism but hadn't the temper to make an issue of it. He rarely made an issue of anything, which was just as well, as it meant that he could settle into the Kilns despite Mrs. Moore's abrasiveness. Lewis loved having his brother around; when all was said and done, Warnie was his closest companion, if not his match in scholarship or creativity. Warnie, for his part, knew the value of escape hatches and fashioned several for himself, to be used whenever the Kilns grew too claustrophobic. Digging into his savings, he bought a two-berth, twenty-foot-long boat that he named the *Bosphorus*, after a vessel in the Boxen tales, and on it he cruised England's rivers and canals. Life on the water was bliss, for "no one ever knows where you are, and you have no mail." Another escape was his diary, in which he could express safely his blossoming dislike of Mrs. Moore. His third escape was booze. Warnie had always been a binge drinker. Stuck at the Kilns or afloat on some quiet river, what better way to pass the time than by opening a bottle? His diary tells the tale. On February 22, 1935, for example, he attends a performance of *Hamlet* produced by Coghill, but finds the lead character to be a "snivelling, attitudinizing, platitudinizing arch bore" and notes that "if I had not been fortified by a double whiskey and soda half way through, I would not have stuck it to the end." A few days later, he observes that the same fortifying beverage had kept his pet dog going during its final days. And so on. Lewis knew of the drinking and was deeply troubled by it, but there was nothing he could do.

If Lewis ranked male friendship as his chief happiness, work ran a close second. He excepted tutoring, however; while he liked and even admired some of his pupils, such as Griffiths, he found others a terrible drain on his time and energy. Dr. Dimble in *That Hideous Strength* speaks for him: "There is my dullest pupil just ringing the bell. I must go to the study, and listen to an essay on Swift beginning 'Swift was born.'" But writing, reading, and lecturing gave him strength. During the 1930s, as always, he absorbed books at a ferocious pace, reading intensively in early English literature while ranging afield into authors as diverse as Kafka, whom he likened to George MacDonald for mythic profundity, and David Lindsay, whose metaphysical space adventure, *A Voyage to Arcturus*, dazzled both him and Tolkien. In 1937, down with the flu, he managed during one "grand week in bed" to read *Northanger Abbey*, *The Moonstone*, *The Vision of Judgment*, *Our Mutual Friend*, the third volume of Ruskin's *Modern Painters*, and *The Egoist* ("There's a good deal of the ass about Meredith—that dreadful first chapter—Carlyle in icing sugar"). As if to balance the ledger, letters poured out at an equally prodigious pace, he cast Virgil into rhyming alexandrines, and, at the invitation of

OUP, commenced work on a major investigation of sixteenth-century English literature for the multivolume *Oxford History of English Literature*. The book's immense labors weighed upon him for many years, and he took to calling the series *OHEL* and, finally, *O HELL*. To top off this frenzy of activity, he fulfilled his pledge to match Tolkien's time-travel tale with a space-travel adventure of his own by writing his first real novel and possibly his most lucid work of fiction: *Out of the Silent Planet*.

A Journey to Malacandra

The model for *Out of the Silent Planet* (1938) was a childhood favorite of Lewis's: H. G. Wells's anti-imperialist *First Men in the Moon* (1901). In this early science fiction tale, which Lewis considered "the best of the sort I have read," a scientist and a young adventurer, working in secret in a remote English country setting, build a spherical spaceship out of gravity-repellent material and travel to the moon, where, captured by insectlike inhabitants who dwell beneath its inhospitable surface, they inadvertently reveal the brutality of the human race and are brought before the "Grand Lunar" for judgment.

Lewis took his scaffolding from this tale, borrowing more than a few details of setting and plot, but the edifice he built upon it was altogether different; for he had been convinced, by reading David Lindsay's *A Voyage to Arcturus*, that the planetary romance could be a vehicle for profound "*spiritual* adventures." He thought he could use this form to counter the materialistic picture of the universe that dominated popular science writing. As an adolescent, Lewis had pored over the scientific potboilers of the Victorian astronomer Sir Robert Stawell Ball, in which the universe was depicted as a vast wasteland where humans are of vanishingly little account. More recently, he had found in Olaf Stapledon's *Last and First Men* (1930) and in the essays of the geneticist J.B.S. Haldane (*Possible Worlds*, 1927) an admirable speculative power allied to chilling schemes of interplanetary colonization, moral and genetic reprogramming, material advancement, and limitless life extension. He had been dismayed to discover that, for some of his own students, such utopian fantasies had supplanted both Christian realism and Christian hope. Lewis hoped, in this novel, to present an appealing imaginative alternative. "I like the whole interplanetary idea as a *mythology*," he told Roger Lancelyn Green, "and simply wished to conquer for my own (Christian) pt. of view what has always hitherto been used by the opposite side."

The novel's hero is Dr. Ransom (identified at first, with a suggestion of allegory, as "the Pedestrian"), a Cambridge philologist on holiday. Tolkien denied that Ransom was based on him, and Lewis put readers off the scent by stating in the epilogue that Ransom was a pseudonym, not the hero's real name. But there are hints to the contrary: as an English surname, Ransom means "Ranolf's son," but as an English noun and verb, Ransom comes from Anglo-Norman for the Latin *redemptio* and savors of English Catholicism. It is under the title of "Our Lady of Ransom" that Catholic Oxford claims the patronage of the Virgin Mary; and the Guild of Ransomers, founded in 1887 for the purpose of asking Our Lady of Ransom to intercede for the conversion of England and Wales, was (and still is) a going concern. A painting of Our Lady of Ransom was (and still is) venerated in a special chapel in Tolkien's parish church. Could there be a more feeling tribute to Tolkien than to create a philologist-hero with such a name? Moreover, Ransom's Christian name, Elwin, Old English for "Elf-friend," completes the tribute and signals the extent to which Lewis would rely on Tolkien's inspiration in developing his un-Wellsian version of Wells.

As the novel begins, Ransom has set out with map and pack on a solo walking tour in the English Midlands. He soon finds his ramble thwarted by a thunderstorm, an unfriendly innkeeper, and a mother worried about her retarded son, who has failed to come home from his job working for a professor and a London businessman in a desolate country house. Ransom agrees to inquire after the boy, but the dwelling is strangely forbidding, and the moment he throws his pack over the gate in order to crawl through the hedge into the garden, he realizes that there is no turning back. Like Lewis the reluctant convert in *Surprised by Joy*, he has been drawn in and is about to be prodigiously interfered with.

On the other side of the hedge, Ransom discovers the missing boy trying to escape from the clutches of two men—the brilliant physicist Dr. Weston and an old schoolmate of Ransom's, the venal, vulgar industrialist Dick Devine. Ransom intervenes and saves the boy, only to become himself a substitute victim. He is drugged, tied up, and bundled onto a spaceship of Weston's design, which takes off for Mars (Malacandra). Weston, he learns, is a Stapledonian raised to the nth power, the architect of a grandiose experiment to tame other worlds for human habitation once Earth's resources run out. Devine's intentions, by contrast, are almost refreshingly crass; he plans to exploit Mars for commercial gain. Ransom is to be offered as a sacrifice to the Malacandrians, whom all three assume to be savages or worse (Ransom pictures insectoid monstrosities).

His expectations are, however, quickly overturned. Space, which he had always imagined to be dark and cold, turns out to be an ocean of living light. The intense heat caresses rather than oppresses, filling him with vigor and sensual delight: "Stretched naked on his bed, a second Danaë, he found it night by night more difficult to disbelieve in old astrology: almost he felt, wholly he imagined, 'sweet influence' pouring or even stabbing into his surrendered body." "Almost he felt, wholly he imagined": the archaism of the language, with its anastrophe (inverted word order) and parallelism characteristic of heigh stile—more muted than in Tolkien's prose, however—and its faint echo of the biblical "almost thou persuadest me to be a Christian," presages Ransom's coming entry into a hieratic and mythic world.

Ransom's first glimpse of Malacandra reveals "nothing but colours— colours that refused to form themselves into things," but he begins to see the landscape more clearly once he opens his soul to it. When he meets his first Malacandrian and realizes that the creature possesses the gift of language, his zeal as a philologist overcomes his fear. Lewis gives a similar account in *Surprised by Joy* of conquering his own insect phobia by developing a scientific interest in entomology. The cure lies in the curiosity: a scientific curiosity that is genuinely objective and disinterested cleanses the vision.

As Ransom discovers the rationality and humanity of the three Malacandrian races—the furry, childlike, poetry-loving *hrossa*, the froglike, technically dexterous *pfifiltriggi*, and the fantastically tall, white-feathered, austerely intellectual *séroni*—so do his own rationality and humanity expand. He exchanges fear for trust and places himself in the Malacandrians' hands. Under their guidance, he comes to understand the high-pitched voice of a fourth type of being, the angel-like *eldila*, learns the value of obedience, and is brought to meet the Oyarsa, the planet's ruling Intelligence, comparable to an archangel or to the planetary archons of Hellenistic and Gnostic lore. The Oyarsa reveals to Ransom a terrible secret, the etiology of all Earth's woe: Ransom's beloved home planet is Thulcandra, the silent planet, estranged from the company of the heavens by the perverse design of the fallen angel who is its ruling Intelligence and by the sin of the archetypal man, Adam. The whole human race is "bent" (*incurvatus*—a word favored by St. Anselm—though created to mirror God, we have become bent, like mirrors in a fun house, reflecting lower things).

Meanwhile, Weston and Divine, driven by lust for knowledge and power, have committed the first Malacandrian murder, slaying Ransom's closest friend among the *hrossa*. Dragged before the Oyarsa, Weston delivers a jingoistic speech in a scene that makes high comedy out of his pose as a noble martyr for science and civilization. The Oyarsa, with perfect justice, sends the three humans back to Earth. Weston and Devine plan to kill Ransom en route, but he narrowly escapes, and returns to tell the tale to his friend, the fictional C. S. Lewis, and to await further angelic instructions. The earth is under siege, but not abandoned, for it has been ransomed by the divine Son, Maleldil; and Ransom's own journey into deep heaven, though seemingly a chance event, is a sign that the siege may be lifting.

Out of the Silent Planet is not difficult to decode, but no less delightful for being transparent. It is largely about seeing: seeing humanity in the nonhuman rational creature; seeing angelic forms just beyond the range of normal perception; and seeing the cosmos just beyond the range of materialistic science, as a place of meaning and purpose. Space is deep heaven (the Anglican mystic Evelyn Underhill wrote to thank Lewis for this idea) and the planets are "mere holes or gaps in the living heaven . . . formed not by addition to, but by subtraction from, the surrounding brightness." It is a revitalized picture of the universe that owes something to Chesterton's "cosy little cosmos," but the details come from what Lewis liked to call the "medieval model," as he put it in the lectures that would become *The Discarded Image*:

> . . . to look out on the night sky with modern eyes is like looking out over a sea that fades away into mist, or looking about one in a trackless forest—trees forever and no horizon. To look up at the towering medieval universe is much more like looking at a great building. The "space" of modern astronomy may arouse terror, or bewilderment or vague reverie; the spheres of the old present us

with an object in which the mind can rest, overwhelming in its greatness but satisfying in its harmony . . . This explains why all sense of the pathless, the baffling, and the utterly alien—all agoraphobia—is so markedly absent from medieval poetry when it leads us, as so often, into the sky.

The "medieval model" was not simply bad science; in many ways it was, Lewis believed, scientifically astute: "Earth was, by cosmic standards, a point—it had no appreciable magnitude. The stars, as the *Somnium Scipionis* had taught, were larger than it. Isidore in the sixth century knows that the Sun is larger, and the Moon smaller than the Earth (*Etymologies*, III, xlvii–xlviii). Maimonides in the twelfth maintains that every star is ninety times as big, Roger Bacon in the thirteenth simply that the least star is 'bigger' than she." There is neither fundamentalism nor flat-earth pseudoscience in the medieval model, nor in Lewis's fictional appropriation of it.

By a happy accident, Lewis found in one of the texts discussed in his lectures, the *Cosmographia* of the twelfth-century Christian Platonist Bernard Silvestris, a conjecture about an "Oyarses" who shapes things in the lower world after the pattern of the higher world. The Magdalen fellow C.C.J. Webb suggested to Lewis that *Oyarses* might be a corruption of *Ousiarches*, "ruling essence"—which appears in the *Asclepius* of Pseudo-Apuleius. Perhaps Oyarses could be the tutelary genius assigned to a planet, after the manner of the angels assigned to the nations. There was room for the pagan gods in Lewis's Christian cosmos, provided they appeared as angels or "middle spirits," archetypes or allegorical figures. Thus, in his alliterative poem, "The Planets" (1935), the planetary gods return as "Lady Luna in light canoe," Mercury "madcap rover," Venus's floral and copper glories, Sol's burning chariot, "Mars mercenary," Jove "calm and kingly," Saturn silent and melancholy.

It was Lewis's inspiration, in the Ransom trilogy, to transpose the medieval model to a modern "scientifictional" frame. Though he was criticized by some readers for being weak on the technological side, his real object, at which he succeeded, was to reimagine the universe as an organic whole, teeming with life and intelligence, hierarchically differentiated, and knit together by an inner telos; as a cosmic order whose microcosm is the rational creature made in the image and likeness of God, marred (in our world) by the Fall, but restored by the deifying light. No achievement of genuine science, Lewis was convinced, can render the essential features of this medieval model obsolete; it is only a crude scientism that makes it seem so. And since crude scientism is a failure of perspective and imagination, imaginative literature would prove to be the best remedy.

Lewis read *Out of the Silent Planet* in draft form to the Inklings. Tolkien approved, but thought it too short and deficient in matters of consistency and philological detail. Lewis quickly revised to accommodate these criticisms and sent the manuscript to Stanley Unwin for consideration. The first report from an external reader was lukewarm: "Mr. Lewis is quite likely, I dare say, to write a worth while novel one day. This one isn't good enough—quite." Unwin sent the report to Tolkien, who, in a letter of March 4, 1938, rose to Lewis's defense. If Lewis's otherworldly creatures were really "bunk," as the external reader had opined, then so was the myth of the Fall of angels and men; and if that myth were bunk, very little of Western literature would be left standing. Thanks to Tolkien's intervention, the book was accepted for publication.

Companions of the Co-inherence

"It was the full Celian sun that uttered to all of me the identical words of Christ: 'I am come that ye may have life, and that ye may have it more abundantly.'" Williams was writing constantly to Phyllis Jones, his Celia, still seven thousand miles away in Java, inundating her with praise and advice. She disliked the island, disdained the racial and cultural snobbery of her husband's oil company coworkers, felt trapped in her marriage, dreamed wistfully of Williams, and asked him, "Am I still Celia?" She would always be Celia, always Beatrice: "Quite clearly, quite certainly," he replied, "You are all that I ever said. I always saw *you* . . . Dear Celia, you are an exactitude of vision." The last sentence is obscure but calls to mind Dante's visions of Beatrice in *La Vita Nuova*. Future letters upped the ante, touching on intimacies physical and spiritual, achieved or simply aspired after. He called Celia "darling," he gloried in "the anatomical articulation of your joints and also the articulation of speech," and declared her "frame" to be the "compressed epigram" of both articulations. Bewildered, unhappy, she sent an equivocal response, and he lashed out, like an overwrought adolescent (he was nearly fifty years old at the time):

"I will not discuss it now. I am too angry at heart . . . I love you . . . Good-bye. O I hate, hate, everything—the world and myself and you—I hate it for months, and it grows. Blessing, be blessed." No wonder Williams's wife resented his never-ending platonic passions. She was plagued by terrible backaches, then fell sick with pneumonia. Despite the presence of little Michael, the Williamses' was not a happy home.

Work provided refuge. Williams plunged into new acquisitions, roping Auden into the fold to produce *The Oxford Book of Light Verse* and—a magnificent coup, his very finest as an editor—steering into print, in December 1936, David F. Swenson's translation of Kierkegaard's *Philosophical Fragments*, the first of the Danish philosopher's works to appear in England, followed soon after by Walter Lowrie's massive biography *Kierkegaard* and Alexander Dru's edition of the great Dane's journals. Many more Kierkegaard volumes would follow, all brought to press by Williams. It was a perfect match of editor and subject, for the two shared not only a liking for multiple personae but the conviction that their work might help to restore the Church to its original promise (Kierkegaard by his attacks upon the Danish Lutheran establishment, Williams by his proselytizing for the Way of Affirmation). "He was," wrote Williams of Kierkegaard but as if describing himself, "the type of the new state of things in which Christendom had to exist." To bring this strange obscure life and work to the attention of the world was an unmitigated joy: "Kierkegaard at any rate," he wrote to Lowrie, "whatever his other influence, has brought one group of his admirers into what is almost a state of love."

He loved Kierkegaard, in addition to the reasons given above, because Kierkegaard wrote at a furious clip. Williams did his best to emulate this practice. Alice Hadfield remembers the intensity of his literary concentration, even when on the premises of Amen House: "He wrote a great deal of poetry early in the day, composing all the way from Hampstead in the privacy and freedom of being alone in crowds. He used to march into Amen House, generally looking very grave because he was thinking verse, go straight upstairs, only raising his gloves in greeting to anyone who passed him, slap the gloves and hat on a peg, drop himself into his chair, scramble for a cigarette and start to write on his little pad."

In 1936, the Friends of Canterbury Cathedral asked him to write a play for their annual Canterbury Festival. Eliot's *Murder in the Cathedral* had been the 1935 production; Williams must have realized, when he received the invitation, that he had finally arrived. The production of *Thomas Cranmer of Canterbury* garnered raves; Eliot attended and invited Williams to "lunch . . . tea . . . dinner . . . supper—or breakfast at any time." The following year, he published another novel, *Descent into Hell*, a supernatural drama of sin and salvation that received a tepid critical and popular reception (although Lewis, at this point enamored of every word Williams wrote, called it "a thundering good book"). His most ambitious book of poetry, *Taliessin Through Logres*, a sequence of dense, elliptical poems on the Arthurian legend, appeared in 1938. Lewis again bubbled with enthusiasm, telling Williams it was "a great work, full of glory" and writing a nine-page review for *Theology*. Other Inklings disagreed. When Williams read the poem to the group, Havard recalled that "I've never listened to anything quite so obscure" and that others were "literally struck dumb like myself." The public, too, withheld their applause. The truth is that *Taliessin* and all of Williams's later Arthurian work, a tangled array of fraught syntax, elevated feelings, and shifting moods, is rarely picked up, more rarely read, and even more rarely enjoyed. When Williams's novels suffer from obscurity, thanks to esoteric illusions and occasionally tortured prose, the plot usually affords enough excitement to carry the reader along. In his poetry, there is no such mediating grace; the poems may reward close reading, but few readers make the effort. Perhaps it doesn't matter; although Williams counted himself a poet (his epitaph reads simply "Poet"), most people read him for his thrilling supernatural clashes of good versus evil and his adventurous theology.

Turning once again to his true strength, in 1938 Williams also published *He Came Down from Heaven*, a potpourri of lively writings on heaven, Adam and Eve, the prophets, the Incarnation, the theology of romantic love, and the city, the latter being Williams's ideal community of love. He dedicated the book, perhaps for expiatory reasons, "To MICHAL, by whom I began to study the doctrine of glory." The next year saw the appearance of what may be his most widely read theological work, *The Descent of the Dove*, a history of the Church in the form of a biography of the Holy Spirit, written in a distinctly Anglican idiom. He had hit his stride and was moving from strength to strength.

These varied volumes from the mid and late 1930s, produced at white-hot speed, cover a plenitude of topics. And yet in a sense they can all be read as one continuous book. This is because a trinity of ideas runs through them all; ideas that Williams had nurtured for many years, fore-shadowing them in his fiction but never before enunciating them at length. These are his three great doctrines of substitution, exchange, and co-inherence.

At its most exalted, substitution refers to Jesus' sacrifice on the Cross, when he offered himself as a sacrificial lamb to atone for our sins. Williams believed that each of us may, in a lesser mode, repeat this divine sacrifice by bearing one another's burdens. Exchange, closely allied to substitution— sometimes Williams used the two terms interchangeably—is a spiritual way, a daily practice in which we offer our time, money, and self-esteem for another's sake. As Williams is quick to point out, this practice de-mands a high degree of humility and love. What makes substitution and exchange possible is co-inherence. God provides us with a divine model of co-inherence: in the Trinity, three Persons (Father, Son, and Holy Spirit) co-inhere in one Godhead. So, too, are we part of one another, co-inhering in our shared human nature and in the Mystical Body of Christ. Roman-tic love, always of intense interest to Williams, is an imperfect expression of co-inherence, flawed because contaminated by fantasy and self-love.

Co-inherence was the ruling principle of Williams's life and the idea for which he is best remembered. He sought by every means to nourish this principle in his own life and that of his fellows; thus his habit of as-signing theatrical titles to employees at Amen House, creating from the clashing temperaments and shifting alliances of a typical large office a company of companions, a co-inherent circle based upon mythical iden-tities and the seminuminous aura engendered. In *The Descent of the Dove*, he speculates about the possibility of a new force within the Church, the Order of the Co-inherence (later, the Companions of the Co-inherence), created to foster "substitutions in love, exchanges in love." Within a year, prompted by requests from friends and devotees, he drew up a skeletal rule for the order. These are the first four decrees (the remainder describe co-inherence, substitution, and exchange):

1. The Order has no constitution except in its members. As it was said: *Others he saved, himself he cannot save.*
2. It recommends nevertheless that its members shall make a for-mal act of union with it and of recognition of their own nature. As it was said: *Am I my brother's keeper?*

3. Its concern is the practice of the apprehension of the Co-inherence both as a natural and a supernatural principle. As it was said: *Let us make man in Our image.*
4. It is therefore, *per necessitatem*, Christian. As it was said: *And whoever says there was when this was not, let him be anathema.*

Readers may note echoes, in the imperious tone, the oracular rhythms, the recommendation of a "formal act of union," the reference to principles natural and supernatural, the presiding Hermetic idea of "as above, so below," of Waite's Order of the Rosy Cross. Williams had learned his lessons well, and until his death his own order co-inhered, its members striving to put into practice their teacher's lessons, turning to him whenever needed for encouragement and direction. The order did some good; according to Hadfield, herself a member, Williams frequently "used the Companions in their proper service of exchange, asking each one to help another when he or she heard of trouble." But the group never attained the status that Williams had envisioned in *Descent*, that of an authorized, sanctified order within the church. It remained a private affair, an exchange of vows and charity among friends, under the eye of a charismatic founder, and perhaps inevitably, it dissolved upon Williams's death. Indeed, if he had lived a few more years, his order might have fallen apart, like so many other private spiritual organizations, by internal backbiting and scandal. For Williams himself, as we will see, had secrets that made him, if not ineligible, at least highly problematic as a spiritual director for his order, or for anyone at all.

The Coming of the Dark

Co-inherence was soon to be sorely tested by events on a larger stage than Oxford. The Inklings had long suspected that war was on the way. Throughout the 1930s, Barfield fumed over England's policy of appeasement toward Hitler. His anger intensified when the Nazi government banned the Anthroposophical Society in 1935. Even the London newspapers, he believed, intended to suppress news of Hitler's misdeeds, and he canceled his subscription to *The Times* in protest. Lewis, by contrast, knew little of political machinations but dreaded the possibility of worldwide bloodshed. Dark forebodings filled his letters as the decade rushed to a close. On September 12, 1938, he wrote to Barfield what reads like a farewell letter, speculating that "our whole joint world may be blown up before the end of the week" and adding, "If we are separated, God bless you, and thanks for a hundred good things I owe to you, more than I can count or weigh. In some ways we've had a corking time these twenty years." He harbored no doubts about the moral legitimacy of taking on the Germans, for, as he told Bede Griffiths, he had "always believed that it is lawful for a Christian to bear arms in war." "Our Lord does not appear to have regarded the Roman soldiers as *ex officio* sinners," he continued; "I cannot believe the knight errant idea to be sinful." Pacifism offered a poor substitute; writing to *Theology*, he observed that "Christendom has made two efforts to deal with the evil of war—chivalry and pacifism. Neither succeeded. But I doubt whether chivalry has such an unbroken record of failure as pacifism." He was ready to cheer on the troops.

Tolkien was primed as well. He, like Barfield, held a personal grudge against the Nazis, for besmirching whatever pride he felt in his German ancestry and for persecuting Jews, many of whom he counted as friends. His feelings boiled over in a magnificent letter addressed on July 25, 1938, to the Potsdam firm of Rütten & Loening, which planned a German edition of *The Hobbit* and had inquired about Tolkien's *arisch* (Aryan) background. "I regret," Tolkien icily responded, "that I am not clear as to what you intend by *arisch* . . . But if I am to understand that you are enquiring whether I am of *Jewish* origin, I can only reply that I regret that I appear to have *no* ancestors of that gifted people." For good measure, he added, with prescience, that if such inquiries continued, "the time is not far distant when a German name will no longer be a source of pride." Five months later, the Foreign Office approached him about working as a cryptographer if war should break out, and from March 27 to 30, 1939, he took the office's four-day cryptography course. In October, however, for reasons that remain obscure but that may be connected to Edith's precarious health, the office told him that his services would not be required.

Predictably, Williams had a more idiosyncratic view of the matter. He was convinced that the British, outmanned and outgunned, would lose to the Germans, and as a result he refused to endorse the war effort. Late one evening, Alice Hadfield spotted Williams and her future husband, an OUP employee, marching together up Oxford Street, Williams chanting

"We don't want to fight for Czechoslovakis" and his companion replying "Hear! Hear!" Prewar gloom had overspread Amen House. Esprit de corps had vanished, due in large measure to Williams's own conflicted views. With palpable confusion and an edge of despair, he confessed to Alice that "if there were war I could wish we could all die together—as it is we shall have to hold separately to the Doctrine by ourselves . . . I am as terrified of my old age as you were of your immediate future, but I reject the terror."

Events outmarched his terror and his defiance. A day or two later, on September 1, Hitler invaded Poland. Warnie, recalled to active service, headed to Yorkshire. The next day, Lewis sent him a letter that he signed, looking ahead and fearing the worst, "God save you, brother." On September 3 at 11:15 a.m., Britain declared war on Germany. Tolkien, just returned from daily Mass, could not hide his agitation from Priscilla. Twenty-four hours later, Amen House and its employees, including Charles Williams, relocated to Oxford.

12

WAR, AGAIN

W hen Charles Williams, his clothes grimy from London soot, stepped off a train onto the Oxford platform on September 4, 1939, he entered a city that had changed dramatically. With the government's proclamation at 11:07 a.m. on August 31 to "Evacuate Forthwith!" Operation Pied Piper had gone into effect, and up to three million children, mothers of young children, pregnant women, and invalids had fled possible German air attacks by moving out of major metropolitan areas. Ten to fifteen thousand child evacuees arrived in Oxford, to be crammed in wherever room could be found, not only in professorial residences like the Kilns but in empty cinemas and university towers. Blackout conditions ruled, plunging the cobbled streets into near-absolute darkness on moonless nights. The Examination Schools became a military hospital, the Ministry of Food commandeered St. John's College, and the Ministry of Agriculture occupied a portion of Pembroke College, delighting Tolkien with a newly erected sign, PESTS: FIRST FLOOR. The university instituted a two-year "war degree," but even that pittance tried the patience of many students who, matriculating at seventeen, joined the armed forces at eighteen and headed to the Continent or farther afield to be mowed down by Axis guns. The death rate was shocking; Jan Morris reports, in a typical instance, that "of the Trinity boat crew which won the Eights Week races in 1939, all but two died." This slaughter notwithstanding, the "bewildered university," as Tolkien described it, carried on as best it could with smaller classes and periodic food shortages, contributing to the war effort not only through enlistees but through faculty research, most notably when Professor of Pathology Howard Florey and his staff developed, in the early 1940s, a technique to process penicillin for clinical use.

In the midst of this transformation the Inklings thrived. War famously induces in those far from carnage, at least for a time, a giddy excitement, a sense of living in suspension, betwixt and between, plucked by the hand of history from the suffocating confines of ordinary life. So it was for many of the Oxford intelligentsia. Lewis, describing to Warnie a Thursday night meeting in November, wrote that "I have never in my life seen Dyson so exuberant—'a roaring cataract of nonsense.'" After dining at the Eastgate Hotel, the troupe returned to Lewis's rooms at Magdalen to hear a chapter from the new *Hobbit*, a nativity play by Williams ("unusually intelligible for him, and approved by all"), and a portion of Lewis's *The Problem of Pain*.

This was the usual fare: at nearly every meeting of the band, as the readings ventured into new territory (Lewis's apologetics, Williams's study of Dante, medical treatises by Havard), the humor delighted, the conversation sparkled, and the beer flowed freely. The exhilaration of these wartime gatherings was due in large measure to Williams. Cast up on Oxford shores, he became a regular on Thursday nights and instantly impressed his hectic personality upon the groups. He declaimed long passages from his plays, novels, and essays; he speculated, challenged, and joked, always in motion, a whirling dervish in mind and body. Lewis started to think along Williamsesque lines, acquiring a fascination for Arthurian myth and weighing the possibility of using Earth rather than outer space as a stage for fantasy fiction (these twin interests would culminate in his 1945 fantasy, *That Hideous Strength*). Dyson ascended to new heights of biting humor; learning of Williams's interest in chastity, he declared that his new friend was "becoming a common chastitute." Some of the quieter Inklings, caught up in the excitement, began to join in more vigorously: Havard read papers on mountain climbing and on the nature of pain, while Adam Fox recited poetry. Warnie, when he returned in May 1940 from the Continent, read from the manuscript of *The Splendid Century: Life in the France of Louis XIV*, his quirky, insightful study of seventeenth-century France, filled with a brooding sense of the dark tidal forces that rule history, altogether a surprise for those who had weighed up the elder Lewis as little more than his younger brother's duller, boozier sidekick. Havard remembered Warnie's reading as "very witty . . . very good . . . It took us out of the theological atmosphere into another world." Nonetheless, Lewis and Tolkien continued to dominate meetings, Tolkien reading sections of the new *Hobbit*, Lewis bits of works in progress, including his translation of the *Aeneid*, a text that survives only in fragments, pieced together and published in 2011 as *C. S. Lewis's Lost Aeneid: Arms and the Exile*.

Visitors, too, breached the gates, now and then generating friction within the core group. One Tuesday morning, Tolkien arrived at the Bird and Baby with Williams in tow and spied "a strange tall gaunt man half in khaki half in mufti with a large wide-awake hat, bright eyes and a hooked nose, sitting in the corner," looking very much like Trotter (Strider's original name) at the Inn of the Prancing Pony in *The Lord of the Rings*, as Tolkien noted in a letter to Christopher on October 6, 1944. The mysterious figure was Roy Campbell, a right-wing Catholic poet who had fought for Franco in the Spanish Civil War and had arrived in Oxford partly in order to meet Lewis. Lewis, however, despised Campbell (whom he had previously parodied in *The Oxford Magazine*), ostensibly for his fascism. Tolkien, who felt some kinship with Campbell over their shared faith, suspected that Lewis's dislike was inspired in part by anti-Catholic bigotry, and he complained bitterly to Christopher that when Lewis heard of Catholic priests being murdered, as happened frequently in Spain during the 1930s, he "really thinks they asked for it." Another odd visitor who attended several Inklings meetings was E. R. Eddison, a childhood pal of Arthur Ransome and author of *The Worm Ouroboros* (1922), a rococo space fantasy set on Mercury. Lewis adored *Ouroboros*, reading it at least six times and praising it and Eddison's other novels as "a new literary species, a new rhetoric, a new climate of the imagination." Eddison had crafted for his novels an artificial, dense, mock-medieval voice, first cousin to Morris's and Tolkien's heigh stile, and he and Lewis took to corresponding with one another in this register. His account of his first Thursday night gathering catches the flavor of the group, of his peculiar manner, and of this curious exchange of letters:

And so to that quincunciall symposium, at ease about your sea-cole fire, in your privat chaumbre, where (as it seemed to mee)

good discourse made night's horses gallop too faste; & so to our
goodnight walke & adieux in the gate under your great Towre . . .
For my self, I tasted wisdome as wel as good ale at your fireside . . .
If our talk were battledore & shuttlecock, what matter? 'Twas merry
talk, & truth will sometimes appere, better than in statu, in the
swift flying to & again of the shuttlecock.

As the gaming analogy shows, Eddison grasped the essence of the Inklings' method: thrashing out the truth through verbal play. But he never
shared their vision of truth, disdaining in his fiction and in his few published letters such Christian virtues as simplicity and poverty. Tolkien,
who vastly admired Eddison's literary skills, ranking him the most gifted
of all inventors of imaginary worlds, described the philosophy that permeates every page of *Ouroboros* and his other novels as a celebration of
"arrogance and cruelty." Tolkien may be unjust in this assessment; Eddison admired grandeur, strength, brooding intelligence, and refined beauty,
qualities that, under Mercury's perverse skies, flourish in lieu of love, compassion, and hobbitlike humility. Perhaps because of Tolkien's objections—
the two butted heads from the start—Eddison never became a regular
among the Inklings.

More significant—and perplexing—were Tolkien's reservations about
Charles Williams. His response to Williams seemed inversely keyed to
Lewis's; the more Lewis admired Williams, the more Tolkien demurred.
Some scholars have put his disaffection down to plain jealousy of the
man who displaced him as Lewis's best friend. There is truth in this; by
1939, Lewis had absorbed most of Tolkien's ideas and literary motifs and
was ready to be dazzled by someone new. In a letter he would write to his
former pupil Mary Neylan shortly after Williams's death, Lewis refers to
him as "my great friend Charles Williams, my friend of friends, the com-
forter of all our little set, the most angelic"; small wonder that the sensitive Tolkien felt elbowed aside.

Nonetheless, Tolkien enjoyed Williams's company and valued his
critical acumen. During the war, he wrote a poem that reveals, if not his
deepest feelings about Williams, at least those he was willing to express;
in it he calls Williams "dear Charles" and lauds his "subtle mind," his
"virtues," and his "wisdom." He and Williams drank together, went on midnight strolls together, regaled one another at Inklings gatherings. Tolkien

went out of his way to help Williams lecture at the university and, most tellingly, loaned him portions of the *Hobbit* sequel while still in manuscript (Williams immediately put his finger on one great strength of the tale: the bucolic peace of the Shire in contrast to the wrenching horrors of war). But mutual affability notwithstanding, Tolkien disdained William's literary works, declaring in 1965 that he found them "wholly alien, and sometimes very distasteful, occasionally ridiculous." Whence the antipathy? Distrusting Williams's penchant for magic, he may have suspected (correctly) that behind these plot devices lay personal occult experience kept strictly hidden from the Inklings. It is easy to understand why, when Lewis wrote in the 1947 Festschrift *Essays Presented to Charles Williams* that "he gave to every circle the whole man," Tolkien scribbled in the margin of his personal copy, "No, I think not."

Visions in War Time

The tensions between Inklings and guests and among Inklings themselves reveal not only ideological friction but the fraught atmosphere of the age. Britain faced an implacable, fanatical foe; as the initial euphoria of war receded, the shadow of pain, privation, disease, and death loomed ever larger. A few weeks before the outbreak of war—as if an augury of things to come—Tolkien had suffered, while on holiday in Worcestershire, a concussion whose baleful effects had lasted for months. At the same time, Edith had fallen dreadfully sick; cancer was suspected. By December, doctors had settled upon a more benign diagnosis, but Tolkien now found himself beset with worries about his children. His first concern was John, who had graduated from Exeter College in the summer of 1939 and in November had arrived at the Venerable English College in Rome to begin studies for the Roman Catholic priesthood. From the start, John's position was precarious. Italy would not declare war upon England until June 1940, but it was already allied with Germany and hostile to British interests. The college authorities decided to evacuate, and on May 16, 1940, six days after the Nazis swept through Belgium, France, Luxembourg, and the Netherlands, John and a contingent of fellow seminarians fled Rome in disguise. They arrived in the French port of Le Havre in the nick of time, catching the last boat before German troops arrived. John's hairbreadth escape did little to end Tolkien's concerns, however, for a few weeks later, his son Michael quit Oxford to join the RAF. He fought as an antiaircraft gunner during the Battle of Britain, received the George Medal, and later saw combat in France and Germany. Christopher, too, entered the Royal Air Force, training as a pilot in South Africa from 1943 to 1945.

In addition to illness and worry, Tolkien felt hemmed in by the domestic routines imposed by war. A portion of the garden now housed a chicken coop, and he spent much time tending to the hens and repairing the structure. His duties as an air raid warden proved exhausting; they included preparing the neighborhood for enemy attack and checking on adherence to blackout regulations, tasks that sometimes entailed all-night encampment at local headquarters. On one occasion his fellow warden, the kindly Jewish historian Cecil Roth, awoke him from a fitful sleep just in time to attend Mass at St. Aloysius; Tolkien thought the service "seemed like a fleeting glimpse of an unfallen world." But Eden proved elusive. As the war ground on, his spirits sank and his letters overflowed with disgust at mankind ("A small knowledge of history depresses one with the sense of the everlasting mass and weight of human iniquity"), at the world ("How stupid everything is!"), and at his own inability to fight, hampered as he was by age and responsibilities ("I feel like a lame canary in a cage").

Still, now and then happiness broke the gloom. New friendships blossomed, notably with Robert Murray, a student at Corpus Christi College and grandson of Sir James Augustus Henry Murray, editor of the *Oxford English Dictionary*. Young Murray soon became a family favorite and under the guidance of Tolkien and others entered the Catholic Church after the war and later joined the Jesuits; Tolkien would give him a prepublication typescript of *The Lord of the Rings* to evaluate, a sign of highest esteem. There was cheerful news within the family as well. Halfway through the war, Michael and his wife, Joan, gave Tolkien and Edith their first grandchild, Michael George Reuel. At around the same time, Tolkien became godfather to David Havard, the Useless Quack's son. Priscilla, a child when the war began, turned sixteen before its end, and Tolkien took great pleasure in observing her intellectual maturation, noting with delight that she, as he did, preferred *Perelandra* (the second volume in Lewis's Space Trilogy) to *Out of the Silent Planet*. He cultivated a remarkable correspondence with Michael and Christopher, writing letters bursting with family gossip, literary asides, and religious reflections. To Christopher he offered what amounts to an abbreviated course in Catholic living, counseling him to recall always his guardian angel, to aspire to Christian tranquillity, and to memorize the canon of the Mass and various prayers so that he would "never need for words of joy." To Michael he unveiled his soul, declaring, in one of the most memorable spiritual passages to be found in his letters, that "out of the darkness of my life, so much frustrated, I put before you the one great thing to love on earth: the Blessed Sacrament . . . There you will find romance, glory, honour, fidelity, and the true way of all your loves upon earth."

Tolkien's Catholic ardor, nearly always at high pitch, intensified yet more during the war, as the Luftwaffe attacked his homeland and his sons flirted with death abroad. His wartime letters on Catholicism, lengthy, closely argued, and deeply felt, sometimes surprise and even shock readers ignorant of the religious roots of his art, those who imagine him a happy pagan or nothing at all. One of the most startling proclamations came in a letter to Christopher dated November 7–8, 1944, in which Tolkien revealed that he had experienced a "sudden vision" or "apperception" of the "Light of God" (the capital letters are Tolkien's) while deep in Eucharistic adoration at Sts. Gregory & Augustine Church on the Woodstock Road. In the vision, he saw God's Light surrounding and bathing "one small mote," which he realized was himself (although it could have been anyone "that I might think of with love"); he realized, too, that the Light linking God and the mote was a Guardian Angel, "not a thing interposed between God and the creature, but God's very attention itself, personalized." This extraordinary event brought with it a "great sense of joy" and "comfort." Tolkien now knew with unshakable conviction that his loved ones lived always under supernatural protection.

During this period, he inundated Christopher with literary as well as spiritual confessions. He considered his youngest son the perfect sounding board on which to test works in progress: bright, insightful, sensitive to language, quick to notice small discrepancies of plot, and trustworthy as only one's own child can be. He told Christopher that he was writing the new *Hobbit* with him in mind and regularly sent him new sections of typescript as soon as they became available. Christopher in turn responded to each installment with steady enthusiasm and trenchant criticism.

While working on his tale, Tolkien continued to experiment with pencil and paint, turning out landscapes, buildings, and other subjects based on the *Hobbit* sequel. Towers, fortresses, and mountains abound, curiously static subjects for such a swiftly moving tale; yet their dark, brooding, militaristic atmosphere reflects the fear and gloom that pervaded England during much of World War II. Scholars have long quarreled over which of the two world wars cast a greater shadow over *The Lord of the Rings*. The consensus favors World War I, for then Tolkien experienced firsthand the horrors of trench warfare, but World War II left its mark as well. Tolkien began writing the new *Hobbit* in December 1937, as prewar anxiety neared a climax, and he worked on it feverishly, albeit in bits and spurts, throughout the six years of active fighting. Parallels between Hitler and Sauron occur to almost every reader of the novel and surely occurred to Tolkien during composition. In his 1966 foreword to the second edition, he goes to great lengths to discount the influence of World War II on the book, declaring that the text contains nothing "topical" and that "little or nothing in it was modified" by the clash between Axis and Allies. One may be excused for discerning in these protestations the author's insistent view of his work as a subcreation, an imaginative exercise in service to God, rather than an allegorical restatement of the politics of his age.

Subcreation, however, is clearly the theme of "Leaf by Niggle," a short story that Tolkien wrote just before the outbreak of war and published in *The Dublin Review* in January 1945. The idea for the tale came to him in a dream or reverie, for one day "I awoke with it already in mind." The story tells of a "little man called Niggle," an artist who, although frustrated by constant interruptions, manages to paint a leaf that becomes a tree that becomes a landscape—an obvious allegorical recounting of the creation of Tolkien's endlessly expanding legendarium. Before Niggle finishes his painting, he goes on a journey (that is, he dies), finds himself in a Workhouse (purgatory), is released, and winds up inside his own canvas, where he discovers his Tree, complete and perfect, its leaves "as he had imagined them rather than as he had made them," and beyond them the Mountains, foretelling "something different, a further stage" (heaven). Niggle, through his long and painful artistic labors, has created something beautiful, intelligible, and good, a finite creation that points to the infinite. Tolkien tells the tale in simple, direct prose—reading Lewis's novels may have proved beneficial—with none of the dense elegiac manner of *The Lord of the Rings*. "Leaf by Niggle" is his most successful short story, an evocative account of the artist's calling and a worthy counterpart to the more theoretical presentation of the same material in "On Fairy-Stories."

"Blue as a Whortle-Berry"

As the war expanded, Barfield trudged to his law office, day by tedious day. He knew by now that law would never replace literature, nor would legal discourse compensate for the loss of philosophical give-and-take with Lewis. He had fallen into a "colorless" existence. During the London Blitz, the firm moved to the suburbs, and for a time he, Maud, and the kids camped in a bus in a Buckinghamshire field. Country sights and smells offered relief from office monotony, but his frustration and boredom intensified. He tried his best to find deep meaning in legal procedures, presenting at an Inklings gathering in the early 1940s "Poetic Diction and Legal Fiction," a paper that draws analogies between the poetic world he had regretfully abandoned and the legal world in which he was now immersed. Both worlds mature through a process Barfield calls *tarning*, the act of "saying one thing and meaning another"—not in the sense of lying but of using figurative language (simile, metaphor, symbol) so that a new or original poetic (or legal) understanding may result. Tarning, then, plays a role in "the long, slow movement of the human mind." Long, complex, and wistful, the essay concludes on a note of frustration as Barfield laments modern culture's failure to grasp the importance of metaphor, the evolution of language, and the blossoming of consciousness. Indeed, Barfield was as frustrated as a man could be, in his legal profession, in his literary vocation, in his inability to convince Lewis and the world of the value of Anthroposophy.

He was discouraged, too, by the failure of so many to grasp the magnitude of Hitler's threat. World War II came to him, according to his grandson, as "a great trauma," not least because of his love for German culture and language. On May 28, 1940, his mother died at the age of seventy-nine (his father had passed away just before the war); Lewis, in a letter of condolence sent a few days later, perceptively linked "this particular desolation . . . to the general one in which we all are." As the war progressed, Barfield's depression deepened; on August 20, 1942, Lewis described his friend as being "blue as a whortle-berry." Barfield did what he could to ameliorate his situation. He wrote a short play on Jason and Medea, which he read before the Inklings in late November 1944. The reading was well received, but Barfield recalled years later making the unsettling discovery, when he had finished his presentation, that "at least three of those present . . . had written poems about Medea themselves in the past"—hardly a circumstance to assuage doubts about one's literary originality.

During the same year, he published *Romanticism Comes of Age* with an obscure Anthroposophical publishing house. In 1945 he and Maud welcomed a third child into the family, Geoffrey Corbett (later Jeffrey Barfield), born June 6, 1940, a refugee from German air raids. Around the same time, he befriended Walter de la Mare, with whom he argued Steiner, poetry, and language at the Athenaeum Club and at de la Mare's residence in Twickenham. Barfield helped his new friend improve at least one poem, "The Traveller," and in turn de la Mare invited Barfield to lunch with T. S. Eliot, who seemed, Barfield thought, to carry around him an "aura of unhappiness"—but perhaps this was only a reflection of Barfield's own pervasive gloom. Whatever the case, these rare upbeat moments served largely to accentuate his growing despair over powers unused, ideas spurned, a voice prematurely silenced.

Williams Unbound

Williams's voice, on the other hand, was now reaching its highest development, in the lecture halls, pubs, and dons' quarters of Oxford. In London he had lectured to night classes and weekend poets. In Oxford, within six months of arrival, he marched under Lewis's auspices into the Divinity School to discourse on Milton's *Comus* (a masque celebrating the inviolability of a true Lady's virtue) and pulled off the remarkable and perhaps unprecedented coup of holding an undergraduate audience rapt with a paean to chastity (this was the talk that had triggered Dyson's scornful remark about Williams being a common chastitute). Lewis, aglow with admiration, proclaimed that "that beautiful carved room had probably not witnessed anything so important since some of the great mediaeval or Reformation lectures. I have at last, if only for once, seen a university doing what it was founded to do: teaching Wisdom."

Williams was overjoyed. Finally he had arrived in the intellectual firmament, a heaven on earth peopled, for once in his life, by men. "Am I only to be followed by the feminine?" he asked his wife on March 5, answering the rhetorical question in the negative before adding, in high-spirited tribute to her, that "you will be attended—you—by the masculine minds, great minds, strong males, brothers of our energy—those who know our work—Lewis & Eliot & Raymond & Tolkien & the young males; and they, having read me, will look for You & walk round you, & admire, & say 'This was the Origin of all, and the continual Friend and Supporter.'" He knew what his wife wanted to hear—sometimes it seemed to him that he knew what every woman wanted to hear—and he bragged to Florence that "it was Anne [Ridler], I think, who once wrote that I was about as aware of women as Jesus Christ; it is (omitting the comparison) largely true."

Male and female alike fell under his spell. He lectured at St. Mary the Virgin, the Taylor Institute, Pusey House, St. Margaret Hall, Reading University, Birmingham University, on Shakespeare, King Arthur, love, hell, religion and drama, whatever ignited his tinderbox mind. Everywhere, he triumphed. T. S. Eliot, who watched him lecture, said that Williams "held his audiences in rapt attention, and left with them the contagion of his own enthusiastic curiosity." Flushed with success, Williams crowed to Florence, "I begin to believe I am a genius." In February 1943, in recognition of his services at OUP, the university awarded him an honorary M.A.; afterward, husband and wife enjoyed "loftily lunching with Cabinet Ministers and V.C.s [vice chancellors]." He was the first editor of OUP's London office to receive the honor: "It's obvious that I'm the best person to start on," he allowed. A less public but possibly even more satisfying triumph came the same year, when he and Tolkien scheduled university lectures for the same time slot. Williams talked on *Hamlet* before a packed house, while Tolkien taught Anglo-Saxon to an audience of one, his other students having migrated to hear Williams. After the event, according to at least one report, the two lecturers celebrated together with drinks. Williams was in high spirits; one wonders what Sauronian thoughts scampered through Tolkien's mind as he lifted his glass.

Throughout these triumphs, Williams worked tirelessly for his beloved employers. Conditions on the job were bad: "We work between
gas-masks and sirens," he complained in a letter most likely written in his
new office, a converted bathroom overlooking a hedge at OUP's Southfield House, near the Headington Road in east Oxford. He insisted on
keeping up appearances, even though he found Oxford to be "a kind of
parody of London," arriving at the office each morning in a sober blue suit,
umbrella, and homburg. Responsibilities at the press consumed most of
his energy; what remained he employed largely in writing. His output,
during the last seven years of his life, was prodigious: plays, poems, a
novel, a study of witchcraft, a biography. A few years before his sudden
death at fifty-eight, he produced his finest book, the luminous *The Figure
of Beatrice* (1942).

The Way of Affirmation

The Figure of Beatrice, like all books about Beatrice Portinari, is primarily about the man who loved her. One cannot think of Beatrice apart
from Dante Alighieri, for all that we know about her comes from him;
she exists for us as the great poet's lover, muse, and means of salvation.
The Figure of Beatrice remains true to this pattern, but one of its charms
is that it takes Beatrice seriously in her own right and paints a plausible
portrait, culled from Dantean verses, of the Florentine maiden, wife, and
object of adoration as a dark-complexioned woman with green eyes, a
sweet, low voice, and a disposition passionate and bright, "full of courtesies, and of *amicitia*." To give the flesh-and-blood Beatrice her due was
no small thing, for the tendency in Dantean studies has always been to
read her as a symbol of virtue or heaven or God. For Williams, she is a
symbol of goodness but also a real woman who exemplifies this goodness
and inspires Dante to seek it. By merging the offices of symbol and of
fleshed reality, she becomes, in Williams's precise lexicon, a *figure*—the
principal figure in world literature—of the Way of Affirmation.

Beginning with *Outlines of Romantic Theology* in the early 1920s,
Williams sought to champion this Way, which, as he understood it, describes God through positive attributes—the Good, the Beautiful—and
seeks God through the things of the world, in contrast to the Way of

Negation, which finds its Christian fountainhead in the writings of Pseudo-Dionysius. "Wherever any love is," Williams writes in *The Figure of Beatrice*, "there is either affirmation or rejection of the image, in one or other form. If there is rejection—of that Way there are many records. Of the affirmation, for all its greater commonness, there are fewer records." *The Divine Comedy* was for Williams the most perfect literary exposition of the affirmative way, a view in keeping with the high modern regard for Dante's masterpiece. (Eliot declared it the greatest of all philosophical poems and, in a remarkably audacious phrase, its final canto "the highest point that poetry has ever reached or ever can reach.")

For Williams, as for Dante, the Way of Affirmation is best pursued through love between the sexes. There may be higher modes—Williams gives Christ's healing miracles as an example—but romantic love remains the most familiar, as men and women glimpse heaven in one another's eyes (Williams notes that "elders" may scoff at such love, adding that the reasons for their cynicism can be found "in the ditches of the *Inferno*"). For Dante, the Way opened at the age of nine, when he first encountered Beatrice and heard a voice say, "Now your bliss has appeared"; his subsequent experience proved a compound of bliss and pain, encompassing Beatrice's death at twenty-four, his own exile from Florence, and the subsequent composition, over fourteen years, of the *Commedia*.

What becomes apparent as one reads *The Figure of Beatrice* is that, in tracing Dante's career, Williams is describing his own. He, like Dante, is a Christian poet, a devotee of the spiritual potential of courtly love; he, like Dante, trembles at the beauty of his beloved (it was his habit to explicitly liken women, especially Florence, to Beatrice, once writing to his wife that "if you substitute 'Michal' for 'Beatrice,' you get the whole thing"). Pondering Dante's attraction, after Beatrice's death, to a second woman, the so-called "Lady in the Window," he declares, as if speaking to himself about Phyllis and his other extramarital passions, that such a "second image of the Beatrician kind" is "not to be denied." He goes so far as to muse wistfully on what might be possible if a wife could learn to tolerate a husband's other chaste ardors: "I do not know what new liberties and powers might not be achieved." Such aspirations are never to be realized on this side of the grave, but in paradise, every longing finds its sanctified fulfillment. There Dante's love for Beatrice is subsumed in the beatific vision. Beatrice fulfills the meaning of her name; she is revealed as not only Dante's bliss but the very Way of his blessedness. Might not Dante's experience be Williams's also?

The Figure of Beatrice is a stunning achievement that drained its author. Upon its completion, he was exhausted and frustrated. He feared that he had proved unequal to Dante's vision; his sins had blocked his genius. The book "has slid from being what it ought to be down to what I could make it. One's past rules one; a hundred immoralities that obscure the high things here." He was right to think that his personal history affected his study, but this truth may be applied to almost any writer, almost any book. Sins hobbled Dante as well, at least until the catharsis of repentance recounted in the Purgatorio cleared the way to the incomparable ecstasies of the Paradiso. Williams, peering into Dante's mind and recognizing a fellow sufferer, had been ideally placed to convey in The Figure of Beatrice his predecessor's agonies and longings, if not his spiritual triumphs.

Reviewers lauded his accomplishment. In The Times Literary Supplement, Dermot Michael Macgregor Morrah praised the work for its "delicate sensitiveness" and for "continually evok[ing] rays of fresh light from facets of Dante's jewel," while Hugo Dyson applauded it in The Spectator; the review by Christopher Hollis in The Tablet, a Catholic newspaper, found that it deserved to be "part of the furniture of the mind." In the long run, the most significant response came from Dorothy L. Sayers. A correspondent and friend of Williams since the 1930s, Sayers read Dante for the first time in the afterglow of Williams's study: in August 1943, she had come across a review of The Figure of Beatrice in the Sunday Times, read the book, and decided to tackle Dante's great poem, a task she had put off for years due to her faulty Italian. The following year, huddled in a backyard shelter during an air raid, she began the Temple Classics dual-language Inferno. Dante's brilliant imagery and lightning pace mesmerized her; she finished the poem in five days and wrote Williams immediately, exclaiming with a schoolgirl's excitement that "I found myself panting along with my tongue hanging out, as though it were a serial thriller," and giving Williams full credit for her new passion. Within a few years, these raptures had settled into an iron determination to translate the Commedia into English terza rima—a daunting task, given the scarcity of English rhymes—with an extensive theological and literary commentary. Her

Hell and *Purgatory,* and her unfinished *Paradise* (completed by her god-daughter, the scholar and translator Barbara Reynolds) remain widely read more than half a century after publication.

Meanwhile, Williams's "hundred immoralities"—he identified a few of them to one young acolyte as jealousy, envy, sullenness, and pride—continued without relief. Behind them lay an inability to be at ease with either sex. Men he must impress, women he must teach or rule. He recognized these shortcomings but could not overcome them, a failure leading to internal conflicts that found outward expression in his shaking hands, his restlessness at the podium, his wandering eye, and, quite possibly, his early death. He felt isolated, estranged from his surroundings and himself. "I become more and more a figure, a name, an influence perhaps; less and less a person," he wrote to Alice Hadfield, detailing a disassociation that grew more acute each year. To Florence he described himself as "a pattern, a voice, a name; not a person. I am Bach's *Ninth Symphony,* Shakespeare's *Tempest,* and Da Vinci's *Madonna of the Rocks*": little more than a set of roles and masks. His letters burn with anger and resentment, as he savages others for his inability to feel close to them: "I dislike people, & I hate being with them"; "You can't imagine how I dislike people's *faces*"; "There are wells of hate in one which are terrifying." The dark notes of intertwined and barely controlled megalomania and alienation are unmistakable.

Curiously, his relationship with Florence improved, almost certainly because of the physical distance between them. His ardor for her was deep and sincere, although, in his last years, largely couched in contemplative or platonic terms, yet another mode of distancing. He addressed her as Madonna and declared his love for her to be *"amor intellectualis"*—an exalted phrase, to be sure, but not one that many women welcome from their lovers. He saw Phyllis, back from Java, and dashed off letters to her laced with ecstasies and incoherencies, disclosing in their rambling intensity the strain of trying to co-inhere his work, his writings, and his multiple Beatrices. More than one passage suggests a mind unraveling ("You go on in my head exactly like a trumpet—yes; a kind of sight instantaneously transmuted into sound—a silent sound, I suppose . . . no, of course, I have it wrong; it is sound transmuted into sight, I now realize that you are a kind of sound . . ."). "O, I wish I were free" of her, he cried to Alice Hadfield in a moment of clarity.

But other enchantments and enchainments waited in the wings. In the summer of 1943, Lois Lang-Sims, a young (twenty-six-year-old) spiritual seeker fascinated by Williams's writings, wrote him a letter about *The Figure of Beatrice*. He responded, as he usually did, with generosity and genuine interest. In October, he and Lang-Sims met at his lodgings at 9 South Parks Road. The young woman thought the great man "deferential and authoritarian"; he poured ideas and observations at her and over her, while she noted with wonder "the constant jerky movements of his limbs and the muscles of his face." Walking home, she decided that Williams's behavior revealed a man "incapable of . . . a human relationship on a personal basis. I sensed that he was totally identified with, and enclosed within, his own myth." But she was drawn to him, and he to her, and some months later the two met for lunch at the Randolph Hotel, where he ticked off on her fingers the initiatory order to "Love—obey—pray—play—and be intelligent." She was henceforth one of his acolytes, a member of the Companions of the Co-inherence, which must have numbered at least a dozen and perhaps many more by now. Soon he gave her additional instructions: to practice substitution, to dot her palm with a pencil mark each time she failed, to write three times "Sir, I am the most exquisite dunce who ever lived." He threatened to beat her for her imperfections. In December, he struck the palm of her hand with a ruler, hard enough to hurt, after which a "torrent of words poured from his lips, while he strode around the room, his head jerking sideways as he talked." Lang-Sims, who had never taken his threatened punishments as more than poetic imagery, was "stunned with shock." Soon after, Williams warned her that "next year of course will be stricter."

And so it was. He bestowed upon her a new name, that of Lalage, the slave girl. He gave her new, virtuous tasks—to pray for friends, to excel in charity. He believed in her potential, both spiritual and poetic, and read to the Inklings her essay on Milton, while carefully omitting those phrases in her text that hinted at his strange relationship with her. But how should he nurture her potential? He ordered her to stand in corners and to bind her own ankles with string. In February 1944, Lang-Sims took the train up from London "in a painfully divided state," still swept off her feet yet confused by Williams's behavior, aware that he "had manoeuvered me into a position where I could not refuse him anything without seeming to refuse him everything." He met her bewildered innocence with another punishment, best told in her own words: "After I had kissed his hand, kneeling on one knee, and he had kissed mine, he told me to bend over a chair and lift up my skirt. When I did so, he took the ruler and struck me hard on the behind."

Lang-Sims returned home "in a state of dangerous exhaustion," and retreated to her bed. She remained there for six weeks. Unable to escape her role as Lalage, she wrote to Williams, declaring that her "punishment had been inadequate." He replied that the thin walls of his room had restrained his hand and that next time "I will play my part with more rigour." But there would be no next time. Lang-Sims had had enough. She confronted Williams in May, accusing him of reducing her to a figure in a myth. He agreed instantly, handed her—as a memento or a bit of spite—his wife's obscure little volume, *Christian Symbolism*, and dismissed her with a "Go with God." Master and acolyte corresponded fitfully and met for lunch a year later, but "nothing was as it had been before."

What led Williams to indulge in ritualized sadistic behavior with a much younger woman unable to determine, much less express, her own wishes in the matter? Lang-Sims, who later authored several books (including *The Christian Mystery: An Exposition of Esoteric Christianity*), believed that Williams was practicing a form of sexual magic to accumulate power. Circumstantial evidence supports her theory. He was, of course, an expert in ritual occultism, experiencing it firsthand as a member of the Fellowship of the Rosy Cross and employing it as a plot device in his novels. In an unpublished 1940 letter to Phyllis, he discusses the sexual energy generated by contemplation of her arms and links it to imagination and intellect. Lang-Sims found parallels to Williams's presumed thought and practice in Tantrism; both offered, she believed, access to "power through sexual transcendence" based upon the interplay of arousal and restraint. A more mundane explanation presents itself, however: that Williams harbored impulses, largely kept under control— he was, after all, a benevolent and generous man—that erupted in the intense stress of the war years, a sexual analogue to his twitching limbs and incoherent letters. There are indications that Lang-Sims may not have been his only victim. Sadism was long a component of his imagination; as early as 1930, he had written to Phyllis that "I am sadistic towards you, but within the sadism is mastery, and within the mastery is government, within the government is instruction, within the instruction, service . . ." and, in a later letter, "I wouldn't hurt a fly unless it made it perfectly clear that it liked it. And then only a little. And then only for the conversation."

All this is painful to read, difficult to assimilate. Only the hopelessly naïve believe that someone who writes beautifully about Christianity (or any religion) is incapable of such behavior; yet invariably it shocks to discover such extreme disconnection between public pronouncement and private life. The revelations of Lang-Sims and others dismayed, when they did not devastate, Williams's admirers. Some felt betrayed, some turned upon the messenger, some said that the disclosures came as no surprise, for everyone is a sinner. Williams, who believed in original sin, would have agreed.

His behavior and his antic letters suggest a mind cracking under immense psychic pressures: not only those occasioned by loneliness, thwarted ambition, and repressed sexuality, but those triggered by his need always and everywhere to keep secret his private life. They show, too, that he was a master of disguise. In *The Listener* of December 1946, T. S. Eliot proclaimed him "a man of unusual genius" and possessor of "an extended spiritual sense"; ten years later, W. H. Auden wrote that "in his [Williams's] company one felt twice as intelligent and infinitely nicer than, out of it, one knew oneself to be." All this is true. But what does one make of Eliot's declaration, in his 1948 introduction to *All Hallows' Eve*, that "I have never known a healthier-minded man than Williams" and that he was "a gay and simple man," or of Auden's observation, after meeting with Williams, that "for the first time in my life [I] felt myself in the presence of personal sanctity," or of Lewis's claim that Williams "was extremely attractive to young women and (what is rare) none of his male friends ever wondered why: nor did it ever do a young woman anything but immense good to be attracted by Charles Williams"?

The truth is, Williams was not simple and happy but complex and tortured. He was not a saint but had his saintly side, which came and went, radiant and sincere as long as it lasted. Lewis came closer to the truth when he described Williams as double-sided, by which he meant that he was a pessimist in feelings, an optimist in faith. The full truth is that Williams was multisided, presenting himself, as it suited him or as his obsessions demanded, in one role or guise or mythological mode after another. Lewis also came close to the mark when he noted that a friend of Williams, whom Lewis does not identify, "always found Williams a reserved man, one in whom, after years of friendship, there remained something elusive and incalculable." Just so. He was to students a mesmerizing classroom performer; to magicians a master magus; to young women a sage, a disciplinarian, a platonic lover; to men of his own age an artist, a thinker, a poet; to all, at one time or another, an inspiration. It may be that no one—not his wife, not even he himself—knew him as he really was. "I am certain as one can be of anything," said Lang-Sims, "that no one ever really penetrated beneath the mask-like image that Charles presented of himself."

Culture in War Time

The Kilns had never been so alive. In addition to Lewis, Warnie, and Mrs. Moore (Maureen had married and departed in 1940), animals galore roamed the property, including two swans (a gift from the president of Magdalen), a dog (the beloved Papworth, who died in 1936 and was replaced by the frequently barking, sometimes incontinent, much despised Bruce), cats, and countless chickens, badgers, foxes, rabbits, birds, snakes, and frogs. Tending these animals was Fred Paxford, caretaker and gardener, who lived in a bungalow on the property. Paxford was a wizard with fruits, vegetables, and chickens, and skilled enough at feeding swans, mending roofs, and burying dead pets, but he was surrounded by a nimbus of gloom, usually expressed in prophecies of impending disaster (later he served as the model for the aptly named Puddleglum in *The Chronicles of Narnia*). A typical Paxfordism, explaining why the Kilns lacked sugar on the table, runs as follows: "Well, you never know when the end of the world will come and we don't want to be left with sugar on our hands. What'll we do with it then, eh?" Warnie disliked him intensely, in part because Mrs. Moore quoted him as an authority on every subject and took to taunting Warnie by calling him Pax-Warnie; he struck back in the safety of his diary with an anemic "Bugger Paxford." The gardener, for his part, had kind words for everyone at the Kilns, notably Mrs. Moore, whom he described as "like a mother to Mr. Jack . . . She was also very good to me . . . She bottled a lot of fruit and gave a lot of it away. She gave a lot of eggs away as well. She had a kind nature. Anyone who came to the Kilns for help nearly always went away with money, and if it was a man, a handful of cigarettes."

The primary source of congestion in this eccentric Noah's Ark was the influx of refugees fleeing London and other big cities. On September 2, 1939, a group of four young girls had arrived at the Kilns. Lewis wrote immediately to Warnie, who had been summoned to active duty and posted to North Yorkshire, that "our schoolgirls have arrived and all seem to me—and, what's more important, to Minto—to be very nice, unaffected creatures and all most flatteringly delighted with their new surroundings." The girls—only girls, a restriction set by Mrs. Moore and the Lewis brothers—came in waves throughout the war. They adored Mrs. Moore, her evident devotion to Lewis, her funny habit of dangling a cigarette from the corner of her mouth. Patricia Boshell, an evacuee who lived at the Kilns in 1940, recalled her as "kind, solicitous, and indeed, most forbearing." Boshell and the other evacuees loved Lewis, too, who greeted them warmly and helped them with their homework. Lewis tutored Boshell in Latin and Greek and arranged to pay her tuition at Oxford University on the condition that the gift remain a secret.

Another evacuee, June Flewett, who arrived in 1943—she would later marry Clement Freud, a member of Parliament and grandson of Sigmund Freud—greatly admired both brothers. Warnie she found "comfy to be with all the time and obviously highly intelligent" and devoted to music: "Almost every Sunday night the brothers listened to a complete symphony on Major Lewis's old gramophone. It had a large, wooden, handmade horn. The sound was good and he was proud of it; no one else was allowed to use it." Lewis's great gift to her, not surprisingly, was books: "what Jack Lewis imposed—I should say unwittingly and continually impressed on me—were ideas and books . . . he told me to go to Blackwell's Bookshop in Oxford, anytime, and buy any book I wanted on his account . . . Lewis was the first person who made me believe that I was an intelligent human being and the whole of the time I was there he built up my confidence in myself and in my ability to think and understand." Flewett's admiration for her hosts was warmly reciprocated; when she prepared to quit the Kilns in 1945 to train as an actress in London, Warnie wrote in his diary that "our dear, delightful June Flewett leaves us tomorrow, after nearly two years . . . She is not yet eighteen, but I have met no one of any age further advanced in the Christian way of life. From seven in the morning till nine at night . . . she has slaved at The Kilns, for a fraction 2d an hour; I have never seen her other than gay, eager to anticipate exigent demands, never complaining, always self accusing in the frequent crises of that dreary house." Lewis gave her a book inscribed with the following note:

Beauty and brains and virtue never dwell
Together in one place, the critics say.
Yet we have known a case
You must not ask her name
But seek it 'twixt July and May.

Lewis not only enjoyed Flewett and the other evacuees; he drew literary inspiration from them, eventually using them as models for the young protagonists in *The Chronicles of Narnia*. But he was unable, when at home, to spend as much time with them as he might have wished. Shortly after Great Britain declared war on the Third Reich, austerity measures swept the nation, and the university suspended all lectureships; his annual income plummeted and he took on the dreaded task of grading School Certificates to compensate for the loss, complaining of the new work to Warnie, now serving at a base supply depot in Le Havre, France. As the war ground on, the niggling tasks multiplied. Lewis made sure that the Kilns met blackout requirements, by means of a "most complicated Arthur Rackham system of odd rags—quite effectively but at the cost of much labour. Luckily I do most of the rooms myself, so it doesn't take me nearly so long as if I were assisted." He tried not to grumble about rationing—in early 1940, butter, sugar, and pork products had become controlled foods, followed soon by other beloved British staples, including tea, cheese, and jam. This led to obsessive hoarding on Mrs. Moore's part, but Lewis fought off panic, writing to Arthur that "I think a great deal of nonsense is talked about rationing. I've never been hungry yet—in fact the only way it affects me is to plunge me back into the pleasures of early boyhood."

He did, however, brood over Warnie's safety. Afraid that prayers might amount to doubting God's providence, he scribbled in his notebook,

"How can I ask thee Father to defend / In peril of war my brother's head to-day." But pray he did, answering his question with additional lines suggesting that prayer is a way to share God's "eternal will." Out of kindness and blood duty and to relieve his own anxiety, he sent Warnie long frequent letters packed with gossip, news, memories, and literary asides. Lewis hated the filial separation, hated the terror and deprivation of armed conflict. Before the war, he had confessed to Griffiths that "if its got to be, its got to be. But the flesh is weak and selfish and I think death wd. be much better than to live through another war." He felt, as Warnie did, a "ghostly feeling that it has all happened before—that one fell asleep during the last war and had a delightful dream and has now waked up again," and wished he could hibernate through the whole affair or wake up from the dream and find himself "safely dead and not quite damned." But once plunged into the wartime ethos, in many ways he found it to be a profound stimulant, as he wrote Arthur: "for me, personally, [the war] has come in the nick of time: I was just beginning to get too well settled in my profession, too successful, and probably self complacent."

As a nearly forty-one-year-old don, responsible for teaching younger undergraduates exempt from service, Lewis had every reason to hope that he would be spared the horrors of battle. A troubling dilemma remained, one faced by all students and teachers at Oxford who stayed behind while others went to die on their behalf, and by the university itself, which might be obliged at any moment to suspend regular operations: How could one justify the intellectual life in time of war? This quandary furnished the subject for Lewis's first sermon, "None Other Gods: Culture in War Time" (later published as "Christians in Danger," then as "Learning in War-Time"), preached at St. Mary the Virgin on October 22, 1939. With a world war once more threatening to derail the education and possibly cost the lives of the undergraduates in the pews, Lewis voiced the inevitable question: "What is the use of beginning a task which we have so little chance of finishing? . . . why should we—indeed how can we—continue to take an interest in these placid occupations when the lives of our friends and the liberties of Europe are in the balance?"

The answer, for Lewis, has to do with the nature of Christian vocation. A Christian may be called to heroic exertion and sacrifice or to more humble tasks. The main thing is to stay at one's post. If the life of a scholar is good in ordinary times, Lewis maintains, it remains good during war;

if it is a frivolity during war, it has no place in a world at peace. "If we had foolish un-Christian hopes about human culture, they are now shattered. If we thought we were building up a heaven on earth . . . we are disillusioned, and not a moment too soon. But if we thought that for some souls, and at some times, the life of learning, humbly offered to God, was, in its own small way, one of the appointed approaches to the Divine reality and the Divine beauty which we hope to enjoy hereafter, we can think so still."

Meanwhile, there were other ways to serve. There were schoolgirls to tend to and anxieties to calm, with Mrs. Moore expecting a German invasion of the Kilns any day and bomb alerts becoming a matter of routine. There were honorable civilian roles; in the summer of 1940, after the fall of France, Lewis joined the recently formed Local Defence Volunteers (later called the Home Guard), which meant spending "one night in nine mooching about the most depressing and malodorous parts of Oxford with a rifle." The real war work for Lewis, however, would be defense of the faith and, nearly as important, defense of the integrity of literary experience. England was under siege from without, but Christianity and Western culture were under siege from within, and that was a battle— a war of attrition for the most part—that Lewis was prepared to fight with every weapon at his disposal. As he put it to Warnie, "I can never forget Tolkien's Spanish friend who, after having several colleges pointed out to him by name from the roof of the Radder [the Radcliffe Camera], observed with surprise 'So this was once a Christian country?'"

"I Am a Very Ordinary Layman . . ."

Lewis had been a Christian for twelve years now, with all the expected peaks and troughs; the war gave him fresh motive for diligence in observing the sacraments and other ordinances of the faith. In October, after much trepidation, he resolved to make his first confession, the Anglican principle being that "none must, all may, some should" confess privately to a priest. This "auricular" confession was a significant step beyond the General Confession that is a regular part of the liturgy, and Lewis worried that it might make him morbidly self-concerned. Fortunately, he found an able and holy confessor in Fr. Walter Adams of the Society of Saint John the Evangelist (the "Cowley Fathers"), the Anglican Benedictine community founded in 1865 by Richard Meux Benson as part of the Anglo-Catholic revival.

Having adopted Father Adams as his spiritual director, Lewis began to go regularly for confession to the Cowley Fathers' motherhouse in Oxford or to the Anglo-Catholic Church of St. Mary Magdalen (known at the time as the "highest church in Oxford"). Although Tolkien gives him no credit for this, Lewis had a strong sense of the unique power and authority of the priest to provide spiritual direction and instruction. To Mary Neylan, his former pupil and friend who regularly poured her troubles into his ear, he expressed doubts about the appropriateness of anyone, other than a priest or doctor, being "told too many of his neighbour's secrets—unless, of course, there is some desperate need." Yet Lewis never identified with the Anglo-Catholic movement, which he pillories in the character of Neo-Angular in *The Pilgrim's Regress*, and in recommending Father Adams as confessor to Mrs. Neylan, he qualified his praise with a single misgiving: that the holy priest was "much too close to Rome."

Nonetheless, Anglo-Catholic influences continued to come his way, one of the most important being his friendship with Sister Penelope Lawson, a nun of the Anglican Community of Saint Mary the Virgin in Wantage, about fifteen miles from Oxford. Sister Penelope first wrote to Lewis in 1939, upon reading *Out of the Silent Planet*, in which she found "bits . . . more lovely and more satisfying than anything I have met before." Lewis thanked her but pointed out that she had placed him on the horns of a dilemma: "Do I become more proud in trying to resist or in frankly revelling in, the pleasure it gives me?" There is no record of her response, but having spent twenty-seven years in a convent, Sister Penelope would have been familiar with the struggle for humility and the many traps set by pride. While never ceasing to laud Lewis's literary efforts, she seemed to be interested primarily in doing what she could to enhance her new correspondent's spiritual life. She sent him copies of her books, which he admired for "the avoidance of that curious *drabness* which characterizes so many 'little books on religion,'" and, more surprisingly, a photograph of a popular Catholic icon, the Shroud of Turin, a linen cloth venerated by those who believe that it bears the image of the crucified Christ. Lewis's initial response was guarded, but soon he warmed to the gift, declaring that "it has grown upon me wonderfully . . . the great value is to make one realize that He was a man, and once even a dead man. There is so much difference between a doctrine and a realisation." He framed the picture and placed it in his bedroom; Sister Penelope was awakening something within him.

As their correspondence blossomed, the two exchanged letters on philology, angelology, dogma and doctrine, the nature of Hell, and a hundred other topics. Perhaps because Sister Penelope dwelled in the cool calm cloisters of prayer rather than the stormy trenches of academic dispute, Lewis opened up to her as he had to few others. She became, for some years, his confidante: it was to her that he expressed his worry that in going to confession he was "merely indulging in an orgy of egoism," a concern assuaged, if not erased, by the event itself: "Well—we have come through the wall of fire and find ourselves (somewhat to our surprise) still alive and even well. The suggestion about an orgy of egoism turns out, like all the enemy propaganda, to have just a grain of truth in it, but I have no doubt that the proper method of dealing with that is to continue the practice, as I intend to do." To her he bared his heart about household troubles ("things are so bad at home that I'm cancelling several of my R.A.F. engagements"), lectured to the junior sisters of her community for Easter, critiqued her writings, and sent her the manuscript of his new novel, *Perelandra*. He dedicated the novel to "Some Ladies at Wantage," which in the Portuguese translation became, to Sister Penelope's delight, "To some wanton ladies." Lewis revealed to this writer-nun, who shared a common theological vocabulary, his views on how to persuade readers (through the imagination, especially when dealing with children) and, importantly, on the spiritual foundations of art. As the years passed, the exchange of ideas became more irregular, the letters briefer, but the deep affection between scholar and nun never ceased.

More tantalizing than Lewis's Anglo-Catholic affinities, but difficult to assess, is the question of whether he was tempted to become a Roman Catholic. According to Guy Brinkworth, a Jesuit who claimed to have corresponded with Lewis during the 1940s but failed to save the letters, Lewis "time and again asked specifically for prayers that God might give him 'the light and grace to make the final gesture.'" Brinkworth reports that Lewis went so far as to ask in a postscript to one of his letters for "prayers that the prejudices instilled in me by an Ulster . . . nurse might be overcome."

He did, to some degree, shed those prejudices. His first postconversion book, *The Pilgrim's Regress*, was free enough of overt anti-Catholic sentiment to make some readers suspect, misinterpreting the figure of Mother Kirk, that Lewis was defending the claims of Rome. Not in the least, he insisted; *The Pilgrim's Regress* was "intended to be a general apologetic allegory for 'all who profess and call themselves Christians,'" a phrase aptly taken from the Collect "For All Sorts and Conditions of Men" in the Book of Common Prayer. The position he took, in addressing himself to all sorts and conditions of men, was not generic Christianity, but Anglicanism through and through, for he saw the Anglican Church as the custodian of all that was best in historic Christianity. As he put it in *The Allegory of Love*: "When Catholicism goes bad it becomes the world-old, world-wide *religio* of amulets and holy places and priestcraft; Protestantism, in its corresponding decay, becomes a vague mist of ethical platitudes." Anglicanism, he believed, avoided both kinds of decadence. As an Anglican, one could be Catholic without idolatry, Protestant without impoverishment, and orthodox where it really mattered, admitting as true "that which has been believed everywhere, always, by everyone" (a formula Lewis liked to cite, from the *Commonitory* of the fifth-century saint Vincent of Lérins).

To an American Episcopalian who was feeling attracted to Catholicism, Lewis spelled out his position, identifying as authentically Catholic "the vast mass of doctrine wh. I find agreed on by Scripture, the Fathers, the Middle Ages, modern R.C.'s, modern Protestants" but rejecting the Roman Church "where it differs from this universal tradition" (e.g., with regard to Mary, the papacy, and the metaphysics of transubstantiation) as constituting "as much a provincial or local *variation* from the central, ancient tradition as any particular Protestant sect is." David Soper recalled Lewis saying in an interview not long before his death that "the difficulty with joining the Roman Church was that you were, so to speak, 'buying a pig in a poke'; you could not possibly know at what hours something new would be added, as essential for salvation, to the worship of Christ as God and Saviour." As a communicant of the Church of England, Lewis believed one could live the full ecclesial and sacramental life, receive Christ fully present in the Eucharist, pray for the dead, go to confession, and submit to the teaching authority of bishops without having to accept newly minted dogmas like the Immaculate Conception.

There was also spiritual benefit in staying at one's post: as a member of the national church one could be ordinary and unpretentious, worship with one's neighbors in the local parish (whether high church or low— Lewis's parish in Headington was a mix), and leave the fine points of ecclesiology to experts. "There is no mystery about my own position," Lewis wrote in his introduction to *Mere Christianity*; "I am a very ordinary layman of the Church of England, not especially 'high,' nor especially 'low,' nor especially anything else." All the evidence confirms that this is exactly what he was, and without any prolonged anxiety as to whether he should become more Catholic or even Roman Catholic. Now that Britain was at war, and all the goods of civilization under siege, it was comforting and a matter of pride to be able to speak, as he repeatedly did, of "my church, the Church of England." As a literary scholar and writer, moreover, Lewis felt he could be imaginatively Catholic, like Spenser, without any thought of submitting to Rome. Wasn't that the whole fun of reading and writing allegory? Allegory often *looks* Catholic, for Catholicism abounds in symbols and images; but the presence of Catholic imagery is no proof of a longing for Roman collars. Quite the contrary, Lewis says: "only a bungler, like Deguileville, would introduce a monastery into his poem if he were really writing about monasticism." Perhaps Lewis protested too much; but it was a constant vexation that people either suspected him of Popish leanings or demanded to know why he was not yet a confirmed Roman Catholic. At Oxford there were rumors that he was not only a closet Catholic but a secret Jesuit—but the many Catholics among Lewis's friends (Tolkien, Hardie, Havard, Griffiths, Fr. Gervase Mathew, Dundas-Grant) and pupils (George Sayer, Christopher Derrick) knew better. "Jack, most of your friends seem to be Catholic. Why don't you join us?" Havard would ask, but to no avail.

13

MERE CHRISTIANS

S ales of *The Pilgrim's Regress* had fallen short of expectations, but the book had caught the eye of the Christian publisher Ashley Sampson, who invited Lewis just before the war to contribute a volume on suffering for the "Christian Challenge" series he was editing for the Centenary Press. This would be the real beginning of Lewis's career as a Christian evangelist. He submitted *The Problem of Pain* under his favorite pseudonym, Nat Whilk (from *nát-hwilc,* "I know not who," used in Old English as the indefinite pronoun, e.g., "someone"), but at the publisher's insistence the book appeared in 1940 under his own name. He dedicated it to the Inklings, to whom he had read chapters as they emerged from his pen; the notes Havard had been reading to Inklings meetings on mental and physical pain appeared as an appendix. While writing the book, Lewis was treating himself with Veganin (paracetamol, codeine, and caffeine) for the sharp pain of a rib injured when he slipped in the bath. Yet *The Problem of Pain*—in contrast to *The Pilgrim's Regress*— has little that could be called autobiographical. It is refreshingly objective. As he said to Warnie, "If you are writing a book about pain and then get some actual pain as I did from my rib, it does *not* either, as the cynic wd. expect, blow the doctrine to bits, nor, as a Christian wd. hope, turn into practice, but remains quite unconnected and irrelevant, just as any other bit of actual life does when you are reading or writing."

The Problem of Pain sets the tone for almost all of Lewis's evangelizing volumes: it is short, conversational, commonsensical, witty, and bristling with logic that usually hits its mark, while sometimes going wildly astray. Lewis displays his trademark style in the first sentence, making the chattiest of remarks about the most profound of subjects: "Not many years ago when I was an atheist, if anyone had asked me, 'Why do you not believe in God?' my reply would have run something like this: . . ." His answer, in a nutshell, is death, matter, meaninglessness, *pain*. "The creatures cause pain by being born, and live by inflicting pain, and in pain they mostly die . . . all life will turn out in the end to have been a transitory and senseless contortion upon the idiotic face of infinite matter." If we come to believe in God, as Lewis did, the problem of pain remains; unknotting it is the purpose of his book.

How do we reconcile human suffering with divine omnipotence and divine goodness? Mostly by understanding these divine attributes in a more clearheaded, rational way—by grasping, for example, that omnipotence does not mean doing the intrinsically impossible (as an example, Lewis imagines God giving and denying creatures free will at one and the same time): "nonsense remains nonsense even when we talk it about God." As for divine goodness, Lewis argues that precisely because God is perfectly good, he wishes us to share in his own perfect, complete, and eternal goodness. God is love, and our highest bliss is to become creatures who can receive this love. But learning to love perfectly is no easy task; pain and suffering are means by which God effects this miraculous transformation. We may revolt at the prospect, but "whether we like it or not, God intends to give us what we need, not what we now think we want." We must see ourselves as we really are, and then die to our old selves through obedience and sacrifice. Pain "gives the only opportunity the bad man can have for amendment"—and we are all, to a greater or lesser extent, bad men. Tribulation is the means of redemption and "cannot cease until God either sees us remade or sees that our remaking is now hopeless." That some people will never reform, actively willing their own damnation, is the reason for hell; but for the rest of us heaven awaits, a place or state of which we now know fleeting hints, echoes, glimpses. Here Lewis is referring to his old standard, Joy, which we know as an unquenchable longing for something beyond—beyond our hopes, beyond our ken—that "is the thing I was made for . . . the secret signature of each soul."

All this is standard orthodox Christianity. The book's success lies in its ability to present these traditional views with humor, down-to-earth metaphors, and no hint of condescension or pretension; it reads like a well-bred, well-educated, well-spoken friend laying out his views in the corner pub. Moreover, like any skilled barroom orator, Lewis has two or three surprises up his sleeve. Consider his reflections on animal pain. He suggests, inter alia, that animals may suffer less pain than we think, for while all undergo pain as raw sensation, they may lack the consciousness to be "standing above the sensations and organising them into an 'experience'" (as Lewis suggests in *Out of the Silent Planet*, they have a sensitive, but not a rational, or *hnau*, soul); that the animal kingdom may have suffered corruption at the hands of Satan long before the Fall of humankind recounted in the Bible; and that, just as human beings go to heaven through their relationship to God, so animals may go to heaven through their relationship to human beings (and thereby to God). These are radical notions, pleasing neither to those who see animals as automatons nor to those who believe they possess immortal souls. Years later, when the philosopher and controversialist C.E.M. Joad (famous as "The Professor" on the BBC radio show *The Brains Trust* and a favorite sparring partner of Lewis's) published a friendly critique in the Jesuit journal *The Month*, Lewis responded by stressing "how confessedly speculative" his chapter on animal pain had been. How could we presume to know what animals experience or what God has in store for them? Our assurance of God's goodness is the only real guide; the rest is guesswork.

Equally provocative is Lewis's assertion, early in the text, that Jesus' claim of divinity "is so shocking . . . that only two views of this man are possible. Either he was a raving lunatic of an unusually abominable type, or else He was, and is, precisely what He said." It was the first of many times he would resort to some version of the *aut deus, aut malus homo* (either God or bad man) argument, a familiar device of nineteenth-century apologetics with forerunners as far back as the church fathers.

Although largely ignored by the popular press, *The Problem of Pain* did receive warm reviews in *The Times Literary Supplement* and in several ecclesiastical journals, including *The Church Times*, *The Guardian*, and *Blackfriars*. Charles Williams, assessing it for *Theology*, was predictably effusive, declaring that "Mr. Lewis's . . . style is what style always is—goodness working on goodness, a lucid and sincere intellect at work on the facts of life or the great statements of other minds." More unexpected was his remark to Lewis, delivered when the two were discussing Job and recalled by Lewis in *Essays Presented to Charles Williams*, that Job's self-righteous comforters were "the sort of people who wrote books on the Problem of Pain."

Two or three months after this first venture in Christian apologetics, Lewis dreamed up a book of considerably more popular appeal. The immediate context is significant. The Battle of Britain had just begun, on July 10—that battle between Britain and Germany for air supremacy, on which, as Churchill said in his "Finest Hour" speech, the survival of Christian civilization would depend. Lewis closed a July 16 letter to Bede Griffiths by saying, "Well: we are on the very brink of the abyss now. Perhaps we shan't be meeting again in this world." Warnie had been evacuated from Dunkirk and was safely stationed in Cardiff, but Lewis found that his closest friends were showing signs of frayed nerves. On July 14, Churchill had delivered his "War of the Unknown Warriors" speech: "now it has come to us to stand alone in the breach, and face the worst that the tyrant's might and enmity can do." On July 19, Lewis had been listening with Havard to a BBC broadcast of Hitler's "Last Appeal to Great Britain" address before the Reichstag, a litany of threats and promises beginning and ending with a call "to reason and common sense." Lewis was intrigued: "I don't know if I'm weaker than other people," he told Warnie, "but it is a positive revelation to me how *while the speech lasts* it is impossible not to waver just a little."

Two days later, the idea for a "useful and entertaining" book came to him as he was (dutifully, but without much relish) attending Sunday communion service at his parish church, Holy Trinity Headington Quarry— a curious, but upon consideration wonderfully apposite birthplace for what he had in mind. As he told Warnie, "It wd. be called *As one Devil to Another* and would consist of letters from an elderly retired devil to a young devil who has just started work on his first 'patient.' The idea wd. be to give all the psychology of temptation from the other point of view."

The result was *The Screwtape Letters*, dedicated "To J.R.R. Tolkien," thirty-one letters from a senior devil named Screwtape to his apprentice, Wormwood, offering him guidance, encouragement, and spleen as he attempts to lead a young Englishman, known as the "patient," into final damnation. Lewis wrote the book effortlessly but paid a price:

. . . though it was easy to twist one's mind into the diabolical attitude, it was not fun, or not for long. The strain produced a sort of
spiritual cramp. The world into which I had to project myself while
I spoke through Screwtape was all dust, grit, thirst, and itch.
Every trace of beauty, freshness, and geniality had to be excluded.
It almost smothered me before I was done. It would have smothered
my readers if I had prolonged it.

Despite Lewis's qualms about the project, the book (which first appeared in weekly installments in *The Guardian*, beginning May 2, 1941)
has freshness, charm, humor, and a certain cockeyed geniality. Screwtape's
inverted values, in which sin is admirable, purity damnable, and God's
love utterly incomprehensible, provide most of the satire; this experienced devil is a master psychologist, delivering during his analysis of
human foibles many memorable aphorisms and devilish insights, along
the lines of "men are not angered by mere misfortune but by misfortune
conceived as injury" and "once you have made the World an end, and
faith a means, you have almost won your man." Screwtape's own worldview is nicely detailed, including his insatiable hunger for human souls,
whom he desires not out of some abstract wish to damn but simply in
order to eat; his bag of poisonous tricks, designed to lead humans to per-
dition by taking advantage of the Law of Undulation, our propensity for
oscillating between happiness and sorrow, energy and enervation; and
the spite and fury bubbling within his breast, ready to erupt at any provocation, most memorably when a German bomb kills Wormwood's patient
before his soul can be claimed for Hell. For all the clever satire, however,
the book does, as Lewis feared, begin to smother the reader by the end.
It is a one-joke affair, however inventive the variations. The devils' names—
Screwtape, Slumtrimpet, Slubgob, Scabtree, Triptweeze, Toadpipe—and
their use of inverted epithets—"Our Father Below" for Satan, "The Enemy" for God—delight and then grow tiresome; so, too, do Lewis's repeated slaps at favorite targets, including psychoanalysis, proponents
of the "Life Force," and overly spiritualized conceptions of prayer
(Coleridge's "sense of supplication" takes a direct hit). It all comes off as
terribly clever but a bit sophomoric. *The Screwtape Letters* is a good,
short book; if it were half as long and half as clever, it might have been
twice as good.

The public, however, roared its approval. The book sold very well upon release and remains one of Lewis's most popular works. *The Manchester Guardian* (February 24, 1942), eager to canonize it, declared that it "should become a classic," while *The Times Literary Supplement* (February 28, 1942) more temperately warned that "time alone can show whether it is or is not an enduring piece of satirical writing." Endured it has; whether that makes it a classic, the next century or two will judge.

Pressed into Service

If the early deprivations of war disturbed Lewis's complacency, the Blitz shook him to his core. "It's like the end of the world," he wrote to Arthur when Belfast was bombed. The Blitz began on September 7, 1940, when over a thousand Luftwaffe planes attacked London in the first wave of an all-out German effort to destroy the British war industry and sow panic among the civilian population. The British government, after some initial sluggishness, responded by opening the Underground as a massive bomb shelter (more than one hundred thousand people took refuge there every night during the height of the raids), with antiaircraft fire and airborne counterattacks by the RAF, and by establishing special programs to boost public morale. According to Charles Gilmore, who ran the RAF Chaplains' School at Magdalene College, Cambridge, the Battle of Britain "had had an extraordinary effect on the nation and a quite miraculous effect on the status of the Royal Air Force . . . For quite a time, the RAF received into its ranks more than its fair share of the cream of the nation." The dean of St. Paul's Cathedral, hoping to inspire these new recruits, decided to fund an RAF chaplaincy lectureship and suggested that Lewis be given the post. On a rainy day in early 1941, Gilmore and the RAF chaplain in chief arrived at Magdalen College to set about convincing him that he was the right man to lecture airmen throughout the UK about the war effort and their place in it. Addressing raw troops, many of whom had not attended a university, was a new challenge for Lewis; after a bit of reasonable hesitation, he agreed, "promising to soar," in Gilmore's words.

The first lectures took place in Abingdon, right outside Oxford. Lewis thought them a "complete failure" and took solace in remembering "that God used an *ass* to convert the prophet," but soon he did soar, providing his listeners, in Gilmore's words, with "a sterling and direct purpose, where before they had found only the confusion of a whirlpool." He traveled up and down the nation, on trips that usually lasted two or three days, followed by a short break at home and then another trip. He complained to Arthur Greeves that "I had never realized how tiring perpetual travelling is (specially in crowded trains)," and yet he rejoiced in the beauty of the landscape and, above all, "the chance in many places to see and smell the sea and hear the sound of gulls again, which otherwise I wd. have been pining for." In Tolkien's eyes, Lewis had shouldered the task *in imitatione Pauli*, "as a reparation; now the least of Christians (by special grace) but once an infidel . . . The acceptance of the RAF mission with its . . . lonely, cheerless, embarrassed journeys . . . all this was in its way an imitation of St. Paul."

A second and more difficult phase of the lectures opened up when Lewis also agreed to address RAF chaplains—many of whom had been doctors, bankers, journalists, or professional ministers prior to the war— on a regular basis at the RAF Chaplains' School. Facing a well-educated audience, Lewis chose as the topic for his first presentation "Linguistic Analysis in Pauline Soteriology"—a subject, as he should have realized, of no interest to men just back from battle or about to join the fray. Charles Gilmore, who attended the talk, recalled Lewis as "feeling for words. Clive Staples Lewis feeling for words! He hummed, and the ill-mannered coughed. A future bishop secretly got on with *The Times*' crossword." Thankfully, Lewis sensed his error before it was too late, dropped the philological analysis, "said something about prostitutes and pawnbrokers . . . and the rest of the morning was full of the clang of steel on steel and the laughter of good fellows, and answers that belonged to life . . . Jack had done his job."

He had indeed, despite his belief that the RAF talks had been a failure. But greater tasks lay at hand. A few months before the first RAF address, he had been approached by James W. Welch, director of religious broadcasting for the BBC, about addressing an even larger audience than British flyboys. Welch, who had read *The Problem of Pain* and found it personally helpful, proposed that Lewis take up religious broadcasting, allowing him to address "a fairly intelligent audience of more than a million." With cinemas, theaters, and the nascent BBC Television Service closed as an emergency measure, the BBC Home Service and its companion Overseas Service had to be the supplier of necessary infor-mation and equally necessary diversion. The broadcast talk, a short, lively, intimate, single-speaker presentation, was a new form invented to meet both needs; and considerably more than a million at home and at the front could be expected to tune in. Two thirds of them, Welch guessed, would be lapsed Christians, if not outright nonbelievers.

When Lewis accepted the assignment, Welch put him in the hands of a BBC staff member named Eric Fenn—a Presbyterian, active in the Student Christian Movement, who had served time in Wormwood Scrubs prison for his pacifist stance and who shared Welch's desire to do some-thing about the appallingly dreary state of religious programming. Fenn coached Lewis in the art of delivering a crisp, fifteen-minute colloquial radio talk, vetted his scripts and passed them on to the censors, worried about the timing (each talk had to fill its precise time slot, to prevent German programming from breaking in), and helped him arrange to have the earnings distributed as charity to various correspondents in need and to the Cowley Fathers.

Initially, Welch suggested two topics for broadcast: the lack of Chris-tian influence in modern literature, or "The Christian Faith as I See It—by a Layman." Lewis countered by proposing a series of talks on natural law, or "objective right and wrong"—a reality, he told Welch, that the Bible takes for granted but that is far from obvious to modern minds. He was convinced that "most apologetic begins a stage too far on. The first step is to create, or recover, the sense of guilt. Hence if I give a series of talks I should mention Christianity only at the end, and would prefer not to unmask my battery till then." Lewis thought of calling the first series "The Art of Being Shocked"; later on, he came up with "Inside Information." Neither title satisfied Welch. Eventually, they agreed on "'RIGHT AND WRONG': A Clue to the Meaning of the Universe?" with the first installment, "Common Decency," broadcast on August 6, 1941, at 7:45 p.m., immediately following "News in Norwegian."

If "The Art of Being Shocked" was what Lewis was after, though, he went about it by an unexpected path, appealing to the intellect rather than the emotions, arguing first for the objective reality of the moral law, then for our chronic failure to obey it, and finally for God as the giver of the law, who alone, by means of the Atonement, is working to repair us. Lewis knew that he would have to make this point in the language of the street, however, and he discovered, with some help from Eric Fenn, that he had a gift for doing so. He began the first evening broadcast:

> Every one has heard people quarrelling. Sometimes it sounds funny and sometimes it sounds merely unpleasant; but however it sounds, I believe we can learn something very important from listening to the kind of things they say. They say things like this: "That's my seat, I was there first"—"Leave him alone, he isn't doing you any harm"—"Why should you shove in first?"—"Give me a bit of your orange, I gave you a bit of mine"—"How'd you like it if anyone did the same to you?"—"Come on, you promised."

It was a brilliant move. The instinct to protest against unfairness is universal, and it emerges very early in childhood. The offended party in such a quarrel, Lewis observes, "is appealing to some kind of standard of behaviour which he expects the other man to know about—and the other man very seldom replies, 'To hell with your standard.'" In other words, the moral law is a principle of accountability that transcends cultural differences and cannot be reduced to herd instinct. As a principle of accountability, the moral law presupposes freedom—*ought* implies *can*. If we fail to live up to the moral law, it can only be because we have freely rejected it; and if we are in the habit of freely rejecting it, we are in serious disarray. Summing up his first fifteen-minute talk, Lewis said, "Well, those are the two points I wanted to make tonight. First, that human beings, all over the earth, have this curious idea that they *ought* to behave in a certain way, and can't really get rid of it. Secondly, that they don't in fact behave in that way. They know the Law of Nature; they break it. These two facts are the foundation of all clear thinking about ourselves and the universe we live in."

So far, Lewis had said nothing especially original or specifically Christian; Kant would have smiled. It was no small achievement, however, to have secured so succinct a moral foundation for the Christian reflections to follow. Lewis was proceeding upon the assumption that what had served as *praeparatio evangelica* (preparation for the Gospel) in his own life might win over his listeners as well. Before he became a Christian, he had been a convinced moral realist. After his conversion, he came to see knowl-

edge of the moral law—called "natural law" or "law of nature" because it
is a universal pattern discoverable by reason—as the best introduction to
the faith, especially for those outside the Church. As St. Paul said, the
natural law is "written on the heart" (Romans 2:14–15) even of Gentiles
who have not known divine revelation. Lewis studied the development of
this idea in the writings of Thomas Aquinas, undisputed master of natural
law theory, whose belief in the fundamental rationality of human beings
Lewis wholeheartedly shared, and also in the works of the sixteenth-
century Anglican divine Richard Hooker, whose adaptation of scholastic
natural law theory laid the foundation for Anglican moral theology.

Some Protestant thinkers have worried that natural law theory gives
too much credit to human reason. But Lewis was convinced that the risk
to moral sanity comes from placing too little, not too much, stock in reason. He opposed, with every fiber of his being, subjectivism, relativism,
utilitarianism, pragmatism, and all views that came, he believed, from
despising the objective, essentially commonsense morality of ordinary
people. Though our minds are fallen instruments, we remain capable of
discerning the difference between right and wrong, and honest self-
appraisal suffices to show us what the revealed law makes even more
transparent, that we are chronic sinners in need of grace. Far from being
the remnant of herd instinct, the introjection of parental scolding, or the
self-sufficient discovery of human reason, the moral law is the closest we
are likely to get in this life to a vision of the God who made us.

Wisely, Lewis did not bring God directly into the argument until his
fourth talk. Even then, he was nervous about losing his audience. To
disarm suspicions, he resorted to a few special rhetorical devices. One
was slang: "There's been a great deal of soft soap talked about God for
the last hundred years. That's not what I am offering. You can cut all that
out." And again: "You may even have thought that I'd played a trick on
you—that I'd been carefully wrapping up to look like philosophy what
turns out to be one more 'religious jaw.'" In revising the *Broadcast Talks*
for publication as *Mere Christianity*, Lewis deleted the contractions, but
the slang remained, giving academic theologians and stylistic purists one
more reason to turn up their noses. He wooed his vast audience further
by deploying, to great effect, the telling analogy and didactic exemplum,
often introduced as a "supposal":

Supposing you hear a cry for help from a man in danger. You will probably feel two desires—one a desire to give help (due to your herd instinct), the other a desire to keep out of danger (due to the instinct for self-preservation). But you will find inside you, in addition to these two impulses, a third thing which tells you that you ought to follow the impulse to help, and suppress the impulse to run away. Now this thing that judges between two instincts, that decides which should be encouraged, can't itself be either of them. You might as well say that the sheet of music which tells you, at a given moment, to play one note on the piano and not another, is itself one of the notes on the keyboard. The Moral Law is, so to speak, the tune we've got to play: our instincts are merely the keys.

These techniques united to create a strong bond between Lewis and his vast audience, and the talks were an instant success. Justin Phillips, a BBC radio journalist and author of *C. S. Lewis in a Time of War*, quotes an RAF officer recalling an episode in the officers' mess, in which Lewis's voice boomed over the radio just as the barman was handing over a drink. "Suddenly everyone just froze listening to this extraordinary voice." At the end of the fifteen-minute talk, "there was the barman with his arm still up there and the other man still waiting for his drink." Letters from listeners poured in: "One gets funny letters after broadcasting—some from lunatics who sign themselves 'Jehovah' or begin 'Dear Mr Lewis, I was married at the age of 20 to a man I didn't love'—but many from serious inquirers whom it was a duty to answer fully. So letter writing has loomed pretty large!"

What Do Christians Believe?

Lewis broadcast his second series of talks—"What Christians Believe"—during January and February 1942. He began by presenting his credentials: he had been chosen to give the talks not because of his special expertise, but because, as a layman and converted atheist, he might be better able than some professional theologians to speak to the concerns of ordinary people. His aim was to express, in five fifteen-minute talks, the lineaments of the classical Christian worldview, or, as he would later call it, after the seventeenth-century English Puritan theologian Richard Baxter, "mere Christianity"—mere, that is, in the older sense of the word, meaning pure, unvarnished, and undistorted by sectarian bias. To that end, he sent his scripts to be vetted by four clergy friends: a Catholic (Bede Griffiths), a Methodist (the RAF padre Joseph Dowell), a Presbyterian (Eric Fenn), and an Anglican (possibly Austin Farrer, according to Walter Hooper).

Lewis's chief concern was to combat the tendency to reduce the faith, as Enlightenment thinkers were wont to do, to nothing but window dressing on the moral law. It's only "after you have realized that there is a real Moral Law, and a Power behind the law, and that you have broken that law and put yourself wrong with that Power—it's *after* all that that Christianity begins to talk." And what Christianity begins to talk about, Lewis expressed with a favorite analogy: that we are living in "enemy-occupied territory," in a world under siege. Christianity is "the story of how the rightful king has landed, you might say landed in disguise, and is calling us all to take part in a great campaign of sabotage. When you go to church you're really listening in to the secret wireless from our friends: that's why the enemy is so anxious to prevent us going." One could hear, amid the groans of liberal theologians who had thought we were done with Devil talk, the echo of Churchill's BBC addresses to a world overshadowed by "the dark curse of Hitler." In wartime, Lewis could count on the siege analogy appealing even to the lapsed Christians in his audience.

The analogy is a powerful one, and perhaps just as effective when encountered in peacetime. Lewis's point was that we are always over-shadowed by a dark curse; it's just that Hitler brought the curse into plain view. Shortly before the first series of radio talks, Lewis had skirmished with C.E.M. Joad in the pages of *The Spectator* over whether the problem of evil has a "new urgency" during wartime.

> . . . *what* new urgency? Evil may seem more urgent to us than it did to the Victorian philosophers—favoured members of the happiest class in the happiest country in the world at the world's happiest period. But it is no more urgent for us than for the great majority of monotheists all down the ages. The classic expositions of the doctrine that the world's miseries are compatible with its creation and guidance by a wholly good Being come from Boethius waiting in prison to be beaten to death and from St Augustine

meditating on the sack of Rome. The present state of the world is normal; it was the last century that was the abnormality.

Whether in war or in peace, questions of religious commitment are always urgent. It is always on "this day" (Deuteronomy 30:15) that we are offered the choice of good or evil, life or death. Lewis's argumentative mind tended to run to such dichotomies in any case, so it seemed natural to set forth the options for belief in pairs of opposites: atheism and theism, pantheism and monotheism, dualism and its Christian alternative. Dualism appealed for its vigor, but Christianity proved the better "fighting religion," contending for the good world God made against the evils that are parasitic on that good.

In the third talk, Lewis restated in plain language the standard free-will theodicy: that it was a greater good for God to have created a world in which his intelligent creatures (angels and men) were free to choose between good and evil than it would have been for God to create a race of automatons, hardwired to choose good. That free creatures might decide to choose evil was the risk God took in creating us—and when they did choose badly, and creation was marred, God determined to rescue us from the ruin, first by giving us an innate knowledge of right and wrong; second, by sending the human race, in the form of myths and cults, "good dreams" of a dying-and-rising god; third, by electing the children of Israel and spending "several centuries hammering into their heads the sort of God He was," and finally by visiting his sorry planet in the person of a Jewish man who said "the most shocking thing that has ever been uttered by human lips." At this point, Lewis resumed the *aut Deus, aut malus homo* argument, converting the dilemma (God or bad man) into a trilemma: lunatic, liar, or Lord:

> I'm trying here to prevent anyone from saying the really silly thing that people often say about Him: "I'm ready to accept Jesus as a great moral teacher, but I don't accept His claim to be God." That's the one thing we mustn't say. A man who was merely a man and said the sort of things that Jesus said wouldn't be a great moral teacher. He'd either be a lunatic—on a level with the man who says he's a poached egg—or else he'd be the Devil of Hell. You must make your choice. Either this man was, and is, the Son of

God: or else a madman or something worse. You can shut Him up
for a fool, you can spit at Him and kill Him as a demon; or you can
fall at His feet and call Him Lord and God. But don't let us come
with any patronising nonsense about His being a great human
teacher. He hasn't left that open to us. He didn't intend to.

Such stark oppositions are often recipes for disaster, and one wonders
that Lewis, who prized logic, brought this one to the table. Other views
of Jesus may be—and have been—offered: that he was sane on the whole
but mistaken on this one point, that he was misled by his handlers into a
false understanding of his identity and mission, that he was a mystic who
spoke in allegorical code. There is also the possibility that Jesus did not
actually claim divinity but was a prophet divinized by his followers after
death.

This last objection was one Lewis did not bother to consider. In his
youth, he had been a great proponent of "higher criticism," writing know-
ingly to Arthur about a "Hebrew philosopher Yeshua" who became the
object of a mystery cult after his death. But for the mature Lewis, higher
criticism had no traction; some years later he wrote, "as a literary historian, I am perfectly convinced that whatever else the Gospels are they
are not legends. I have read a great deal of legend and I am quite clear that
they are not the same sort of thing. They are not artistic enough to be
legends." Not artistic enough for mythology, yet filled with small details—
like Jesus scribbling in the dust—that only the modern realistic novel
would think to include. The so-called "historical Jesus" has proven to be
an elusive figure, each version supplanting its predecessor; but the Jesus
of the Gospels gives every indication of being conscious of his divinity,
forgiving sins, casting out demons, uttering "I AM" sayings that echo
the tetragrammaton (YHWH), and promising to return as judge at the
end of time.

In the original broadcast, though not in the published versions, Lewis
anticipated the historicist objection: "Of course you can take the line of
saying He didn't say these things, but his followers invented them. But
that's only shifting the difficulty. They were Jews, too: the last people who
would invent such a thing, the people who had never said anything of the
sort about Moses or Elijah. That theory only saddles you with twelve in-
explicable lunatics instead of one." It was just as well that he removed

this passage, for it would not withstand a deep study of Christian beginnings in the Jewish and Mediterranean world. Lewis's impression of Judaism rested largely on his reading of the Old Testament, viewed through the lens of a general philosophical monotheism; but it was not unusual for Jewish thinkers during the Second Temple period, in which Christianity took shape, to dream of quasi-divine, or angelomorphic, prophets and saints. Moreover, that God sometimes chose to become manifest to his people, whether in the still, small voice or as an overwhelming angelic presence, was a fundamentally Jewish belief. The Incarnation was a new idea, but not an alien one; as Lewis himself notes, the Jews were being prepared from the moment of their election for just such a saving invasion of history.

Lack of historical nuance is understandable in a fifteen-minute popular radio talk; the question remains of whether Lewis's trilemma succeeds on logical grounds. No doubt, if Jesus had been lying about his identity—and on the strength of that lie inducing his closest friends to follow him to the gallows—it was the act of a moral monster. But what of the "lunatic—on a level with the man who says he's a poached egg"? Lewis's flippancy here grates modern sensibilities (and sounds strange coming from a man who had witnessed two genuine mental breakdowns); it helps to know that the poached egg madman is a stock figure, a sort of urban legend, that dates back at least to the turn of the century. "Wants a Slice of Toast," a typical example of this trope, was the headline of a human-interest piece in *The Philadelphia Inquirer* of November 26, 1900, reprinted verbatim in English-language papers as far as New Zealand. Arnold Bennett speaks of the poor fellow in 1908, Chesterton mentions him prominently in *Orthodoxy* (also 1908) as well as in several subsequent publications, and Bertrand Russell refers to him in 1945, in the context of a critique of David Hume in *A History of Western Philosophy*.

The key point, about which Lewis is deadly serious, is that anyone so massively mistaken about his identity cannot be trusted as a font of moral teachings. Yet it is at least conceivable that Jesus could have been deluded without being fundamentally unsound. Millions outside the Christian fold admire Jesus for his wisdom, courage, compassion, and self-sacrifice, while thinking he was mistaken about his identity. Millions within the Christian fold (and other major world religions) have a comparable opinion of the Dalai Lama, considering him mistaken in his belief that he is the reincarnation of the previous thirteen Dalai Lamas and ultimately of the celestial bodhisattva Chenrezig (Avalokiteśvara), but admiring him nonetheless as a moral teacher and public leader.

Lewis's *aut Deus, aut malus homo* argument is not without its virtues, however. For those wavering on the threshold of belief in the divinity of Christ, it has at least a suggestive force. Nowhere does the New Testament propose that the truth of the Incarnation is logically self-evident or patently obvious; rather, we are told that the signs of God's presence will be recognized by those graced with the eyes to see them. If the argument succeeds, it does so by evoking the experience, so characteristic of the Gospels, of being confronted with the question "Who do you say that I am?" A personal decision is called for; the matter is too urgent and a lifetime too fleeting to wait for all the evidence to come in.

In the fourth talk of the series, Lewis wrestled with various models of the Atonement, noting that orthodox Christianity has countenanced more than one way of understanding how it is that Christ, by dying, has achieved reconciliation between God and human beings. Lewis's preference is for a substitutionary model—think of Aslan dying in Edmund's place—but the key point for him is that "in Christ, a new kind of man appeared: and the new kind of life which began in Him is to be put into us" by means of baptism, communion, and assent to the faith of the apostles.

Two more radio series would follow. One, on the practical aspects of morality, which had to be cut down to ten-minute segments, Lewis published in 1943 under the title *Christian Behaviour.* His focus was on the virtues as distinguished from abstract "ideals" and political or therapeutic programs. He analyzed the master sin of pride and corrected common misunderstandings of its antidote, humility; and he tackled contested questions of sexual morality, setting forth without hectoring the basic Christian understanding of ordered and disordered sexual practices and affections. In a final series, published in weekly installments in *The Listener,* and in 1944, with additional chapters, as the book *Beyond Personality,* Lewis offered "first steps in the doctrine of the Trinity," concluding with an account of what it means to share in the life of the Triune God. Now that he had moved beyond the argumentative preambles and into the heart of his Christ-centered vision of man, Lewis could soar. One might think another Augustine was speaking:

Give up yourself, and you will find your real self. Lose your life and you will save it. Submit to death, death of your ambitions and favourite wishes every day and death of your whole body in the end: submit with every fibre of your being, and you will find eternal life. Keep back nothing. Nothing that you have not given away will be really yours. Nothing in you that has not died will ever be raised from the dead. Look for yourself, and you will find in the long run only hatred, loneliness, despair, rage, ruin, and decay. But look for Christ and you will find Him, and with Him everything else thrown in.

Thus he completed his final assignment for the BBC—to "take some of the more abstruse theological doctrines and show what sort of difference they make, both to thought and to conduct," as Eric Fenn had proposed. Listeners who wrote to the BBC registered strong reactions: "They obviously either regard you as 'the cat's whiskers,'" Eric Fenn said, "or as beneath contempt."

Most of the reviewers were of the cat's whiskers persuasion. All three volumes, *Broadcast Talks*, *Christian Behaviour*, and *Beyond Personality* received glowing reports in such periodicals as *The Times Literary Supplement*, *The Tablet*, *Time and Tide*, and *The Clergy Review*. An October 1944 review of *Beyond Personality* in *The Times Literary Supplement* is representative: "Mr. Lewis has a quite unique power of making theology an attractive, exciting and (one might almost say) an uproariously fascinating quest." In the July 22, 1945, issue of *The New York Times*, P. W. Wilson, a British journalist and Liberal MP, had this to say of *Beyond Personality*: "With the BBC for his pulpit . . . Mr. Lewis, the layman of Oxford, continues to be the major apostle of Christian faith for the man in the street . . ."; Wilson also accurately predicts how future critics would react to Lewis's apostleship: "There will be those who will say of him what was said of a certain Bishop Magee—that he made religion so simple that he must be wrong . . ." On the other hand, George Orwell, who was ardently anti-Catholic and uneasy about Anglicanism, thought *Beyond Personality* a typical example of "the silly-clever religious book," in the tradition of R. H. Benson, G. K. Chesterton, and Ronald Knox, "which goes on the principle not of threatening the unbeliever with Hell, but of showing him up as an illogical ass, incapable of clear thought and unaware that everything he says has been said and refuted before." He found Lewis's language insufferably patronizing with its "homey little asides like 'you know' and 'mind you,' or Edwardian slang like 'awfully,' 'jolly well,' 'specially' for 'especially,' 'awful cheek' and so forth. The idea, of course, is to persuade the suspicious reader, or listener, that one can be a Christian and a 'jolly good chap' at the same time." In Orwell's opinion, Lewis's "chummy little wireless talks" succeeded because of their reactionary implications. "They are not really so unpolitical as they are meant to look."

The Club Is Long Overdue

During the 1940s, as John Wain reports in his memoirs, Lewis was at the height of his fame: "People whose lives had been torn apart by war and suffering, who needed something to cling to, devoured his series of popular theological books, tuned into his broadcasts, flocked at every opportunity to hear him speak." If the BBC talks constituted Lewis's electronic bully pulpit, other venues supplied him with a live audience. He was in demand as a preacher (a role Tolkien considered highly inappropriate for a layman), and he was invited on a few occasions to occupy Oxford's most visible pulpit: the University Church of St. Mary the Virgin.

No one who saw Lewis ascend the pulpit of St. Mary the Virgin could fail to recall the storied image of John Henry Newman climbing the same elegant, narrow staircase. The similarities were not lost on the press; *The Daily Telegraph* called Lewis "Modern Oxford's Newman." Like Newman in his Anglican period, Lewis treated the sermon as a literary art, and, like Newman, he applied that art to inciting the desire for personal holiness, though Lewis would often insist that, not being a priest, he felt called upon to compare notes rather than to instruct. His sermons are really hybrids, part lecture, part homily, graced with an evangelical fervor and a philosophical economy not found in his longer, more teacherly books.

Two of these sermons—"The Weight of Glory," preached to a packed congregation at St. Mary the Virgin during Solemn Evensong on June 8, 1941, and "Transposition," preached to a Congregationalist chapel at Mansfield College on the Feast of Pentecost 1944—are among the best of Lewis's religious writings and recapitulate or anticipate nearly all his grand themes: the unquenchable desire that tells us we are made for heaven, the error of mistaking proximate for ultimate goods, the complementarity of rational freedom and trust in authority, the solemn merriment that characterizes Christian life, and the realization that "there are no *ordinary* people"—we are all immortals whose mortal pilgrimage will end either in the beatific or the "miserific" vision. During his Mansfield College sermon, which united under the theme of "transposition" the Incarnation, the real presence of Christ in the Eucharist, the descent of the Holy Spirit, the resurrection of the dead, and our faltering human efforts to conceive this inconceivable splendor, Lewis suddenly found himself overcome with emotion. The choir had to sing a hymn while he collected himself before he could resume speaking.

There was another forum, however, in which Lewis could engage in cheerful, manly, sunlit combat with adversaries of the faith. In late 1941, Stella Aldwinckle, chaplain to women students at Oxford, posted a notice at Somerville College, one of the first women's colleges at Oxford, inviting "all atheists, agnostics, and those who are disillusioned about religion or think they are" to meet with her in the Junior Common Room to address their concerns. From this initial gathering sprang the Socratic Club, a university-wide organization dedicated to promoting Christianity through weekly discussions—more realistically, debates—between believers and skeptics. Aldwinckle, who was reading *The Problem of Pain* at the time, wrote Lewis inviting him to serve as faculty sponsor and first president. He jumped at the offer, declaring that "this club is long overdue!" How could he not? The Socratic Club joined in perfect union two of his great loves: Christian witness and intellectual battle. "Those who founded it do not for one moment pretend to be neutral," Lewis wrote in the club digest. "It was the Christians who constructed the arena and issued the challenge." Nonetheless, he believed that the rules insured a fair fight: "We never claimed to be impartial. But argument is. It has a life of its own. No man can tell where it will go. We expose ourselves, and the weakest of our party, to your fire no less than you are exposed to ours." It was, moreover, a fight whose weapons were those of unfettered rational dialectics: "Here a man could get the case for Christianity without all the paraphernalia of pietism and the case against it without the irrelevant *sansculottisme* of our common anti-God weeklies." Usually two speakers—one Christian, one atheist—addressed a single topic (when

C. S. Lewis (Used by permission of the Marion E. Wade Center, Wheaton College, Wheaton, IL)

J.R.R. Tolkien (© Douglas R. Gilbert)

Owen Barfield (Used by permission of the Owen Barfield Literary Estate, Owen A. Barfield, trustee)

Charles Williams (Used by permission of the Marion E. Wade Center, Wheaton College, Wheaton, IL)

J.R.R. Tolkien at age fifteen with the King Edward's School cadets (Courtesy of the Governors of the Schools of King Edward VI in Birmingham, by the kindness of John Garth and Alison Wheatley, who have confirmed the identity of Tolkien in this 1907 photograph)

Tolkien, 1911 (Private collection / Bridgeman Images)

Tolkien and H.V.D. ("Hugo")
Dyson, from a 1954
photograph of the Fellows of
Merton College (From the Inklings
collection of Harry Lee Poe)

Tolkien and his wife, Edith, at 76 Sandfield Road, Oxford, 1961

Lewis family portrait, ca. 1899: (left to right) Florence Augusta Hamilton Lewis (mother) holding Warren Lewis, Albert Lewis (father), Richard Lewis II (grandfather), Martha Lewis (grandmother), Eileen Lewis (cousin), Agnes Lewis (aunt) holding C. S. Lewis (Used by permission of the Marion E. Wade Center, Wheaton College, Wheaton, IL)

Father and son: formal portrait of Albert Lewis and C. S. Lewis, ca. 1918 (Used by permission of the Marion E. Wade Center, Wheaton College, Wheaton, IL)

C. S. Lewis (left) and Warnie on holiday at Annagassan, County Louth, Ireland, ca. 1952 (Used by permission of the Marion E. Wade Center, Wheaton College, Wheaton, IL)

C. S. Lewis at the Royal Air Force Chaplains' School, 1944 (RAF Chaplaincy Branch Archive, RAF Museum, Hendon, London)

Lewis and the Moores on holiday at St. Agnes Cove, Cornwall, September 1927: (left to right) Maureen Moore, the family dog Baron Papworth, C. S. Lewis, Mrs. Janie Moore

(Used by permission of the Marion E. Wade Center, Wheaton College, Wheaton, IL)

Lewis and his wife, Joy, with their dog Susie, photographed by Michael Peto, 1958

(© University of Dundee, The Peto Collection)

Charles Williams, ca. 1910, formal portrait
(Used by permission of the Marion E. Wade Center, Wheaton
College, Wheaton, IL)

Florence Conway in 1908 (before her
marriage to Charles Williams) in Tudor
costume (Used by permission of the Marion E. Wade
Center, Wheaton College, Wheaton, IL)

Williams (left) with William Butler Yeats, 1917 (Used by permission of the Marion E. Wade Center, Wheaton College, Wheaton, IL)

Williams in the snow, heading down the long driveway from the Oxford University Press offices at Southfield House, ca. 1940–43 (Used by permission of the Marion E. Wade Center, Wheaton College, Wheaton, IL)

Owen Barfield, ca. 1915, as a Highgate schoolboy playing chess (Used by permission of the Owen Barfield Literary Estate, Owen A. Barfield, trustee)

Owen Barfield, ca. 1920–25, probably at Oxford (Used by permission of the Marion E. Wade Center, Wheaton College, Wheaton, IL)

C. S. L.

Βιογραφία Θεολογικά

Ἰδοῦ ἦν φιλόσοφός τις, καὶ ἔγνω ἑαυτὸν ὁ φιλόσοφος ὅτι εἷς ἐστι. καὶ ὁ λόγος ἐν τῷ φιλοσόφῳ γενόμενος ἦν εἰς θεός. καὶ ὁ λόγος ἦν τὸ φῶς τῆς φιλοσοφίας αὐτοῦ· καὶ τὸ φῶς ἐν τῇ φιλοσοφίᾳ φαίνει, καὶ ὁ φιλόσοφος αὐτὸ οὐκ ἔγνω. ἐν τῷ φιλοσόφῳ ἦν καὶ ἡ φιλοσοφία δι᾽ αὐτοῦ ἐγένετο, καὶ ὁ φιλόσοφος αὐτὸ οὐκ ἔγνω. καὶ δὴ καὶ οὐκ ἔφη ὁ φιλόσοφος ὅτι οὐδεὶς δύναται τὸ φῶς οὔποτε οὐδαμῶς θεάσθαι. καὶ θεασάμενος τὸ φῶς ἐλάλησεν ὁ φιλόσοφος ὅτι ὄνομα αὐτῷ κύριος. καὶ ἑρμήνευσεν ἡ φιλοσοφία περὶ τοῦ φωτὸς ὅτι λόγος καὶ ζωὴ τῶν ἀνθρώπων ἐστι καὶ περὶ τοῦ φιλοσόφου ὅτι οὐκ ἐξ αἱμάτων οὐδὲ ἐκ θελήματος σαρκὸς οὐδὲ ἐκ θελήματος ἀνδρὸς

οὐδὲ δι᾽ ἐντολῆς κυρίου ἀλλ᾽ ἐκ θεοῦ ἐγεννήθη. καὶ ὁ φιλόσοφος τὴν μαρτυρίαν οὐ κατέλαβεν.

Date uncertain, but almost certainly between 1941 and 1946. I don't think I ever showed it to him, though I felt a strong impulse to do so. If I did, then he paid scant attention to it; if I didn't, it was because I was afraid of his paying scant attention to it.

O. B. Aug. 1969

Owen Barfield, "C.S.L.: Biographia Theologica," handwritten in Greek, ca. 1941–46, with note by Barfield, dated August 1969: "I don't think I showed it to him . . ." (Used by permission of the Owen Barfield Literary Estate, Owen A. Barfield, trustee)

Barfield and his wife,
Maud, with the family
cat in front of their
home in Surrey, ca. 1969
(Used by permission of the Marion
E. Wade Center, Wheaton College,
Wheaton, IL)

Barfield in his study, early 1980s (Used by permission of the Owen Barfield Literary Estate, Owen A. Barfield, trustee)

Magdalen College panorama with a view toward the New Building and Addison's Walk

The Eagle and Child
("Bird and Baby") pub,
49 St. Giles, Oxford

A walking tour, Wales, ca. 1935, photograph presumably taken by Owen Barfield: (left to right) Alfred Cecil Harwood ("Lord of the Walks," according to Lewis), C. S. Lewis, Walter O. ("Wof") Field (Anthroposophist and close friend of Harwood and Barfield), W. Eric Beckett (Fellow of All Souls, friend of Barfield and Harwood, later knighted for his service as legal adviser to the Foreign Office), Arthur Alan Hanbury-Sparrow (friend of Barfield, author of the World War I memoir *The Land-locked Lake*, and an Anthroposophist) (Used by permission of the Marion E. Wade Center, Wheaton College, Wheaton, IL)

Inklings at the Trout Inn (near the Godstow Bridge in Wolvercote, north of Oxford), ca. 1947: (left to right) Commander James Dundas-Grant, Colin Hardie, Dr. Robert E. Havard, C. S. Lewis, Peter Havard (Used by permission of the Marion E. Wade Center, Wheaton College, Wheaton, IL)

(Alan) Bede Griffiths, 1926 (Used by permission of Kathryn Spink, courtesy of Adrian Rance-McGregor)

Sr Penelope Lawson, CSMV (Courtesy of the Community of St. Mary the Virgin, Wantage, Oxfordshire)

Dorothy L. Sayers, studio portrait, ca. 1926 (Used by permission of the Marion E. Wade Center, Wheaton College, Wheaton, IL)

Lord David Cecil and Rachel MacCarthy on their wedding day, at St. Bartholomew the Great, West Smithfield, London, October 13, 1932 (© TopFoto / The Image Works)

Nevill Coghill with Richard Burton and Elizabeth Taylor at Merton College on October 14, 1967, eve of the premier of the Oxford University Drama Society production of *Doctor Faustus* (© TopFoto / The Image Works)

Gervase Mathew, O.P. (© Douglas R. Gilbert)

John Barrington Wain, October 1958 (© Mark Gerson / National Portrait Gallery, London)

atheists proved in short supply, as sometimes happened, Christians with differing views filled the bill). Questions and comments from the audience followed the presentations. Meetings were held every Monday during term, from 8:15 to 10:30 pm.

As president, Lewis opened most of the sessions, and he served also as principal speaker or respondent over two dozen times, on topics ranging from the matter-of-fact "Christianity and Aesthetics" to the evocative "Is Theology Poetry?" (not exactly, Lewis decided; better poetry can be found outside theology's precincts, where it does not have to contend with historical facts, yet theology includes poetry much as waking includes dreams). Lewis also brought in other Inklings to speak. Dr. Havard addressed the very first gathering, on January 26, 1942, delivering a paper with the ungainly title of "Won't Mankind Outgrow Christianity in the Face of the Advance of Science and of Modern Ideologies?" Havard's answer was a resounding *sed contra*, declaring that Christianity will endure while our confidence in science and modern ideologies will fade.

Other speakers included C.E.M. Joad ("On Being Reviewed by Christians"—a joust with Lewis that attracted an overflow crowd), Charles Williams ("Are There Any *Valid* Objections to Free Love?" Answer: yes, if free love means licentiousness; no, if it means love informed by faithfulness and guided by will), Fr. Gervase Mathew, Colin Hardie, and para-Inklings like Dorothy L. Sayers (who so admired the Socratic Club that she attempted, without success, to open a London counterpart) and the Anglican theologian Austin Farrer, a friend of both Tolkien and Lewis. Still, it was Lewis's show. To John Wain, the club was "a kind of prize-ring in which various champions appeared to try conclusions with Lewis, who week after week put on a knock-down-and-drag-out performance that really was impressive. Our time has produced no better debater . . . I can remember packed meetings in stifling college common-rooms where the atmosphere was positively gladiatorial." Farrer seconds Wain on the skill of the president's mental fisticuffs:

> He was a bonny fighter . . . I was occasionally called upon to stop a gap in the earlier programmes . . . I went in fear and trembling, certain to be caught out in debate and to let down the side. But there Lewis would be, snuffing the imminent battle and saying "Aha!" at the sound of the trumpet. My anxieties rolled away.

Whatever ineptitude I might commit, he would maintain the cause; and nobody could put Lewis down.

It may be, as Wain suggests, that many club members were "simple-minded undergraduates" eager to hear Christianity defended "in a straight-forward, manly way, by somebody who wasn't a parson and didn't resemble the Soapy-Sam chaplains of their schooldays." Lewis fulfilled this role admirably. But he also attracted to the club many of the smartest and most learned skeptics of the time—A. J. Ayer, Antony Flew, Gilbert Ryle, J.B.S. Haldane—and the debates that ensued often brought out the best on both sides. Under Lewis's aegis and that of Aldwinckle (who served as chairman and moderated many meetings), the Socratic Club was the most thrilling undergraduate club at Oxford. In its apologetic aim, its take-no-prisoners ambience, and its sparkling high seriousness, it was for some years a lively stepchild of the Inklings.

Lewis also seized what occasions he could to take his arguments afield. A noteworthy opportunity arose in February 1943, when he delivered the Riddell Memorial Lectures at King's College, Newcastle, then part of the University of Durham. Warnie, who had returned to Oxford in May 1940 to serve in the Home Guard, accompanied him. The voyage up north was a welcome one for both brothers: in January, Lewis had been lamenting to Arthur, "Minto is laid up with one of her terrible varicose ulcers, but W. and I are alright. But it's a weary world, isn't it?" For Warnie, it was a blissful interlude, "a little oasis in the dreariness" of war and of strife at the Kilns ("that horrid house," he called it), the domestic clashes directly traceable, he believed, to Mrs. Moore's grasping, bullying ways. He spent as much time as possible away from her presence, usually sequestered in Lewis's rooms at Magdalen, where he continued his study of the Sun King and acted as Lewis's secretary, typing on his portable Royal his brother's scrawled correspondence—which had ballooned to spectacular proportions thanks to the BBC lectures—sometimes adding a sentence or two of his own and now and then signing letters in his brother's name.

The Riddell Lectures were established in memory of Sir John Walter Buchanan-Riddell, the 11th Baronet of Riddell, who had been high sheriff of Northumberland and active in Christian and academic causes; their subject was to be some facet of the relation between religious thought and modernity. For Lewis, it was a chance to defend, against relativizing trends in education, philosophy, and literary criticism, the reality of the universal moral code inherent in all human beings. What surprised many readers, when the three lectures ("Men Without Chests," "The Way," and "The Abolition of Man") appeared in book form near the end of 1943 as *The Abolition of Man*, was how friendly the great Christian apologist was toward other religions, at least when he contrasted them to modern Philistinism. He chooses a non-Western term, *Tao*, to emphasize the universality of moral reasoning. He begins with an epigram from Confucius's *Analects* and concludes with an appendix citing illustrations from a vast array of cultures, including Norse, Egyptian, Babylonian, Hebrew, Greek, Roman, American Indian, and Hindu. Many of these come from Hastings's great twelve-volume *Encyclopaedia of Religion and Ethics*, which he pored through in preparation for the lectures.

This wideness of outlook did not, however, as some might have wished, signal a relaxation of his belief in Christianity as the sole final repository of universal truth; instead, it buttressed his argument that the moral law, precisely because it is natural, flourishes wherever it finds soil to grow. He had grown more favorable toward paganism, which seemed, in some of its forms, to adumbrate Christian ideas of immortality, and more distant from Hinduism, which once he had considered to be the only serious alternative to Christianity. But both were tainted: "I am inclined to think," he told Bede Griffiths a few years after the Riddell Lectures, "that Paganism is the primitive revealed truth corrupted by devils and that Hinduism is neither of divine nor diabolical origin but profoundly and *hopelessly* natural." The gold in these religions lay in their adherence to the Tao, to universal axioms of goodness and justice. The teachings vary here and there, as God's truth is more fully realized in one culture, less in another, but the spirit of the Tao is everywhere the same and everywhere indispensable: "In the *Tao* . . . we find the concrete reality in which to participate is to be truly human: the real common will and common reason of humanity, alive, and growing like a tree, and branching out, as the situation varies, into ever new beauties and dignities of application."

The book received a warm welcome, especially in religious periodicals. *The Hibbert Journal* lauded "the fineness of Mr. Lewis's thought," while *The Churchman* called it "a most thought-provoking book." Barfield, too, liked it greatly. No doubt he especially enjoyed Lewis's concluding paragraphs, in which this stalwart critic of Anthroposophy speculates on the possibility of a new kind of science faithful to the Tao, allowing that "I hear rumours that Goethe's approach to nature deserves fuller consideration—that even Dr Steiner may have seen something that orthodox researchers have missed." Moved by this unexpected concession, Barfield wrote to Lewis in an ecstasy of praise, declaring *The Abolition of Man* "a real triumph. There may be a piece of contemporary writing in which precision of thought, liveliness of expression and depth of meaning unite with the same felicity, but I have not come across it."

Such praise from friends always gratified Lewis, although he tried not to be swept away on tides of self-approbation. He worried about being egotistical, knowing how thoroughly he had wallowed in amour propre during his youth. He valued friends who supported him without fawning over him, who challenged him to improve as a thinker, artist, and Christian. Barfield, Tolkien, Williams, Sayers, and Sister Penelope fit this description. In particular, he worried that apologetics might be bad for his faith. He could not discuss this sensitive question with Tolkien, but to comrade-in-apologetics Dorothy L. Sayers he confessed that "a doctrine never seems dimmer to me than when I have just successfully defended it." To Sister Penelope, as usual, he entrusted his misgivings in full, sending her in 1942 his "Apologist's Evening Hymn":

> From all my lame defeats and oh! much more
> From all the victories I have seemed to score;
> From cleverness shot forth in Thy behalf,
> At which, while angels weep, the audience laugh;
> From all my proofs of Thy divinity,
> Thou, who would'st give no sign, deliver me.
> Thoughts are but coins. Let me not trust, instead
> Of Thee, the thumb-worn image of Thy head;
> From every thought, even from my thoughts of Thee,
> Oh thou fair Silence! fall and set me free.
> Lord of the straight way and the needle's eye,
> Take from me all my trumpery lest I die.

Hell Is Locked on the Inside

Beginning in the spring of 1944, Lewis wrote a little book that would take his evangelizing in a new direction—not exactly theology, not exactly apologetics, not exactly fiction, but an imaginative "supposal" about the journey from this world to the next. He read chapters at Inklings meetings during April and May under the working title "Who Goes Home." Tolkien's assessment was lukewarm. In an April 13 airgraph to Christopher in South Africa, he describes a Thursday Inklings meeting with Lewis, Warnie, Williams, and the Useless Quack in attendance, during which he enjoyed "the chapter of Major Lewis' projected book— on a subject that does not interest me: the court of Louis XIV; but it was most wittily written (as well as learned)," but did "not think so well of the concluding chapter of C.S.L.'s new moral allegory or 'vision,' based on the medieval fancy of the Refrigerium, by which the lost souls have an occasional holiday in Paradise." After appearing in *The Guardian* in weekly installments under the title "Who Goes Home? Or The Grand Divorce," the book was published as *The Great Divorce*—an answer to William Blake's *Marriage of Heaven and Hell*, itself a reaction against Swedenborg's *Heaven and Its Wonders and Hell from Things Heard and Seen*. Swedenborg's vision of the afterlife came straight from God, or so he claimed; but Lewis's vision, like Dante's, is a conscious literary creation, a moral satire rather than a mystical revelation, and if Swedenborg is an influence, it is only indirectly, through George MacDonald.

The opening scene is quintessentially English: "I seemed to be standing in a busy queue" at twilight, in a "grey town" in the rain. As in *The Divine Comedy*, the narrator is the same as the author, yet not quite the same, and characters present themselves as the narrator sees them: "a little waspish woman," "the Short Man," "the Big Man," a "Tousle-Headed Poet," "the Intelligent Man" who talks business in a bowler hat, an Anglican bishop of progressive views. Not so English, but unmistakably human, the people in the queue quarrel, whine, swagger, and worm their way to the top, some cheated out of their place, some leaving in a snit. "Well, this is hardly the sort of society I'm used to as a matter of fact."

A bus arrives "blazing with golden light, heraldically coloured," and lifts the passengers above the wet roofs of the grey town through a vast expanse of searing light to a grassy meadow, a variant of the *locus amoenus* of classical and medieval mythology, a place of pure being and light. "I had the sense of being in a larger space, perhaps even a larger *sort* of space, than I had ever known before." Against this saturated landscape, men look like ghosts. Flowers are diamond-hard; grass does not bend beneath one's feet. Lewis's dream reveals a heaven that is anything but dreamlike, an ethereal region more materially dense than the earth below. He mentions in a preface that he got this idea from a story in an American science fiction magazine in which a traveler to the past finds "raindrops that would pierce him like bullets and sandwiches that no strength could bite." The Tolkien scholar Douglas A. Anderson has identified the story as "The Man Who Lived Backwards," by Charles F. Hall, which appeared in the summer of 1938 in *Tales of Wonder*, a British science fiction magazine.

Seeing the grass through his own feet, Lewis realizes that he, too, is a phantom. "'Golly!' thought I, 'I'm in for it this time.'" In fact, all the passengers are ghosts: the Tousle-Headed Poet had jumped under a train when society refused to acknowledge his gifts. One by one, the ghosts are met by bright spirits, gloriously naked or resplendently attired, always wonderfully solid. Overhearing their conversations, Lewis realizes that the spirits are assigned to ghosts whom they had known in life, with the aim of helping them to overcome their besetting sins, their self-importance, self-pity, melancholy, lust. Offered the chance to be made fit for heaven, almost all the ghosts make excuses: "Of course I should require some assurances," the Bishop says. "I should want a guarantee that you are taking me to a place where I shall find a wider sphere of usefulness . . ." But there are no guarantees; one must be remade, and that can be painful. "I came here to get my rights, see?" says the Big Man, "Not to go snivelling along on charity tied onto your apron-strings." Almost all hold fast to their sins, decline the offer of remediation and forgiveness, refuse the promised joy as an all-too-easy answer to their problems or an insult to their dignity, and eventually return to the grey town to be consumed by their resentments. A cynic is certain this is all a con game run by a secret cabal, an artist must return to publish manifestos against "those damned Neo-Regionalists" who have eclipsed his fame, a social climber who drove her husband to a nervous breakdown will stay only if she can have further opportunities to improve him. And so on. The easiest sin to cure is lust—in Lewis's view, far less insidious than envy or pride, and more capable of submitting to the death and resurrection that all natural loves must undergo.

The sound of a Scottish accent and the sight of a resplendent being introduces Lewis to his own guiding spirit: George MacDonald. Mac-Donald is to Lewis at once Virgil and Beatrice, for it was he who carried Lewis from a bookstall at the Leatherhead Station to the threshold of the New Life. In paying tribute to his mentor, Lewis rehearses the conversion story he would later tell in *Surprised by Joy*, and fictionalizes Mac-Donald, who in life was a universalist (believing in the salvation of all), by having him offer a doctrine of hell and a theodicy more compatible with orthodox Christianity. The grey town is the Valley of the Shadow of Death. "To any that leaves it, it is Purgatory." But for those who, refusing every offer of salvation, are bent on returning to it, it "will have been Hell even from the beginning." The Valley of the Shadow of Life, where they now dwell, is a precinct of heaven to those who choose to remain. And just as heaven works backward, turning all past suffering into glory, so Hell works backward, turning all past pleasures into ash, so that "at the end of all things, when the sun rises here and the twilight turns to blackness down there, the Blessed will say, 'We have never lived anywhere except in Heaven,' and the Lost, 'We were always in Hell.' Hell, though, is smaller than an atom of the Real World; the damned soul fits in Hell by being "nearly nothing . . . shrunk, shut up in itself."

"My Roman Catholic friends would be surprised," the fictional Lewis remarks, "for to them souls in Purgatory are already saved. And my Protestant friends would like it no better, for they'd say that the tree lies as it falls.'" To which Lewis's version of MacDonald replies, in the spirit of *Mere Christianity*, "'They're both right, maybe. Do not fash yourself with such questions. Ye cannot fully understand the relations of choice and Time till you are beyond both. And ye were not brought here to study such curiosities. What concerns you is the nature of the choice itself: and that ye can watch them making.'" The nature of the choice, the ordering and disordering of love, was always what concerned Lewis most, and what he was most skilled at representing. His life with the increasingly irritable Janie Moore gave him firsthand knowledge of the process by which small choices can carry the soul into a small hell of its own making. From the crucible of daily domestic miseries, Lewis emerged as an expert in the deep devices of the human heart.

Paradise Rehabilitated

Lewis was now the foremost Christian apologist in the English-speaking world and firing on all cylinders as a literary scholar and a fantasist. Diverse as his writings were, all touched on one great subject—the Fall of Man, arguably the central theme of English poetry from Spenser, Milton, and Dryden, to Shelley, Coleridge, and Blake. Though Enlightenment thinkers reinterpreted the Fall in secular terms, as the corruption, by social forces, of a human nature originally pure, or as a freely willed rejection of the universal moral law, and though Romantic thinkers succeeded for a brief time in describing the Fall as a glorious Promethean defiance or a necessary stage in the liberation of human consciousness, no English writer of any stature surrendered the idea in favor of unalloyed optimism. One has only to think of Joseph Conrad and William Golding to realize that this fundamental platform of Christian doctrine belongs as much to the English literary mainstream as it did to the Inklings.

It fell to Lewis, in these dark times, to interpret the English literary tradition of the Fall and to defend the doctrine as the compelling truth about "the sort of universe in which we have all along been living." But interpreting this literary tradition meant, first of all, interpreting John Milton, the poet English modernists love to hate. This was a task Lewis relished, for he had long loved *Paradise Lost*—perhaps as far back as his ninth year, when he read the epic poem for the first time. Under Kirkpatrick's tutelage, Lewis devoted many of his blissful hours of ad-lib reading to Milton's poems, enthusing about his discoveries in letters to Arthur Greeves. Thrilled with his purchase of a fine edition of *Paradise Lost*, he wrote to him in July 1916, "Don't you like the Leopard witches? How you will love Milton some day!" A week later, he was more cautious: "I don't think I should advise Milton: while there are lots of things in him you would love—the descriptions of Hell and Chaos and Paradise and Adam and Eve and Satan's flight down through the stars, on the other hand his classical allusions, his rather crooked style of English, and his long speeches, might be tedious." By March 1917, all such hesitations were gone: "I have finished 'Paradise Lost' again, enjoying it even more than before. Really you must read it sometime soon. In Milton is everything you get everywhere else, only better. He is as voluptuous as Keats, as romantic as Morris, as grand as Wagner, as wierd [sic] as Poe, and a better lover of nature than even the Brontës."

And that was before Lewis became a Christian. Before his conversion, Lewis loved Milton without sharing his convictions, much as the Romantics loved Milton (Blake thought Milton "a true Poet and of the Devil's party without knowing it" and Shelley admired the "energy and magnificence" of Milton's Satan as passionately as he detested the vindictiveness of Milton's God). It fell to Lewis to rescue *Paradise Lost* from the Romantics who loved Milton for the wrong reasons as well as from the new generation of poets and critics—notably John Middleton Murry and T. S. Eliot—who disliked Milton for a host of reasons: his indigestible epic style, his repellent portrait of God, his political opinions. To Eliot, writing in 1936, Milton was a major poet but a bad moralist, theologian, psychologist, political philosopher—and man—who exerted a corrupting influence on English language and literature from which it was still struggling to recover. As the redoubtable Cambridge critic F. R. Leavis put it, thanks to T. S. Eliot, "Milton's dislodgement . . . was effected with remarkably little fuss."

Perhaps Milton had been dislodged in the circles Leavis knew, but in Oxford, with the arrival of Charles Williams, things were very different. Williams didn't just love Milton, he channeled him. His Hilary term 1940 lectures on Milton, as Lewis said in *A Preface to Paradise Lost*, which he dedicated to Williams, "partly anticipated, partly confirmed, and most of all clarified and matured, what I had long been thinking about Milton," namely, "that when the old poets made some virtue their theme they were not teaching but adoring, and that what we take for the didactic is often the enchanted." The lectures are not extant, but Williams distilled them in a preface for the 1940 World's Classics edition of *The Poetical Works of Milton*, in which he attributes opposition to Milton to ignorance of Christian doctrine, whether it concerns chastity ("that great miracle of the transmutation of the flesh proposed in *Comus*") or obedience ("the proper order of the universe in relation to . . . the law of self-abnegation in love" that is the real theme of *Paradise Lost*). In just twenty three-by-five-inch pages, Williams achieved, according to Lewis, "the recovery of a true critical tradition after more than a hundred years of laborious misunderstanding."

It was during the period of Milton's disgrace and Williams's triumph that Lewis received an invitation from the University College of North Wales in Bangor to deliver the Ballard Mathews Lectures (named for a first professor of mathematics at Bangor, the polymath George Ballard Mathews) on a subject of his choosing. Lewis chose *Paradise Lost*. From these lectures, given on the first three days of December 1941, came his book *A Preface to Paradise Lost*, with a handsome testimony to what Williams had done to rescue Milton for modern readers: "Apparently the door of the prison was unlocked all the time; but it was only you who thought of trying the handle. Now we can all come out."

Though his debt to Williams was real, Lewis's approach to the appreciation of *Paradise Lost* was characteristically his own. The first task, Lewis said, is to understand the *genre* with which one is dealing. *Paradise Lost* is an epic poem, a genre that has its roots in oral recitation and is never merely "original" or idiosyncratic. The "primary epic" (Homer, *Beowulf*) tells of heroic adventures; the "secondary epic" (Virgil, Milton) treats "great subjects," events by which the world is forever changed, and uses an elevated style to convey the momentousness of its theme.

W. W. Robson, among others, was of the opinion that Lewis was so intent on defending *Paradise Lost* that he lost touch with "any of the normal standards and criteria which it is usual to apply to poetry traditionally considered great" and in his "frenzy of special pleading" inadvertently called attention to Milton's faults. But was it special pleading? That there are defects in Milton's verse, Lewis freely admits. That there are unattractive elements in Milton's theology and that he could have done a better job portraying unfallen sexuality, Lewis also admits. But Lewis was convinced that understanding *Paradise Lost* as an epic meant reading it differently from the way one would read a lyric poem or any essentially private work of art.

In *Paradise Lost*, Milton took on the greatest of all great subjects, the fundamental Christian story: that God made all creation good while knowing that it would be marred by Satan's rebellion and mankind's Fall. For that purpose an elevated style and a high didacticism is certainly in order. To approach the poem through a film of modernist assumptions (the "normal standards and criteria") is inevitably to miss the point. F. R. Leavis was a good judge of Milton's verse but a bad judge of Milton's universe: "It is not that he and I see different things when we look at

Paradise Lost. He sees and hates the very same that I see and love. Hence the disagreement between us tends to escape from the realm of literary criticism. We differ not about the nature of Milton's poetry, but about the nature of man, or even the nature of joy itself."

When Eric Fenn wrote to suggest a radio broadcast about *Paradise Lost*, Lewis declined, arguing that the listening audience would not derive any pleasure from Milton. But another possibility suggested itself: a way of defending, not the seventeenth-century Puritan poet himself, but the essential Christian vision of his poem, by transmuting it into a very different kind of story. Fiction can make an argument more compelling than even the best criticism (hence Lewis told T. S. Eliot that Charles Williams would do more good "if only he cd. be induced to write more fiction"—like *Descent into Hell*—"and less criticism!"). It was time to return to Ransom.

Voyage to Venus

The parting words of Ransom in the fictional letter that concludes *Out of the Silent Planet* suggest that Lewis did not plan to send his hero on another planetary voyage: "Now that 'Weston' has shut the door, the way to the planets lies through the past; if there is to be any more space-traveling, it will have to be time-traveling as well . . . !"

Tolkien's attempt to write a time-travel novel had been abortive; now Lewis thought he would give it a try. Sometime during 1938 or 1939, he began *The Dark Tower*, a sequel to *Out of the Silent Planet*, discovered in unfinished form by Walter Hooper years after Lewis's death. Its authenticity, once questioned, is now accepted by the great majority of Lewis scholars; Alastair Fowler remembers having seen it in Lewis's rooms, and Fr. Gervase Mathew said that Lewis read it to an Inklings meeting in 1939 or 1940. *The Dark Tower* picks up where *Out of the Silent Planet* leaves off, beginning with a Cambridge don named Orfieu saying "'Of course . . . the sort of time-travelling you read about in books—time-travelling in the body—is absolutely impossible.'" Orfieu invents a "chronoscope" by means of which his friends (among them Ransom) first observe and eventually interact with the alien, mutagenic, parallel universe of Othertime. Perhaps Lewis thought the tale too weird to continue. In any event, he dropped it after a few scenes and instead reopened the door Weston had shut, sending Ransom on another planetary journey, this time to Venus.

The new Ransom adventure enabled Lewis to grapple with a question frequently raised about *Paradise Lost* and only half-answered in his *Preface*: Did Milton succeed—can anyone succeed—in making plausible the Fall of Man? Can one convincingly portray, can one even coherently imagine, the temptation of a wholly innocent being? What chink could there be in Eve's armor of holiness and bliss that would make an opening for the serpent's fatal suggestion? Conversely, can one convincingly portray, can one even coherently imagine, an Eve who is genuinely tempted yet ultimately prevails, a Paradise nearly, yet not finally, lost? To answer these questions, to defend Milton—and with Milton the entire classical Christian Augustinian tradition—called for another imaginative supposal. Venus, *Perelandra* in the Old Solar tongue, would be a young planet at the Adam-and-Eve stage, Lewis told Arthur; and Ransom would arrive "in time to prevent their 'falling' as *our* first pair did."

A November 1941 letter to Sister Penelope indicates that the story was in medias res and already at a troubling crux: "I've got Ransom to Venus and through his first conversation with the 'Eve' of that world: a difficult chapter." The difficulty was that "this woman has got to combine characteristics which the Fall has put poles apart—she's got to be in some ways like a Pagan goddess and in other ways like the Blessed Virgin." Meanwhile, Lewis himself was in medias res and feeling rather like a moral failure; he accused himself of relapsing into old (unspecified) sins and asked the nun, "Have you room for an extra prayer? Pray for *Jane* if you have. She is the old lady I call my mother and live with (she is really the mother of a friend)—an unbeliever, ill, old, frightened, full of charity in the sense of alms, but full of uncharity in several other senses. And I can do so little for her."

Venus had an obvious appeal for Lewis, who knew better than any man alive all her attributes in pagan, medieval, and Renaissance mythology; he loved to observe the planet in the morning and evening sky and point out its splendors to his friends, as in this April 1940 note to Warnie: "Every night Venus grows more spectacular. It is true *Chaucerian* weather! How impossible not to believe, after so many disappointments, that it *means* what it says." If one imagines, as Ransom suggests in *Perelandra*, that the things we hear of in myths are "scattered through other worlds as realities," the planet Venus, afloat in the ocean of Deep Heaven, younger and closer to the sun than Mars, is an obvious location for the blessed island realms of ancient lore—the Fortunate Isles, the Celtic Tír na nÓg, the Garden of the Hesperides.

But how to connect this book to *Out of the Silent Planet?* A frame narrative solves the problem by having Lewis recapitulate Ransom's initial journey. Now it is Lewis who is the Pedestrian, grudgingly making his way to Ransom's cottage in answer to his friend's urgent wire, growing more anxious with every step, fearful of meeting the unearthly *eldila*, of being "drawn in," of going mad: He is experiencing, as he soon discovers, a barrage by the *eldila* of the Dark Lord, not unlike the way Christian monks of the desert were bombarded by demonic *logismoi*. The attack is in the open now because the great siege is drawing to its end. The forces of good and evil (Allies and Axis, Lewis obviously intends us to think) have started to emerge "in something a little more like their true colours," and ordinary people are being called upon to do the fighting.

Lewis's part in this engagement "with principalities and powers and depraved hypersomatic beings" is small. He is to help Ransom climb naked and blindfolded into a casket that the Oyarsa of Malacandra will send to Venus; in contrast to *Out of the Silent Planet*, there is no effort here to construct a plausible technology for space travel; preternatural means suffice. Lewis is also charged with summoning the "four or five people whom we can trust"—Inklings, in other words—to convene whenever he returns, with "Humphrey" (another nickname for Dr. Havard, who seemed to invite them) to provide any necessary medical support. Not knowing the details of his mission or why he was chosen for it, Ransom climbs into his "celestial coffin" with a self-abandonment that is at once trusting and despairing. Lewis closes the coffin lid, goes into the house, and is sick.

After a little more than a year, during which "we had raids and bad news and hopes deferred and all the earth became full of darkness and cruel habitations," Ransom returns. He emerges from his coffin like St. Antony from his cave, glowing with vitality and wondering why his friends look so pale. The only injury he bears is a wound that bleeds incessantly from the heel, suggesting an affinity with the Fisher King, a mirror of Christ. Conversations with B. (Barfield) and "a sceptical friend of ours called McPhee" elicit the unsettling fact that Ransom has "seen" the Platonic Form of Life itself, has had a taste of Paradise and a fore-taste of the Resurrection—a reality "too *definite*" to be put into words, in which bodily experience is not transcended but "engulfed."

This Paradise roofed by a golden sky is indeed a world to be sensed and tasted—a swooning landscape of islands floating on a sweet-water green-gold ocean, lush vegetation, bubble-trees that drench body and soul, and great clusters of fruit that fall into the hand, so delicious that "for one draught of this on earth wars would be fought and nations be-trayed." Remembering what he learned on Malacandra, Ransom resists the temptation to reach for more of this ecstatic refreshment. The "itch to have things over again . . . was it possibly the root of all evil?" After a reassuringly comical first encounter with a sentient being, a small dragon that likes to have its belly stroked, Ransom meets the Green Lady, who is queen of the realm, newly created by Maleldil and green in every sense of the word. She is naked, innocent, as spontaneous as the floating is-lands on which she dwells; they undulate freely to every wave Maleldil sends, while she absorbs whatever He desires her to know. Ransom and the Green Lady converse in Old Solar, and the dialogue prospers—until interrupted by the arrival of Weston, armed with gun and provisions.

No longer the positivistic scientist with imperialistic designs on other planets, Weston has embraced the philosophy of the Life Force, wor-shipped as a "blind, inarticulate purposiveness thrusting its way upward and ever upward." This new, spiritual Weston is a great deal worse than the old materialist Weston; he is so committed to serving the Life Force that he invites that most spiritual of beings, the Devil, to take up resi-dence within him, to the ruin of his personality and selfhood. His trans-formation into the "Unman" is, one reviewer wrote, "the most terrifying and convincing instance of diabolical possession in English letters since Benson's *The Necromancers*." Foregoing sleep, the Unman makes a relent-less verbal assault on the innocence of the Green Lady, interrupted only by vacant interludes spent eviscerating small frogs, urging her to disobey a seemingly arbitrary divine command against sleeping on the Fixed Land.

Ransom counters with the case for obedience, speaking of the joy of surrendering one's own will; the Unman presses the paradox that to dis-obey will be to give up her *deepest* will. The debate continues until Ran-som realizes that the contest will not be won with words; he must fight the Unman physically, to the death, just as "far away on Earth . . . men were at war, and whitefaced subalterns and freckled corporals who had but lately begun to shave, stood in horrible gaps or crawled forward in deadly darkness, awaking, like him, to the preposterous truth that all really depended on their actions." Battle ensues, Perelandra is saved, and the Oyarsas of Malacandra and Perelandra descend in an operatic finale to crown the queen and her king (largely absent from the narrative) in a scene whose bridal mysticism owes much to Charles Williams's Way of Affirmation.

To some readers, the conclusion of *Perelandra* was over the top; others felt that Lewis had produced "an inspired litany of love and homage" on the level of Dante. The poet Ruth Pitter (whose friendship with Lewis is discussed below) was so taken with the ending that she transcribed it into "irregular Spenserian stanzas" in order to memorize it. Alistair Cooke, by contrast, found the reverence for chastity so galling that he could only assume that Lewis's "secret fear that unchastity is the best pleasure" was its real subtext: "It is at this point that an earthly book-reviewer must uncross his gross legs and tiptoe out, leaving Mr. Lewis to the absorbed serenity of his dreams." This seems an eccentric—or deliberately provocative—reading of a book so full of delight in unfallen sensuality that one feels at times that one is bathing nude along with Lewis in Parson's Pleasure.

Lewis justly regarded *Perelandra* as his best book to date and was overjoyed to hear from readers who understood it. In this novel, more completely than in any of his other works, all the Lewises—the literary scholar, the philosopher, the moral psychologist, the satirist, the critic, the fantasist, the evangelist—are present and working in harmony. On the cover of *The Saturday Review of Literature* for April 8, 1944, a wood engraving by the well-known portraitist Frances O'Brien Garfield shows a dreamy, contemplative Lewis set against a backdrop of stars, planets, and a hieratic dragon, with the caption "C. S. Lewis has gone down again into his bottomless well of imagination for a captivating myth." The portrait is a poor likeness, but the caption is correct.

A Kingdom Hidden in the Heart of Britain

By the time *Perelandra* appeared in 1943, a sequel, *That Hideous Strength: A Modern Fairy-Tale for Grown-Ups*, was almost ready for the printers, thus bringing to completion the *commedia* that began on a spaceship headed for Mars. The title came from a verse about the Tower of Babel ("the schaddow of that hidduous strenth") by one of Lewis's OHEL figures, the sixteenth-century Scottish poet Sir David Lyndsay. During a time "vaguely 'after the war,'" the Shadow looms over a small university town in the English Midlands, as an academic squabble becomes a full-scale engagement with powers and principalities. Upon this stage, Lewis unfolds a broadly satirical supernatural tale that packs in the multitudinous moral and social concerns he had addressed in *The Abolition of Man* and in his controversial essays of the postwar years: the miseducation of young minds; the evils of eugenics, vivisection, social engineering, "humane" rehabilitation of misfits, and police-state propaganda; the encroachment on the humanities of the fetish for "research" and practical results; the nature of true fellowship; and the value of hierarchy. Barfield's observation about Lewis that "somehow what he thought about everything was secretly present in what he said about anything" is amply confirmed.

At the same time, *That Hideous Strength* is the Lewis novel most clearly indebted to Charles Williams: the Arthurian themes, the esoteric Christianity, and the mundane setting all testify to Lewis's fascination with his visionary friend. Readers expecting another planetary romance were puzzled and even offended by what seemed an indiscriminate blending of realism with science-fantasy. But Lewis was attempting a third kind of novel altogether, in which, as he explains while writing of Williams's works, there is a "violation of frontier" and the everyday world finds itself "invaded by the marvellous."

Ransom has changed; his spiritual transformation complete, he has become director of a small company reminiscent of Williams's Companions of the Co-inherence and a figure of Arthurian legend. The bleeding heel at the end of *Perelandra* had already signaled his identification with the Fisher King. Now an even greater mystery is revealed: he is none other than the Pendragon, successor to King Arthur and sovereign over all that remains of the Arthurian kingdom of Logres, the true, spiritual England that lies buried in the heart of Britain and haunts its history. Ransom remains offstage for the most part, as the action centers on two parallel tales of temptation and conversion: that of Jane Studdock, a would-be scholar with an unfinished doctoral thesis on Donne's "triumphant vindication of the body," and her husband, Mark, a fellow in sociology at venerable Bracton College, founded in 1300 near an ancient walled woodland (Bragdon Wood) at whose center, paved in Roman-British masonry, is "Merlin's well." Despite the setting, Bracton College is a modern institution, increasingly in the hands of the "Progressive Element" who hold the key to Mark's advancement.

In sketching Mark Studdock's character, Lewis traces the process by which the desire to belong to the "Inner Ring" (as Lewis called it in a 1944 address to undergraduates at King's College, London) gradually chokes out other interests. The desire for the Inner Ring, Lewis maintained, is "one of the great permanent mainsprings of human action," a temptation more insidious than ambition or lust, more "skillful in making a man who is not yet a very bad man do very bad things," more liable to take over one's personality. "Unless you take measures to prevent it," Lewis warned the students in his audience (who might have hoped to hear a pep talk rather than a jeremiad), "this desire is going to be one of the chief motives of your life, from the first day on which you enter your profession until the day when you are too old to care."

Mark lacks the resources to hold this desire in check. Thrilled to hear himself included in the "we" of the Progressive Element, he allows himself to be manipulated by Lord Feverstone, a fellow of the college, who turns out to be Weston's former business partner Dick Devine, now come up in the world. Lord Feverstone recruits Mark for the National Institute of Co-ordinated Experiments (NICE), a social-engineering think tank with plans "to make man a really efficient animal." NICE's eventual aim, as Mark learns too late—here the novel departs from Orwellian political satire into Lovecraftian fantasy—is to place humanity under the control of hyperintelligent Macrobes (the fallen *eldila*), who communicate by means of the organization's Head—the severed head of an executed murderer, kept alive in the lab.

The Head in a vat was a macabre joke on Lewis's part, but he was convinced that scientists were on the point of creating monstrosities no less chilling. "It is commonly done with cats' heads in Oxford laboratories," Lewis told the poet Herbert Palmer, "and was really tried (unsuccessfully) on a human head in Germany. One can hardly satirise these people—the reality is always more incredible than what one invents."

Mark is also wanted because NICE has its eye on his wife, who is troubled by clairvoyant dreams. This is Lewis's first novel in which the hero is a woman, and in highlighting her flaws as well as her virtues, he offended some feminist readers. Jane "wasn't meant to illustrate the problem of the married woman and her own career in general," he assured the Harwoods; "rather the problem of everyone who follows an *imagined* vocation at the expense of a real one." Like Ransom in the first pages of *Out of the Silent Planet*, like the fictional Lewis in the first pages of *Perelandra*, and like Lewis himself, as he tells us in *Surprised by Joy*, Jane wishes above all else to do her academic work and fears above all else to be "drawn in."

Jane *is* drawn in, of course, for she has a vital role to play; increasingly disturbed by her dreams, she finds refuge in a manor house where she joins Ransom's motley company, including an Arthurian scholar, a housemaid, the skeptical Ulster Scot MacPhee (called McPhee in *Perelandra*, modeled on Kirkpatrick), and Mr. Bultitude, last of the seven bears of Logres, who is, according to Tolkien, a good likeness of Lewis himself. The prophet Merlin Ambrosius, who has been sleeping in the barrow beneath Bragdon Wood since the fifth century, awakens and joins their ranks; though a Christian, he is permitted to use magical means to battle evil because he represents—in a Barfieldian note—"the last vestige of an old order in which matter and spirit were, from our modern point of view, confused." The reign of Belbury, like that of Babel, collapses in a confusion of tongues; the liberated laboratory animals find love; the Studdock marriage is healed; and the Head and its followers meet their end in a dénouement Orwell found "so preposterous that it does not even succeed in being horrible in spite of much bloodshed." As in *Perelandra*, there is a festal conclusion; the planetary deities descend in a joyous tumult; "opera-bouffe," Barfield called it.

That Hideous Strength bears a dedication to Janie McNeil, an old family friend from Belfast. Unfortunately, she hated the book: "I wish he'd dedicated any book other than this to me!" She was not alone in her disdain. Lewis told Sayers that the book "has got a more unanimous chorus of unfavourable reviews than any book I can remember. Apparently reviewers *will not* tolerate a mixture of the realistic and the supernatural. Which is a pity, because (a) It's just the mixture I like, and (b) We have to put up with it in real life." A little later, after more reviews came out, he told Sister Penelope, "*That Hideous Strength* has been unanimously damned by all reviewers." Lewis himself had had doubts about the book while writing it, telling Eddison in April 1943, "I have just read through what is already written (about 300 sheets) and come to the uncomfortable conclusion that it is all rubbish. Has this ever happened to you?" In May, he was still struggling, telling Barfield that "the novel at present in progress is bosh," while in an illustrated Christmas 1944 letter to his godson Laurence Harwood, he reported, "I'm writing a story with a Bear in it [a little drawing of the bear is in the margin] and at present the Bear is going to get married in the last chapter. There are also Angels in it. But sometimes I don't think it is going to be very good."

We are not obliged to agree. Though each volume of the Space Trilogy is markedly different in style and theme, the whole possesses a mythopoeic unity that lends strength and beauty to each part. The trilogy begins with an invasion of unfallen worlds by wicked men and ends with an invasion of our fallen world by planetary angels. Souls are continually in motion, ascending to ultimate happiness in the beatific vision or descending to ultimate despair: the "miserific vision." Taken as a whole, the trilogy's portrait of salvation and damnation was Lewis's most ambitious attempt before Narnia to write a convincing theological anthropology and recover a sacramental cosmos in which moderns could live.

Critics at War

In the years from 1939 to 1945, Lewis became the leading Christian voice (popes aside) of the twentieth century and did much of his best work in mythopoeic fantasy and moral satire. In addition, he flourished as a historian of medieval and Renaissance poetry and prose and as a defender of the traditional English canon. Was he, then, a literary critic? Not exactly; the very idea of criticism and of "theory" made him uncomfortable. Nonetheless, as in the case of *Paradise Lost*, there were critical controversies that Lewis couldn't resist, for they had implications for the future not only of university education but of Christian culture.

The first of these critical battles, a lively but gentlemanly debate with the Milton scholar E.M.W. Tillyard, published as *The Personal Heresy: A Controversy* (1939), was Lewis's chance to air his disapproval of the fatal subjectivism of critics who treat poetry as covert autobiography. The sparks really flew, however, when Lewis joined battle with an influential school of criticism seated in the colleges and lecture halls of Cambridge

University. By 1931, as we have seen, Lewis and Tolkien had successfully fended off a modernist revision of the Oxford English syllabus (though skirmishes would continue until the 1960s). The English faculty at Cambridge, by contrast, was more open to innovation; the syllabus had been revised in 1917 to encompass modern and even international studies, and a radical new approach to reading, evaluating, and teaching English literature was gathering momentum.

The historic rivalry between Oxford and Cambridge played a part in shaping these differences; and a bit of background is needed to see where the battle lines would be drawn. Ever since Isaac Newton's days, Cambridge had been the dominant force in mathematics and natural philosophy. The Apostles, an undergraduate secret society founded in 1820 to foster debate on the topics of the day, counted among its members a pantheon of physicists, economists, historians, politicians, philosophers, theologians, poets, and critics. During and after the Edwardian period, many of the Apostles had ties to the Bloomsbury Group, and shared in Bloomsbury's devotion to social radicalism and destabilizing aesthetic and sexual experiences. In this atmosphere of scientific positivism and iconoclastic aestheticism, I. A. Richards, a student of G. E. Moore, developed a bold theory of poetry and criticism.

Richards was a charismatic teacher, an early champion of T. S. Eliot and Ezra Pound, developer with C. K. Ogden of an international "Basic English" (Orwell's "Newspeak"), a polymath and adventurer who climbed mountains and mastered Chinese in his spare time. He was also a communist, with a particular admiration for Mao. His aim as a scholar and teacher was to establish literary studies on a sound scientific footing, freed from vague and obscurantist metaphysical notions. Drawing upon psychoanalysis, neurophysiology, linguistics, and analytical philosophy, Richards developed the method of "Practical Criticism," involving close reading, analysis of the multiple meanings present in a text, and observation of the effects such meanings have on the attentive reader. In a post-Christian, morally rudderless world (as Richards diagnosed the situation), when poetry was all that remained of the mythopoeic faculty, it fell to criticism to address the great needs of culture. "To set up as a critic," Richards wrote in 1924, "is to set up as a judge of values." This was Matthew Arnold with a distinctly modern, positivistic spin. Richards trained his students to distinguish the emotive language of poetry from the fact-language of science, to analyze the number and range of "appetencies" that a poem is able to satisfy, and to detect and uproot the "stock responses" and "doctrinal adhesions" that stand in the way of an authentic response to poetry—and to life.

Richards's following at Cambridge was fervent; huge crowds attended his lectures on Practical Criticism; as the halls filled up, he took to lecturing in the streets. Christopher Isherwood, who attended Richards's lectures before dropping out of Cambridge, described the phenomenon in a 1938 memoir:

> Here, at last, was the prophet we had been waiting for . . . he was infinitely more than a brilliant new literary critic: he was our guide, our evangelist, who revealed to us, in a succession of astounding lightning-flashes, the entire expanse of the Modern World . . . Poetry wasn't a holy flame, a fire-bird from the moon; it was a group of interrelated stimuli acting upon the ocular nerves, the semi-circular canals, the brain, the solar plexus, the digestive and sexual organs. It did you medically demonstrable good, like a dose of strychnine or salts. We became behaviourists, materialists, atheists. In our conversation we substituted the word "emotive" for the word "beautiful."

Oxford was slower to appreciate Richards. When he visited Magdalen College in the late 1920s or early '30s and was placed in Lewis's hands, his reception was decidedly chilly—if we can trust Richards's own account many years later to a biographer. Lewis, it seems, had forgotten to reserve lodgings for his distinguished guest, and so, as a makeshift, placed Richards in R. G. Collingwood's temporarily vacant rooms. Before retiring for the night, Lewis brought Richards his own annotated copy of Richards's masterpiece, *Principles of Literary Criticism* (1924), saying, "Here's something that should put you to sleep." But Richards passed a restless night after reading Lewis's detailed critical comments in the margins.

Lewis's relationship with F. R. Leavis was even more fraught. For a time a passionate disciple of Richards, Leavis was every bit as charismatic in the lecture hall; "when Leavis read poetry during a lecture," one admirer said, "it could seem as if for the moment the world stopped." Though for most of his career he was connected only peripherally to the

Cambridge English faculty, he was, in John Wain's words, the "one man who has, almost single-handed, turned the university study of 'English' from a placid, rather stagnant ornamental lake to a choppy and sometimes tempestuous sea." As one former student put it, Leavis trained his followers to read critically "as if our very lives depended upon it." Although Leavis gave warm encouragement to his own students, he was acutely sensitive to perceived slights from colleagues and delighted in uncovering the deficiencies of his literary adversaries; he "cultivated to perfection the sneer which he used like an oyster knife," as Noel Annan said.

In 1932, Leavis founded the quarterly review *Scrutiny*, editing the journal with his wife, Q. D. "Queenie" Leavis, until 1953. The journal's name—taken from Edgell Rickword's *Scrutinies*, a two-volume anthology of iconoclastic criticism—has a religious connotation, calling to mind the Lenten Scrutinies, a searching self-examination intended to fortify the faithful against corrupting influences. As such, *Scrutiny* carried out a thoroughgoing revaluation of the English literary canon, discrediting Milton (see above), exalting Donne and Marvell, and admitting a small number of more modern authors (Jane Austen, George Eliot, Henry James, Joseph Conrad, and D. H. Lawrence) to the empyrean that Leavis called the Great Tradition. Evaluative criticism, as the Leavises practiced it, was a moral crusade. They and their disciples would be the "saving remnant" of which Matthew Arnold spoke, exposing the degradation of "mass culture," industrialization, consumerism, and technocracy, lamenting the loss of organic communal life, and training their disciples in a discipline of fine discrimination that would stem the rising tide of philistine vulgarity. Not just literary excellence, but the future of civilization, depended upon such criticism.

John Wain recalled engaging "in several long conversations with Leavisites before I realized that all they were doing was to get me to condemn myself out of my own mouth, so that they could go back to Cambridge and add mine to the row of wax images over the slow fire." Lewis figured prominently among those wax images; to the Leavis circle, he was a romantic nationalist, "nostalgically addicted" to the Anglo-Saxon past, whose zeal for Christianity had warped his critical faculties. When Lewis published *Rehabilitations* in 1939—a rejoinder to the "Revaluations" series in *Scrutiny*—contributing editor L. C. Knights of *Scrutiny* slammed the book for combining "a distaste for 'highbrow' literature with an aversion from radical enquiries concerning the academic *status quo.*" *The Great Divorce* should be censored by church authorities, one reviewer wrote, not for heresy, but for the worse sin of "persistent nourishment of false attitudes." Worst of all, Lewis seemed to the Leavis circle to be a privileged insider, the very embodiment of the Oxford English faculty, with all the power and entitlements of the academic literary establishment at his disposal, while they remained persecuted and misunderstood outsiders. As Queenie Leavis (a formidable critic in her own right) wrote in a 1943 issue of *Scrutiny*:

> *Rehabilitations* was warmly received in academic quarters, where Mr. Lewis was credited with brilliant wit and a powerful intellect, and from thence came assertions that a blow had been struck for the cause. A really up-to-date intellectual, combining the scholarly virtues with critical genius, had taken service under them, we were given to understand. If there had been the slightest indication of originality in Mr. Lewis's outlook or of criticism of the *status quo* in his programme, what outraged bellows would have come from that herd instead! We may conclude that the academic club will go on recruiting its kind so long as it has a stranglehold on appointments in nearly every university.

It was high time, said Mrs. Leavis, to take English studies "out of the hands of the old-style academic." English studies "must be cut free from the classical-scholarly tradition in every respect and at every level; must point out firmly that the ability to edit texts and make piddling comments on them is no more qualification by itself for an English university post than a certificate of librarianship." The doors must be opened to admit "new and uniquely equipped specialists" who will remake not just English studies but the whole university curriculum. *Scrutiny* eschewed political ideology and had as many partisans on the Right as on the Left, as well as a significant Catholic following; but where the cause of English studies was concerned, it was *To the barricades!* "Can anyone be so optimistic as to believe," wrote Queenie Leavis, "that any university reform less violent than a bloody revolution would make such a programme possible?"

A third major figure in the new critical movement, William Empson, was a gifted and witty critic and a fine poet, a disciple of Richards who wrote his masterpiece, *Seven Types of Ambiguity*, when he was only twenty-two, but was banished from Cambridge upon the discovery of condoms in his Magdalene College rooms. Kingsley Amis had the impression, during the war years in Oxford, that everybody was reading either *Seven Types of Ambiguity* or *The Allegory of Love*—presumably revealing their true colors by the choice they made. Yet Empson himself greatly admired *The Allegory of Love*, wrote a gracious unsigned review of *Studies in Words* in which he takes special delight in Lewis's rebuttal of "Professor Empson," and made it plain that he liked Lewis personally ("I wish I had seen more of C. S. Lewis," he once said). He just couldn't fathom how such a decent man as Lewis could worship the vindictive Christian God, let alone compose apologetic tracts on His behalf. In July 1945, alarmed by a rumor that Lewis was in the running to succeed Sir Arthur Quiller-Couch as King Edward VII Professor of English Literature at Cambridge, Empson wrote to Richards to say, "The gossip is that C. S. Lewis is going to get it, and I cannot forgive him for believing that pet animals live for ever because they have been taught nice feelings by their owners. He seems to have no interests now except his moralising." Those disgusting "neo-Christians" (Empson's term) were all around.

The three major prophets of the new critical movement—Richards, Leavis, Empson—only sporadically agreed with one another and in the end were not on speaking terms. Yet something like a school did emerge from their efforts. By the 1940s, their principles and methods were carried by disciples into secondary education, shaping curricula and examinations and producing textbooks like *The Control of Language* by Alec King and Martin Ketley—Lewis's target under the name *The Green Book* in *The Abolition of Man*. In American English departments, New Criticism acknowledged Richards as a spiritual father, and the technique of "close reading" proved to be a lasting contribution to English studies on both sides of the Atlantic. At Oxford, F. W. Bateson and W. W. Robson (a devoted student of David Cecil, an admirer of Chesterton, and a not unsympathetic critic of Lewis and Williams) offered a version of Leavisism without the melodrama.

Was there, then, an Oxford School to counteract this incursion from Cambridge? Not so much a school, John Wain recalled, as an *ethos*: "When I was an Oxford undergraduate I was taught simple appreciation; I read an enormous number of authors, in rapid succession, and in each case I learnt to pick out what could be 'said for' the man. Nobody taught me, as Cambridge undergraduates seem to be taught, that every author has to get through a kind of sieve, called Criticism, before he is considered worth reading." Only at Oxford would a candidate in English encounter the examination question "What seems to you lastingly delightful in *Paradise Lost?*"

What seems to you lastingly delightful? For all their differences, the Inklings and the Cambridge critics shared an interest in the lastingly delightful (even if the Cantabridgians downplayed it in formal study). They believed with all their heart and soul in the power of the literary imagination to create a world worth living in. When the battle between these two camps heated up during the last years of Lewis's life (see chapter 18), the contest was all the more bitter because of their underlying agreement.

14

LOSS AND GAIN

As the war wound down, so did Charles Williams. "I'm even more of a . . . prophet? priest? something—more of a Voice and less of a man everywhere except at home," he wrote Florence in mid-February 1945. "I am always aware of a gulf. My voice—or my style—goes across it, but my heart doesn't." He was tired, lonely, unable to escape the disparity between outward eloquence and inward uncertainties.

Once he had rejoiced in Oxford's intellectual glamour, but now he longed for home. "I wish you and I were spending a cosy evening alone," he told his wife, expanding this desire a few weeks later into "all I want in this world is you, a bearable place to live, some money & enough distant publicity to bring in the money and be amusing. Nothing more." He turned to his old acolyte, Alice Hadfield, for long walks on the High Street and long talks in the King's Arms. He spun for her his dazzling web of words, telling of dreams unrealized, of books on Milton and Wordsworth that in his straitened circumstances he could not afford to write, of hopes for self-improvement that he could not afford to relinquish. Mostly he seemed preoccupied with former days. An old man (old at fifty-eight!), he rehearsed his life, as the ancient do. Some of this was simply exhaustion: in 1944, in addition to his full-time editing post at OUP, he had delivered forty-seven lectures and written part or all of multiple books, including a new novel entitled *All Hallows' Eve*, a study of Arthurian legend, and a biography of the Reverend W. H. Flecker, headmaster of Dean Close School in Cheltenham and father of the Georgian poet James Elroy Flecker. The insignificance of this last project tells us how much Williams had thinned out. Great themes had fled him; his prose was now little more than journalism. As *All Hallows' Eve* rushed to a conclusion, he declared himself "bitterly disappointed in it."

He suspected that death was near. "I am, I think, somehow and obscurely warned," he told Alice, and quoted Wordsworth to the effect that every effort comes "with a weight / Heavy as frost and deep almost as life." He arranged for Fr. Gervase Mathew to celebrate a Catholic Mass at Blackfriars Hall in St. Giles', Oxford, "for anyone I have ever loved in any way"—a most unusual request from a devout Anglican, and one with overtones of farewell. In early February, Eliot asked him when the Arthurian book might be ready. Not soon, for, as Williams told Florence, he had made little headway, producing "3000 words . . . out of 90,000." Such a huge project was beyond him now. He could still write letters, though, and those to his wife during the late winter and early spring of 1945 overflow with tenderness: "I do love you. I also badly need you"; "Bless you for everything. I love you"; "O sweet, to what a labour you committed us both when you first admired the *Silver Stair* . . . you have always been the first and great Influence."

All the while, great events shook the world. In February, Allied leaders met in Yalta to divide up the postwar world. In April, Roosevelt died of a cerebral hemorrhage, Mussolini was slaughtered by Italian partisans, Hitler committed suicide, and the Reichstag fell to Allied troops. Williams exulted in the Axis defeat: "I am very glad the fighting has been so heavy in Berlin; and may it be fifty years before it's built again." He praised Florence extravagantly for her part in the war effort: "They've failed; they've been broken. And you—especially—have helped to do it. Victory depended on you." The triumph seemed to rejuvenate him, and new projects bubbled up. He told Florence that he had in him "one more novel, which my faithful public will not like . . . There will be no black magic, no dancing figures, and no supernatural beings wandering through its pages." To Father Mathew, he described a projected *Life of Jesus*, eliciting from him the quip, as Williams relayed it to Florence, that the project would be "quite simple: all I had to do was to have the 4th Gospel typed out & sent it in as mine," for "nothing was a more exact C.W. style than

'In the beginning was the Word.'" This was, for Williams, absolutely true; from his earliest days the Word and words, lyrical, magical, and mystical, had meant all to him. But now silence descended. On May 8, he wrote Florence that "it's very quiet & silent now. It's also pouring with rain. I'm sitting on the balcony alone in the house . . . The mourning & the burying are done . . . it is nice to be done."

Compiling a list of new projects proved to be his final creative act. On May 10, the same day that Tolkien was hosting an "A.R.P. R.I.P." ("Air Raid Precautions Rest in Peace") victory party for fellow air wardens at his Northmoor Road home, Williams doubled over with pain. Florence was contacted and rushed up from London to escort her husband to the Radcliffe Infirmary. On May 14, he underwent surgery. The next morning, John Wain, who had become a devotee of Williams's lectures, was on his way to class when

> a girl I knew by sight came pedaling fast and agitatedly on her bicycle round the corner from New College Lane. "John," she called out, "Charles Williams is dead." She had never spoken to me before, and normally would have avoided using my Christian name. But this was a general disaster, like an air-raid, and the touch of comradeliness was right. I asked her for details, but she knew nothing except that he was dead. In any case, she could not talk; she was only just not crying.
>
> I walked on towards St. John's. The war with Germany was over. Charles Williams was dead. And suddenly Oxford was a different place. There was still much to enjoy, much to love and hate, much to get used to; but the war-time Oxford of my undergraduate days had disappeared. Its pulse had stopped with the pulse of Williams.

Warnie was at his desk at Magdalen when the news arrived:

> At 12.50 this morning I had just finished work on the details of the Boisleve family, when the telephone rang, and a woman's voice asked if I would take a message for J—"Mr. Charles Williams died in the Acland this morning." One often reads of people being "stunned" by bad news, and reflects idly on the absurdity of the

expression; but there is more than a little truth in it. I felt just as if I had slipped and come down on my head on the pavement.

Distraught, he rushed out for a consoling drink, "choosing unfortunately the King's Arms, where during the winter Charles and I more than once drank a pint after leaving Tollers at the Mitre." Writing in his journal later the same day, he wept over the death of this man he much admired, lamenting that "there will be no more pints with Charles: no more 'Bird and Baby': the blackout has fallen, and the Inklings can never be the same again . . . I hear his voice as I write, and can see his thin form in his blue suit, opening his cigarette box with trembling hands . . . so vanishes one of the best and nicest men it has ever been my good fortune to meet. May God receive him into His everlasting happiness."

Soon other Inklings learned of Williams's passing. Tolkien immediately wrote a letter to Florence: "I share a little in your loss, for in the (far too brief) years since I first met him I had grown to admire and love your husband deeply, and I am more grieved than I can express." That Tolkien ever loved Williams deeply, or at all, is doubtful, and his words are best read as an appropriate condolence to a new widow. He was utterly sincere, however, in adding that "I shall have you all in my prayers immediately and continually." He arranged for Father Mathew to celebrate a Mass for the repose of Williams's soul on the following Saturday, at which he participated as altar server.

But it was Lewis who felt most keenly the blow of Williams's death, and who dramatized the loss most strikingly. While Warnie and Tolkien situated their friend's death in a conventional religious frame, Lewis cast it as a great discovery of hitherto unrealized truths, almost a holy revelation, experienced not only by himself but by his entire circle. He had dropped by the Acland on May 15, planning to lend Williams a book and cheer him up, but instead had learned of his death, news he had anticipated "as little (almost) as I expected to die that day myself." It was a Tuesday, and the Inklings were gathering at the Eagle and Child. Lewis hurried over, noticing en route that "the very streets looked different," and presented the grim news to his astonished colleagues: "I had some difficulty in making them believe or even understand what had happened. The world seemed to us at that moment primarily a *strange* one." This sense of strangeness continued long afterward. For Lewis it never went away, for Williams's death confirmed for him and the others the reality of eternal life:

> We now verified for ourselves what so many bereaved people have reported; the ubiquitous presence of a dead man, as if he had ceased to meet us in particular places in order to meet us everywhere. It is not in the least like a haunting. It is not in the least like the bitter-sweet experiences of memory. It is vital and bracing; it is even, however the word may be misunderstood and derided, exciting . . . No event has so corroborated my faith in the next world as Williams did simply by dying. When the idea of death and the idea of Williams thus met in my mind, it was the idea of death that was changed.

In a letter to Florence written soon after the event, Lewis underscored the transformative effect of her husband's death: "I believe in the next life ten times more strongly than I did. At moments it seems quite tangible. Mr. Dyson, on the day of the funeral, summed up what many of us felt, 'It is not blasphemous,' he said, 'to believe that what was true of Our Lord is, in its less degree, true of all who are in Him. They go away in order to be *with* us in a new way, even closer than before.' A month ago I would have called this silly sentiment. Now I know better."

The Ranks Expand

These subtle perceptions notwithstanding, it was the acute reality of Williams's absence that claimed attention when the Inklings next convened, the unavoidable gap in the circle, the void once filled by that antic energy, that puckish, dead-serious mind that reeled off ancient poetry and new ideas with a rapidity and accuracy that only Lewis could match, that brought to each gathering goodwill, comradeship, and an earnest intelligence that rarely outran its expressive skills. As Warnie said, "The Inklings [would] never be the same." And yet Wain's claim that "the group had begun to spiral downwards from the time Williams died; one after another, people fell away . . ." overstates the case. Williams had been a brilliant addition to the group, but only for a while had his personality dominated. He was irreplaceable, not indispensable. Lewis and Tolkien continued to hold the center; the Inklings had met before Williams arrived and continued to meet after he departed.

In addition to the familiar crew—Lewis, Warnie, Tolkien, Dyson, Havard—new figures swelled the ranks in the years just before and after Williams's death. These novices chimed in with a splendid variety of voices. Wain, a budding poet and critic and a future biographer, playwright, and novelist, seemed promising but proved a lukewarm Christian and disliked fantasy, arguing that "a writer's task . . . was to lay bare the human heart, and this could not be done if he were continually taking refuge in the spinning of fanciful webs." He never became a full-blooded member. Steadier participation came from young Christopher Tolkien, who in late 1945, although only twenty, was invited by his father, with the group's hearty approval, to join as "a *permanent member*, with right of entry and what not quite independent of my presence or otherwise." He reentered Trinity College, Oxford, to complete his degree, reading English under Lewis, and became an active Inkling. Christopher was an ideal recruit, gentle, well-spoken, intelligent, likable, and especially close to his father. From early boyhood, he had loved his father's writings and had obsessed, like his father, over textual inaccuracies and contradictions; Michael recalled him exclaiming, at the age of four or five, "Last time, *you* said Bilbo's front door was blue, and *you* said Thorin had a golden tassel on his hood, but you've just said that Bilbo's front door was green, and the tassel on Thorin's hood was silver." Years later, in South Africa during the war, Christopher had performed a similarly eagle-eyed service, not only critiquing installments of *The Lord of the Rings* but drawing maps and making fair copies. With his clear, melodious voice, a welcome contrast to his father's hopeless mumbling, he now became the official reader of the elder Tolkien's work, to everyone's satisfaction.

The group also enjoyed an influx of Roman Catholic members. It is unclear when Father Gervase Mathew (Gervase was his religious name; his birth name was Anthony) joined, but by the time of Williams's death, this Dominican priest, theologian, and lecturer in Byzantine history had become a valued member, much liked for his gentleness and air of distracted dowdiness; Warnie dubbed him "the universal aunt." The Lewis brothers admired Mathew's scholarship, although Lewis ribbed his work in a clerihew (a four-line ditty, invented by the novelist Edmund Clerihew

Bentley and much in vogue among English Christians during the first half of the twentieth century):

> Father Gervase
> Makes inaudible surveys
> On little-known sages
> Of the Middle Ages

The more ardently Protestant Inklings refrained from sniping at Mathew, perhaps in deference to his priestly office. But they were not always so ecumenically serene. Lewis's difficulties with Catholicism have been detailed above; Warnie, equally unsettled by a Roman collar, proclaimed that "there has always been something sinister, a little repulsive, almost ogreish, about the practice of the R.C. religion." He never let his ingrained bias stand in the way of friendship, however. When the medievalist J.A.W. Bennett attended his first meeting at Tolkien's invitation, on August 15, 1946, Warnie wrote in his diary of his "dismay" at Bennett's presence, both because he was a "dull dog" and because he was "an R.C." Warnie's objection, in this case, was not so much because he disliked Catholics per se, but because he worried about Hugo Dyson's reaction to Bennett's faith. As it happens, he was wrong about Bennett, who would not become a Catholic for some years, but he was right about Dyson. The latter was continually irked by Tolkien's religion and had threatened more than once to quit the Inklings if any more Catholics joined. It may be that his disdain for *The Lord of the Rings*, which grew pronounced as the years passed, originated in animosity (conscious or not) to its Catholic undercurrents. Notwithstanding Warnie's edginess and Dyson's bias, however, Bennett fit in nicely, becoming a regular and well-liked member of the group.

Another new member was Commander James Harold Dundas-Grant, a Catholic of Scottish descent, who first encountered one of the Inklings in Magdalen's Senior Common Room in October 1944, while billeted at the college as head of the University Naval Division:

> At the far side of the table, I saw a baldish head deeply ensconced in *Punch*, so I helped myself to porridge, picked up *The Times*, and sat down. There was a rustle of *Punch*, and I found a pair of merry,

friendly eyes looking at me. "I say," then in a whisper, "do you talk at breakfast?" "By training, no; by nature, yes," I replied. Down went *Punch*. "Oh good," he said. "I'm Lewis." "Not 'Screwtape'?" I blurted out. "I'm afraid so; yes" . . . There was a step outside; the door was flung open; a tall, gaunt figure stalked in. Up went *Punch*; up went *The Times*. We ate in silence.

Soon after that morning encounter, Dundas-Grant asked Lewis to accept him and four fellow officers as informal tutees in philosophy. Lewis instantly responded, "I'm your man," delighted at the chance to teach mature students (Dundas-Grant was nearly fifty at the time). A rigorous course of weekly compositions and meetings started up. "He couldn't have taken more trouble with us," Dundas-Grant remembered, "had we been graduates reading for a doctorate. True, he tore our essays to pieces but so gently that he could put the pieces together again in proper form and solve the argument. The great thing was he made us *think*." A bit later, Lewis invited him to a ham dinner, a rarity during this time of rations. There Dundas-Grant met Tolkien, "tall, sweptback grey hair, restless," along with Warnie, Hardie, and Havard. He soon found himself at other gatherings with his new friends, enjoying the company but rarely chiming in, for "it was at these sessions that I found out how much one learned just sitting and listening." Lewis admired Dundas-Grant's unfeigned humility, and after the war, at about the time that Dundas-Grant and his wife converted a house on the Iffley Road into a residence for Catholic undergraduates, Lewis invited him to attend Tuesday morning meetings at the Bird and Baby. There "acquaintance turned to friendship . . . We sat in a small back room with a fine coal fire in winter. Back and forth the conversation would flow. Latin tags flying around. Homer quoted in the original to make a point. And Tolkien, jumping up and down, declaiming in Anglo-Saxon."

Tolkien, Agonistes

"Wars are always lost, and The War always goes on," wrote Tolkien to Christopher near the end of the war. The worldwide carnage embittered him, as did the jingoistic jubilation of British citizens as Allied troops pressed forward to victory:

There seem no bowels of mercy or compassion, no imagination, left in this dark diabolic hour. By which I do not mean that it may not all, in the present situation, mainly (not solely) created by Germany, be necessary and inevitable. But why gloat! We were supposed to have reached a stage of civilization in which it might still be necessary to execute a criminal, but not to gloat, or to hang his wife and child by him while the orc-crowd hooted.

Dark futures began to proliferate in his mind, steeped not only in the horrors of the European and Pacific theaters but in the equivalent if imaginary monstrosities that threatened Middle-earth. He wrote to Christopher in quasi-apocalyptic tones, calling World War II "the first War of the Machines," an assault by technology upon human values "leaving, alas, everyone the poorer, many bereaved or maimed and millions dead, and only one thing triumphant: the Machines." A few months later, again addressing his son, he railed against the RAF and its warplanes and expressed his "grief" that Christopher had been obliged to work with these deadly inventions: "My sentiments are more or less those that Frodo would have had if he discovered some Hobbits learning to ride Nazgûl-birds, 'for the liberation of the Shire.'" He denounced the Pacific War, for which he felt not "a glimmer of patriotism" and to which he "would not subscribe a penny . . . let alone a son, were I a free man." The jeremiad continues on August 9, this time lambasting the atomic bombing of Japan by "lunatic physicists"; God, he warned, "does not look kindly on Babel-builders."

In these shocking tirades, one hears a man nearing the end of his tether. Illness, work, war, and worry over Edith and his children had taken their toll. The Allies, with their great engines of destruction, had become tools of Morgoth. World War II was drawing to a close, but Tolkien foresaw a greater one looming against the Machines, by which he meant not only mechanization but a panoply of evil acts and inventions epitomized by automation and automatism, by Satanic disconnection from soil, family, and faith. The truth is, he badly needed a vacation, but he refused to leave Oxford and Edith. Instead, he took refuge in work, toiling, mostly at night, on the new *Hobbit*, a project that by now had taken on, in its wild ambition, gargantuan size, and interminable construction, more than a few similarities to the Tower of Babel he had condemned to Christopher.

During March, he had written Unwin, confiding that he had "squandered" his precious spare time by penning letters to his son, explaining that the *Hobbit* sequel is "simply is not the kind of stuff for odd moments," and assuring him—as usual, he was wildly off the mark—that "three weeks with nothing else to do—and a little rest and sleep first—would probably be sufficient" to complete the project.

The longed-for serenity, sleep, and spare time arrived months later, the sequel to a momentous change. In the summer of 1945, Tolkien resigned as Rawlinson and Bosworth Professor of Anglo-Saxon (he was replaced by fellow Inkling Charles Wrenn) in order to become Merton Professor of English Language and Literature, thus transferring his academic associ-ation to Merton College. The move was liberating. True, it irked him that Dyson, elected to a Merton fellowship at the same time, had secured the very rooms Tolkien had desired, overlooking the meadow. But, as he crowed to Christopher, he found it "incredible belonging to a real college (and a very large and wealthy one)." To Unwin he explained that, as he was no longer professor of Anglo-Saxon, "I shall not be left all alone to try and run our English School." Moreover, "for the first time in 25 years, except the year I went on crutches (just before The Hobbit came out, I think), I am free of examining . . . I hope after this week actually to—write."

He encountered, when he returned to his manuscript, an unexpected obstacle. Repeated interruptions had weakened his grasp on the book's vast, intricate architecture, and "I shall now have to study my own work in order to get back to it." Nonetheless, he promised Unwin that the book would be completed "before the autumn term, and at any rate before the end of the year." For a while it looked as though he could meet his pledge, and on September 30 he informed Unwin that "I picked it up again last week and wrote (a good) chapter." But soon the interruptions returned. A few weeks before Christmas, he wrote to say that the family was relocat-ing to a smaller house, a Merton College rental requiring less time and effort to manage. Nonetheless, his "magnum opus" would be finished and delivered, he predicted, "before long, or before January." Seven months later, Book I—a small portion of the whole—arrived in Unwin's hands.

The publisher immediately turned it over to his son Rayner, who as a boy of ten, eleven years earlier, had reported so glowingly on *The Hob-bit*. Rayner didn't disappoint, calling the new typescript "a brilliant and gripping story" in which "the tortuous and contending currents of events in this world within a world almost overpower one." He added, with a touch of his father's practicality, that "quite honestly I don't know who is expected to read it." Tolkien wrote to thank him and to assure the elder Unwin that there would be readers, for "those that like this kind of thing at all, like it very much, and cannot get anything like enough of it, or at sufficiently great length to appease hunger." He concluded with a cri de coeur and a new resolve, declaring that the tale was "written in my life-blood, such as that is, thick or thin; and I can no other. I fear it must stand or fall as it substantially is. It would be idle to pretend that I do not greatly desire publication, since a solitary art is no art . . . yet the chief thing is to complete one's work, as far as completion has any real sense."

Quenched Spirits

While Tolkien soldiered on with his magnum opus, the Inklings gathered, declaimed, and drank copiously, just as they had done throughout the war. Warnie jotted down abbreviated minutes for each meeting in his diary. On Thursday, March 28, 1946: "a good meeting of the Inklings, although scantily attended. Present, J and I, Christopher, Humphrey, Colin Hardie, Gervase Mathew. Interesting discussion on the possibility of dogs having souls." Five days later: "To the Bird and Baby where I was joined by Humphrey, Tollers, and Chris. Tollers looking wonderfully improved by his restcure at Stonyhurst, and in great spirits (having packed his wife off to Brighton for ten days)." Thursday, August 8: "We went on to Magdalen, where there was a well attended Inklings—Stanley Bennett of Cambridge, who had been dining with J, Humphrey, Ronald, Gervase. But not the sort of evening I much enjoy, mere noise and buffoonery, although Hugo as improvisatore was very funny at times." Special dinners supplemented or occasionally replaced the standard Tuesday-Thursday program. Thus in late July, Warnie and his brother traveled "to dine with the Hugo Dysons in their new house, 12 Holywell—very reluctantly, for with all my army experience I am still as shy of women as a hobbledehoy: and also it would otherwise have been an Inkling night." His trepidations proved baseless, for successive glasses of sherry, hock, and whiskey along with a delicious fish salad provided a helpful buffer, and he found both Mrs. Dyson and the Dyson's house appealing "after our slatternly straggling Kilns." He brooded on the contrast: "I have now endured the Kilns for over fifteen years, and it is no more 'home' now than it was when I first entered it; I still have the feeling that it is a billet which I have marched into late in the evening and will be leaving for ever after an early breakfast." The warmth and lavishness of the Dysons' hospitality cast aside the shadows, and even the appearance of "two she-tutors" after dinner couldn't mar the evening.

Attendance at lectures and brief trips afield expanded the group's repertoire, although the great walking tours of the 1930s had ended, as Lewis's college and domestic responsibilities, especially tending an aging Mrs. Moore, kept him on a short leash. One July evening in 1946, Warnie and Lewis visited St. Hugh's College to hear Father Mathew talk on Byzantine civilization; he declared, as Warnie recalled it, that "Charles [Williams] . . . had managed to give a much truer account of Byzantium in *Taliessin* than that given by Gibbon." Earlier that year, the Lewis brothers and Dyson had taken a train to Liverpool, where Lewis was appearing on the BBC's *Brains Trust* program. They visited a church or two, and in the evening, Warnie watched his brother and Dyson clash over art and philosophy until "towards the end of the first hour J and Hugo discovered that they were talking about different subjects. Each side then restated its war aims, and they set to again. When or how the argument ended I don't know, for it was still going strong when I went to bed at eleven." In April 1947, the same three visited Mrs. Moore's daughter, Maureen, at her home in Malvern, where they hiked the hills. Dyson "blossomed out as a walker" and, fortified by wine and gin, burst into song and generally "treated the place as a rather unusually noisy Inklings. What Bernard [Maureen's 'French factotum'] made of the spectacle of a grey haired 'professeur' roaring out 'Ta-ra-ra-boom-dy-ay' with appropriate high kicks I don't suppose we shall ever know."

Warnie controlled his drinking on this visit but it wasn't to last. The difficulties of life at the Kilns, which meant tending for his adored younger brother while fending off Mrs. Moore's carping ways, overwhelmed him, and in June 1947 he escaped to Ireland "feeling very guilty at leaving poor J alone with that horrid old woman in that abominable house." The motherland, however, proved a second prison. His rental cottage had, he discovered, bad feng shui (a Chinese system used to balance subtle forces in the landscape). The term comes oddly from the mouth of a Lewis, but we must remember that Warnie passed two tours of duty, a total of more than four years, in China. Soon "great waves of depression" poured over him, which he combated with great waves of alcohol, mixed with "*methylated spirit*" (ethanol plus poisonous additives). By June 20, he was deathly ill and checked himself into a Catholic hospital run by the Medical Missionaries of Mary in Drogheda. The doctor in charge wired for Lewis, who arrived three days later, "anxious and travel stained." Warnie was overjoyed to see his brother; his spirits rallied, and within a few days he was out of danger, although he remained frail for several more weeks.

Despite the crisis, Warnie continued to drink, although moderating his intake. His first move upon leaving the hospital was to obtain a room at the nearby White Horse pub, where he could order stout before meals and sherry before bed. When Jack left for England a few days later, the bereft older brother sipped his fortified wine and brooded over "the haunting fear that is so often with me—suppose J were to die before I did. And a sheer wave of animal panic spread over me at the prospect of the empty years; but I pulled myself together, said my prayers, and tumbled into bed." His dipsomaniacal collapse had terrified him, but the aftermath had helped him vanquish an old bogeymen. The "holy and very loveable" nuns of Drogheda had shown him, by their "radiant happiness" and the selflessness of their tender ministrations, the folly of seeing Catholicism as "almost ogreish" and a convent of nuns as "something grey and secret, with sad faced women gliding about noisily." Warnie remained a committed Anglican, but his heart softened toward Catholics. A few days later, when Tolkien sent a letter filled with good wishes and the news that he had prayed to St. Bernadette of Lourdes to speed Warnie's healing, he took the news without a hint of rancor. Tolkien, perhaps sensing an opening—or even two, for if he persuaded Warnie of the faith's validity, he might sway Lewis—followed up with a letter thick with Catholic theology. Warnie's response, again, was measured and conciliatory. He would no longer blast the Catholic Church, now that its ministering angels had saved his life. He returned to the Kilns, more or less recovered, at the end of July, but not before a farewell visit to the Mother Superior, who greeted him warmly and plied him with cakes and coffee. "This holiday has been worth while," Warnie wrote in his diary that night, "if only for meeting her."

Agapargyry and Bettiana

Success forges its own chains, one of which is importuning by the unsuc-
cessful. Lewis was now famous and well-off, and beggars knocked regularly on his door. "He is certainly a fool and perhaps a lunatic: but he
seems v. miserable," he wrote to Barfield near the end of the war, describing a man who had contacted him for a handout. Always a soft touch
thanks to his warmheartedness, his indifference to the accumulation of
wealth, and his Christian principles, Lewis decided to help, even though,
as he admitted to Barfield, "Almost anyone but you wd. say I was as mad as
he for taking any notice of such a rhapsody." As the rhapsodies sounded
more loudly, however, and not only from fools and lunatics, he and
Barfield felt the need to come up with a ready response. They devised a
charitable trust called the Agape Fund, known also as the Agapony and
the Agapargyry. The last is a typical Lewisian/Barfieldian witticism, a
pun on St. Paul's use in 1 Timothy 6:10 of *philargyria* (*philos*+*argyros*,
love+silver) to mean the love of money, the root of all evil. "Agapargyry"
(*agape*+*argyros*) also means love of money, but with *agape* (self-giving love)
replacing *philos*, the term reverses the meaning to one of charity rather
than avarice.

Lewis had asked Barfield to establish the Agape Fund in 1942, soon
after receiving an enormous tax bill from the government To avoid any
future surprises, Lewis put two-thirds of all future royalties into the
trust, to be dispensed, usually anonymously, to needy cases, particularly
widows and orphans. Over the years, the fund handed out huge sums,
customarily in small portions, to innumerable recipients; typical was
Lewis's 1946 request that Barfield send seventy-five pounds to "a poor
gentlewoman forced to move house and transport invalid mother by hired
ambulance." In a letter to Cecil Harwood, Lewis explained the principle
behind the fund: "The fund is in a most flourishing condition and there
is no reason to stint yourself. You understand that nothing you draw
impoverishes me, for all the money in that fund is already given away
from me, tho' the question '*To* whom?' is answered at my direction from
time to time."

Barfield liked administering these charitable donations; it was, in
fact, one of his few pleasures during these years. The law office, with its

rituals and petty intrigues and interminable paperwork, swallowed up time and stifled imagination; at home, Maud still decried the truth and even the value of Anthroposophy. The entry of Geoffrey into the family as a foster child had pleased both Barfield and his wife, but moments of domestic bliss failed to overcome his despair at the throttling of his creative talents. He wrote a brief essay on the Psalms, lectured on Hamlet, translated some Steineriana—all activities within the small, safe Anthroposophical orbit—and placed a review and a number of poems under the pseudonym of G.A.L. Burgeon with *The New English Weekly*, a magazine founded by A. R. Orage and best known for publishing portions of T. S. Eliot's *Four Quartets*. Barfield's poems were frothy, forgettable affairs, some of them ("Cosmetics," "The Doppelganger") revolving around the elusive charms of a woman named "Betty." These works delighted Lewis, who termed them "Bettiana," and wrote "there's something v. wrong" when a publisher declined to print more of them.

The Bettiana failed to advance Barfield's reputation or assuage his sorrows. Nor did Lewis's sudden willingness in August 1948 to reopen for a brief time the "Great War" make much difference. Lewis's change of heart may have sprung from a dawning recognition of Barfield's unhappiness or from the pleasure derived from a recent mock literary joust with Barfield, during which the two had exchanged letters in the personae of law firms, Barfield representing King Mark of Cornwall and Lewis Sir Tristram, figures drawn from Malory's Arthurian romances, which Lewis had just reviewed for the *TLS*. This was just the sort of banter that Lewis loved and may have reminded him of the fun to be had in battling with his old friend. In any event, he and Barfield began corresponding again about the nature of creation, reason, and the like, but the skirmish was controlled and short-lived. So, too, was the apparent revival of Barfield's dramatic career in a September 1948 production of his verse play *Orpheus* by the Sheffield Education Settlement, a Christian organization with a Steinerian tilt. Lewis wrote a glowing blurb for the program notes, praising the work for "a variety almost as rich as that of the *Shepherd's Calendar*" (eclogues by Spenser) and declaring that "I await with great interest the public reaction to a work which has influenced me so deeply as Barfield's *Orpheus*." The public reaction, as for all of Barfield's output during these dark years, was a smattering of applause followed by a discouraging silence.

A Gift for Williams

The dappled shadow of Charles Williams, bestowing darkness or light depending upon one's memories, still loomed over the Inklings and their activities. Lewis busied himself preparing an edition of his friend's unpublished Arthurian prose; Warnie continued to miss the boozy warmth of the many pub visits he and Williams had enjoyed together; others among the Inklings still felt acutely, with regret or relief, the absence of the man's high-pitched, eccentric energies. In 1947, as homage, memorial, and final farewell, five Inklings joined forces to produce the only significant pan-Inklings publication in the group's long history: *Essays Presented to Charles Williams*. Lewis had come up with the idea long before Williams's death, intending to produce a Festschrift to be presented to Williams upon his return to London at the end of the war. Now the volume would serve other purposes, as a memorial and as a fund-raiser for Florence, who was to receive all profits.

Lewis, as editor, already had in hand suitable pieces by himself, Barfield, and Tolkien. Two days after Williams's passing, he wrote to T. S. Eliot and Dorothy L. Sayers, soliciting from each a contribution; he also asked Eliot if Faber & Faber would take on the book. Eliot declined to publish it, recommending instead that Lewis approach Sir Humphrey Milford at Oxford University Press, but he did agree to supply an essay. Apparently he did so reluctantly, for despite repeated pleas by Lewis, who told him that "your absence would in our view cripple the book," the promised piece never appeared. In desperation, Lewis suggested instead that Eliot contribute a poem—an astonishing request, considering how little Lewis liked Eliot's poetry, and an indication of how much he valued Eliot's name as a magnet for readers and of how willing he was to thrust his own tastes aside to honor his friend. In any event, the poem also failed to materialize, and a frustrated Lewis finally sent a curt note to Eliot suggesting that "perhaps you will find your own way of honouring our friend later and no less effectively."

Many of Williams's former companions did come through, however, producing a volume that offers a revealing cross-section of the Inklings and their thought in the late 1940s. The work underscores both the group's eclecticism and its common interests. "In this book," Lewis writes in his preface, "the reader is offered the work of one professional author, two dons, a solicitor, a friar, and a retired army officer"—that is, Dorothy L. Sayers, C. S. Lewis, J.R.R. Tolkien, Owen Barfield, Gervase Mathew, and W. H. Lewis. This group constituted for Williams, wrote Lewis, "a fairly permanent nucleus among his *literary* friends. He read us his manuscripts and we read him ours: we smoked, talked, argued, and drank together (I must confess that with Miss Dorothy Sayers I have seen him drink only tea: but that was neither his fault nor hers)." As Lewis had informed Eliot, at least some of the essays also share a common nucleus: "They are . . . concerned with *story*, or if you will *mythopoea*: in fact with that element in literature wh. nearly all criticism between Aristotle and Maud Bodkin has left entirely alone. Their connection with Charles is that this was rather his own long suit."

The anomaly among these contributors is, of course, Sayers, author of the acclaimed Lord Peter Wimsey mystery novels and two influential books of Christian apologetics, *The Mind of the Maker* (1941) and *Creed or Chaos?* (1947). She is the only non-Inkling on the title page. What is she doing there? As we know, she was excluded in principle from membership in the group by virtue of her sex. Did Lewis, by this singular honor, intend to confer on her the title of honorary Inkling? Was she, as many critics claim, almost an Inkling or "not quite an Inkling"? We can dismiss as meaningless the claim that if she had been a man she would have been an Inkling, for if she had been a man she would not have been Dorothy L. Sayers. Equally unhelpful is the speculation of one Sayers biographer that if her candidacy had been seriously proposed, some Inklings "might have been disturbed by the inclusion . . . of Dorothy's transsexual mind and not-very-stimulating body."

Sexual politics aside, however, Sayers had much in common with Lewis and Tolkien's circle, including a love of orthodox Christianity, traditional verse, popular fiction, and debate. In *The Mind of the Maker* (1941), she presents a theory of artistic creation as an image of the Trinity that closely parallels Tolkien's idea of subcreation. Tolkien, it is true, came to detest her aristocratic sleuth, Lord Peter Wimsey, telling Christopher that "I conceived a loathing for him (and his creatrix) not surpassed by any other character in literature known to me . . . ," but his objections, likely based upon Wimsey's dandyism and Sayers's affinity for strong female characters, seem not to have transferred wholesale to other Inklings. Lewis,

for example, praised her Jesus play, *The Man Born to Be King*, a wartime
BBC radio drama, which he reread "every Holy Week since it first appeared and never re-read . . . without being deeply moved." She, in turn,
admired his writing and was, Lewis said, "the first person of importance
who ever wrote me a fan letter."

Sayers's most significant association among the Inklings, however,
was with Charles Williams. Their friendship was long and deep, and it
was chiefly for this reason that Lewis included her in the memorial volume (that she, like Eliot, would attract a flock of readers was a welcome
bonus). In 1933, Williams had written to the publisher Victor Gollancz
an exuberant letter upon reading an advance copy of Sayers's *The Nine
Tailors*, declaring, "Your Dorothy Sayers . . . ! Present her some time
with my profoundest compliments. It's a marvellous book; it is high
imagination . . . the ending is unsurpassable." This glowing tribute was
relayed to the author, who wrote Gollancz that "I only hope he isn't pulling
my leg—it sounds too good to be true!" He wasn't, it wasn't. The two writers met, hit it off, and continued to dine together periodically for several
years.

In 1937, Williams wrote the play *Thomas Cranmer of Canterbury* for
the annual Canterbury Festival and proposed Sayers as the festival's next
playwright. Sayers accepted the invitation and wrote *The Zeal of Thy
House* for the 1938 season; her play, about William of Sens, the architect
who rebuilt the Canterbury Cathedral choir after a devastating fire in
1174, received good notices and gave her prominence as a Christian artist
as well as a creator of elegant mysteries. A few years later (as we saw
in chapter 12), Williams unwittingly did Sayers a yet more profound
favor by sparking her passion for Dante. Her contribution to *Essays Presented to Charles Williams* is to a great extent a summary of the many
enthusiastic letters that she sent Williams during the early days of her
Dante mania. Most notable and Inklings-like is her vigorous defense of
story: Dante "was simply the most incomparable story-teller who ever set
pen to paper"; the *Commedia* is, first and foremost, "a story of adventure,"
and it is this that allows it to be also "a satire, a love-romance, a spiritual
autobiography"; Dante succeeds because "nobody had taught him the
strange theory of the early twentieth-century novelists, that one is a better story-teller for having no story to tell"; the *Commedia* possesses "that

quality without which a tale may indeed take captive the imagination but can never root itself in the affections—the power to create a whole universe of breathing characters." Lewis or Tolkien might have written these lines, which could serve as an aesthetic manifesto for the Space Trilogy and *The Lord of the Rings*, although the two Inklings might have adopted a more studied, less breathless tone (Lewis told Barfield that he found Sayers's essay "perhaps a trifle vulgar in places").

As it happens, a donnish or professorial tone emerges in *Essays* on the very heels of Sayers's contribution, for it is followed by Tolkien's "On Fairy-Stories" and Lewis's "On Stories." Together, the contributions of Sayers, Tolkien, and Lewis constitute a closely reasoned, richly illustrated defense of fantasy, Faërie, children's literature, and the mythopoeic imagination: that is to say, the literature of the Inklings and their colleagues. Tolkien's essay, contending that Faërie offers "Fantasy, Recovery, Escape, Consolation," and "Enchantment," and that fantasy allows the artist to "assist in the effoliation and multiple enrichment of creation," is an expanded version of his 1939 Andrew Lang Lecture. Lewis approaches the same theme from a different angle than does Tolkien or Sayers, examining neither a particular story nor a single genre but rather "Story itself" (the capital letter is Lewis's) and those literary forms in which "everything else"—characters, social analyses, propaganda—"is there for the sake of the story." He rejects the popular notion that story exists to create excitement; if this were so, then *The Three Musketeers*, which is nothing but a torrent of thrills, would be the greatest of all stories. Lewis never states exactly what Dumas lacks that a good story possesses; instead, he contrasts such tales with those that join excitement to that special frisson—"sense of wonder" may be the best term for it—induced by a giant, a pirate, or an otherworldly landscape. These marvels stimulate the "deeper imagination"; they offer "something other than a process and much more like a state or quality." H. Rider Haggard, David Lindsay, Walter de la Mare, and J.R.R. Tolkien are modern writers who have achieved this elemental quality; Charles Williams is not, for his stories remain, "despite their free use of the supernatural, much closer to the novel; a believed religion, detailed character drawing, and even social satire all come in." Children's literature, on the other hand, is specifically dedicated to evoking the sense of wonder, and Lewis's argument is also a defense of this maligned genre (and thus of Tolkien's *The Hobbit* and Barfield's *The*

Silver Trumpet). "No book is really worth reading at the age of ten which is not equally (and often far more) worth reading at the age of fifty—except, of course, books of information . . . A mature palate will probably not much care for *crème de menthe*: but it ought still to enjoy bread and butter and honey."

The final essays in the book go in other directions. Barfield's "Poetic Diction and Legal Fiction" (see chapter 12) links the author's twin vocations of literature and law. Gervase Mathew contributes an essay on marriage and courtly love in fourteenth-century England, while Warnie closes the volume with an account of the horrors of French galley life during the reign of Louis XIV, the Sun King being a subject that vastly interested Williams as well ("these two, and Mr. H.V.D. Dyson of Merton, could often be heard in a corner talking about Versailles, *intendants*, and the *maison du roy*," remembers Lewis in his preface).

Signs of Decline

Essays Presented to Charles Williams was the Inklings' collaborative high-water mark; the tide soon began to ebb. In 1946, Merton College commenced a search for a new professor of English literature. Tolkien, one of the electors, favored Lewis or possibly Lord David Cecil for the post, but after fierce opposition from the English faculty, the position went to Lewis's old tutor F. P. Wilson. Everyone knew the reason: the faculty feared that Lewis would turn the professorship into a bully pulpit for Christian evangelization. A month or so earlier, he had received an honorary doctor of divinity degree from the University of St. Andrews; during the ceremony, the presiding dean had said that "with his pen and with his voice on the radio Mr. Lewis has succeeded in capturing the attention of many who will not readily listen to professional theologians, and has taught them many lessons concerning the deep things of God." At St. Andrews this passed muster, but at Oxford some academics doubted whether Lewis, now an international celebrity, would pay sufficient attention to the many vexing details that accompanied a professorship, while others fretted over how it would look to grant the author of *The Screwtape Letters*, an embarrassingly popular novel, such a prestigious chair. Tolkien's lobbying failed to overcome these obstacles, and Christina Scull and Wayne G. Hammond speculate that his failure may have "slightly sour[ed] relations between" him and Lewis "for a while." If so, it foreshadowed greater rifts to come.

All the while, the Inklings continued to attract new members. In 1947, C. E. Stevens, historian, fellow of Magdalen, and a warm, rambunctious figure—a born Inkling, by all accounts—joined the group. Stevens had worked for British intelligence during the war and had conceived the brilliant notion of using the celebrated opening notes of Beethoven's Fifth, *da da da daa*, which also happens to spell "V" (for Victory) in Morse code, as the BBC's propaganda theme. He, Lewis, and Warnie had been friends for years, but he had never been invited to the Thursday night gatherings, perhaps because his war work often took him away from the university. Lewis finally proposed Stevens's membership at a meeting on October 23, 1947, to general acclamation. It was "the smallest Inkling we have had for a long time," Warnie noted significantly— only he, his brother, Tolkien, and Havard attended—and the beverage was green tea. Clearly, change was in the air. The following Thursday, the same core group showed up. Stevens finally appeared on November 27 and made a good impression; "A very pleasant meeting," declared Warnie. Other small pleasures arrived as well. Dr. Warfield M. Firor, a renowned surgeon at Baltimore's Johns Hopkins University and an admirer of Lewis's writings, began to send him ham and other delicacies to alleviate the postwar food rationing. On March 11, 1948, these gifts resulted in a grand Inklings assembly, featuring not only Dr. Firor's ham but fillet of sole, pâté, soup, and assorted wines. For Warnie, at least, the feast was a brilliant success, "which I enjoyed as much as anything of the sort I have ever attended . . . We sat down eight to dinner, all in the highest spirits . . . There was just the right amount of everything, including drink." The somewhat inebriated celebrants sent a "Ham Testimonial" to the good doctor, inscribed by all—the core four plus Christopher Tolkien, Dyson, Cecil, and Hardie. Dinner completed, the party raffled off a tuxedo, a gift from yet another overseas fan. For one night, at least, it was just like old times.

Beneath the bonhomie, however, tensions festered. Five or six weeks before the Ham Testimonial, Tolkien had sent to Lewis a long letter that amounted to an apologia—in the dual sense of apology and justification— for having disparaged an unspecified work by Lewis read aloud at an Inklings meeting. The attack had upset Lewis greatly, and the two had exchanged letters on the subject. Tolkien piles up the mea culpas: "I regret causing pain, even if and in so far as I had the right; and I am very sorry indeed still for having caused it quite excessively and unnecessarily . . . I have been possessed on occasions (few, happily) with a sort of *furor scribendi*, in which the pen finds the words rather than head or heart; and this was one of them." This bald apology seems to discomfit him, however, for he adds notes of defense (he had not realized at the time that Lewis was offended), attack (Lewis reads too much and too analytically), and presumptuous advice (Lewis's suffering "will do good rather than harm, but that is between you and God. It is one of the mysteries of pain that it is, for the sufferer, an opportunity for good, a path of ascent however hard"). He then backtracks, advancing into Williamsian territory by asking Lewis to "do me the great generosity of making me a present of the pains I have caused, so that I may share in the good you have put them to." This is the sort of behest that one can only make of someone who shares one's deepest beliefs, a friend to whom one can confess one's sorrows, and this is just what he does, revealing that he is "suffering . . . from 'suppressed composition'" and is in consequence a "savage creature, a soreheaded bear." It is a tender moment; the comradeship he feels for Lewis is palpable. Yet he wraps up the letter on a note of aggressive jocularity that undercuts the closeness: "But I warn you, if you bore me, I shall take my revenge . . . I sometimes conceive and write other things than verses or romance! And I may come back at you." The bright flash of exposed nerve is unmistakable.

Dyson's Roar

The tensions between Inklings had many causes. One of them showed up at almost every meeting: the ever vexatious Hugo Dyson, who relished any opportunity to create a ruckus. Recently, Dyson had broadcast the rumor that Tolkien disliked Lewis's boisterousness during meetings. "Nay!" Tolkien assured Lewis. "That is largely a self-defensive rumour put about by Hugo. If it has any basis (for him), it is but that noise begets noise." Warnie noted Dyson's loudness in his diary for March 4: "Hugo's voice was booming through the fog in the Quad, inviting a party of undergraduates up to his rooms, he really can be very irritating at times." Tolkien was right in his assessment, for Dyson was the clangorous provocateur

at Inklings gatherings. He bristled at anything he disliked, most notably
The Lord of the Rings; Christopher Tolkien has described him as "lying
on the couch, and lolling and shouting and saying, 'Oh God, no more
Elves'"—a bowdlerization of the funnier, more devastating, and more
Dysonesque actual jibe, usually given as "Oh God, not another fucking
elf!" Eventually, Dyson bullied his way into the censor's seat and managed to ban all readings of *Lord* while he was present. One should add, in
his favor, that he was not the only Inkling who disapproved of Tolkien's
epic: Barfield put it aside unfinished, and John Wain poured on the scorn:
"When Tolkien came through the door at a meeting of the Inklings with
a bulging jacket pocket, I winced because I knew we were in for a slab of
Gandalf and Bilbo Baggins and the rest of it. I wished him no harm, but
would have preferred him to keep his daydreams within bounds and not
inflict them on us."

Dyson, despite his knack for obnoxiousness, was generally liked for
his conviviality and wit, and he and Tolkien had been allies, not least in
the late-night discussion along Addison's Walk that had led to Lewis's
conversion. His disapprobation stung Tolkien deeply. "I remember this
very vividly, my father's pain, his shyness, which couldn't take Hugo's
extremely rumbustious approach," recalled Christopher. Lewis intervened
whenever possible to soften the blow, shouting, "Shut up, Hugo . . . Come
on Tollers," but it did little good. Dyson got his way. The source of his
rudeness is not hard to discern: his mind outran his manners. To Warnie,
who adored him for his humor (and because a day with Dyson meant a
day with drink), he gave "the impression of being made of quick silver: he
pours himself into a room on a cataract of words and gestures, and you
are caught up in the stream." Dyson would seize any opening for a quip;
one evening he and Warnie downed some glasses of sherry at the Mitre
Tap and then walked to the courtyard, where they saw a boy slip on the
cobbles. "Don't do that, my boy: it hurts you and distresses us," Dyson
shouted. His humor and impudence went hand in hand:

> Councillor Brewer arrived [at the King's Arms Pub] and put his
> vast bulk in the chair facing Hugo across the table: it was plain
> that Hugo had never spoken to him before, but he leant forward
> and addressed him with an almost servile deference—"you will
> pardon the liberty, Sir; I trust you don't think I presume: but I

shall call you Fred. You look the sort of man who ought to be called Fred." This the Councillor took well, and conversation became general: but a minute later, Hugo, gazing intently at his huge pale face, broke in again—"You'll excuse me sir, but am I looking at your full face or your profile?"

Dyson's rudeness was a slow-acting poison. First it amused, then it exasperated, finally it destroyed. His aggressiveness intensified with the years; by 1949, Warnie noted in his diary that "at a ham supper in J's rooms, H bellows uninterruptedly for about three minutes, and as he shows no signs of stopping, two guests at the bottom of the table begin a conversation: which being observed by Hugo, he raises his hand and shouts reproachfully—'Friends, friends, I feel it would be better if we kept the conversation *general*.'" One detects in this remark, as in Dyson's overall antics, both insecurity and envy. His genius lay in idle repartee and back-slapping friendship rather than scholarly pursuits. He published but a handful of notable books: *Pope: Poetry and Prose*; *Augustans and Romantics* (coauthored with John Butts); and *The Emergence of Shakespeare's Tragedy*. The introduction to his Pope anthology is telling; he singles out the poet's "freshness and vigour of execution," his "colour and movement," and, in regard to his greatest work, *The Rape of the Lock*, its tone of "sophisticated malice-flecked delight," all attributes of Dyson's own persona. When *Augustans and Romantics* appeared, Lewis remarked, "It is, as one would expect, almost too bright, but some of the sparks are admirable"—a splendid summing up of Dyson's gestalt. Others, too, admired Dyson's writings, but he never attained the popular acclaim poured so lavishly upon other Inklings. In the mid-1960s, he appeared in the John Schlesinger film *Darling* as a celebrated author, a white-haired owlish man with clever, shifting eyes, tossing off bons mots of which the most memorable is "It's true I have always preferred to be a mouse off by itself rather than a member of a group of literary lions." The line carries a full measure of truth: Dyson, although a key member of the pride, often stood apart, too prickly and insecure (like all who demand their own way) to mesh perfectly with others. His contrariness exacted its price: when he vetoed *The Lord of the Rings*, it was no longer a case of Inklings against the world, but of Inkling against Inkling, another stage in the breaking of the circle.

15

MIRACLES

S ome people believe in God because they believe in miracles; other people believe in miracles because they believe in God. Lewis was the latter sort. Miracles made sense to him only after he had embraced a God who transcends the natural order. Once he became a Christian, however, he began to notice that believer and nonbeliever alike say very odd things about miracles, as if there are only two positions one can take, credulity or skepticism. In 1942, in the first of two talks on the subject for an Evensong "Voices of the Laity" series at the London church of Saint Jude-on-the-Hill, Lewis proposed a third possibility: a rational belief in miracles supported by careful philosophical inquiry.

The following year, Dorothy L. Sayers wrote to him wondering why there weren't any books about miracles that could help her fend off the objections of an atheist correspondent: "Has Physics sold the pass? Or is it merely that everybody is thinking in terms of Sociology and international Ethics? Please tell me what to do with this relic of the Darwinian age who is wasting my time, sapping my energies, and destroying my soul." Lewis answered immediately with a copy of his first "Voices of the Laity" talk, and he assured Sayers that a book on the subject was in the works. He completed it in May 1945 and published it under the title of *Miracles: A Preliminary Study* two years later, by which time he had also produced the essay "Meditation in a Toolshed" and addressed Magdalen

College ("*De Futilitate*") and the Socratic Club ("Is Theology Poetry?" and "A Christian Reply to Professor Price") on the same theme.

Lewis's intent in writing *Miracles* was not to justify indiscriminate belief in spiritual prodigies, for which a healthy skepticism can often be the better part of piety, but to defend miracles against the naturalist who automatically and hence unphilosophically rules claims of the miraculous out of court. The locus classicus for the naturalistic view that he wished to combat is the essay "Of Miracles" in *An Enquiry Concerning Human Understanding* by the eighteenth-century Scottish philosopher David Hume. A miracle, according to Hume, is "a violation of the laws of nature," and we can never possess evidence for such a violation strong enough to outweigh our "firm and unalterable experience" of nature's regularity.

But a miracle need not be seen as a *violation* of nature's laws, Lewis points out; indeed, that is not how Christian philosophers have tradition-ally understood the matter. Rather, a miracle interrupts or invades the system of nature, without disrupting its fundamental laws. The natural-ist thinks he knows in advance that such an invasion can never occur, because nature is "the whole show." But for the supernaturalist—that is, for anyone who admits a reality beyond the system of nature—the port-cullis is open. On a supernaturalist account, miracles *might* occur. Whether they really do is a matter for further investigation.

Odd as it may seem at first glance, Lewis sets out to justify this su-pernaturalist account by an appeal, not to revelation or religious experi-ence, but to reason alone. To the naturalist, he observes, logical thinking is a useful behavior evolved, like all behaviors, under the influence of ir-rational causes; as such, Lewis argues, it has no purchase on objective truth. Nothing can shield naturalism itself from being explained naturalis-tically, so that, judged by its own criteria, naturalism self-destructs. This, at least, is the way Lewis put it in the third chapter of the original 1947 edition of *Miracles* on "The Self-Contradiction of the Naturalist":

> . . . no account of the universe can be true unless that account leaves it possible for our thinking to be a real insight. A theory which explained everything else in the whole universe but which made it impossible to believe that our thinking was valid, would be utterly out of court. For that theory would itself have been

reached by thinking, and if thinking is not valid that theory would, of course, be itself demolished. It would have destroyed its own credentials. It would be an argument which proved that no argument was sound—a proof that there are no such things as proofs—which is nonsense.

It was a Chestertonian move. In *Orthodoxy*, G. K. Chesterton had similarly observed that "evolution is either an innocent scientific description of how certain earthly things came about; or, if it is anything more than this, it is an attack upon thought itself"; more aphoristically: "the sceptics, like bees, give their one sting and die." Lewis thought that by focusing on logical inference rather than on thought or consciousness in general, he had made the case more compelling. Barfield, for one, disagreed; in a note he inserted in his copy of *Miracles* (and may or may not have sent to Lewis), he expressed his doubt that a reasoning process that, as Lewis put it, "has grown up gradually since my birth and is interrupted for several hours each night" could secure our access to the supernatural. Supersensible cognition (of the sort Steiner experienced) is where one should look for evidence of the supernatural.

Lewis's view faced its most formidable criticism on February 2, 1948, at a Monday evening meeting of the Socratic Club, when G.E.M. (Elizabeth) Anscombe, a Catholic convert, student of Wittgenstein, and arguably the most brilliant moral philosopher of her generation, read a paper to the Socratic Club pointing out, as a fatal flaw in Lewis's argument, his conflation of *irrational* with *nonrational* factors in belief-formation, and arguing that reasoning, considered as a process or event, can be described naturalistically without prejudice to a judgment of rational validity:

Whether [a man's] conclusions are rational or irrational is settled by considering the chain of reasoning that he gives and whether his conclusions follow from it. When we are giving a causal account of this thought, e.g. an account of the physiological processes which issue in the utterance of his reasoning, we are not considering his utterances from the point of view of evidence, reasoning, valid argument, truth, at all; we are considering them merely as events. Just *because* that is how we are considering them, our description has in itself no bearing on the question of "valid," "invalid," "rational," "irrational," and so on.

Anscombe noted other ambiguities as well, and Lewis conceded some of them: "veridical" might have expressed his meaning better than "valid," and "cause" should have been distinguished from "ground." The minutes of the meeting concluded that "in general it appeared that Mr Lewis would have to turn his argument into a rigorous analytic one, if his notion were to stand the test of all the questions put to him."

For a 1960 edition of *Miracles*, Lewis made revisions with Anscombe's criticisms in mind, changing the title of his third chapter from "The Self-Contradiction of the Naturalist" to "The Cardinal Difficulty of Naturalism," substituting "non-rational" for many occurrences of "irrational," and clarifying the cause-effect/ground-consequent distinction. Anscombe remained unconvinced by Lewis's arguments but noted that "the fact that Lewis rewrote that chapter, and rewrote it so that it now has these qualities, shows his honesty and seriousness."

As of this writing, the jury is still out on the soundness of Lewis's "argument from reason," as it is now called, even in its improved 1960 form, but it has its notable defenders, among them the philosopher Alvin Plantinga. While Lewis failed to consider naturalism in all its varieties, he successfully refuted naturalism of the most virulent kind—eliminative materialism. In place of this crude and unsatisfying worldview, *Miracles* paints a portrait of the harmony between mind and reality, and between faith and reason, that should encourage scientists and believers alike: "The rightful demand that all reality should be consistent and systematic does not therefore exclude miracles . . . By definition, miracles must of course interrupt the usual course of Nature; but if they are real they must, in the very act of so doing, assert all the more the unity and self-consistency of total reality at some deeper level . . ." This sense of a deep harmony achieved by the sovereignty of reason over nature and of God over all was what Lewis wanted most to convey, and Anscombe's valid criticisms do not diminish this insight.

Nonetheless, he was bruised by the debate. Derek Brewer, his student at the time, remembered Lewis speaking of the event "with real horror": "His imagery was all of the fog of war, the retreat of infantry thrown back under heavy attack." Brewer also recalled hearing Dyson say, with sympathy, that Lewis "had lost everything and was come to the foot of the Cross." Some biographers, missing the hyperbole in these descriptions, have advanced the view that Lewis was so devastated by the Anscombe affair that he abandoned apologetics and retreated into children's fantasy. This belief has gained traction in recent years, but there are good reasons to reject it. For one thing, it does not match Anscombe's impression. "My own recollection," she wrote later, "is that it was an occasion of sober discussion of certain quite definite criticisms, which Lewis' rethinking and rewriting showed he thought were accurate. I am inclined to construe the odd accounts of the matter by some of his friends—who seem not to have been interested in the actual arguments or the subject-matter—as an interesting example of the phenomenon called 'projection.'" For another, it overlooks Lewis's enjoyment of a good fight. When Stella Aldwinckle asked him to nominate speakers for the 1951 Socratic Club season, Anscombe was his first choice: "The lady is quite right to refute what she thinks bad theistic arguments, but does this not almost oblige her as a Christian to find good ones in their place: having obliterated me as an Apologist ought she not to *succeed* me?"

The truth is, as we saw in chapter 13, Lewis had been worrying for many years about the baleful effects of apologetics upon the apologist. In *The Great Divorce*, completed by the summer of 1944, nearly four years before the Anscombe debate, the Teacher (George MacDonald) warns Lewis about Christians so caught up in proving God's existence that they ignore the living God. "It is," MacDonald says, "the subtlest of all the snares." Lewis picked up the theme again in an address to Anglican clergy in 1945, telling his audience that "nothing is more dangerous to one's own faith than the work of an apologist." The problem, as he saw it, was that a successful debater for Christ, aware of the flaws in his arguments, may come to see what he has defended as "spectral" and "unreal." The only hope, Lewis said, is for the believer to turn "from Christian apologetics into Christ Himself."

A few remarks in Lewis's letters might seem to support the picture of a demoralized Lewis abandoning the intellectual defense of Christianity, but they need not be so construed. Thus, in a letter to the BBC declining to participate in a series of broadcast dialogues on the evidences for Christianity, Lewis begged off by saying that "like the old fangless snake

in *The Jungle Book*, I've largely lost my dialectical power." Fatigue, the
tedium that such a project would promise for anyone who has already
performed in that circus, polite humor, and the wisdom of late middle
age more than account for the self-deprecation. In a similar spirit, he
declined an invitation to write for the American evangelical magazine
Christianity Today: "My thought and talent (such as they are) now flow in
different, though I think not less Christian, channels, and I do not think
I am at all likely to write more *directly* theological pieces. The last work
of that sort which I attempted had to be abandoned. If I am now good for
anything it is for catching the reader unawares—thro' fiction and symbol. I have done what I could in the way of frontal attacks, but I now feel
quite sure those days are over." The abandoned work to which he refers
here is not *Miracles*, but a projected book of private prayers for the use of
the laity. As any experienced writer knows, abandoning books when they
fail to gel is no defeat but a crucial part of the creative process.

Lewis still had a great deal of theological and philosophical writing
ahead of him. Though 1948 marked the end of his most productive period
in Christian apologetics, he continued to publish polemical and medita-
tive essays expounding and defending Christian doctrine from different
angles, many of which appeared in collections like *The World's Last Night*,
Christian Reflections, and *Undeceptions* (*God in the Dock* in the United
States). In books still to come, such as *The Four Loves* and *Letters to
Malcolm*, the Christian apologist is alive and well; and in *Surprised by Joy*
he would present, under the guise of autobiography, a winning articulation
of the case for theism. *Miracles* was a capstone, not a swan song, as Lewis
himself suggested in a whimsical note to the poet and Arthurian scholar
William L. Kinter in 1953: "It's fun laying out all my books as a cathedral.
Personally I'd make *Miracles* and the other 'treatises' the cathedral school:
my children's stories are the real side-chapels, each with its own little
altar." What went on in the side-chapels—*The Chronicles of Narnia*—
will be explored in the next chapter.

Other Friendships

Dorothy L. Sayers was not the only woman who might have made a
splendid Inkling. Sister Penelope, with her skill in Latin and Greek, her
puckish humor, and her outpouring of works on Christian doctrine, each

one better than the previous in Lewis's estimation, perfectly fit the mold. An equally strong case could be made for the poet and painter Ruth Pitter (1897–1992). Pitter came within the orbit of the (future) Inklings as early as 1932, when David Cecil read her poetry collection *A Trophy at Arms* and dashed off a laudatory letter. "I must tell you how very beautiful I think your poems," he wrote. "I read them last week in a fit of drab depression brought on by the condition of the world: and I cannot tell you what a ray of light spread out on my horizon to discover that someone cared still to write such firm spontaneous glowing poetry—could feel the essential normal beauties of soul & body, so freshly, so strongly, so unsentimentally."

At the time, Pitter was in her late thirties, a friend of Belloc, Orwell, AE, and Orage, struggling to make ends meet by comanaging a company that sold painted furniture. Her poetry was just the sort that Cecil loved, with its precise traditional forms and Christian values (later, L. P. Hartley described her poems as "closely-worked, carved like gems, and immediately intelligible," and John Wain declared her "a poet of the full singing voice," of the "high style"—the latter a very Inklingesque compliment). Cecil became a lifelong friend, and thanks in large measure to his support, *A Trophy at Arms* won the 1937 Hawthornden Prize.

A few years later, Pitter forged her most important Inklings bond, befriending C. S. Lewis. He had first heard of her early during the war, when Cecil had showed him her poetry. Lewis had been "deeply struck," Cecil wrote Pitter, "& went off to buy your poems." The following year, she read *The Screwtape Letters* and told Cecil that the book had "excited me more than anything has done for a long time." When she heard Lewis's BBC broadcasts, excitement turned into something more significant:

> There were air raids at night. The factory was dark and dirty. And I remember thinking—well—I must find somebody or something because like this I cannot go on . . . sometime afterwards I heard the broadcast talks of C. S. Lewis, and I at once grappled them to my soul, as Shakespeare says . . . I had to be intellectually satisfied as well as emotionally . . . and I was satisfied at every point.

The radio talks worked their magic and "driven to it by the pull of C. S. Lewis and the push of misery," she formally entered, a few years later, the English Church.

Thanks to the poet Herbert Palmer, a mutual friend who acted as go-between, Pitter finally met the great evangelizer at his Magdalen digs on the morning of July 17, 1946. "My visit to you has discountenanced all the gypsy's warnings of people who say 'never meet your favourite authors,'" she wrote happily to her new friend that evening. He replied a few days later, having just read *A Trophy of Arms*: "I was prepared for the more definitely mystical poems, but not for this cool, classical style . . . I meant to send you something of mine but I shan't. It all sounds like a brass band after yours . . . Why wasn't I told you were as good as this?" Five days later he did mail her a handful of his own poems, confessing that he had doubts about their value: "I know (or think) that some of these contain important thought and v. great metrical ingenuity . . . But are they real poems or do the content and the form remain separable—fitted together only by force?" Pitter assured him that they were indeed real; to a friend she remarked that she hadn't known that poetry (in any language!) could blend such metrical brilliance and deep thought. Lewis was "greatly relieved" by her assessment—he was far more assured of his skill with prose than with poetry—and admitted that "I often lust after a metre as a man might lust after a woman."

This satisfying round of congratulations and assurances initiated one of the significant artistic friendships of Lewis's life. He and Pitter exchanged scores of letters and met dozens of times. He visited her at home in Chelsea, invited her to lectures and debates, and introduced her to other Inklings, including Warnie, Barfield, and Dyson—but never, of course, to an official Inklings meeting, the prohibition against women remaining unbreachable. During their lunches, the two friends discussed faith, fellow writers, what to read, and what to write. Their correspondence flourished. Lewis's letters, less confessional than those to Sister Penelope, combine banter with serious reflections on a variety of topics, including the fall of the angels, the beauties of nature, and the space romances of David Lindsay. They couldn't stop talking about poetry: "The important thing is that we put the individual poet firmly in his place," Lewis said. "He is not the creator, only the mother, of something whose father is the Universe or Time." He continued to seek Pitter's advice on his verse, on at least one occasion sending her two versions of a poem ("Two Kinds of Memory") and asking which she preferred. If she had said neither, he would have agreed, for he still doubted that his poems were "real" and wondered whether her praise came from "kindness and liking for my prose work." Pitter later saw the legitimacy of Lewis's qualms; he had the tools of a poet, but his obsession with technique hampered his expression. "Did he ever," she mused, "catch some floating bit of emotional thistledown & go on from that?"

While corresponding with Pitter, Lewis started up yet another episto-lary exchange, in this instance with someone who differed from him "in place, nationality, language, obedience and age." Don Giovanni Calabria, an Italian Catholic priest and founder of the Poor Servants of Divine Providence, initiated the letters, writing to Lewis from Verona on September 1, 1947, that he had just read *Le Lettere di Berlicche* (*The Screwtape Letters*) and wished to consult the author on "a problem of the greatest importance," that of the schism between Catholics and Protes-tants. Not knowing English, he addressed Lewis in Latin. Delighted, Lewis rose to the challenge and replied in kind, apologizing for any rust in his delivery. Ecumenical issues were, for him, too, "a source of grief and a matter for prayers." However, he thought himself unqualified to tackle such subtle matters, which should be addressed by "bishops and learned men." He preferred to concentrate on "those things which still, by God's grace, after so many sins and errors, are shared by us." This may sound disingenuous, given his willingness to pronounce on many theo-logical issues for which he had no professional training (a practice that irked Tolkien mightily, as the reader will recall), but there is an appealing note of humility in Lewis's voice, an echo of Don Giovanni's own self-deprecating tone. Carried on until Don Giovanni's death in 1954, the exchange covered many conventional but heartfelt themes, such as the love of God, moral darkness, the threat of atheism, and prayers of encouragement. Lewis enjoyed the correspondence and revered the cor-respondent; on September 13, 1951, after hearing that Don Giovanni was ill and fearing that he may be dead, he wrote that "never in the least did I cease from my prayers for you; for not even the River of Death ought to abolish the sweet intercourse of love and meditations." These letters reveal Lewis at his most tender, kind, and conciliatory; the bullying don and bullheaded debater annihilated by love through his encounter with the saintly Italian (Don Giovanni was canonized by Pope John Paul II on April 18, 1999).

"Uton Herian Holbytlas"

"I actually wept at the denouement," Tolkien recalled, years later. His great epic was finished. Well might he weep, as eleven years of intense creation, interrupted by seasons of terrible stagnation, drew to a close. In the late summer of 1948, he sequestered himself at Payables Farm, his son Michael's nineteenth-century home at the Oratory School in the Chiltern Hills, and completed a working draft of *The Lord of the Rings*. Then came further revisions. He fiddled and fussed with this passage and that and produced much new material that would become part of a prologue and various appendices. On October 31, 1948, he wrote to Hugh Brogan, a schoolboy correspondent, that he was "happy to announce that I succeeded at last in bringing 'the Lord of the Rings' to a successful conclusion. Also, it has been read and approved by Rayner Unwin, who (the original reader of the 'Hobbit') has had time to grow up while the sequel has been made, and now here at Trinity. I think there is a chance of it being published although it will be a massive book far too large to make any money for the publisher . . ."

Another year would pass, however, before he completed a fair copy of the text. The intervening months saw transition, disruption, and disappointment. Priscilla moved from the family home into Lady Margaret Hall as an Oxford undergraduate, leaving her parents with an empty nest for the first time in over thirty years. Despite the extra free time this afforded, Tolkien remained frustrated, complaining to Brogan that "this university business of earning one's living by teaching, delivering philological lectures, and daily attendance at 'boards' and other talk-meetings, interferes sadly with serious work." On February 10, 1949, he contacted university officials about the possibility of a leave of absence, in order "to complete a number of writings I have on hand" and—less exalted but equally pressing—to arrange for the removal of all his teeth, "which are said to be poisoning me."

The university granted a sabbatical for Trinity term 1949 (mid-April to the end of June), but it came to naught, thanks to unavoidable teaching and committee responsibilities. Tolkien then requested and received a lengthier leave, covering the fall and winter of 1949–50. In June 1949, he traveled for the first time to Ireland, serving as an external examiner for the National University of Ireland, work that he enjoyed, thanks to Ireland's "curious shabby, happy-go-lucky, tumbledown charm" and, of course, its fervent Catholicism. Throughout these months the fair copy of *The Lord of the Rings* lay heavily upon his mind. When not abroad, he spent much of his spare time preparing the typescript, bending over a machine balanced on a bed in the attic of his home, a herculean task completed only in October. Instantly he passed the finished copy to Lewis for evaluation. "*Uton herian holbytlas* [let us praise hobbits] indeed," Lewis responded on October 27. "I have drained the rich cup and satisfied a long thirst. Once it really gets under weigh the steady upward slope of grandeur and terror . . . is almost unequalled in the whole range of narrative art known to me." He added a few objections, for instance, that "many passages I cd. wish you had written otherwise or omitted altogether"— Lewis possessed a finer ear for literary music and a sharper eye for overripe prose than his friend—but he hastened back to praise: "I congratulate you. All the long years you have spent on it are justified. Morris and Eddison, in so far as they are comparable, are now mere 'precursors.'"

Nor was this the end of Tolkien's literary triumphs in this glorious month of October 1949. On the twentieth, Allen & Unwin published *Farmer Giles of Ham*, his first book to see print in twelve years, a fantasy novella about a farmer named Giles who conquers a dragon named Chrysophylax, collects the beast's treasure horde, and becomes a king. Tolkien had thought it up on the spot in the 1920s, to entertain his children as the family huddled under a bridge during a passing storm. After Allen & Unwin had accepted *The Hobbit* in 1936, Tolkien had sent them *Farmer Giles* for consideration, but it had been rejected as too brief to publish, despite a favorable report from Rayner Unwin. A year later, Tolkien had read a different version of the tale to the Lovelace Society at Worcester College and had been delighted to see that the audience "was apparently not bored—indeed they were generally convulsed with mirth." One attendee recalled that Tolkien, in response to an undergraduate's query about the truth of dragons and other legends, declared that behind such tales invariably lies something real; he then dug into his pockets and pulled out, along with a ball of string and other detritus, a small green shoe, thin and pointed in the toe, made of a leathery substance that felt like reptile skin, and declared it, "stoutly and with apparent sincerity," to be a leprechaun's shoe.

He pulled a rabbit out of his hat with *Farmer Giles of Ham*. In final form, it is not only a comic romp but a knowing satire, packed with philological jokes, invented etymologies, a pseudo-scholarly foreword, bits of Latin, and insider references to the "Four Wise Clerks of Oxenford" (the four editors of the *OED*). The full title of the book, setting the tone for what follows, is *Aegidii Ahenobarbi Julii Agricole de Hammo Domini de Domito Aule Draconarie comitis Regni Minimi regis et basilei mira facinora et mirabilis exortus* or in the vulgar tongue *The Rise and Wonderful Adventures of Farmer Giles, Lord of Tame, Count of Worminghall and King of the Little Kingdom*. When, after the war, Allen & Unwin reversed its decision and decided to publish, they insisted on illustrations to beef it up to acceptable size. The first artist did not work out, but Tolkien struck gold when, during a visit to the firm's offices, he spied some delightful watercolor-and-ink illustrations based upon the whimsical grotesqueries of the fourteenth-century Luttrell Psalter. The illustrator, Pauline Baynes, a young woman who had been born in East Sussex and raised in India, was soon assigned to *Farmer Giles of Ham*. Her line drawings for the book, playing off medieval conventions without ridiculing them, enraptured Tolkien "beyond even the expectations aroused by the first examples. They are more than illustrations, they are a collateral theme."

The End of Thursday Nights

October 1949 was a watershed not only for Tolkien but for all the Inklings. As the decade waned, Thursday night meetings continued at Lewis's Magdalen rooms or at Merton under Tolkien's auspices, but attendance was sparse. It seemed that every week, half the group had something else to do; only Tolkien, the Lewis brothers, and possibly Havard or Hardie could be relied on to make a regular appearance. Sometimes one or two less active members swelled the ranks, such as George Sayer, an English teacher at Malvern College and friend of Lewis and Tolkien, or Ronald B. McCallum, a fellow of Pembroke. The wine flowed, as did the talk, ranging from the poetics of T. S. Eliot to the ethics of cannibalism, but it was evident all around that interest was flagging. On October 27, 1949, Warnie noted in his diary: "Dined with J at College . . . No one turned up after dinner, which was just as well, as J had a bad cold and wanted to go to bed early." No one would turn up ever again. From now on, Tuesday mornings at the Bird and Baby—a brilliant social hour but nothing more—would have to suffice; the Thursday night meetings had died from neglect.

What brought to an end those shining hours, rivaling or surpassing at their peak the gatherings of those magnificent eighteenth-century clubs of Johnson and Reynolds, Pope and Swift? No doubt the loss of Williams played a part, even if not as decisive a part as John Wain perceived (see chapter 14). Four years removed, his early demise still stung, and none of the new enrollees, however accomplished, could replace his feverish, enchanting mind. Lewis, ever faithful to his old friend, in 1948 had published *Arthurian Torso*, a literary diptych of Williams's incomplete prose study of the Arthurian legend and Lewis's commentary on Williams's Arthurian poems. Most of the reviews ranged from lukewarm to cold. For the Shakespeare scholar Molly Mahood, writing in the *Modern Language Review*, the book's strength lay in the idiosyncratic appeal of Williams's poetry and theology; those seeking instruction in the history of Arthurian romance should look elsewhere. In *The Review of English Studies*, the Arthurian scholar John E. Housman declared that Williams's share of the work "will . . . discredit the memory of an accomplished poet, because of its utter disregard for research and its lack of the most elementary principles of scholarship." Few cared, really. Williams's star, never very bright, was fading, and among the Inklings perhaps only Lewis held out hope for a Williams revival, telling Sayers that he wished to "be only the starting point of *Williamswissenschaftslehre*" (the scientific doctrine, or knowledge-theory—an expression favored by German idealists—of Williams). He never stopped boosting his friend; in *Essays Presented to Charles Williams*, he proclaimed, in an egregious example of loyalty trumping taste, Williams's Arthurian poems to be "among the two or three most valuable books of verse produced in the century." Lewis, of all Inklings, felt most acutely the absence of that mercurial man on Thursday evenings.

There were other things amiss with Thursday night meetings. Readings had ground almost to a halt. Tolkien, wearied by Dyson's carping, no longer presented any of his work, and Lewis followed suit by withholding portions of his new children's book, *The Lion, the Witch, and the Wardrobe*. Perhaps he, too, anticipated a Dysonian assault; certainly he had qualms about reading the work in front of Tolkien, who already had heard parts of it in private session and had been repelled by its patchwork mythology. Without the readings and the subsequent critiques, Thursday night had become, in effect, Tuesday morning: an opportunity to chat with chums. Why not, then, drop Magdalen entirely for the Bird and Baby, with its dark, cozy, beery atmosphere? Tolkien, for one, had been thinking along these lines for some time; in his Septuagesima Sunday 1948 letter to Lewis on Dyson's transgressions, he had made no mention of Magdalen (or the occasional Merton) gatherings but had signed off by declaring, "I know no more pleasant sound than arriving at the B. and B. and hearing a roar, and knowing that one can plunge in."

A few Inklings specialists, notably Humphrey Carpenter, see yet another force at work, suggesting that Christianity had lost its cachet at Oxford by the late 1940s and that the resulting climate of religious indifference played a role in the demise of Magdalen meetings. But there is evidence to offset this view. When William Empson returned from his Asian travels in 1952 to take up a professorship in English literature at Sheffield, he was shocked by the resurgent Christianity among the British intelligentsia, a calamity he attributed to the influence of T. S. Eliot's conversion and Lewis's BBC talks and apologetic books. Kathleen Nott, a prominent poet and critic, registered her dismay at this state of affairs in her 1953 book, *The Emperor's Clothes: An Attack on the Dogmatic Orthodoxy of T. S. Eliot, Graham Greene, Dorothy Sayers, C. S. Lewis, and Others*. At Oxford, the Student Christian Movement (SCM) continued to thrive, as did the Roman Catholic chaplaincy; church attendance remained high, and retreats, prayer meetings, charitable associations, and missions proliferated.

It would be more accurate to say that Lewis's rise to fame as a Christian apologist (especially in the United States: he appeared on the cover of *Time* magazine on September 8, 1947, just two years before the Thursday evening lights went out) and Williams's death were two aspects of the same overriding reason for the Inklings' sea change: the membership was aging. In 1949, Tolkien was fifty-seven, Warnie fifty-four, Lewis and Barfield fifty-one; each was approaching that stage when many men settle into themselves and long for the armchair as much as the podium. Tolkien had finished *The Lord of the Rings*; no major projects beckoned apart from refining *The Silmarillion*, now in its fourth decade of composition; the home nest was empty of hatchlings; to complete the image of autumn setting in, he was about to acquire a full set of dentures. Lewis was smoking heavily and prone to flu, worn down by Mrs. Moore's incessant demands and frightened by Warnie's alcoholic binges. Barfield, with his dancer's body, remained in excellent health but locked in literary limbo. None of these core members harbored doubts about the value of their long association with the group. It was simply time for a change.

"Why Should Not We Wake Up Sometimes?"

"I've read your poem with interest and sympathy, but we are obliged at present to keep our poetry list down to the shortest we can . . . I am therefore returning it with profound regrets." So wrote T. S. Eliot to Barfield on June 1, 1948, rejecting his proposal that Faber & Faber publish his long narrative work, "The Unicorn." Despite "profound regrets" and a few personal remarks ("I have been glad to see your occasional appearance in *The New English Weekly*"), Eliot's refusal amounted to little more than a formal rejection letter and must have come as a bitter blow, especially as Barfield had convinced himself—and had notified Lewis—that publication was assured. In the event, "The Unicorn" never saw the light of day. Laid low by this letdown, by his general failure to publish, by domestic tensions, and by a job he disliked, Barfield confessed to Lewis that he was suffering from depression. Lewis, eager to buck up his friend, replied that this realization might well "mark an advance in self criticism and objectivity—i.e. that the very same experiences wh. wd. once have led you to say 'How nasty everyone (or the weather, or the political situation) is at present' now leads you to say 'I am depressed.'" This newfound self-awareness, Lewis continued, amounted to "a Copernican revolution."

He was right, Barfield was seeing things more objectively, but clear-sightedness only increased his misery. He began to question everything: his relationship with Maud, his work as a solicitor, his writings, his religious views. His spirits spiraled downward over the next several months, and he grew irritable as well as depressed. In the early spring of 1949, he sent Lewis a touchy note accusing him of not answering letters, a charge that Lewis responded "has caused me more shame and pain that it is at all likely you intended." Once again, Lewis tried to cheer up his friend, this time with a clumsy joke crackling with resentment: "Did I ever mention that Weston, Devine, Frost, Wither, Curry and Miss Hardcastle [villains from the Space Trilogy] were all portraits of you? (If I didn't, that may have been because it isn't true. By gum, tho', wait till I write another story.)"

Clearly, Lewis was exasperated, but it is doubtful that he realized the extent of Barfield's anguish. "I was under very heavy pressure at my office," Barfield said later. "And it was after my father's death, and there was also some domestic misunderstanding or trouble at home . . . I think I was really on the verge of a nervous breakdown." Faced with collapse, the artist in him came to the rescue; he picked up his pen and produced his only successful mainstream novel, *This Ever Diverse Pair*, a work that "staved off" the impending disaster.

The story has a clever premise: a London solicitor, closely based on Barfield, harbors two personalities: one a dreamy, poetic, philosophically minded literary type named Burgeon, the other a plodding, detail-oriented, matter-of-fact sort named, with unfortunate heavy-handedness, Burden. Burgeon tells the tale. He explains at the outset why he is doing this: "I must now write about something or die." He must write because he is an artist trapped in a law office; he writes about his oppressive alter ego and the occupation they share, because "the only thing upon which I am allowed, and indeed expected, to fix my attention, is Burden." This is, of course, Barfield describing the occupational trap that, of his own volition, he has constructed, stepped inside, and snapped shut. He allows that "it was *my* doing that we ever went into the law at all," but now Burden has become "a sort of Frankenstein," living only for his profession and dragging the erstwhile poet along with him into "a complex of responsibilities from which there may be no way out until the shadows lengthen, the busy world is hushed and our world is done."

Divorce, real estate, inheritance, and other legal cases reinforce the trap, each complication presented in high satirical mode, as Burgeon and Burden combat law firms like Pauncefoot & Mecklenburgh for the doubtful rights of their dubious clients. One chapter, "The Things That Are Caesar's!" features a certain Ramsden (a thinly disguised Lewis, echoing "Ransom"), "a rather extraordinary sort of chap" with whom Burgeon once shared "a period of intellectual intercourse long since woven into the stuff of our lives and taken up into whatever we can claim of wisdom and insight." Ramsden, like his real-life model, suffers from profligate generosity; in lieu of royalties, he "just writes to his publisher and says . . . 'Pay the next lot to the Home for Retired Professors of Ichthyosophy.'" This practice leads (as it did with Lewis) to a staggering tax bill and an amusing account of how Burgeon's intervention saves the day.

The legal escapades make for entertaining farce, but as the Burgeon/ Burden conflict continues, the tale darkens and turns surreal. Burden finds himself "like Alice Through the Looking Glass . . . out of breath with running at full speed in order to keep up with himself remaining in the same place." He—and through him Burgeon—develops rhemato-phobia (from the Greek *rhema*, utterance or word), a fear and loathing of the spoken word—a disease, incidentally, unrecognized by both the medical profession and the *Oxford English Dictionary*. Rhematophobia afflicts the ability to absorb and grasp language: "The moment of pain is the effort required to convert sound into meaning and to unite that meaning . . . with the meanings of the preceding words and of those which are to follow." This fantastic ailment, one of Barfield's brightest inventions, is a psychic inversion of his own youthful stammering; instead of struggling to get the words out, one struggles to get them in. Burgeon's deterioration accelerates, until one day he snaps and assaults his partner/ alter ego with a trash can and ruler; in turn, Burden announces to Burgeon, with icy certainty, "I'm going to kill you."

At this desperate moment—corresponding to the real-life moment when Barfield found himself facing mental collapse—Burgeon suddenly sees the way out. It comes to him that, precisely as a poet, he is indis-pensable to Burden, that without poets "the very profession itself, and the law which it helps to administer, would not be there. For if it is the Burdens of this world who keep traditions alive, it is the Burgeons who create them." Well, then, why must "we Burgeons need always remain *sleeping* partners. Why should not we wake up sometimes and take a hand once more in the practice both of law and of life?" A modus vivendi is achieved, a modus operandi initiated: Burgeon and Burden, art and business, inspiration and drudgery, will advance hand in hand, in a fruitful if uneasy conjunction of opposites. The ending is weak, Burgeon's sudden self-understanding dawning as no more than a deus ex machina. It doesn't matter—not for the tale, which is lighthearted and implausible enough to sustain this final narrative collapse, and not for Barfield, for whom the writing was as much therapy as art, paving the way to continue his legal practice without killing his creative soul.

This Ever Diverse Pair had little difficulty in attracting a publisher, especially after Barfield's old friend Walter de la Mare consented to write the introduction. On April 29, 1949, Sheila Hodges of the firm of Victor Gollancz bid for the book, stating that it had "enchanted" Gollancz, who was "most anxious to meet the author," and offering a small advance. Lewis, receiving the news, was delighted. Soon he heard tidings that gave him even greater joy. A few weeks after Gollancz accepted *This Ever Diverse Pair*, Barfield decided to enter the Anglican Church, arranging to be baptized on June 25 at St. Saviour's Church in Uckfield, East Sussex. Lewis, although recovering from a high fever, wrote to congratulate him, declaring that "I am humbled (I think that is the right word) by your great news. I wish I cd. be with you. Welcome and welcome and welcome."

He assured Barfield, oddly, that his baptism didn't mean the end of the "Great War"—a sop to a friend, one presumes, for as far as Lewis was concerned, the war had ended decades ago—and mentioned that he didn't resent being passed over as godfather. What he failed to bring up, although he must have wondered about it, was why Barfield had decided upon baptism after so many years outside the church, and whether this decision meant an end to his Anthroposophical involvement. Barfield's answer to the second question would have been a very firm "no." He remained dedicated to the cause, contributing essays and reviews to *The Golden Blade*, an Anthroposophical journal, and promulgating Steiner's works; the very year of his baptism, he published a revised edition of Steiner's *World-Economy: The Formation of a Science of World-Economics*. Why, then, get baptized? He may have joined the Anglican Church as a gift to Maud, to show her that Anthroposophy and Christianity were not antithetical. But his act was a gift to Lewis as well, who read the event as nothing less than Barfield's spiritual rebirth. To think that his dear friend had finally entered the faith! He dashed off a letter to Bede Griffiths, asking him to pray for the new Christian and mentioning that "I have two lists of names in my prayers, those for whose conversion I pray, and those for whose conversion I give thanks. The little trick of *transferences* from List A to List B is a great comfort."

The baptism must have brought comfort to Barfield as well. Just as *This Ever Diverse Pair* signaled an accommodation between art and law, so did his baptism signal a détente between the Anglican orthodoxy that surrounded him and his own Steinerian esotericism. Accommodation and détente, however, are far from permanent peace. *This Ever Diverse Pair* was a small triumph but an artistic dead end, for Barfield was not a satirist. He was too sincere and ardent for that. He was a true believer. Despite embracing Anglicanism, his spiritual home remained Anthroposophy, which entailed beliefs—reincarnation, akashic realms, the evolution of consciousness, and the rest—that have never found a home in Christian orthodoxy. He remained uneasy, uncertain of what to do, whom to turn to. His friends praised *This Ever Diverse Pair*, Ruth Pitter saying that "your prose works are . . . so full of meat one could spend years on them." Lewis told the world the same, writing in *Time and Tide* that the novel was "a high and sharp philosophic comedy, more fully a work of art and more original than anything I have read for a long time." But these were sops tossed by friends, and Barfield remained frustrated and depressed.

He also remained, despite the friendly review, vexed with Lewis. For many years, Barfield had harbored "the impression of living with, not one, but two Lewises"—one the old, direct, sincere Lewis, the other, as Barfield expressed it, somehow *"voulu,"* taking part in a sort of deliberate role-playing. One of the best accounts of Lewis's strange behavior, Barfield would suggest many years later, could be found in Alan Watts's 1971 study of mysticism, *Behold the Spirit*, which describes Lewis as exhibiting "a certain ill-concealed glee in adopting an old-fashioned and unpopular position." This impression of two Lewises, the real and the contrived, disturbed Barfield greatly, until finally it "became something like an obsession." Around 1950, he decided to address the problem through literature, just as he had addressed the problem of the law in *This Ever Diverse Pair*. He composed a long poem, "The Mother of Pegasus" (also known as "Riders of Pegasus"), a retelling of Greek myth in which two figures, Perseus and Bellerophon, represent the two aspects of Lewis's personality. As Barfield summarized it, Perseus "after going through a great many difficulties arising out of a preference he had developed for dealing with the reflections of things rather than with the things themselves . . . made peace with . . . his 'creative eros,'" while Bellerophon wound up "in increasing obscurity as a kind of aging, grumbling, earthbound, guilt-obsessed *laudator temporis acti* [praiser of times past]." As several Barfield scholars have remarked, the message is far from clear. Perseus appears to be Lewis face-to-face with reality and achieving a belated maturity, and Bellerophon Lewis hollowed to a shell by his taste for role-playing. But whether Barfield meant one of these to represent the "real" Lewis or whether each portends a possible future not yet determined is difficult to discern.

The murkiness, one can't help feel, reflects Barfield's literary limitations as well as his confused feelings about his friend, and indeed he wrote that he may have been "on the wrong track altogether," giving vent to "a common bit of overelaborated psychology à la mode, our twentieth century rococo." There is, however, no mistaking the clashing tides of love and resentment in his views of Lewis. It must have pained him, too, that no one seemed interested in publishing "The Mother of Pegasus." His friend George Rostrevor Hamilton, a critic and poet well placed in literary circles, warned him that "it is a particularly unfavorable season for poetry, and you have had the boldness to defy fashion by writing (a) a long poem (b) a poem on a Classical subject and (c) a poem which is neither in the mode nor in an easy convention," and then offered the coup de grâce by adding that "fine though the poem is . . . it is likely to frighten most of the cautious tribe of publishers." It was a familiar story. With *This Ever Diverse Pair*, Barfield had reopened the possibility of being both solicitor and artist; but to what avail, if no one would accept his art?

"MAKING UP IS A VERY MYSTERIOUS THING"

y house is unquiet and devastated by women's quarrels,"
Lewis confided to Father Calabria in January of 1949. "I
have *to dwell in the tents of Kedar.*" He was quoting Psalm
120, which begins with the piercing cry, "In my distress I cried unto the
Lord," as the psalmist laments his prolonged stay among the nomadic
Kedar, a tribe that "hateth peace." The Kedar had pitched their tents in
the Kilns: Mrs. Moore's arthritic legs had given out and she was confined
largely to her bedroom, from which she unleashed what Warnie described as a "stifling tyranny" of demands and denunciations. "Every day
had to have some kind of domestic scene or upheaval, commonly involving the maids." Her goddaughter, Vera, over from Ireland to help with
domestic chores, was sucked into the fray, as was the next-door neighbor,
Miss Griggs, who on one occasion burst into Mrs. Moore's bedroom to
berate her for selfishness. Lewis, trapped and miserable, spent much of
each day as her dog walker, nurse, and houseboy. She tightened her stranglehold by forbidding him afternoon access to the study, ostensibly to
economize on fuel but in reality to force him into the dining room where
she could keep a closer watch on him.

"How long, oh Lord, how long," wailed Warnie in his diary. He, at least,
had an escape, albeit a poisonous one, and he used it often. In February,
he awoke from another alcohol-induced stupor to find himself in Acland
Nursing Home, a small hospital on the Banbury Road. While consigned
to his hospital bed, he mulled over his plight and concluded that he was

the victim of a cycle of "insomnia-drugs-depression-spirits-illness." He feared, however, that his brother construed it—as Lewis correctly did—as "spirits-insomnia-drugs-depression-spirits-illness." Like many alcoholics, Warnie refused to see "spirits" as the active agent of his dissolution and convinced himself that with proper care he could drink safely and pleasurably. At least he held no illusions about the Kilns, preferring the Acland's friendship and warmth to his home's cold comforts. Once back under Mrs. Moore's roof, he tried to pray but "found the line 'dead.'"

In June, Lewis, too, entered the Acland, suffering a nasty streptococcal infection that left him feverish and delirious; Dr. Havard, who tended him, told Warnie that it was "a serious illness for a man of fifty." The underlying problem, said Havard, was exhaustion, and the cure a long vacation. Lewis agreed—it would be his first in fifteen years—and asked Arthur to find him a room for a month near Belfast. Preparations went forward until it dawned on Warnie that while Lewis recuperated in Ireland, he would be left alone at the Kilns with Mrs. Moore. This proved too much to bear, the bottle rematerialized, and by July 1 he had drunk himself back into a hospital bed. Immediately Lewis canceled his vacation to oversee his brother's recovery, which proved a complicated process that entailed a brief stay in Warneford hospital, a mental asylum, when the Acland doctor declared Warnie too "out of control" to treat. Warnie responded to Lewis's kindness with an act of consummate (and probably unconscious) irony: shortly after leaving the hospital, he set off on his own Irish holiday, booking into his favorite Drogheda tavern to test, with initial success, his new theory that he could safely manage a nip now and then. Lewis, meanwhile, resigned himself to the Kilns, writing Arthur that "as long as [Warnie] is a dipsomaniac, it *seems* impossible for me to get away for more than a v. few days." In effect, he had now not one jailor, but two.

How did Lewis respond to these calamities? With anxiety, as one might expect, but also with forbearance and humor. As he told Dorothy L. Sayers just before Warnie's July collapse, those who believe in easy cures often turn dour, while those who recognize ills as deep-rooted maintain a brighter disposition, "wh. is not really a paradox. If one is hurrying a hurt man into an ambulance with the knowledge that he can be saved if you get him to hospital in time, of course one doesn't joke. But if one is alleviating (year in, year out) the sufferings of an invalid who will never be quite well till the Resurrection, then for his sake as well as one's own cheerfulness, even gaiety, must be encouraged . . . the importance of *not* being earnest."

In addition to this fortunate outlook, Lewis possessed, like his brother, his own private means of escape: he could quit at once the Kilns, the Acland, and the shackles of his complex relationships by picking up his pen. Absorbed in narrative rapture, he would travel effortlessly to Mars, Venus, or whatever otherworldly realm beckoned, there to pursue, in a virgin landscape untouched by personal sorrows, the same theological and social themes that occupied him in the real world of tutorials, Inklings gatherings, and Bodleian research. He found the making of fiction so involving that for him it bypassed the ordinary analytical faculties, at least in its first stages: "a man writing a story is too excited about the story itself to sit back and notice how he is doing it," he said.

Nonetheless, Lewis bristled at accusations that his writing was no more than escapism. He told the science fiction writer Arthur C. Clarke that he had shed all worries about the issue after a friend (surely Tolkien) had pointed out that the only people who condemn escape are jailers. But unlike Tolkien, Lewis emphasized the didactic power of fantasy, and in turning from apologetics to fairy stories and children's literature (the genres are distinct yet overlapping), he was conscious of advancing, rather than shirking, his cause. The Anscombe debate was of minor importance in this awareness. Lewis knew there were better ways than heated debate to communicate the truths of the faith; he would title a later essay "Sometimes Fairy Stories May Say Best What's to Be Said." Writing in September 1947 to Mrs. E. L. Baxter, an Episcopalian in Kentucky who along with her husband had been sending care packages of tea and food, Lewis remarked, "Don't the ordinary fairy tales really already contain much of the Spirit, in solution? Does not Cinderella give us *exaltavit humiles*, and is not Redemption figured in *The Sleeping Beauty*?" It was only as a grown-up that he came fully to appreciate children's fantasy; *The Chronicles of Narnia*—his seven-part otherworld fantasy with gospel overtones—was almost the inevitable next move. Indeed, there is evidence, in the form of a fragment discovered by Walter Hooper among Lewis's posthumous papers, that he may have taken a stab at something like a Narnia tale as early as World War II, while young evacuees packed the Kilns and he was immersed in his BBC talks and other explicitly apologetic projects. The fragment, which does date from the war years, contains what appears to be a raw version of the first paragraph of *The Lion, the Witch, and the Wardrobe*:

> This book is about four children whose names were Ann, Martin, Rose and Peter. But it is most about Peter who was the youngest. They all had to go away from London suddenly because of Air Raids . . . They were sent to stay with a kind of relation of Mother's who was a very old Professor who lived all by himself in the country.

Apparently Lewis set the manuscript aside. In September 1947, responding to Mrs. Baxter's suggestion that he should write his own children's stories, he said, "I have tried one myself but it was, by the unanimous verdict of my friends, so bad that I destroyed it." Curiously enough, there is no record of any of Lewis's friends reading such a story. In any event, within a year of his exchange with Mrs. Baxter, he had plunged into the tale that would become *The Lion, the Witch, and the Wardrobe: A Story for Children*.

Through the Wardrobe

Lewis set his new fiction—the adventures of four young siblings (Peter, Susan, Edmund, and Lucy, in descending order of age) evacuated to a country house during the London Blitz, who pass through a bedroom wardrobe into a magical land—in a precinct of Faërie that he called Narnia. He took the name, as he told Walter Hooper, from an Umbrian town ("Narni") on an atlas of ancient Italy. The idea of the tale first came as an image, appearing unheralded in his mind: "a Faun carrying an umbrella and parcels in a snowy wood." The picture had arisen when he was sixteen, and he had nurtured it for more than thirty years. He never could determine its origin or antecedents; he believed that such ignorance was commonplace among artists: "I don't know where the pictures came from. And I don't believe anyone knows exactly how he 'makes things up.' Making up is a very mysterious thing."

In the summer of 1948, Lewis told the American poet and literary scholar Chad Walsh (author, in 1949, of *C. S. Lewis: Apostle to the*

Skeptics) that he was in the midst of writing the memoir that would become *Surprised by Joy*—he had gotten as far as the end of World War I—and was planning to finish a book he had begun "in the tradition of E. Nesbit." This conjunction is worth noting: if *Surprised by Joy* was a way for Lewis to confess and come to terms with the spiritual crises of his youth, Narnia was a way to reclaim the best parts of his youth in the light of the spiritual convictions of his Christian maturity, freed from the burdens of the past; Narnia and *Surprised by Joy* are two sides of the same conversion story. Almost a year after Walsh's visit, Lewis read two chapters of the completed manuscript of his first children's fantasy to his former tutee Roger Lancelyn Green, whose earlier story, "The Wood That Time Forgot" about three children magically transported into a preternatural forest, had been an encouragement and a minor influence. In his diary, Green declared the chapters "very good indeed, though a trifle self-conscious." Dr. Havard's daughter, Mary Clare, announced her approval, as a representative child reader.

Tolkien's assessment, by contrast, was apoplectic; he declared to Green, "it really won't do, you know! I mean to say: '*Nymphs and their Ways, the Love-Life of a Faun.*' Doesn't he know what he's talking about?" It was bad enough that Lewis had borrowed the Númenor legend (Tolkien's retelling of the Atlantis story) for incidental use in *That Hideous Strength*—changing the spelling to Numinor (suggestive of "numinous")—before Tolkien had had a chance to publish the legend himself. But what really irked Tolkien about Narnia was that he saw Lewis as deploying, for a pious allegory, bits and pieces of classical and Tolkienesque mythology, instead of undertaking the long labor required to create a fully realized mythological world. Had Tolkien's opinion prevailed, the series would have been stillborn. But it would be wrong to view Narnia as Middle-earth Lite or as a mere jumble of mythological motifs. It is a more fully and consciously *other* otherworld than Tolkien's Middle-earth, and as such holds up a mirror to Lewis's own broadly erudite mind and catholicity of taste. There was ample room in Lewis's monotheistic world, if not for the old high gods, then for a host of lesser deities to play supporting parts. Bacchus, Silenus, fauns, satyrs, dryads, naiads, and centaurs roam freely in Narnia, detached from their Greek and Roman origins, their wildness (and, in the case of fauns or satyrs, their lechery) subdued. So do dwarfs, giants, and werewolves, of Germanic, Celtic, or uncertain provenance, as well as talking beasts and walking trees, earthmen, sea-people, and mono-pods, river gods and singing stars, and wholly fanciful beings like the Marsh-wiggle. These inconsistencies are not fatal; they remind us that the gradual Christianization of Europe was also a matter of assimilating and reframing local and classical myths. Lewis found a way to gather the "good dreams" (as he put it in *Mere Christianity*), the hints scattered throughout world mythology of divine and preternatural truth, and create for them an imaginal habitat—for what is Narnia if not the imagination made real?—in which they can convincingly coexist.

Jarring notes do intrude. Some of the humor is self-consciously pa-tronizing and whimsical—a literary sin Tolkien would also commit in the first chapter of *The Lord of the Rings*—and would have been worse if Green had not persuaded Lewis to rein in colloquialisms like "Crikey!" The sudden appearance of Father Christmas, as the tide is turning in *The Lion, the Witch, and the Wardrobe*, sends an all-too-obvious signal to seek out the Christian message. Green urged Lewis to drop Father Christ-mas. Tolkien was appalled. But on this matter, Lewis stuck to his guns; no other figure of legend would convey so fully to an English audience all that is truly festal in the celebration of Christ's birth, overcoming the secular commercialization of Christmas on the one hand and the puri-tan prohibition of the holiday on the other, embodying the triumph of warmth and light over the long dark hours of a northern winter and of cheerful abundance amid the deprivation that lingered after the war. *The Lion, the Witch, and the Wardrobe* has as much to say about war and its aftermath—about collaborators, traitors, and heroes of resistance, about ordinary people caught up in a geopolitics they can't fathom, about the harm even a vanquished enemy can cause, and about rationing and the fragile goodness of domestic life—as it does about the Christian myster-ies. The four children who take refuge from the London Blitz in the country home of an eccentric professor are reluctant pilgrims, like Ran-som, lifted out of a world at war into a realm where myths are real.

Just as H. G. Wells, in *First Men on the Moon*, provided a structure for Lewis to adapt to the more profound narrative that is *Out of the Silent Planet*, so did E. Nesbit (a friend of Wells, and like Wells a Fabian social-ist) provide a structure for the first Narnia book. Though consciously modeling *The Lion, the Witch, and the Wardrobe* on the Psammead and other Nesbit tales he had loved since childhood, Lewis had forgotten, until Green brought it to his attention, a minor Nesbit story that must have been an unconscious influence. In "The Aunt and Amabel," a young girl, wrongly punished for some innocent mischief, discovers that the great wardrobe in a spare bedroom is actually a magical railway station called Bigwardrobeinspareroom where all times are Now; she boards a crystalline train bound for Whereyouwantogoto—a land of pure desire (everything is crystal, silver, or white) and instant gratification (with Whatyouwantoeat, Whatyouwantodrink, and Whatyouwantoread always on offer) whose citizens are the People Who Understand.

The parallels do not run deep, however; Nesbit's story is a one-dimensional morality tale, with an ironic twist that could not be more different from the tone and purpose of *The Lion, the Witch, and the Wardrobe*. There is nothing in it like the numinous lion-god of Narnia. This majestic figure, as Lewis recalled, occurred to him long after the image of the faun with the umbrella—he had been dreaming of lions—but once present in the story as "Aslan" (Turkish for lion), quickly acquired a majesty and solar splendor suggestive of Christ, Lion of the tribe of Judah (Revelation 5:5). As Lewis said later, "I don't know where the Lion came from or why He came. But once He was there He pulled the whole story together, and soon He pulled the six other Narnian stories in after Him."

Out of the Silent Planet had been Lewis's apprenticeship in the art of didactic fantasy, but in Narnia, addressing himself to children, he came of age. The new series gave Lewis the freedom to drop the science fiction framework entirely and transfer the great themes of his planetary romance and the central arguments of his Christian apologetics to a more purely fantastic otherworld whose laws could be completely of his own invention, with no worries about scientific plausibility. It would not be a work in code, but an integrated work of mythopoeic imagination, more like Spenser's *Faerie Queene* than Bunyan's *The Pilgrim's Progress*.

Lewis thought that the best way to appreciate Spenser would be to encounter him first "in a very large—and, preferably, illustrated—edition of *The Faerie Queene*, on a wet day, between the ages of twelve and sixteen . . ." Reading *The Faerie Queene* thus, as a "mere wonder-tale," would trigger a sense of having "met all these knights and ladies, all these monsters and enchanters, somewhere before"—and that would be literary magic enough for a child. Only later, as one grows up with *The Faerie*

Queene in possession, would one discern layer upon layer of Spenser's Christian and Platonic symbolism, without obscuring the initial, unanalyzed delight. Such a reading of *The Faerie Queene* is possible because it is allegory at its best, drawn from the reservoir of natural symbols rooted in the psyche and of scriptural symbols equally connatural to the Christian soul.

The same approach recommends itself for Narnia; for *The Lion, the Witch, and the Wardrobe* is an allegory in the Spenserian sense alone, and as such repays both childish and adult investment. Lucy, the youngest of the children, represents the ideal of faithful reason, in just the way that real individuals often do embody a particular virtue and make it real for others. She is innocent and trusting, sensitive and inquisitive, but also essentially levelheaded. Her credentials as a witness, when her siblings doubt the reality of Narnia, pass the trilemma test Lewis had famously applied to Christ himself. Is Lucy a habitual liar? No. A lunatic? No. Then the conclusion is inescapable:

> "Logic!" said the Professor half to himself. "Why don't they teach logic at these schools? There are only three possibilities. Either your sister is telling lies, or she is mad, or she is telling the truth. You know she doesn't tell lies and it is obvious that she is not mad. For the moment then and unless any further evidence turns up, we must assume that she is telling the truth."

To the Professor—named Kirke, a thoroughly converted version of the ultrarational Kirkpatrick and something of a Gandalf figure (odd-looking, slightly alarming, in possession of a secret knowledge)—impeccable logic is the natural companion to Platonic metaphysics and, though this is unstated, to Christian faith. A well-formed mind, the Professor suggests, would find it eminently reasonable that there should be entrances to Faërie in the spare room of a great country house; to paraphrase Dryden, great reason is to great imagination near allied.

And great imagination is to moral vision near allied—this was the lesson of *Out of the Silent Planet.* Lucy, as her name suggests, is lucid; her vision is wide-angle, her dreams rational, her communication with other talking species (beginning with the faun, Tumnus) immediate and unimpeded. Peter is sympathetic to Lucy's lucidity yet burdened by his responsibility for making the wise decisions, while Susan is kindly and affectionate but in too great a hurry to grow up, to talk and eventually to look just like Mother. Edmund is a grouch; when we find him, in the first pages of *The Lion, the Witch, and the Wardrobe*, reacting with exasperation to Susan's affectation, scoffing at Lucy's childish fears, and grumbling that the rain will spoil their fun, we are already witnessing the seeds of his downfall. Unwilling to admit that he is exhausted and scared, Edmund can see only what his own desires and resentments enable him to see; after a seemingly motiveless betrayal of Lucy, he lays himself open to manipulation by the White Witch, fails to see the essential goodness of the Badger family, and recoils in horror at the name of Aslan—all marks of the corruption of his affections and will. He is Mark Studdock with a sweet tooth; and Susan is Jane Studdock in training heels. Both embody faults Lewis detected in himself, confessed in *Surprised by Joy*, and hoped to absolve by the means of grace his Christian faith afforded.

By December 1949, *The Lion, the Witch, and the Wardrobe* was ready to be published. Lewis thought he might like to do the illustrations himself, but made the wiser decision to employ Pauline Baynes, the illustrator for Tolkien's *Farmer Giles of Ham*. Unfortunately, Lewis never quite grasped the nature of her genius; though politely encouraging (for he found her a gentle creature, easily demoralized by criticism), he complained to friends that her human faces were vacant and her animals anatomically incorrect. He had pictured a realistic lion; what Baynes produced instead was a heraldic lion, along with a splendid array of medievalesque miniatures whose delicate drollery invites rather than imposes belief.

Throughout the Narnian books, the Lion is a living portrait of holiness, akin to the theophanies and angelophanies of biblical literature, at once terrifying and desirable beyond all desires; Lewis was indebted to Rudolf Otto's *The Idea of the Holy* for this conception of a *mysterium tremendum et fascinans*. More concretely, Aslan is an icon of Christ, "son of the great Emperor-beyond-the-Sea," who gives his life to pay a sinner's debt, and in so doing confounds the enemy, releases the "deeper magic from before the dawn of time," and breaks the rule of sin and death. When pressed to identify himself directly, the Lion echoes the great "I AM" three times, suggesting the three Persons of the Trinity: "'Myself,' said the voice, very deep and low so that the earth shook: and again 'Myself,' loud and clear and gay: and then the third time 'Myself,' whispered so softly you could hardly hear it, and yet it seemed to come from all round you as if the leaves rustled with it." In a messianic breakfast near the world's end, the Lion becomes the Lamb, echoing the Book of Revelation and the Gospel according to St. John. All this, Lewis said, was not allegory but imaginative "supposal": "Suppose there were a Narnian world and it, like ours, needed redemption. What kind of incarnation and Passion might Christ be supposed to undergo there?"

By March 1951, Lewis had written *Prince Caspian: The Return to Narnia*—the original title was *Drawn into Narnia*—a time-travel adventure in which the Pevensie children are magically summoned to the ruins of their former castle, more than a thousand years after their reign, to aid the young heir against his uncle, an evil usurper, during a dark period when the very existence of Aslan is doubted; *The Voyage of the* Dawn Treader, the most mythically rich of the tales, in which the younger Pevensies, Edmund and Lucy, joined by their priggish cousin Eustace, are drawn into Narnia by way of a ship at sea, and sail with Caspian, now king, on a mission to recover seven lords exiled by Caspian's usurper; *The Horse and His Boy*, originally *To Narnia and the North*, the title echoing the cry of a Narnian prince and his horse fleeing in advance of an invasion by soldiers from the south in whose realm they had been forced to dwell; and *The Silver Chair*, originally *Night Under Narnia*, featuring Eustace and a school chum named Jill Pole, along with a sage and melancholy Marsh-wiggle, Puddleglum. By March 1953, Lewis had finished his Apocalypse, *The Last Battle: A Story for Children*, in which an Antichrist ape persuades a befuddled donkey to dress up as Aslan and deceive the masses, and Eustace and Jill return in time to uncover the fraud and experience the world's end. Last to be finished, and longest in the writing, was Lewis's version of Genesis, *The Magician's Nephew*, in which Aslan sings Narnia into existence, only to be challenged by Eustace's uncle Andrew, a second-rate magician in thrall to the queen who would eventually conquer Narnia as the White Witch.

If, in Narnia, Lewis recast his great themes into a form suited to the nursery, he did little to dilute their potency or to dull the edge of his satire. Uncle Andrew is much like Weston in *Out of the Silent Planet*—a self-important Edwardian man of science thwarted in his attempt to corrupt a new world. Like Weston, he willfully makes himself incapable of understanding divine speech ("If I spoke to him, he would hear only growlings and roarings"). The difference is that conversion remains possible for him; he is cured after a brief humiliation and a long sleep. Other conversion stories are more poignant; in *The Lion, the Witch, and The Wardrobe*, the traitor Edmund is redeemed by the sacrificial death of Aslan, and in *The Voyage of the* Dawn Treader, the prig Eustace submits to a painful undragoning suggestive of purgatory. By the tender and terrible mercy of the Lion, both Edmund and Eustace emerge from their ordeals as saints, forever chastened and grateful; and if Uncle Andrew is not sanctified, he is at least softened by his upending.

In a 1956 essay for the Children's Books section of *The New York Times Book Review*, Lewis explained that his aim in writing the Narnia books had been to recover an instinct for sacred things from the moralistic sentimentality by which it had been deadened:

> I thought I saw how stories of this kind could steal past a certain inhibition which had paralysed much of my own religion in childhood. Why did one find it so hard to feel as one was told one ought to feel about God or about the sufferings of Christ? I thought the chief reason was that one was told one ought to . . . But supposing that by casting all these things into an imaginary world, stripping them of their stained-glass and Sunday school associations, one could make them for the first time appear in their real potency? Could one not thus steal past those watchful dragons? I thought one could.

Stealing past the watchful dragons, Lewis was able to portray a Christian cosmos sung into being ex nihilo, marred in its beginning, redeemed by divine self-sacrifice, and finally dissolved, at the eschaton, into the real Narnia and the real England, into the story "which goes on forever: in which every chapter is better than the one before." He was able to render this didacticism delightful by associating it with talking beasts, magical portals, healing elixirs, and courtly gentilesse. Stealing past the pedestrian Christians, he could satisfy the indelible human desire to speak with beings of a different kind, to know fauns, Arabian princesses, monopods, and a Marsh-wiggle, to discover one's hidden royal identity, to visit the faraway realm seen from the nursery window, across the green

Castlereagh Hills. Reepicheep the chivalrous mouse is no allegorical figure, yet in many ways the spiritual heart of the Narniad is his quest for the world's end, his deepest longing since, as an infant mouse, he had heard the dryad's song: "Where sky and water meet, / Where the waves grow sweet, / Doubt not, Reepicheep, / To find all you seek, / There is the utter East."

Reviews in the popular and Christian press were straightforwardly appreciative. On the assumption that the books were written for boys and girls, criticism of the series was light. Most reviewers read the Christian symbolism accurately, without taking offense, while Christian educators were quick to appreciate the value of the tales for winning young hearts. Charles A. Brady, a professor at Canisius College and author of a historical novel about St. Thomas More, reviewed the series in the Jesuit magazine *America*, calling it the "greatest addition to the imperishable deposit of children's literature since the Jungle Books" and noting the value to Catholic children in particular of an author who "evangelizes through the imagination." Soon letters from adoring young readers began to pour in (to continue, long after Lewis's death and even to the present day). But among the non-Christian literary and academic vanguard, Narnia only intensified resentment against its author; that admirers like Brady characterized Lewis as leader of an "Oxford Circle" of evangelizers scarcely helped the situation.

A Bad Patch

"I don't like to hear of that 'bad patch' at all, at all," wrote Walter de la Mare to Barfield on June 14, 1950, "but if the desire you mention is at all persistent—though it is ten to one that you didn't mean it literally—then I'm sure there is something *physically* wrong." By now the friends had exchanged dozens of letters discussing, with humor and growing intimacy, fellow authors, mutual friends, Anthroposophy, and closely held hopes and dreams (thus de la Mare, on November 16, 1949: "Between you and me I have a particular and forlorn hope—just once before I depart hence—to see a dryad, a naiad, an oread, sylph or a Nereid—in this England of ours"). By 1950, de la Mare would address Barfield as "My dear Obee" and sign his letters "All blessings and my love."

In his June 14 letter, however, warmth and high spirits give way to fear and foreboding. Barfield's "bad patch," his ominous but unspecified "desire," and de la Mare's anxiety about his friend's mental and physical state, indicate that despite the success of *This Ever Diverse Pair*, Barfield remained in serious distress. The failure to find a home for "The Mother of Pegasus" had been just the latest in a series of stinging defeats. His poetry attracted few readers, and his primary literary outlets had dwindled to a few Steinerian house organs. He gave two talks on the BBC Third Programme, "Goethe and Evolution" on December 1, 1949, and "The Influence of Language on Thought: The Poetic Approach" on January 10, 1951, but these opened no new doors. Reconciled to the legal profession, he still despised its daily grind.

His friendships, too, were undergoing more painful changes. Lewis, to his eyes, had half-disappeared behind a mask, although his generosity remained undiminished. Daphne Harwood had fallen terribly ill; on June 5, 1950, a concerned Lewis wrote to Cecil Harwood that "you must be incurring a good many unusual expenses at present: and there may be other—alleviations—wh. you wd. like to incur for Daphne," and invited him to plunge into the Agape Fund, adding in a second letter four days later, "Dip and spare not." Daphne died of cancer on July 14, leaving behind her husband and five children. To cap this calamity afflicting one of his closest friends, Barfield faced an Anthroposophical Society fractured by ideological rifts and packed with members who found it hard to face the modern world with its rampant skepticism and materialism. "It is . . . within my knowledge," he said in a lecture to the society, "that there are people within this Movement who feel that they have just about reached the end of their tether, who really do not know which way to turn; to whom life appears to be one long series of seemingly meaningless frustrations; people for whom . . . life really does, in one way or another, wear the mask of something like a living death." He might have been talking about himself, although he later denied this.

Meanwhile, he was increasingly exposed to the intimate troubles of others. Thanks to his rising prominence in Steinerian circles and his reputation as a kindly man, he received a stream of letters begging advice on matters Anthroposophical and personal. Some of the latter concerned marital difficulties. In 1951 he responded to a letter from a distraught woman regarding a situation in which, as he put it, "an appreciable number of married women, among our members, are finding themselves as they grow older"—that of a straying husband. He advised his correspondent to "get some mutual friend or relative to see him on your behalf and tell him (if that is the fact) that you are still fond of him and wish to . . . re-establish the marriage in the ordinary human sense. I would not recommend your explicitly insisting on absolute fidelity as a condition, but it is obvious that the present liaison would have to cease . . . there would have to be a genuine resolution on his part to make a true household with you . . ." This counsel, seemingly that of a sagacious bystander far beyond the fray, reflects Barfield's own agonies of heart; for his marriage with Maud was in perilous disarray.

By 1951, Barfield was in his early fifties, Maud in her midsixties. Their marriage had lasted thirty years, during which Maud's animosity toward Steiner and his teachings had, if anything, intensified. In 1927, Lewis had recorded in his diary a conversation between Maud and Mrs. Moore: "Mrs. B has apparently been having a heart-to-heart with D. She 'hates, hates, hates' Barfield's Anthroposophy, and says he ought to have told her before they were married: wh. sounds ominous." Twenty-four years later, despite Barfield's conversion to Anglicanism, Maud remained implacably opposed to her husband's esoteric interests. The two maintained a peaceful veneer by avoiding all discussion of religion or metaphysics, and especially of Anthroposophy, but this scarcely constitutes a prescription for marital bliss. Frustrated in his art, unhappy in his career, uninspired in his marriage, Barfield longed desperately for . . . well, he hardly knew what.

Change arrived unexpectedly, as it often does; in this case, according to the Barfield scholar Simon Blaxland–de Lange, through a chance encounter with a young woman. Susan Josephine Grant Watson, known familiarly as Josephine, was twenty-five years old and the daughter of E. L. Grant Watson, a novelist, essayist, and naturalist who admired Jung and Steiner, harbored strong reservations about Darwinian evolution, and had read with pleasure *Romanticism Comes of Age*, an enthusiasm that he had passed on to his daughter. Barfield and Josephine Grant Watson caught each other's eye at an Egyptology lecture in London, discovered their mutual interests, and embarked upon a relationship pursued through meetings and letters and culminating in a sub rosa Spanish holiday. Barfield pondered divorce but was forestalled when the skittish Josephine ended the liaison and soon married another Anthroposophist, the teacher John Dymott Spence.

Maud remained unaware of this brief idyll, according to Blaxland–de Lange. Nor did she know of another relationship that followed upon its heels, as Barfield, rejected by Grant Watson, grew close to the Anthroposophist Marguerite Lundgren, founder of the London School of Eurythmy (an Anthroposophical dance mode). Ten years older than Grant Watson, Lundgren was a committed follower of Steiner; she was also an exceptionally gifted dancer, which may have awoken in Barfield something akin to what Mircea Eliade has termed nostalgia for paradise, a yearning for lost innocence and bliss—in Barfield's case, a rediscovery, on the threshold of old age, of the beauty, energy, and beatific abandon of those long vacations as an Oxford undergraduate dancing with Maud and Cecil Harwood on the Cornwall circuit. One of Lundgren's chief students, Annelies Davidson, has provided a breathless account of her teacher's magnetism that helps to explain Barfield's interest: "Her mobility was exceptional . . . In a piece by Dag Hammarskjöld from his book *Markings* she took space into herself, transforming from a physical to an etheric level to such an extent that one person commented that she "consumed" the space around her . . . the way Marguerite placed herself in space could irradiate it delicately or fill it with a blaze of light." She and Barfield seemed a perfect match. But in the end, his nostalgia for paradise kept him faithful to his union with Maud. He refused to dissolve his marriage, and Lundgren wound up in the arms of the recently widowed Cecil Harwood, whom she married.

Despite this outcome, Barfield's influence upon Lundgren, and upon the curious art of Eurythmy that she helped to pioneer, was substantial. An introductory text on the subject coauthored by Harwood, Lundgren, and Marjorie Raffé describes it as "the apotheosis of the dance" and contends that "whereas the experience of movement in Modern Dance is confined to the earth, Eurythmy balances earthly with spiritual and cosmic experience" as "one of the channels through which the spirit is again revealing itself to human consciousness." High claims, indeed; in more mundane terms, Eurythmy is a performance art in which a dancer's gestures and movements accompany and express the inner meaning of words or music. Eurythmists cloak themselves in loose, flowing robes, often of a single color—orange, yellow, blue, white—and dance with sinuous or rhythmic movements that resemble other spiritualized dances of the twentieth century, such as Dalcroze Eurhythmics and Gurdjieff's Movements. To casual observers, these varied modes may bring to mind ancient temple rituals, Conan Doyle's prancing fairies, or almost anything in between. Lundgren's particular aim—here is where Barfield's influence becomes most apparent—was to reveal, through the Eurythmic expression of passages from Shakespeare, Blake, Coleridge, and others, with particular attention to the kinesthetic manifestation of the inner life of consonants and vowels, the "spiritual soul" or "consciousness soul," as Steiner called it, of the English people. This ambition runs, albeit in a different medium, very close to Barfield's lifelong desire to demonstrate through philology and grammar, with particular attention to English words, the history of consciousness. Dance, for Barfield, was ever a royal road to spiritual truth.

The Dawning of Joy

"Oh the mails," complained Lewis to Dorothy L. Sayers during the last days of 1949. "Every bore in two continents seems to think I *like* getting letters." One new correspondent proved anything but a bore. On January 10, 1950, a letter arrived from a thirty-four-year-old American, a former atheist, now a Christian convert, Mrs. W. L. Gresham, who wrote books under her maiden name of Joy Davidman. A child of secular Jews, Joy had rejected God by the age of eight; by fifteen she had learned that "men . . . are only apes. Virtue is only custom. Life is only an electrochemical reaction. Mind is only a set of conditioned reflexes . . . Love, art, and altruism are only sex." She became a Communist and preached revolution. She might have remained on the radical fringe, but poetry, marriage, and the demands of offspring eventually opened her eyes to another world.

Joy's own poems proved exceptional, winning the Yale Series of Younger Poets award in 1938 and appearing in print as *Letters to a Comrade* the following year. She spent summers at New Hampshire's MacDowell Colony for artists and writers, where she wrote her first novel, *Anya*, set among nineteenth-century Ukrainian village Jews; it debuted in 1940 to considerable applause ("a powerful, well-written novel," ran the generic but, to the author, surely heady review in *The New York Times*, by, as it happened, a former lover of Dorothy L. Sayers). In 1942 she married William Lindsay Gresham, a writer, womanizer, and alcoholic. Gresham, himself a former Communist, helped Davidman clarify her doubts about the Party. They had two boys, David and Douglas; the children grounded her, and she realized "what neglected, neurotic waifs the children of so many Communists were." In 1946, Gresham suffered an alcoholic nervous breakdown; the episode drove Davidman to despair and thence to a spiritual awakening: "All my defenses—the walls of arrogance and cocksureness and self-love behind which I had hid from God—went down momentarily. And God came in . . . There was a Person with me in the room, directly present to my consciousness—a Person so real that all my previous life was by comparison mere shadow play. And I myself was more alive that I had ever been; it was like waking from sleep."

All at once Davidman saw that "God had always been there, and that, since childhood, I had been pouring half my energy into the task of keeping him out." She learned to pray; she forgave her enemies, or at least "some" of them—she, like Lewis, enjoyed a good battle—and, oddly, she returned to the Communist Party out of her newborn sense of "moral responsibility." It didn't last. She perceived the fallacies in dialectical materialism, in socialist realism, in the Soviet Union's claim to be a worker's paradise, until finally communism "blew away like a withered tumbleweed." She and her husband turned religious—their new path bolstered by reading C. S. Lewis—and in time, partially through her authorial instincts ("Not Shakespeare himself could have invented the Synoptic Gospels"), she became a Christian. Her writing career continued; in 1949, the *New York Post* ran, over several days, her long account of her conversion from hammer and sickle to cross, under the lurid title of "Girl Communist." In 1950, Macmillan published her second novel, *Weeping Bay*, a somewhat cynical, somewhat anti-Catholic portrayal of religious life on the Gaspé Peninsula; the *New York Times* reviewer faulted the story's characterization but found it made "an enduring impression," while *Catholic World* accused it of "pamphleteering" and *Library Journal* of "bursts of blasphemy." She was becoming a figure on the American literary scene. Nonetheless, Warnie later remembered in his diary that "neither of us had ever heard of her . . . she appeared in the mail as just another American fan," who "stood out from the ruck by her amusing and well-written letters." Soon this bright, tart-tongued fan would shake Lewis's life to its roots.

"I Am, I Fear, a Most Unsatisfactory Person"

On March 9, 1950, after a year's delay, Tolkien underwent the dentist's knife to have his perilously decayed teeth removed. Four weeks later he was fitted with a full set of dentures, which would cause problems of its own; rumor has it that once, as Tolkien opened his celebrated *Beowulf* lecture with his customary *"Hwaet!,"* the dentures flew from his mouth and clattered to the floor. In any case, another extraction proved far more vexing. By late 1949, Fr. Gervase Mathew had introduced Tolkien to Milton Waldman, a senior editor at the publishing house of William Collins, Sons, who expressed great admiration for Tolkien and his work, leading him to consider withdrawing from his long relationship with Allen & Unwin. He still resented Unwin's refusal, in the prewar years, to publish *The Silmarillion*, which he considered irrevocably linked to the still-unpublished *The Lord of the Rings*. The two works, he felt, must see print in tandem. He sent portions of *The Silmarillion* to Waldman, who offered to publish it once the manuscript was complete, a pledge that inspired Tolkien to begin enlarging and refining many of its pivotal tales, including those of Túrin Turambar, and Beren and Lúthien, along with key sections on Elves, Dwarves, and Valinor. When Waldman subsequently read *The Lord of the Rings*, praised it, and promised to take it on as long as there was "no commitment either moral or legal to Allen & Unwin," the die was cast. "I certainly shall try to extricate myself, or at least the *Silmarillion* and all its kin, from the dilatory coils of A. and U.," Tolkien promised Waldman on February 5, 1950, in a draft for a now-lost letter that indicates his confused feelings about the affair. "I should . . . be glad to leave them, as I have found them in various ways unsatisfactory. But I have friendly personal relations with Stanley (whom all the same I do not much like) and with his second son Rayner (whom I do like very much) . . ."

This letter marked the opening salvo in Tolkien's campaign to repel the Unwins and shift his literary future to Waldman, a sly endeavor that shows him in a not entirely favorable light. He avoided a point-blank declaration of intentions, instead sending a string of messages to Stanley

Unwin denigrating himself and his work. On February 24, he told Unwin that "I am, I fear, a most unsatisfactory person." He derided *The Lord of the Rings*, declaring that "my work has escaped from my control, and I have produced a monster: an immensely long, complex, rather bitter, and very terrifying romance, quite unfit for children (if fit for anybody) . . ." This ungainly work, he insisted, was "tied to the Silmarillion," and "ridiculous and tiresome as you may think me, I want to publish them both . . . in conjunction or in connexion"; he therefore refused to undertake major rewriting or restructuring and assured Unwin that no offense would be taken "if you decline so obviously unprofitable a proposition." Never did Casanova so artfully separate himself from an unwanted lover.

Unwin was not easily dissuaded. He advanced the possibility of publishing *The Lord of the Rings* and *The Silmarillion* together, but only if divided into three or four volumes, and he added the discouraging news that *Farmer Giles of Ham* had sold less than half of its first printing, a poor showing. Unwittingly, his reply played right into Tolkien's hands. Instantly rejecting Unwin's proposal, Tolkien agreed sarcastically that a large work could be chopped into parts—giving as an example *OED* divisions like "'ONOMASTICAL-OUTING' and 'SIMPLE to SLEEP,'" before declaring that "the whole Saga of the Three Jewels and the Rings of Power has only one natural division into two parts (each of about 600,000 words)." Following this broadside, he again disparaged his project, speculating that few beyond his friends would tolerate so long a book, and that Unwin would likely fail to recoup the cost of publication. As compensation he offered, should Unwin decide against handling the vast opus, to produce something briefer when time allowed. Later the same day, he wrote to Waldman, detailing his letter to Unwin and declaring, "I profoundly hope that he will let go without demanding the MS. and two months for 'reading.'"

Unwin continued the chess match on April 3, informing Tolkien that he had discussed the matter with his son Rayner, now a student at Harvard University. Rayner wrote to his father, suggesting that an editor might incorporate the more pertinent material from the vast legendarium into *The Lord of the Rings*, but "if this is not workable, I would say publish *The Lord of the Rings* as a prestige book, and after having a second look at it, drop *The Silmarillion*." Tolkien, incensed by this, countered with an ultimatum demanding an immediate yes or no to his requirement that the two works be published together. Boxed in and sensing Tolkien's unwillingness to compromise, Unwin conceded defeat on April 17, declaring himself "bitterly disappointed" and saying "the answer is 'no'; but it might well have been yes given adequate time and the sight of the complete typescript."

Tolkien's triumph was total—but terribly short-lived. A month or two later, Milton Waldman traveled to Oxford, bearing the devastating news that the Collins editors had decided that *The Lord of the Rings* needed severe pruning. A period of delays ensued, occasioned in part by illness and Italian sojourns on Waldman's part, and by late 1951 the project remained in limbo. Finally Tolkien sent to Waldman, at the latter's request, a ten-thousand-word document explaining the genesis, development, and meaning of his entire fictional oeuvre—*The Silmarillion, The Hobbit,* and *The Lord of the Rings*—a magnificent summa commencing with the poignant observation that "it is difficult to say anything without saying too much: the attempt to say a few words opens a floodgate of excitement." Revealingly, he utilizes near the end of this letter the same arguments he had deployed to rid himself of Unwin: "It is . . . only too likely that I am deluded, lost in a web of vain imaginings of not much value to others— in spite of the fact that a few readers have found it good, on the whole. What I intend to say is this: I cannot substantially alter the thing. I have finished it, it is off my mind; the labour has been colossal; and it must stand or fall, practically as it is." On some level he may already have realized that Waldman would not publish the book. In the event, his letter failed to rescue the project. In the spring of 1952, exasperated and discouraged, Tolkien insisted that Collins publish *The Lord of the Rings* at once or lose the right to do so. The firm responded by rejecting both it and *The Silmarillion.*

Tolkien was stranded now, without publisher or agent, his two books— representing more than thirty years of work—moldering on the shelf. One hope remained. In late November, Rayner Unwin had sent him a letter, stating that he still believed in the value of Tolkien's vast creation and asking to see *The Silmarillion.* Tolkien responded the following June, in a message rife with kindness (he had always liked Rayner), lament, and remorse. He had "behaved badly" by not writing earlier; "disaster" had struck, in the form of summer examinations; he had suffered a "terrible bout of fibrositis and neuritis," he had been "too downhearted" to take further steps toward publishing. But now he had "modified" his views. The unspoken truth, of course, was that time was fleeting and he feared his work would come to naught. "Better something than nothing!" he exclaimed. Yes, *The Lord of the Rings* and *The Silmarillion* belonged together, but he would rejoice to see any portion of the work in print: "Can anything be done . . . to unlock gates I slammed myself?"

Rayner threw open the gates eight days later, replying that his firm remained eager to publish *The Lord of the Rings*. Tolkien's very own eucatastrophe had arrived. Letters and meetings ensued, notable for the marked change in his account of his writings: now he found *The Lord of the Rings* "a great (though not flawless) work" and, contradicting his earlier dire predictions to Milton Waldman and Stanley Unwin, assured Rayner that a "larger number of people than might be supposed" loved books of this type and length and might be expected to buy it. Newly confident, he busied himself by fixing chronological and narrative inconsistencies in the text. During this time, he also visited his friends George and Moira Sayer in Malvern. There he recorded, after exorcising the tape recorder (the first he had seen) by reciting the Lord's Prayer in Gothic, portions of *The Hobbit* and *The Lord of the Rings*. He volunteered to help Sayer in his garden, which led to this telling reminiscence from his host: Tolkien "chose an area of about two square yards, part flower border and part lawn and cultivated it perfectly: the border meticulously weeded and the soil made level and exceedingly fine; the grass cut with scissors closely and evenly. It took him quite a long time to do the job, but it was beautifully done. He was in all things a perfectionist."

More good news followed. On September 19, 1953, Rayner and his wife traveled to Oxford to collect the revised typescript; in early November, Rayner telegrammed his father, now in Asia, to say that the book might lose the firm a thousand pounds but that it was a work of genius; Stanley replied, "*If* you believe it is a work of genius, *then* you may lose a thousand pounds." On November 10, Allen & Unwin officially tendered an offer to publish. Tolkien immediately passed the great tidings on to Lewis, who replied by describing an "inward chuckle of deep content." The news meant the prospect of "having the book to read and re-read"; it also meant that "so much of your whole life, so much of our joint life, so much of the war, so much that seemed to be slipping away quite *spurlos* into the past, is now, in a sort made permanent." The eucatastrophe embraced not only Tolkien but his friends, his generation, and the world. Oblivion had been averted; is it surprising that Lewis closed the letter "God bless you"?

Changes at the Kilns

At the same time, Lewis was watching his own world slip away. Mrs. Moore, now seventy-eight and spending her days in an immobilized fury, confined to bed by arthritis and senility, was removed on April 29, 1950, to the aptly named Restholme, a private nursing home on the Woodstock Road where Warnie had lodged recently while recovering from his increasingly frequent binges. She reacted to her new environs with expected fury, lambasting the nurses and demanding, as Warnie reports in his diary, "to know how soon she will be able to escape from this hell on earth in which she is imprisoned." She would never escape; Restholme would remain her home until death. Lewis rejoiced and despaired over the change, telling Arthur that "it will be an enormous liberation for me" yet fretting over the cost, five hundred pounds a year, so that "I hardly know how I feel—relief, pity, hope, terror, & bewilderment have me in a whirl. I have the jitters!"

The jitters soon fled. He visited Mrs. Moore every day, a "grievous" burden, but otherwise he reveled in his new freedom, as if released from a binding spell. How could he not? The Kilns, formerly his prison, had become his manor, free of a scolding woman and yelping dogs. He urged Arthur to come to Oxford, chirped about his own improved health now that he was at liberty to swim regularly in the local river, and assured his friend that his home was "*now* a house less horrible to stay in than I know it was before." During the summer, he also invited George Sayer ("We cd. read the whole *Aeneid* together") and Cecil Harwood to visit. His letters lost the plaintive note that had crept in as his home life had collapsed around him. When Mrs. Moore died on January 12, 1951, nearly nine months had passed since she had entered Restholme, and Lewis's freedom had come to term. He barely recorded her death in his voluminous correspondence, apart from a terse remark to Arthur ("Minto died a fortnight ago. Please pray for her soul") followed immediately by details of his long-delayed, now-impending sojourn in Ireland. He would breathe again the air of his childhood. He would, in a sense, begin his life again. Warnie was far more outspoken in his own diary, seething over Mrs. Moore's role in "the rape of J's life" and of Lewis's "crushing misfortune" in meeting her.

Even Lewis's failure to win an Oxford professorship did not dampen his spirits. On February 8, less than a month after Mrs. Moore's death, the university elected, as it did every five years, a chair of poetry. The two leading candidates were Lewis and another Irish-born poet-novelist, C. Day-Lewis. The latter, a former Communist and future poet laureate (as well as future father of actor Daniel Day-Lewis), was a lyrical nature poet as well as the author, under the pseudonym of Nicholas Blake, of a series of popular mystery novels. Many of C. S. Lewis's closest friends, including Warnie, Barfield, Havard, Bennett, and David Cecil, gathered at the Royal Oxford hotel to await returns, which proved as close as the two candidate's names, C. Day defeating C.S. by 21 votes out of 367. Warnie blamed the loss on atheists, Communists, and voters with "Slav and Balkan names," and it is probably true that Lewis's Christian bully-pulpit image did him in; one elector told Dyson he planned to vote against Lewis because of *Screwtape*.

The loser, however, seemed indifferent to the outcome: life without Mrs. Moore shone too brightly for a momentary eclipse to matter. Nor did it upset him when, later that year, he felt obliged to turn down a CBE from Churchill's Conservative government, fearing that it would encourage "knaves" and "fools" to read his Christian writings as right-wing screeds. The proposed honor gratified, but a Christian must recognize the ephemerality of earthly fame, and, anyway, more acute pleasures—especially that of wielding the pen—beckoned. The Narnia series flowed on, book after book, with scarcely a hitch; Magdalen had granted him a year's sabbatical to work on *OHEL*; and to cap this litany of joys, Joy Davidman had reentered his life.

Lewis had responded with gusto to Joy's first letter. He always welcomed aggressive intellectuals, especially those who showed wit and bite—Barfield had been the greatest example—and Joy, although female, looked as if she might qualify. She, for her part, treasured his ripostes.

"Just got a letter from Lewis in the mail," she told Chad Walsh. "Lord, he knocked my props out from under me unerringly; one shot to a pigeon. I haven't a scrap of my case left. And, what's more, I've seldom enjoyed anything more . . . what I feel is a craftsman's joy at the sight of a superior performance." The correspondence flourished. For Joy, it offered not only friendly exchange with a famous Christian writer but escape from her collapsing marriage to Bill Gresham, who continued to drink and womanize as his career advanced (his 1946 novel of carnival hucksterism and psychic scams, *Nightmare Alley*, had become a 1947 Hollywood film with Tyrone Power in the lead). Joy no longer loved her husband; the romance evaporated, she told a friend, "as a result of something [Bill] did"—the unnamed transgression was an affair—"when I was seriously ill." This behavior was characteristic of Gresham, whose rakish charm was small compensation for a roving eye and a quick fist that threatened both wife and offspring.

In August 1952, Joy sailed alone for England, leaving her family in New York, harboring plans to meet Lewis. Did she, even then, have designs on him as a mate? Years later, Gresham told Lewis that this had been the case, that Joy had confessed to him, "she was in love with you and had to get to know you," and that this long-distance infatuation—with a man she had never met—had triggered her flight to England. Gresham's account cannot be taken on face value; he was not always truthful and, when making this disclosure, had reason to paint his wife in the worst possible light. But it is not implausible. Joy admired Lewis greatly, prized her correspondence with him, and was miserable in her current state. Her husband was, in many ways, her Mrs. Moore; Lewis, a bachelor, a scholar with an enchanting mind, three thousand miles from the wreckage of her marriage, may well have been the symbol, if not yet the realized means, of her release.

Soon after arriving in England, Joy invited Lewis to join her and a London friend, Phyllis Williams, for lunch on September 24 at Oxford's Eastgate Hotel. No record remains of this first encounter. It must have been successful, however, for Lewis returned the invitation by asking the pair to lunch with him at Magdalen College. George Sayer, present at the second meeting, remembers Joy as "of medium height, with a good figure, dark hair, and rather sharp features. She was an amusingly abrasive

New Yorker, and Jack was delighted by her bluntness and her anti-American views" as well as her curt dismissal of modern literature: "Mind you, I wrote that sort of bunk myself when I was young."

The friendship fast intensified, but not without mishap. In December, Joy arrived at the Kilns. To Lewis's surprise, she encamped for three weeks, thrice longer than he had anticipated. Again he took pleasure in her quick mind and quirky ways, but complained to Laurence Harwood, Cecil's son, that he felt "completely 'circumvented'" by a guest who "asked for one week but [is] staying for three, who talks from morning to night . . . I can't write (write? I can hardly think or breathe. I can't believe it's all real)." But Warnie, who warmed to anyone who warmed to him, seemed to have no regrets, recalling later the "many merry days" of her visit. He liked her spunk, her smarts, and her uninhibited humor, and he nonetheless found her "intensely feminine." To others, like Chad Walsh, "there was nothing feminine about her." In addition to her sharp tongue, she looked vaguely froglike with her curved spine and bulging eyes, the result of childhood hyperthyroidism. Warnie told George Sayer that the visit had been a success because "we treated her just as if she were a man."

Joy quit the Kilns after Christmas and sailed for America in early January. She had been away for five months. Before boarding ship, she was shocked to receive a long letter from her husband declaring the marriage over, for he had fallen in love and begun an affair with Joy's cousin, Renée. He worried about Joy's reaction, unnecessarily as it proved; by the end of January, she was gaily describing to Chad Walsh her Lewisian adventures, her Anglophilia, and her eagerness to begin writing again; by the end of February, she was calling the imminent divorce "a blessed release," telling Walsh that "Lewis strongly advised me to divorce Bill; and has repeated it even more strongly since I've been home." Lewis was appalled by Joy's account of her husband's philandering and violence; he inclined toward a lenient view on divorce, although he accepted the Anglican Church's ban against divorced persons remarrying. Joy's letters to friends rang with criticism of her wayward husband and with revelations, sometimes unwitting, of the desperate disorder that gripped her family ("Davy's quite eager for me to divorce his father—talked to me like a Dutch uncle: 'There is a point at which patience stops being a virtue!' says he. And lots more, all very adult and shrewd—uncanny in a child not yet nine."). One wonders if David had witnessed one of his father's outbursts, which recommenced as soon as Joy returned home: "Bill greeted me by knocking me about a bit . . . Two days after he'd half choked me, he asked in all seriousness, 'Have you ever known me to do a brutal or unkind thing?'" Divorce loomed, the sooner the better.

17

THE LONG-EXPECTED SEQUEL

T his charming house has become uninhabitable—unsleepable-in, unworkable-in, rocked, racked with noise, and drenched with fumes. Such is modern life. Mordor in our midst." The immediate cause of Tolkien's wretchedness, retailed to Rayner Unwin a few weeks before hearing the rapturous news that Allen & Unwin would publish *The Lord of the Rings,* was the unbearable traffic outside 99 Holywell Street. The racket and stink angered him and sickened Edith, who was already in precarious health. On doctor's orders, the couple began to search for a more peaceful, less polluted locale; on March 30, 1953, they moved to 76 Sandfield Road in Headington, a mile and a half from the Kilns, an upheaval that entailed ten days of "endless labour."

The deeper source of Tolkien's complaint, however, was his growing hatred of machines, especially what he liked to call "the 'infernal combustion' engine." His antipathy had been aroused by firsthand experience of mechanized warfare during World War I, accelerated by the terrible devastation of World War II, confirmed by the atomic bomb, which he described to Rayner as a "billowing cloud" unleashed "by persons who have decided to use the Ring for their own (of course most excellent) purposes," and underscored by the industrialization of Oxford, where cars now circled the dreaming spires while trees fell and factories rose in the once-bucolic outskirts. Failure to perceive the false allure of industrial progress, he had written Christopher in 1944, was "almost a world wide mental disease." In this same letter, he drew a stark opposition between machines and art, the first an attempt to seize power in the primary world, the second an attempt to create beauty in the secondary world of subcreation. Lewis had addressed the first half of this equation in *The Abolition of Man*, pointing out that conquest of nature, which he exemplified by the airplane, the radio, and contraceptives, are expressions of power that result in one group of human beings controlling another (by bombs, by propaganda, by manipulating the future). Tolkien upped the ante, giving distrust of machinery a theological foundation. Just as art points to God, machines point to Satan—or, in Tolkien's legendarium, to the cosmic tyrant Morgoth and his followers. The monstrosity of machines lies in the hubris and pride of their inventors, who savage God's truth, beauty, and goodness with tools that bring ugliness, pain, and lies (witness the small lie that automation improves upon handcrafted work and the great lie that power offers more than love).

Mechanophobia aside, however, Tolkien had reason to rejoice. True, he was exhausted from moving house, overwhelmed by college chores, and afflicted by various ailments—including bouts of flu, neuritis, fibrositis, lumbago, laryngitis, and sciatica—and *The Silmarillion* remained in limbo. But nothing could suppress the exaltation of knowing that *The Lord of the Rings* would soon see print. And he was traveling more, enjoying different landscapes and cultures. He returned to Ireland in 1950 and 1951 (and would go again in 1958), serving again as an external examiner for the National University, which would grant him an Honorary D. Litt. in July 1954. In 1951 he summered with Edith and Priscilla in County Kerry, where he sketched nine landscapes. *Summer in Kerry*, in colored pencil, eschews the sharp contours and geometric patterns of his legendarium-based illustrations for soft, melting masses of olive-green cloud, daubed with white, lowering over a range of gray-green-yellow mountains. Unfortunately, this promising new direction was not followed up, and these Irish landscapes seem to have been his last. He also traveled to the Continent, visiting the University of Liège several times to attend academic festivities, delivering a paper on the Middle English word *losenger* ("deceiver," "flatterer," "liar"—i.e., the type of scoundrel that figures in many of his tales), and receiving another honorary doctorate.

Tolkien's reputation as a Middle English scholar advanced yet more when he delivered the 1952–53 W. P. Ker Lecture at the University of Glasgow on *Sir Gawain and the Green Knight*. The lecture was scheduled for April 15, just two weeks after the disruptive move to Sandfield Road, and Tolkien rushed to complete the text as the train steamed toward Glasgow. He grumbled about the result, but the published version, which appeared posthumously, holds considerable interest for its stalwart defense of fairy story as the supreme vehicle for moral instruction. *Sir Gawain*, Tolkien argues, is at heart a moral study, in which Gawain's temptation to adultery, his hesitation between courtly politesse and Christian virtue, and his final triumph over sin play out against a background of Faërie that serves to "enlarge the scene and the actors," transforming a bedroom tug-of-war between a befuddled knight and a lascivious lady into a battle for personal salvation.

Throughout his lecture, Tolkien quotes from his translation of *Gawain*, begun when he was a fledgling instructor at Leeds but only recently completed. In 1953 the novelist P. H. Newby, at this time a producer at the BBC, proposed that the translation might make a fine Christmas broadcast, especially if someone like Dylan Thomas read the text. Tolkien, perhaps still dazzled by his own performance while recording portions of *The Hobbit* and *The Lord of the Rings* on George Sayer's tape recorder, suggested that he himself might be the right man for the job. He auditioned on September 1 and, with a glint of the vanity that sometimes peeped forth—as in his fondness for ornamental waistcoats—declared that "it sounded to me better than most things I have listened to of the sort— more *interesting* (more variable and unexpectable)." Tolkien's delivery held little charm for others, however, and the BBC settled for a professional, multivoice presentation, to be broadcast in four segments over the course of December. The author was invited to introduce the first broadcast and discuss the poem at length in a special January program.

His translation of *Gawain* was published posthumously in 1975. It was not well received. Tolkien had argued in the W. P. Ker Lecture that a translation should retain "the original metre and alliteration, without which translation is of little value except as a crib" (a view also upheld by T. S. Eliot, who argued that Dante, for one, could only be properly translated in terza rima, for "a different metre is a different mode of thought . . . and a poem should be translated as nearly as possible in the same thought-form as the original"). But transforming into modern verse the long-abandoned thought-forms of the *Gawain* poet proved beyond Tolkien's ability. To the American critic Roger Sale, writing in *The Times*

Literary Supplement, the work suffered from "constructions that are straightforward in Middle English but awkward now," forcing Tolkien to employ "an idiom that is neither medieval nor twentieth-century—just as he does in *The Lord of the Rings*." In *The Times Higher Education Supplement*, the medievalist A. C. Spearing agreed, remarking that the "style and diction have an archaic quality that produces a quite different effect from that of the originals—not of ancient grandeur, but of faded romanticism laced with awkwardness."

More successful was *The Homecoming of Beorhtnoth Beorhthelm's Son*, a dramatic dialogue that Tolkien had worked on intermittently throughout the 1930s and '40s and eventually published in the English Association's *Essays and Studies 1953*. He based this short, dark work on the Old English poem "The Battle of Maldon," which celebrates the heroic ethos while telling of a crushing Anglo-Saxon defeat at the hands of Viking invaders in A.D. 991 (in Lewis's *Perelandra*, Ransom shouts out a line from the poem while throttling the demonic Unman). Tolkien, however, focuses on the battle's aftermath, as two servants search the carnage for the body of the fallen hero Beorhtnoth (or Byrhtnoth: the name in Old English means "bright courage"). While the Old English poem lauds Beorhtnoth for his nobility in allowing the Vikings to move to a more advantageous location, Tolkien interprets this move as a disastrously foolhardy act prompted by *ofermod*, over-spirit, or "overmastering pride" (as Tolkien translates it). As in his *Gawain* translation, Tolkien retains the dense alliteration of the original, but here, unhampered by the strict requirements of translation, his method works, and the servants' terse, gritty conversation offers a modern gloss upon the values of the original poem by emphasizing the violence, ugliness, confusion, and horror of war. Since its publication, the drama has received mixed notices from medievalists, some of whom challenge Tolkien's interpretation of historical events. Nonetheless, the work enhanced his literary reputation. In early 1954, still enamored of his own thespian skills, he tape-recorded it in his study, assaying all the parts himself and adding home-brewed sound effects, and then proposed to P. H. Newby that the BBC mount a professional production. When the Third Programme broadcast the play some months later, Tolkien, always seeking perfection, criticized it harshly, but with the twin productions of *Gawain* and *Homecoming*, his Old English and Middle English labors had, against all expectations, reached a wide audience.

By then it scarcely mattered. A far more important event was unfolding: the great epic of Middle-earth was about to see the light of day. The production process had been long and arduous. Tolkien had promised Rayner Unwin that the book would be delivered in final form by March 25, 1953. This deadline he had failed to meet. He submitted the text as quickly as he could, adding maps and appendices, improving spelling, grammar, and chronological consistency. Various titles came and went, some of them smacking of old radio serials: *The Return of the Shadow* for what would become *The Fellowship of the Ring*; *The Shadow Lengthens* for *The Two Towers*. Finally the great labor came to a close, and on July 29, 1954, Unwin published *The Fellowship of the Ring*, followed on November 11, 1954, by *The Two Towers*, and on October 20, 1955, by *The Return of the King*: approximately 475,000 words in total, one of the longest novels in modern English literature.

On July 30, 1955, Tolkien and his daughter, Priscilla, set out by train and boat for Italy, while Edith departed for a Mediterranean cruise with friends. Husband and wife had long accepted their differing tastes and temperaments in the matter of friends and pastimes, and separate vacations of this sort seemed in order. For Tolkien, the voyage afforded an opportunity to step back for two weeks from the tensions and trials of guiding his masterwork into print, while also allowing him to set foot in a land he had admired from afar and to revel in a language that he found lovely but spoke haltingly, although he had studied it while recovering from gastritis during World War I. It came as a "linguistic shock," when he arrived on Italian soil, to learn that Italians, contrary to reputation, "dislike exaggeration, superlatives, and adjectives of excessive praise. But they seem to answer to colour and poetic expression, if justified." This opalescent language worked its magic: after his return, he wrote Christopher that "I remain in love with Italian, and feel quite lorn without a chance of trying to speak it! We must keep it up . . ."

Italy and magic seemed synonymous. Venice, the first significant stop, where the travelers were met by Christopher and his wife, Faith, proved bewitching, otherworldly, with its intersecting canals, crumbling palaces, and mysterious plazas, "elvishly lovely—to me like a dream of Old Gondor, or Pelargir of the Númenorean ships, before the return of the Shadow." The enchantment arose from more than the cityscape: Italy was saturated with Catholicism—a far cry from England, with its history of anti-Catholic murder and riot—and Tolkien felt like "an exile from the borders and far provinces returning home, or at least to the home of his fathers." Especially welcoming were the many chapels that housed the Blessed Sacrament, buildings that emanated "a curious glow of dormant life and Charity." Tolkien rejoiced also in Venice's lack of cars, a brief respite from "the cursed disease of the internal combustion engine of which all the world is dying." Assisi, too, was a revelation. He and Priscilla stayed in a convent, awoke to the "tremendous babel of bells" at 5:30 a.m., strolled around the church of San Damiano, "soaked with a sense of the personality of St Clare, and of St Francis," and attended a Mass at the Basilica of San Francesco and a High Mass at the church of Santa Chiara, where, Tolkien thought, "the great choir of friars sang magnificently, to my thinking, with enormous controlled power—capable of lifting the roof even of Santa Chiara instantaneously and without effort." Like all trips, this one also offered irritations and disappointments: too much rain, some architectural monstrosities, a friar who preached an interminable sermon, and clouds of mosquitoes, who savagely bit Tolkien's face, hands, and legs, resulting in swellings and blisters.

Overall, however, the voyage proved an extraordinary success. Those lucky enough to read the *Giornale d'Italia*—which remains lamentably unpublished, languishing in a bin at the Bodleian—cannot help but be impressed by the extent to which Tolkien, on vacation, far away from the university, his great literary labor in its final stages, bursts loose in glorious descriptive passages, using words as splashes of paint to capture, impressionistically, the moods of this bewitching land. Tolkien was always more immersed in the visual arts than most of his readers realize. Here is Tolkien the watercolorist, registering the tones of Venice; Tolkien the art critic, passing judgment on medieval and Renaissance paintings. Of Venice: "it is much paler and less hard and clear in colour than I expected: black, white, pale pink, grey," and "heartrendingly lovely after so short a stay, so soon to end. Still no hard or deep colours. Clear but pale sky, glass-grey glinting water, light olive-greenness." As for Italian art, the famous frescoes ascribed, perhaps erroneously, to Giotto in the Basilica of San Francesco in Assisi struck him as too dependent upon shades of red ("ochre, brick-red, scarlet, crimson"), while in Venice's Gallerie dell'Accademia he admired the Tintorettos and was "much moved" by Bassano's *St. Jerome* (1556), which depicts the elderly saint in a cave, wearing a loincloth, surrounded by books. Perhaps he read in Jerome's suffering and scholarship something of his own life. To Titian's *Assumption of the Virgin* (1516–18) in the Franciscan Church of Santa Maria Gloriosa dei Frari, also in Venice, he had a complicated response, approving its bright colors but put off by its histrionics, its startled Virgin and wildly gesticulating apostles, commenting that "it has nothing whatever to say to me about the Assumption: which means that with that in mind it is offensive (to me)."

This raised questions about the relation of religion to art: "Can a picture concerned with religion be satisfactory on one side only? Spiritual but bad art; great art but irreligious?" Many would answer positively, at least to the second clause—after all, Picasso, the most important artist of the twentieth century, was relentlessly irreligious, even in his *Crucifixion* (1930)—but to Tolkien, it was "impossible to disentangle the two. Easier perhaps for the irreligious." For him religiosity in art was a subtle business, best handled indirectly; in 1953 he had written to Fr. Robert Murray that "*The Lord of the Rings* is of course a fundamentally religious and Catholic work; unconsciously so at first, but consciously in the revision. That is why I have not put in, or have cut out, practically all references to anything like 'religion,' to cults or practices, in the imaginary world. For the religious element is absorbed into the story and the symbolism."

Lightning from a Clear Sky

Tolkien's best argument that it is impossible to disentangle great art from religion is *The Lord of the Rings* itself; no other twentieth-century fiction comes close to Tolkien's fusion of invented mythology, imagined history, high fantasy, and deep piety. His admirers cannot resist comparing him to Dante, Malory, or Blake, with the necessary proviso that Tolkien is incomparable. Thus Lewis in "The Gods Return to Earth," a review of *The Lord of the Rings* for *Time and Tide*: "This book is like lightning from a clear sky; as sharply different, as unpredictable in our age as *Songs of Innocence* were in theirs . . . Nothing quite like it was ever done before . . ." To the "predestined readers" of Tolkien's heroic romance—the only readers who would be prepared to understand—Lewis prophesied, "here are beauties which pierce like swords or burn like cold iron;

here is a book that will break your heart. They will know that this is good news, news beyond hope."

Years earlier, commenting on the slow progress of his friend's *Hobbit* sequel, Lewis had observed that Tolkien "works like a coral insect." It was a stock image: the Victorians likened missionaries to coral insects building up the majestic reefs by their ceaseless, unseen, and unrewarded labor, *soli Deo gloria*. The divine drudgery of this coral-insect labor was rewarded by moments of serendipitous discovery: "I met a lot of things on the way that astonished me," Tolkien told Auden. "Tom Bombadil I knew already; but I had never been to Bree. Strider sitting in the corner at the inn was a shock, and I had no more idea who he was than had Frodo. The Mines of Moria had been a mere name; and of Lothlórien no word had reached my mortal ears till I came there. Far away I knew there were the Horse-lords on the confines of an ancient Kingdom of Men, but Fangorn Forest was an unforeseen adventure. I had never heard of the House of Eorl nor of the Stewards of Gondor. Most disquieting of all, Saruman had never been revealed to me, and I was as mystified as Frodo at Gandalf's failure to appear on September 22."

It had been clear from the outset that the settled happiness of *The Hobbit*'s conclusion would have to be overturned and Bilbo would have to step aside—the sequel demanded an heir, and the heir would need a new rationale for venturing beyond the secure confines of the Shire. "Make return of ring a motive" occurred early on to Tolkien, as we have seen, but the nature of this ring was still unclear to him; in the original version of *The Hobbit*, Bilbo had stumbled upon a magic ring that conferred invisibility and helped him through various scrapes, but initially Tolkien thought of this ring as "not very dangerous, when used for good purpose."

As Tolkien labored on, however, the story turned more ominous as well as more profound. Figures familiar from *The Hobbit* become much stranger in the sequel. The Dwarves disclose their character as a people apart—like the Jews, Tolkien thought, "at once native and alien in their habitations, speaking the languages of the country, but with an accent due to their own private tongue . . ." The Necromancer from *The Hobbit* becomes the Dark Lord Sauron (so named, Tolkien told a correspondent, from an Elvish word for "detestable"), Morgoth's lieutenant, maker of the Rings of Power, and intent upon conquering Middle-earth by means of the master Ring into which he poured his *libido dominandi*. And with Morgoth and Sauron come a vast procession of beings from Tolkien's master myth: the longeval High Elves, survivors of the epic wars of the past, who linger in Middle-earth, conscious that their glory is fading; the dreadful Orcs (tortured and corrupted beings, akin to goblins) and Uruk-hai (warrior Orcs crossbred with Men); the langorous Ents ("giants" in Old English), tree-shepherds assigned by the godlike Valar to protect the primeval forests; and the Istari ("wise ones") clad in the bodies of aged Men, among them Saruman (his name means "Craft-Man"), chief of the Order and bent on domination, and Gandalf ("Staff-Elf") the Grey Pilgrim, who wanders Middle-earth giving aid and counsel, now unveiled as the keeper of the primordial Secret Fire ("his joy, and his swift wrath, were veiled in garments grey as ash, so that only those that knew him well glimpsed the flame that was within.")

While the Men of Bree regularly mingle with Hobbits, Men are for the most part strange, aloof, oversized; their motivations and values—the medieval Germanic shame/honor culture of the Rohirrim, the Byzantine grandeur of Gondor, the clandestine fellowship of the Dúnedain—inscrutable, even alien, when seen through ordinary Hobbit eyes. Clearly the reader is meant to identify with small Hobbits rather than with great Men. Tolkien's deeply Catholic understanding of the Magnificat theme—the exaltation of the humble, already present in *The Hobbit*, as we have seen, and adumbrated in all his writing—would be fully realized here.

How to frame the story, now that it was so much more complex than *The Hobbit*, was a real puzzle. Tolkien was torn between different authorial registers. In a foreword to the first edition, he begins by speaking as the (fictional) chronicler of the history of Middle-earth, but ends by speaking as the real-world author, dedicating *The Lord of the Rings* to his children and fellow Inklings. But it didn't work; the two voices clashed. For the second edition, published in 1965, he produced a new foreword in his real-world voice, explaining why it had taken so long to write the book (and, incidentally, dropping the dedication to the Inklings); this was followed by a prologue by the unnamed scholar who, within Tolkien's secondary world, is responsible for the book known in English translation as *The Lord of the Rings*.

The unnamed scholar, we are given to believe, is a compiler, redactor, and translator of prodigious text-critical skills who has mined the Matter of Middle-earth from *The Red Book of Westmarch* and other documentary sources, reconciling manuscript variants, transcribing runic and alphabetic scripts, and rendering in various shades of modern English the idioms, accents, musicality, and poetic diction of the languages of Elves, Men, Dwarves, Ents, Orcs, and Valar. To take just one example: Sam's real name, transliterated from the Mannish vernacular called Westron, is Banazîr ("halfwise") Galbasi (*galab* is "game" and *bas* is a suffix used in place names), for which Samwise Gamwich is an English approximation, devolving into Samwise Gammidgy, or Gamgee. Shire place-names, similarly, are represented by English place-names, most of which have recognizably Midlands roots. Tolkien's invented nomenclature thus enabled him to locate the Shire in a region replete with nostalgic significance—the region of his lost childhood home, which was also, as he argued in his study of the *Ancrene Wisse*, a sanctuary for Anglo-Saxon language and culture during the centuries after the catastrophe of 1066.

వ౨

A translator must perforce be an interpreter of cultures; hence a good deal of the fictional prologue is taken up with Hobbit ethnography, much of it tongue in cheek. The Hobbits are "an unobtrusive but very ancient people" who "love peace and quiet and good tilled earth" and enjoy their six meals a day, though they are capable of enduring extraordinary privation at need. Like most traditional peoples, they have a keen interest in genealogies and family histories. Though on better terms with the natural world than we moderns, their preference is for nature cultivated rather than wild, for the products of small-scale farming and artisanship and for civilized pleasures like the smoking of pipe-weed. The Shire is not a medieval town so much as a nineteenth-century hamlet ("more or less a Warwickshire village of about the period of the Diamond Jubilee," Tolkien told Allen & Unwin), a gossipy, provincial, preindustrial little world, rather like Cure Hardy in *That Hideous Strength*, which is attractive "in spite of all its obvious absurdities" and deserves to be saved. As Gandalf will say, "It would be a grievous blow to the world, if the Dark Power overcame the Shire; if all your kind, jolly, stupid Bolgers, Hornblowers, Boffins, Bracegirdles, and the rest, not to mention the ridiculous Bagginses, became enslaved." Even more so than in *The Hobbit*, the very anachronisms in the tale—like Bilbo's pocket handkerchiefs and Sam's fish and chips—can be understood most profitably as acts of translation meant to convey the homely goodness of the Shire, and all that deserves to be saved, by means of quintessentially English comforts.

The story opens with a comic explosion in the form of an antic "long-expected party"—an ironic inversion of the "unexpected party" with which *The Hobbit* begins. The occasion is Bilbo's "eleventy-first" and Frodo's thirty-third birthday, and Gandalf has arrived with fireworks to crown the occasion. A last gasp of *Hobbit* silliness and facetiousness (regretted by Tolkien and his critics alike) marks the moment of transition from a children's story to the tremendous narrative that is about to unfold. Bilbo makes a mocking valedictory speech, puts on the Ring that he had obtained during the adventures of *The Hobbit*, and abruptly vanishes, leaving Frodo to distribute the gifts and preside as heir in his place. Bilbo returns to Bag End and prepares to take to the open road again; yet when it comes to surrendering the Ring—the hidden purpose of the whole affair—he shows an unwillingness that arouses Gandalf's suspicion.

Seventeen years later, amid rumors of dark stirrings outside the Shire, Gandalf returns to give Frodo the true story of Bilbo's finding of the Ring, saying just enough to make Frodo thoroughly alarmed. From now on, the reader is in the hands of an omniscient narrator who folds into a third-person, real-time account—by means of a great deal of talking—an array of first-person voices recalling past or offstage events. With Frodo, we find out that the prize Bilbo took from Gollum was the One Ring, chief among the Great Rings of Power forged by Sauron during the Second Age as a means of enslaving all of Middle-earth.

Far from being a conventional magical device, however, the Ring proved to be an active and intelligent power. After lying hidden in the mud for more than two thousand years, it found Gollum, used him, and abandoned him. Nor was Bilbo immune to its addictive power; he would undoubtedly have been consumed by the Ring had he kept it much longer. Gandalf admits that he had initially failed to recognize the extent of the danger; now he means to terrify Frodo for his own good, warning him that the possessor of the Ring "does not grow or obtain more life, he merely continues, until at last every minute is a weariness. And if he often uses the Ring to make himself invisible, he *fades*: he becomes in the end invisible permanently, and walks in the twilight under the eye of the Dark Power that rules the Rings."

Though Tolkien indignantly rejected the comparison, there is more than a passing resemblance to the ring of power in Wagner's *Ring of the Nibelung*, cursed by its maker, the dwarf Alberich, to destroy its possessor, "des Ringes Herr als des Ringes Knecht" (the lord of the ring as the ring's slave). Tolkien's Ring cannot be hidden for long; nor can it be destroyed except by casting it into the fires in which it was forged, in the volcanic heart of Mount Doom, at the center of Mordor. "Doom"—Tolkien uses the Old English word a hundred times in *The Lord of the Rings*, registering its full range of meanings: a fate decreed, a judgment pronounced, a world destroyed.

But the most terrifying news Gandalf brings is his discovery that Gollum has revealed to Sauron the existence of Hobbits and the probable location of the Ring. The news prompts Frodo to cry out, "What a pity that Bilbo did not stab that vile creature, when he had a chance!" to which Gandalf responds, "Pity? It was Pity that stayed his hand. Pity, and Mercy: not to strike without need. And he has been well rewarded, Frodo. Be sure that he took so little hurt from the evil, and escaped in the end, because he began his ownership of the Ring so." It is one of Gandalf's many prophetic statements, and signals a major underlying Christian theme: "Blessed are the merciful: for they shall obtain mercy."

Frodo resolves to take the Ring and leave his beloved home—his first sacrificial act—thereby saving the Shire from attack. The gardener Samwise Gamgee, caught eavesdropping, is drafted to accompany him as his servant and helper; Tolkien would liken Sam to "the privates and my batmen I knew in the 1914 War, and recognized as so far superior to myself." The growing mutual dependence of Frodo and Sam does not erase this class difference, but Sam is ennobled by his perseverance, humility, love for Frodo, and inveterate delight in Elvish marvels. Frodo, Sam, and a few Hobbit friends set out on their journey, with the terrifying Black Riders (the "Nazgûl," once-powerful mortals, now deathless "ring-wraiths" enslaved to Sauron) close on their heels.

And so the pattern is established for the rest of the book. From here on it is all recapitulation: a dedicated company hastily formed and soon divided; a desperate flight "from deadly peril into deadly peril" followed by a temporary sanctuary and fleeting taste of domestic comfort. As the pattern recurs, the gravity of the danger and the solemnity of the mission become more evident and sharply focused, though the joys of table and bath are not diminished.

Such recapitulation of actions and themes is typical of epic narratives—think of Homer or Gilgamesh. For Tolkien, it was a way to link *The Hobbit* to its sequel, to govern the otherwise ungovernable tale he had worked on for so long and to express, in terms suited to a pre-Christian world, a distinctively Christian vision of history as a movement from types and figures toward fulfillment in the incarnate Redeemer who recapitulates all things past and future in his own Person. To the Greeks and Romans, recapitulation (Greek *anakephalaiosis*, Latin *recapitulatio*) was a rhetorical device, but for Christian writers beginning with Irenaeus, the second-century bishop and martyr, it was an essential key, revealing the Bible's narrative of redemption. It is the pattern of recapitulation that makes the Book of Revelation (Greek: Apocalypse) an intelligible vision rather than a mad tumult of avenging angels, dragons, and worlds unmade. It serves the same function in Tolkien's tale.

Perhaps Tolkien came upon his recapitulation design by accident, for he was initially sailing without coordinates. It is a measure of the difficulty he experienced in finding momentum for his plot, Tom Shippey suggests, "that Frodo has to be dug out of no less than five 'Homely Houses' before his quest is properly launched: first Bag End, then the little house at Crickhollow with its redundant guardian Fredegar Bolger, then the house of Tom Bombadil, then the *Prancing Pony*, and finally Rivendell, with its 'last Homely House east of the Sea.'" It is a mark of Tolkien's genius that he makes a virtue out of successive literary defeats.

Some interludes serve the tale by being almost wholly serendipitous; thus the encounter with Tom Bombadil and his wife, Goldberry the river daughter, taken from Tolkien's 1934 poem. Critics point out that this episode is not well integrated into the story; if so, that is part of its charm. Tom Bombadil is Nature personified, an impartial and independent power immune to the Ring and the terrors of history. He plays his part precisely by not having a part in the unfolding history, and his interventions on behalf of the Hobbits—rescuing them from the clutches of an evil willow tree and from certain death at the hands of ghostly barrow-wights—

come at no personal cost. Frodo, by contrast, has to accept great personal cost. When he and his companions are imprisoned in the cairns of the Barrow-downs, he resists the impulse to use the Ring to save himself, chants one of Tom's rhyming songs, and throws himself on the mercy of providence or fate. The lesson is not lost on Frodo: in the very moment when his courage awakens, so does his awareness of the need to call upon others. The episode transposes to a more somber key the encounter with trolls and the timely intervention of Gandalf in *The Hobbit*; here, too, a cache of charmed weapons comes to light. At the Inn of the Prancing Pony, Frodo and his companions learn, after a dangerous indiscretion, that they must be wise as serpents and innocent as doves, suspicious of strangers, and yet—when the alarming figure of Strider offers his assistance—capable of trust.

The journey is just beginning, but the Christian themes of *The Lord of the Rings* are already in play: pity and mercy, faith and trust, humility, self-sacrifice, the powers of the weak, providence (disguised as chance), freedom (deformed by sin), and grace when all seems lost. Though the story is set in a distant epoch when (as Tolkien explained in a letter drafted but never sent to an inquisitive reader), "the Fall of Man is in the past and off-stage; the Redemption of Man in the far future," the intimations of the Gospel are unmistakable. Fr. Robert Murray was right, Tolkien said, to detect a fundamental sympathy between *The Lord of the Rings* and the perennial Catholic vision of the "order of Grace."

At Rivendell, the Elven sanctuary, the flight from the Shire turns into a Quest; in a council of Elves, Dwarves, Men—and Frodo—convened by Elrond, Half-elven lord of the realm, the decision is taken to bring the Ring to the very heart of the Enemy's territory and there cast it into the fiery chasm of Mount Doom to be unmade. It is a strategy to confound Sauron, who knows only the calculus of power and self-interest. Frodo is to be the Ring-bearer—it is his fate, or chance, or providentially ordered vocation—assisted by Gandalf, the hobbits Sam, Merry, and Pippin, the elf Legolas, the dwarf Gimli, and two men, Boromir and Strider (later revealed as Aragorn, the long-awaited king). Together they constitute a Company of Nine Walkers, the Fellowship of the Ring, uniting the free races of Middle-earth.

The Company advances through one adventure after another, involving monsters, magicians, prodigies of nature, epic battles, bold kings, ethereal queens, and underworld descents, including the death and resurrection of Gandalf. One is reminded of the heroic quest pattern common to the world's myths and folktales—but there is a difference: in this case, the quest is not to seek a treasure but to lose one, and the chief responsibility falls upon an insignificant hobbit rather than a great hero. If *The Hobbit* undermines the hero paradigm, *The Lord of the Rings* utterly overturns it. If Bilbo Baggins in *The Hobbit* is a version of Grimm's brave little tailor, Frodo Baggins in *The Lord of the Rings* breaks the mold: he is brave without bravado, clever without dissembling, and, once committed to his task, so self-sacrificing that there is no place for him on the standard motif lists of folklore and mythology. Strangest of all, at the critical moment his quest miscarries; having arrived, utterly spent, at the "Cracks of Doom" (the expression is pure apocalyptic), Frodo declares, "I do not choose now to do what I came to do. I will not do this deed. The Ring is mine!"

Tolkien was at pains to explain the deeper meaning of this seeming rebellion on Frodo's part. "I do not think that Frodo's was a *moral* failure," he told one reader. Like all who consent to be placed in "'sacrificial' positions," Frodo should be judged by the "motives and disposition" with which he began; in his case, by his humility, his desire to save those he loved, his willingness to extend that love even to the unlovable Gollum, and his consent to suffering and death, if need be. He had fulfilled his contract with every ounce of his strength.

By the end of the tale, however, Frodo's will is so damaged that it is difficult to call it unambiguously free. The meaning lies in the ambiguity. In a discarded version, Tolkien had him say "But I cannot do what I have come to do" and there is only a hair's breadth of a difference—for Tolkien is working within the Augustinian tradition, which will brook no Pelagian optimism about the perfectibility of the human will. The power of the Ring to enslave is beyond measure, and men of goodwill can be broken even by lesser enchantments. Choices made with the best intentions can founder or seem to do so: witness the recurring lament, voiced by Frodo, Aragorn, Sam, and others, "All my choices have proved ill." Many of the characters are fated to repeat the deeds of their forerunners; recapitulation is tinged with fatalism in this pre-Christian epoch, and resignation is the better part of wisdom. There remains only just that spark of freedom sufficient to enable the characters at key moments to respond to the lot they are given.

We are in a pagan world, consoled—like the philosopher Boethius in his prison cell—by intimations of Gospel hope, rumors of grace. Hence, though the wise are monotheists who believe in divine providence, they do not expect God to show his hand; nor, for that matter, does a wise Christian claim knowledge of the exact workings of grace. Help comes "unlooked-for"—a homely expression Tolkien prefers to abstract theological words like "providence"; "unlooked-for" occurs sixteen times in *The Lord of the Rings*, and with mounting frequency—twice in *The Fellowship of the Ring*, six times in *The Two Towers*, eight times in *The Return of the King* (as well as eight times in *The Silmarillion*, but not at all in *The Hobbit*).

Other key words are "dwindle," which occurs thirty times in *The Lord of the Rings*, and "diminish," which occurs sixteen times. The Men of Westernesse were diminished when their hero fell to the Orcs at the beginning of the Third Age; and by the latter days of Third Age, in which the events of *The Lord of the Rings* unfold, all the Free Peoples of Middle-earth (Dwarves, Elves, Ents, Hobbits, and Men) have been diminished by wars, plagues, departures, and betrayals. The corrupt figures—Sauron the Dark Lord and Saruman the wizard—cannot bear to accept their own diminishment; they are consumed by a diseased will to power and by the wrath and envy that their failures provoke. Throughout Tolkien's mythology this theme recurs, as power-wielders among each of the several kinds of beings—Morgoth among the Valar, Fëanor among the Elves, Túrin Turambar among Men, and the idolatrous Númenóreans—succumb to the *ofermod*, overmastering pride, for which Tolkien blamed Beorhtnoth at the Battle of Maldon. In contrast, the faithful among the Valar, Elves, and Men accept their place in the created order and humbly repent when they err. Galadriel, the visionary Elven queen with the light of the Two Trees in her golden hair, has so far conquered her will as to refuse the One Ring when Frodo offers it to her and to declare, in words reminiscent of John the Baptist (John 3:29), "I will diminish, and go into the West, and remain Galadriel."

In other words, optimism must die so that hope unlooked-for—or, in Lewis's words, "good news, news beyond hope"—may live. There is no room for the illusion that victory in war is a guarantee of perpetual peace or that evil can be permanently subdued in this world. Death itself is an indelible feature of a world whose redemption is in the far future. The Elves, immortal while the world lasts, experience nostalgia for death; the Númenóreans, envious of Elvish immortality, are destroyed by their disordered craving; and for mortals like Frodo who are deeply wounded, the only cure is to die from this world and pass into the next. "All this stuff," Tolkien told Milton Waldman, "is mainly concerned with Fall, Mortality, and the Machine."

Perhaps it needs saying that even if the whole work serves (like all fairy tales, if Tolkien is right) as *praeparatio evangelica*, there is no unambiguous Christ figure in *The Lord of the Rings*—rather, there are several partial Christ figures: Strider/Aragorn is Christ as anointed healer and king who travels the paths of the dead to bring victory and peace, and the Half-elven Arwen is his Christ-like bride; Gandalf is Christ as prophet and priest transfigured and risen from the dead; Frodo is Christ in Gethsemane and on the Cross bearing the sins of the world, and Sam is Christ refracted in the saints of the Church militant, typifying the servant-saint who remains at his post till the last. As for the Virgin Mary, whose veneration was so central to Tolkien's Catholicism ("Our Lady, upon which all my own small perception of beauty both in majesty and simplicity is founded," as he put it in his 1953 letter to Fr. Robert Murray), her light is refracted in all the lovely Elven and Half-elven women of legend, in Arwen, and above all in the power and humility of Galadriel— yet even Galadriel can only partially foreshadow the glorious Queen of Heaven.

Tolkien found the early reviews of *The Fellowship of the Ring*, which began appearing in August 1954, "a great deal better than I feared." Lewis may have been right to warn him that his endorsement might do Tolkien more harm than good, given the hostility to Lewis in some literary circles. But as Tolkien told Rayner Unwin, "I should not have wished other than to be associated with him—since only by his support and friendship did I ever struggle to the end of the labour." Lewis's dust-jacket endorsement would stand:

If Ariosto rivalled it in invention (in fact he does not), he would still lack its heroic seriousness. No imaginary world has been projected which is at once so multifarious and so true to its own inner laws; none so seemingly objective, so disinfected from the taint of an author's merely individual psychology; none so relevant to the actual human situation yet so free from allegory. And what fine shading there is in the variations of style to meet the almost endless diversity of scenes and characters—comic, homely, epic, monstrous, or diabolic!

There were similarly ecstatic blurbs by Richard Hughes, the poet, novelist, and screenwriter for Ealing Studios, comparing *The Fellowship of the Ring* to *The Faerie Queene*, and Naomi Mitchison ranking it with Malory.

Jack Walter Lambert, the literary and arts editor for *The Sunday Times* (London), was among the early reviewers who, unfortunately, took the measure of *The Fellowship* from the blurbs on the dust jacket and the impressions created by its first, Hobbit-centered, chapter: "On the jacket Ariosto, Malory and Spenser are evoked: skirting these peaks, glorious but seldom climbed, it may be more helpful to suggest that those who enjoy, say, the Brothers Grimm, Peacock in 'The Misfortunes of Elphin,' 'The Wind in the Willows,' or T. H. White's 'The Sword in the Stone,' will find this bizarre enterprise very much to their taste." The most he was willing to say was that the book "sweeps along with a narrative and pictorial force which lifts it above" the level of "whimsical drivel with a message." Alfred Duggan, the historical novelist and stepson of Lord Curzon, wrote in *The Times Literary Supplement* that he admired the "sound prose and rare imagination," but thought it odd that Hobbits, obviously meant for light entertainment fare, "had intruded into the domain of the Nibelungs" and gotten mixed up in what looked like an anti-Soviet allegory. In reviews of the subsequent volumes, though he remained generally appreciative, he registered his disappointment that the allegory didn't gel. Peter Green, fiction editor at *The Daily Telegraph* (and a classicist who would later write an important history of the Hellenistic age as well as a biography of Kenneth Grahame), regarded *The Fellowship* as "a bewildering amalgam of Malory, Grimm, the Welsh *Mabinogion*, T. H. White, and 'Puck of Pook's Hill.' The style veers from pre-Raphaelite to Boy's Own Paper. And yet this shapeless work has an undeniable fascination especially to a reviewer with a severe cold in the head." "I must say that I was unfortunate in coming into the hands of the D. Telegraph, during the absence of Betjeman," Tolkien told Rayner Unwin. "My work is not in his line, but he at any rate is neither ignorant nor a gutter-boy. Peter Green seems to be both. I do not know him or of him, but he is so rude as to make one suspect malice."

There were a few reviewers, however, who on the basis of *The Fellowship* alone could foresee the total pattern of *The Lord of the Rings* and avoid facile misreadings. The celebrated journalist and broadcaster Bernard Levin, writing in the magazine *Truth* under the pen name "A. E. Cherryman," considered Lewis's dust-jacket endorsement a piece of "buffoonery," but was hardly less subdued than Lewis in his praise: "it may be that in years to come the Death of Gandalf is placed beside the Death of Hector in its power to stir the mind and heart" and "it seems almost as though he has added something, not only to the world's literature, but to its history." Edwin Muir, the poet, critic, and novelist from Orkney, loved *The Fellowship* for its consistent realization of an imagined world, but considered Tolkien's portrayal of good and evil oversimplified and his style ("alternating between the popular novel and the boy's adventure story") unequal to his great theme; yet he was intrigued enough to review the subsequent volumes as they appeared and defend them against the debunkers. Above all, there was W. H. Auden, confessing in *The New York Times Book Review* that "no fiction I have read in the last five years has given me more joy than 'The Fellowship of the Ring'" and telling readers of *Encounter* that "the suspense of waiting to know what happens to the Ring Bearer is intolerable."

As the subsequent volumes appeared, reviews became increasingly polarized, leading Tolkien to observe that "some critics seem determined to represent me as a simple-minded adolescent, inspired with, say, a With-the-flag-to-Pretoria spirit, and wilfully distort what is said in my tale." Reviewing the final volume in *The New York Times Book Review*, Auden said he could "rarely remember a book about which I have had such violent arguments"; Tolkien wrote a lengthy response, which he apparently never sent, in which he thanks Auden for the review but rebukes him for interpreting *The Lord of the Rings* as in part autobiographical. Edmund Wilson, whose review for *The Nation* will go down in history as one of the great unintentional parodies of scorched-earth literary criticism

("Oo, Those Awful Orcs!"), blamed Tolkien's "infatuated admirers" for inflating *The Lord of the Rings* into something more than "an overgrown fairy story, a philological curiosity." Auden's love of Quest literature must have blinded him to the bad writing, Wilson surmised, but even as Quests go, *The Lord of the Rings* was a failure:

> The hero has no serious temptations; is lured by no insidious enchantments, perplexed by few problems. What we get here is a simple confrontation—in more or less the traditional terms of British melodrama—of the Forces of Evil with the Forces of Good, the remote and alien villain with the plucky little home-grown hero. There are streaks of imagination: the ancient tree-spirits, the Ents, with their deep eyes, twiggy beards, rumbly voices; the Elves, whose nobility and beauty is elusive and not quite human. But even these are rather clumsily handled. There is never much development in the episodes; you simply go on getting more of the same thing. Dr. Tolkien has little skill at narrative and no instinct for literary form. The characters talk a story-book language that might have come out of Howard Pyle, and as personalities they do not impose themselves. At the end of this long romance, I had still no conception of the wizard Gandalph [sic], who is a cardinal figure, had never been able to visualize him at all. For the most part such characterizations as Dr. Tolkien is able to contrive are perfectly stereotyped: Frodo the good little Englishman, Samwise, his dog-like servant, who talks lower-class and respectful, and never deserts his master.

The success of "these long-winded volumes of what looks to this reviewer like balderdash" Wilson attributed to the fact that "certain people—especially, perhaps, in Britain—have a lifelong appetite for juvenile trash."

Other prominent mainstream critics agreed, considering the case against Tolkien open and shut, with Philip Toynbee writing in *The Observer* in 1961, with remarkably deficient prophetic skill,

> There was a time when the Hobbit fantasies of Professor Tolkien were being taken very seriously indeed by a great many distinguished literary figures. Mr. Auden is even reported to have

claimed that these books were as good as *War and Peace*; Edwin Muir and many others were almost equally enthusiastic. I had a sense that one side or the other must be mad, for it seemed to me that these books were dull, ill-written, whimsical and childish. And for me this had a reassuring outcome, for most of his more ardent supporters were soon beginning to sell out their shares in Professor Tolkien, and today those books have passed into a merciful oblivion.

Tolkien wisely ignored such remarks. "The only criticism that annoyed me," he told Houghton Mifflin, "was one that it 'contained no religion' (and 'no Women,' but that does not matter, and is not true anyway)"—referring to the review by J. W. Lambert.

In November 1955, the BBC Third Programme began a six-episode radio broadcast of *The Fellowship of the Ring*, with Norman Shelley, the well-known voice of Winnie-the-Pooh, speaking the parts of Gandalf and Tom Bombadil; it was followed a year later by a six-part adaptation combining *The Two Towers* and *The Return of the King*. Predictably, Tolkien wasn't pleased: "I think the book quite unsuitable for 'dramatization,' and have not enjoyed the broadcasts—though they have improved. I thought Tom Bombadil dreadful—but worse still was the announcer's preliminary remarks that Goldberry was his daughter (!), and that Willowman was an ally of Mordor (!!)."

A Circle of Friends

When Dr. Havard watched his wife, Grace, lose her battle with cancer in 1950, "both J and I warned him," wrote Warnie in his diary, "of the disaster of P's [Pudaitabird, Albert Lewis] sliding into solitude after Mammy's death." Sliding into solitude, or at least into small isolated units, imperiled all the Inklings throughout the 1950s. "My brother and I took a day off last week, put sandwiches in our pockets, and tramped sixteen miles or more along the old Roman road—now a mere track—which runs from Dorchester Abbey to Oxford," Lewis wrote ten days after Grace's death. The walk epitomized the new situation, which followed close on the heels of the final Thursday evening gathering in autumn 1949 and would run, with peaks and troughs, until Lewis's death fourteen years later:

long walking tours with a throng in attendance had become a memory; now the two brothers strolled apart from the others, along the green swards of Northern Ireland or close by the Kilns. Still, Tuesday mornings at the Bird and Baby continued, and they could be riotous affairs, even if they lacked the intensity and intimacy of Thursday evenings; sometimes they included new faces who fit in well enough, although the old guard never considered them full-blooded members. Often the best conversation arose when one Inkling met another in a neutral (non-Inkling) venue, over dinner at home or in a hotel, or at church, or at a faculty gathering. Wain's cabal was becoming, in its early senescence, what Lewis always claimed it to be: no more than a circle of friends.

Happily, the loosening of the band did not foretoken any diminishment in the Inklings' individual achievements. Tolkien's *Lord of the Rings* and Lewis's *Chronicles of Narnia* spearheaded the decade's great accomplishments, but several members produced notable, even outstanding, works. Warnie's *The Splendid Century: Life in the France of Louis XIV*, dedicated "To My Brother," appeared in Britain in 1953 and America in 1954; *The New York Times* gave it two reviews, the daily edition declaring it "extremely well-written . . . social history at its best," the Sunday edition praising the author as a "conscientious scholar as well as a delightful writer." David Cecil continued his string of splendid biographies with *Lord M, or the Later Life of Lord Melbourne* (1954), and John Wain came into flower with his first novel, *Hurry on Down* (1953), a comic tale of disaffected youth that misled critics into naming him one of the Angry Young Men, although on balance he exhibited, like Kingsley Amis and others so misidentified, far more wit than anger.

During this decade, Lewis completed not only *Narnia* but also a second gargantuan undertaking: *English Literature in the Sixteenth Century, Excluding Drama*, his contribution to the fifteen-volume *Oxford History of English Literature* (a.k.a. *OHEL*). He had shouldered the assignment in 1935, and by 1938 he was staggering under its weight, telling one of the two general editors of the *History*, Frank Percy Wilson, who had been his English tutor and who would later best him for the Merton professorship in English literature, that "The O HELL lies like a nightmare on my chest . . . I shan't try to desert—anyway, I suppose the exit is thronged with dreadful faces and fiery arms—but I have a growing doubt if I ought to be doing this." He signed the letter "Yours, in deep depression . . ." The problem lay in the sheer immensity of the task, which entailed surveying, with impeccable scholarship, a full century of the richest literature in the world. Later in 1938, Lewis reported to Wilson that he had already covered "Platonism, Douglas, Lyndsay, Tottel, Mulcaster's Elementarie, Sir Thomas More, Prayer-book, Sidney, Marlowe (non-dramatic), Nashe, Watson, Barclay, Googe, Raleigh (poems), Shakespeare (poems), Webbe; and among other sources Petrarch and Machiavelli," but even so would welcome a chance to withdraw if a suitable pretext could be found.

Eventually Lewis scoured the complete works of every important author of the century, perhaps two hundred in all. He also pored over all the relevant secondary literature he could find, including "ploughing through back numbers of learned periodicals less in the hope of fresh knowledge than in the fear I've missed something . . . In any forgotten article the really illuminating thing might lie hid: tho' about 90 to 10 against. So that I mostly pass the hours reading rubbish." The prodigious research and writing advanced or flagged as he pounced on other projects, but he never lost the thread (unlike Tolkien with his epic tale), and by May 1952, the book was finished. As it wended its way through the Oxford production labyrinth, Lewis burbled with pleasure. "Joy, joy, my task is done" he told Sister Penelope. The nightmare was off his chest at last.

The great labor produced a masterpiece. When the book appeared in print two years later, John Wain wrote in *The Spectator* that "Mr. Lewis, now as always, writes as if inviting us to a feast." Ruth Pitter, writing in her journal, approached the work as nearly a universal palliative, declaring it "dear and delectable, to read for enjoyment, for relaxation, for the sense of balance & just appraisal, bringing unction." Dame Helen Gardner summed up the book's achievement in her 1966 memoir of Lewis for the British Academy: "The merits of this book are very great indeed. It is, to begin with, a genuine literary history . . . The book is also brilliantly written, compulsively readable, and constantly illuminated by sentences that are as true as they are witty. Who else could have written a literary history that continually arouses delighted laughter?" The cascade of praise notwithstanding, *OHEL* remains one of Lewis's least-read books. Who, in an age of instantly available digitized data, troubles to read seven-hundred-page works on literature five centuries old?

৵৹

Joy Davidman returned to England in November 1953, this time with her boys in tow, and settled into an apartment in the annex of a Hampstead hotel. A month later, she and her children arrived at the Kilns for a four-day pre-Christmas stay. The assembled company loped across the Headington hills, ascended Magdalen Tower, and, for a breather, read or played chess, a regimen that left the worn-out hosts, already dazzled by the mother's unbridled tongue, marveling at the boys' boundless vigor. It was as tiring as surf-bathing, Lewis told more than one correspondent.

He and Joy lived in separate cities and saw one another rarely, but they shared, via letters, their ideas and enthusiasms, and the friendship ripened. Lewis paid for the boys' schooling (room, board, tuition). Joy shepherded into print her new book, *Smoke on the Mountain*, a popular study of the Ten Commandments. Lewis wrote the foreword, which contains one or two unfortunate declarations—including "To us Christians the unconverted Jew (I mean no offense) must appear as a Christian *manqué*"—but otherwise offers a thoughtful analysis of the book as "a true bill against Western civilization," a civilization that, it is difficult to deny, falls flat when measured against the decrees from Sinai. One suspects that his account of Joy's literary manner ("the Jewish fierceness, being here also modern and feminine, can be very quiet; the paw looked as if it were velveted, until we felt the scratch") is drawn from life. She had a temper, cut people badly, suffered fools poorly. Many of Lewis's friends, feeling or fearing her scratch, rejected her. She was too American, too bold, and, at least to some, too Jewish. One could imagine Dorothy L. Sayers as an Inkling, but Joy would have never passed muster: her sex, nationality, ethnicity, and impending divorce (finalized on August 5, 1954) made her a walking catalogue of disqualifications. Of the Tuesday morning, Thursday night crowd, only the Lewis brothers embraced her.

This was in marked contrast to the way in which Lewis's friends, especially Barfield, Cecil, and Dyson, took to Ruth Pitter. She was in so many ways Joy's inverse: English, shy, with soft features, and a far more gifted poet than Joy. *The Ermine: Poems 1942–1952* cemented her reputation, an effusive review (by the children's book author Theresa Furse) in *The Times Literary Supplement* calling it "perhaps Miss Pitter's most beautiful book." Lewis was bowled over, pouring on her the sort of praise he had reserved for Charles Williams: "Bright Angel! I'm in a sea of glory! . . . the new volume is an absolute Corker."

With these accolades ringing in her ears, Pitter decided to move to Oxford. Was she in love with Lewis? There is no concrete evidence to support this conjecture, but it's likely that Pitter admired him as much as or more than she did any other man, save perhaps David Cecil. After months of searching, she and her friend and business partner, Kathleen O'Hara, moved into a villa at Long Crendon, where Barfield had once resided. "Welcome to what Tolkien calls the Little Kingdom," wrote Lewis. He and Pitter met soon after for lunch at the Eastgate Hotel. Conditions were perfect for a romance to blossom—barring one enormous impediment: Joy Davidman was present at the lunch. Pitter and Joy did not hit it off; Lewis, no doubt sensing the friction, chose to direct his attentions to Joy. In 1955 he told George Sayer (as Sayer later remembered it) that "if he were not a confirmed bachelor, Ruth Pitter would be the woman he would like to marry. 'One could have with her the kind of relationship described by Patmore in *The Angel in the House*,' he said. 'It's not too late,' I commented. 'Oh yes it is,' he said, 'I've burnt my boats.'"

The burnt boats, about which Sayer knew nothing, refer, of course, to his commitment to Joy, a lively companion whom no one mistook for Patmore's idealized portrait of the sweet, selfless wife. Lewis may have tried, gently and discreetly, to convey the reality of the situation to Pitter. In August, he and Sayer visited Long Crendon, hoping to surprise her at home but finding only her housemate. "The one miss out of a thousand days that wd. have been hits," he wrote Pitter, "certainly suggests Providence Herself, moving in a more than usually mysterious way." The Lewis-Pitter friendship, never brought to the boil for which some Inklings wished ("Jack should have married Ruth Pitter," Colin Hardie told his wife and Walter Hooper in 1969), settled down to occasional visits and letters. Pitter's regard for Lewis remained high (matched by a bitter and outspoken resentment of Joy), and some years after his death she defended his relations with women, writing Hooper that "if he was mistrustful of women, it was not hatred, but a burnt child's dread of fire . . . I would say he was a great & very perspicacious lover of women."

Meanwhile, Providence Herself, pursuing her own inscrutable aims, was engineering a tremendous change in Lewis's life. In the spring of 1954, Cambridge University had established a new chair in Medieval and Renaissance Literature. The electors included several friends and supporters of Lewis, including his old tutor F. P. Wilson, the medievalists David Knowles and Henry Stanley Bennett, Lewis's amiable adversary and coauthor, E.M.W. Tillyard, and, not least, J.R.R. Tolkien. This group decided, unanimously, to offer their mutual friend the post, although he had expressed no interest in it. Lewis declined the offer, tendering flimsy arguments about losing a precious servant (Fred Paxton) by moving to Cambridge, about standing in the way of another candidate (G. V. Smithers, a University College philologist who was never seriously considered for the post), and about his own flagging energies. The truth is, he was worried about Warnie, who surely would spiral down into drunken disaster if abandoned at the Kilns. The university re-tended its offer; Lewis turned it down again. At this stage, the electors approached their second choice, Dame Helen Gardner.

But this was not the end. Tolkien, dismayed at Lewis's refusal and convinced that life in Cambridge would revitalize him emotionally as well as physically, took the offensive. On the field of friendship, this was his shining hour. He forcefully countered Lewis's objections, assuring him that Smithers was ineligible for the professorship, which had been earmarked for a literary scholar rather than a philologist, and that the university would be content if he shuttled to and from the Kilns, living in supplied rooms in Cambridge four days of each week and passing the remainder at home in Oxford. Tolkien may also have mentioned that Lewis's salary would triple in the new post, and that he would be quit of tutoring, a ball and chain for the past thirty years. Elated by these revelations, Lewis wrote a letter accepting the chair, adding that he had already begun composing suitable lectures in his head. The electors swallowed hard and, through the university vice-chancellor, informed him that the backup candidate had been offered the job. The situation seemed hopeless—until another eucatastrophe unfolded. Gardner turned down the post, without specifying why. The answer emerged in her 1966 memorial memoir for Lewis, in which she wrote, gracefully disguising her own role in the matter, that "fortunately, the 'second string' declined, partially on account of having heard that Lewis was changing his mind, for it was obvious that this ought to be Lewis's chair."

Lewis's chair it became; but what was to become of his Magdalen College tutorship? Herein lies a mystery. According to Barfield, when

Lewis accepted the Cambridge position, he selected Barfield as his Oxford replacement, arranged a transfer with the Master of Magdalen, and "fixed up a kind of farewell dinner for himself and an introductory dinner for me, all together." All seemed set until the proposal was put before the dons and was voted down. So Barfield remembered the sequence of events, years later. The real reason for the rejection, he suspected, was antagonism toward Lewis, but the proffered excuse was that Barfield was close to retirement age and a new search would have to be instituted soon after his arrival. Oddly, there is no substantial corroboration for Barfield's account in Lewis's papers; the situation is furthermore muddled by Barfield's belief that all this transpired in the late 1950s, several years after Lewis's retirement. Whatever the precise details, for Barfield the result was "a pretty big disappointment, because I'd looked forward very much to living in Oxford, to the kind of society you get there—my wife was also looking forward to it very much." It was another blow in a life of blows.

War Against Williams

Charles Williams, many years dead, lived still in the hearts of his friends and the spleen of his enemies. His was not a happy legacy. The first significant attack had come in 1950, in the otherwise upbeat, celebratory pages of the immensely popular *Penguin Book of Contemporary Verse*. The editor, poet Kenneth Allott, chose for his collection all the obvious candidates—Eliot, Yeats, Joyce—and added Charles Williams to the list, reprinting "The Calling of Arthur" from *Taliessin Through Logres*. Why this selection?

According to Allott, artistic merit had nothing to do with it. Williams's poems constitute "a literary oddity of great interest" that influenced Auden, Eliot, and Ridler; beyond this faint praise, Allott offers only condemnation. Lewis's evaluation of his friend's work is "wildly off the mark." Lewis has "been hypnotized by his memories of the man" into seeing in the poems things that are "barely half-said" and poorly at that, in an Arthurian narrative so garbled that "all Mr. Lewis's ingenuity" is needed to sort it out. Williams is "at times . . . metrically clumsy and in expression uncouth and, more rarely, bathetic." One recoils at the ferocity of this onslaught, which appears, after all, in a book ostensibly dedicated to the work of the best modern poets. Nor does Allott offer any reason for his decision to guard the precincts of Parnassus with a merciless sword and make Williams his exemplary victim. And yet his conclusions seem, for the most part, incontestable. Most will agree that Lewis, blinded by friendship, passed from praise to adulation when assessing Williams's poetry, and few will disagree with T. S. Eliot and many others that to read Williams's Arthurian works is to enter a nearly impenetrable thicket of obscurities.

The motives behind the next major attack, launched a year later, were more transparent. The aggressor was F. R. Leavis, the means his collection of essays, largely culled from *Scrutiny*, called *The Common Pursuit*. It appears that Leavis simply transferred his dislike of Lewis and his allied discomfort with much of Christian orthodoxy to Williams. "I can see no reason for being interested in Charles Williams," he begins, shutting the door in his opening move. Williams "hadn't begun to be a poet"; his analysis of Milton is "the merest attitudinizing and gesturing of a man who had nothing critically relevant to say." These are broad judgments, made contemptuously and without textual support. Other observations, perhaps unwittingly, hit the mark. Leavis contends that Williams is not the best advertisement for Christianity, that his "preoccupation with the 'horror of evil' is evidence of an arrest at the schoolboy (and -girl) stage rather than of spiritual maturity," a perspicacious remark that we can now buttress with evidence of which Leavis was almost certainly unaware, including Williams's ritualistic behavior with his OUP colleagues and his participation in Waite's Fellowship of the Rosy Cross. His assertion that Williams's "dealings in 'myth,' mystery, the occult, and the supernatural belong essentially to the ethos of the thriller," can be guardedly embraced. As a critic and historian, especially in *The Figure of Beatrice* and *The Descent of the Dove*, Williams is a sophisticated and judicious explorer of supernatural themes, but his novels, excepting *The Place of the Lion* and *All Hallows' Eve*, rarely rise above highbrow pulp. Leavis's claim that Williams is "a subject worth attention from the inquirer into the 'sociology' of contemporary literature" is belittling but correct: he indeed deserves attention for his unusual character and interests; that this is the only reason for studying him is doubtful.

Williams's prominence as a specifically Christian author occasioned the third major assault on his reputation, unleashed by the poet and historian Robert Conquest in *Essays in Criticism, 1957*. Conquest's offensive differs radically from those of Allott and Leavis. He gives Williams some high marks as a poet, declaring him possessed of "in many ways an admirable talent," producing works of genuine quality and sporadic technical brilliance. For Conquest, Williams's sin lies elsewhere: he is a totalitarian. By this, Conquest—who would later attain fame for *The Great Terror* (1965), his study of Stalinist atrocities—does not mean, as most readers might assume, that Williams is Fascist or Communist. What he means is that Williams is an orthodox Christian, foisting on others a "closed system" of thought, an "ideological straightjacket." In this perceived coercion, Conquest discerns deliberate hypocrisy or self-deception on Williams's part, for "nowadays" all "intelligent people" know perfectly well that such systems are "ridiculous and wrong" and that "definite research exists which makes nonsense of them." As Williams's exegete and defender, Lewis also comes under Conquest's scourge; both Inklings are guilty of "the tendency to terrorism," of "smug self-congratulation," and "the pitying sneer," which they employ "as a substitute for the unattainable whip and labour camp." This, then, is the voice of 1950s skepticism at high pitch and full volume, smugly confident of its own closed certainties, willing, just like the totalitarian-inspired Soviet Realism that Conquest abhors, to condemn a work on ideological as well as aesthetic grounds.

Conquest's anti-Christian arguments did little to dent Williams's stature. On the other hand, neither did Williams's friends accomplish much in their many efforts to enhance his poetic reputation. Lewis and Dorothy L. Sayers spoke and wrote on his behalf; even Eliot chipped in, calling *Taliessen Through Logres* "absorbing after we have got the hang of what he is after." In 1955 the poet John Heath-Stubbs published a laudatory booklet on Williams for the British Council and the National Book League, but he was obliged, in the very first sentence, to say of his subject that "it is very difficult to arrive at a balanced estimate of his place in modern English literature." A few other voices joined the pro-Williams choir, but few listened, while many who did, after turning to the poems themselves, gave up in bewilderment. Williams's gravestone identifies him as "Poet," but following Allott's initial backhanded salute, no major collection of modern English verse has included his work. *Arthurian Torso* and *Taliessen Through Logres* flicker in and out of print, always difficult to obtain, but within fifteen years of Williams's death, his fame came to rest upon his novels, a few works of theology and literary criticism—and his membership in the Inklings.

18

THE DIALECTIC OF DESIRE

There may be times when what is most needed is, not so much a new discovery or a new idea as a different 'slant'; I mean a comparatively slight readjustment in our *way* of looking at the things and ideas on which attention is already fixed." The opening line in Barfield's *Saving the Appearances* (1957), with its gentle incitement to new perspectives, addressed the need for Western culture to acquire a new understanding of consciousness. At the same time, Barfield was talking of himself and his own desperate readiness for transformation. The patterns of a lifetime were ready to break asunder; his *vita nuova* was about to commence.

What triggered the metamorphosis? The answer may lie in the accumulating pressure of thirty years of literary frustration, of watching Lewis, de la Mare, Eliot, and other friends achieve lasting fame while he remained entombed in the sepulcher of trust-and-property law. Or it may be discerned in his awareness that Maud was turning seventy while he neared sixty, driving home the frightening truth that his time was now or never. Whatever the cause, during the mid-1950s he cut back his law hours and instead frequented the British Museum Reading Room, taking copious notes on whatever caught his fancy—philology, philosophy, anthropology, history of science—with no definite plan in mind. He began to write a new book but abandoned it after one chapter, displeased by its lack of focus. His frustration mounted, until one happy day he stumbled upon the phrase "saving the appearances" in Garvin Ardley's *Aquinas and Kant*

(1950), a now-forgotten study of early science. "Somehow," Barfield recalled, "around that [phrase], all these unconnected notes I'd made . . . from different parts of the mental world, seemed to crystallize."

The newly precipitated crystals took literary form as *Saving the Appearances*. Barfield had not attempted a full-length presentation of Anthroposophical ideas since *Poetic Diction*, written during his twenties, nearly thirty years before. The skills of a solicitor—close reasoning, attention to detail, verbal agility, aggressiveness, unflagging effort—which had driven him half-mad in legal affairs, now proved invaluable in literary forensics. *Saving the Appearances* is sharply argued and elegantly phrased. In it, Barfield ventures far beyond the philological speculation of his earlier works, diving into philosophy, theology, occultism, prophecy, and ancient, medieval, and modern history in order to mount his fullest exposition to date of the evolution of consciousness.

He begins with epistemology. How do we apprehend the world around us? He calls our experience a *collective representation*, the result of sense data interacting with the mind of the perceiver (these representations are the "appearances" of the title). "When I 'hear a thrush singing,'" Barfield writes, "I am hearing, not with my ears alone, but with all sorts of other things like mental habits, memory, imagination, feeling, and . . . will." He appeals to modern physics, which recognizes that the act of observation modifies what is observed; thus we condition our view of what we call reality. This process, of constructing the world from raw sense data interpreted by the mind, he calls *figuration*. So far, Barfield's account is largely uncontroversial, resting squarely upon Kant's insistence that we cannot get hold of the "thing-in-itself."

Ever the evolutionist, however, Barfield takes a further step: he argues that figuration changes over time. "Primitives"—a term that he leaves largely undefined—experienced the world differently from us; they apprehended it through what Barfield calls *original participation*, an intimate, extrasensory connection with the phenomena around them. Primitives were closely linked to the reality they perceive. This gave them a spiritual awareness that we have lost, a knowledge that beyond the phenomenal world (beyond collective representations) lies something deeply mysterious—a life force, gods, God—to which we are profoundly related.

With us moderns it is different. Human consciousness has evolved and original participation has vanished, replaced by morbid self-consciousness and distancing from the world around us. We experience our collective representations (the world as we know it) as disconnected and remote from ourselves. We believe in a world *out there*, open to scientific investigation. Here Barfield adds another term to his specialized vocabulary, calling this kind of investigation *alpha-thinking*. For Barfield, alpha-thinking is fundamentally flawed, even delusional, leading to patent falsehoods, most notably in our account of evolution: "It can do no harm to recall occasionally that the prehistoric evolution of the earth, as it is described for example in the early chapters of H. G. Wells's *The Outline of History*, was not merely never seen. It never occurred." When Wells, or any modern scientist, describes the events of prehistory—the formation of the solar system, the appearance of life on earth, the rise of trilobites and dinosaurs, and so on—what he recounts is not what *really* happened, but rather what a modern person, with a modern person's cramped, detached, self-conscious mode of figuration, would have perceived as happening if he or she had been a witness to prehistory. If a "primitive," the possessor of an entirely different set of collective representations, had witnessed the same events, "we should then have to write a different pre-history altogether."

This is, of course, a wholesale rejection of almost all of modern science and its findings. Barfield's objections apply equally well to disciplines other than prehistory. In astronomy, for example, experts predicate conditions in other galaxies upon data received and interpreted through modern modes of figuration. Are we, then, trapped in an illusory universe—a universe of idols, as Barfield puts it? Is everything we know a lie? For Barfield, the startling answer, to a considerable degree, is yes.

There are, however, signs that humanity is awakening from its long, troubled collective dream. The recognition of the observer effect in quantum mechanics gives hope. We now face a choice between idolatry—enslavement to our common representations—and a conscious effort to awaken a new form of participation, *final participation*, through which, by means of "goodness of heart and a steady furnace in the will," we will heal our perceptions and cultivate a renewed awareness of God. This forthcoming state of consciousness will truly "save the appearances."

Barfield's spiritual reading of evolution, presented more lyrically and succinctly than ever before in *Saving the Appearances*, stands far outside the main current of modern thought. Few readers will rush to accept his radical rejection of orthodox science, epitomized by his scorn for standard accounts of prehistory; as he himself observes, the views of quantum physicists on the role of the observer have not been adopted by most other scientists, much less the world at large, which remains wedded to dualistic subject-object epistemology. Nor will many embrace his account of final participation, a state of consciousness brought into play, for each of us, via personal *metanoia* unfolding through successive reincarnations. Like other esoteric accounts of the world, Barfield's spins in its own orbit, attracting the occasional adventurer into its eccentric field of influence but having little or no effect upon the masses. At the same time, it possesses its own coherence, internal logic, and beauty, incorporating some of humankind's greatest religious myths—a past golden age, a present tribulation, a future new heaven and new earth— into a strange but lovely narrative, in which the powers of the imagination (in the exact Blakean sense of perceiving invisible realities) may yet save the world. As such, it takes its place, at the very least, as a remarkable example of mid-twentieth-century apocalyptic, a modern philosophical prose variant of Blake's *Jerusalem*. For its author, it was a definitive breakthrough, a regrouping and expansion of scattered talents, a return to the battlefield, a harbinger of things to come.

Saving the Appearances attracted few reviews; Barfield had been out of the literary scene far too long for his work to draw notice. The fullest response came from a clearly dissatisfied Lewis, who read the work in manuscript. He declared it "full (of course) of sap and strength, and v. much yours," then added several pages pinpointing its weaknesses, leavened by the occasional "splendid" and "V. good." When the book appeared in print, he told Barfield that it was a "stunner" but offered no further analysis. T. S. Eliot, on the other hand, wrote Barfield, three years after publication, to declare his "very high opinion" of the book, which he thought "too profound for our feeble generation of critics." Barfield would later tell Valerie Eliot (the poet's wife) that he valued this letter "highly."

Sufferings and Celebrations

"I am feeling as flat as a burst tyre," Tolkien had written to Naomi Mitchison in mid-1955. He was referring to his immediate workload at the time, especially his lecturing and the burden of shepherding *The Return of the King* into print, but the hyperbolic metaphor depicts fairly his state not only then but in ensuing years. He was becoming an old man, quit of his great work, feeling his creative energies dwindle. He marveled at his achievement and increasingly worried about his legacy. "[My] chief biographical fact," he wrote to a fan, ". . . is the completion of *The Lord of the Rings*, which still astonishes me . . . I still wonder how and why I managed to peg away at this thing year after year, often under real difficulties, and bring it to a conclusion. I suppose, because from the beginning it began to catch up in its narrative folds visions of most of the things that I have most loved or hated." He would spend his remaining years elucidating to family, friends, and readers, in a vast epistolary torrent, the intricacies of these narrative folds, guiding others to see his masterpiece as he did and to share in his hates and loves.

Taken en masse, Tolkien's late letters constitute his *Apologia pro vita sua*. Gripping, generous (he would answer complete strangers at great length), revelatory in their exposition of a Catholic aesthetic built upon Mary and the Eucharist, and obsessive, almost balmy, in their attention to the minutest details of Middle-earth history, folklore, geography, archaeology, linguistics, and mores, they become a platform on which Tolkien corrected misreadings of his texts, misunderstandings of his aims, and misconceptions about his life. The task was prodigious. One example—there are scores—concerned the Swedish translator of *The Lord of the Rings*, who gave Hobbits "*feathery*" soles, compared the book to Wagner's Ring, and invented fanciful tales of Tolkien walking the Welsh borderlands during his youth. The outraged author wrote to Allen & Unwin, decrying the first error as "absurd," the second as "a farrago of nonsense," and answering the third with a shout that many a celebrated author would gladly echo: "Why must I be made an object of fiction while still alive?"

The letters let off steam while correcting the record, but they also consumed Tolkien's time and impeded his creativity. He published no new fiction for years, although "Imram," a poem based on St. Brendan's mythical voyages and dating, in its original version, to *The Notion Club Papers*, appeared in *Time and Tide* in December 1955. He continued to rewrite *The Silmarillion*, expanding or contracting earlier tales, deepening the theological subcurrents, resolving vexing problems regarding the nature, power, and destiny of Melkor, Elves, Men, and Orcs. But all this work remained, for the time, unpublished, and he complained to Rayner Unwin about the difficulty of finding time for the project. Unwin wanted to publish *The Silmarillion* more than ever, anticipating good sales on the coattails of *Lord*'s success, but he harbored reservations about the portions he had seen so far. On New Year's Eve of 1957, he warned the author that he found the text "a bit uncompromising for the general reader," with a "somewhat undigested form" that reminded him of the Book of Numbers, and that he was "not attracted by the rather rudimentary narrative form . . . nor of the variable archaism of language . . . [which] gave a somewhat precious feeling to the narrative." The ameliorating adverbs cushioned the blow without disguising the message: Tolkien's publishers were deeply worried about the future of their bestselling author's most personal and long-lived project.

Tolkien had no intention of giving up on *The Silmarillion*. Still, Unwin's letter must have stung badly, and soon after receiving it, instead of diving back into his rewrite, he put it aside to attempt a sequel to *The Lord of the Rings*. He labored on *The New Shadow* sporadically from the late 1950s until at least 1968. Only a handful of pages resulted, with three separate versions of an aborted tale about secret societies, underground plots, and adolescent "orc-cults." The extant fragments exude a brooding Augustinianism, not only in their unrelenting sense of ancient evil pressing in from all sides, but in their adaptation of the most famous story of Augustine's childhood, in which the future saint and his companions wantonly eat stolen pears to satiety and beyond; here a group of boys, pretending to be Orcs, strip an orchard of unripe apples out of sheer perversity. Tolkien, unable to control the text, watched it turn in directions "sinister and depressing" and concluded the tale was "not worth doing." His great tale of Hobbits and Elves, Wizards, and Men had already been told; only the dregs remained. Ten or twenty years earlier, he might have pulled it off, but age and illness had taken their toll.

Both he and Edith suffered from ill health during the tail end of the 1950s. Edith, beset by arthritis and rheumatism, required regular medical attention. In February 1958, she underwent a serious operation, requiring lengthy recuperation in a nursing home and then in Bournemouth. That autumn she fell and broke her arm, requiring Tolkien to rescind a promise to write a ten-thousand-word essay for the British

Council on *Beowulf*. A few months later, he fainted from weariness and stress. Doctors ordered him into a nursing home, but instead he returned to Bournemouth with Edith for additional rest. He complained, during these years, of a medley of aches and pains. Almost certainly some of his ailments were psychosomatic; Rayner Unwin observed that "sometimes the less specific complaints seem to have been associated with worry." He believed, however, that the source was usually a recognizable illness or injury. "His catalogue of physical woes grew year by year," said Unwin. "As his retirement approached there was a crescendo, and thereafter illness was never far away . . . None of these ailments were life-threatening, but they were certainly distractions."

Another unwelcome diversion came in the form of a plan, floated in 1957 by the Californian science fiction and horror entrepreneur Forrest J. Ackerman (who would go on to found *Famous Monsters of Filmland*, a garish magazine beloved by generations of American boys), to mount a cartoon version of *The Lord of the Rings*. At first Tolkien approved, largely for "the glint of money" it portended, but he balked upon seeing the written treatment, which wreaked havoc upon the book. A series of angry letters ensued, in which he denounced the proposed version in devastating detail: "Why does Z [the screenwriter] put beaks and feathers on *Orcs*!? (*Orcs* is not a form of *Auks*.)" In 1959, having destroyed Tolkien's equanimity and consumed much of his free time, Ackerman abandoned the project.

During this creatively fallow period, Tolkien traveled three more times to Ireland. His 1958 sojourn proved especially exhausting, providing fodder for a litany of complaints sent by Tolkien to Robert Burchfield, a linguist and lexicographer whose D.Phil. he had supervised: "On Sept. 24 I was involved in an alarming tempest at sea, and began to think I should suffer the fate of Lycidas King. I arrived 5 hours overdue in Dublin at noon on 25, rather battered; and I have since crossed Eire (E-W and N-S) about 6 times, read 130 lb. (avd) of theses, assisted in the exams of 4 colleges, and finally presided at fellowship-vivas in Dublin before re-embarking (doubled up with lumbago)." He also hoped, around this time, to visit Marquette University in Milwaukee, Wisconsin, a Jesuit institution that had just purchased, for £1500, the manuscripts of *The Hobbit*, *The Lord of the Rings*, *Mr. Bliss*, and *Farmer Giles of Ham*, and had offered him $600 per lecture plus travel expenses. But he was forced to scuttle the arrangement, pleading illness and exhaustion, and he never did manage to visit America.

In spite of these problems, gratifications multiplied. *The Lord of the Rings* sold well, and the Tolkiens' lifelong concern about money abated. In April 1957, Tolkien was elected to the Royal Society of Literature, and in August *The Lord of the Rings* won the International Fantasy Award, besting future Nobel Prize winner William Golding's *Lord of the Flies*, along with John Christopher's *The Death of Grass*. At the festive awards lunch, Tolkien received what he described to Christopher and his first wife, Faith, as "a massive metal 'model' of an upended Space-rocket (combined with a Ronson lighter)." The clunky trophy amused him; his fame was spreading. The following spring, he sailed to Rotterdam for a "Hobbit Dinner," sponsored by Dutch booksellers and attended by over two hundred fans, featuring clay pipes and pipe-weed, "maggot-soup," "Fricandeau À La Gimli" (it was Friday, but the Rotterdam Catholic diocese had released the guests from the meatless Friday rule), and an avalanche of laudatory speeches, capped by remarks by Tolkien in English, Dutch, and Elvish. He found the event "remarkable" and "extremely enjoyable."

Further enhancing his happiness, and Edith's as well, their children had matured into flourishing adulthood. John, now a Catholic priest, settled down to parish life in Stoke-on-Trent; Michael was married with three children; Priscilla had acquired certificates in social science and applied social studies at the London School of Economics. Christopher, pursuing a modified version of his father's academic path, had become a lecturer and tutor in English at Oxford. In 1958 he delivered a talk on "Barbarians and Citizens," suffusing his father with "great delight" and "parental pride"; the latter, Tolkien hastened to tell his son, was "a legitimate satisfaction with the least possible of egotism in it." A few years later, Christopher published a translation of the Icelandic *Saga of King Heidrek the Wise*; he had become, like many another Inkling, a full-fledged Nordophile.

Tolkien derived pleasure, too, from a project that fell unexpectedly into his lap in early 1957. At the end of January, Fr. Alexander Jones, an admirer of *The Lord of the Rings*, wrote to ask if Tolkien would be willing to join the translation team for *The Jerusalem Bible*, a new Catholic English translation of scripture for which Jones was the overall editor.

The translation was to be drawn in part from an existing French version and in part from original Hebrew and Greek texts. Tolkien disliked French for its phonological and structural hauteur; he also blamed it for contaminating Old English after the Norman invasion; but he read it well enough and couldn't pass up the opportunity to contribute to what would become the basis of the English Lectionary of the Mass for decades to come. He dashed off a translation of Isaiah 1:1–31 to Father Jones to indicate his level of competency. Father Jones, delighted with the result, asked Tolkien to tackle the Book of Jonah, a short text that he completed in about two weeks.

Tolkien then offered to try his hand at Joshua, Judges, and a few other texts, but nothing came of this. According to Father Jones's nephew, the philosopher Anthony Kenny, Tolkien was a "difficult collaborator"; Tolkien himself ascribed his failure to translate other texts to overwork. When published in 1966, *The Jerusalem Bible* received mixed reviews. Critics applauded its literary felicities while questioning, inter alia, the unfortunate use of "Yahweh," a vocalization of the Hebrew tetragrammaton (YHWH), considered sacrilegious by many and, since 2008, forbidden in Catholic liturgical services, as well as the decision to jettison the exquisite traditional greeting of Gabriel to the Virgin, "Hail [Mary], Full of Grace," in favor of the more literal but disconcertingly Cecil DeMille–esque "Rejoice, so highly favored!" Tolkien's Jonah translation adheres closely to the original but is curiously sedate; compare his rendition of Jonah 2:9, "the vow I have made, I will fulfil / Salvation comes from Yahweh" to the Revised Standard Version's "What I have vowed I will pay. Deliverance belongs to the LORD!"

A Live Dinosaur

"Yesterday I went up to Cambridge for Jack's inaugural address—there was damn near as much fuss about that as a Coronation," wrote Joy to Bill Gresham on November 30, 1954. "I lurked modestly in the crowd and didn't go near him—he was walled about with caps and gowns and yards of recording apparatus. A great success . . . I don't know how the dons liked it but the students ate it up. But I think, for once, he was sacrificing accuracy in the interests of a good show."

Lewis put on more than a good show: his talk, *"De Descriptione Temporum"* ("On the Description of Times"), was audacious, original, and contrarian. His argument was that the commonly held classification of historical periods into Antiquity, the Dark Ages, the Middle Ages, the Renaissance—epochs divided by frontiers or chasms—is "greatly exaggerated, if indeed it was not a figment of Humanist propaganda." Though such sharp demarcations, Lewis grudgingly concedes, can be useful, even necessary, for the convenience of professional historians (he is, after all, the first occupant of the new Chair in Medieval and Renaissance Literature), it is far more important to recognize the cultural, religious, and ethical continuity (or "continuity-in-mutability") of "Old Western Culture." There is, however, one genuinely cataclysmic break in the historical record, one division between eras that must be acknowledged: this fault line cuts across the early nineteenth century, immediately following the time of Jane Austen and Walter Scott, isolating all that comes after—the Victorians, the Edwardians, all that we call modern or postmodern—from all that came before: "somewhere between us and the Waverly Novels, somewhere between us and *Persuasion*, the chasm runs."

Lewis begins assembling his evidence for this extraordinary claim with a look at poetry. In the past, poems, even difficult ones, could be readily understood; readers agreed on what they meant. But now poetry has gone adrift. Consider, Lewis says, a recent symposium of seven experts—two of them Cambridge scholars—that had assembled to analyze the little poem "A Cooking Egg" by T. S. Eliot. The experts could find "not the slightest agreement among them as to what, in any sense of the word, it means." Modern poetry's rejection of meaning is, Lewis argues, unprecedented "in the whole history of the West," comparable only to a similar revolution in the visual arts, exemplified by Cubism, Surrealism, Dadaism, and the work of Picasso. Lewis perceives, too, a parallel disruption in the history of religion, manifested by the split between Christian and post-Christian cultures. But these examples pale beside what Lewis calls his "trump card": the nineteenth-century emergence of industrialization, with its obsequious worship of progress, its enthrallment to "a new archetypal image . . . of old machines being superseded by newer and better ones." The rise of the machines—one hears echoes of Tolkien's great fear—spells the fall of tradition. Today new trumps old;

future, past; change, permanence; and "the very milestones of life are technical advances."

"De Descriptione Temporum" heralds, with vigor and wit, a tectonic shift in our understanding of history. For the assembled scholars squirming in their seats, many of whom had devoted their lives to detailing that old historical outline that the lecturer had just erased, this was inflammatory enough. Lewis proceeded to heap salt on the wound, however, by situating himself on the wrong side of his new map of the past. "I myself belong," he told the Cambridge guardians of conventional wisdom, "far more to that Old Western order than to yours." This was, he hastened to add, not a drawback but a golden opportunity. "If a live dinosaur dragged its slow length into the laboratory, would we not all look back as we fled? What a chance to know at last how it really moved and looked and smelled and what noises it made!" Henceforth, Lewis would be the dinosaur in Cambridge's laboratory, the antiquated spokesman of a rejected past—and he would do this, paradoxically, by being the revolutionary creator of a new vision of time—and thus a thing as rare and precious as any living fossil. "Use your specimens while you can," he exhorted the crowd, digging the knife in a little deeper. "There are not going to be many more dinosaurs."

Lewis was pleased with his talk and agreed to repeat it on the BBC's Third Programme (calling it "The Great Divide") the following April. Joy told Chad Walsh that "it was brilliant, intellectually exciting, unexpected, and funny as hell . . . Athanasius contra mundum, or Don Quixote against the windmills." Others demurred. Secular humanists on the Cambridge faculty began to panic over the presence in their midst of so many prominent Christians, who now included David Knowles, exclaustrated Benedictine monk and scholar of monastic history; Basil Willey, professor of English and author of *Christianity Past and Present*; and Herbert Butterfield, fellow of Peterhouse College, who in *The Origins of Modern Science, 1300–1800* anticipated Lewis's theory of history by proposing that the Renaissance and Reformation were "mere episodes, mere internal displacements, within the system of medieval Christendom." Marshaling their forces, the combined opposition struck back through *The Twentieth Century*, a humanist journal that devoted its February 1955 issue to deploring Lewis's talk and all that it represented.

E. M. Forster led the charge. Earlier, during a World War II radio talk, Forster had called Lewis "as clever as they make 'em," comparing him to Chesterton. But the celebrated novelist no longer cared—if he ever had—for Lewis's brand of cleverness and now warned, in his soft, elegant Bloomsbury manner with its undercurrent of despair, of the incoming tide of "obscurantism" and "authoritarian fundamentalism" threatening intellectual and social life. He singled out Lewis, and perhaps Butterfield, as the culprits, noting that things had degenerated so far that humanism's "stronghold in history, the Renaissance, is alleged not to have existed." Lewis shrugged off the broadside in a note to Ruth Pitter on March 5, charging that these self-proclaimed humanists were really atheists and that Forster was "the silliest of the lot." In a letter to the mystery novelist Katharine Farrer a month later, Lewis again lambasted Forster, this time as one of those "high-minded old twaddlers" who think paganism would be a splendid thing. In the April 1955 issue of *The Twentieth Century*, he delivered his own broadside against the humanist idolatry of culture (and misuse of "humanism," a word that once had real meaning). He was relishing the combat.

Lewis felt at home in Cambridge. At Oxford, he had been a celebrity without honors; his new university, aware of the slight, granted him not only a professorship but superb fifteenth-century rooms in Magdalene College's Old Court. He moved in on January 7, 1955. He was cautious at first, feeling out his new surroundings; Richard W. Ladborough, a lecturer in French who would eventually become Lewis's closest friend at Cambridge, found him shy and insecure and, as a result, too eager to showcase his brilliance. But as this phase passed, Lewis made friends and settled into a comfortable daily round: an early walk in the Fellow's Garden, chapel matins at 8:00 a.m., breakfast, letter writing, lunch, work on essays and books, an afternoon ramble, dinner in the Senior Common Room, more writing, and evening tea. His responsibilities included lecturing on medieval cosmology, religion, and literature, on the nature and meaning of words, on Spenser.

In addition, Lewis shouldered numerous administrative chores, from supervising graduate research to serving on prize and appointment committees and the faculty board—the sort of academic busywork that Tolkien had come to abhor but that Lewis, formerly a mere don, had rarely tasted. This manifold activity brought him into frequent contact with F. R. Leavis. In 1956, Lewis backed Leavis for the faculty board in English, a magnanimous gesture that hid a cunning if benevolent agenda: Lewis wrote Basil Willey about his "wild idea of Leavis," asking, "Is it just possible that if his nose were once rubbed in the actual working of the Faculty, if he were once the target of criticism instead of the critic, he might be cured? Of course we should suffer: but then we suffer already. I know it's risky: but malcontents have before now been tamed by office." But it was not to be.

Lewis's was, in many ways, a nearly ideal bachelor existence, made even better by the weekly run to Oxford. Every available weekend and vacation, he would return to the Kilns. To accommodate his schedule, the Inklings obligingly moved their meetings to Monday mornings, after which Lewis would stroll to the train station, accompanied often by Havard and others, to catch the 2:34 back to Cambridge. Sometimes one or more of his companions would ride with him for dinner and an overnight stay at Magdalene, before returning to Oxford on Tuesday morning.

The incessant travel and change in vista did nothing to impede Lewis's literary output. During his time at Cambridge, he published at least a dozen books, including his autobiography, occasional essays, studies of love, words, reading, and the psalms, along with children's fantasies and a novel. Warnie, too, benefited from the change, at least in terms of output, and took advantage of the empty hours created by his brother's absence to establish himself more firmly as a historian of sixteenth- and early seventeenth-century France with a prodigious flow of biographies and cultural studies, all bearing enticing titles like *The Sunset of the Splendid Century* (1955), *Assault on Olympus* (1958), *Louis XIV: An Informal Portrait* (1959), *The Scandalous Regent* (1961), and *Levantine Adventurer* (1962). He wrote daily in the Kilns's study, while complaining about the irritation of "hearing Paxford bellowing about the place all day." Warnie missed the sheltered silence of Magdalen and, of course, Jack's daily presence, but he believed that his brother was "undoubtedly happier and healthier" in his new environment and, in retrospect, should have chosen Cambridge over Oxford upon his return from World War I, for, despite their reputations, "it is not Cambridge, but Oxford which is the hardboiled materialistic, scientific university."

One of the more unexpected of Lewis's literary productions, during his Cambridge years, was his 1956 novel, *Till We Have Faces*, a retelling of the Cupid and Psyche tale from Apuleius's second-century Latin fantasy, *The Golden Ass*. It is the most controversial of Lewis's fictions, intensely disliked by many of his readers, extravagantly praised by a few, an anomaly among his works with its female narrator, its bleak landscapes, its bitter, ironic tone—more than a few passages might have come from Camus or Sartre—its complex plot, its cultivated obscurities, and its uncertain conclusion. Lewis was aware of the adverse reaction: "A complete flop, the worst flop I've ever had," he described it to a former pupil on August 8, 1959, and a year later, writing to thank Anne Scott (a former pupil and a good friend of Charles Williams) for her appreciative words, he confessed that, while he regarded *Till We Have Faces* as "far and away the best I have written," he still ranked it as "my one big failure both with the critics and with the public."

The book had a protracted and difficult gestation. Lewis began re-tooling the myth (which he believed predated Apuleius's version) while still an undergraduate; by the time it appeared in print, as he wrote in the first edition, he had "worked at it most of his life." The breakthrough came in the spring of 1955, when Joy was visiting at the Kilns and, in her words, she and Lewis "kicked a few ideas around till one came to light. Then we had another whisky each and bounced it back and forth between us." In *The Golden Ass*, Psyche, the youngest and most beautiful of three daughters, falls in love with an unseen god (Cupid), breaks her promise never to look at his face, and consequently undergoes a series of punishing trials, which ends when Cupid forgives her and Jupiter makes her a goddess. In Lewis's novel, the focus shifts from Psyche to her oldest sister, Orual, queen of the drought-and-plague-ridden land of Glome. Orual, ugly but brilliant, narrates the tale, which amounts to her indictment of the gods, who bring us happiness only "when they are preparing some new agony. We are their bubbles; they blow us big before they prick us." Orual is consumed by anger, resentment, and jealousy; where Psyche sees the palace of the god, she sees only barrenness; Orual's spiritual blindness leads to great suffering for both herself and her sister. The situation, Lewis told Katharine Farrer, is comparable to that of "every nice, affectionate agnostic whose dearest one suddenly 'gets religion,' or even every luke warm Christian whose dearest gets a Vocation." At the end,

Orual acquires enough wisdom to understand that God does not reveal himself or his motives readily; directly addressing God, she concedes that "I know now, Lord, why you utter no answer. You are yourself the answer. Before your face questions die away." In her impotence and queenly power, her self-love and self-hate, her consuming rage and final understanding, she is Lewis's most completely realized character, male or female. And yet the book's presiding darkness and relentless melancholy make it a struggle to read and nearly impossible to cherish. "Most reviewers," observed Walter Hooper, "had difficulty understanding the book." Even T. H. White—a writer deeply sympathetic to modern retellings of ancient myth—caviled over Lewis's "mumbo-jumbo." *Till We Have Faces* remains, for all its brilliances, the Lewis novel most readers turn to last and slog through with grudging admiration.

By mid-March 1955, Lewis had also finished *Surprised by Joy*, and sent it to Jocelyn Gibb, managing director at Geoffrey Bles and a devoted custodian of Lewis's publishing career, to check for libel risk. The title came from Wordsworth: "Surprised by Joy—impatient as the Wind." It was not an autobiography so much as a spiritual testament, written, Lewis said, "partly in answer to requests that I would tell how I passed from Atheism to Christianity and partly to correct one or two false notions that seem to have got about."

The path to writing *Surprised by Joy* was well grooved. In *The Pilgrim's Regress*, Lewis had already allegorized his conversion, and in the process worked out everything he would ever want to say on the subject of Joy. In his imaginative fiction, Lewis had made preliminary sketches of several memorable characters and themes; as we have seen, Kirkpatrick would step into a role already prepared for him in the Ransom trilogy and *The Lion, the Witch, and the Wardrobe*. Lewis's favorite arguments for the existence of God—from morality and from reason—accompanied by his favorite Romantic theme, the "dialectic of desire," are present throughout the narrative of his adolescent moral agonies, his discovery of sound reasoning, and his longing for an elusive Joy. A series of tableaux fans out like a Tarot deck: the first stab of beauty in the biscuit-tin garden, the Green Hills beyond the nursery window, the "long corridors, empty sunlit rooms, upstairs indoor silences, attics explored in solitude, distant noises of gurgling cisterns and pipes" and endless books; the flowering currant bush, *Squirrel Nutkin*, and "Tégner's Drapa"; the nightmare sounds and smells of his mother's dying; the miseries of bad teeth and physical clumsiness; his father's follies, fits, and "wheezes"; friends, bullies, and idols at school; Joy receding and then returning on wings of Northernness; the deliverance by Kirkpatrick; the discovery of Arthur ("'Do *you* like that?'"); the encounter with Barfield, "as fascinating (and infuriating) as a woman"; Oxford and war; and finally a succession of philosophical worldviews attempted and abandoned; leading to the picture of Lewis on his knees, checkmated by "My Adversary"—"the most dejected and reluctant convert in all England."

Many readers were puzzled by the disproportionate attention Lewis gave to his boyhood, the searing light shone on his besetting sins, the comparative neglect of his wartime experience and his romantic entanglements, and the abrupt, unsentimental ending. As Dorothy L. Sayers noted in her review for *Time and Tide*, the "latter stages of that journey, from Rationalism, through Philosophic Idealism and Pantheism, to Theism and finally to Christianity, are . . . related with a businesslike brevity." But it was by no means Lewis's intention to pour his experiences uncensored onto the page; the book is, rather, a carefully shaped literary meditation, much like Augustine's *Confessions*, though Lewis declined the comparison; and like the *Confessions*, its theme is the disordering and reordering of desire. "In a sense," Lewis said, "the central story of my life is about nothing else." Had Lewis been a less gifted memoirist, *Surprised by Joy* would have followed the dialectic of desire along conventional lines, as a journey from experience to experience in search of God. Instead, Lewis opted to make himself the object of God's pursuit, so that he could say, with Chesterton, "I am the fool of this story." He falters, though, Sayers noted, in introducing his "hound of heaven" theme too peremptorily at the end.

These minor flaws notwithstanding, *Surprised by Joy* is a spiritual masterpiece and enjoyed a warm reception in the mainstream and church press. The Anglican poet Norman Cornthwaite Nicholson, reviewing it in *The Times Literary Supplement*, was thrilled by the chess-game ending: "God moves, indeed, in a mysterious way, and this book gives a brilliant account of one of the oddest and most decisive end-games He has ever played." Praising the "delightful and humorous candour" of *Surprised by Joy*, Sayers concluded her review by saying, "The limpidity of these waters may disguise their depth, so clearly do they reveal the bottom. But any illusions about this can be quickly dispelled by stepping into the river."

The Sweet Humiliation of Incarnation

Despite the manifold pleasures of Cambridge, Lewis's heart remained in Oxford. Nostalgia was not the cause. He had little interest in memories for their own sake; in writing *Surprised by Joy*, he had revisited the past not for the pleasure of reminiscence but to understand for himself and to convey to others a conversion that was still unfolding. Even Charles Williams, for most of the Inklings little more now than a fading set of images and words, remained for Lewis a living event, someone whose presence in eternity had become a central fact of his own Christian faith.

He cared for Oxford, in part, because Warnie lived there. The fraternal bond had never frayed, despite the strain of Warnie's drinking and his own departure to Cambridge. The presence of other Inklings counted, too. But the real reason for his undying attachment to this city was Joy Davidman, who had worked (some would say wormed) her way into his life and was now awakening in him, not just affection, but love. A watershed arrived in late summer 1955, when she and her two boys moved from London to Headington, passing a hot August at the Kilns—she could see nearby stucco houses "shimmering in the heat haze on a cloudless day"—and then, in September, settling about a mile away at 10 Old High Street, a drab semidetached house with a pleasant garden producing tomatoes and cabbages, apples and plums. There she patched together a small income from typing, checks sent by Bill, and the rare small advance from her agent. It wasn't enough, but this didn't really matter, as Lewis paid the rent and helped with other expenses. He visited her every day and often stayed until late in the evening. A casual onlooker might have assumed that Joy was Lewis's mistress; this onlooker could not know that, given the couple's mutually reinforced Christian principles, the relationship was chaste, nor that Lewis, who had almost no extended experience of women apart from Mrs. Moore, was feeling his way like a blind man beginning to see. Eva Walsh, who had visited Lewis with her husband, Chad, during the summer, "smelled marriage in the air." To Warnie, "it was now obvious what was going to happen."

Happen it did, a few months later, after the British Home Office denied Joy a renewal of her visa. (According to Sheldon Vanauken, an American friend of Lewis, this was because of Joy's Communist background.) Deportation loomed—unless she married a British citizen. Lewis, who had anticipated the quandary, made swift arrangements, and on April 23, 1956, he and Joy were married at the Oxford Registry Office. In Lewis's mind, the wedding was no more than an official convenience, a ceremony doubling as a visa stamp. He informed few friends (and no Inklings apart from Warnie) of the event, assuring those in the know that things remained as before, that he and Joy had married in name only and would retain separate addresses and lives. Warnie, a wily observer of human motives, knew better. He noted that "Joy, whose intentions were obvious from the outset, soon began to press for her rights." By now he felt great affection for this boisterous American, whose warm informality and cutting intelligence he enjoyed as much as his brother did. But the irony of the situation—Joy as the new, albeit more favored, Mrs. Moore—did not escape him, and he remarked that "the gap between the end of the Ancien Regime and the Restoration had lasted for less than four years."

Joy, just turned forty-one, basked in her new marital status, the end of eight years of upheaval, the culmination—perhaps—of eight years of planning. Lewis continued to visit her at 10 Old High Street but, worried about neighborhood gossip, soon agreed that she and the boys should move into the Kilns. Meanwhile, Joy worked on a new book, *The Seven Deadly Virtues*, but made snail-like progress. She doubted its worth and had written Bill Gresham to ask, "How did I get into this theology racket anyway? The trouble is that while I like Christianity well enough, I hate Churchianity." History seemed a viable alternative, and she researched a life of Madame de Maintenon, Louis XIV's second wife, tentatively entitled *Queen Cinderella*, but this project made little headway also. The problem lay in a mismatch between her talents and her chosen subjects. Her novels, although dotted with religious imagery, reveal her real strength to lie in raw, rich portraits of village life. She switched to theology under Lewis's spell, while the idea for a book on Madame de Maintenon came from Warnie, who originally proposed it as a collaboration. But if Joy's literary career took a wrong turn when she encountered the Lewis brothers, the sacrifice paled beside the reward. She was Lewis's wife and would soon become his housemate, and she and Warnie enjoyed a warm, merry friendship, admiring one another and loving the same man.

Meanwhile, Joy's circle of friends enlarged. The Inklings continued to avoid her, rudely and blatantly, but those among Lewis's intimates who had been told of the marriage welcomed her, especially Katharine Farrer and her theologian husband, Austin Farrer. Joy landed a job typing Katharine's latest mystery novel, *Gownsman's Gallows*. She started to make her mark on the university community; in February, she had addressed undergraduates on Charles Williams and had the students doubled over with laughter. Her family was blossoming, especially David, who was learning to read the Greek New Testament under Lewis's enthusiastic tutelage. To crown this burgeoning happiness, Lewis approached the Bishop of Oxford—Harry James Carpenter, father of the future biographer Humphrey Carpenter—for permission to be wed in the Church of England. Previously, Lewis had rejected such a marriage, believing, in keeping with ancient Christian tradition, that Joy, as a divorcée, could not remarry. But he had reassessed the situation and now believed that Joy's first marriage had been invalid, as Bill had been married and divorced before marrying her, and that therefore she was free to marry in the church. Bishop Carpenter disagreed, however, and the matter was dropped for now.

A professorship, a wife, a surfeit of love, a season of glorious fecundity during which Lewis had published *Surprised by Joy*, *Till We Have Faces*, *The Magician's Nephew*, and *The Last Battle*, the latter completing the Chronicles of Narnia, and was now hard at work on several more projects. He had rarely been happier. In August 1956, leaving Joy in Oxford, he and Warnie vacationed in Ireland, staying at a bungalow in a "place of unearthly beauty," across a bay from "the most fairy-tale mountains you cd. ask for." He then joined up with Arthur in Donegal, "a v. fine, wild country with green mountains, rich secretive valleys, and Atlantic breakers on innumerable desolate sands." Hidden valleys, mysterious mountains; Lewis now was seeing life as a fulfilled fairy tale. He returned to England in mid-September. A month later, he found himself charmed by a season tinged by magic: "a 'St. Luke's summer': which means autumn at its very best—warm, coloured days, but cold nights, and usually misty mornings, every cobweb on the hedge turned into a necklace by the heavy dew." The idyll ended, as idylls must. On October 18, the same day that Lewis was reveling in "autumn at its very best," Joy tripped over a telephone wire and was unable to get up. She had been suffering from hip aches, which she attributed to rheumatism, but the fall opened a new abyss of pain. "I have got something really hellish the matter with my left hip and am being carted off to the hospital this afternoon on a stretcher," she managed to write Bill. In Wingfield-Morris Orthopaedic Hospital, an old Headington army clinic, doctors discovered cancer in her left femur, left breast, right shoulder, and right leg. "The X-rays showed the bone looking 'moth-eaten,'" she told Bill, "and they are talking of carcinomas or leukemia. In short, it is fairly probable that I am going to die." She was only forty-one.

Joy underwent radiation and three operations, during which doctors removed her ovaries and a small tumor in her breast and patched up her femur. "I never have loved her more than since she was struck down," wrote Warnie, putting the best possible face on the nightmare. "Her pluck and cheerfulness are beyond praise, and she talks of her disease and its fluctuations as if she was describing the experiences of a friend of hers." The truth is that during these months of treatment, Joy shuttled headlong between hope and despair, now trusting in the radiation to work a cure, now praying for grace, now feeling the grave close in, now undergoing "physical agony . . . combined with a strange spiritual ecstasy," so that she knew "how martyrs felt." When the radiation therapy failed, the demon of doubt wreaked havoc: "I am trying very hard to hold on to my faith, but I find it difficult; there seems such a gratuitous and merciless cruelty in this." Lewis, however, refused to give up. He contacted Peter W. Bide, a former pupil of his, an Anglican priest in Sussex with a reputation as a faith healer, and asked him to visit Joy and perform a laying on of hands. When Bide arrived in Headington, Lewis immediately raised the possibility of a Christian wedding. Bide—a theological liberal—complied, thereby violating church regulations in what Warnie described as "a notable act of charity, for he is not of this Diocese, and had no right to do so without the Bp's authority." The wedding took place at 11:00 a.m. on March 21, 1957, at Joy's hospital bedside. "I found it heartrending," Warnie wrote, "and especially Joy's eagerness for the pitiable consolation of dying under the same roof as J: though to feel pity for anyone so magnificently brave as Joy is almost an insult."

The laying on of hands took place the same day. It proved but an early stage in Lewis's quest for a miraculous cure. He began to pray that he might be allowed to assume Joy's pain, in the sort of substitutionary miracle that Charles Williams had taught his followers to seek. Shortly after initiating these prayers, Lewis came down with osteoporosis—not an uncommon problem, especially among those who smoke heavily and weigh too much, as Lewis did. More puzzling was the simultaneous improvement in Joy's condition. According to Nevill Coghill, hardly the most gullible of men, Lewis's disease and Joy's healing both issued from Lewis's substitutionary action. It was, Coghill later reported, "a power which Lewis found himself . . . to possess, and which, he told me, he had been allowed to use to ease the suffering of his wife, a cancer victim, of whom the doctors had despaired." Coghill asked him point-blank, "You mean that her pain left her, and that you felt it for her in your body?" Lewis replied, "Yes, in my legs. It was crippling. But it relieved hers." At times the pain was so bad that Lewis screamed. He ceased his beloved rambles and took to wearing a surgical belt, a sort of corset that, he joked, "gives me a wonderfully youthful figure." Photos of him and Joy taken at the time reveal the ravages of illness on both their faces; Lewis described one such image, which appeared in *The Observer*, as "a spiritualist picture of the ectoplasms of a dyspeptic orangutan and an immature Sorn."

Coghill believed that Lewis's uncanny healing skills were but one aspect of his "life-giving generosity," which manifested itself as well in his widespread charity, about which he also kept silence. Lewis, however, urged caution in claiming a miracle. To Sheldon Vanauken, writing on November 27, 1957, he urged, "One dreams of a Charles Williams substitution! Well, never was a gift more gladly given; but one must not be fanciful." His expressed view of the matter fluctuated depending upon whom he was addressing. To one correspondent he wrote, after the cancer had subsided, that there was "hardly any hope for the long term issue." To Bede Griffiths he said that Joy's condition "has improved, if not miraculously (but who knows?) at any rate wonderfully." To an American correspondent, however, he dropped his defenses and declared that "the improvement in my wife's condition is, in the proper use of the word, miraculous," while to R. W. Chapman, he called it "almost miraculous." Warnie makes no mention of a substitutionary miracle in his diary or memoir, but then he was not always privy to his brother's religious reflections; one wonders, then, whether he ever shared with his brother something he had learned some years ago from Tolkien: Tolkien's dentist, it seems, had the experience of suffering, in place of his young patient, the agony of the surgery he had to perform on her infected jaw—a phenomenon which Warnie felt could only be accounted for "by supposing Charles's theory of Substitution to be fact and not fantasy." It seems likely that Warnie would have related this story to his brother.

The truth is that Lewis, a firm believer in miracles, longed to believe that Joy had been the recipient of one, but he feared false optimism, as well as unwarranted claims upon God's mercy, and so decided to guard his tongue, especially about a "Charles Williams substitution." He did not refrain, however, from declaring how happy he was, wrapped in a felicity with beatitude at the core but bordered by tragedy. "My heart is breaking and I was never so happy before," he told Dorothy L. Sayers. He assured Sister Penelope that she "wd. be surprised (or perhaps you would not?) to know how much of a strange sort of happiness and even gaiety" he and his wife now enjoyed, and he told Cecil Harwood that "we are often a great deal happier, merrier, delighted, than you wd. think possible." He could see now, as he put it to Bede Griffiths, the great arc of his love as "something which began in Agape, proceeded to Philia, then became Pity, and only after that, Eros. As if the highest of these, Agape, had successfully undergone the sweet humiliation of an incarnation." He, too, was becoming more enfleshed, by his carnal love for Joy and by his pains.

He became a brawling defender of her—now his—family. Bill Gresham, getting wind of Joy's condition, had written to tell her that "naturally I shall want [the boys] to be with me in the event of your death." Immediately Lewis dashed off a response, informing Bill that the boys opposed his plan, that they "remember you as a man who fired rifles thro' ceilings to relieve his temper, broke up chairs, wept in public, and broke a bottle over Douglas's head." Evidently dissatisfied that this would do the trick, Lewis wrote again the same day, blasting Bill's behavior toward Joy ("You have tortured one who was already on the rack"), underscoring the boys' rejection of their father ("certain scenes . . . make you a figure of terror to them"), and then baring his teeth: "If you do not relent, I shall of course be obliged to place every legal obstacle in your way." The tongue-lashing and teeth baring worked; Bill dropped the idea of reclaiming his sons.

It was shortly after this that Lewis began work on *Reflections on the Psalms*. The timing is apposite, for the wrenching emotions, among the most violent of his life, that he experienced during Joy's illness and Bill's aggression—the violent, clashing tides of anger and gratitude, fear and peace, despair and exaltation—parallel those expressed in the Psalter. Lewis knew the psalms intimately from his long experience with morning and evening prayer. Richard Ladborough remembers that he always showed up for weekday Matins at chapel, "the center of his life in college," and this was true at Oxford as well, where he had attended services since 1933, despite his intense dislike for hymn singing. In addition, he read the evening psalms on a daily basis. Now he set to work to puzzle out, in all their lyrical and strident glory, these 150 ancient Hebrew songs of praise, thanksgiving, lament, and execration.

Here Lewis writes, in patient and pellucid prose, "for the unlearned about things in which I am unlearned myself . . . one amateur to another." This studied pose means that much of his presentation is introductory, as he explains the role of allegory, prophecy, and literary devices like parallelism. More compelling is his discussion of judgment, a major theme in the psalms, as he observes that while "Christians cry to God for mercy instead of justice; *they* [the ancient Israelites] cried to God for justice instead of injustice." Christians see themselves as criminals; ancient Jews see themselves as plaintiffs. This is true, to a degree—in many psalms, the innocent party pleads divine redress for earthly transgression—but it is a partial truth, as the psalms offer self-incrimination as well ("Who can understand his errors? cleanse thou me from secret faults"—Psalms 19:12, KJV). When Lewis refers to "that typically Jewish prison of self-righteousness," one winces at the adverb. His discussion of the multitudinous cursing psalms is more rewarding, both in its gratitude to Israel (to whom, he says, we "are indebted . . . beyond all possible repayment") and in its argument that these songs, rife with hatred, echo God's own anger at human sin. Other sections, on the psalmist's understanding of death, nature, the law, and so on, instruct the novice and entertain the learned. Most notable, for the light it sheds on all Lewis's religious writings, is his rejection of biblical literalism and his embrace of the manifold meaning of scripture, as well as its partial origin in earlier mythical models. The "Father of Lights," he insists, is behind all "good work," including the entirety of the revealed Word. By and large, reviewers saluted *Reflec-*

tions on the Psalms for its warmth and clarity, although a reviewer for *Blackfriars*, the Dominican Catholic journal, wished that "a little more technical equipment" had been employed—Lewis used almost none—and thought that the result had "only the most tenuous connection with the psalms." This seems excessive, unless one insists upon advanced scholarship in any religious discussion; Lewis, precisely because he wrote as an amateur to amateurs, penetrated to the heart of the psalms.

Soon after completing *Reflections*, Lewis received an invitation from the Episcopal Radio-TV Foundation of Atlanta, Georgia, to prepare some tape recordings for American broadcast. He agreed, indicating that he would talk about love in its assorted major forms, which "bring in nearly the whole of Christian ethics." Lewis made the recordings in London on August 19–20, 1958, under the direction of the organization's founder, Caroline Rakestraw, a formidable woman whose meddling manner irked both Lewis and Joy, the latter labeling her "insufferable" and the former christening her "Cartwheel," a quasi-anagram, perhaps a reference to the contortions she tried to put him through. When Lewis resisted her editorial intrusions, which included an attempt to transform his direct "Today I want to discuss" into the hesitant "Let us think together, you and I," she demanded that he "sit absolutely silent before the microphone for a minute and a half 'so they could feel his living presence.'" Whether the sponsoring bishops enjoyed this moment of mystical communion is not recorded, but they vigorously objected to Lewis's bold discussion of eros, the third love in his typology, and canned the series. Lewis, of course, immediately converted the tape recordings (which the foundation has since offered for sale as *Four Talks on Love*) into a book, which he completed in June 1959.

The Four Loves sustains the avuncular tone of the recorded talks, as Lewis analyzes four forms of love: affection, friendship, eros, and charity. The first three, arising in the natural order of things, may be beautiful or good but have the potential to be twisted into something ugly and destructive. Thus *storge*, or affection, the warm animal love between mother and child or dog and master, may become a tyrannous stranglehold, as Lewis explains in a passage that may reflect his experiences with Mrs. Moore: "If people are already unlovable a continual demand on their part (as of right) to be loved—their manifest sense of injury, their reproaches, whether loud and clamorous or merely implicit in every look and gesture of resentful self-pity—produce in us a sense of guilt (they are intended to do so) for a fault we could not have avoided and cannot cease to commit." Friendship, too, may be perverted into exclusivity, yet it offers incomparable joys, as in Lewis's glowing account of male friends gathering in an inn after a "hard day's walking," which doubles as an idealized portrait of the Inklings. "Those are the golden sessions . . . when our slippers are on, our feet spread out towards the blaze and our drinks at our elbows; when the whole world, and something beyond the world, opens itself to our minds as we talk; and . . . all are freemen and equals as if we had first met an hour ago, while at the same time an Affection mellowed by the years enfolds us. Life—natural life—has no better gift to give. Who could have deserved it?"

Eros, too, which binds two individuals together, transforming them into lover and beloved, harbors its deadly snares, such as obsession and uncontrolled passion. Charity, however, stands alone. Charity (*agape*) is supernatural, a sheer gift, "Love Himself working in a man." It allows us to do what we would not ordinarily do: to embrace our enemies, kiss lepers, give away money, take on the sufferings of others. Through charity we draw close both to God and to our fellow human beings. Lewis rejects the idea, which he discerns in Augustine's account of the loss of his friend Nebridius, that one must beware of creaturely love and embrace only God, who never dies; instead, he stands with Charles Williams (without mentioning him by name), arguing that human and divine love complement and complete one another, and that in the Beatific Vision, the culmination of charity, we will find our earthly beloveds in their completion and consummation, united in God.

The Four Loves received predictable reviews, acclaimed by most religious periodicals and praised, a tad less fervently, by their secular counterparts. The Jesuit philosopher Fr. Martin D'Arcy (whose book *The Mind and Heart of Love* had been published in 1945 by T. S. Eliot at Faber & Faber), writing in *The New York Times Book Review*, found Lewis's categories rather "vague and fluid" but applauded the author for merging "a novelist's insights into motives with a profound religious understanding"— a serviceable but bland comment that could apply equally well to any of Lewis's apologetic works.

Meanwhile, Joy's recovery continued apace. She walked with a bad limp—surgery had shortened one leg by three inches—but otherwise was in fine fettle; the doctors declared the damaged bones reknit; to Lewis, the healing was "more like resurrection." Joy, back at the Kilns, refurbished the ragged décor, ordering the ceiling restored and the walls painted, and hobbled around the grounds with a cane, waving a starting pistol at trespassers. She and Lewis dared a belated honeymoon in Ireland, where they became, in his words, "drunk with blue mountains, yellow beaches, dark fuchsia, breaking waves, braying donkeys, peat-smell, and the heather just then beginning to bloom."

This second idyll—a brief spell in an enchanted garden encircled by ravening beasts—ended as well. In October 1959, Joy's cancer reappeared, X-rays revealing spots throughout her bones. Lewis told Roger Lancelyn Green that it was "like being recaptured by the giant when you have passed every gate and are almost out of sight of his castle." He prayed for a second miracle but there would be none. The couple kept up appearances as best they could, mingling with friends, answering letters, checking proofs. In April, they traveled with Green and his wife, June, to Greece, feasting on fish, cheese, retsina, sunlight, and the sun-drenched landscape. Green noted in his travel diary that "Joy was often in pain, and alcohol was the best alleviation: so I had become adept at diving into the nearest taverna, ordering 'tessera ouzo,' and having them ready at a convenient table by the time June had helped Jack and Joy out of coach or car and brought them in." For Joy, it was a glorious escape, and she returned to Oxford, wrote Lewis, "in a *nunc dimittis* frame of mind, having realized, beyond hope, her greatest lifelong, this-worldly, desire." The final collapse followed swiftly. The breast cancer returned in force and in May, Joy, as she put it, was "made an Amazon." She weakened and made several visits to the Acland Nursing Home. Here she befriended Edith Tolkien, also a patient (for rheumatism), and met, for the first and only time, Tolkien. What passed between them is not recorded. On July 13, 1960, she was taken by ambulance to the Radcliffe Infirmary to die. She received final rites from Austin Farrer, bequeathed her fur coat to Katharine Farrer, asked for cremation, and told Lewis, in a final burst of plain speaking, "Don't get me a posh coffin; posh coffins are all rot." Five days later, a funeral was held in Headington and her ashes scattered over the crematorium's rose garden. Austin Farrer presided, with Katharine in attendance. None of Lewis's other friends showed up.

A Seminal Work, A Second Birth

Invigorated by his work on *Saving the Appearances*, Barfield knew that only continued production, entailing a dramatic change in his daily routine, would prevent relapse into the despair and silence of past decades. He needed to retire from the law or at least restructure his job. In 1957 he wrote the firm a poignant letter, asking permission to relinquish his current responsibilities and ease into semiretirement as an advising director "on the basis that there is *prima facie* evidence that the literary, or more strictly philosophical, work I could do, given freedom from grind, between now and my death may be of lasting importance to the community." He added, somewhat unconvincingly, that whatever the response "I shall survive, unembittered," but pressed his case by observing that "it does often strike me as preposterous and wrong that my nose should be kept so long and so firmly to the grindstone, and even more preposterous and wrong that it should remain there for the rest of my life." In 1959 he finally left the firm and plunged headlong into full-scale authorship.

The first fruit of Barfield's retirement was *Worlds Apart (A Dialogue of the 1960's)*, an entertaining transposition into fictional form of many of the ideas from *Saving the Appearances*. Burgeon, a solicitor—the same Burgeon who serves as Barfield's mouthpiece in *This Ever Diverse Pair*—troubled by the specialization and insularity of intellectual disciplines (thus the "worlds apart" of the title), invites a group of intellectuals from different fields to spend a weekend together at a Dorchester cottage for a serious exchange of ideas. A theologian (closely based on Lewis), a psychiatrist, a philosopher, a schoolmaster, and three scientists—a biologist, a physicist, and a rocket scientist—constitute the ensemble, which resembles the Inklings in its pipe-and-flannels geniality, its male-only membership, its diversity of professions, and its love of argument.

Spurred on by Burgeon, the group tackles epistemology, the evolution of consciousness, the nature of religious revelation, and a host of other topics. The theory of *polarity*—an idea that would occupy Barfield increasingly in the years to come—receives much attention. Simply put, the theory states that aspects of reality can be usefully described as two poles—heaven/earth, male/female, constancy/change, act/potency, conscious/unconscious, literal/figurative, subject/object, poetic/prosaic, and so on—interpenetrating one another in a mutually dependent relationship. The poles "exist by virtue of each other *as well as* at the expense of each other . . ." The fundamental polarity that defines reality is that of "the subjectivity of the individual mind and the objective world which it perceives"; the result of the interplay between these two elements is the world we inhabit. Polarity operates on the local level, too, affecting our personal actions and relations; Barfield considered his youthful decision to lay aside literature for the law to be a prime example of polarity; another was his adversarial but richly productive relationship with Lewis. The theory is not, of course, entirely new; aspects of it can be seen in Hegelian dialectic and, further afield, in the combinational tensions and harmonies revealed by the Chinese classic the *I Ching*, as well as in the manifold clashing and reconciling forces of Taoist alchemy. Barfield traced his own elaboration of the theory, which in its fullest form he called objective idealism, to the influence of Steiner, for whom polarity is not an explicit teaching but rather the unstated "basis of his whole way of interpreting the world." The idea receives some attention in *Saving the Appearances*, in a discussion of the contrapuntal balance of *actus* and *potentia* at the heart of Scholastic thought, and a richer, more nuanced treatment in *Worlds Apart*, where the polarities of will/thought and conscious/unconscious lie at the basis of many of the key arguments about human nature.

For the most part, *Worlds Apart* unfolds as dialogue, with disputes between the theologian (Lewis) and the biologist—some of which bring to mind clashes between Ransom and Weston in Lewis's Space Trilogy—dominating the first half, and Anthroposophical insights by the schoolmaster providing resolution in the second half. The narrative ends most curiously, with the theologian recounting a recent dream, in which a set of massive bronze doors open before him and three figures emerge: first a man with a head like a "round box" with "light . . . blazing out of its eyeholes" (resembling a Halloween pumpkin), then a man with a lion's head, and finally a man without a head. In later years, Barfield would offer an interpretation of this dream, which he had based upon one told to him by Lewis: the first man represents ordinary human consciousness, the second a consciousness that combines mind and heart, and the third consciousness with "final participation," that apotheosis in which human beings will experience fully self-aware rapport with the cosmos.

Worlds Apart, or at least its Steinerian conclusions, discomfited some of the author's friends. Lewis, by now utterly familiar with Barfield's lines of argument, sent him a short note declaring the work "so exciting that I can't help reading it far too quickly" before dishing out petty complaints ("Your language sometimes disgruntles me. Why must it be *polyvalence* instead of *multivalence*? And why do you use base as an intransitive verb . . ."). T. S. Eliot offered a blurb that pointedly sidestepped assessment of Barfield's thesis, calling the book "an excursion into seas of thought which are very far from ordinary routes of intellectual shipping." Real encouragement came from an unexpected and perhaps not entirely welcome source: the American theologian Thomas J. J. Altizer, just a year away from international fame for his controversial "death of God" theology. Altizer reviewed *Worlds Apart* and *Saving the Appearances* in the *Journal of Bible and Religion* for October 1964, and, after the astonishing gaffe of describing Barfield as "recently deceased," praised the author for his "delightful and gracious style," his "fully coherent and logically forceful mode of thinking," and his "mastery of history"—"all of which," Altizer noted, "are absent in his master Steiner." *Saving the Appearances*, he wrote, is "potentially one of the truly seminal works of our age," and *Worlds Apart*, although the lesser work, nonetheless forged "a fascinating link between a mystical form of theology and the natural sciences."

Barfield may have resented Altizer's slur against Steiner, but he surely enjoyed the applause directed at himself. As for his reported demise, he laughed it off, for he knew that he was undergoing, if anything, a second birth. He possessed a new, inspired proficiency and fluency; he recognized his mission and trusted his skills as never before; and, to cap it off, by the time Altizer's review appeared in print, he had quit the cold comforts of England for America's welcoming embrace: a new continent for a new beginning. Stanley Hopper, professor of philosophy and dean of the graduate school at Drew University in Madison, New Jersey, read and enjoyed "Poetic Diction and Legal Fiction" and arranged for Barfield to teach at the school as a visiting professor in philosophy and letters, focusing upon "metaphor, symbol, language, and problems of communication." This voyage to the New World, Barfield remarked, was "like starting a new life . . . a strange experience, rather like the 'ugly duckling.'" Out of the blue, he had become the hero of his own fairy tale: the duckling was turning into a swan.

An Act of Will Inspired by Love

"Hwaet! We Gardena in geardagum . . ." Tolkien bellowed the opening lines of *Beowulf*, as he had done for so many decades before so many students, as he strode into a packed Merton College Hall at 5:00 p.m. on June 5, 1959, to deliver his valedictory address to the University of Oxford. He began his talk with a whimsical jest, a sly reference to his proclivity for tardiness, noting that he had never given an inaugural lecture and that he was "now about 34 years behind." Other self-deprecatory remarks followed. He had "nothing special to say"; he was an "amateurish person" who knew nothing of the "wide view, the masterly survey." A bit disingenuous, all this, coming from the creator of *The Silmarillion*, an account of the origin and early history of the cosmos and, as such, one of the twentieth century's extreme instances of the "wide view, the masterly survey." But it was true that Tolkien loved minutiae, especially of the philological stripe; his address consisted in a stirring defense of the discipline of philology as "the foundation of humane letters" and an impassioned attack upon those who would ban it from the curriculum. He blasted "the B.Litt. sausage-machine," regretted "the degeneration of real curiosity and enthusiasm," and called for research motivated by love of knowledge rather than hunger for a job. Suitably warmed up, he turned to the "lang.-lit." debate and decried its existence, arguing that these two disciplines go hand in hand, each encompassing the other; he compared their divorce to the apartheid policies of his native South Africa. His jeremiad then faded into a nostalgic mist of memories, as he recalled Joseph Wright, William Craigie, George Stuart Gordon, and other old friends, before concluding with a valedictorian's perfect wistful-yet-optimistic fare-thee-well, rejoicing, in words reminiscent of the Old English poems he had contributed to the 1936 collection produced with E. V. Gordon, *Songs for the Philologists*, that "the *duguð* [noble company] has not yet fallen by the wall, and the *dréam* [revelry] is not yet silenced." The *Oxford Mail* called his presentation "vigorous," which it was, but "disputative," even "crotchety" suit as well. It was an old man's talk, descrying the fallen battlements, raising the torn standards, sniping at the enemy, giving thanks for past and present blessings.

Tolkien *was* old. His body was betraying him: he suffered now from frequent bouts of arthritis, and in February 1959, four months before the valedictory address, went under the knife to remove a diseased appendix, surgery that depleted him for several weeks. Retirement he found "in many ways a melancholy proceeding"; one reason was the loss of his Merton office, which forced him to convert the garage at 76 Sandfield into a makeshift study. He saw less of his colleagues and friends, suffered the common ills—loneliness, bitterness, depression, lack of energy—of the newly retired, and by July of 1960 wrote Rayner Unwin that "I am in fact utterly stuck—lost in a bottomless bog, and anything that would cheer me would be welcome." Ostensibly freed from scholarly chores, he was chained to his desk ten hours a day in a desperate effort to wrap up his edition of the *Ancrene Wisse*—now nearly thirty years in the making— while laboring on *The Silmarillion* and dealing with assorted domestic crises, not least Edith's fading health. His prickliness intensified; when in September Lewis sent him a copy of his latest work, *Studies in Words*, Tolkien wrote to Christopher that Lewis's "ponderous silliness is becoming a fixed manner. I am deeply relieved to find I am not mentioned." Matters hadn't improved by the following April. "Forgive my chattiness," he wrote to Robert Burchfield of the Early English Text Society (and later chief editor of the *OED*), "I am rather isolated, and it is a relief to chat even by way of typewriter to someone who has any interest in the work." The isolation intensified in the fall, when the Tolkiens' housekeeper quit, leaving the aging couple without adequate help.

Still, publishing triumphs helped offset the encroaching gloom. *The Lord of the Rings* was selling extremely well, so much so that Stanley Unwin declared it the most important and successful book in his firm's history. In October 1961, Tolkien's aunt, Jane Neave, wrote to him suggesting that he produce a small book about Tom Bombadil; he seized on the idea and the volume appeared on November 22, 1962, as *The Adventures of Tom Bombadil and Other Verses from the Red Book*, with illustrations by Pauline Baynes. Tolkien thought it "a very pretty book." He praised the illustrations, telling Baynes that "I do not think that they could have been more after my own heart" (although during production he had objected to her drawing of a dragon, telling Rayner Unwin that the figure itself was "excellent" but complaining that "of course no dragon, however decrepit would lie with his head away from the entrance"). Alfred Duggan, reviewing it in *The Times Literary Supplement*, found the verses "ingenious" but too alike with their "hurrying rhythm and a fondness for feminine endings." The poet Anthony Thwaite, writing in *The Listener*, by contrast, called the book "something close to genius," praising the same technique that Duggan derided, and declaring that it had made a convert of him. Tolkien was pleased with both reviews—he had anticipated only contempt from the literary establishment—but by now his attention was on another, even happier literary event: the appearance of a Festschrift in his honor, entitled *English and Mediaeval Studies Presented to J.R.R. Tolkien on the Occasion of His Seventieth Birthday*, prepared in secret by C. L. Wrenn and Norman Davis, with contributions by several Inklings (Lewis, Coghill, Bennett) and many other friends and colleagues. Tolkien received the book at a Merton College celebration on December 5. To crown this fecund autumn, the Early English Text Society published, in conjunction with the release of the Festschrift, Tolkien's long delayed edition of the *Ancrene Wisse*. The book received little or no attention in the popular press, but Arne Zettersten, a Swedish medievalist and friend of Tolkien, had kind words for it in a 1966 issue of the professional journal *English Studies*, and it has served since as the basis for the only scholarly concordance of this important Christian anchoretic text.

That Tolkien's major contribution to Christian scholarship appeared at this late stage in his life was felicitous, for old age and its cargo of worries had driven him to renewed reflection upon his faith. He continued to explain to readers the veiled place of Catholicism in *The Lord of the Rings* and to puzzle out its role in *The Silmarillion*. During this period, he wrote his most explicit statement of religious belief, a messy tangle of theology, history, memoir, apology, political invective, and paternal love, sent as a letter to his son Michael, who had recently told his father that he had been suffering from depression and "sagging faith." Michael's depression may have been occasioned by the shell shock he had suffered during World War II; even so, low spirits, Tolkien advises his son, are "an occupational affliction" among those, like Michael, who teach school and endemic among those Michael's age (forty-three), just old enough to realize the hypocrisy that infects all institutions. Recalling his own experiences, he rails against administrative shortsightedness, against being forced to teach what one does not love, against professionals in school and church who dishonor their calling out of exhaustion, insincerity, and greed. However, he assures Michael, "men's hearts are not often as bad as their acts, and very seldom as bad as their words."

After this prolonged outburst with its faintly cheering coda, Tolkien turns to what he perceives as Michael's deeper problem, his crisis of faith. He begins with superbly crafted apothegms of considerable psychological penetration: "Faith is an act of will inspired by love"; "'scandal' at most is an occasion of temptation—as indecency is to lust, which it does not make but arouses." Michael's faith, it seems, had fallen victim to the scandals of sinful clergy. As readers will surely note, this is a long-standing problem, perhaps never to be resolved, and Tolkien recounts his own suffering at the hands of "stupid, tired, dimmed, and even bad priests." But, he adds, this is scarcely reason to leave the Church, a move that would mean turning one's back on Jesus: an inconceivable act. He echoes Lewis's lunatic/liar/Lord trilemma, arguing that either Jesus is who he claimed to be, or he is a "demented megalomaniac." The correct choice he considers obvious; in any event, no one with critical intelligence will swallow the canards that Jesus never existed or that his sayings were forged by others.

How, then, can one shore up one's faith? Through Holy Communion. The core of this remarkable letter is a sustained paean to the Eucharist. Tolkien tells his son that he "fell in love with the Blessed Sacrament from the beginning—and by the mercy of god never have fallen out again." He urges frequent communion (he himself communicated daily whenever possible), preferably in difficult or distracting circumstances: "Choose a snuffling or gabbling priest or a proud and vulgar friar; and a church full of the usual bourgeois crowd"; it is the Eucharistic miracle that matters, not its setting. He refers to "the greatest reform of our time," by which he means Pope Pius X's recommendation of daily communion as the path to personal and societal salvation. The Eucharist is the center of the Church, of the faith, of the hope of all believers; Tolkien is Roman Catholic because Rome has always safeguarded the Eucharist, scrupulously abiding by Jesus' last command to Peter, "Feed my sheep" (John 21:16–17).

Rarely has Tolkien been so impassioned or personal. The stakes are high: he is fighting for his son's soul. Having presented his case, he admits that "this is rather an alarming and rambling disquisition to write! It is not meant to be a sermon!" But alarm, if such he imparted, surely originated in his numerous personal confessions, not his homiletics. The letter is riddled with admissions: He is "an ignorant man, but also a lonely one." He nearly abandoned God; he is a bad parent: "I brought you all up ill and talked to you too little . . ." He casts all this in biblical terms, as "one who came up out of Egypt." He concludes these revelations with a cri de coeur that God may heal his defects "and that none of you shall ever cease to cry *Benedictus qui venit in nomine Domini.*" These twin prayers, for himself and for his children, say much: what had begun as a letter of assistance to his child ends as a plea to God for mercy on himself and all his flesh. His sorrow, bitterness, and depression nearly take command, nearly overwhelm the beautiful theology, diseased briars choking the rose. One wonders what Michael made of this epistle.

The Clerk's Tale

Lewis responded to Joy's death as one might expect: he grieved, he comforted his stepchildren, he notified Joy's few friends and family of her passing—and he wrote a book. *A Grief Observed* stands apart from Lewis's other works: it is a raw, choppy assemblage of about 120 jottings, ranging from a line to a page or more, largely stripped of literary effects, tracking the contours of his grief over the first few weeks of bereavement. The text was almost complete by early September, three months after Joy's demise, when Roger Lancelyn Green perused it during a visit to the Kilns. Lewis, realizing the work was sui generis, decided to publish it under a pseudonym and settled on Dimidius, Latin for "halved." When he turned in the manuscript to Faber & Faber, however, T. S. Eliot and others at the firm guessed the author's identity and suggested that a "plausible English pseudonym" might make a better disguise. Lewis concurred and settled upon N. W. Clerk—N. W. for Nat Whilk ("I know not who"), the pen name he had used in the past, and Clerk for scholar.

Walter Hooper believes *A Grief Observed* was "not written with publication in mind," but another view is possible. Near the book's end, Lewis explains that he wrote it for two reasons: as "a defence against total collapse, a safety-valve," and to "describe a *state*; make a map of sorrow." The therapeutic motive, a private concern, accords with Hooper's evaluation, but it is difficult to imagine that Lewis, born to communicate, would chart sorrow in all its shades and not wish to pass his discoveries on to others, especially as he saw his discoveries as terra incognita. Just eight days after Joy's death, he wrote Katharine and Austin Farrer that "there are a lot of things about sorrow which no one (least off all the tragedians) had told me. I never dreamed that, in between the moments of acute suffering, it wd. be so like somnambulism or like being slightly drunk. Nor, physically, often so like fear." Moreover, *Grief* possesses qualities that suggest considerable shaping on Lewis's part. Granted, it displays the fragmentation and staccato of an unplanned text, and we know that its length, at least, was not predesigned but determined by how much Lewis could squeeze into four small notebooks he found lying around the Kilns. Nonetheless, the book follows a clear trajectory, from undigested shock and confusion at the outset to conditional acceptance at the end, and it concludes with a poignant quotation from Dante, *"Poi si tornò all'eterna fontana"* (then turned again to the eternal fountain—*Paradiso* XXXI), marking the instant when Beatrice—and thus Joy, Lewis's Beatrice—departs her lover to return to heaven. This ending is not only a radiant tribute to Joy but also, inter alia, an homage to Charles Williams; it is just the sort of rhetorical flourish at which Lewis excelled—when addressing others.

Lewis divides *Grief* into four sections, each marking a stage in the process of his grieving for "H" (Helen, Joy's first name). In the first section, Lewis's self-censoring mechanism has broken down, ravaged by his loss, and what we get is undiluted anger, misery, self-pity, and doubts about God, along with flashes of the old evangelist ("For those few years H. and I feasted on love . . . If God were a substitute for love we ought to have lost all interest in him"). In the second section, self-criticism returns, and Lewis discovers that his jottings to date, focused on his reactions to H's death rather than H herself, "appall" him. Can he be thinking of the real H, or only of her remembered, distorted image? Her reality was "the most precious gift" of his marriage, and he prays piteously for its return. Does she exist anywhere? Where? When? "She is, like God, incomprehensible and unimaginable." He is inconsolable, and God seems to be the "Cosmic Sadist." In part three, the pressure of grief alleviates, just slightly. Lewis still erupts in anger, confusion, and sorrow, but something new happens. He is sleeping better, the weather has improved, and one morning he receives "an instantaneous, unanswerable impression" of H—something almost akin to a meeting. In the fourth and final movement of this symphony of bereavement, genuine hope dawns: "Turned to God, my mind no longer meets that locked door; turned to H., it no longer meets that vacuum." He feels called to praise both God and H, "Him as the giver . . . her as the gift," each in His or her stark reality "Not my idea of God, but God. Not my idea of H., but H."

A *Grief Observed* was published on September 29, 1961. The novelist Sylva Norman, reviewing it for *The Times Literary Supplement*, praised its "strange, firm magnetism" but hesitated over its religious conclusions ("Religion—reassurance—seems to conquer. But on what basis does the resolution rest?"); otherwise, the book received little notice beyond the Christian press, which, unsurprisingly, admired its courage and honesty. It remains an oddity, unique in Lewis's oeuvre but not in English letters, for it carries distant echoes, in its personal anguish and resilient devotion, of John Donne's *Devotions* and Samuel Johnson's *Prayers and Meditations*.

Lewis published two other books while working on *A Grief Observed*. In September 1960, he released *Studies in Words*, based upon his 1950s university lecture series, "Some Difficult Words," which traces the etymology of various terms—chief among them being "nature," "sad," "wit," "free," "sense," "simple," "conscience," "conscious," "world," and "life"—with a rich cargo of meaning and implication. *Studies* is a minor work, witty, erudite, and rarely read, although Lewis, in his publicity notes for the publisher, suggested that it belonged alongside Barfield's most popular work, *Poetic Diction*. William Empson applauded the work's "easy tone" and the author's "continually interesting" details in the course of an unsigned *TLS* review so convoluted that Lewis judged it "unintelligible." Few other reviewers—and almost as few book buyers—paid it any attention, and the volume is remembered mostly for Tolkien's negative reaction, noted above, in his September 12 letter to Christopher.

Against the Vigilants

Lewis also published, in 1960, an article in the Cambridge *Broadsheet* about the characteristic vices of undergraduate literary criticism. These include, he said, favoring radical over time-honored interpretations, lacking a foundation in biblical and classical learning, treating literary texts "as a substitute for religion or philosophy or psychotherapy," and in all these vices "imitat[ing] that which, in their elders, has far less excuse." High dudgeon was the inevitable response; an article in *Delta: The Cambridge*

Literary Magazine accused Lewis of "Pecksniffian disingenuousness," "shabby bluff," and "self-righteousness," ad hominem remarks to which Lewis fired back:

> Do not misunderstand. I am not in the least deprecating your insults; I have enjoyed these twenty years *l'honneur d'etre une cible* and am now pachydermatous. I am not even rebuking your bad manners; I am not Mr. Turveydrop and "gentlemanly deportment" is not a subject I am paid to teach. What shocks me is that students, academics, men of letters, should display what I had thought was an essentially uneducated inability to differentiate between a disputation and a quarrel. The real objection to this sort of thing is that it is all a distraction from the issue. You waste on calling me liar and hypocrite time you ought to have spent on refuting my position.

But the fact was that Lewis was growing tired of *l'honneur d'être une cible* (the honor of being a target). He was sufficiently roused to devote an entire book—*An Experiment in Criticism* (1961)—to a critique of the Leavisites, under the name of the "Vigilant School." He would omit the names of his adversaries, "shrinking a little, it may be, from their 'insular ferocity,'" as Frank Kermode put it in a review, but no one familiar with the period could fail to recognize Lewis's intent.

Lewis characterizes the Vigilant School as a cultural militia always on patrol, subjecting literary taste to the prejudices of the day ("Tell me the date of your birth and I can make a shrewd guess whether you prefer Hopkins or Housman, Hardy or Lawrence"), placing whole genres (such as fantasy, detective novels, and Westerns) under embargo, and encouraging a suspicion that is fatal to literary experience: "No poem will give up its secret to a reader who enters it regarding the poet as a potential deceiver, and determined not to be taken in. We must risk being taken in, if we are to get anything."

Lewis's "experiment," then, is to turn Vigilant criticism on its head. If literary works must be evaluated, let us evaluate them by the kind of reading they generate. A good book would be one that "permits, invites, or even compels good reading." A bad book would be one that is incapable of eliciting such a response. Despite the title, *Experiment* is not a methodology designed to be implemented in salons or schools: it is a manifesto. Lewis exhorts us to become the kind of generous readers he himself was: capable of enjoying works of vastly differing genres, idioms, and periods; quick to appreciate but slow to declare a work unfit; distrusting one's negative reactions as indications of bias; and extending the franchise of aesthetic judgment to everyone who loves to read. We read, Lewis says, not primarily to appraise an author's worth, but to seek "an enlargement of our being." "Literary experience heals the wound, without undermining the privilege, of individuality . . . ," he writes. "In reading great literature I become a thousand men and yet remain myself. Like the night sky in the Greek poem, I see with a myriad eyes, but it is still I who see. Here, as in worship, in love, in moral action, and in knowing, I transcend myself; and am never more myself than when I do."

Viewed from the distance of half a century or more, Lewis's paean to reading continues to enchant, but his polemic against Leavisite criticism beats a dead horse. Just two years after *Experiment* appeared, the Leavisite school received its definitive send-up in *The Pooh Perplex: A Student Casebook*, a satire by Frederick Crews in which "Simon Lacerous," editor of the literary journal *Thumbscrew*, revalues *Winnie-the-Pooh*, determining that it is "Another Book to Cross Off Your List." No intellectual movement that has made itself so easy to parody could long survive. Lewis, on the other hand, set up no theory to tilt at and offered no practical technique for disciples to use or abuse. His critical program was largely a corrective against the excesses of other peoples' programs—and it may be that he overcorrected. Who can really abstain, as Lewis proposed in *A Personal Heresy*, from all consideration of an author's biography? Who can really set aside all prior commitments and approach a literary work in naked surrender?

The irony is that Lewis and his Cambridge literary adversaries agree about a good many things: that civilization is in a dire state, that the Industrial Revolution has produced a mechanized consumer culture estranged from its roots, that things have been getting worse since the Great War, that literature, and university study of literature, has a vitally important moral influence, that scientism should be opposed, and more. As a Coleridgean, Richards would come out with statements ("The saner and greater mythologies are not fancies; they are the utterance of the whole soul of man") that could have been spoken by Lewis himself. Similarly,

Leavis could describe the ideal critic of poetry as one who permits himself "not to 'think about' and judge but to 'feel into' or 'become'" the poem, and advocated "a kind of responsiveness that is incompatible with the judicial, one-eye-on-the-standard approach."

A reviewer of Lewis's *Experiment in Criticism* in *The Times Literary Supplement*, citing these words of Leavis, observed that "Professor Lewis's own credo is not, after all, very far removed from that of Dr. Leavis" and concluded by saying, "By all means let us have an end to acrimony: and if the critical alliance is led by a compound figure, it does not matter whether we call him C.S. Leavis or F.R. Lewis." But there would be no end to acrimony. Summing up the history of the conflict in a 1962 letter to J. B. Priestley, Lewis had this to say:

> The actual history of Eng. Lit. as a "Subject" has been a great disappointment to me. My hope was that it would be primarily a historical study that wd. lift people out of (so to speak) their chronological provincialism by plunging them into the thought and feeling of ages other than their own: for the arts are the best Time Machine we have. But all that side of it has been destroyed at Cambridge and is now being destroyed at Oxford too. This is done by a compact, well-organised group of whom Leavis is the head. It now has a stranglehold on the schools as well as the universities (and the High Brow press). It is too open and avowed to be called a plot. It is much more like a political party—or the Inquisition.

As for Leavis, Lewis concluded that he was

> a perfectly sincere, disinterested, fearless, ruthless fanatic. I am sure he would, if necessary, die for his critical principles: I am afraid he might also kill for them. Ultimately, a pathological type—unhappy, intense, mirthless. Incapable of conversation: dead silence or prolonged, passionate, and often irrelevant, monologue are his only two lines. And while he is in fact the head of the most powerful literary Establishment we have ever had since Boileau, he maddeningly regards himself as a solitary martyr with his back to the wall.

A year later, when Lewis died, Leavis announced the fact to his students at Cambridge: "C. S. Lewis is dead . . . They said in the *Times* that we will miss him. We will *not*. We will *not*."

The Encircling Darkness

While publishing at a breathless pace, Lewis was engaged in other literary work, including a regular stream of essays, a book on prayer in the form of letters to an imaginary correspondent (*Letters to Malcolm: Chiefly on Prayer*), and *The Discarded Image: An Introduction to Medieval and Renaissance Literature*, based on lectures dating back to the 1920s and '30s. Both books would appear posthumously, to friendly reviews that doubled as memorials, Helen Gardner, in *The Listener*, praising Lewis's "wonderful gusto, the clarity of his style, the wit of his comments and analogies, the range of his learning and the liveliness of his mind," commending the gentler style of his rhetoric once the "hot-gospelling" days were past, paying homage to his gift for allegory (ideas became "almost persons" for him), and declaring, in high epitaphic style, that "whether we were his pupils in the classroom or no, we are all his pupils and we shall not look upon his like again."

During these years, he also served on an Anglican commission charged with revising Miles Coverdale's sixteenth-century translation of the Psalter, used in the Book of Common Prayer. Other commission members included the Archbishops of Canterbury and York and, of all people, T. S. Eliot. The mix of Lewis and Eliot portended a glorious literary duel, but the two adversaries, tired out, one foot already in eternity (Eliot was seventy when the commission first convened at Lambeth Palace in 1959), had sheathed their swords. Writing to Eliot regarding the Psalter, Lewis displayed a level of jocularity unknown in the stiff exchanges of earlier years; he pointed out that the two shared "(a.) Having educated Betjeman, (b.) Not having given evidence about *Lady C.*" (D. H. Lawrence's *Lady Chatterley's Lover*, whose publisher was on trial at the Old Bailey in 1960 for obscenity). He told Walter Hooper that "I never liked Eliot's poetry, or even his prose. But when we met this time [at Lambeth] I loved him." Late did Lewis love Eliot—and could have loved him sooner if he had allowed himself to realize that, poetry aside, they were kindred spirits in the fight against philistine secularism.

But to love Eliot now, to love the man who represented almost all one disliked in modern poetry: this as much as anything signaled the beginning of Lewis's dying. He had achieved a mellow old age at the disconcertingly young age of sixty-two. Heavy smoking played a part in the premature decline, as did a lifelong diet of beef and beer. The primary reason may lie, however, in Joy's death; with her went his only sustained experience of romantic bliss, and he knew there would never be another. This realization has led more than one man to an early grave. Nonetheless, he soldiered on, with a fortitude inspired less by a traditional British sense of duty than by belief in the importance of kind attention to others. Few events exemplify his devotion to this principle more than his activity on the day after Joy's death. The musician Donald Swann, unaware of the tragedy, came with a colleague to the Kilns that day to consult with Lewis about a projected opera based on *Perelandra*: "It was a quiet morning and we went to Lewis's home in Oxford for breakfast. We strolled around his lovely garden with him, talking about the opera. After about an hour he said: 'I hope you will excuse me. I must go now because my wife died last night.' He left us. I was very moved. Quite overcome. It is just another story of this very gracious gentleman who always looked after his guests. I mean, at a time like that! What did we matter?"

Within a week, Lewis was writing to an American correspondent on the nature and knowledge of God; within two weeks, he was advising another American on the best source for secondhand British books. He spent a great deal of time tending to Joy's two boys—when David, the older, developed a passionate interest in Judaism, Lewis arranged Hebrew lessons for him—and served as a buffer between them and their father, who visited Oxford during the August after Joy's death (Gresham would commit suicide two years later, after developing cancer of the tongue and throat). Warnie, in stark contrast to his brother, collapsed after Joy's death, fleeing to his beloved Drogheda, where he drank himself once again into the care of the gentle nuns at Our Lady of Lourdes Hospital. His journals for these years make painful reading, as he meticulously notes his pattern of intoxication and sobriety: "During the year which ended today I have been a teetotaller for 355 days" (October 20, 1961); "I drank from 22 June until 27 August while I was in Ireland, then was again a teetotaller from 28 August to 31 December, 126 days. So out of 365 days I was T.T. for 298 days. A poor performance compared with

1961" (January 2, 1963). At least Lewis had learned to expect no better and even to joke about his brother's malady, telling a correspondent on January 17, 1962, of "a dipsomaniac retired major I once knew who refused the suggestion that he shd. try A.A. on the ground that 'it would be full of retired majors'!"

As the post-Joy months ticked by, Lewis's body went into steady decline. In 1961 his prostate enlarged, his kidneys balked, his blood soured. He wore a catheter, slept in a chair, could not climb stairs, and underwent multiple blood transfusions. When Tolkien in 1962 invited Lewis to his Festschrift celebration, Lewis declined with a dark jest, explaining that "I wear a catheter, live on a low protein diet, and go early to bed. I am, if not a lean, at least a slippered, pantaloon" (a reference to the decrepitude of the sixth age of man, as described in *As You Like It*, II, vii: "The sixth age shifts / Into the lean and slipper'd pantaloon / With spectacles on nose and pouch on side / His youthful hose, well saved, a world too wide / For his shrunk shank . . ."). As Lewis could not travel easily, his friends, including Barfield, Arthur Greeves, Ruth Pitter, John Wain, and George Sayer, came to him at the Kilns. Whenever possible, Havard and Dundas-Grant drove him on Mondays to the Bird and Baby, and, beginning in 1962, to the Lamb and Flag, to meet with Hardie, McCallum, Mathew, and a few others. Lewis called these gatherings "Inklings," but they lacked the fire, if not the friendship, of former days.

By early 1963, he was fading fast. He continued to teach at Cambridge, however, and this proved his undoing, at least in Dr. Havard's estimation, as the strain resulted in his bladder poisoning his kidneys. If Lewis had taken a leave of absence, Havard told George Sayer, he might have lived another decade or two. Instead, on July 15, he entered the Acland for a blood transfusion, had a heart attack, and fell into a coma. The Acland staff, convinced he was dying, summoned a priest to administer last rites. However, Lewis recovered sufficiently to return to the Kilns. There he took on a new personal secretary, Walter Hooper, who would become in later years a leading light in Lewis studies, and enjoyed a visit from Tolkien and his son John; the two old Inklings discussed *Le Morte d'Arthur* and the death of trees. This was their last encounter. Lewis wrote a farewell letter to Arthur: the last sentence of their forty-nine-year-long correspondence runs "But oh Arthur, never to see you again! . . ."

Now he and Warnie stood alone against the encircling darkness. "By early October it became apparent to both of us that he was facing death," wrote Warnie. "Once again,—as in the earliest days—we could turn for comfort only to each other. The wheel had come full circle: once again we were together in the little end room at home . . . 'I have done all I wanted to do, and I'm ready to go,' he said to me one evening." He went on November 22, around 5:30 p.m., collapsing and dying in his bedroom at the Kilns; John F. Kennedy was assassinated in Texas and Aldous Huxley passed away of laryngeal cancer in California on the same day, the former death relegating Lewis's obituary to the inner pages, if not the next day's edition, in newspapers around the world. Lewis's funeral was held four days later at Headington's Church of the Holy Trinity. Close friends flocked to the service, including Barfield, Havard, Dundas-Grant, and the Farrers. Douglas Gresham turned up, along with Christopher Tolkien and his father, who earlier in the morning had served at a Mass for Lewis at St. Aloysius, the Jesuit church on the Woodstock Road. There was one startling absence: Warnie, who had railed bitterly about those who skipped Joy's funeral, remained at the Kilns, lost in grief and memories, emptying his bottle.

19

INKLINGS FIRST AND LAST

Moral compass, intellectual catalyst, best of companions: Lewis in his passing was remembered as these and more. Those close to him, reeling with loss, offered tributes brimming with admiration for their fallen friend and with self-pity for themselves. Writing to Priscilla on the day of the funeral, Tolkien recalled the "time of close communion" he and Lewis had shared but emphasized his own pain: "So far I have felt the normal feelings of a man of my age—like an old tree that is losing all its leaves one by one: this feels like an axe-blow near the roots." Warnie suffered most, as one would expect, and he poured his anguish into his diary: "My life continues very desolate, and I seem to miss my dear SPB more rather than less as time goes on. I have no one to *chat* with." Nor was the "perpetual ache of J's absence" his only burden; deeply depressed, he lost track of finances and discovered again the haunting fear of impoverishment that had afflicted both brothers since childhood, along with new worries about his mental acuity: "I forget quite important names in French history even." He slept poorly, grew bored, and drank himself in and out of the hospital (in 1964 it was discovered that he had stashed hundreds of empty whiskey bottles in the hollowed-out tops of his bookcases at the Kilns). He prayed that a stroke would kill him while he slept. Barfield, more restrained, apotheosized Lewis as "the absolutely unforgettable friend, the friend with whom I was in close touch for over forty years, the friend you might come to regard hardly as another human being, but almost as a part of the furniture of my existence," while at the same time composing the pessimistic, self-absorbed "Moira" (Greek: fate, destiny), a poem linking Lewis's death to his own and contrasting his friend's posthumous enlightenment to his own earthbound ignorance: "You came to him: when will you come to me? / He knows what matters from what matters not. / I hurry to and fro and seem to be."

Yet Barfield in his mourning stood apart from Tolkien and Warnie, despite their common loss. The two older men lived in the past as much as the future: Tolkien revising his work, refining his legacy, elucidating Middle-earth minutiae to an awestruck, sometimes cranky readership; Warnie drinking, poring over memories of his brother, squeezing out one more book on French history (*Memoirs of the Duc de Saint-Simon* appeared in 1964), and awaiting his death. As they folded up at the edges, Barfield entered the great adventure of his life. Having set foot in America less than a year after Lewis's death, he was aflame with hope and trepidation. "I find the prospect exciting, especially as I have never before crossed the Atlantic, but wish I were a bit younger," he told Philip Mairet, a British writer and admirer who claimed to have read *Saving the Appearances* four times. At Drew University, his first port of call, he contracted to deliver "2 lectures a week, ranging as I like over the stuff in my books, and to take a seminar on Coleridge and Romanticism." The salary was $7,200, which he "rather jumped at," along with a travel stipend of $800. He made quick use of the latter, visiting, during his first months abroad, the evangelical stronghold of Wheaton College in Illinois, and Beloit College in Wisconsin, where he "spoke of Jack for an hour to an audience variously estimated at 800 and 1000" and basked in their "really wonderful attentiveness, warmth and response." One attendee, he told Cecil Harwood, "flew from Los Angeles to hear the lecture, returning the following day."

Wherever Barfield went, crowds gathered. At first they came to see him not for his sake but for Lewis's. Barfield's fame, such as it was, depended upon the passage in *Surprised by Joy* in which Lewis identifies him as the "Second Friend," with whom "you go at it, hammer and tongs, far into the night, night after night . . . out of this perpetual dogfight a community of mind and a deep affection emerge." He never resented Lewis's prominence. Many times Lewis had gone out of his way to laud him and his writings, and he was happy to return the favor. In talks, writings, and interviews, he focused on aspects of Lewis's life that he alone knew well: their early friendship, the "Great War," Lewis's rejection of Anthroposophy. The presentations, eventually gathered into *Owen Barfield on C. S. Lewis* (1989), seesawed between love for his friend and exasperation at the RUP ("residue of unresolved positivism," a favorite catchphrase) that blocked Lewis's perception of spiritual realities. He came to see the long, warm, adversarial friendship as another example of polarity; in Barfield's eyes, the "Great War" had never ended, nor should it have: *in bello, veritas*.

The public, won over by his quiet manner and colorful memories, soon began to lend an ear to his unusual philosophical and religious views. At Drew he met Howard Nemerov, former and future United States poet laureate (holding the post twice, in 1963–64 and 1988–90), who declared himself a disciple, at least in regard to the evolution of consciousness and the dangers of positivism. Barfield in turn anointed Nemerov his "ambassador at the court of contemporary poetry." Many other American writers and scholars contacted him, suddenly eager to discuss his work. Encouraged and inspired by this unexpected groundswell of enthusiasm, he commenced a major new project, a study of Samuel Taylor Coleridge that would come to complete fruition in 1971 with *What Coleridge Thought* (see below). As early as 1919, reading the *Biographia Literaria*, he had discerned "a strong affinity" between his own thought and that of the great poet. Now, reading extensively through Coleridge's lesser-known works, he discerned, in the poet's sometimes obscure presentations, foreshadowings of his own cherished views on mind and nature. Coleridge, Barfield came to believe, also thought in terms of polarity and anticipated, although he never quite realized, the truth of the evolution of consciousness. Here was a man after his own heart; even the poet's celebrated dithering appealed to him. He perceived in it an underlying unity of thought, consisting of harmonies too complex to be passed on readily to others. He believed that Coleridge "had a muddled life but not a muddled mind" and would liken his sometimes impenetrable philosophical passages to a conceptual stammer, in veiled allusion to his own painful impediment.

He realized, with gratitude and amazement, that against all odds, against the fierce current that was sweeping his friends into exhaustion or death, he was enjoying tremendous new intellectual and creative vitality.

In February 1965, he received an invitation to be a visiting professor at Brandeis University in Waltham, Massachusetts. Immediately he wrote for advice to Cecil Harwood, still his closest friend, weighing the lure of England—"even my unsatisfactory children count for something"— against the promise of America: "I like the work and the *milieu* it invokes and have a sort of blossoming feeling . . . why do they *want* me so ruddy badly over here? . . . If I do reject it, I may never cease kicking myself spiritually, psychically and financially . . ."

Barfield accepted the offer and stayed in America. Maud joined him for a time, as did their daughter Lucy, now thirty, who taught piano in Cambridge, Massachusetts, while he lectured at Brandeis, conducted a seminar on Coleridge, and gave talks published two years later as *Speaker's Meaning.* For the most part, his Brandeis lectures address familiar themes of philology, polarity, and evolution. But thanks to his study of Coleridge and, no doubt, to renewed self-confidence, he assumed the role of prophet and began to elaborate with increased specificity upon the immediate past and future of consciousness. Barfield argues in *Speaker's Meaning* that a turning point in human thought took place with the Romantics, a transformation whose initial stages involved, in Coleridge's words, "an interpenetration . . . of spontaneous impulse and voluntary purpose"—that is, of desire and will, resulting in the triumph of active imagination over passive inspiration. Through imagination, the poet—and, in his wake, human consciousness as a whole—is learning for the first time truly to do, to make, to create. This fundamental change in the nature of thought, coupled with earlier evolutionary advances, pro- vides Barfield with ample evidence that history has a "plot," and a plot driven not by matter but by mind. Our ordinary understanding must be turned inside out. Science teaches us that matter precedes mind (first a barren planet, then the emergence of life, then of mind), but the truth, argues Barfield, is that mind has always been here. It is the evolution of mind, not of matter, that lies at the heart of the story of the world.

Barfield also wears the prophet's mantle in his novel *Unancestral Voice* (1965), his strangest work, published during his Brandeis stint. Burgeon, the author's alter ego whom we first encountered in *This Ever Diverse Pair*, begins to receive messages from a disembodied spirit known as a Meggid, a figure drawn from the mystical experiences of the sixteenth- century Jewish seer Joseph Karo. In between discussions of *Lady Chat-*

terley's Lover, Arnold Toynbee, and the evils of Descartes, the Meggid promotes, as one expects in any Barfield book, the evolution of consciousness. This mysterious spirit also advances some of Anthroposophy's more outré claims, such as the neognostic division of human history into angelic ages (humankind has recently progressed from the "age of Gabriel" to the "age of Michael") and the astonishing two-Jesus theory, which asserts that the New Testament records the birth and childhood of two Jesuses—each born in Bethlehem of parents named Mary and Joseph— who merged into one at about the age of twelve. As presented by Steiner in his lecture series *From Jesus to Christ*, although not mentioned in *Unancestral Voice*, one Jesus is the reincarnation of Zarathustra, the other permeated by the spiritual influence of Buddha. The climax of *Unancestral Voice* comes at a lecture on quantum mechanics, as the Meggid takes control of the speaker and declares that the future of physics lies in the study of "non-spatial relationships between hierarchies of energetic beings"—in effect, in Steiner's Spiritual Science. As the journalist/politician Ivor Thomas noted in his review for *The Times Literary Supplement*, *Unancestral Voice* offers "no lack of topics" and is "stimulating and not infrequently entertaining"; for many, it is also too thick with esoteric proselytizing and too reliant upon Meggidian *angelus ex machina* to satisfy as a novel. Barfield never attempted another book-length fiction.

The Inklings, Scattered

"The events and troubles of this year have defeated me," wrote Tolkien on May 28, 1964, to Rayner Unwin, who had become by now a principal recipient of his more plaintive letters, cushioning the news by adding that "I am at last recovering health and some kind of mental equilibrium." Not least among these "events and troubles" had been Lewis's death, which had engendered in him complex, conflicting thoughts and feelings. He sealed his lips regarding public assessment of his friend, declaring that "I feel his loss so deeply that I have since his death refused to write or speak about him." But in private he revealed both intense loyalty and disquieting bitterness. To some he protested Lewis's posthumous treatment by the popular press ("He was a great man of whom the cold-blooded official obituaries only scraped the surface, in places with injustice"), while he disclosed to a few select correspondents the depth of his scorn for Lewis's religious writings. This was nothing new; previously he had declined an invitation to prepare an obituary of Lewis (newspapers and magazines stock such items years in advance of a person's death), declaring that "a Catholic could not possibly say anything sincere about Jack's books without giving widespread offence." But his simmering resentment, stoked over the years not only by Lewis's Ulster biases but also by the latter's friendship with Williams, came to a boil with the posthumous publication in January 1964 of Lewis's *Letters to Malcolm: Chiefly on Prayer*. Composed during the last six months of Lewis's life, this book consists of letters from Lewis to a fictional correspondent on topics like the afterlife, God, and, of course, prayer. Like many of his other popular works, it offers affable common sense laced with sentimentality, as in this account of heaven: "And once again, after who knows what aeons of the silence and the dark, the birds will sing and the waters flow, and lights and shadows move across the hills and the faces of our friends laugh upon us with amazed recognition." Despite the occasionally weak imagery, *Letters to Malcolm* strikes most readers as a solid, pleasant presentation of fundamental Christian themes.

Tolkien saw it differently. To him, *Letters to Malcolm* was a monstrosity. He wrote to a Jesuit priest that "I personally found *Letters to Malcolm* a distressing and in parts horrifying work. I began a commentary on it, but if finished it would not be publishable." This commentary has never been released and is presumably lost. A. N. Wilson notes, however, that Tolkien's personal copy of *Malcolm* contains the marginal observation that the book is not "about prayer, but about Lewis praying." This sniping by Tolkien is not only based on an old-fashioned Catholic's objection to the views of an amateur Protestant theologian, as Wilson points out; it expresses also the drear state of his mind at the time. He was still mired in the bottomless bog that he had described to Unwin in 1960, trapped fast by illness, overwork, and anxiety over his wife's health, his children's faith, and his own failing powers. Exhaustion and depression lowered his inhibitions and loosened his tongue, allowing festering resentments to pour forth, as they had in his earlier objection to Lewis's "ponderous silliness" in *Studies in Words*. The sad truth is that the Tolkien-Lewis friendship fell victim to the insecurities of both men.

At least one event alleviated Tolkien's gloom. In May 1964, George Allen & Unwin published *Tree and Leaf*, a compendium of "Leaf by

INKLINGS FIRST AND LAST

485

Niggle" and a revised version of "On Fairy-Stories." Tolkien supplied the cover illustration, a line drawing of the Tree of Amalion with its serpentine truck and ornate leaves, an invention that, he told Rayner Unwin, "crops up regularly at those times when I feel driven to pattern-designing." Most reviewers praised the work, discerning in its twinned essay-and-tale expressions of the same rich, imaginative worldview that had informed *The Lord of the Rings*. By now, that monumental epic had made its author a small-scale celebrity, leaving him both gratified and irked. Like any writer, he enjoyed being read and praised, but he was troubled by those who borrowed names without permission from his invented cosmos, and he railed against the cross-Channel hydrofoil, christened *Shadowfax* after Gandalf's great, gray stallion. Still, his budding fame led to amusing anecdotes—some at his own expense—that he retailed with glee. In November 1964, he attended a lecture by Robert Graves ("a remarkable creature, entertaining, likeable, odd, bonnet full of wild bees, half-German, half-Irish, very tall, must have looked like Siegfried/Sigurd in his youth, *but* an Ass") and was introduced to a friendly young woman, with whom he chatted merrily until Graves interrupted to declare, "it is obvious neither of you has ever heard of the other before." The woman turned out to be Ava Gardner, the world-famous actress, utterly unknown to Tolkien "till people more aware of the world informed me that she was a film-star of some magnitude, and that the press of pressmen and storm of flash-bulbs on the steps of the Schools were not directed at Graves (and cert. not at me) but at her."

Money, by contrast, was never a laughing matter. Tolkien was greatly distressed when in 1965 the American science fiction publishing house Ace Books, on technically murky but possibly legal grounds, released an unauthorized version of *The Lord of the Rings* for which Tolkien received no royalties. His official British and American publishers protested loudly, as did the aggrieved author, who appended a note to his American correspondence urging a boycott of the Ace edition. The press soon learned of the controversy and a transcontinental uproar ensued. Tolkien prepared a lightly revised version of the book for copyright purposes, remarking to Rayner Unwin, while making changes, that "my admiration for the tightness of the author's construction is somewhat increased. The poor fellow (who now seems to me only a remote friend) must have put a lot of work into it." The revised, authorized version appeared in October as a Ballantine Book paperback, with the following biting statement, signed by Tolkien, on the cover: "This paperback edition, and no other, has been published with my consent and co-operation. Those who approve of courtesy (at least) to living authors will purchase it and no other." Ace caved in, paid Tolkien a royalty, and ceased reprinting its edition. Some might suggest that Tolkien owed Ace the royalty, for the brouhaha made his fortune, transforming his epic from a literary curiosity into an enormous cause célèbre. Young readers, avid consumers of fantasy, now learned of the trilogy's existence and devoured it in droves. By 1966, it sat atop the *New York Times* paperback fiction bestseller list.

Meanwhile, *The Silmarillion* languished in utero. Tolkien continued to alter the text, refining its cosmogony and cosmology and bringing the assorted tales into harmony with *The Lord of the Rings*, but the work resisted final revision. Nonetheless, on September 12, 1965, Tolkien wrote to a member of the Tolkien Society of America, describing the book's state as "confused" but expressing hope—an echo sounding down the decades!— that a portion might be published in 1966. This hope brightened a few months later, albeit briefly, when Clyde S. Kilby, an American professor at Wheaton College (Illinois) who had hosted talks by Barfield and had founded the C. S. Lewis Collection (which would later become the Marion E. Wade Center, devoted to research on Lewis, Tolkien, Williams, Barfield, MacDonald, Chesterton, and Sayers), volunteered to assist as needed on *The Silmarillion*. Tolkien accepted gratefully, and Kilby spent most of the following summer in Oxford on a mission of mixed fruits, as Tolkien spurned most of his visitor's editorial suggestions while basking in his admiration. In the event, *The Silmarillion* continued its prodigious gestation.

On March 22, 1966, Tolkien and Edith marked their golden wedding anniversary with a double celebration at Merton College: a luncheon on March 22 and a dinner the following evening at which the British composer Donald Swann performed, with the singer William Elvin, portions of a song cycle based on *The Lord of the Ring* (the cycle was published in 1967 as *The Road Goes Ever On*). As a follow-up, in mid-September the couple departed on a Mediterranean cruise. This voyage, a second honeymoon considerably more adventurous than the couple's original week-long stay in 1916 in Clevendon, a Victorian-era seaside resort, seemed jinxed from the start. Edith fell on board soon after the ship left port, injuring her arthritic leg, and later on, Tolkien developed a throat infection. As a result of these setbacks, the couple rarely left the boat but did arrange to set foot on Asian soil in Izmir, Turkey; Tolkien also managed to attend a Mass at St. Mark's in Venice. Like Kilby's visit to Oxford a few months earlier, the Mediterranean tour was a happy occasion that failed to meet expectations. Unadulterated joy, Tolkien was reminded as his life wound down, thrived only within the precincts of the Eucharist. Every human effort, even subcreation, was vulnerable to loss and sorrow.

This lesson suffuses *Smith of Wootton Major*, his last completed work of fiction, published in November 1967. He had begun the novella in late 1964, after receiving an invitation from Pantheon Books in New York to write a preface to a new edition of George MacDonald's fairy tale, "The Golden Key." Tolkien accepted the assignment only to discover, upon re-reading the story, that he despised its vision of Faërie, which was sweeter, thinner, and less numinous than his own (Kilby recalls that during his summer in Oxford, Tolkien "frequently fired verbal cannonades at George MacDonald"). When Tolkien sat down to write his preface, he decided to illustrate the qualities of good fairy fiction by supplying a freshly minted example of his own. Soon this composition so captured him that he jettisoned the preface, which was never completed, and instead produced *Smith of Wootton Major*. The book recounts the adventures of the titular hero, a boy who eats a fairy star hidden in a Great Cake. When the star falls out of his mouth some months later, he fixes it to his forehead. It becomes his passport to Faërie, where he wanders at will, meeting a young maiden, the fairy queen in disguise, who dances "on a lawn beside a river bright with lilies" in a scene reminiscent of Edith's dance for Tolkien in the woods half a century earlier. Through these and other encounters, Smith acquires humility, kindness, and insight, enabling him to make the great sacrifice of bidding farewell to Faërie and passing the star on to another deserving young boy.

Smith of Wootton Major received mixed reviews. The American writer Robert Phelps, in *The New York Times Book Review*, called it "a good tale, dense and engrossing," but Naomi Mitchison, who had been an early defender of *The Lord of the Rings*, wrote in the *Glasgow Herald* that "Tolkien needs a bigger canvas and harder work on it if one is to become involved and convinced." The book proved popular with the public, despite widespread disappointment that it was not a tale of the Shire; when Tolkien read the story before publication at Blackfriars, Oxford's Dominican Hall and Studium, more than eight hundred people showed up in the pouring rain. By now, his name had become a magical lure and anything by him glittered. *Smith* appealed also to many scholars, who ventured a number of fanciful interpretations. Some saw in the hero a likeness to Tolkien, or perhaps to Anodos, MacDonald's protagonist in *Phantastes*, while others read the story as an apology for the author's failings as a philologist, or as a Christian allegory (despite Tolkien's repudiation of that genre), or a fictional valedictory, or even a commentary upon Vatican II. In a letter to Roger Lancelyn Green, Tolkien describes it as "an old man's book, already weighted with the presage of 'bereavement.'" With this in mind, Smith's surrender of the fairy star is the crux of the tale; we must let go of even the most precious things, when our time has come and gone.

The Inklings, too, at least as a corporate entity, had reached its end. A handful of gatherings were held after Lewis's death, attended by the stalwart few, but without the maestro's ebullient presence they proved poor pantomimes of the original and soon ceased. From now on, members would meet one another for a beer or lunch or dinner or by chance. Ironically, just as the Inklings dwindled away, the first significant study of the group appeared, *The Precincts of Felicity* (1966) by Charles Moorman, an American English professor, medievalist, and Arthurian scholar. Dubbing his subjects the Oxford Christians, Moorman concentrates on Lewis, Tolkien, Williams, T. S. Eliot and Dorothy L. Sayers; the last two, he claims, may be usefully located on the "periphery" of the group. This is inaccurate, markedly so in the case of Eliot, but Moorman manages to introduce readers to the Tuesday morning and Thursday night meetings, provides a roster of the chief participants, and, among some wild hazards (predicting, for instance, that Beat writers Jack Kerouac and Allen Ginsberg would prove a passing fad), accurately foresees that the Inklings may become "in days to come . . . a movement."

Warnie, for one, disliked Moorman's book, as he did all accounts of the Inklings that depicted them as anything more than like-minded fellows raising glasses and voices in joyful fellowship. He called the book "silly," misread Moorman's account of literary alliances as suggesting a "group mind" among the Inklings, and found the inclusion of Eliot and Sayers to be, correctly, "frankly absurd." His negative assessment should be taken with a grain of salt, however, as he was still engulfed in grief and deeply sensitive about his brother's legacy. Lewis haunted his thoughts, day and night. Just a few days after blasting Moorman, Warnie wrote in his diary of hearing a song that swept him into the past, when he and his brother idled in the shrubbery at Little Lea, smoking cigars and listening to the gramophone; a week after that, he jotted down a dream in which he and Lewis "died at the same instant and found ourselves walking hand in hand in twilight over an immense featureless plain," until a mysterious force drew them apart, Lewis "holding out both hands to me until the last when he was absorbed into white light which gave out no radiance."

No radiance: so it was, so it would be. The world had become a dark, dreary void. Rereading his diary, he stumbled on an old account (from June 1947) of panic at imagining "the empty years" if his brother should die first. "But little did I realize," he added, in the inescapable gloom of the present, "how empty they were to be." He fought the sorrow as best he could, even moving out of the Kilns for a time to alleviate his misery. His anguish intensified, and then his body broke down as if rent by grief. He developed terrible insomnia, then a slipped disk, and in 1965 suffered a stroke that impaired his speech and partially paralyzed his right hand. On New Year's Day 1966, he awoke in the "Hell-hole," his term for Warneford mental hospital. "The hospital atmosphere is killing me, and I am seriously worried at my mental decay," he writes. "I often find myself wishing that God would send me another stroke which would carry me off painlessly in my sleep. God help me!"

Warnie's suffering included continued regret at not having kept a better diary. He was pleased with his histories of France, but he knew that his brother had been the finest thing in his life and still lamented his failure to "Boswellise" him while he could. In partial reparation he wrote a biography of Lewis, on the model of the seventeenth-century French "life and letters" memoir, interspersing brief narrative accounts with letters, diary entries, and poems representing the successive periods of Lewis's life. The original resides as a 471-page typescript in the archives of the Marion E. Wade Center at Wheaton College, Illinois. Jocelyn Gibb, who acquired the rights to this material for Geoffrey Bles, hired the writer Christopher Derrick to transform the book into a collection of letters, prefaced by a heavily edited version of Warnie's memoir. When it appeared in this reworked form in 1966, Warnie was livid; he considered Derrick a

"busybody" and a "fool" and blamed him (though the decision had actually been Gibb's) for adding to the collection letters from Lewis to Barfield
consisting of "withering discourse on the nothingness of the utterness or
some similar topic."

His French research completed, his memorials to his brother rebuffed
or radically altered, Warnie withdrew into a narrow round of bad sleep,
meals, naps, television, reading, visits to neighbors, and long bouts of
boredom. His brother's fans interrupted his solitude while imparting no
pleasure, and he worried in his diary that "on my death bed—or at any
rate the day before—I shall have some verbose American standing over
me and lecturing on some little observed significance of J's work. Oh
damn, damn, DAMN!" In 1966, Clyde Kilby came to call, the two became friends—Warnie, whose diary sketches had grown increasingly
acerbic, describes Kilby as "that nice type of American . . . [having] something of the dog which with wagging tail appeals to you to like him"—
and together they visited Whipsnade Zoo. But such interruptions were
rare; for the most part, *no radiance* ruled the day.

"A Very Lucky Man"

"It is rather queer, after a lifetime of writing (in so far as it was spent in
writing at all) almost unread, as it seemed, and usually very nearly unpublished books, to keep on being told at the age of 70 that they have
really meant something to quite a few people," remarked Barfield to the
American scholar R. J. Reilly in 1969. "I think perhaps I was a very lucky
man." Luck, or reward for years of uncompensated effort, was flying his
way at last. After his Brandeis stint, he returned home to England for a
year, then traveled back to America to teach, again at Drew University
and then at Hamilton College, which awarded him an honorary doctorate. Hamilton's small size and its original aim of turning "Red Indians
into Christian gentleman," as Barfield put it to Harwood, added a "not
unpleasingly Gilbert & Sullivan touch to the whole proceeding, but that
doesn't prevent it from tickling my vanity." Every bit as gratifying was an
essay by G. B. Tennyson, an English professor at UCLA, in *The Southern
Review* (Winter 1969) on "Owen Barfield and the Rebirth of Meaning."
This was the first serious academic appraisal of Barfield's work. Tennyson
provides a genial summary of his subject's career, laying out Barfield's views

on philology and consciousness—including a dose of Anthroposophy—while contending, with an enthusiasm that edges into advocacy, that "his researches into the nature of poetry and inspiration have repeatedly taken him to the secret places of the spirit."

His self-confidence growing yet stronger from these intoxicating endorsements, Barfield began to renew his contact with other Inklings. Nevill Coghill expressed thanks for a "charming" message and passed along the disclosure, undoubtedly an eye-opener to Barfield, that he, too, suffered from self-doubts, and that they had crippled his chances of getting as close to Lewis as Barfield and Williams had managed to do: "I always felt that there was too little I could contribute in exchange for the time it took from him," Coghill wrote. "Towards the end . . . we had more frequent meetings. But it was too late to establish *new* kinds of insight and sympathy." Barfield, continuing his Inkling outreach, traveled at least twice to the Kilns during the late 1960s for overnight stays with Warnie. During a visit on July 29–30, 1969, he shocked his host by admitting to a firm belief in reincarnation. That this essential feature of Anthroposophy came as news to Warnie tells us just how innocent he had been of his brother's intellectual battles, including the Lewis-Barfield "Great War." In the late 1970s, Barfield also revived his correspondence with Colin Hardie, who wrote that "I am so glad to hear from you again. I cannot remember when we last corresponded, but only that you deplored my acceptance of evolution" (one imagines this was not the first time Barfield received that particular response). Hardie continued, in an old man's vein, that "since the *Times* (fortunately to reappear, at what price?, next week) vanished"—the newspaper was on strike—"one hasn't known who is alive, and I am glad that you are and are still writing and thinking about Coleridge . . . I am feeling a slow decay (e.g. of memory and teeth)."

Letters, in these halcyon days of the late 1960s and '70s, now poured in to Barfield from ardent admirers, some of them major figures in the countercultural thinking that had mesmerized a large portion of the American intelligentsia. Theodore Roszak told him of the nation's hunger for spiritual rebirth, David Bohm discussed quantum physics and polarity, and Norman O. Brown, author of the mantic, enigmatic *Love's Body*, wrote that he was rereading Steiner's *Cosmic Memory* and hunting for a commentary on root-races and Atlanteans. Intellectual revolution was in the air, and the soft-spoken English lawyer-philosopher who preached the evolution of consciousness fit right in. Barfield was invited to teach at the University of Missouri (Columbia), and, in later years, at SUNY Stony Brook and the University of British Columbia. Harwood wrote to say that "I heard from Walter Hooper that you were getting VIP treatment in America." Readers sent him political manifestos, accounts of their dreams and visions, requests for spiritual guidance, and an avalanche of bulky manuscripts, many mad, poorly written, or both; he answered all courteously, often at length. Maud, impressed by her husband's newfound fame, reassessed her rejection of his esoteric path and came to see, as he recalled, "that I wasn't just a fanatic or a fool . . . when it came to anthroposophy." Now in her eighties, she was aging rapidly and weighed down by worries, especially over their daughter Lucy, who had fallen victim to multiple sclerosis and become a shut-in. "She is not well enough to *do* anything or *go* anywhere," wrote Barfield to an American correspondent. "What a life for a young woman of 35 or so. The thought of it gnaws at my vitals all the time."

Still, the fight against RUP must go on, along with the broader battle to demonstrate the spiritual basis of mind and matter. In 1971, Barfield advanced his campaign by publishing *What Coleridge Thought*, his last major book and the summing-up of decades of research and analysis. In what may well be his magnum opus, he sets out to demonstrate that Coleridge's work presents an original and coherent philosophy that offers a key to the nature of consciousness. Barfield proceeds thematically, exploring—often by looking at literary fragments passed over by many earlier scholars—Coleridge's views on thinking, nature, life, imagination, understanding, reason, law, God, society, and so on. He concludes that Coleridge's philosophy is neither a haphazard by-product of opium, poetizing, and an overheated imagination, nor a rehash of Platonism, Protestantism, and idealism, but a rich, completely satisfying worldview resting squarely upon the law of polarity.

That Coleridge believed in such a law seems incontestable, given this passage from his 1818 "Treatise on Method": "Contemplating in all Electrical phenomena the operation of a Law which reigns through all Nature, viz. the law of *polarity*, or the manifestation of one power by opposite forces." Barfield emphasizes that Coleridge's view of polarity has little in common with the reconciliation of opposites so frequently evoked in modern literary and psychological studies; Barfield dismisses the latter as an academic abstraction, whereas polarity, in the Coleridgean sense, is a living, creative, fructifying power. As Barfield describes it, "Where logical opposites are contradictory, polar opposites are generative of each other—and together generative of new product."

Interpenetrating opposites generating a "new product" is, of course, also a description of sexual reproduction, and, from a broader perspective, of the process of evolution. Barfield argues that Coleridge provides the receptive modern thinker with "a full-fledged theory of evolution alternative to, and largely incompatible with, the one he has been taught to revere." The incompatibility is twofold. It resides not only in the mechanism of evolution, which Coleridge ascribes to intermingling forces rather than random mutation, but also in the realization—very hard for most modern thinkers to swallow—that in nature everything, rocks as well as animals, evolves. To accept these truths requires an act of imagination, in the special (Steinerian) sense of perceiving subtle spiritual truths. Meditating on polarity leads to such truths, for "the apprehension of polarity," Barfield argues, "is itself *the basic act of imagination* [Barfield's italics]," and leads to astonishing discoveries. For example, according to Barfield, Coleridge realized, in the course of his reflections, that nature and mind are inseparable. It was no idle fancy when the poet imagined a major force in evolution to be a *"Yearning"* that is "hallowing, sanctifying." This means, as Barfield explains in one of those explosive observations that he tends to unleash almost in passing, that scientific materialism is dead, that "the whole Laplace-Lyell-Darwin, closed-system universe (together with its fancied billions of earth-years and millions of 'light-years')" must be jettisoned.

What takes its place, according to Barfield's reading of Coleridge, is a spiritual vision of polar forces—God/man, man/nature, will/reason, and many more—suffusing the evolutionary process, with Christ's advent as the pivotal event in the process. Coleridge, in other words, "Like Hegel . . . was moving on from the notion of a history of thought ('history of ideas' as it is commonly called) towards that of an evolution of consciousness." Coleridge failed to attain this holy grail of understanding because the required imaginative leap was too great, the old way of thinking too imbedded. Nonetheless, Barfield concludes, Coleridge anticipated and came close to attaining the visionary breakthrough achieved a century later by Steiner, whose presence, as readers familiar with Barfield's work will have perceived long ago, informs so much of the book.

Many critics enthused over *What Coleridge Thought*. In the *Journal of the American Academy of Religion*, the historian of religion Antony C. Yu praises Barfield's presentation as "orderly and lucid," while in *Studies in Romanticism*, the literary critic G. A. Cevasco calls it (along with the highly controversial *Coleridge: The Damaged Angel* by Norman Fruman, which paints the poet as a plagiarist and liar) "quite indispensable to serious students of Coleridge." Neither reviewer, however, confronted the radical conclusions of Barfield's argument. Another Coleridge expert by the name of John Colmer did, and his report in *Modern Language Review* bristles with caveats. He applauds Barfield for his "admirable grasp of the totality of Coleridge's thought" but accuses him of slighting the complexities of Coleridge's philosophical arguments. Yet more damagingly, Colmer asserts that Coleridge was "being used" by Barfield "to combat all the aspects of modern materialism that the author most dislikes." Colmer challenges in particular the "uncritical coupling" of Coleridge and Steiner, "minds of such dissimilar quality." Barfield could not have been happy with this review. He welcomed intellectual disagreements but chafed at those that he thought misrepresented his views; a report in *The Review of English Studies* by the Wordsworth scholar W.J.B. Owen so incensed him with its failure to grasp his argument that he shot off protest letters to the author and to the editor of the journal.

Despite the objections of Colmer and Owen, Barfield scored a major triumph with *What Coleridge Thought*. He had made his mark in Coleridge studies—while in his seventies!—and, by so doing, had sailed out of the backwaters of Anthroposophical argumentation and philological-historical analysis into the mainstream of English literary criticism, establishing himself as a serious, astute analyst of one of Romanticism's most enigmatic poets and essayists. His scholarly stature grew apace, and for much of the next two decades he taught, lectured, and wrote with sterling credentials as an intellectual celebrity in his own right, rather than solely as Lewis's bosom friend. He made no further advances in Coleridge studies, however. In the late 1970s, he agreed to edit the poet's "Lectures on the History of Philosophy" for *The Collected Works of Samuel Taylor Coleridge*, but his contribution foundered, a victim of his advanced years and his lack of expertise in scholarly editing. *What Coleridge Thought* struck gold, and in doing so, exhausted the vein.

Into the Dark

On July 19, 1967, Tolkien traveled to London to receive, along with Dame Rebecca West, the A. C. Benson Silver Medal from the Royal Society of Literature. He told the audience at the ceremony that, of all the rewards of writing *The Lord of the Rings*, "I think that receiving this silver medal is the most astonishing as it is the most delightful." De rigueur politeness aside, he meant it. The Royal Society was an arbiter of British literary taste; however loudly his detractors scoffed, the medal spoke more loudly still. He was now and would be forevermore a recognized figure in the history of English letters. The pleasure surrounding this triumph was in part personal, the satisfaction of someone who, considering himself an amateur "in a world of great writers," had bested the field. But it was also sheer joy at the triumph of his kind of narrative, replete with heroes, villains, fantastic beings, imaginary lands, and an absorbing plot. "And after all that has happened," he told two reporters for *The Daily Telegraph Magazine*, speaking of himself and Lewis, "the most lasting pleasure and reward for both of us has been that we provided one another with stories to hear or read that we really liked." The decades of doubt had ended; he knew now that the world liked them, too.

Yet still he kept the world at bay. Besieged by journalists, photographers, and readers, he "found none of them pleasant, nearly all of them a complete waste of time." The portcullis descended, he refused to be photographed in his house, and he complained bitterly about interviews, even those that his publishers believed would boost sales. During the summer of 1968, Tolkien and Edith moved out of Oxford to Poole, a seaside resort on the English Channel, adjacent to Bournemouth, where they had vacationed since the early 1950s. Edith rejoiced in the change; she had felt isolated among the Oxford intelligentsia, while in Bournemouth she had friends who shared her interests in family, music, and the like. For Tolkien, the move meant the loss of friends, especially in academia, a painful sacrifice; still, he relished the prospect of escaping city bustle and, even more important, intrusions from nosy fans. He was at home in Oxford, preparing for the move, when on June 17 he tumbled down a flight of stairs. The accident resulted in an immediate operation at Nuffield Orthopaedic Centre. After a month in the hospital, fretting and fussing (and, at least at first, terrified that his leg would be amputated), he moved to Bournemouth, his leg encased in a plaster cast, where he rejoined Edith, who had preceded him.

The Tolkiens inhabited a small bungalow at 19 Lakeside Drive in Poole for more than three years. Tolkien likened it to "a ship or ark," an appropriate image for a haven of escape from Oxford turmoil. Seen from the garden, the house resembled a ship, surrounded by roses instead of water. During his residence there, Tolkien produced several philological, etymological, and historical studies on his legendarium, covering such arcane themes as Númenórean measurement, Rohan's military matters, and Elvish reincarnation. Many of these pieces remained unfinished, some decaying into what Christopher Tolkien called "chaotic and illegible or unintelligible notes and jottings." Wearing down, Tolkien was determined to pass on to the world as much knowledge of Middle-earth as possible. He longed to compile grammars of Quenya and Sindarin, and he continued to draw, in colored pencils and pen, curious Elvish heraldic designs and flowering or paisley doodles. "'Stories' still sprout in my mind from names," he told his son Michael, asking for prayers that he might live long enough to record them.

During this time, he became increasingly upset over certain developments in the Catholic Church. The liturgical changes in the wake of Vatican II disturbed him deeply. He furiously objected to the adoption of the vernacular during Mass and cringed at the casual attitude of many Catholics toward dress, prayer, and pious practices; Clyde Kilby records that the failure of some people to genuflect once distressed Tolkien so much that he "made his way awkwardly to the aisle and there made three very low bows, then stomped out of the church." He continued to communicate, to family and friends, his own deeply held beliefs; one of the most interesting letters of his final years is addressed to Camilla Unwin, Rayner's young daughter, who had written Tolkien to ask the purpose of life. He begins his lengthy response by pointing out that the question is really about the purpose of human beings and the "things they design and make" (that is, subcreation, although Tolkien does not employ the term). Inevitably, he continues, the discovery of design or pattern leads to the discovery of Mind, and from there to the discovery of God. Life's purpose, then, is to know, praise, and thank God, a truth he underscores by quoting, in English and Latin, key passages of the *Gloria in excelsis Deo*, a Christian hymn dating to the fourth century or earlier and sung to this day in the liturgy of the Catholic Mass. Presumably, Camilla was a bright child who knew her Latin; surely, she must have been delighted by this long, eloquent testament from such a famous man, with its kindly yet serious tone and its delightful way of proceeding in logical leaps and bounds from her fundamental question to the heights of faith.

In July 1969, Tolkien complained of pain and depression. His doctor diagnosed a diseased gallbladder and placed him on a fat-and-alcohol-free diet. This strict regimen was modified once X-rays proved negative; nonetheless, the episode left him feeling isolated, helpless, brooding over his health and that of his wife. Edith's arthritis continued to worsen, and in April 1970, she slipped in the bath, fracturing her shoulder. The injury healed, after a stint in an arm sling, and she and Tolkien were able to resume for a while their quiet Bournemouth habits, he working with diminished energies on *The Silmarillion* and related projects, she enjoying the company of friends. Rayner Unwin came to visit, as did Pauline Baynes, bringing along a painted map of Bilbo's journey in *The Hobbit*. In October 1971, Tolkien lost his appetite and took to his bed; he remained unfit until Christmas and told Michael he had dropped more than a stone (fourteen pounds) in weight. But the great blow fell on November 19 of that year, when Edith's gallbladder became inflamed. After more than a week in the hospital, during which she grew better and then relapsed, she died, age eighty-two, on November 29. Three days later, a Requiem Mass was held at 9:00 a.m. in Bournemouth, and the same afternoon she was buried in Wolvercote Cemetery, Oxford. "I am utterly bereaved, and cannot yet lift up heart, but my family is gathering round me and many friends," wrote Tolkien the day she died. By Christmas Eve, he was still engulfed in mourning and unable to work, writing to a correspondent that "she was my *Lúthien Tinúviel*"—the lovely Half-elven princess who exchanged her immortality for the love of the mortal hero Beren—"with her raven hair and fair face and bright starry eyes." Almost immediately, he looked for a means to return to Oxford. A solution emerged when Christopher wrote to the warden of Merton College, describing his father's predicament and asking for help; the school responded by offering

Tolkien a resident fellowship that encompassed a suite of rooms at the school and the assistance of a caretaker and his wife. Tolkien traveled back to Oxford in March, riding with the movers in their furniture van. He dove happily into college life, reveling in the Fellows' Garden, ablaze with butterflies and flowers, and in renewed contact with academic friends. He began to climb out of his sorrow.

On March 22, the *Oxford Mail* ran a cheerful interview with him in which he said what he had been saying for decades, that *The Silmarillion*, or a part of it, would be published "before very long." On March 27, he traveled to London to receive the next day the CBE (Commander of the British Empire, the same award that Lewis had rejected in 1951) from Queen Elizabeth. In June, Oxford University awarded him an honorary doctorate of letters, in a ceremony at the Sheldonian with a tribute in Latin by Colin Hardie, who was by now public orator of the university. Hardie's address ended with the ringing if quixotic aspiration that "as the Road goes ever on, he [Tolkien] will produce from his store Simarillion and scholarship." But as the honors accrued, creativity diminished, and Tolkien found it increasingly difficult to focus on his work. *The Silmarillion* would not appear during his lifetime.

In spite of his dwindling powers, however, Tolkien fulfilled perfectly, during this first year at Merton, the role of paterfamilias and famous if aging author. He made the rounds of his scattered family, including his brother Hilary in Evesham, with whom he imbibed whiskey and television shows; donated to charity the desk upon which he had written *The Hobbit*; visited the offices of Allen & Unwin, who treated him royally, as befitted their principal source of income; and dealt with hundreds of letters and gifts from admirers, including a steel goblet that bore, in Sauron's Black Speech, the "terrible words seen on the Ring. I of course have never drunk from it, but use it for tobacco ash."

Warnie, meanwhile, had heard of Edith Tolkien's death by reading the *Telegraph*. "Peace to her ashes," he wrote in his diary, where he often brooded over his own death and postmortem fate. The diary itself was dying, visited only at long intervals: twelve entries in 1970, six in 1971, six in 1972. He had brought his drinking under control but was prone to poor circulation and dizzy spells, which increased when a pacemaker was implanted in January 1972. The following August he sailed to Ireland for a month of rest and companionship with the sisters at Our Lady of Lourdes Hospital in Drogheda. While there, he developed gangrene in his feet, underwent surgery, and remained abroad for most of a year. The following April 9, back at the Kilns, he collapsed, died, and was buried beside his brother in Headington.

Three miles away in Merton College, Tolkien was under siege. "I have been assailed by hosts of people, and worse, have been invaded by criminals, so that I live behind locked doors, and under the eye of the local C.I.D." The assailants, as usual, were fans and journalists; the invaders were thieves, who stole his CBE medal and some of Edith's jewelry. In addition to these aggravations, he was oppressed by physical frailty and failure to complete *The Silmarillion*. To a long-term friend and correspondent he confessed that he had "lost confidence," comparing himself to an "old man" who "sits cold and unable to muster courage to go out on a journey that his heart desires to make." During August 1973, he managed some notes revising the history of Galadriel; Christina Scull and Wayne G. Hammond speculate that this may have been the last addition to his vast creation. The same month, he sat for his last photograph, taken by his grandson Michael George in Oxford's Botanical Garden: an image of an old man with cane, dressed in tweed jacket, flannel pants, and ornamental waistcoat, leaning against a *Pinus nigra*, a tree cultivated in Great Britain and South Africa, thus linking his first and final days. Three weeks later, on August 31, while in Bournemouth visiting friends, he was hospitalized with a bleeding ulcer. John and Priscilla rushed to his bedside (the other children were on the Continent). A chest infection developed, and Tolkien succumbed on September 2. After a funeral Mass in Headington concelebrated by John, Fr. Robert Murray, and the local parish priest, he was laid alongside Edith in Wolvercote Cemetery. Creation and subcreation, history and story merged into one, as the granite gravestone read "Edith Mary Tolkien, Luthien, 1889–1971. John Ronald Reuel Tolkien, Beren, 1892–1973."

An Unexpected Friendship

As Barfield's reputation continued to expand, a new crop of friends, colleagues, and acolytes emerged. The most famous—and, at first glance, one of the most unlikely—was the American novelist Saul Bellow, whose sprawling seriocomic novels would garner him the Nobel Prize in

Literature in 1976. On June 3, 1975, he wrote to Barfield from Chicago, explaining that he had studied *Saving the Appearances* and *Unancestral Voice* and wished to consult with Barfield about "the Meggid and about Gabriel and Michael and their antagonists." He added, as if concerned that Barfield might suspect his motives or worry that a popular novelist lacked the delicacy of mind to apprehend spiritual truths, that "I am, I assure you, very much in earnest." Although Barfield did not know it at the time, Bellow's earnestness had been amply expressed in his latest novel, *Humboldt's Gift*, which teemed with Anthroposophical musings.

Barfield responded favorably, and the two met for lunch a few weeks later in London at Barfield's club, the Athenaeum. The meeting went well, the American sitting at the Englishman's feet, the humble disciple querying the master. "I was a totally unknown quantity," Bellow wrote Barfield afterward, "and felt that I had failed to show why I should be taken seriously." A telling moment occurred at this session, or possibly during a second lunch in London before Bellow returned to the States, when Barfield asked Bellow his age. Bellow answered "Sixty," to which Barfield, with a smile, said "Sixteen?" Bellow, convinced of his spiritual immaturity, took this as an "entirely justified" joke, whereas the truth was simply that Barfield had misheard his response. As it happened, however, Barfield did harbor doubts about Bellow. He described them on October 25, writing that "of course there's no guarantee that he will not lose interest and go on to something else. But I make that remark as applicable to any exceptionally volatile mind capable of producing 'best-sellers,' not as arising from my actual impression of him."

Despite these hesitations, the relationship mellowed into a warm, if brief, friendship. Bellow pored over Steiner's works and tackled his spiritual exercises, which Barfield had sent him. This practice gave him "a certain daily stability," but he found it a struggle at his age to change his ways and reimagine the world in Steiner's visionary terms. Barfield, firmly set in his own ways, read *Humboldt's Gift* and told Bellow that "I couldn't get up enough interest in enough of what was going on to be held by it. If it's any comfort to you . . . I had very much the same experience with the Lord of the Rings." But Bellow had no interest in *The Lord of the Rings*, and Barfield's comment stung. He took it with grace, however, as a good student must, and continued his esoteric research, highlighted by a university seminar during which he led discussions of *Saving the Appear-*

ances and *Worlds Apart*. He also shipped Barfield a Parker Knoll armchair as an expression of gratitude and affection. Barfield, however, maintained his criticism of Bellow's fiction and on August 15, 1979, the latter put his foot down, telling Barfield that "I can't easily accept your dismissal of so much investment of soul . . . You don't like novels? Very well. But novels have for forty years been my trade; and if I do acquire some wisdom it will inevitably, so I suppose, take some 'novelistic' expression. Why not?" Barfield wrote back immediately, saying that he had meant no harm, that he had assumed that criticizing the novels of a Nobel Prize winner was akin to the "damage . . . a peashooter will do to an armored car." Bellow responded in kind, happy to return to his subordinate role, declaring that "four or five years of reading Steiner have altered me considerably" and hoping that by the time he died "I will have made some progress . . . and you won't have to be quite so severe with me."

After this embarrassing kerfuffle, the correspondence dried up for three years. Then, in 1982, Barfield agreed to review Bellow's new novel, *The Dean's December*, for the U.S.-based Anthroposophical journal, *Towards*. His evaluation, largely a convoluted retelling of the story, is unforgiving and at times hostile. He complains that the tale has too little plot, too much "excruciating" self-consciousness, too many metaphors, and summarizes it, in a creaky metaphor of his own, as "a journey through fascinating country in a jerky, stopping-and-starting wagon." As if aware that he had gone too far, he tacks on a conciliatory final sentence, noting that the book makes "a deep and lasting impression."

The damage had been done. Bellow, who received an advance copy of the review, was deeply wounded. He wrote to Barfield, offering the customary obeisance ("perhaps your understanding of the book is better than my own"), and then advising him that "you failed to find the key, the musical signature without which books like mine can't be read." Barfield and he inhabited different worlds: "I was aware from our first meeting that I was far more alien to you than you were to me"; Barfield knew nothing of the American Jewish sensibility and next to nothing about modern fiction; as a result he misread a "hard, militant and angry book" as an indulgent exercise in self-consciousness.

The assessment is hard to dispute. The two men had attempted to traverse a perhaps unbridgeable chasm. Bellow painted the world, Barfield parsed it; Bellow sought meaning, Barfield had found it. The two had little more in common than Tolkien and Ava Gardner, and Bellow and Barfield's friendship, although sustained for seven years rather than a single hour, produced little more in the way of lasting fruit. After the *Towards* review, they never spoke to each other again.

Waning and Waxing

Meanwhile, the ranks of the Inklings thinned rapidly. C. L. Wrenn died in 1969, Warnie, Tolkien, and R. B. McCallum in 1973, Hugo Dyson in 1975, along with Barfield's and Lewis's close friend Cecil Harwood. Fr. Gervase Mathew passed on in 1976, Adam Fox in 1977. Nevill Coghill died in 1980, after achieving, late in life, notoriety for codirecting *Doctor Faustus*, a film adaptation of Marlowe's play with Richard Burton declaiming and Elizabeth Taylor disrobing, and accolades for cowriting a modern English musical of Chaucer's *Canterbury Tales* that pleased critics and audiences in London's West End and around the world.

As the Inklings diminished in number, however, their fame multiplied. *The Lord of the Rings* and the Narnia books continued to enjoy spectacular sales; in 1975, Barfield learned from a correspondent that Crown Princess Michiko of Japan was reading his books, along with those of Lewis and Tolkien. Two years later, *The Silmarillion* appeared in print and became an international bestseller. It had fallen to Christopher Tolkien to create a publishable book out of the mountain of manuscript and typescript, fragmentary and finished *Silmarillion* tales that his father had left behind: a nearly overwhelming task. His desire to do justice to his father's legacy is palpable. Christopher had lived in the world of *The Silmarillion* since childhood; as he expressed it in an interview with *Le Monde*, "Si étrange que cela puisse paraître, j'ai grandi dans le monde qu'il avait créé . . . Pour moi, les villes du Silmarillion ont plus de réalité que Babylone" ("Strange as it may seem, I grew up in the world he created . . . For me, the cities of the Silmarillion possess more reality than Babylon"), and he had played a key part in every stage of its unfolding. A dream he remembered having after his father's death speaks volumes: "J'étais dans le bureau de mon père, à Oxford. Il entrait et se mettait à chercher quelque chose avec une grande anxiété. Alors je réalisais avec horreur qu'il s'agissait du Silmarillion, et j'étais terrifié à l'idée qu'il découvre ce que j'avais fait" ("I was in my father's office in Oxford. He came in and began searching for something with great anxiety. Then I realized with horror that it was the Silmarillion he was after, and I was terrified by the idea that he might discover what I had done"). *The Silmarillion* was the first fruit of his heroic labor. An unexpected harvest followed, as a vast corpus of *Silmarillion* material, along with other major elements of the legendarium, assembled with text-critical apparatus and commentary by Christopher from his father's writings, would appear in the twelve-volume *History of Middle-earth* (1983–96). Fittingly, *The Silmarillion* (book) did not exhaust the contents of the *Silmarillion* mythology.

In 1975, meanwhile, Barfield had written his only science fiction work, the novella *Night Operation*, a dark satire in which the human race, in Morlock fashion, has retreated underground, replacing the three Rs of traditional education with the three Es of a degenerate culture: ejaculation, (d)efecation, and eructation. Jon, a young man whose mind has been awakened by studying the nature of words, leads a few others to the Aboveground, where they undergo a mystical experience akin to Steiner's final participation. *Night Operation* is familiar in its dystopian miasma and didactic in its quasi-autobiographical unfolding, but it does manage to condense familiar Barfieldian occupations into a brief, engaging narrative. The same is true of Barfield's last fictional foray, *Eager Spring*, written in 1985, which examines Steinerian ideas in the context of ecological and environmental concerns. *Night Operation* appeared in *Towards*, while *Eager Spring* remained unpublished during Barfield's lifetime.

Throughout the 1970s and the first years of the '80s, Barfield stayed active on the American lecture and conference circuit as one of the more profound voices in an arena still heavily populated, in that volatile era, by flamboyant countercultural figures. He talked and wrote about Lewis, about Coleridge, and above all, about the nature of consciousness. His American followers continued to respond as they had never done in England. "North America has shown at least ten times as much enthusiasm for my stuff as has the UK," he wrote in a 1985 note addressed to his future literary executors. A Festschrift with the neatly encapsulating title of *Evolution of Consciousness: Studies in Polarity* appeared in 1976, edited, fittingly, by an American scholar, Shirley Sugerman. In 1978, Barfield delivered three talks at the University of British Columbia; the series appeared in 1979 as *History, Guilt, and Habit*, bearing on the cover of the paperback edition a blurb by Saul Bellow: "a clear, powerful thinker, and a subtle one."

At the same time, his personal life underwent significant change. Following the death of Cecil Harwood in 1975, he grew close to Marguerite, Cecil's widow, and by 1977 she was writing him from Cornwall to declare her love. Three years later, Maud died, age ninety-four. She had faded greatly, following a stroke that had put an end to her work as a dance instructor. Photos from this era show a hunched-up woman with a cane, supported by an erect, trim husband; the two resemble mother and son. Soon after Maud's death, Josephine Grant Watson (now Josephine Spence), with whom Barfield had remained friendly after their 1950s relationship had foundered, asked him—he was now eighty-two—why he didn't marry Marguerite. He gave the practical reasons—"I just can't imagine myself taking on the vast upheaval it would involve, house removal and all that, let alone the responsibility"—before acknowledging the most significant one, that "I suspect M. has a certain need of me . . . she is strenuous and energetic and determined, but there are times when all that fails her . . ." Barfield refers, in the same letter, to his strong feelings for Josephine, telling her that "Zwei *Damen* wohnen ach! in meiner Brust" ("two ladies live ah! in my breast"), wondering whether this means that "I am a bit of a blighter" and whether Josephine might conclude the same. Josephine, however, appeared content to guide and comfort Barfield in this matter as in others. In 1983, Marguerite died, closing the issue.

Now death surrounded Barfield, as it does all octogenarians. J.A.W. Bennett, who, upon Lewis's death, had succeeded him as Cambridge's professor of medieval and Renaissance literature, died in 1981; Dr. "Humphrey" Havard and James Dundas-Grant in 1985. Lord David Cecil passed away on New Year's Day 1986, after unleashing in his waning years a slew of biographical studies examining, with sympathetic eye and witty tongue, the life and art of Samuel Palmer and Edward Burne-Jones, Max Beerbohm, Jane Austen, Charles Lamb, and others. Cecil's had been a happy life, braced by deep Christian faith and a loving marriage. Gerard Irvine, a family friend, described him as one of William James's "once-born," those who, in James's words, "see God not as a strict Judge, not a Glorious Potentate; but as the animating Spirit of a beautiful harmonious world, beneficent and kind, merciful as well as pure." If he had attended Inkling meetings more regularly, he might have been the fifth focus of this book. Later that same year of 1986, Barfield moved to the Walhatch, a retirement home in East Sussex. Here he continued to hold court for visiting scholars, writers, and devotees of his own work as well as that of Steiner and Lewis. As his autumn whitened into winter, he turned out an occasional Anthroposophical piece, along with *Owen Barfield on C. S. Lewis*, a compilation of essays, talks, and poems on the friend with whom he would be forever tied. Reporters visiting him in the 1990s would find him, as if in conscious echo or parody of both Lewis and Tolkien, wreathed in smoke, pipe in hand, happily discoursing on the pleasures of tobacco and the nature of consciousness. In 1997 he told Walter Hooper that "I don't fear death, I fear dying." Above all he dreaded the physical ordeal: "I'm so tired," he told Hooper. "Imagine that someone arrives and says, 'Get up old man, you've got to go to China!' And off you go." "He was thinking," Hooper remarked, "of a Chinese junk, months and months on a choppy sea." On December 14, 1997, he passed away, at home, of bronchopneumonia. Hooper was at his side and comforted the dying man by saying, "I know what you're sad about—that trip to China! It's here, it's started, but it's not going to be choppy seas, it's going to take just a minute, and you *know* what's going to happen. The pearly gates open, you enter, C. S. Lewis and you will start all over again, all the things you wanted to argue about, you'll have it now." Barfield smiled—and died. Colin Hardie would last another ten months, expiring on October 17, 1998, but when Barfield closed his eyes, the life of the great Inklings came to an end.

EPILOGUE:
THE RECOVERED IMAGE

W hat, then, were the Inklings? Was John Wain right to call them (as we reported on the first page of this study) "a circle of instigators, almost of incendiaries, meeting to urge one another on in the task of redirecting the whole current of contemporary art and life"? Were they, rather, just a circle of friends, sharing talk, drink, jokes, and writings? Something in between or something other? The question vexed the Inklings themselves, their supporters, and their detractors during the group's existence and after its demise.

In 1955, David Cecil opened an informed and reasonable window upon the matter while exploring, "one fine evening in May amid the Gothic shades of New College," in conversation with the novelist Rachel Trickett, the possible existence of an "Oxford School"; he later published a summary in dialogue form in the journal *The Twentieth Century*. If not exactly a school, Cecil thought, "there *is* something one might call an Oxford atmosphere," and it had to do with a wide range of ideas "entertained imaginatively" in a "tradition of non-specialized cultured conversation," a "relaxed, humane atmosphere" that gives writers room to breathe, in which bitter controversies are relatively rare. Within this happy climate, many different kinds of writers flourished; but Cecil could think of only one instance of a coherent, if informal, group or circle: the Inklings.

The Inklings, Cecil explained, "combined voluminous learning . . . with a strong liking for fantasy. But this fantasy was not indulged independently of their ideas; it was fantasy *about* their ideas." And it was, in the best sense of the word, "boyish fantasy; the imagination of a romantic, adventurous kind of boy." The Inklings, then, constituted "Oxford's nearest recent approximation to a 'school' . . . a school of ideas expressed through adventurous but learned fantasy." In addition to erudition and boyish fantasy, Cecil thought, there was a third and paramount factor that united them: their Christianity.

Cecil noted that "when I read writers in the Cambridge number of *The Twentieth Century* apparently showing pained surprise that distinguished intellectual persons should avow a belief in God, I cannot help reflecting that in Oxford this has never been at all unusual." Rachel Trickett agreed: in Oxford, a "savour of grave and gracious piety," as she put it, still lingered. Lewis had the impression, too, that the soldiers returning to Oxford from World War II were more likely to be Christian than the returning soldiers of his own generation.

Of course there were Christians at Cambridge and modernists at Oxford, and plenty of anomalies on both sides (like T. S. Eliot, both Christian and modernist, and F. W. Bateson, both Christian and Leavisite). Moreover, Lewis himself warned against making too much of Oxford's Christian revival, pointing out in a 1946 article for *The Cherwell* that it could not be counted on to last: "Sooner or later it must lose the public ear; in a place like Oxford such changes are extraordinarily rapid. Bradley and the other idealists fell in a few terms, the Douglas scheme even more suddenly, the Vorticists overnight . . . Whatever in our present success mere Fashion has given us, mere Fashion will presently withdraw. The real conversions will remain: but nothing else will." Lewis was well aware, too, that a Christian atmosphere is no protection against preening egos. That the Inklings may have been on the whole more decent and less vain than many other literary coteries can only be because they made a conscious effort to follow the path of real conversion.

Lack of vanity is one reason why the Inklings vigorously resisted any account of the group as a formal school or movement. In a 1956 essay in *Books on Trial*, the novelist Charles A. Brady named Lewis, Tolkien, Williams, and Dorothy L. Sayers as members of an "Oxford Circle." "Lor' bless you," Lewis wrote to Brady in reply, "those dear friends of mine were never 'my school.' They were all older than I. Miss Sayers was an established author before I was heard of. Charles influenced me, not I him. And as for anyone influencing Tolkien, you might as well (to adapt the White

King) try to influence a bandersnatch." Lewis repeated this view just two months before his death in a letter to an American correspondent who was looking for clarification on this point: "I don't think Tolkien influenced me, and I am certain I didn't influence him. That is, didn't influence *what* he wrote. My continual encouragement, carried to the point of nagging, influenced him v. much to write at all with that gravity and at that length. In other words I acted as a midwife not as a father. The similarities between his work and mine are due, I think, (a) To nature—temperament. (b) To common sources. We are both soaked in Norse mythology, Geo. MacDonald's fairy-tales, Homer, *Beowulf*, and medieval romance. Also, of course, we are both Christians (he, an R.C.)."

All this seems definitive, although one must bear in mind that friends shape each other in myriad ways, obvious and subtle, and not always detectable to the principals involved. Tolkien and Lewis were comrades-in-arms during the Oxford English syllabus wars and planned—before their parting of ways—to coauthor a book on *Language and Human Nature* intended to exorcise the influence of I. A. Richards and his colleagues at Cambridge. *Out of the Silent Planet* might have been stillborn without Tolkien's intervention; so, too, *The Lord of the Rings*, but for the persistent support and timely critiques of Lewis and others. Both Lewis and Tolkien acknowledged a debt to Owen Barfield's *Poetic Diction*; and while Lewisian traces in Williams's books may be more elusive than the Williamseque motifs that saturate *That Hideous Strength*, Lewis's encouragement buoyed Williams tremendously. We know that the two friends discussed two literary collaborations, neither carried to term: one a "short Xtian Dictionary (about 40 Headings)" for a "library of Christian knowledge," the other "a book of animal stories from the Bible, told by the animals concerned."

In any event, the dispute over the exact nature of the Inklings—cabal or club?—has faded as history has stepped in with a third alternative: that whatever the Inklings may have been during their most clubbable years, today they constitute a major literary force, a movement of sorts. As symbol, inspiration, guide, and rallying cry, the Inklings grow more influential each year. This acclamation has led to much grinding of teeth, not least because the Inklings never achieved the formal brilliance of the greatest of their contemporaries, such as Joyce, Woolf, Nabokov, Borges, or Eliot.

The Australian critic Germaine Greer famously declared that "it has been my nightmare that Tolkien would turn out to be the most influential writer of the twentieth century. The bad dream has materialized . . . The books that come in Tolkien's train are more or less what you would expect; flight from reality is their dominating characteristic." And much to the chagrin of those who share Greer's viewpoint, the books and spinoffs of various kinds that come in the Inklings' train are legion. Without the Inklings there would be no Dungeons and Dragons (and the whole universe of online fantasy role-playing it produced), no Harry Potter, no Philip Pullman (in his role as the anti-Lewis). Hollywood, the voice and arbiter of popular culture, has shifted dramatically toward mythopoeic tales; this is widely recognized to be the legacy of Tolkien, whose influence was disseminated by the sixties ("Frodo Lives!") drug culture, itself a neo-Romantic movement that soon overflowed its banks.

Fan fiction, derivative fantasy novels, and sophomoric imitations aside, it is plain that Tolkien has unleashed a mythic awakening and Lewis a Christian awakening. Tolkien fans are often surprised to discover that they have entered a Christian cosmos as well as a world of Elves and Hobbits; fans of Lewis's apologetic writings, on the other hand, are often discomfited when they learn about their hero's personal life, his relationship with Mrs. Moore, his hearty appetite for drink and ribaldry, and his enduring affection for the pagan and planetary gods. But Tolkien's mythology was deeply Christian and therefore had an organic order to it; and Lewis's Christian awakening was deeply mythopoeic and therefore had an element of spontaneity and beauty often missing from conventional apologetics.

The Inklings' work, then, taken as a whole, has a significance that far outweighs any measure of popularity, amounting to a revitalization of Christian intellectual and imaginative life. They were twentieth-century Romantics who championed imagination as the royal road to insight and the "medieval model" as an answer to modern confusion and anomie; yet they were for the most part Romantics without rebellion, fantasists who prized reason, for whom Faërie was a habitat for the virtues and literature a sanctuary for faith. Even when they were not on speaking terms, they were at work on a shared project, to reclaim for contemporary life what Lewis called the "discarded image" of a universe created, ordered, and shot through with meaning.

Lewis's work was all of a piece: as literary scholar, fantasist, and apologist, he was ever on a path of rehabilitation and recovery. Tolkien, like Lewis, claimed to be a living anachronism—"I am in fact a *Hobbit* (in all but size)"—but anyone who troubles to create new languages and surround them with new myths for the sake of reenchanting English literature can hardly be accused of living in the past. In his fiction, Charles Williams reclaimed mysterious, numinous objects—the Holy Grail, the Stone of Suleiman, a Tarot deck, Platonic archetypes—from past epochs and relocated them in modern England to demonstrate the thinness, even today, of the barrier between natural and supernatural. His best nonfiction studies sustain this work of recovery; thus *The Figure of Beatrice* tells not only of the influence of a thirteenth-century Florentine girl upon a great poet, but of the lessons of this poet for modern life. Owen Barfield excavated the past embedded within language, secreted in the plainest of words, in order to illuminate the future of consciousness in all its esoteric, scarcely imaginable glory.

There is another point that may explain the hostility of critics like Germaine Greer: the Inklings were, one and all, guilty of the heresy of the Happy Ending. A story that ends happily is, some believe, necessarily a sop to wishful thinking, a refusal to grow up. In "On Fairy-Stories"— the closest we come to a manifesto for the Inklings' aesthetic—Tolkien turns this charge on its head, arguing that our deepest wishes, revealed by fairy stories and reawakened whenever we permit ourselves to enter with "literary belief" into a secondary world, are not compensatory fantasies but glimpses of an absolute reality. When Sam Gamgee cries out, "O great glory and splendour! And all my wishes have come true!" we are not in the realm of escapism, but of the Gospel, in all its strangeness and beauty.

Yet although the Inklings were guilty of the heresy of the Happy Ending, they were not optimists; they were war writers who understood that sacrifices must be made and that not all wounds will be healed in this life. Their belief in the Happy Ending was compatible with considerable anguish and uncertainty here below. One may be as gloomy as Puddleglum or as convinced as Frodo that "All my choices have proved ill" without losing hope in a final redemption.

And it is on the strength of this hope that the Inklings' project of recovery continues to unfold. Though surpassed in poetry and prose style by the very modernists they failed to appreciate, though surpassed in technical sophistication by any number of distinguished academic philosophers and theologians, the Inklings fulfilled what many find to be a more urgent need: not simply to restore the discarded image, but to refresh it and bring it to life for the present and future.

Literary revolutions leave many in their wake; but some of those who excoriate the Inklings may come to see that Tolkien, Lewis, Barfield, Williams, and their associates, by returning to the fundamentals of story and exploring its relation to faith, virtue, self-transcendence, and hope, have renewed a current that runs through the heart of Western literature, beginning with Virgil and the *Beowulf* poet; that they have recovered archaic literary forms not as an antiquarian curiosity but as a means of squarely addressing modern anxieties and longings. From our present vantage point this looks like a signal and even unprecedented achievement; but what permanent place the Inklings may come to occupy in Christian renewal and, more broadly, in intellectual and artistic history, is for the future to decide.

NOTES

PROLOGUE: DABBLERS IN INK

3 "a circle of instigators": John Wain, *Sprightly Running: Part of an Autobiography* (New York: St. Martin's, 1962; London: Macmillan, 1962), 181.

3 "a pleasantly ingenious pun": J.R.R. Tolkien, *The Letters of J.R.R. Tolkien*, a selection edited by Humphrey Carpenter with the assistance of Christopher Tolkien (Boston: Houghton Mifflin, 1995), 388.

6 "whispering from her towers": Matthew Arnold, Preface to the First Edition of Essays in Criticism [First Series] (London: Macmillan, 1865), in Matthew Arnold, *Essays, Letters, and Reviews*, ed. Fraser Neiman (Cambridge, Mass.: Harvard University Press, 1960), 98.

6 "Did I ride, one sunset": Max Beerbohm, "Diminuendo," in Max Beerbohm, *The Works of Max Beerbohm*, ed. John Lane (London: John Lane, The Bodley Head, 1921), 151–52.

7 "the Oxford Christians": Charles Moorman, *The Precincts of Felicity: The Augustinian City of the Oxford Christians* (Gainesville: University of Florida Press, 1966). See especially the epilogue, assessing the character of the "Oxford Christians" as a movement, 137–39.

7 "an organized group": W. H. Lewis, *Brothers and Friends: The Diaries of Major Warren Hamilton Lewis*, ed. Clyde S. Kilby and Marjorie Lamp Mead (San Francisco and New York: Harper & Row, 1982), 268.

7 "as organically Christian": Jan Morris, *Oxford* (Oxford: Oxford University Press, 1993), 164.

8 "the Victorian crisis of doubt": Timothy Larsen, *Crisis of Doubt: Honest Faith in Nineteenth-Century England* (Oxford and New York: Oxford University Press, 2006).

8 "like monasteries": Victor Gollancz, *My Dear Timothy: An Autobiographical Letter to His Grandson* (New York: Simon and Schuster, 1953), 416. Quoted in *The Oxford Book of Oxford*, ed. Jan Morris (Oxford and New York: Oxford University Press, 2002), 336.

8 The Oxford University Roll of Service: For more information on the number of Oxford students who perished in World War I, see Richard Tames, *A Traveller's History of Oxford* (New York and Northampton: Interlink Books, 2003), 240.

8 "on or about December 1910": Virginia Woolf, *Mr. Bennett and Mrs. Brown* (London: L. and Virginia Woolf, 1924), 4.

8 severing ties: The standard view of the cultural impact of the Great War is summed up by Samuel Hynes as follows: "a generation of innocent young men, their heads full of high abstractions like Honour, Glory, and England, went off to war to make the world safe for democracy. They were slaughtered in stupid battles planned by stupid generals. Those who survived were shocked, disillusioned and embittered by their war experiences, and saw that their real enemies were not the Germans, but the old men at home who had lied to them. They rejected the values of the society that had sent them to war, and in doing so separated their own generation from the past and from their cultural inheritance." In *A War Imagined: The First World War and English Culture* (New York: Atheneum, 1991), xii.

8 "higher literary aspirations": Anthony Burgess in *The Observer*, November 26, 1978, quoted in Tom Shippey, *J.R.R. Tolkien: Author of the Century* (Boston: Houghton Mifflin, 2002), 308.

1. "A STAR SHINES ON THE HOUR OF OUR MEETING"

15 "My dear Mr. & Mrs. Tolkien . . . when he's very much *un*dressed": A reproduction of the letter from which these quotations are taken appears in John and Priscilla Tolkien, *The Tolkien Family Album* (Boston: Houghton Mifflin, 1992), 17.

16 gigantic size: In a June 7, 1955, letter to W. H. Auden, Tolkien denied any connection between his childhood spider bite and his adult spider-monsters. This is in keeping with his intense dislike of any effort to read into *The Lord of the Rings* events in his own life or in the outer world. However, it is easy to imagine that the attack in Africa may have left a subconscious scar, eventually recorded in his fictional universe.

17 "The dragon had the trade-mark *Of Faërie*": J.R.R. Tolkien, "On Fairy-Stories," *Tree and Leaf* (London: George Allen & Unwin, 1964), 39–40.

18 "attend mass regularly for a time to note well the mummeries thereof": Charlotte Brontë, in Margot Peters, *Unquiet Soul: A Biography of Charlotte Brontë* (New York: Atheneum, 1986), 109, quoted in Patrick Allitt, *Catholic Converts: British and American Intellectuals Turn to Rome* (Ithaca, N.Y.: Cornell University Press, 2000), 23.

18 "why, if people must have a religion": Virginia Woolf, *The Voyage Out* (New York: George H. Doran, 1920), 95.

20 "there is no hurt among all the human hurts deeper": Leon Edel, *Bloomsbury: A House of Lions* (Philadelphia: Lippincott, 1979), 20.

20 "gifted lady of great beauty": Tolkien, *Letters*, 54.

20 "worn out with persecution": Ibid., 353–54.

20 "If you have these by heart": Ibid., 66.

20 Catholic prayers: Published in two parts in the journal *Vinyar Tengwar*: "'Words of Joy': Five Catholic Prayers in Quenya," ed. Patrick Wynne, Arden R. Smith, and Carl F. Hostetter, *Vinyar Tengwar* 43 (January 2002): 4–38; *Vinyar Tengwar* 44 (June 2002): 5–20.

20 "a devout and strict old-fashioned Catholic": George Sayer, "Recollections of J.R.R. Tolkien," in *Proceedings of the J.R.R. Tolkien Centenary Conference*, Keble College, Oxford, 1992, ed. Patricia Reynolds and Glen H. GoodKnight (Milton Keynes: Tolkien Society; Altadena, Calif.: Mythopoeic Press, 1995), 23.

21 "The Church is the mother": *Catechism of the Catholic Church* (Vatican City: Libreria Editrice Vaticana, 1994), chap. 3, article 1, 181.

22 "all the responses very loudly in Latin": Simon Tolkien, "My Grandfather," *The Mail on Sunday*, February 23, 2003.

23 "the first [language] to take me by storm": J.R.R. Tolkien, "English and Welsh," in J.R.R. Tolkien, *The Monster and the Critics and Other Essays*, ed. Christopher Tolkien (London: HarperCollins, 1997), 191–92.

23 Ruginwaldus Dwalakōneis: Tolkien, *Letters*, 357.

23 "it was your works": Elizabeth Mary Wright, *The Life of Joseph Wright by Elizabeth Mary Wright* (London: Oxford University Press, 1931), vol. 2, 651.

23 What was this discipline: For further insight into Tolkien's love affair with philology (itself a love affair with words and their histories), see the works of the medievalist and Anglo-Saxonist Tom Shippey, who held Tolkien's former post at Leeds, and went on to produce the pioneering study of Tolkien's scholarly mythopoeia in *The Road to Middle-earth*, which accomplished for Tolkien what John Livingston Lowes did for Coleridge in *The Road to Xanadu: A Study in the Ways of the Imagination* (1927). Tom Shippey, *The Road to Middle-Earth: [How J.R.R. Tolkien Created a New Mythology]*, rev. and exp. ed. (Boston and New York: Houghton Mifflin, 2003).

23 "the love and knowledge of words": C. S. Lewis, *Studies in Words*, 2nd ed. (Cambridge, UK: Cambridge University Press, 1967), 3.

24 "exists to communicate": Ibid., 313.

24 "*O felix peccatum Babel!*": Tolkien, "English and Welsh," 194.

24 "sound only": Tolkien, *Letters*, 310.

24 "cellar door" . . . "in Welsh": Tolkien, "English and Welsh," 190–91. According to the lexicographer Grant Barrett, encomiums to the beauty of "cellar door" go back at least as far as Cyrus Lauron Hooper's 1903 novel, *Gee-Boy*, and are widely circulated. Mencken spoke of the musical effect of "cellar door" in 1920. As Barrett notes, Lewis discusses the theme in a letter to a young writer dated July 11, 1963 ("I was astonished when someone first showed that by writing cellar door as Selladore one produces an enchanting proper name") and Norman Mailer carries on the tradition in a more scatological vein in his 1967 novel, *Why Are We in Vietnam?* (New York: Putnam, 1967), 150. Grant Barrett, "On Language: Cellar Door," *The New York Times Magazine* (February 14, 2010): 16.

25 "native language": Tolkien, "English and Welsh," 190.

25 "Supposing you say some quite ordinary words": Bill Cater, "We Talked of Love, Death, and Fairy Tales," *The Daily Telegraph* (November 29, 2001): 23.

26 *Elen síla lúmenn' omentielmo*: Tolkien, *Letters*, 265. Tolkien later changed the spelling to *omentielvo*.

26 unraveled the fellowship: The best study of Tolkien's life as it was shaped by his early friendships and by the devastation of World War I is John Garth's biography *Tolkien and the Great War: The Threshold of Middle-earth* (Boston: Houghton Mifflin, 2003).

26 "'Friendship to the Nth power,'": Tolkien, *Letters*, 10.

27 "consist of Such men": M. Waingrow, ed., *The Correspondence and Other Papers of James Boswell Relating to the Making of the Life of Johnson*, 2nd ed. (Edinburgh: Edinburgh University Press; New Haven: Yale University Press, 2001), 209, quoted in James Sambrook, "Club (*act.* 1764–1784)," *Oxford Dictionary of National Biography*, Oxford University Press, http://www.oxforddnb.com/view/theme/49211 (accessed July 4, 2014).

2. HEAVEN IN A BISCUIT TIN

29 "'appeared' sitting in a chair": J. B. Phillips, *Ring of Truth: A Translator's Testimony* (New York: Macmillan, 1957), 118–19.

30 "verging on the shabby . . . reflected the warmth": Luke Rigby, O.S.B., "A Solid Man," in *C. S. Lewis at the Breakfast Table: And Other Reminiscences*, new ed., ed. James T. Como (New York: Harcourt Brace Jovanovich, 1992, 1979), 39. (Republished as *Remembering C. S. Lewis: Recollections of Those Who Knew Him* [San Francisco: Ignatius Press, 2005].)

30 "I'll tell you": Alastair Fowler, "C. S. Lewis: Supervisor," *The Yale Review* 91, no. 4 (October 2003): 78.

30 "thick lips": From a diary kept during the Christmas holidays of 1907 and incorporated by Warnie Lewis into "The Lewis Family Papers or Memoirs of the Lewis Family" (1850–1930) [unpublished typescript], edited by Warren Hamilton Lewis in 11 volumes, 1933–1935, held at the Marion E. Wade Center, Wheaton College, Wheaton, Illinois, and the Bodleian Library, Oxford.

31 "I have seen landscapes": C. S. Lewis, "On Stories," in C. S. Lewis, *On Stories and Other Essays on Literature*, ed. Walter Hooper (New York: Harcourt, Brace, 1982, 1966), 8.

31 "They were not very far off": C. S. Lewis, *Surprised by Joy: The Shape of My Early Life* (New York: Harcourt, 1955), 7.

31 "an author exactly after my own heart": Letter to Arthur Greeves, June 5, 1914, in C. S. Lewis, *The Collected Letters of C. S. Lewis*, vol. 1: *Family Letters 1905–1931*, ed. Walter Hooper (New York: HarperCollins, 2004), 59.

31 "I am often surprised": Letter to Arthur Greeves, November 4(?), 1917, in ibid., 342.

31–32 "in whom even the exacting memory . . . Through Lizzie we struck our roots": Lewis, *Surprised by Joy*, 5.

32 "I see the great tree of English literature": AE, 1895 letter to John Eglinton (William Magee), "Unpublished Letters from AE to John Eglinton," *Malahat Review* (April 1970): 84–107, quoted in Henry Summerfield, "AE as a Literary Critic," in *Myth and Reality in Irish Literature*, ed. Joseph Ronsley (Waterloo, Ontario: Wilfrid Laurier Press, 1977), 47.

32 "Remember that the great minds": Lewis, *Collected Letters*, vol. 1, 394.

32 "The flatness! The interminableness! . . . seemed like the voices of demons": Lewis, *Surprised by Joy*, 24.

33 "I'm more Welsh than anything": George Sayer, *Jack: A Life of C. S. Lewis* (Wheaton, Ill.: Crossway Books, 1994), 21.

33 "sentimental, passionate, and rhetorical . . . The Hamiltons were a cooler race": Lewis, *Surprised by Joy*, 3.

34 "an endless and one-sided torrent": Warren Lewis, "Memoir of C. S. Lewis," *Letters of C. S. Lewis: Edited and With a Memoir by W. H. Lewis, Revised and Enlarged Edition Edited by W. H. Lewis* (New York: Harcourt, 1966, 1983), 26.

34 "miracle . . . all done by cords": "The Lewis Family Papers or Memoirs of the Lewis Family" I:312, quoted in Walter Hooper, *C. S. Lewis: A Complete Guide to His Life & Works* (San Francisco: HarperSanFrancisco, 1996), 693.

35 "I always thought . . . I wonder do I love you?": "Lewis Family Papers" II: 248–49, quoted in Hooper, *C. S. Lewis*, 695.

35 On enjoying seaside holidays without Albert: Warren Lewis, "Memoir of C. S. Lewis," 22.

35 "strange smells . . . ill and crying": Lewis, *Surprised by Joy*, 18–19.

35 "all settled happiness": Ibid., 21.

36 "the brightest jewel in the week": Ibid., 126.

36 "infallibly and invincibly wrong": Ibid., 30.

36 "had more capacity for being cheated": Ibid., 10.

36 "It was axiomatic . . . more power of confusing": Ibid., 120–22.

37 "uncomfortable and embarrassing": Ibid., 4.

37 "What time would you like lunch?": Ibid., 125.

37 "I never met a man": Warren Lewis, "Memoir of C. S. Lewis," 42.

38 "I would not commit the sin of Ham": Lewis, *Surprised by Joy*, 123.

38 "devastatingly cruel": A. N. Wilson, *C. S. Lewis: A Biography* (New York and London: W. W. Norton, 1990), 31.

38 "the unfortunate man": Lewis, *Surprised by Joy*, 19.

38 "brought into the nursery . . . the first beauty": Ibid., 7.

38 "to a child it seemed less like a house": Ibid., 10.

38 "atrociously uneconomical": Warren Lewis, "Memoir of C. S. Lewis," 23.

39 "I am a product of long corridors . . . I had always the same certainty": Lewis, *Surprised by Joy*, 10.

39 "KING BUNNY": C. S. Lewis, *Boxen: The Imaginary World of the Young C. S. Lewis*, ed. Walter Hooper (San Diego: Harcourt Brace Jovanovich, 1985), 26.

39 "India": Lewis, *Surprised by Joy*, 6.

39 "a prophetic portrait": Ibid., 80.

40 "Neither of us ever made any attempt . . . 'I'll be seeing that fellow Arrabudda'": W. H. Lewis, *C. S. Lewis: A Biography* (unpublished), quoted in W. H. Lewis, *Brothers and Friends: The Diaries of Major Warren Hamilton Lewis*, ed. Clyde S. Kilby and Marjorie Lamp Mead (San Francisco: Harper & Row, 1982), 6, note 13.

40 "Papy of course is the master . . . Hoora!! Warnie comes home": "My Life during the Exmas Holadys of 1907," "Lewis Family Papers" III:88–92, quoted in Hooper, *C. S. Lewis: A Complete Guide*, 5–6.

41 "the most courteous": John Wain, *Sprightly Running*, 184.

41 By the age of twelve: In this light, it's interesting to note the remarks, upon reading *Surprised by Joy*, of the Welsh poet and artist David Jones (1895–1974) in a 1956 letter: "I was astounded how virtually *identical* were things he read and thought about as a child and young man . . . with those which I read etc. It was quite peculiar—almost uncanny—to find item after item . . , From Everyman's Library, the Home U Library, the Temple Classics and even going to Denny's

bookshop in the Strand to get them, all is the same. And then Chesterton later and the *Dream of the Rood* and then Langland . . . in just those early years the similarity of taste is extraordinary." David Jones, *Dai Greatcoat: A Self-Portrait of David Jones in His Letters*, ed. René Hague (London and Boston: Faber & Faber, 1980), 171–72.

41 "he has read more classics": William T. Kirkpatrick, quoted in Roger Lancelyn Green and Walter Hooper, *C. S. Lewis: A Biography*, rev. and exp. ed. (London: HarperCollins, 2002, 1974), 28.

41 "The great thing is to be always reading": Fowler, "C. S. Lewis: Supervisor," 75.

42 "Joy" . . . "It troubled me": Lewis, *Surprised by Joy*, 16.

42 "I heard a voice that cried": In *Surprised by Joy*, Lewis says that he found these lines after thumbing through "The Saga of King Olaf"—which appears as "The Musician's Tale: The Saga of King Olaf" in *Tales of a Wayside Inn* (London: Routledge, Warne & Routledge, 1863; Boston: Ticknor & Fields, 1863); but these lines are the beginning of "Tégner's Drapa" (inspired by the Norse themes in the poetical works of the Swedish bishop Esaias Tégner) from *The Seaside and the Fireside*. Possibly he was reading a volume of Longfellow's collected works.

43 "the banks of Styx": Lewis, *Surprised by Joy*, 24.

44 "I think I shall like this place . . . My dear Papy": Lewis, *Collected Letters*, vol. 1, 6–7.

44 "All schools": "Lewis Family Papers" III:140, quoted in Hooper, *C. S. Lewis: A Complete Guide*, 640.

44 "I do not like church here . . . In this abominable place": Diary, November 1909, quoted by Hooper in Lewis, *Collected Letters*, vol. 1, 8.

44 "the doctrines of Christianity": Lewis, *Surprised by Joy*, 33.

45 "coarser . . . ravenous": Ibid., 35.

45 "the text-book case": C. S. Lewis, "The Mythopoeic Gift of Rider Haggard," *On Stories*, 97.

45 "You have never refused me anything Papy": Warnie in "Lewis Family Papers" III:146, quoted in Hooper, *C. S. Lewis: A Complete Guide*, 7.

45 "I find school very nice . . . in spite of all": Lewis, *Collected Letters*, vol. 1, 9.

45 "grave melancholy": Lewis, *Surprised by Joy*, 53.

46 "realization . . . a certain vividness": Ibid., 61.

46 "the universe was, in the main, a rather regrettable institution": Ibid., 63.

47 "a fop, a cad, and a snob . . . sexual temptation": Lewis, *Surprised by Joy*, 68.

47 On "Pogo," see also Lewis's 1918 letter to his father, Lewis, *Collected Letters*, vol. 1, 357. Oddly enough, Harris turned up again in Lewis's life as captain of his company in the Somerset Light Infantry. "He impressed me in those days, but I find him very disappointing," Lewis told his father, "I suppose these things are to be expected." In fact, Harris, who left Exeter College without a degree, was twice decorated for his acts of valor. See National Archives WO 339/24756, Captain Percy Gerald Kelsall HARRIS, Prince Albert's (Somerset Light Infantry) and Walter Hooper's note in Lewis, *Collected Letters*, vol. 1, 357, note 11.

47 "Siegfried . . . almost like heartbreak": Ibid., 72–73.

47 "secret, imaginative": Ibid., 78.

47 "nothing to do with each other": Ibid., 119.

48 "all the prefects detest me": Lewis, *Collected Letters*, vol. 1, 50.

48 "I was big for my age": Lewis, *Surprised by Joy*, 94.

48 "gloom and boredom": Warren Lewis, "Memoir of C. S. Lewis," 4.

48 "I had an idea": Warnie in "Lewis Family Papers" IV: 156–57, quoted in Lewis, *Collected Letters*, vol. 1, 52.

48 "I find it very difficult to believe": Warren Lewis, "Memoir of C. S. Lewis," 4.

49 "'Norse in subject' . . . Why should creatures have the burden of existence": Lewis, *Surprised by Joy*, 114–15.

49 "dog-tired": Ibid., 96.

49 "Please take me out of this": Lewis, *Collected Letters*, vol. 1, 51.

50 "'Do *you* like that?'": Lewis, *Surprised by Joy*, 130.

50 "You know how I would love": Lewis, *Collected Letters*, vol. 1, 176.

50 "neither of us had any other outlet": C. S. Lewis, *The Collected Letters of C. S. Lewis*, vol. 2: *Books, Broadcasts, and the War, 1931–1949*, ed. Walter Hooper (New York: HarperCollins, 2004), 101.

50 "The story that you have a headache after being drunk": Lewis, *Collected Letters*, vol. 1, 319–20. In editing the Lewis letters, Hooper reinstated passages that Arthur Greeves had attempted to blot out; the reinstated text appears within these brackets: < >. See Lewis, *Collected Letters*, vol. 1, x.

50 "Terreauty": Ibid., 176.

51 "Niflheim and Asgard, Britain and Logres, Handramit and Harandra": Lewis, *Surprised by Joy*, 154. Handramit and Harandra are the lower and upper regions of Malacandra (Mars) in Lewis's first space fantasy novel, *Out of the Silent Planet* (New York: Scribner, 1938; reprint ed., 2003).

51 "crowing cocks and gaggling ducks . . . 'spirit grocers'": Lewis, *Surprised by Joy*, 154.

51 "I learned charity": "Lewis Family Papers" X: 218–20, quoted by Hooper in Lewis, *Collected Letters*, vol. 1, 995.

51 homosexual inclination: Lewis addresses this kind of speculation in the chapter on friendship in *The Four Loves*: "This imposes on me at the outset a very tiresome bit of demolition. It has actually become necessary in our time to rebut the theory that every firm and serious friendship is really homosexual . . . Kisses, tears and embraces are not in themselves evidence of homosexuality . . . On a broad historical view it is, of course, not the demonstrative gestures of Friendship among our ancestors but the absence of such gestures in our own society that calls for some special explanation. We, not they, are out of step." C. S. Lewis, *The Four Loves* (New York: Harcourt, Brace, 1960), 60–63.

51 "Do you ever wake up in the morning": Ibid., 94.

51 "With the Chaucer I am most awfully bucked": Ibid., 187.

51 "I feel my fame as a 'Man-about-the-Gramaphone' greatly put out": Ibid., 116.

52 "feelings ought to be kept for literature": Ibid., 117.

52 "I am a coarse-grained creature": Ibid., 205.

52 "You are interested in a brand of *That* . . . Let us talk of these things when we want": Ibid., 287, 288.

52 "'however great an evil in itself": Lewis, *Surprised by Joy*, 109–110. Lewis's discussion of pederasty in *Surprised by Joy* gives many of his Christian acolytes pause; he refused to condemn it, even though he considered it sinful, partially because it was a temptation he never experienced and therefore could not speak about with authority, and partially because the cruelty of Malvern he found far more depraved than the lust; any activity touched by Eros, he suggests, still carries "the traces of

his divinity" (Lewis, *Surprised by Joy*, 110). This seems remarkable for a middle-aged heterosexual man in the 1950s.

53 Kirkpatrick: See Ian Wilson, "William Thompson Kirkpatrick (1848–1921)," *Review: Journal of the Craigavon Historical Society* 8, no. 1 (April 2008), www.craigavonhistoricalsociety.org.uk/rev/wilsonikirkpatrick.html (accessed August 6, 2014).

53 "simply out of his proper environment . . . there would be no one there except Mr and Mrs K": "Lewis Family Papers" IV: 156–57 and 160, quoted by Hooper in Lewis, *Collected Letters*, vol. 1, 52.

53 "hopelessly rotten": Lewis, *Collected Letters*, vol. 1, 65.

54 "Stop!" . . . "Do you not see, then, that you had no right to have any opinion": Lewis, *Surprised by Joy*, 134, 135.

54 "the great Rubicon": Ibid., 141.

54 "I suppose I reached as much happiness": Ibid., 147.

54 "If ever a man came near to being a purely logical entity": Ibid., 135.

55 "I have repeatedly explained": C. S. Lewis, *That Hideous Strength: A Modern Fairy-Tale for Grown-Ups* (New York: Scribner, 2003), 166.

55 "a man of unusual mental power . . . he became an almost incomparable teacher": Robert M. Jones, in Joseph R. Fisher and John H. Robb, *Royal Belfast Academical Institution: Centenary Volume, 1810–1910* (Belfast: McCaw, Stevenson & Orr, 1913). Cited in Wilson, "William Thompson Kirkpatrick (1848–1921)," and in Hooper, *C. S. Lewis: A Complete Guide*, 685.

55 "*Je soupçonne*": Lewis, *Collected Letters*, vol. 1, 545.

55 "firstly, I am very happy . . . It seems a great pity": Ibid., 87, 93.

56 "You ask me my religious views": Ibid., 230–31.

3. ADVENT LYRICS

58 "Tolkien, if we are to be guided by the countless notices on his mantelpiece": Oxoniensis (pseud.), "Oxford Letter," *King Edward's School Chronicle*, December 1912, quoted in Christina Scull and Wayne G. Hammond, *The J.R.R. Tolkien Companion and Guide: Reader's Guide* (Boston and New York: Houghton Mifflin, 2006), 954.

58 his allowance from Father Francis: That Father Francis was underwriting Tolkien's university career is suggested by Tolkien's remark, reported by Humphrey Carpenter, that when Father Francis learned that Tolkien had been seeing Edith, he "threatened to cut short my University career." Humphrey Carpenter, *Tolkien: The Authorized Biography* (Boston: Houghton Mifflin, 1977), 43.

58 "two people . . . capable of bouts of profound despair": Carpenter, *Tolkien*, 31.

59 "the Finnish language is still in so unsettled and fluid a condition": Charles Eliot, *A Finnish Grammar* (Oxford: Clarendon Press, 1890), 5.

59 "deserves its undesirable reputation": Charles Eliot, *Finnish Grammar*, xxxvii.

59 "quite intoxicated me": Tolkien, *Letters*, 214.

60 "gasping out of deep water": Ibid., 347.

60 Tolkien's new art: For discussion of these visionary pictures, with reproductions, see Wayne G. Hammond and Christina Scull, *J.R.R. Tolkien: Artist & Illustrator* (Boston and New York: Houghton Mifflin, 1995), 35–40.

62 "Name him not!": J.R.R. Tolkien, *The Lord of the Rings*, 50th Anniversary One-Volume Edition (London: HarperCollins, 2005; Boston: Houghton Mifflin, 2005), Part 2: *The Two Towers*, book 3, 501.

62 "incomparably easier and clearer": C. S. Lewis, "William Morris," *Rehabilitations and Other Essays* (London: Oxford University Press, 1939), 39.

63 "I am trying to turn one of the stories": Tolkien, *Letters*, 7.

63 "that very primitive undergrowth . . . I would that we had more of it left": Quoted in John Garth, *Tolkien and the Great War: The Threshold of Middle-earth* (Boston: Houghton Mifflin, 2003), 52.

63 "an attempt to reorganize": Tolkien, *Letters*, 214.

63 "a curious thrill": quoted in Carpenter, *Tolkien*, 64.

64 *Éarendel . . . eorendel*: For *eorendel* as John the Baptist, see *The Blickling Homilies*, ed. Richard J. Kelly (London: Continuum, 2010), XIV "The Birth of John the Baptist," 116–17, section 45: Ond nu seo Cristes gebyrd set his aeriste, se niwa eorendel Sanctus Johannes. Ond nu se leoma Þære soÞan sunnan, God selfa, cuman wille. "The birth of Christ occurred at his appearing; John the Baptist heralded the new dawn. Now the ray of the true Sun, God Himself, will come."

64 astral myth: See Tolkien's explanation of the astronomical associations with Éarendel (and its variants), in a draft letter to "Mr. Rang" (Gunnar Urang, who later published *Shadows of Heaven: Religion and Fantasy in the Fiction of C. S. Lewis, Charles Williams, and J.R.R. Tolkien*), dated by Tolkien August 1967, in *Letters*, 385 and note.

64 "not a Redeemer": Shippey, *Road to Middle-earth*, 246.

65 she agreed to switch altars: Robert Murray, S.J., personal interview, July 12, 2006.

65 "the moving force": Tolkien Papers, Bodleian Library, quoted in Scull and Hammond, *J.R.R. Tolkien Companion and Guide: Reader's Guide*, 1001.

65 "Council of London . . . I *never* spent happier hours": Tolkien Papers, Bodleian Library, quoted in ibid., 1001.

66 "to drive from life, letters, the stage and society . . . to reestablish sanity, cleanliness, and the love of real and true beauty": Tolkien Papers, Bodleian Library, quoted in ibid., 1001.

66 "had been granted some spark of fire": Letter to G. B. Smith, August 12, 1916, Tolkien, *Letters*, 10.

67 "those grey days": Carpenter, *Tolkien*, 78.

67 "Edith Mary Tolkien": *J.R.R. Tolkien: Life and Legend. An Exhibition to Commemorate the Centenary of the Birth of J.R.R. Tolkien*, ed. Judith Priestman (Oxford: Bodleian Library, [1992]), 30.

68 "O lonely, sparkling isle, farewell!": J.R.R. Tolkien, "The Lonely Isle" (or "Tol Eressëa"), first published as "The Lonely Isle" in *Leeds University Verse 1914–1924*, quoted in Garth, *Tolkien and the Great War*, 144–45. See Michael D. C. Drout, "Tol Eressëa," in *J.R.R. Tolkien Encyclopedia: Scholarship and Critical Assessment*, ed. Michael D. C. Drout (New York: Routledge, 2007), 651.

68 "Theoretically . . . it would have been possible to walk from Belgium": Paul Fussell, *The Great War and Modern Memory* (New York: Oxford University Press, 1975), 37.

68 "one of the most interesting in the whole long history of human disillusion": Fussell, *Great War and Modern Memory*, 29.

68 "I see men arising": Henry Williamson, *The Wet Flanders Plain* (London: Faber & Faber, 1929), 3, quoted in Fussell, *Great War and Modern Memory*, 29.

69 "hungry and lonely . . . a mere individual": Tolkien, *Letters*, 10.

69 "spark of fire . . . testify for God": Ibid.

70 "you might scribble something": From an interview with Philip Norman, "'More Than a Campus Craze; It's Like a Drug Dream'; The Prevalence of Hobbits: Thirty Years After They Were Invented by a Bored Oxford Don, the Hobbits—'a Benevolent, Furry-Footed People'—Have Taken a New Generation by Storm," *The New York Times*, January 15, 1967.

70 "in grimy canteens": Tolkien, *Letters*, 78.

71 "It is plain": Tolkien, "On Fairy-Stories," *Tree and Leaf*, 54.

71 "being huddled up in a little dog-kennel": Siegfried Sassoon, *Memoirs of an Infantry Officer* (London: Faber & Faber, 1930), 64.

71 "The child alone a poet is": Robert Graves, "Babylon," *Fairies and Fusiliers* (New York: Alfred A. Knopf, 1918), 14.

4. HARD KNOCKS AND DREAMING SPIRES

72 "I am desperately in love": Letter to Arthur Greeves, November 22, 1916, in Lewis, *Collected Letters*, vol. 1, 256.

72 "will be an improvement": Lewis, *Collected Letters*, vol. 1, 257.

73 "He hardly realizes": Kirkpatrick quoted in "Lewis Family Papers," quoted by Walter Hooper in Lewis, *Collected Letters*, vol. 1, 178.

73 "He is always cheerful": Kirkpatrick quoted in "Lewis Family Papers," quoted in Walter Hooper, preface to *Spirits in Bondage: A Cycle of Lyrics*, by C. S. Lewis, (San Diego, New York, London: Harcourt, Brace & Company, 1984), xvii.

73 Among letters that speak of suicide, see also "My father seemed in very poor form when I got home, and fussed a lot about my cold: so everything is beastly, and I have decided—of course—to commit suicide again," September 18, 1916. Lewis, *Collected Letters*, vol. 1, 222.

73 "the rod": Lewis, *Collected Letters*, vol. 1, 283, 271.

73 "the recognized scientific account": Ibid., 231.

73 "as an old Saxon thane": Ibid., 244.

74 "Leopard witches . . . He is as voluptuous as Keats": Ibid., 290.

74 "the place has surpassed my wildest dreams": Ibid., 262.

74 "Oxford is absolutely topping": Ibid., 266.

74 "in a way we have spoiled our paradise": Ibid., 288.

76 "a really ripping kind of person": Ibid., 310. Such cultured female society is "a great anodyne in a life like ours," he told Arthur (Lewis, *Collected Letters*, vol. 1, 325). So much for the charge that Lewis avoided the company of intellectual women.

76 "Of course, mind you, I am not laying down as a certainty that there is nothing outside the material world": Ibid., 231.

76 "ardent Newmanite . . . He came into my rooms last night": Ibid., 307.

77 "do not actually prove the agency of real spirits": Ibid., 313–14. The book, according to Walter Hooper, was *Psychical Research* by William Fletcher Barrett, [1911]; ibid., 313, note 96.

77 "one of our few philosophers": Lewis, *Collected Letters,* vol. 1, 326. Lewis started reading *Principles of Human Knowledge* June 12 and finished it June 14, 1924. C. S. Lewis, *All My Road Before Me: The Diary of C. S. Lewis,* ed. Walter Hooper (San Diego, New York, London: Harcourt, 1991), 329, 332.

77 "royally drunk" . . . Butler and Dodds: Lewis, *Collected Letters,* vol. 1, 319.

78 "good fellow . . . very decent": Ibid., 319, 322.

78 "immensely": Ibid., 334.

79 "Don't understand telegram": Quoted in ibid., 345.

79 "the frights, the cold . . . I have gone to sleep marching": Lewis, *Surprised by Joy,* 197–98.

80 "dear Sergeant Ayres . . . turned this ridiculous": Ibid., 196. See Everard Wyrall, *History of the Somerset Light Infantry 1914–1919* (London: Methuen, 1927), 295.

80 "west country farmers": Lewis, *Surprised by Joy,* 193.

80 Siegfried Sassoon: Consider, for example, Sassoon's famous war poem, "The General" (1917): " 'Good-morning; good-morning!' the General said / When we met him last week on our way to the line. / Now the soldiers he smiled at are most of 'em dead, / And we're cursing his staff for incompetent swine. / 'He's a cheery old card,' grunted Harry to Jack / As they slogged up to Arras with rifle and pack. / But he did for them both by his plan of attack."

80 "shows rarely": Lewis, *Surprised by Joy,* 196.

81 "a boy lay asleep on a bank": Warnie in "Lewis Family Papers" V: 109–110, quoted in K. J. Gilchrist, *A Morning After War: C. S. Lewis & WW I* (New York: Peter Lang, 2005), 27.

81 "ghastly dreams": Lewis's diary entry for July 19, 1915, quoted in Walter Hooper, preface to *Spirits in Bondage,* xxi.

81 "Long leagues on either hand the trenches spread": Lewis, "French Nocturne (Monchy-Le-Preux)," *Spirits in Bondage,* 4.

82 "This is War . . . Here is a man dying": Lewis, *Surprised by Joy,* 196–97.

82 "that there was a fully conscious 'I' ": Ibid., 197–98.

83 "something purely spiritual": Lewis, *Collected Letters,* vol. 1, 372.

83 "a self-caressing luxury": Lewis, *Surprised by Joy,* 168.

83 "a particular hill walk": Ibid., 166.

84 "to care for almost nothing but the gods and heroes": Ibid., 174.

84 "the passion for the Occult": Ibid., 60.

85 "a superabundance of mercy": Ibid., 178. March 4, 1916, is the date indicated in Lewis's letter of March 7, 1916, to Arthur (Lewis, *Collected Letters,* vol. 1, 169). But Lewis places this event in October in *Surprised by Joy.*

85 "bright shadow . . . Holiness": Lewis, *Surprised by Joy,* 179.

85 "transforming all common things . . . baptized": Ibid., 181.

86 "its thought is not daring": T. S. Eliot on Arthur Clutton-Brock's *The Ultimate Belief,* quoted in Donald J. Childs, *T. S. Eliot: Mystic, Son, and Lover* (New York: St. Martin's Press, 1997), 63.

86 "god-imposed . . . an object": Lewis, *Collected Letters,* vol. 1, 343.

86 "Most people in England": Arthur Clutton-Brock, *The Ultimate Belief* (New York: E. P. Dutton, 1916), 20.

87 highbrows: For an apposite portrait of the sort of highbrow Lewis has in mind, see Ian Hay (pseudonym for John Hay Beith), *The Lighter Side of School Life* (Edinburgh: Ballantyne Press, 1914), 107–108:

> Then comes the Super-Intellectual—the "Highbrow." He is a fish out of the water with a vengeance, but he does exist at school—somehow. He congregates in places of refuge with others of the faith; and they discuss the English Review, and mysterious individuals who are only referred to by their initials—as G. B. S. and G. K. C. Sometimes he initiates these discussions because they really interest him, but more often, it is to be feared, because they make him feel superior and grown-up. Somewhere in the school grounds certain youthful schoolmates of his, inspired by precisely similar motives but with different methods of procedure, are sitting in the centre of a rhododendron bush smoking cigarettes. In each case the idea is the same—namely, a hankering after meats which are not for babes. But the smoker puts on no side about his achievements, whereas the "highbrow" does. He loathes the vulgar herd and holds it aloof. He does not inform the vulgar herd of this fact, but he confides it to the other highbrows, and they applaud his discrimination. Intellectual snobbery is a rare thing among boys, and therefore difficult to account for. Perhaps the pose is a form of reaction. It is comforting, for instance, after you have been compelled to dance the can-can in your pyjamas for the delectation of the Lower Dormitory, to foregather next morning with a few kindred spirits and discourse pityingly and scathingly upon the gross philistinism of the lower middle classes. No, the lot of the æsthete at school is not altogether a happy one, but possibly his tribulations are not without a certain beneficent effect. When he goes up to Oxford or Cambridge he will speedily find that in the tolerant atmosphere of those intellectual centres the prig is not merely permitted to walk the earth but to flourish like the green bay-tree . . .

See also Lewis's November 4, 1917, letter to Arthur (Lewis, *Collected Letters,* vol. 1, 342).

87 "immediate conquest . . . God is": Lewis, *Surprised by Joy,* 190–91.

88 "to relish energy": Ibid., 198.

89 "the Junior Common Room": Lewis, *Collected Letters,* vol. 1, 428.

89 "household gods": Ibid., 447.

90 "After breakfast I work": Ibid., 425.

90 "most of them vile": Lewis, *All My Road Before Me,* 252–53.

90 "She is old enough to be his mother . . . The daily letter business": "Lewis Family Papers" VI: 129, quoted by Walter Hooper in Lewis, *Collected Letters,* vol. 1, 451–52.

91 "fast becoming unbearable": Lewis, *Collected Letters,* vol. 1, 455.

91 "Haven't heard from my esteemed parent": Ibid., 454.

91 "On 6 August he deceived me": "Lewis Family Papers" VI: 167, quoted in Lewis, *Collected Letters,* vol. 1, 462. There followed a series of letters in which Lewis attempted to justify himself and to make peace.

91 "the blackest chapter of my life": Quoted in A. N. Wilson, *C. S. Lewis*, 68, from Bodleian Library Ms. Fas.d.264, f.140.

91 "a strange fellow . . . right up our tree": Leo Baker, "Near the Beginning," in Como, *C. S. Lewis at the Breakfast Table*, 3.

91 "where everyone . . . I like and admire him": Lewis, *Collected Letters*, vol. 1, 495.

91 "amateur disciple in mysticism . . . presently I could hardly see anything else": Ibid., 472–73.

91 "in every way the best person": Ibid., 488.

93 "counterblast": Ibid., 492. The Vorticist movement takes its name from the short-lived journal *Blast: The Review of the Great English Vortex* (only two issues appeared, in 1914 and 1915), founded by Wyndham Lewis and Ezra Pound as a showcase and manifesto for modernist poetry and art.

93 "I was interested in contemporary events . . . You take too many things for granted": Baker, "Near the Beginning," 4.

93 "some sort of God": Lewis, *Collected Letters*, vol. 1, 509.

93 "Were you much frightened in France?": Baker, "Near the Beginning," 6.

93 "with deep and uncontrollable hatred": Ibid., 4.

93 "to try and pick up some of the old links": Lewis, *Collected Letters*, vol. 2, 161.

94 "we are all young once": Walter Hooper, preface to Lewis, *Spirits in Bondage*, xi.

94 "our b——y lyrical poet": Lewis, *Collected Letters*, vol. 1, 400.

95 "I was at this time living": Lewis, *Surprised by Joy*, 115.

95 "matter's great enemy": Lewis, *Collected Letters*, vol. 1, 374.

95 "driven and hurt beyond bearing . . . Country of Dreams!": C. S. Lewis, "Death in Battle," *Spirits in Bondage*, 74–75.

95 "considered opinion of his own youth": Warnie quoted in Walter Hooper, preface to *Spirits in Bondage*, xxvii.

95 "Beyond the western ocean's glow": Lewis, "Ballade Mystique," *Spirits in Bondage*, 54.

95 "I am the flower . . . I am the spider": Lewis, "Satan Speaks," *Spirits in Bondage*, 3.

95 "Come let us curse our Master": Lewis, "De Profundis," *Spirits in Bondage*, 20. Compare Housman: "We for a certainty are not the first / Have sat in taverns while the tempest hurled / Their hopeful plans to emptiness, and cursed / Whatever brute and blackguard made the world." A. E. Housman, "The chestnut casts his flambeaux," in *Last Poems* (1922).

95 "the curse against God": G. K. Chesterton, "The Defendant," *The Defendant* (New York: Dodd, Mead, 1902), 2.

96 "But lo!, I am grown wiser": Lewis, "Ode for New Year's Day," *Spirits in Bondage*, 14.

96 "Thank God that there are solid folk": Lewis, "In Praise of Solid People," *Spirits in Bondage*, 42.

96 "Can it be true": Lewis, "The Ass," *Spirits in Bondage*, 51–52.

96 "emotional glooming . . . the thought, when closed with": quoted in Hooper, *C. S. Lewis: A Complete Guide*, 144.

96 "purely academic . . . he is young": letters between Warnie and Albert in "Lewis Family Papers" VI: 98, quoted by Walter Hooper in Lewis, *Collected Letters*, vol. 1, 443, note 44.

97 "I have been moved": Lewis, *Collected Letters*, vol. 1, 569.

97 "I am glad to have met Mrs. M": W. H. Lewis, *Brothers and Friends*, 10, 12–13.

97 "notably domineering": Warren Lewis, "Memoir of C. S. Lewis," 33.

97 "he is as good as an extra maid": Ibid., 37.

98 "the Second Friend . . . has read all the right books": Lewis, *Surprised by Joy*, 199–200.

5. "WORDS HAVE A SOUL"

99 "The good are befriended": Ralph Waldo Emerson, "Compensation."

99 "every word was once a poem": Emerson, "The Poet." Barfield's library included several books annotated by him, including an edition of Emerson's essays; for details, see the Marion E. Wade Center website: www.wheaton.edu/~/media/Files/Centers-and-Institutes/Wade-Center/RR-Docs/Non-archive%20Listings/Barfield_Library.pdf (accessed July 13, 2014).

99 "I remember that awfully well": Simon Blaxland–de Lange, *Owen Barfield: Romanticism Come of Age, A Biography* (Forest Row, UK: Temple Lodge, 2006), 12.

99 "always surrounded with music": Shirley Sugerman, "A Conversation with Owen Barfield," *Evolution of Consciousness: Studies in Polarity* (Middletown, Conn.: Wesleyan University Press, 1976), 4.

100 "I chalked on the wall": Blaxland–de Lange, *Owen Barfield*, 12.

100 "*Cato, octoginta annos natus* . . . the actual moment": Ibid., 28.

101 "a great shadow . . . couldn't say anything": Ibid., 13.

101 "Sleep has a brother": Ibid., 13.

101 "I was rather well developed": Ibid., 22.

101 "Poetry . . . had the power to change one's consciousness": Barfield, "Owen Barfield and the Origin of Language," *Towards* 1, no. 1 (June 1978): 3. *Towards* was founded by the Waldorf educator Clifford Monks in 1977 as "a magazine for all who are striving for clarity and direction in meeting today's challenges. It exists to explore and make better known the work of Owen Barfield, Samuel Taylor Coleridge, Wolfgang von Goethe, Rudolf Steiner, and related authors. Implicit and explicit in their work are achievements and goals which offer profound insight, guidance, and hope for all who are struggling with the essential challenges of modern life."

102 "the sort of thing my mind was full of": Blaxland–de Lange, *Owen Barfield*, 24.

103 "a vivid experience . . . It was very strong": Ibid., 22.

103 "It was a kind of new world . . . delightful": Ibid., 23.

103 "the idea of love . . . being caged in the materialism of the age": Ibid., 20.

103 "I have been seeing practically no-one": Ibid., 299.

104 "pondering the problem of existence . . . acute depression": Ibid., 301.

104 "Sophia experience . . . suddenly one evening": Ibid., 20.

105 "would be able to find all the beauty": Ibid., 20.

105 "led into the whole shape and development": Ibid., 21.

106 "Hey-diddle-diddle . . . the poet's material": Owen Barfield, "Form in Poetry," *New Statesman* (August 7, 1920), 501–502.

107 "words have a soul . . . grows subtler and subtler": Owen Barfield, "'Ruin,'" *The London Mercury* 7 (December 1922): 164–70.

108 "Steiner had obviously forgotten volumes more": Owen Barfield, introduction to *Romanticism Comes of Age* (Middletown, Conn.: Wesleyan University Press, 1967), 13.

108 "stature . . . we observe, actually beginning to occur, the transition": Owen Barfield, "Introducing Rudolf Steiner," *Towards* 2, no. 4 (Fall–Winter 1983): 42–44.

109 "The essence of Steiner's teachings": Astrid Diener, *The Role of Imagination in Culture and Society: Owen Barfield's Early Work*, Appendix: "An Interview with Owen Barfield" (Glienicke, Berlin: Galda+Wilch Verlag, *Leipzig Explorations in Literature and Culture* 6, 2002), 186–87.

109 "*il maestro*": Owen Barfield, *Romanticism Comes of Age*, 1st ed. (London: Anthroposophical Publishing, 1944), 11.

110 "We went at our talk like a dogfight": Lewis diary entry January 26, 1923, in W. H. Lewis, *Letters of C. S. Lewis*, 179.

110 "a reputation among my own friends of being argumentative . . . Most people— here, especially, Lewis was different—are apt to flinch at the verbal aggression": Owen Barfield, *Owen Barfield on C. S. Lewis*, ed. G. B. Tennyson (Middletown, Conn.: Wesleyan University Press, 1989), 127.

110 "a summoned voice": Cecil Harwood, *The Voice of Cecil Harwood: A Miscellany*, ed. Owen Barfield (London: Rudolf Steiner Press, 1979), 8.

111 "We got into conversation on fancy and imagination": Lewis, *All My Road Before Me*, 59–60. Lewis and Barfield called wish-fulfilling fantasies "Christina Dreams" after Christina Pontifex in Samuel Butler's *The Way of All Flesh*.

111 "felt change of consciousness": Blaxland–de Lange, *Owen Barfield*, 260.

112 "in which with prodigality [Barfield] squirts out the most suggestive ideas": Lewis, *All My Road Before Me*, 275.

112 "one of the best new fairy stories": "Stories for Little Children," *The Times Literary Supplement* 1245 (November 26, 1925): 811.

112 "I lent the *Silver Trumpet* to Tolkien": Lewis, *Collected Letters*, vol. 2, 198. See Blaxland–de Lange, *Owen Barfield*, 171–72.

112 "Steiner seems to be a sort of panpsychist": Quoted by Walter Hooper in "The 'Great War' Letters," appendix to C. S. Lewis, *The Collected Letters*, vol. 3: *Narnia, Cambridge, and Joy, 1950–1963*, ed. Walter Hooper (New York: HarperCollins, 2007), 1596.

113 "I was hideously shocked": Lewis, *Surprised by Joy*, 206.

113 "an almost incessant disputation . . . the 'Great War'": Ibid., 207. For an in-depth study, see Lionel Adey, *C. S. Lewis' 'Great War' with Owen Barfield* (Wigton, UK: Ink Books, 2002).

113 "we used to foregather": Nevill Coghill, "The Approach to English," in *Light on C. S. Lewis*, ed. Jocelyn Gibb (New York and London: Harcourt Brace Jovanovich, 1965), 54–55.

114 *Clivi Hamiltonis Summae Metaphysices . . . Commentarium in Tractatum De Toto et Parte*: From the unpublished "Great War" material in the manuscript collections of the Marion E. Wade Center. C. S. Lewis, MS *Clivi Hamiltonis Summae Metaphysices Contra Anthroposophos Libri II* [November 1928–1929], the Marion E. Wade Center CSL / MS-29 / X. C. S. Lewis, MS ["De Bono et Malo"] [1930], the Marion E. Wade Center CSL / MS-34 / X. C. S. Lewis, "Commentarium in Tractatum *De Toto et Parte*" [1931], the Marion E. Wade Center CSL / MS-30. Owen Barfield, MS "Replicit Anthroposophus Barfieldus" and "Autem" [1929], the Marion E. Wade Center, OB / MS-101 / X. Owen Barfield, MS *De Toto et Parte* (rough

draft) [1930], the Marion E. Wade Center, OB / MS-7; MS *De Toto et Parte* [1930], the Marion E. Wade Center, OB / MS-8 / X.

114 "We must be content to feel the highest truths 'in our bones'": A. C. Harwood, "About Anthroposophy," in Como, *C. S. Lewis at the Breakfast Table*, 26; letter dated October 28, 1926.

114 three sketches: Reproduced in "The 'Great War' Letters," appendix to Lewis, *Collected Letters*, vol. 3: 1601–1603.

115 "words may be made to disgorge the past": Owen Barfield, *History in English Words* (London: Methuen, 1926; rev. ed., London: Faber & Faber, 1962), 13.

115 "Sir John Cheke": Ibid., 62.

115 "for the Romans themselves": Ibid., 90.

116 "The scientists who discovered": Ibid., 13.

116 "No one who understands": Ibid., 135.

116 "new element": Ibid., 125.

116 "Perhaps . . . it can best be expressed": Ibid., 127–28.

116 "when our earliest ancestors": Ibid., 85.

116 "there came": Ibid., 140.

116 "self-consciousness": Ibid., 165.

117 "a change": Barfield, *Owen Barfield on C. S. Lewis*, 109–10.

117 when the human being achieved self-awareness: Jacob Burckhardt, *Die Cultur der Renaissance in Italien: Ein Versuch* (1860; Vienna: E. A. Seemann, 1885), 143.

117 "perfect clearness": Lewis, *Collected Letters*, vol. 3, 1498.

118 "learned, imaginative, moving": Cyril Connolly, "Telling Words," *The Sunday Times* (January 24, 1954): 5.

118 "not merely a theory of poetic diction": Owen Barfield, *Poetic Diction* (Middletown, Conn.: Wesleyan University Press, 1973), preface to 2nd ed., 14.

118 "They decided it wasn't . . . whether Coleridge had": Blaxland–de Lange, *Owen Barfield*, 28.

119 "in the infancy of society": Barfield, *Poetic Diction*, 58.

119 "meant neither *breath*, nor *wind*": Ibid., 81.

119 "a re-creating, registering as *thought*": Ibid., 103.

119 "felt change": Ibid., 48.

119 "in addition to the moment or moments of aesthetic pleasure . . . Now my normal everyday experience": Ibid., 55.

120 "had a permanent effect": Alan Bede Griffiths, O.S.B., "The Adventure of Faith," in Como, *C. S. Lewis at the Breakfast Table*, 13.

120 "Your conception of the ancient semantic unity": Lewis, *Collected Letters*, vol. 3, 1509.

120 For Barfield's influence on Tolkien, see Verlyn Flieger, *Splintered Light: Logos and Language in Tolkien's World* (Kent, Ohio, and London: The Kent State University Press, 2002) and *A Question of Time: J.R.R. Tolkien's Road to* Faërie (Kent, Ohio: Kent State University Press, 1997).

120 "there are no words left to describe his staggerment": J.R.R. Tolkien, *The Hobbit, or There and Back Again* (Boston and New York: Houghton Mifflin, 1997), chapter 12, "Inside Information," 194.

121 "marvelously absurd . . . obviously unable to make anything": Lewis, *Collected Letters*, vol. 1, 761.

121 "careful and sensitive . . . minor poet": Edmund Blunden, "Mechanisms of Poetry," *The Times Literary Supplement* 1372 (May 17, 1928): 375.

121 "I see no other way of studying the history of thought": Arthur Waley, *The Way and Its Power: A Study of the Tao tê ching and Its Place in Chinese Thought* (London: Allen & Unwin, 1934), 29–30.

121 "among the few poets and teachers of my acquaintance": Howard Nemerov, fore-word to Barfield, *Poetic Diction*, 1.

122 Lewis places the land of *Anthroposophia* next to that of *Occultia*: A. C. Harwood, "About Anthroposophy," in Como, *C. S. Lewis at the Breakfast Table*, 25.

122 "a reassuring German dullness": Lewis, *Surprised by Joy*, 207.

122 "think responsibly and logically": Blaxland–de Lange, *Owen Barfield*, 29.

6. A MYTHOLOGY FOR ENGLAND

123 "He is improving but requires hardening": Quoted from the archives of the Public Record Office by Christina Scull and Wayne G. Hammond, *The J.R.R. Tolkien Companion and Guide: Chronology* (Boston and New York: Houghton Mifflin, 2006), 96.

123 "small woodland glade . . . In those days": Tolkien, *Letters*, 420.

124 "if you do come out in print": Tolkien Papers, Bodleian Library, quoted in Scull and Hammond, *J.R.R. Tolkien Companion and Guide: Chronology*, 96.

125 "become indeed the poet of my race": James Joyce, letter of September 5, 1909, to Nora Barnacle, in *Selected Letters of James Joyce*, ed. Richard Ellman (London: Faber & Faber, 1975; reprint ed., 1992), 169. A good test of one's artistic inclinations is to ask oneself whether Joyce or Tolkien better achieved this ambition.

125 "I was from early days grieved": Tolkien, *Letters*, 144.

125 "polysyllabic barbarities": Gerald Seaman, "France and French Culture," in Drout, *J.R.R. Tolkien Encyclopedia*, 219, quoting Carpenter, *Tolkien*, 40.

125 "too lavish . . . the known form of the primary 'real' world": Tolkien, *Letters*, 144. Nonetheless, in the 1930s Tolkien attempted an Arthurian verse, only to abandon it soon after. The fragment appeared in J.R.R. Tolkien, *The Fall of Arthur*, ed. Christopher Tolkien (London: HarperCollins, 2013).

126 "a new world . . . revel in an amazing": Scull and Hammond, *J.R.R. Tolkien Companion and Guide: Reader's Guide*, 440.

126 "I am driven by my longing": *Kalevala: The Land of Heroes*, translated from the original Finnish by W. F. Kirby, vol. 1 (London: J. M. Dent, 1907), 1.

126 "cool and clear . . . fair elusive beauty": Tolkien, *Letters*, 144.

127 "as 'given things'": Carpenter, *Tolkien*, 92.

127 "*Nu we sculon herigean*" ("Now must we praise"): Caedmon's Hymn, the West Saxon version appended to Bede's Latin version in his *Ecclesiastical History of the English People*.

128 "objectively real world": Tolkien, *Letters*, 239.

128 "High School Exercise . . . One who dreams alone": Tolkien, "The Cottage of Lost Play," *The Book of Lost Tales*, part 1 (*The History of Middle-earth*, vol. 1), ed. Christopher Tolkien (Boston: Houghton Mifflin, 1984), 13–14.

128 "broad and woody plain": Tolkien, "Cottage of Lost Play," 13.

129 "The Music of the Ainur . . . mighty melodies": Tolkien, "The Music of the Ainur," *The Book of Lost Tales*, part 1, 53.

129 The net effect: For Tolkien's defense of his archaisms, see the draft letter of September 1955 to his longtime fan and correspondent Hugh Brogan, *Letters*, 225–26.

130 "facts seemed to run round": From the obituary by sometime Inkling C. L. Wrenn, "Sir W. Craigie: Stimulus to Study of Germanic Languages," *The Times* (September 9, 1957): 10.

131 words from "waggle" to "waggly": It's not difficult here to see glimmerings of later Tolkien inventions; his hobbits, for instance, wear waistcoats, use wains, live among wolds, venture into wilds (at least Bilbo and his relatives do); while it may be that any random list of English words will apply to hobbits, it is also true that throughout his life Tolkien obsessively recycled his work.

131 "learned more . . . than in any other": Scull and Hammond, *J.R.R. Tolkien Companion and Guide: Reader's Guide*, 726.

131 "not only to read texts": Tolkien, *Letters*, 406.

132 "natural niggler . . . I compose only with great difficulty": Ibid., 257, 313, 113.

132 "the ordinary machinery of expression . . . exceptionally full treatment": J.R.R. Tolkien, "Note," *A Middle English Vocabulary Designed for Use with SISAM'S Fourteenth Century Verse and Prose* (Oxford: Clarendon Press, 1922), 2.

132 "a mole-hill glossary . . . accumulated domestic distractions": Letter to John Johnson, University Printer, quoted in Scull and Hammond, *J.R.R. Tolkien Companion and Guide: Reader's Guide*, 588.

132 "curses on my head": Tolkien, *Letters*, 11.

132 "a piece of work . . . exhaustive textual references": Margaret L. Lee, "Middle English," in *The Year's Work in English Studies*, vol. 2, 1920–1921, edited for the English Association by Sir Sidney Lee and F. S. Boas (London: Oxford University Press, 1922), 42–43.

133 "terrible to recall": Tolkien, *Letters*, 11.

133 "complete cycle of events in an Elfinesse . . . very graphically and astonishingly told": Scull and Hammond, *J.R.R. Tolkien Companion and Guide: Chronology*, 110.

133 "what Gondolin was": John Garth, "Tolkien, Exeter College and the Great War," in *Tolkien's The Lord of the Rings: Sources of Inspiration*, ed. Stratford Caldecott and Thomas Honegger (Zurich and Jena: Walking Tree Publishers, 2008), 53.

133 "Mrs. Tolkien . . . North Pole": J.R.R. Tolkien, *Letters from Father Christmas*, ed. Baillie Tolkien, rev. ed. (Boston: Houghton Mifflin, 1999), 6.

134 "rotted the curtains . . . change his collar": John and Priscilla Tolkien, *Tolkien Family Album*, 45.

134 "more like a man": Lewis, *All My Road Before Me*, 240–41.

134 "It is not often in 'universities,'": Tolkien, *Letters*, 56–57.

134 "his name is a disadvantage": George Stuart Gordon, *The Letters of George S. Gordon, 1902–1942* (London and New York: Oxford University Press, 1943), 146.

135 "industrious little devil . . . my devoted friend": Carpenter, *Tolkien*, 104–105.

135 Tolkien composed poems and songs for the revels: Douglas A. Anderson, "An Industrious Little Devil: E. V. Gordon as Friend and Collaborator with Tolkien," in *Tolkien the Medievalist*, ed. Jane Chance (New York: Routledge, 2003), 23.

135 "not so much a staff as a Club!": Mary C. Biggar Gordon, *The Life of George S. Gordon 1881–1942* (London: Oxford University Press, 1945), 67.

135 "team fired not only with a departmental esprit de corps": Tolkien, *Letters*, 56–57.

135 "the proportion of 'language' students is very high": Ibid., 11.

135 "provide the student": J.R.R. Tolkien and E. V. Gordon, *Sir Gawain and the Green Knight* (Oxford: Clarendon Press, 1925).

135 "clearness, conciseness": Cyrill Brett, review of *Sir Gawain and the Green Knight* by J.R.R. Tolkien and E. V. Gordon, *The Modern Language Review* 22, no. 4 (October 1927): 451–58.

136 "standing by my bedside": Carpenter, *Tolkien*, 106.

137 "I have never consulted him without gaining an illumination": Scull and Hammond, *J. R. R. Tolkien Companion and Guide: Reader's Guide*, 1.

137 "there is no philological (or literary) scholar of his generation from whom I have learned so much": Ibid., 349.

137 "for many years I have felt strongly": Eugène Vinaver quoted in Peter H. Sutcliffe, *The Oxford University Press: An Informal History* (Oxford: Clarendon Press, 1978), 270.

138 "wickedness and sloth . . . I regret those days bitterly": Tolkien, *Letters*, 340.

138 "the spirit of the (vanishing) Oxford": Ibid., 26.

139 "a thousand whispering trees": Tolkien, "Cottage of Lost Play," 33.

139 "The Coming of the Valar": *Book of Lost Tales*, part 1, 72–73.

139 "torture . . . murder": In an indignant letter to the editor of *The Daily Telegraph*, responding to an article in which overgrown forests are described as places of "a kind of Tolkien gloom, where no bird sings." Tolkien, *Letters*, 420. See Matthew Dickerson, "Trees," in Drout, *J.R.R. Tolkien Encyclopedia*, 678.

139 "a great-limbed poplar": Tolkien, "Introductory Note," *Tree and Leaf*, 5.

139 "a row of coloured Quink": John and Priscilla Tolkien, *Tolkien Family Album*, 56–57.

140 his speech was often incomprehensible: The authors once heard the following anecdote from a close friend of Tolkien: "I was visiting him one day and asked him what he really thought of C. S. Lewis. He said, 'I'll tell you, but let's go on a walk while I talk.' So we walked for twenty or thirty minutes around North Oxford, and he spilled out his heart to me, or so I believed, telling me his real views on his close friend. But the truth is, I have no idea what he said. He was mumbling so much I couldn't make out a word."

140 "I do not remember a single word": W. H. Auden, "Making, Knowing and Judging," Inaugural Lecture as Professor of Poetry, Oxford, June 11, 1956, in *The Dyer's Hand and Other Essays* (London: Faber & Faber, 1963), 41–42.

140 "could turn a lecture room into a mead hall": J.I.M. Stewart quoted in Philip Norman, "'More Than a Campus Craze; It's Like a Drug Dream; The Prevalence of Hobbits: Thirty Years After They Were Invented by a Bored Oxford Don, the Hobbits—'a Benevolent, Furry-Footed People'—Have Taken a New Generation by Storm," *The New York Times*, January 15, 1967.

140 earning one hundred pounds by grading exams: Tolkien, *Letters*, 24.

141 "the great indiarubber trunks": J.R.R. Tolkien, *Roverandom*, ed. Christina Scull and Wayne G. Hammond (Boston and New York: Houghton Mifflin, 1998), 59.

141 "the Mountains of Elvenhome": Ibid., 74.

141 "poems and major legends": Tolkien, *Letters*, 342.

141 "Tolkien's ultimate tree": Hammond and Scull, *J.R.R. Tolkien: Artist and Illustrator*, 64.

141 "I have exposed my heart to be shot at": Tolkien, *Letters*, 172.

142 "a new starting-point": Christopher Tolkien, "The Earliest 'Silmarillion,'" in J.R.R. Tolkien, *The Shaping of Middle-Earth: The Quenta, the Ambarkanta, and the Annals, Together with the Earliest "Silmarillion" and the First Map*, vol. 4: *The History of Middle-earth*, ed. Christopher Tolkien (Boston: Houghton Mifflin, 1986), 11.

142 "*Tinúviel* meets with qualified approval": Scull and Hammond, *J.R.R. Tolkien Companion and Guide: Chronology*, 134.

7. WANTED: AN INTELLIGIBLE ABSOLUTE

144 "purpose of worshipping devoutly": Lewis, *Collected Letters*, vol. 1, 468.

144 "little twinkling man like a bird": Ibid., 531.

144 "sham romance": Ibid., 525.

144 "I have seldom felt less at my ease . . . Kod": Ibid., 565–66. Lewis uses the slang expression "Kod" (or its variants, "cod," "codotta," "kodotta") in many of his early letters, and gave the title "Metrical Meditations of a Cod" to the notebook of poems he wrote at the Kirkpatricks'—including poems that would be incorporated into *Spirits in Bondage*.

145 "if he were now alive": C. S. Lewis, "Preface by the Author to the 1950 Edition" of *Dymer*, in C. S. Lewis, *Narrative Poems*, ed. Walter Hooper (San Diego: Harcourt, 1969), 6.

145 "Poor old Kirk!": Lewis, *Collected Letters*, vol. 1, 535.

145 "is so indelibly stamped": Ibid., 539–40.

146 "I wish life and death were not the only alternatives": Lewis, *All My Road Before Me*, 18.

146 "whiff of what I used to call the 'real joy'": Ibid., 406.

146 "A greater bore I have never met": Ibid., 115.

146 "Smudge": Ibid., 65.

146 they would send her off to church by herself: A. N. Wilson mentions this as a personal communication from Maureen (Lady Dunbar), *C. S. Lewis*, 66.

147 "In the midst of all this confusion": Lewis, *All My Road Before Me*, 104.

147 "very characteristically": Ibid., 427.

147 "Found D and Dorothy": Ibid., 245–46.

148 "we sat in judgement on Headington": Ibid., 145.

148 "that foul hag . . . the Bitch": Ibid., 85 et passim.

148 "was generous": Sayer, *Jack: A Life of C. S. Lewis*, 155.

148 "that fatal tomb": Lewis, *Collected Letters*, vol. 1, 528.

149 "hostility to the emotions": Lewis, *Surprised by Joy*, 198.

149 an admirer of Tolkien: Three years earlier, Coghill had sat in the audience as Tolkien introduced his mythology in March 1920 to the Exeter College Essay Club.

149 "[Coghill] was a big man built on generous lines": John Wain, quoted in Nevil Coghill, *The Collected Papers of Nevill Coghill: Shakespearian and Medievalist*, ed. Douglas Gray (Sussex: Harvester, 1988), vii.

150 "you countenanced": W. H. Auden, "To Professor Nevill Coghill upon his retirement in A.D. 1966," in *To Nevill Coghill from Friends*, collected by John Lawlor and W. H. Auden (London: Faber & Faber, 1966), 155.

150 "a tutor in whom": Auden, *Dyer's Hand and Other Essays*, vii.

150 "a good looking fellow": Lewis, *All My Road Before Me*, 189.

150 Coghill's accusation: Ibid., 190.

150 "In Oxenford": Nevill Coghill's minutes, quoted by Walter Hooper in the preface to C. S. Lewis, *Selected Literary Essays*, ed. Walter Hooper (Cambridge: Cambridge University Press, 1969), x–xii.

150 "combative pleasure . . . was certainly the best": Nevill Coghill, "The Approach to English," in Gibb, *Light on C. S. Lewis*, 52.

151 "was a world he could inhabit and believe in": Ibid., 51–52.

151 Even the gods: Ibid., 55.

151 "a continuous intoxication . . . we were uninhibitedly happy": Ibid., 52.

151 Coghill . . . was a Christian: Lewis, *Surprised by Joy*, 212.

152 the Real Presence: N.K.H.A. Coghill, "The Sacraments of the Church and the Presence of God in Nature," *Report of the Anglo-Catholic Congress, Subject: The Holy Eucharist, London, July, 1927* (London: Society of SS. Peter and Paul, 1927; Milwaukee: Morehouse Publishing, 1927), 32–43. Other lay speakers included Evelyn Underhill, A. E. Taylor, and Will Spens.

152 "You stranger": Lewis, *Narrative Poems*, 7.

153 "development by self-destruction . . . redemption by parricide": Lewis, *Collected Letters*, vol. 1, 664.

153 "At Dymer's birth no comets scared the nation": Lewis, *Dymer*, in C. S. Lewis, *Narrative Poems*, 8.

154 "that country clothed with dancing flowers": Ibid., 91.

154 "To 'get it again'": Lewis, *Surprised by Joy*, 169.

154 "new psychology . . . unmask and defeat": C. S. Lewis, "Preface by the Author to the 1950 Edition" of *Dymer*, in C. S. Lewis, *Narrative Poems*, 4.

154 "My desire then contains two elements": Lewis, *Collected Letters*, vol. 1, 929–30.

154 AE . . . had kind things to say: "Note from Coghill today saying that the 'V.O.,' whose favourable review of *Dymer* in the *Irish Statesman* had seemed to me not 'good' in any sense except that of being favourable, is really A.E. (Russell)," in Lewis, *All My Road Before Me*, 453.

155 "great poem": "A good review from G.K's Weekly arrived by the morning post, signed by a man called Crofte-Cooke, where Dymer figures as 'a great poem' for the first time* in print"; "* and last" reads a note Lewis added later. Lewis, *All My Road Before Me*, 436.

155 "notable because it is in the epic tradition": *The Times Literary Supplement* (January 13, 1927), 27. Lewis told his father,

> Fausset's review really says as big things as I could, with any reason, wish for. The question "Is epic now possible?" has been a stock question for years. Taking the word "epic" to mean his sense, there is no candidate between Milton and our own times. He puts up Masefield as a possible, and prefers me. He says I have brought back under modern conditions something that has seemed impossible since the days of myth—for I think he includes the Miltonic along with the Spenserian . . . I don't mean of course that he thinks I am better than Milton and Spenser, but that I have brought back something lost before (and during) their time. If what he said

were true, it wd. mean that I was a very considerable turning point. Of course he is wrong . . .

Lewis, *Collected Letters*, vol. 1, 680.

155 "silly": Lewis, *All My Road Before Me*, 446.

155 "the metrical level is good": Ibid., 438.

155 "Pre-Raphaelite stained glass": Coghill, "Approach to English," 58–59.

155 "from the age of sixteen onwards I had one single ambition": Lewis, *Collected Letters*, vol. 1, 925.

156 "The Queen of Drum": Hooper, *C. S. Lewis: A Complete Guide*, 160.

156 "a meaningless dance": Lewis, *Surprised by Joy*, 172.

156 "an old, dirty, gabbling . . . The whole question of immortality": Ibid., 201–202.

156 the descent into madness of Mrs. Moore's brother, John "Doc" Askins: Lewis, *All My Road Before Me*, 202–18.

157 "a sort of horrible sympathy": Ibid., 203.

157 An ardent spiritualist friend: Ibid., 221.

157 "it was to this . . . Safety first": Lewis, *Surprised by Joy*, 203.

157 "Keep clear of introspection": Lewis, *Collected Letters*, vol. 1, 605–606.

157 "satisfied an emotional need . . . No more Avalon": Lewis, *Surprised by Joy*, 204.

158 art was a sphere of its own: This was a Romantic axiom; Lewis found it in Schopenhauer, among others, and wrote to tell Arthur about this discovery in October 1918. Lewis, *Collected Letters*, vol. 1, 407.

158 "as rock-bottom reality": Lewis, *Surprised by Joy*, 208–209.

159 hard philosophical work: As he later acknowledged: "I have been astray among second rate ideas too long . . ." (January 19, 1927), in Lewis, *All My Road Before Me*, 432.

159 "as if the Absolute came to eat out of your hand": Bernard Bosanquet, *Some Suggestions in Ethics* (London: Macmillan, 1918), 80.

159 "out here, where I see spirit continually dodging matter": Lewis, *Collected Letters*, vol. 1, 371.

159 For further reflections from Lewis on his journey from realism to idealism and beyond, see C. S. Lewis, *The Pilgrim's Regress*, preface to 3rd ed. (London: Geoffrey Bles, 1943; reprint ed., London: HarperCollins, 1977), 9–12. See also Mathieu Marion, "Oxford Realism: Knowledge and Perception I," *British Journal for the History of Philosophy* 8, no. 2 (2000): 299–338.

160 a disproportionate swath: See J. M. Winter, *The Great War and the British People*, 2nd ed. (Basingstoke, UK, and New York: Palgrave Macmillan, 2003), on the demographic data that supports the widespread belief that there were disproportionate numbers of casualties among the officers (drawn from the educated upper classes), and especially among young officers.

160 On the generational shifts in English philosophy, see the famous essay by Gilbert Ryle, "Fifty Years of Philosophy and Philosophers," *Philosophy* 51, no. 198 (October 1976): 383.

160 "WANTED IMMEDIATELY, for Teaching Purposes, an INTELLIGIBLE ABSOLUTE": *Mind! A Unique Review of Ancient and Modern Philosophy*, ed. A. Troglodyte [F.C.S. Schiller] (London: Williams and Norgate, 1901), 142.

160 "the Absolute cannot be made clear . . . mystifications": Lewis, *Surprised by Joy*, 222–23.

160 "quasi-religion . . . We could talk religiously": Ibid., 210. See Barfield, *Owen Barfield on C. S. Lewis*, 8.

161 "cannot be lived": Ibid., 226.

161 "wasn't a *subject* to Plato": Ibid., 225.

161 "pure applesauce . . . constitutionally incapable": Barfield, *Owen Barfield on C. S. Lewis*, 10. It's a typical rhetorical strategy on Lewis's part, to make himself look the fool, or the callow worldling, in order to set off an insight more effectively, or heighten the dramatic tension of his conversion narrative.

161 "mind was no late-come epiphenomenon": Lewis, *Surprised by Joy*, 209.

161 "And so the great Angler": Ibid., 211.

161 "very attractive": Lewis, *Collected Letters*, vol. 1, 625.

162 "in a strange state of excitement": Lewis, *All My Road Before Me*, 293.

162 "I went up to [Jack's] room": Albert Lewis, diary, May 20, 1925, quoted by Walter Hooper in Lewis, *Collected Letters*, vol. 1, 642.

162 "my audience had dwindled to two": Lewis, *All My Road Before Me*, 348. This "old parson" must be the same as the "aged parson" Lewis speaks of in a letter to his father of February 11, 1925 (Lewis, *Collected Letters*, vol. 1, 638). The "aged parson" was the Reverend Frank Nightingale, ordained an Anglican priest in 1894, now in retirement, auditing classes at Oxford.

163 "I have come to think if I had the mind, I have not the brain": Lewis, *Collected Letters*, vol. 1, 648.

163 "It will be a comfort to me": Ibid., 649.

163 "annihilated . . . I was off once more": Lewis, *Surprised by Joy*, 217.

164 *Space, Time, and Deity*: Discussed by Lewis in *All My Road Before Me*, 301, and *Surprised by Joy*, 217–18.

164 "bearded and deaf . . . cosmic creation": Lewis, *All My Road Before Me*, 403–404.

164 "My class was completely unruffled": Ibid., 394.

164 "I saw that all my waitings . . . all images and sensations": Lewis, *Surprised by Joy*, 219–20. "It appeared to me," Lewis had written long ago in a preface to *The Pilgrim's Regress*,

> that if a man diligently followed this desire, pursuing the false objects until their falsity appeared and then resolutely abandoning them, he must come out at last into the clear knowledge that the human soul was made to enjoy some object that is never fully given—nay, cannot even be imagined as given—in our present mode of subjective and spatio-temporal experience. This Desire was, in the soul, as the Siege Perilous in Arthur's castle—the chair in which only one could sit. And if nature makes nothing in vain, the One who can sit in this chair must exist.

Lewis, *Pilgrim's Regress*, preface to 3rd ed., 15.

165 "I asked the earth": Augustine, *Confessions* 10:6, trans. Sheed.

165 "region of awe": Lewis, *Surprised by Joy*, 221.

165 "beautiful beyond expectation": Lewis, *Collected Letters*, vol. 1, 650.

165 "a kneeling affair": Ibid., 647.

166 "Contempt is his ruling passion": From an account Lewis gave of nine of his Magdalen colleagues, quoted by Walter Hooper in an appendix to *All My Road Before Me*, 482–83.

166 "rowing, drinking": Lewis, *Collected Letters*, vol. 1, 778.

166 "a pleasant change": Ibid., 661. His first lecture at the University College, "The Good, its position among values," had only four in the audience.

166 His most famous lectures: Lewis's twice weekly "Prolegomena lectures" formed the basis of *The Discarded Image* (published posthumously in 1964); and in a letter to Sister Mary Madeleva (Wolff), C.S.C., Lewis says that they were a runoff from material he collected for *The Allegory of Love*: Lewis, *Collected Letters*, vol. 2, 140–41.

166 red face and booming voice: John Wain, "C. S. Lewis as a Teacher," in *Masters: Portraits of Great Teachers*, ed. Joseph Epstein (New York: Basic Books, 1981), 250.

166 a trademark style: George Watson, who attended Lewis's lectures in 1948 (against his tutor's wishes), recalls, "You could have taken dictation from his lectures, and some (including myself) did." Watson, "The Art of Disagreement: C. S. Lewis (1898–1963)," *The Hudson Review* 48, 2 (Summer 1995): 229. A detailed record is preserved in the notes of William Jarvis, catalogued in the Bodleian Library as "Notes on C. S. Lewis's lectures for undergraduates, 'Prolegomena to the Study of Medieval Poetry,' taken by William Jarvis, 1936" (shelfmark: MS. Eng. D. 2567).

166 "Thickening": Walter Hooper, "The Lectures of C. S. Lewis in the Universities of Oxford and Cambridge," *Christian Scholars Review* 27, no. 4 (1998): 441.

166 "girls squatting": Paul Johnson, "A.J.P. Taylor: A Saturnine Star Who Had Intellectuals Rolling in the Aisles," *The Spectator* (March 11, 2006): 31.

166 "as a lecturer he was the biggest 'draw'": Harry Blamires, quoted in Warren Lewis, "Memoir of C. S. Lewis," 38.

167 Sister Mary Madeleva: From a letter to Holy Cross Superior General Mother Vincentia Fannon. Gail Porter Mandell, *Madeleva: A Biography* (Albany: State University of New York Press, 1997), 136.

167 "avuncular informality": Alastair Fowler, "C. S. Lewis: Supervisor," *The Yale Review* 91, no. 4 (October 2003): 74.

167 "I have been bothered": Lewis, *Collected Letters*, vol. 1, 667. These were seven scholars from Lady Margaret Hall.

167 "ladies of St. Hugh's . . . man's man": Stephen Schofield, *In Search of C. S. Lewis* (South Plainfield, N.J.: Bridge, 1983), 62.

168 John Betjeman, future poet laureate: A. N. Wilson, *Betjeman: A Life* (New York: Farrar, Straus and Giroux, 2006), 55. See also Bevis Hillier, *Young Betjeman* (London: John Murray, 1988), for a detailed account of Lewis's relations with Betjeman.

168 parodies of T. S. Eliot poems: Lewis, *All My Road Before Me*, 410.

168 "super-undergraduates . . . absolutely silent": Ibid., 437.

168 "luncheons, luncheons": John Betjeman, *Summoned by Bells* (1960), in *Collected Poems* (New York: Farrar, Straus and Giroux, 2006), 461.

168 "creditable": Lewis, *All My Road Before Me*, 402.

168 "he hasn't been able to read": Ibid., 433.

169 "'Objectively, our Common Room": John Betjeman, "A Hike on the Downs," in *Continual Dew* (1937), in *Collected Poems* (New York: Farrar, Straus and Giroux, 2006), 30.

169 "rude and incompetent": Quoted in Jeremy Treglown, *Romancing: The Life and Work of Henry Green* (New York: Random House, 2000), 46.

169 became for a while a close friend: For more on the Green-Coghill friendship, see Treglown's superb biography of Green, *Romancing*, 50–80.

169 "thought nothing of": Maurice Bowra, *Memories*, 163, quoted in Treglown, *Romancing*, 46.

169 "Lewis's abrasiveness [and] Henry's passivity": Treglown, *Romancing*, 46. We are grateful to Treglown for pointing out the friction between Lewis's and Green's literary tastes.

169 "He cut short my apologies": John Lawlor, *C. S. Lewis: Memories and Reflections* (Dallas: Spence, 1998), 6.

169 "He looked more like an angler": Joan O'Hare, "Intellectual Development," in *We Remember C. S. Lewis: Essays and Memoirs*, ed. David Graham (Nashville, Tenn.: Broadman & Holman, 2001), 42.

169 "implacable criticism": Martin Lings, "A Debt Repaid," in Graham, *We Remember C. S. Lewis*, 54.

169 "happy but incompetent": Alan Rook, "The Butcher," in Schofield, *In Search of C. S. Lewis*, 11.

169–70 "Lewis did not want to bully anyone": W. W. Robson, "The Romanticism of C. S. Lewis," *The Cambridge Quarterly* (1966), reprinted in *Critical Essays* (London: Routledge & Kegan Paul, 1966), 73.

170 "the best read man": A. N. Wilson, *C. S. Lewis*, 161.

170 "If only you could smoke": Lewis, *Collected Letters*, vol. 1, 750.

170 "wall of stillness . . . To sit opposite": Helen Gardner, "Clive Staples Lewis," *Proceedings of the British Academy*, 1966, 419.

171 "*Cum bove bos . . . Necnon ridicula*": J. D. Mabbott, *Oxford Memories* (Oxford: Thornton's of Oxford, 1986), 77–78. As Laurence Harwood (son of Cecil Harwood and Lewis's godson) points out, however, this verse appears to have been composed previously by Barfield and Lewis together. Laurence Harwood, *C. S. Lewis, My Godfather* (Downer's Grove, Ill.: IVP Press, 2007), 53–54. The manuscript is included in the Owen Barfield Papers at the Bodleian Library (shelfmark: Dep. c. 1104, folio 3) under the title 'Poema de XVI Animalibus arcem Noam intrantibus,' with the legend "HAEC FECIT BARFIELD OVENS ET CLIVUS HAMILTON," and initialed "CSL, AOB, Jan. 1929."

172 "smooth, pale fluent little chap": Lewis, *All My Road Before Me*, 393.

8. A MEETING OF MINDS

173 "can't read Spenser . . . no harm in him": Lewis, *All My Road Before Me*, 393.

174 "The school of English Lang. and Litt.": Scarlett Baron, "A Short History of the English Faculty," Christ Church, 2005, http://english.nsms.ox.ac.uk/sites/default /files/History%20of%20Eng%20Fac.pdf (accessed July 15, 2014).

174 "the thousand years . . . a main source": J.R.R. Tolkien, "The Oxford English School," *The Oxford Magazine* 48, no. 21 (May 29, 1930): 778–82.

175 "an intrinsic absurdity . . . the student who wants": C. S. Lewis, "Our English Syllabus," *Rehabilitations and Other Essays*, 91.

175 "if any question of the value": C. S. Lewis, "The Idea of an English School," *Rehabilitations and Other Essays*, 64.

175 "a sense of language": Ibid., 72.

176 "next year is the first exam . . . How long will it take us to become corrupt": Lewis, *Collected Letters*, vol. 2, 9.

176 the views of Tolkien and Lewis . . . prevailed: Tolkien would look back upon these contretemps in his "Valedictory Address to the University of Oxford," delivered at Merton College on the occasion of his retirement. J.R.R. Tolkien, "Valedictory Address to the University of Oxford, 5 June 1959," in *J.R.R. Tolkien, Scholar and Storyteller: Essays in Memoriam*, ed. Mary Salu and Robert T. Farrell (Ithaca and London: Cornell University Press, 1979), 16–32. A slightly different version appears in J.R.R. Tolkien, *The Monsters and the Critics and Other Essays*, ed. Christopher Tolkien (London: George Allen & Unwin, 1983); see discussion by Scull and Hammond, *J.R.R. Tolkien Companion and Guide: Reader's Guide*, 1074–76.

177 "a wild dream": Lewis, *Collected Letters*, vol. 1, 701.

177 "the gods & giants & Asgard": Ibid., 838.

177 "of the 2 class": Ibid., 969.

177 "sense of reality . . . I sat up late last night": Quoted by Christopher Tolkien in an introduction to *The Lay of Leithian*, in J.R.R. Tolkien, *The Lays of Beleriand* (*The History of Middle-earth*, vol. 3), ed. Christopher Tolkien, 151.

177 "For perfect construction": J.R.R. Tolkien, "A Secret Vice," *The Monsters and the Critics*, 210–11.

178 "Roses all the way": Albert's diary, quoted in Lewis, *All My Road Before Me*, 425.

178 "We will resolve them into their elements": Lewis, *Collected Letters*, vol. 1, 866.

178 "J and I went out . . . such stuff": W. H. Lewis, *Brothers and Friends*, 58.

179 C. S. Lewis, *The Allegory of Love: A Study in Medieval Tradition* (London: Geoffrey Cumberlege, Oxford University Press, 1936; reprinted with corrections, 1938). Lewis didn't like the title: "I've also an old grudge against the Clarendon Press for making me call my first book The Allegory of Love when I wanted a sober academic title like The Allegorical Love Poem" (Lewis, *Collected Letters*, vol. 3, 1115).

179 "TO OWEN BARFIELD": The capital letters are Lewis's. In the original, Barfield's name appears in larger type than the rest of the dedication.

179 " . . . I saw him coming slowly towards me": Coghill, "Approach to English," 60–61. Or as Lewis would put it later, "our legend of the Renaissance is a Renaissance legend." C. S. Lewis, *English Literature in the Sixteenth Century Excluding Drama: The Completion of the Clark Lectures* (1944), in the *Oxford History of English Literature*, ed. F. P. Wilson and Bonamy Dobrée (Oxford: Clarendon Press, 1954), 56. In *Surprised by Joy*, Lewis says that the Renaissance is a construct, in which scholars project onto the fifteenth century a dim memory of their own reawakening after the "dark ages" or latency period of adolescence (71).

179 *The Romance of the Rose* "and its school": Lewis, *Collected Letters*, vol. 1, 754, note 18.

179 "I have actually begun the first chapter": Ibid., 766–67.

179 "I . . . wrote nearly the whole": Lewis, *Collected Letters*, vol. 3, 1342.

180 "that long-lost state of mind": Lewis, *Allegory of Love*, 1.

180 "the greatest among the founders": Ibid., 360.

180 "Humanity does not pass through phases": Ibid., 1.

181 "French poets": Ibid., 4.

182 "the very nature of thought . . . To ask how these married pairs": Ibid., 44.

183 "life's golden tree": Ibid., 316.

183 "literary toy": C. S. Lewis, "Edmund Spenser, 1552–99," *Studies in Medieval and Renaissance Literature*, collected by Walter Hooper (Cambridge, UK: Cambridge University Press, 1966), 137.

183 "There is nothing 'mystical'": Lewis, *Allegory of Love*, 48.

183 "the allegorist leaves the given": Ibid., 45.

183 "affords excellent reading . . . If his work lacks": Howard Rollin Patch, *Speculum* 2, no. 2 (April 1937): 272–74.

184 "undoubtedly one of the best books": G. L. Brook, review of *The Allegory of Love*, *Modern Language Review* 32, no. 2 (April 1937): 287–88.

184 "it is rarely that . . . Mr. Lewis is a critic alive": Kathleen Tillotson, review of *The Allegory of Love*, *The Review of English Studies* 13, no. 52 (October 1937): 477–79.

184 "for surely to be indulgent": Lewis, *Allegory of Love*, 89–90.

184 "something between the last of the medieval poets": "On Reading 'The Faerie Queene,'" *Studies in Medieval and Renaissance Literature*, 48. Originally published as "Edmund Spenser," in *Fifteen Poets* (Oxford: Oxford University Press, 1941).

185 believed in a personal God: Lewis, *Surprised by Joy*, 225.

185 "I became aware": Ibid., 224.

185 "I was to be allowed to play at philosophy no longer": Lewis, *Surprised by Joy*, 228–29.

186 "terrible things are happening": Lewis, *Collected Letters*, vol. 1, 882–83. Walter Hooper makes the point that "Lewis appeared to be having the very experience he later described in *Surprised by Joy* XIV."

186 revised dating: Alister McGrath, *C. S. Lewis—A Life: Eccentric Genius, Reluctant Prophet* (Carol Stream, Ill.: Tyndale House, 2013), 141–46.

186 "Adversary": Lewis, *Surprised by Joy*, 216.

186 "a zoo of lusts": Ibid., 226.

187 "And so the great Angler": Ibid., 211.

187 "the tension of these final chapters": *The Times Literary Supplement* (October 7, 1955). Quoted by David Jasper, "*The Pilgrim's Regress* and *Surprised by Joy*," in *The Cambridge Companion to C. S. Lewis*, ed. Robert MacSwain and Michael Ward (Cambridge, UK: Cambridge University Press, 2010), 228–29.

187 "To know God": Lewis, *Surprised by Joy*, 231–32.

187 "sense of honor . . . the fussy": Ibid., 233–34.

187 "Where has religion reached . . . Paganism had been only the childhood": Ibid., 235.

188 As a result: Lewis, *Collected Letters*, vol. 1, 911–12.

188 "I started to say my prayers again . . . the inherent improbability": W. H. Lewis, *Brothers and Friends*, 80.

188 "To one . . . 'breathed through silver'": J.R.R. Tolkien, "Mythopoeia," *Tree and Leaf* (new ed.; London: HarperCollins, 2001), 83. Humphrey Carpenter's reconstruction of the Addison's Walk conversations is based on a series of letters Lewis wrote

to Arthur Greeves, combined with some of the lines in Tolkien's poem "Mythopoeia."

189 "Rum thing": Lewis, *Surprised by Joy*, 223–34. Walter Hooper identifies Weldon as the atheist in question; see Lewis, *Collected Letters*, vol. 1, 763, note 44.

189 "the ecstasy": Ibid., 970.

189 "When we set out I did not believe": Lewis, *Surprised by Joy*, 237.

189 Joy "lost nearly all interest": Ibid., 238.

189 "I have just passed": Lewis, *Collected Letters*, vol. 1, 974.

189 *The Pilgrim's Regress*, written in a white heat: According to Hooper (*C. S. Lewis: A Complete Guide*, 182), Lewis wrote the whole of *The Pilgrim's Regress* in August 1932, while he was simultaneously working on *The Allegory of Love*. He published *Regress* in 1933.

189 "a sweetness and a pang": Lewis, *Pilgrim's Regress*, 33.

189 "needless obscurity": Lewis, *Pilgrim's Regress*, preface to 3rd ed., 9.

189 "Oriental pessimism": Lewis, *Pilgrim's Regress*, 174.

189 "Globol obol": Ibid., 69.

191 "the character of the planets": C. S. Lewis, "The Alliterative Metre," *Lysistrata* 2, (May 1935); reprinted in Lewis, *Selected Literary Essays*, 24.

191 "the twilight of the gods": Lewis, *Allegory of Love*, 52.

191 planetary symbolism is the key: Michael Ward, *Planet Narnia: The Seven Heavens in the Imagination of C. S. Lewis* (New York: Oxford University Press, 2008).

192 "an uninterrupted feast": Lewis, *Collected Letters*, vol. 1, 856.

192 "Barfield doesn't really taste": Ibid., 857.

192 "had the feeling that something was broken . . . I don't think I ever heard him speak": Blaxland–de Lange, *Owen Barfield*, 175.

192 "Lo, there was a certain philosopher": Owen Barfield, "C.S.L.: Biographia Theologica." Owen Barfield Manuscripts, Marion E. Wade Center, OB / MS-6. Translation by John Zaleski.

193 "I don't think I ever showed it": Ibid., note on verso.

9. INKLINGS ASSEMBLE

194 "prove more lasting": Tolkien, *Letters*, 387.

194 "unpublished compositions . . . immediate criticism": Ibid., 388.

195 "undetermined and unelected": Ibid., 388.

195 "philosophical discussion": Lewis, *Collected Letters*, vol. 1, 692.

195 "one of the pleasantest spots . . . Sometimes we talk": Lewis, *Collected Letters*, vol. 2, 16.

195 "ridiculously combative": Owen Barfield, foreword, *VII [Seven]: An Anglo-American Literary Review* 1 (March 1980): 9.

196 "Had I known": Warren Lewis, *C. S. Lewis: A Biography*, unpublished draft, Marion E. Wade Center, Wheaton College, quoted in Colin Duriez, *C. S. Lewis: A Biography of Friendship* (Oxford: Lion Hudson, 2013), 134.

196 "red-brick universities": Warren Lewis, "Memoir of C. S. Lewis," 34.

196 "surprisingly successful": Owen Barfield, "The Inklings Remembered," *The World & I* 5, no. 4 (April 1990): 549.

196 "quite unreal": Lyle W. Dorsett, oral history interview with Dr. Robert E. Havard, July 26, 1984, in the Marion E. Wade Collection, Wheaton College, Wheaton, Illinois (1986), 37.

197 "but better known" . . . "a poet . . . intolerant": J.R.R. Tolkien, *The Notion Club Papers*, in *Sauron Defeated: The End of the Third Age* (*The History of The Lord of the Rings*, Part Four); *The Notion Club Papers; and The Drowning of Anadûnê* (*The History of Middle-earth*, vol. 9), ed. Christopher Tolkien (London: Harper-Collins, 1992), 159.

197 He identified Ramer as "Self": Christopher Tolkien's commentary, Tolkien, *Notion Club Papers*, in *Sauron Defeated*, 150.

197 "not to look for their own faces": Tolkien, *Notion Club Papers*, in *Sauron Defeated*, 149.

198 "read aloud . . . was highly approved": Tolkien, *Letters*, 29.

198 "a feeling for literature": David Cecil, "Oxford's Magic Circle," *Books and Bookmen* 24, no. 4 (January 1979): 10, quoted by Scull and Hammond, *J.R.R. Tolkien Companion and Guide: Reader's Guide*, 429.

198 "There's no sound I like better": From a biographical sketch Lewis provided at the request of his American publisher, Macmillan; quoted and discussed by Alan Jacobs in the introduction to his Lewis biography: Alan Jacobs, *The Narnian: The Life and Imagination of C. S. Lewis* (New York: HarperSanFrancisco, 2005), xviii–xix.

199 "In each of my friends": C. S. Lewis, *The Four Loves* (New York: Harcourt, Brace, 1960; reprint ed. (Orlando: Harcourt, 1991), 61–62.

199 a mutual interest in Thomas Aquinas: On Havard's first meeting with Lewis, see Lyle W. Dorsett, oral history interview with Dr. Robert E. Havard, 17.

199 "Occasionally he would hold a note": Jenifer Wayne, *The Purple Dress: Growing Up in the Thirties* (London: Gollancz, 1979), 65–66, quoted in Scull and Hammond, *J.R.R. Tolkien Companion and Guide: Reader's Guide*, 1124.

200 "elegant yet at the same time spontaneously gauche . . . David and Rachel": Rachel Trickett, "Cecil, Lord (Edward Christian) David Gascoyne- (1902–1986)," rev. ed. *Oxford Dictionary of National Biography* (Oxford, New York: Oxford University Press, 2004); Oct. 2006 online ed., www.oxforddnb.com/view/article/39801 (accessed July 17, 2014).

200 "the pleasure of poetry": Adam Fox, *Poetry for Pleasure: An Inaugural Lecture Delivered Before the University of Oxford, 2 November, 1938* (Oxford: Oxford University, 1938), 7, 13.

200 "were always made by the way": Oral history interview with R. E. Havard, conducted by Lyle W. Dorsett for the Marion E. Wade Center, July 26, 1984, quoted in Colin Duriez, *Tolkien and C. S. Lewis: The Gift of Friendship* (Mahwah, N.J.: HiddenSpring, 2003), 83.

201 "The ritual of an Inklings . . . no rules": Warren Lewis, "Memoir of C. S. Lewis," 34. It is not entirely clear whether this description covers also the earliest Inklings meetings.

201 "the talk might turn . . . the cut and parry": C. S. Lewis, preface, *Essays Presented to Charles Williams* (London, New York, Toronto: Geoffrey Cumberlege, Oxford University Press, 1947), x–xi.

201   "sold his birthright": Barfield, "Inklings Remembered," 549.

201   "His whole manner": Oral history interview with R. E. Havard, conducted by Lyle W. Dorsett for the Marion E. Wade Center, July 26, 1984, quoted in Duriez, *Tolkien and C. S. Lewis*, 83.

201   "We smoked": Lewis, preface, *Essays Presented to Charles Williams*, v.

201   also read works in progress: Inklings scholar David Bratman has compiled an impressive list of "Published works known to have been read or heard by other Inklings prior to publication," but it is not clear how many of these works were actually read aloud at Inklings meetings, www.dianaglyer.com/scholarship/the -company-they-keep/supporting-bibliographic-material/ (accessed July 25, 2014). This and other supporting bibliographies were compiled by Bratman in connection with Diana Pavlac Glyer, *The Company They Keep: C. S. Lewis and J.R.R. Tolkien as Writers in Community* (Kent, Ohio: Kent State University Press, 2007).

202   "Since term began": Lewis, *Collected Letters*, vol. 2, 96.

203   "only slightly taller": The Tolkien children loved hearing about Snergs, and Michael set about creating Snerg stories of his own. In a letter to Auden, Tolkien says that *The Marvellous Land of Snergs* was "probably an unconscious source-book! For the Hobbits, not of anything else" (Tolkien, *Letters*, 215 footnote).

203   other creative and scholarly work: This would include translating *Beowulf*; preparing the 1936 Israel Gollancz lecture ("*Beowulf*: The Monsters and the Critics"); an alliterative verse retelling of the Norse lays of Sigurd the Völsung and the fall of the Niflungs (unfinished; but edited with extensive commentaries by Christopher Tolkien and published in 2009 as *The Legend of Sigurd and Gudrún* [London: HarperCollins, 2009]); an (unfinished) *Lay of Leithian* telling the story of Beren and Lúthien; the 1930 *Quenta Silmarillion*; and *First Annals*.

203   John and Michael remembered: Scull and Hammond, *J.R.R. Tolkien Companion and Guide: Reader's Guide*, 386.

203   "wrote it ages ago": Christopher Tolkien, foreword to *The Hobbit*, 50th-anniversary ed. (Boston: Houghton Mifflin, 1987), vi–vii.

203   "In a hole in the ground": Tolkien's account in a BBC interview, quoted in Douglas A. Anderson, *The Annotated Hobbit*, rev. and exp. ed. annotated by Douglas A. Anderson (Boston: Houghton Mifflin, 2002), 11. See also the June 7, 1955 letter to W. H. Auden, in which Tolkien relates the same story, in Tolkien, *Letters*, 215.

204   "Babbitt": Tolkien's suggestion in an interview: see Michael N. Stanton, "Hobbits," in Drout, *J.R.R. Tolkien Encyclopedia*, 280.

204   "rabbit": Tom Shippey sees some merit in the "rabbit" connection: Shippey, *Road to Middle-earth*, 67–70; see Tolkien's letters on this subject, *Letters*, 30, 406–407.

204   a single instance of "hobbit": In Michael Aislable Denham, *The Denham Tracts*, Publications of the Folk-Lore Society 35 (London: D. Nutt, 1895). Discussed by Anderson, *Annotated Hobbit*, 9, and Marjorie Burns, "Tracking the Elusive Hobbit (in Its Pre-Shire Den)," *Tolkien Studies* 4 (2007): 200–11. See John D. Rateliff, *The History of the Hobbit*, part 2, appendix 1, "The Denham Tracts" (Boston: Houghton Mifflin Harcourt: 2007), 841–54.

204   very little about Tolkien's creative process: Shippey, *Road to Middle-earth*, 66–67.

204 "had been inside language": C. S. Lewis, unsigned obituary for Tolkien (written far in advance of Tolkien's death), "Professor J. R. R. Tolkien: Creator of Hobbits and inventor of a new mythology," *The Times* (London), September 3, 1973.

204 *Oxford English Dictionary*: Tolkien discusses the *OED* entry for Hobbit in his 1971 letter to Roger Lancelyn Green, *Letters*, 406–407. Hobbit (n.) first appeared in the *OED* in 1976, along with hobbitish (a.), hobbitomane (n.), and hobbitry (n.); so far no etymology is provided, but future updates are promised. As far as capitalization is concerned, Tolkien is not entirely consistent, but his rule of thumb seems to have been to capitalize words like Hobbits, Elves, Men, Dwarves, where the reference is to a race—to Mankind, and its analogues—but to use lowercase when it is a matter of referring to one or more individual members. See his December 1937 letter on this subject to Allen & Unwin: Tolkien, *Letters*, 28; we have generally followed this practice.

204 Several scholars have labored mightily: Since Humphrey Carpenter made the first attempt in his 1977 Tolkien biography, and Tom Shippey followed the trail in *The Road to Middle-earth* (which first appeared in 1982), the problem has been studied by Christina Scull and Wayne G. Hammond, by Douglas A. Anderson, who established the work's publication history and created *The Annotated Hobbit* (1988; rev. and exp. ed., 2002), and by John D. Rateliff, who spent nearly twenty years piecing together the earliest draft from manuscripts at Marquette, producing a two-volume *History of the Hobbit* (Boston: Houghton Mifflin Harcourt, 2007), a project initiated by the Tolkien scholar Taum Santoski (before his death in 1991), modeled in part on Christopher Tolkien's twelve-volume *History of Middle-earth*.

205 Beorn: Either "man" or "warrior" in Old English but suggestive of *bjorn* for "bear" in Old Norse, and of Berserker legends.

205 Tolkien borrowed the names for the dwarves from the *Dvergatal*:

> 10. There was Motsognir | the mightiest made
> Of all the dwarfs, | and Durin next;
> Many a likeness | of men they made,
> The dwarfs in the earth, | as Durin said.

> 11. Nyi and Nithi, | Northri and Suthri,
> Austri and Vestri, | Althjof, Dvalin,
> Nar and Nain, | Niping, Dain,
> Bifur, Bofur, | Bombur, Nori,
> An and Onar, | Ai, Mjothvitnir.

> 12. Vigg and Gandalf [=*Magic Elf*] | Vindalf, Thrain,
> Thekk and Thorin, | Thror, Vit and Lit,
> Nyr and Nyrath,— | now have I told—
> Regin and Rathsvith— | the list aright.

> 13. Fili, Kili, | Fundin, Nali,
> Heptifili, | Hannar, Sviur,

Frar, Hornbori, | Fræg and Loni,
Aurvang, Jari, | Eikinskjaldi *[=Oak Shield]*.

From *The Poetic Edda*, trans. Henry Adams Bellows (Princeton: Princeton University Press, 1936). See Rateliff, *The History of the Hobbit*, part 2, appendix 3: "The *Dvergatal* (The Dwarf Names)," 866–71.

205 "a low philological jest . . . hole-dweller": Tolkien, *Letters*, 31. A fanciful etymology would come later, as part of the work of retrofitting necessitated by the *Hobbit* "sequel," *The Lord of the Rings*. Reasoning backward from "hobbit" in search of plausible archaic roots, Tolkien notes in the final appendix to *The Lord of the Rings* that the Shire-folk originally called themselves *kuduk*, a "worn-down form" of *kûd-dûkan*, which means "hole-dweller" in the tongue of Rohan; translating *kûd-dûkan* into (imaginary) Old English yields *holbytla*, from which "hobbit" would have evolved by a similar erosion, if the word had actually existed in our own language. Tolkien, *The Lord of the Rings*, appendix F, 1130, 1138. The necessarily speculative character of this etymology helps to create the effect Tom Shippey calls "asterisk reality" (*Road to Middle-earth*, 19–22). See also John William Houghton on "asterisk cosmogony," in *Tolkien the Medievalist*, ed. Jane Chance, 171–82.

205 the very Smaug-like dragon: See Tolkien's 1949 letter to Naomi Mitchison in which he says that he prefers Fáfnir to the dragon in *Beowulf*, and that "Smaug and his conversation obviously is in debt there." Tolkien, *Letters*, 134.

205 a battle of wits with a loquacious dragon: See Ármann Jakobsson, "Talk to the Dragon: Tolkien as Translator," *Tolkien Studies* 6 (2009): 27–39.

206 "more praiseworthy than the professionals": Tolkien, *Letters*, 215.

206 "from fairy-tale to the noble and high": Ibid., 159.

206 "And what would you do": Tolkien, *Hobbit*, 8. See letter (draft) to Walter Allen, *New Statesman*, April 1959, Tolkien, *Letters*, 297.

207 Mirkwood (Old Norse *Myrkviðr*): William Morris anglicized *Myrkviðr* into "Mirkwood" in his 1899 prose and verse fantasy, *A Tale of the House of the Wolflings and All the Kindreds of the Mark*.

207 this bridging of worlds: See Shippey's insightful discussion of Tolkien's use of anachronism in "The Bourgeois Burglar," chapter 3 of *The Road to Middle-earth*.

207 "lying about in a nunnery": February 1937 letter from Tolkien to the *Beowulf* scholar R. W. Chambers, quoted by Douglas A. Anderson from Caroline Chabot, "Raymond Wilson Chambers (1874–1942)," *Moreana* 24, no. 94 (June 1987): 88, in Douglas A. Anderson, "R. W. Chambers and The Hobbit," *Tolkien Studies* 3 (2006): 140.

207 "Bilbo Baggins was a hobbit": Quoted in Carpenter, *Tolkien*, 180–81.

208 "wholly original story": Richard Hughes, "Books for Pre-Adults," *New Statesman and Nation*, December 4, 1937, quoted in Scull and Hammond, *J.R.R. Tolkien Companion and Guide: Reader's Guide*, 399.

208 "there and back again": The first version Lewis read stopped short with the death of a dragon, leaving undeveloped the "there and back again" theme that would be so salient a feature of the final tale.

208 "The publishers claim": C. S. Lewis, "A World for Children," *The Times Literary Supplement* 1861 (October 2, 1937): 761. Reprinted in Lewis, *On Stories*, 81.

208 "the truth is that in this book": "Professor Tolkien's 'The Hobbit,'" unsigned review by Lewis in *The Times* (London) 47810, October 8, 1937, p. 20.

209 "I must respect his opinion . . . I rather wish I had used": Tolkien, *Letters*, 23–24.

209 woolly mammoths, woolly rhinoceroses, and goblins: Hammond and Scull, *J.R.R. Tolkien: Artist and Illustrator*, 76.

209 "Some . . . are very good": J.R.R. Tolkien, *Letters from Father Christmas*, ed. Baillie Tolkien (December 23, 1932), 78.

210 "I brought you all up ill": Tolkien, *Letters*, 340.

210 "He would like to take us out for walks": Michael Tolkien interview, *Minas Tirith Evening-Star* (Journal of the American Tolkien Society) 8, no. 1 (Spring 1989): 9.

210 "a nervy, irritable, cross-grained": Quoted in Carpenter, *Tolkien*, 169.

211 "receptive . . . real soul mate": Tolkien, *Letters*, 49–51.

212 "made him a pessimist . . . a man of extreme contrasts": Carpenter, *Tolkien*, 129.

213 "I am in fact a *Hobbit*": Tolkien, *Letters*, 288.

213 "in its day and to its users a natural, easy, and cultivated speech": Tolkien, preface, *The Ancrene Riwle*, ed. and trans. M. B. Salu (London: Burns & Oates, 1955), v.

214 "*Vilitas et asperitas*": *Ancrene Wisse: Guide for Anchoresses*, trans. Hugh White (Harmondsworth: Penguin, 1993), 163–64.

214 "crimes of omission . . . My edition of the prime MS.": Tolkien, *Letters*, 301–302. Tolkien's critical edition finally appeared in 1962: J.R.R. Tolkien, *Ancrene Wisse: The English Text of the Ancrene Riwle*, edited from MS, Corpus Christi College, Cambridge 402 (London and New York: Published for the Early English Text Society by the Oxford University Press, 1962).

215 "The Historical and Legendary Tradition": Michael D. C. Drout, in J.R.R. Tolkien, *Beowulf and the Critics*, ed. Michael D. C. Drout (2nd ed., rev.; Tempe, Ariz.: ACMRS [Arizona Center for Medieval and Renaissance Studies], 2011), 4.

215 "an unforgettable experience": Carpenter, *Tolkien*, 133.

215 "It is of their nature": Tolkien, "*Beowulf*: The Monsters and the Critics," *The Monsters and the Critics*, 9.

215 "a history of Sweden": Ibid., 7.

215 "carvings and inscriptions . . . from the top of that tower": Ibid., 8.

216 "as if Milton": Ibid., 13.

216 "the hostile world . . . its lofty tone": Ibid., 18–19.

216 "glimpses the cosmic . . . we look down": Ibid., 33.

216 "a Christian was": Ibid., 22.

216 "You must not delete": Bodleian Library MS Tolkien 4, fol. 58. Quoted in Drout, *Beowulf and the Critics*, 4.

216 "myth is alive": Tolkien, "*Beowulf*: The Monsters and the Critics," 15.

217 "a very lively and happy child": Barfield, quoted in Hooper, *C. S. Lewis: A Complete Guide*, 758.

217 "Why not take": Owen Barfield, foreword, *Orpheus: A Poetic Drama*, ed. John C. Ulreich, Jr. (West Stockbridge, Mass.: Lindisfarne, 1983), 7.

217 "shall ascend Parnassus awake": Barfield, *Orpheus: A Poetic Drama*, act 4, scene 3, 112.

217 "simply superb": Lewis, *Collected Letters*, vol. 2, 223.

217 "H is for Hume": *The Oxford Magazine* 52 (November 30, 1933): 298.

218 "A is for [Acland]": Don W. King, *C. S. Lewis, Poet: The Legacy of His Poetic Impulse*, rev. and exp. ed. (Kent, Ohio: Kent State University Press, 2001), 171.

218 "under eclipse": Sugerman, "Conversation with Owen Barfield," 9.

219 "In the afternoon J and I": Warren H. Lewis, unpublished diary entry for November 5, 1933, in the collection of the Marion E. Wade Center, Wheaton College, Wheaton, Illinois, quoted in Colin Duriez, *The C. S. Lewis Chronicles* (New York: BlueBridge, 2005), 162.

219 "blood feast": According to Barfield, quoted in Hooper, *C. S. Lewis: A Complete Guide*, 714.

219 "in much the same way": W. H. Lewis, *Brothers and Friends*, 128.

219 "a woman of very limited mind": Warren Lewis, "Memoir of C. S. Lewis," 33.

219 "false picture . . . a normal and reasonably happy": Owen Barfield, foreword to Lewis, *All My Road Before Me*, x.

219 "An outside friend": C. S. Lewis, "The Trouble with 'X' . . . ," in C. S. Lewis, *God in the Dock: Essays on Theology and Ethics*, ed. Walter Hooper (Grand Rapids, Mich.: Wm. B. Eerdmans, 1970), 151–55. First published in the *Bristol Diocesan Gazette* 27 (August 1948): 3–6.

10. ROMANTIC THEOLOGY

221 "Williams!": Wain, *Sprightly Running*, 147.

221 "No man whom I have known": Lewis, preface, *Essays Presented to Charles Williams*, ix.

221 "I think he was a man of unusual genius": T. S. Eliot, "The Significance of Charles Williams," *The Listener* 936 (December 19, 1946): 894.

221 "liked to beat them with a ruler": Lois Lang-Sims, personal interview, July 17, 2006.

221 "His face we thought ugly . . . This double-sidedness": Lewis, preface, *Essays Presented to Charles Williams*, ix–xii.

222 "He was nothing if not a ritualist": Ibid., ix.

222 "Why, you come into the room": Dylan Thomas, quoted by Anne Ridler in introduction to Charles Williams, *The Image of the City and Other Essays*, selected by Anne Ridler (London: Oxford University Press, 1958), xx.

223 "trembling . . . staccato eagerness": Theodore Maynard, "The Poetry of Charles Williams," *The North American Review*, 210, 766 (September 1919): 401–411.

223 "He was never still": T. S. Eliot, introduction to Charles Williams, *All Hallows' Eve* (New York: The Noonday Press / Farrar, Straus and Giroux, 1971), xii.

223 "I go to my daily work": Alice Mary Hadfield, *An Introduction to Charles Williams* (London: Robert Hale Limited, 1959), 28.

223 "He used to march into church": Alice Mary Hadfield, *Charles Williams: An Exploration of His Life and Work* (New York and Oxford: Oxford University Press, 1983), 5.

224 "the asps of blindness": Williams uses the expression in his poem "Divorce," dedicated to his father; quoted in Hadfield, *Charles Williams*, 10.

224 "a sort of running drama . . . Most of the boys tolerated": Hadfield, *Introduction to Charles Williams*, 19.

225 "all the good I knew": Charles Williams, "Divorce," quoted in Hadfield, *Charles Williams*, 9.

226 "[Williams's] affection for the Oxford University Press": Sutcliffe, *Oxford University Press: An Informal History*, 203–204.

226 "For the first five minutes": Michal Williams, "Appendix: As I Remember Charles Williams," in Charles Williams, *To Michal from Serge: Letters from Charles Williams*

to His Wife, Florence, 1939–1945, ed. Roma A. King, Jr. (Kent, Ohio, and London: Kent State University Press, 2002), 260.

226 "I used to say that": Charles Williams, Letters to Lalage: The Letters of Charles Williams to Lois Lang-Sims, with commentary by Lois Lang-Sims, introduction and notes by Glen Cavaliero (Kent, Ohio, and London: Kent State University Press, 1989), 19–20.

227 "attitude to her husband . . . married a cross": Glen Cavaliero, introduction to Williams, Letters to Lalage, 7.

227 "Why, I believe": Hadfield, Charles Williams, 16.

227 "How else so long": Charles Williams, "Of the purpose of Cities," The Silver Stair (London: Herbert & Daniel [1912]), book I, X.

227 "Fair women": Charles Williams, "He praises the diverse beauty of Women," The Silver Stair, book I, XI.

228 "All lives of lovers": Charles Williams, "An Ascription," The Silver Stair, book III, LXVII.

229 "real poetry": Hadfield, Charles Williams, 19.

229 "very kindly": Ibid., 24.

230 "a path of symbolism . . . true light of understanding": "The Fellowship of the Holy Cross, Constitution & Laws," in R. A. Gilbert, A. E. Waite: Magician of Many Parts (Wellingborough: Crucible, 1987), Appendix E: (I), 183–84.

230 "seated on his throne . . . be ye transmuted": "The Ceremony of Consecration on the Threshold of Sacred Mystery," in Gavin Ashenden, Charles Williams: Alchemy and Integration (Kent, Ohio: Kent State University Press, 2008), 34–36.

231 "not . . . much affected": Hadfield, Charles Williams, 30.

231 "wholly unsympathetic": Tolkien, Letters, 361.

231 Lois Lang-Sims . . . believed that Williams's obsession with magic never left him: Lois Lang-Sims, personal interview, July 17, 2006.

232 "probably affect profoundly": Quoted in Alice M. Hadfield, "Introduction: The Writing of 'Outlines of Romantic Theology,'" in Charles Williams, Outlines of Romantic Theology, edited and introduced by Alice Mary Hadfield (Grand Rapids, Mich.: Wm. B. Eerdmans, 1990), xii.

232 "is capable of being assumed": Williams, Outlines of Romantic Theology, 9.

232 theology has paid scant attention: Other reasons would be presented by C. S. Lewis, in his Allegory of Love (1936), where he maintains (to a degree that he later regretted) that during the Middle Ages marriage was primarily an economic transaction, romantic love being a matter of platonic longing or illicit adulterous love. Hence a theology of romantic married love, although adumbrated by Dante and Spenser, was not possible at the time.

232 "the whole company": Williams, Outlines of Romantic Theology, 31.

233 "until this study": Williams, Outlines of Romantic Theology, 17–18.

233 "I fear this": Hadfield, Charles Williams, 45.

233 "a child is": Ibid., 39.

234 "Christhood": Ashenden, Charles Williams: Alchemy and Integration, 211.

234 "a radiance rising": Hadfield, Charles Williams, 66.

234 "my saint, my hero": Ibid., 73.

234 "Celian moment . . . the moment which": Charles Williams, ed., The New Book of English Verse (London: Victor Gollancz, 1935), 12–13.

235 "the effect of the Masque": Hadfield, *Introduction to Charles Williams*, 73.

235 "an extraordinary state": Ibid., 72.

235 "In some former existence": Charles Williams, *Poetry at Present* (Oxford: Clarendon Press, 1930), 163.

236 "We are told": Charles Williams, *The English Poetic Mind* (Oxford: Clarendon Press, 1932), 3.

236 "he always boiled": T. S. Eliot, introduction to Williams, *All Hallows' Eve*, xii.

236 "two feet or more . . . 'O glory, glory'": Charles Williams, *The Place of the Lion* (London: Faber & Faber, 1952), 40–43.

237 "a sound as": Williams, *Place of the Lion*, 198–202.

237 "I have just read": Lewis, *Collected Letters*, vol. 2, 180.

238 "I never know . . . informal club": Ibid., 183.

238 "If you had delayed": Hooper, *C. S. Lewis: A Complete Guide*, 740–41.

11. SECONDARY WORLDS

239 "a humble hobbit-fancier . . . dozens": Arthur Ransome, *Signalling from Mars: The Letters of Arthur Ransome*, edited and introduced by Hugh Brogan (London: Jonathan Cape, 1997), 249–51.

240 "Tollers, there is too little": Tolkien, *Letters*, 378.

240 "excursionary 'Thriller'": Ibid., 29.

240 a great, deadly wave: The drowning of Númenor appears in several of Tolkien's works, including *The Notion Club Papers* and *The Silmarillion*.

240 "a hopeless proposition": Tolkien–George Allen & Unwin Archive, quoted in Scull and Hammond, *J.R.R. Tolkien Companion and Guide: Reader's Guide*, 563.

240 "of a very thin": Edward Crankshaw, Tolkien–George Allen & Unwin archive, quoted in Scull and Hammond, *J.R.R. Tolkien Companion and Guide: Reader's Guide*, 895.

240 "my chief joy": Tolkien, *Letters*, 26.

240 "I don't much approve": Tolkien, letter to G. E. Selby, December 14, 1937, quoted in Christopher Tolkien, foreword to J.R.R. Tolkien, *The Return of the Shadow: The History of the Lord of the Rings*, Part One (*The History of Middle-earth*, vol. 6), ed. Christopher Tolkien (London: HarperCollins, 1993), 7. G. E. Selby was an occasional correspondent with an interest in Faërie, perhaps a trifle overbearing in his queries about Middle-earth, who was connected to the College of the Venerable Bede, a teacher-training school in Durham.

241 "Goodness knows what . . . Tom Bombadil": Tolkien, *Letters*, 26.

241 "A long expected party": Ibid., 27.

241 The first version: See Scull and Hammond, *J.R.R. Tolkien Companion and Guide: Reader's Guide*, 531–32.

241 "squandered": Tolkien, *Letters*, 29.

241 "lost my favour": Ibid., 38.

242 "flowing along": Ibid., 40.

242 "Prof. Tolkien spoke . . . one can only stand": *Oxford Mail* (August 4, 1938), quoted in Scull and Hammond, *J.R.R. Tolkien Companion and Guide: Chronology*, 219.

242 March 8, 1939: Not 1938, as Tolkien claims in "Introductory Note," *Tree and Leaf*, 5.

243 a theory of folklore: The original text of Tolkien's talk has been lost. The description that follows is based upon the first published version of the talk, a revision that Tolkien prepared in the early 1940s, which was eventually published in 1947 in *Essays Presented to Charles Williams*.

243 "the realm or state . . . when we are enchanted": Tolkien, "On Fairy-Stories," *Essays Presented to Charles Williams*, 42.

244 "not actually present": Ibid., 66.

244 "we make in our measure": Ibid., 72. This echoes the "Man, Sub-Creator" theme of *Mythopoeia*.

244 "the living Power": Samuel Taylor Coleridge, *Biographia Literaria*, chap. 13. Closer to home, though not in contact with Tolkien, Dorothy L. Sayers was pursuing the same idea. It would appear as the theme of her play *The Zeal of Thy House* and her best nonfiction book, *The Mind of the Maker*.

245 "not a lower . . . elvish craft": Tolkien, "On Fairy-Stories," *Essays Presented to Charles Williams*, 67–68.

245 "inner consistency": Ibid., 66.

245 "story-making in its primary": Ibid., 68.

245 "freed from the drab blur": Ibid., 74.

246 "a sudden and miraculous grace . . . a far-off gleam": Tolkien, "On Fairy-Stories," epilogue, *Essays Presented to Charles Williams*, 81–83. In September 2008, "eucatastrophe" was admitted into the *OED*.

246 "who would never . . . shocked and puzzled": Owen Barfield, introduction to *Romanticism Comes of Age* (Middletown, Conn.: Wesleyan University Press, 1967), 17.

247 "Imagination . . . exact results": Ibid., 15–16.

247 "was nothing less": Ibid., 14.

247 "lost the inestimable": Owen Barfield, introduction to the 1st ed., *Romanticism Comes of Age* (London: Anthroposophical Publishing House, 1944), 12.

247 "nauseating . . . a private outpouring": Blaxland–de Lange, *Owen Barfield*, 291–93.

248 "sword through the marriage knot": Ibid., 291.

248 "very fiery meeting . . . rather flung the stone": Ibid., 36.

249 "Friendship is the greatest": Lewis, *Collected Letters*, vol. 2, 174.

249 "my chief companion": Lewis, *Surprised by Joy*, 234.

249 "I was probably nearer": Alan Bede Griffiths, O.S.B.,"The Adventure of Faith," in Como, *C. S. Lewis at the Breakfast Table*, 11.

250 "I think that it": Ibid., 19.

250 "once and for all . . . any of the questions": Lewis, *Collected Letters*, vol. 2, 135. See also Walter Hooper's discussion of the relationship in his biographical note on Griffiths, in *Collected Letters*, vol. 2, 1042–49.

250 "I think your specifically": Lewis, *Collected Letters*, vol. 2, 178.

250 "[Obedience] appears to me": Ibid., 177.

250 "was a great embarrassment": Griffiths, "Adventure of Faith," 19.

251 "my wretched man . . . was up till this": Lewis, *Collected Letters*, vol. 2, 204.

251 biography of the Prophet: Martin Lings, *Muhammad: His Life Based on the Earliest Sources*, rev. ed. (Rochester, Vt.: Inner Traditions, 2006).

251 "bog-rats . . . bog-trotters": Humphrey Carpenter, *The Inklings: C. S. Lewis, J.R.R. Tolkien, Charles Williams and Their Friends* (London: HarperCollins, 1997), 51.

We can't help but wonder whether Tolkien's initial choice of "Trotter" as the name for his *Lord of the Rings* hero (discussed below) may be a subtle way of pushing back; while Lewis's choice of "Ransom" as the name for his Space Trilogy hero (also discussed below) is a friendly gesture toward Tolkien's Catholicism, and perhaps a way of making amends for their friction.

251 "it is papist": Lewis, *Collected Letters*, vol. 2, 213.

251 "I don't much like": Ibid., 213, 170.

252 "no one ever knows": W. H. Lewis, unpublished letter of April 4, 1966, to American friend Mrs. Betty Jones, quoted by Clyde S. Kilby and Marjorie Lamp Mead, in W. H. Lewis, *Brothers and Friends*, 174.

252 "snivelling . . . if I had not": W. H. Lewis, *Brothers and Friends*, 169.

252 "There is my dullest": Lewis, *That Hideous Strength*, 31.

252 "grand week in bed . . . There's a good deal": Lewis, *Collected Letters*, vol. 2, 210.

253 "the best of the sort": Ibid., 237.

253 "*spiritual* adventures": January 4, 1947, in ibid., 753.

253 materialistic picture of the universe: See Lewis's discussion of H. G. Wells and the Victorian astronomer Sir Robert Stawell Ball, *Surprised by Joy*, 65. In Lewis's day, fear about the cosmic insignificance of human beings was already an old ailment, thus the "ontological wonder-sickness" of William James and the *infini-rien* of Pascal's *Pensées*: "When I consider the short duration of my life, swallowed up in the eternity before and after, the little space which I fill, and even can see, engulfed in the infinite immensity of spaces of which I am ignorant, and which know me not, I am frightened and am astonished . . ." (W. F. Trotter, trans. [London: J. M. Dent & Sons, 1908], 61).

253 "I like the whole": Lewis, *Collected Letters*, vol. 2, 236–37.

254 a philologist-hero with such a name: Ransom would learn the significance of his name in the 1944 sequel, *Perelandra*: "'It is not for nothing that you are named Ransom,' said the Voice . . . All in a moment of time he perceived that what was, to human philologists, a merely accidental resemblance of two sounds, was in truth no accident . . . 'My name also is Ransom,' said the Voice." C. S. Lewis, *Perelandra: A Novel* (New York: Scribner, 1944; reprint ed., 2003), 125–26.

255 "Stretched naked": Lewis, *Out of the Silent Planet*, 33.

255 "nothing but colours": Ibid., 43.

256 "mere holes": Ibid., 41.

256 "cosy little cosmos": "A man may say, 'I like this vast cosmos, with its throng of stars and its crowd of varied creatures.' But if it comes to that why should not a man say, 'I like this cosy little cosmos, with its decent number of stars and as neat a provision of live stock as I wish to see'?" Gilbert Keith Chesterton, *Orthodoxy* (London: John Lane, The Bodley Head, 1908), 113.

256 "to look out": C. S. Lewis, *The Discarded Image: An Introduction to Medieval and Renaissance Literature* (Cambridge, UK: Cambridge University Press, 1994), 99.

257 "Earth was, by cosmic standards": Ibid., 97.

257 angels assigned to the nations: See Daniel 10:13–21, the Greek version of Deut. 32:8, and Acts 17:26.

257 "middle spirits": Though not sympathetic to Lewis's Christian viewpoint, William Empson has much of interest to say about Lewis's scholarly and imaginative treatment of "middle spirits." He sees Lewis as sanitizing the tradition. See Empson,

Essays on Renaissance Literature, vol. 2, ed. John Haffenden (Cambridge, UK: Cambridge University Press, 1994), 155–57, 187–191, 196–97, and Haffenden's note on 266–67.

257 "Lady Luna . . . calm and kingly": C. S. Lewis, "The Alliterative Metre," *Selected Literary Essays*, 24–26.

258 "Mr. Lewis is quite likely . . . bunk": Quoted in Tolkien, *Letters*, 32.

258 "It was the full . . . Dear Celia": Hadfield, *Charles Williams*, 129.

258 "the anatomical articulation . . . compressed epigram": Ibid., 133.

259 "I will not discuss": Ibid., 134.

259 "He was": Charles Williams, *The Descent of the Dove: A Short History of the Holy Spirit in the Church* (London, New York, Toronto: Longmans, Green, 1939), 212.

259 "Kierkegaard at any rate": Charles Williams to Walter Lowrie, letter of December 27, 1937, Walter Lowrie Papers, Princeton University, quoted by Michael J. Paulus Jr., "From a Publisher's Point of View: Charles Williams's Role in Publishing Kierkegaard in English," in *Charles Williams and His Contemporaries*, ed. Suzanne Bray and Richard Sturch (Newcastle upon Tyne, UK: Cambridge Scholars Publishing, 2009), 27.

259 "He wrote a great deal": Hadfield, *Introduction to Charles Williams*, 118–19.

260 "lunch . . . tea": Hadfield, *Charles Williams*, 140.

260 "a thundering good book": Lewis, *Collected Letters*, vol. 2, 219.

260 "a great work": Ibid., 249.

260 "I've never listened . . . literally struck dumb": Lyle W. Dorsett, oral history interview with Dr. Robert E. Havard, 32.

260 "To MICHAL": Charles Williams, *He Came Down from Heaven* (Berkeley: Apocryphile Press, 2005), 7.

261 "substitutions in love": Charles Williams, *Descent of the Dove*, 236.

261 "The Order has": Charles Williams, "The Order of the Co-inherence" (1939), in *Charles Williams: Essential Writings in Spirituality and Theology*, ed. Charles Hefling (Cambridge, Mass.: Cowley Publications, 1993), 149.

262 "used the Companions": Hadfield, *Charles Williams*, 217.

263 "our whole joint world . . . I cannot believe": Lewis, *Collected Letters*, vol. 2, 232–34.

263 "Christendom has made": Ibid., 252.

263 "I regret . . . the time is not far distant": Tolkien, *Letters*, 37–38.

264 "if there were war . . . I am as terrified": Hadfield, *Introduction to Charles Williams*, 164.

264 "God save you, brother": Lewis, *Collected Letters*, vol. 2, 271.

12. WAR, AGAIN

265 "of the Trinity": Morris, *Oxford Book of Oxford*, 381.

265 "bewildered university": Tolkien, *Letters*, 44.

266 "I have never . . . unusually intelligible": Lewis, *Collected Letters*, vol. 2, 288–89.

266 "becoming a common chastitute": Dyson, quoted in ibid., 360.

267 "very witty": Lyle W. Dorsett, oral history interview with Dr. Robert E. Havard, 27.

267 translation of *The Aeneid*: C. S. Lewis, *C. S. Lewis's Lost Aeneid: Arms and the Exile*, ed. A. T. Reyes (New Haven: Yale University Press, 2011).

267 "a strange tall gaunt man . . . really thinks": Tolkien, *Letters*, 95–96.

267 "a new literary species": C. S. Lewis, "A Tribute to E. R. Eddison," *On Stories*, 29.

267 "And so to that": Quoted by Hooper in Lewis, *Collected Letters*, vol. 2, 554.

268 "arrogance and cruelty": Tolkien, *Letters*, 258.

268 "my great friend": Lewis, *Collected Letters*, vol. 2, 652.

268 "dear Charles . . . wisdom": Tolkien's poem about Charles Williams, quoted in Carpenter, *Inklings*, 123–26.

269 "wholly alien": Tolkien, *Letters*, 362.

269 "he gave to every circle": Lewis, preface, *Essays Presented to Charles Williams*, x.

269 "No, I think not": Carpenter, *Inklings*, 121. Further information about this marginal note is supplied in John D. Rateliff, "'And Something Yet Remains to Be Said': Tolkien and Williams," *Mythlore* 45 (Spring 1986): 51 and accompanying note no. 17.

270 "seemed like a fleeting glimpse": Tolkien, *Letters*, 67.

270 "A small knowledge": Ibid., 80.

270 "How stupid": Ibid., 73.

270 "I feel like": Ibid., 55.

271 "never need": Ibid., 66.

271 "out of the darkness": Ibid., 53.

271 "sudden vision . . . comfort": Ibid., 99.

271 sent him new sections of typescript: As Christopher Tolkien remarked in an interview for the French newspaper *Le Monde*: "J'étais pilote de chasse. Quand j'atterrissais, je lisais un chapitre" (I was a fighter pilot. Whenever I made a landing, I would read a chapter), "Tolkien, l'anneau de la discorde," *Le Monde* Héritages 2/10 (July 7, 2012).

272 "topical . . . little or nothing": Tolkien, *Lord of the Rings*, foreword to the 2nd ed., xxii–xxv.

272 "I awoke": Tolkien, "Introductory Note," *Tree and Leaf*, 5.

272 "little man called Niggle": J.R.R. Tolkien, "Leaf by Niggle," *Tree and Leaf*, 73.

272 "as he had imagined them . . . something different": Ibid., 85–86.

273 "colorless": *A Barfield Reader*, edited and with an introduction by G. B. Tennyson (Hanover: University Press of New England, 1999), xix.

273 "saying one thing": Owen Barfield, "Poetic Diction and Legal Fiction," in Lewis, *Essays Presented to Charles Williams*, 111.

273 "the long, slow movement": Ibid., 127.

273 "a great trauma": Owen A. Barfield, personal interview, June 20, 2009.

273 "this particular desolation": Lewis, *Collected Letters*, vol. 2, 418.

274 "blue as a whortle-berry": Ibid., 531.

274 "at least three": Barfield, "Inklings Remembered," 549.

274 Jeffrey Barfield: See Hooper, *C. S. Lewis: A Complete Guide*, 759; and Marjorie Lamp Mead, "Owen Barfield: A Biographical Note," published as the "Afterword" to Owen Barfield, *The Silver Trumpet* (Longmont, Colo.: Bookmakers Guild, 1986), 117–23.

274 "aura of unhappiness": Quoted in Theresa Whistler, *Imagination of the Heart: The Life of Walter de la Mare* (London: Duckworth, 1993), 400.

274 "that beautiful carved room": Lewis, *Collected Letters*, vol. 2, 346.

275 "Am I . . . you will be attended": Williams, *To Michal from Serge*, 50–51.

275 "it was Anne": Ibid., 56

275 "held his audiences": T. S. Eliot, introduction to Williams, *All Hallows' Eve*, xii.

275 "I begin to believe": Williams, *To Michal from Serge*, 52.

275 "loftily lunching," Ibid., 150.

275 "It's obvious": Quoted in Carpenter, *Inklings*, 188.

275 celebrated together with drinks: See Duriez, *Tolkien and C. S. Lewis: The Gift of Friendship*, 121.

276 "We work between": Hadfield, *Charles Williams*, 176–77.

276 "a kind of *parody*": Ibid., 197.

276 "full of courtesies": Charles Williams, *The Figure of Beatrice: A Study in Dante* (London: Faber & Faber, 1943), 105.

277 "Wherever any love is . . . there is": Ibid., 252.

277 "the highest point": T. S. Eliot, *Dante* (London: Faber & Faber, 1929, 1965), 27.

277 "elders . . . in the ditches": Williams, *The Figure of Beatrice*, 21.

277 "if you substitute": Williams, *To Michal from Serge*, 165.

277 "second image . . . I do not know": Williams, *The Figure of Beatrice*, 49–50.

278 "has slid from being": Hadfield, *Charles Williams*, 211.

278 "delicate sensitiveness . . . continually evok[ing]": Dermot Michael Macgregor Morrah, "Dante's Beatrice: Knower, Known, and Knowing," *The Times Literary Supplement* 2164 (July 24, 1943): 358.

278 "part of the furniture": Quoted in Carpenter, *Inklings*, 188.

278 "I found myself panting": Dorothy L. Sayers, *The Letters of Dorothy L. Sayers, 1944–1950: A Noble Daring*, ed. Barbara Reynolds (Cambridge, UK: Dorothy L. Sayers Society, 1998), 45–47.

279 "I become more": Hadfield, *Charles Williams*, 218.

279 "a pattern": Williams, *To Michal from Serge*, 222.

279 "I dislike people . . . There are wells of hate": Williams, *To Michal from Serge*, 7.

279 "*amor intellectualis*": Williams, *To Michal from Serge*, 125.

279 "You go on": Ashenden, *Charles Williams: Alchemy and Integration*, 221.

279 "O, I wish": Hadfield, *Charles Williams*, 180.

280 "deferential and authoritarian . . . the constant jerky movements": Williams, *Letters to Lalage*, 31.

280 "incapable of . . . Love—obey": Ibid., 33.

280 "Sir, I am": Ibid., 44.

280 "torrent of words . . . next year": Ibid., 48–49.

280 "in a painfully divided state . . . I will play": Ibid., 67–70.

281 "Go with God": Ibid., 80.

281 "nothing was": Ibid., 86.

281 "power through sexual transcendence": Ibid., 69.

281 his only victim: See Candice Fredrick and Sam McBride, *Women Among the Inklings* (Westport, Conn.: Greenwood Press, 2001), 40.

281 "I am sadistic . . . I wouldn't hurt": Hadfield, *Charles Williams*, 104–105.

282 "a man . . . an extended": T. S. Eliot, "The Significance of Charles Williams," *The Listener* 936 (December 19, 1946): 894.

282 "in his [Williams's]": W. H. Auden, "Charles Williams: A Review Article," *The Christian Century*, May 2, 1956, 552–54.

282 "I have never known . . . a gay": Eliot, introduction to Williams, *All Hallows' Eve*, xv–xviii.

282 "for the first time": Hadfield, *Charles Williams*, 141.

282 "was extremely attractive . . . always found Williams": Lewis, preface, *Essays Presented to Charles Williams*, x.

283 "I am certain": Williams, *Letters to Lalage*, 19.

283 "Well, you never know": Quoted in Walter Hooper, *Past Watchful Dragons: The Narnian Chronicles of C. S. Lewis* (New York: Collier Books, 1979), 82.

283 "Bugger Paxford": W. H. Lewis, *Brothers and Friends*, 122.

283 "like a mother": Fred W. Paxford, "He Should Have Been a Parson," in *We Remember C. S. Lewis*, ed. David Graham (Nashville, Tenn.: Broadman & Holman, 2001), 123.

284 "our schoolgirls": Lewis, *Collected Letters*, vol. 2, 270.

284 "kind, solicitous": Patricia Heidelberger, "Part A: With Girls at Home," in Schofield, *In Search of C. S. Lewis*, 53.

284 "comfy to be with . . . what Jack Lewis imposed": Jill Freud, "Part B: With Girls at Home," in Schofield, *In Search of C. S. Lewis*, 57.

284 "our dear, delightful June Flewett": W. H. Lewis, *Brothers and Friends*, 180–81.

285 "Beauty and brains": Quoted in Jill Freud, "Part B: With Girls at Home," in Schofield, *In Search of C. S. Lewis*, 59.

285 "most complicated Arthur Rackham": Lewis, *Collected Letters*, vol. 2, 273.

285 "I think a great deal of nonsense": Ibid., 487.

286 "How can I ask thee . . . eternal will": Green and Hooper, *C. S. Lewis: A Biography*, 217.

286 "if its got to be": Lewis, *Collected Letters*, vol. 2, 258.

286 "ghostly feeling": Ibid., 274.

286 "safely dead": Ibid., 278.

286 "for me, personally": Ibid., 274.

286 "What is the use": C. S. Lewis, "Learning in War-Time," in C. S. Lewis, *The Weight of Glory and Other Addresses*, ed. Walter Hooper, rev. and exp. ed. (New York: Collier Books / Macmillan, 1980), 20.

287 "If we had": Ibid., 32.

287 "one night in nine": Lewis, *Collected Letters*, vol. 3, 153.

287 "I can never forget": Lewis, *Collected Letters*, vol. 2, 368.

287 morbidly self-concerned: See his letter to Sister Penelope of October 24, 1940, in ibid., 450–52.

288 "told too many . . . much too close": Lewis, *Collected Letters*, vol. 2, 481–82.

288 "bits . . . more lovely": Ibid., 1057.

288 "Do I become": Ibid., 261.

288 "the avoidance of": Ibid., 479.

288 "it has grown": Ibid., 495.

289 "merely indulging . . . Well—we have come": Ibid., 452–53.

289 "things are so bad": Ibid., 586.

289 "time and again . . . prayers that the prejudices": Guy Brinkworth, S.J., "C. S. Lewis," letter to *The Tablet* (December 7, 1963): 1317.

290 "intended to be . . . When Catholicism goes bad": Lewis, *Allegory of Love*, 322–23.

290 a formula: See letter to Sister Penelope, October 24, 1940, in Lewis, *Collected Letters*, vol. 2, 449.

290 "the vast mass . . . as much a provincial": Lewis, *Collected Letters*, vol. 2, 646–47.

290 "the difficulty": David Wesley Soper, *Exploring the Christian World Mind* (New York: Philosophical Library, 1963; London: Vision Press, 1964), 69.

291 "There is no mystery": Lewis, *Mere Christianity* (New York: HarperCollins, 2001), viii.

291 imaginatively Catholic: Allegory is similar to Catholic sacramentalism, Lewis notes, in that "it consists in giving an imagined body to the immaterial." Thus, in *The Faerie Queene*, the exiled Una (personifying the true church) is dressed like a nun, the House of Holinesse resembles a convent, and Penaunce wields a whip— all in the service of allegory; but Lewis makes a point of saying that Spenser was no unconscious Catholic. Lewis, *Allegory of Love*, 321–23.

291 "only a bungler": Lewis, *Allegory of Love*, 323.

291 "Jack, most of your friends seem to be Catholic": Sayer, *Jack: A Life of C. S. Lewis*, 421. For two staunchly Catholic perspectives on Lewis's attitude toward Roman Catholicism, see Christopher Derrick, *C. S. Lewis and the Church of Rome: A Study in Proto-Ecumenism* (San Francisco: Ignatius Press, 1981), and Joseph Pearce, *C. S. Lewis and the Catholic Church* (San Francisco: Ignatius Press, 2003). For a more broad-based view of Lewis's ecclesial thinking, see the essays in *C. S. Lewis and the Church: Essays in Honour of Walter Hooper*, ed. Judith Wolfe and Brendan N. Wolfe (London: T & T Clark, 2012).

13. MERE CHRISTIANS

292 the "Christian Challenge" series: Williams published *The Forgiveness of Sins* (also dedicated to the Inklings) in the same series in 1942. Charles Williams, *The Forgiveness of Sins*, Christian Challenge Series (London: Geoffrey Bles, 1942).

292 "If you are writing": Lewis, *Collected Letters*, vol. 2, 302.

293 "Not many years ago . . . The creatures cause pain": C. S. Lewis, *The Problem of Pain* (San Francisco: HarperSanFrancisco, 2001), 1–3.

293 "nonsense remains nonsense": Ibid., 18.

293 "whether we like it or not": Ibid., 46–47.

293 "gives the only opportunity": Ibid., 93.

293 "cannot cease": Ibid., 107.

293 "is the thing I was made for": Ibid., 151.

294 "standing above the sensations": Ibid., 136.

294 "how confessedly speculative": "The Pains of Animals: A Problem in Theology," Lewis, "The Reply," *God in the Dock*, 170.

294 "is so shocking": Lewis, *Problem of Pain*, 13.

294 "Mr. Lewis's . . . style": Charles Williams, review of *The Problem of Pain*, *Theology* 42 (January 1941): 62–63.

295 "the sort of people": Lewis, preface, *Essays Presented to Charles Williams*, xiii.

295 "Finest Hour" speech:

> . . . the Battle of Britain is about to begin. Upon this battle depends the survival of Christian civilization. Upon it depends our own British life,

and the long continuity of our institutions and our Empire. The whole fury and might of the enemy must very soon be turned on us. Hitler knows that he will have to break us in this Island or lose the war. If we can stand up to him, all Europe may be free and the life of the world may move forward into broad, sunlit uplands. But if we fail, then the whole world, including the United States, including all that we have known and cared for, will sink into the abyss of a new Dark Age made more sinister, and perhaps more protracted, by the lights of perverted science. Let us therefore brace ourselves to our duties, and so bear ourselves that, if the British Empire and its Commonwealth last for a thousand years, men will still say, "This was their finest hour."

Winston Churchill speech before the House of Commons, June 18, 1940, in Randolph S. Churchill and Martin Gilbert, *Winston S. Churchill*, vol. 6: *Finest Hour, 1939–1941* (London: Heinemann, 1983), 571.

295 "Well: we are on the very brink": Lewis, *Collected Letters*, vol. 2, 423.

295 frayed nerves: In a letter to Warnie, Lewis assessed the damage: "Dyson is in very poor form these days. On the whole I should say that Fox and he are the two among my acquaintance who are bearing up least well. Dyson I should have expected it of, for he's obviously all on wires at any time, but I'm surprised at Fox. The truth is he was *too* tranquil before, with a tranquillity born of inexperience . . ." Lewis, *Collected Letters*, vol. 2, 425.

295 "I don't know": Ibid. Among Hitler's concluding remarks in this very long speech are the following:

Mr. Churchill should . . . place trust in me when as a prophet I now proclaim:
    A great world empire will be destroyed. A world empire which I never had the ambition to destroy or as much as harm. Alas, I am fully aware that the continuation of this war will end only in the complete shattering of one of the two warring parties. Mr. Churchill may believe this to be Germany. I know it to be England.
    In this hour I feel compelled, standing before my conscience, to direct yet another appeal to reason in England. I believe I can do this as I am not asking for something as the vanquished, but rather, as the victor. I am speaking in the name of reason. I see no compelling reason which could force the continuation of this war.

Max Domarus, *Hitler: Speeches and Proclamations, 1932–1945: The Chronicle of a Dictatorship*, vol. 3: *The Years 1939 to 1940* (Wauconda, Ill.: Bolchazy-Carducci, 1997), 2062.

295 "useful and entertaining . . . It wd. be called": Lewis, *Collected Letters*, vol. 2, 426.

296 "though it was easy": C. S. Lewis, "Screwtape Proposes a Toast," *The Screwtape Letters: With Screwtape Proposes a Toast* (New York: HarperCollins, 2009), 183.

296 "men are not angered": Lewis, *Screwtape Letters*, 111.

296 "once you have made": Ibid., 34.

297 "should become a classic . . . time alone can show": Quoted in Hooper, *C. S. Lewis: A Complete Guide*, 275–76.

297 "It's like the end": Lewis, *Collected Letters*, vol. 2, 485.

297 "had had an extraordinary effect" . . . "promising to soar": Charles Gilmore, "To the RAF," in Como, *C. S. Lewis at the Breakfast Table*, 186–87.

297 "complete failure": Lewis, *Collected Letters*, vol. 2, 485. A reference to the biblical story of Balaam and the ass, Numbers 22:28.

298 "a sterling and direct purpose": Gilmore, "To the RAF," 188.

298 "I had never realized . . . the chance in many places": Lewis, *Collected Letters*, vol. 2, 504.

298 "as a reparation": Tolkien, unpublished letter in the possession of Christopher Tolkien, quoted in A. N. Wilson, *C. S. Lewis*, 179.

298 "feeling for words . . . Jack had done his job": Gilmore, "To the RAF," 186–89.

298 "a fairly intelligent audience": Quoted in Justin Phillips, *C. S. Lewis in a Time of War: The World War II Broadcasts That Riveted a Nation and Became the Classic Mere Christianity* (New York: HarperSanFrancisco, 2002), 80.

299 "most apologetic begins": Lewis, *Collected Letters*, vol. 2, 470.

300 "Every one has heard . . . is appealing to": Lewis, *Broadcast Talks* (London: Geoffrey Bles, Centenary Press, 1942), 9.

300 "Well, those are the two points": Ibid., 13.

301 "There's been a great deal . . . You may even have thought": Ibid., 27–29.

302 "Supposing you hear a cry": Ibid., 19.

302 "Suddenly everyone just froze . . . there was the barman": Phillips, *C. S. Lewis in a Time of War*, 119.

302 "One gets funny letters": Lewis, *Collected Letters*, vol. 2, 504.

303 "after you have realized": Lewis, *Broadcast Talks*, 32.

303 "enemy-occupied territory . . . the story of how": Ibid., 46.

303 "the dark curse of Hitler": Winston Churchill, July 14, 1940, BBC broadcast, in Winston Churchill, *Into Battle: Speeches by the Right Hon. Winston S. Churchill* (London: Cassell, 1941), 251. The complete sentence runs "This is a War of the Unknown Warriors; but let all strive without failing in faith or in duty, and the dark curse of Hitler will be lifted from our age."

303 "*what* new urgency?": C. S. Lewis, "Evil and God," *The Spectator* CLXVI (February 7, 1941): 141. Reprinted in C. S. Lewis, *God in the Dock: Essays on Theology and Ethics*, ed. Walter Hooper (Grand Rapids, Mich.: Wm. B. Eerdmans, 1970), 22.

304 "fighting religion": Lewis, *Broadcast Talks*, 39.

304 "good dreams . . . the most shocking thing": Ibid., 49–50.

304 "I'm trying here": Ibid., 50–51.

305 "Hebrew philosopher Yeshua": Lewis, *Collected Letters*, vol. 1, 231.

305 "as a literary historian": Lewis, "What are we to make of Jesus Christ?" Reprinted from *Asking Them Questions*, 3rd series, ed. Ronald Selby Wright (Oxford University Press, 1950), 47–53, in Lewis, *God in the Dock*, 158.

305 "Of course you can take the line": Quoted by Hooper, *C. S. Lewis: A Complete Guide*, 308.

307 "in Christ": Lewis, *Broadcast Talks*, 57. Note that this "new man" is on an altogether different model from the Nietzschean or Theosophical "higher man."

308 "Give up yourself": Lewis, *Mere Christianity*, 226–27.

308   "take some . . . They obviously": Hooper, *C. S. Lewis: A Complete Guide*, 310–13.

308   "With the BBC . . . There will be": P. W. [Philip Whitwell] Wilson, "Prophecy Via BBC," *The New York Times* (July 22, 1945): 98.

308   "the silly-clever . . . They are not really": George Orwell, "As I Please," *Tribune* (October 27, 1944), reprinted in George Orwell, *The Collected Essays, Journalism, and Letters of George Orwell*, ed. Sonia Orwell, Ian Angus, and George Orwell (Boston: David R. Godine, 2000), 264–65.

309   "People whose lives": Wain, *Sprightly Running*, 138.

310   "there are no *ordinary* people": C. S. Lewis, "The Weight of Glory," *Weight of Glory*, 19.

310   "this club": Walter Hooper, "Oxford's Bonny Fighter," in Como, *C. S. Lewis at the Breakfast Table*, 138.

310   "Those who founded it . . . We never claimed": Lewis, preface to *Socratic Digest* 1, reprinted as "The Founding of the Oxford Socratic Club" in *God in the Dock*, 128.

310   "Here a man": Lewis, "The Founding of the Oxford Socratic Club," *God in the Dock*, 127.

311   "a kind of prize-ring . . . I can remember": Wain, *Sprightly Running*, 140–41.

311   "He was a bonny fighter": Austin Farrer, "The Christian Apologist," in Gibb, *Light on C. S. Lewis*, 25–26.

312   "simple-minded undergraduates . . . in a straightforward, manly way": Wain, *Sprightly Running*, 140.

312   "Minto is laid up": Lewis, *Collected Letters*, vol. 2, 549.

312   "a little oasis . . . that horrid house": W. H. Lewis, *Brothers and Friends*, 181.

313   "I am inclined": Lewis, *Collected Letters*, vol. 2, 771.

313   "In the *Tao*": C. S. Lewis, *The Abolition of Man* (New York: HarperSanFrancisco, 2001), 74–75.

314   "I hear rumours": Ibid., 79.

314   "a real triumph": Quoted in Hooper, *C. S. Lewis: A Complete Guide*, 341.

314   "a doctrine never seems": Lewis, *Collected Letters*, vol. 2, 730.

314   "From all my lame": Ibid., 527. The poem was later published as "The Apologist's Evening Prayer" in C. S. Lewis, *Poems*, ed. Walter Hooper (London: Geoffrey Bles, 1964), 129.

315   "the chapter of Major Lewis' projected book . . . not think so well": Tolkien, *Letters*, 71.

315   "I seemed to be standing in a busy queue . . . the Big Man": Lewis, *The Great Divorce* (London: Geoffrey Bles, 1946; New York: HarperCollins, 2001), 1–3.

315   "Tousle-Headed Poet": Ibid., 4, 7–9.

315   "the Intelligent Man": Ibid., 9, 48–49.

315   an Anglican bishop of progressive views: Ibid., 16, 34–44.

315   "Well . . . this is hardly the sort of society I'm used to": Ibid., 2.

315   "blazing with golden light": Ibid., 3.

316   "I had the sense of being in a larger space": Ibid., 20.

316   "raindrops that would pierce him like bullets": Ibid., x.

316   identified the story: See Douglas A. Anderson, *Tales Before Narnia: The Roots of Modern Fantasy and Science Fiction* (New York: Del Rey, 2008), 283–84. The story is reprinted here, 284–300.

316   "'Golly!' thought I": Lewis, *Great Divorce*, 21.

316 bright spirits: Brightest among the spirits is a Sarah Smith, who had lived an ordinary but unstintingly saintly life in Golders Green, a London neighborhood known
for its Jewish population, suggesting that Lewis intends her to be Jewish.
316 "Of course I should require some assurances": Lewis, *Great Divorce*, 39.
316 "I came here to get my rights": Ibid., 31.
317 "To any that leaves . . . will have been Hell": Ibid., 68.
317 "'at the end of all things . . . We were always in Hell": Ibid., 69.
317 "nearly nothing": Ibid., 139.
317 "My Roman Catholic friends would be surprised . . . 'They're both right'": Ibid., 71.
318 "the sort of universe": Lewis, "Learning in Wartime," 32.
318 "Don't you like": Lewis, *Collected Letters,* vol. 1, 215.
318 "I don't think": Ibid., 220.
318 "I have finished": Ibid., 290.
319 the new generation: See J. Middleton Murry, "Milton or Shakespeare?" *The Nation
and the Athenaeum* 28 (March 26, 1921): 916–17, and T. S. Eliot, "A Note on the
Verse of John Milton," *Essays and Studies by Members of the English Association* 21
(Oxford: Clarendon Press, 1936), 32–40.
319 "Milton's dislodgement": F. R. Leavis, "In Defence of Milton," *Scrutiny* (June
1938): 104–114; reprinted in F. R. Leavis, *The Common Pursuit* (London: Chatto
& Windus, 1952), 33–43.
319 "partly anticipated . . . that when the old poets": C. S. Lewis, *A Preface to Paradise
Lost* (London: Oxford University Press, 1942), v.
319 "that great miracle . . . the proper order": Charles Williams, introduction, *The English Poems of John Milton*, from the edition of H. C. Beeching, The World's Classics 182 (London: Oxford University Press, 1940), ix.
319 "the recovery of . . . Apparently the door": Lewis, *Preface to Paradise Lost*, v–vi.
320 "any of the normal . . . frenzy of special pleading": W. W. Robson, "Mr. Empson on
Paradise Lost," *The Oxford Review*; reprinted in Robson, *Critical Essays*, 87.
320 "It is not": Lewis, *Preface to Paradise Lost*, 134.
321 "if only he": Lewis, *Collected Letters*, vol. 2, 561–62.
321 "Now that 'Weston' has shut": Lewis, *Out of the Silent Planet*, 158.
321 in Lewis's rooms: Alastair Fowler, personal interview, October 13, 2006. For the
Matthew testimony, see Hooper, *C. S. Lewis: A Complete Guide*, 215.
321 "'Of course . . . the sort of time-travelling'": C. S. Lewis, "The Dark Tower," in C. S.
Lewis, *The Dark Tower and Other Stories*, ed. Walter Hooper (San Diego: Harcourt, Brace & Company, 1977), 17.
322 "in time to prevent their 'falling'": Lewis, *Collected Letters*, vol. 2, 503.
322 "I've got Ransom to Venus . . . Have you room for an extra prayer?": Ibid., 496.
322 "Every night Venus": Ibid., 397.
322 "scattered through other worlds": Lewis, *Perelandra*, 40.
323 "in something . . . with principalities": Ibid., 21.
323 "four or five people": Ibid., 25.
323 "Humphrey": It was Dyson who came up with "Humphrey" as a nickname when he
couldn't remember Havard's first name. Lyle W. Dorsett, oral history interview
with Dr. Robert E. Havard, 8.
323 "celestial coffin": Lewis, *Perelandra*, 29.
323 "we had raids": Ibid., 26.

323 "a sceptical friend . . . engulfed": Ibid., 29–30.

324 "for one draught": Ibid., 42.

324 "itch to have things": Ibid., 43.

324 Life Force . . . "blind, inarticulate purposiveness": Ibid., 78. As Lewis suggests in *Studies in Words*, the word "life" and all its compounds (life force, life-affirming) had in his day a mystical aura attached to it that made it off-limits to criticism. See "Life," *Studies in Words*, 2nd ed. (Cambridge, UK: Cambridge University Press, 1967), 304–305.

324 "the most terrifying": Charles Andrew Brady, "C. S. Lewis: II," *America* 71 (June 10, 1944): 270.

324 "far away on Earth": Lewis, *Perelandra*, 121.

325 "an inspired litany": Victor Hamm, "Mr Lewis in Perelandra," *Thought* 20 (June 1945): 271–90.

325 "irregular Spenserian stanzas": *The Letters of Ruth Pitter: Silent Music*, ed. Don W. King (Newark, Del.: University of Delaware Press, 2014), 158, note 73.

325 "secret fear . . . It is at this point": Alistair Cooke, "Mr. Anthony at Oxford," *The New Republic* 110, no. 17 (April 24, 1944).

326 "The schaddow of that hidduous strenth": Lewis, *English Literature in the Sixteenth Century Excluding Drama*, 104.

326 "somehow what he thought": Owen Barfield, "The Five C. S. Lewises," *Owen Barfield on C. S. Lewis*, 22.

326 "violation of frontier . . . invaded by": C. S. Lewis, "The Novels of Charles Williams," *On Stories*, 22.

326 Logres: Lewis, *That Hideous Strength*, 191–92; Lewis's character MacPhee quotes a line from Williams's Arthurian poem *Taliessin Through Logres*.

327 "one of the great . . . this desire": C. S. Lewis, "The Inner Ring" [the annual Commemoration Oration, King's College London, December 14, 1944], originally published in C. S. Lewis, *Transposition and Other Addresses* (London: Geoffrey Bles, 1949); quoted here from *The Weight of Glory and Other Addresses*, 100–103.

327 "to make man": Lewis, *That Hideous Strength*, 40.

327 "It is commonly done": Lewis, *Collected Letters*, vol. 2, 717.

328 "wasn't meant to illustrate": Ibid., 669–70.

328 "drawn in": Lewis, *That Hideous Strength*, 81, 112.

328 Mr. Bultitude: Lewis told Sayers that "Mr. Bultitude is described by Tolkien as a portrait of the author, but I feel that is too high a compliment (Lewis, *Collected Letters*, vol. 2, 682). More likely, Lewis is paying homage to F. Anstey's *Vice Versa*, in which Mr. Bultitude is the father who under an enchantment exchanges bodies with his son and finds out what boarding school life is really like.

328 "the last vestige": Lewis, *That Hideous Strength*, 282.

328 "so preposterous": George Orwell, "The Scientists Take Over," *Manchester Evening News*, August 16, 1945, reprinted in *The Complete Works of George Orwell*, ed. Peter Davison, Vol. XVII (1998), No. 2720 (first half), 250–51. This is Orwell's review of *That Hideous Strength*.

328 "opera-bouffe": Owen Barfield, introduction to Gibb, *Light on C. S. Lewis*, xvi.

328 "I wish he'd dedicated": Hooper, *C. S. Lewis: A Complete Guide*, 706.

328 "has got a more unanimous": Lewis, *Collected Letters*, vol. 2, 682.

328 *"That Hideous Strength"*: Ibid., 701.

329 "I have just read": Ibid., 571.

329 "the novel at present": Ibid., 574.

329 "I'm writing a story": Ibid., 634.

330 The Apostles: Members included F. D. Maurice; James Clerk Maxwell; Alfred, Lord Tennyson; Henry Sidgwick; the mathematician G. H. Hardy and his Brahmin prodigy, Srinivasa Ramanujan; Roger Fry; Alfred North Whitehead; J.M.E. McTaggart; Bertrand Russell; G. E. Moore; Ludwig Wittgenstein; Leonard Woolf; Lytton and James Strachey; E. M. Forster; Desmond MacCarthy; Rupert Brooke; and John Maynard Keynes.

330 "To set up as a critic": I. A. Richards, *Principles of Literary Criticism*, 2nd ed. (London: Routledge and Kegan Paul, 1926; reprint ed., London and New York: Routledge, 2001), 54.

331 "appetencies": Ibid., 42–43 et passim.

331 "stock responses . . . doctrinal adhesions": I. A. Richards, *Practical Criticism: A Study of Literary Judgment* (New York: Harcourt, Brace, 1929), 14.

331 huge crowds: See John Paul Russo, *I. A. Richards: His Life and Work* (Baltimore: The Johns Hopkins University Press, 1989), 93.

331 "Here, at last": Christopher Isherwood, *Lions and Shadows: An Education in the Twenties* (London: L. & Virginia Woolf at the Hogarth Press, 1938), 121.

331 his reception was decidedly chilly: See Russo, *I. A. Richards: His Life and Work*, 795, note 28.

331 "when Leavis read poetry": George Watson, *Never One for Theory: England and the War of Ideas* (Cambridge, UK: Lutterworth Press, 2000), 72.

332 "one man who has": Wain, *Sprightly Running*, 174.

332 "as if our very lives": David Ellis, *Memoirs of a Leavisite: The Decline and Fall of Cambridge English* (Liverpool: Liverpool University Press, 2013), 25.

332 "cultivated to perfection": Noel Annan, *Our Age: English Intellectuals Between the World Wars—A Group Portrait* (New York: Random House, 1990), 318.

332 the future of civilization: Queenie Leavis's 1932 *Fiction and the Reading Public* (based on the doctoral thesis she wrote under the supervision of I. A. Richards) traced the pathways by which mass culture—following Gresham's Law—was driving out good culture. Q. D. Leavis, *Fiction and the Reading Public* (London: Chatto & Windus, 1932).

332 "in several long conversations": Wain, *Sprightly Running*, 176–77.

332 "a distaste": L. C. Knights, "Mr C S Lewis and the Status Quo," *Scrutiny* 8 (1939): 92.

333 "persistent nourishment": E.K.T. Dock, "Mr. Lewis's Theology," *Scrutiny* 19 (June 1946): 53–58.

333 "*Rehabilitations* was warmly received . . . Can anyone be so optimistic": Q. D. Leavis, "The Discipline of Letters: A Sociological Note," *Scrutiny* 12 (1943): 22–26, reprinted in *The Importance of Scrutiny: Selections from* Scrutiny: *A Quarterly Review, 1932–1948*, ed. Eric Bentley (New York: New York University Press, 1964), 51–55.

333 William Empson: See John Haffenden's magisterial two-volume biography of Empson: *William Empson: Among the Mandarins* (Oxford: Oxford University Press, 2005), and *William Empson: Against the Christians* (Oxford: Oxford University Press, 2006). A full-length study of the relations between Empson and Lewis is greatly to be desired.

334 *Seven Types of Ambiguity* or *The Allegory of Love*: Kingsley Amis, "Bare Choirs?" [review of Empson, *Argufying*], *Sunday Telegraph* (November 29, 1987), cited in Haffenden, *William Empson: Among the Mandarins*, 3.

334 gracious unsigned review: "Professor Lewis on Linguistics" [review of *Studies in Words*], *The Times Literary Supplement* 3057 (September 30, 1960): 627. Discussed in Haffenden, *William Empson: Against the Christians*, 709, note 28.

334 "I wish I had seen more": John Horder, "William Empson, Straight," *The Guardian* (August 12, 1969), quoted in *Selected Letters of William Empson*, ed. John Haffenden (Oxford: Oxford University Press, 2006), 142, note 3. See Empson's review of *The Allegory of Love*, "Love and the Middle Ages," *The Spectator* (September 4, 1936), reprinted in William Empson, *Argufying: Essays on Literature and Culture*, edited with an introduction by John Haffenden (Iowa City: University of Iowa Press, 1987).

334 "The gossip is that C. S. Lewis is going to get it": Haffenden, *Selected Letters of William Empson*, 145.

334 "neo-Christians": Haffenden, *William Empson: Against the Christians*, 331 et passim.

334 "When I was an Oxford undergraduate": John Wain, *Preliminary Essays* (London: Macmillan; New York: St. Martin's, 1957), 192.

335 "What seems to you": Jose Harris, "The Arts and Social Sciences, 1939–1970," in *The History of the University of Oxford*, vol. 8: *The Twentieth Century*, ed. Brian Howard Harrison (Oxford: Clarendon Press, 1994), 239.

14. LOSS AND GAIN

336 "I'm even more . . . I am always aware": Williams, *To Michal from Serge*, 249.

336 "I wish you . . . all I want": Ibid., 239–45.

337 "bitterly disappointed": Ibid., 200.

337 "I am": Hadfield, *Introduction to Charles Williams*, 201.

337 "for anyone I have ever loved": Hadfield, Ibid., 208.

337 "3000 words": Williams, *To Michal from Serge*, 248.

337 "I do love you . . . O sweet": Ibid., 243–49.

337 "I am very glad . . . There will be no black magic": Ibid., 257–59. In regard to Williams's mention of "one more novel," fragments remain of a unfinished novel entitled *The Noises That Weren't There*, set in post-WWII England, which he apparently started shortly before his death.

337–38 "quite simple . . . "it's very quiet": Williams, *To Michal from Serge*, 258.

338 "a girl I knew": Wain, *Sprightly Running*, 152.

338 "At 12:50 this morning": W. H. Lewis, *Brothers and Friends*, 182.

339 "choosing unfortunately the King's Arms . . . there will be no more pints": Ibid., 182–83.

339 "I share a little . . . I shall have you all": Tolkien, *Letters*, 115.

339–40 "as little (almost) . . . We now verified for ourselves": Lewis, preface, *Essays Presented to Charles Williams*, xiv.

340 "I believe in the next life": Quoted in Carpenter, *Inklings*, 204.

340 "the group had begun": Wain, *Sprightly Running*, 185.

341 "a writer's task": Ibid., 182.

341 "a *permanent member*": Quoted in Carpenter, *Inklings*, 205.

341 "Last time, *you* said": Christopher Tolkien, quoted in John and Priscilla Tolkien, *Tolkien Family Album*, 58.

342 "Father Gervase": Lewis's clerihew is quoted in Luke Rigby, O.S.B., "A Solid Man," 40. Carpenter cites a slightly different version, attributed to Tolkien: Carpenter, *Inklings*, 186.

342 "there has always been something sinister": W. H. Lewis, *Brothers and Friends*, 201.

342 "dismay . . . an R.C.": W. H. Lewis, *Brothers and Friends*, 193.

342–43 "At the far side of the table . . . acquaintance turned to friendship": James Dundas-Grant, "From an Outsider," in Como, C. S. *Lewis at the Breakfast Table*, 229–31.

343 "Wars are always lost": Tolkien, *Letters*, 116.

344 "There seem no bowels of mercy": Ibid., 111.

344 "the first War of the Machines . . . leaving, alas, everyone the poorer": Ibid., 111.

344 "grief . . . does not look kindly": Ibid., 115–16. The Nazgûl are the monstrous winged steeds of the Enemy's servants.

345 "squandered . . . three weeks": Ibid., 112–14.

345 "incredible belonging . . . for the first time": Ibid., 116–17.

345 "I shall now have to study . . . before long": Ibid., 118–19.

345–46 "a brilliant . . . quite honestly": Quoted in ibid., 119–20.

346 "those that like this . . . written in my life-blood": Ibid., 121–22.

346 "a good meeting . . . We went on": W. H. Lewis, *Brothers and Friends*, 188–93.

346–47 "to dine . . . two she-tutors": Ibid., 192.

347 "Charles [Williams]": Ibid., 192.

347 "towards the end": Ibid., 187.

347 "blossomed out . . . treated the place": Ibid., 199–200.

347–48 "feeling very guilty . . . anxious and travel stained": Ibid., 201.

348 "the haunting fear": Ibid., 203.

348 "holy and very loveable . . . something grey and secret": Ibid., 201–202.

348 "This holiday": Ibid., 207.

349 "He is certainly a fool . . . Almost anyone": Lewis, *Collected Letters*, vol. 2, 621–22.

349 "a poor gentlewoman": Ibid., 711.

349 "The fund": Lewis, *Collected Letters*, vol. 3, 31.

350 "Bettiana": Lewis, *Collected Letters*, vol. 2, 974.

350 "there's something v. wrong": Ibid., 974.

350 "a variety almost . . . I await": Ibid., 872.

351 "your absence . . . perhaps you will find": Ibid., 704–709.

351–52 "In this book . . . a fairly permanent nucleus": Lewis, preface, *Essays Presented to Charles Williams*, v.

352 "They are . . . concerned with *story*": Lewis, *Collected Letters*, vol. 2, 655.

352 "not quite an Inkling": Fredrick and McBride, *Women Among the Inklings*, 20. For more on this issue, see pp. 20–24 in their excellent study.

352 "might have been disturbed": James Brabazon, *Dorothy L. Sayers: A Biography* (New York: Scribner, 1981), 236.

352 "I conceived a loathing": Tolkien, *Letters*, 82.

353 "every Holy Week": C. S. Lewis, "A Panegyric for Dorothy L. Sayers," *On Stories*, 93.

353 "the first person": C. S. Lewis, "Wain's Oxford," *Encounter* 20, no. 1 (January 1963): 81, quoted in Hooper, C. S. *Lewis: A Complete Guide*, 34.

353 "Your Dorothy Sayers . . . I only hope": Quoted in Dorothy L. Sayers, *The Letters of Dorothy L. Sayers: 1899–1936: The Making of a Detective Novelist*, ed. Barbara Reynolds (New York: St. Martin's Press, 1995), 339–40.

353 "was simply the most incomparable . . . nobody had taught him": Dorothy L. Sayers, "'. . . And Telling You a Story': A Note on *The Divine Comedy*," in Lewis, *Essays Presented to Charles Williams*, 2–4.

353–54 "that quality without which": Ibid., 15.

354 "perhaps a trifle": Lewis, *Collected Letters*, vol. 2, 817.

354 "Fantasy, Recovery, Escape, Consolation . . . Enchantment": Tolkien, "On Fairy-Stories," in Lewis, *Essays Presented to Charles Williams*, 66–70.

354 "assist in the effoliation": Ibid., 84.

354 "Story itself . . . is there for the sake of the story": C. S. Lewis, "On Stories," in Lewis, *Essays Presented to Charles Williams*, 90.

354 "deeper imagination": Ibid., 96.

354 "something other than a process": Ibid., 103.

354 "despite their free use": Ibid., 104.

355 "No book is really worth reading": Ibid., 100.

355 "these two, and Mr. H.V.D. Dyson": Lewis, preface, *Essays Presented to Charles Williams*, vi.

355 "with his pen": *St. Andrews Citizen*, June 29, 1946, quoted in Duriez, *C. S. Lewis Chronicles*, 223.

355–56 "slightly sour[ed] . . . for a while": Scull and Hammond, *J.R.R. Tolkien Companion and Guide: Chronology*, 305.

356 "the smallest Inkling": W. H. Lewis, *Brothers and Friends*, 212.

356 "A very pleasant meeting": Ibid., 216.

356 "which I enjoyed": Ibid., 218–19.

356 a long letter: the letter is dated Septuagesima 1948, the third Sunday before Advent, which fell that year on January 25.

357 "I regret causing pain . . . But I warn you": Tolkien, *Letters*, 126–28.

357 "Nay!": Ibid., 128.

357 "Hugo's voice was booming": W. H. Lewis, *Brothers and Friends*, 218.

358 "lying on the couch": from *J.R.R.T.: A Study of John Ronald Reuel Tolkien, 1892–1973*, directed by Derek Bailey, written and produced by Helen Dickinson, narrated by Judi Dench (VHS video; London: Visual Corporation, 1992).

358 "Oh God, not another fucking elf!": A. N. Wilson, in his biography of Lewis, records Dyson's remark as "Oh fuck, not another elf!" (A. N. Wilson, *C. S. Lewis*, 217). In an article in *The Telegraph*, referring to Dyson's words as "Oh no! Not another fucking elf!," Wilson states that the "fucking elf" story came from Christopher Tolkien himself. A. N. Wilson, "Tolkien Was Not a Writer," *The Telegraph* (November 24, 2001).

358 "When Tolkien came through the door": "John Wain," in *Contemporary Authors: Something About the Author* (Detroit, Mich.: Gale Research, 1986).

358 "I remember this very vividly": From *J.R.R.T.: A Study of John Ronald Reuel Tolkien, 1892–1973*.

358 "Shut up, Hugo": From ibid.

358 "the impression of . . . Don't do that": W. H. Lewis, *Brothers and Friends*, 97–98.

358 "Councillor Brewer arrived": Ibid., 220.

359 "at a ham supper": Ibid., 230.

359 "freshness and vigour . . . sophisticated malice-flecked delight": Alexander Pope, *Pope: Poetry and Prose, with Essays by Johnson, Coleridge, Hazlitt, &c.*, with an introduction and notes by H.V.D. Dyson (Oxford: Clarendon Press, 1933), v–vii.

359 "It is": Lewis, *Collected Letters*, vol. 2, 360.

15. MIRACLES

360 "Has Physics sold the pass?": May 13, 1943, letter from Dorothy L. Sayers, quoted in Hooper, *C. S. Lewis: A Complete Guide*, 343.

361 a miracle need not be seen as a *violation*: For Thomas Aquinas, "those things are properly called miracles which are done by divine agency beyond the order commonly observed in nature (*praeter ordinem communiter observatum in rebus*)." *Summa Contra Gentiles* III.

361 "the whole show": C. S. Lewis, *Miracles: A Preliminary Study*, rev. ed. (San Francisco: HarperSanFrancisco, 2001), 6.

361 "no account of the universe": C. S. Lewis, *Miracles, A Preliminary Study*, 1st ed. (London: Geoffrey Bles, Centenary Press, 1947), 26.

362 "evolution is either an innocent": Chesterton, *Orthodoxy*, 60.

362 "the sceptics, like bees": G. K. Chesterton, *Alarms and Discursions* (Dodd, Mead, 1911), 227.

362 "has grown up gradually": Lewis, *Miracles*, 42. Barfield's remarks on a letter dated June 19, 1947, inserted in his personal copy of the first edition of *Miracles* (1947): Barfield Library Publications and Inserts, Marion E. Wade Center, Wheaton College, Wheaton, Illinois.

362 "Whether [a man's] conclusions": "A Reply to Mr. C. S. Lewis' Argument that Naturalism is Self-Refuting" reprinted from *The Socratic Digest* 4 (1948): 7–15 as "C. S. Lewis on Naturalism," in G.E.M. Anscombe, *The Collected Philosophical Papers of G.E.M. Anscombe*, vol. 2 (Oxford: Blackwell, 1981), 227. The exchange between Lewis and Anscombe—and its effect on Lewis's subsequent revision of *Miracles*—has been carefully analyzed by Lewis's Dutch translator, Arend Smilde, in a special issue of *The Journal of Inklings Studies* devoted to this topic: Arend Smilde, "What Lewis Really Did to *Miracles*: A Philosophical Layman's Attempt to Understand the Anscombe Affair," *The Journal of Inklings Studies* 1, no. 2 (October 2011): 9–24. See also the supporting material Smilde provides in appendices on his website: www.lewisiana.nl/787olkien787/appendices.pdf (accessed August 17, 2014).

363 "veridical" might have expressed his meaning: Lewis's reply to Anscombe, from the Socratic Club minutes, *The Socratic Digest* 4 (1948): 15, reprinted in Lewis, *God in the Dock*, 146.

363 "in general it appeared": Socratic Club minutes, *The Socratic Digest* 4 (1948): 15, reprinted in Lewis, *God in the Dock*, 145–46.

363 "the fact that Lewis rewrote": G.E.M. Anscombe, preface, *Collected Philosophical Papers*, vol. 2, x.

363 notable defenders: Alvin Plantinga, "Is Naturalism Irrational?" chap. 12 of *Warrant and Proper Function* (New York: Oxford University Press, 1993), 216–37. For a

sustained defense, see Victor Reppert, *C. S. Lewis's Dangerous Idea: In Defense of the Argument from Reason* (Downers Grove, Ill.: IVP Academic, 2003); for a critique, see Peter van Inwagen, "C. S. Lewis' Argument Against Naturalism," *The Journal of Inklings Studies* 1, no. 2 (October 2011): 25–40.

363   "The rightful demand": Lewis, *Miracles*, 97.

363–64 "with real horror . . . had lost everything": Derek Brewer, "The Tutor: A Portrait," in Como, *C. S. Lewis at the Breakfast Table*, 59. Brewer also notes that five of those present when Lewis described Anscombe's critique "had been infantry officers at the age of nineteen and had seen action"—which is, as he notes, "a curious commentary on English scholarly life in the twentieth century," but may also help to account for why such language of defeat under siege would come naturally to Lewis.

364   "My own recollection": G.E.M. Anscombe, preface, *Collected Philosophical Papers*, vol. 2, x.

364   "The lady is quite right": Lewis, *Collected Letters*, vol. 3, 35.

364   "the subtlest of all the snares": Lewis, *Great Divorce*, 74.

364   "nothing is more dangerous . . . from Christian apologetics": Lewis, "Christian Apologetics," *God in the Dock*, 103.

364   "like the old fangless snake": Lewis, *Collected Letters*, vol. 3, 129.

365   "My thought and talent": Ibid., 651.

365   "It's fun": Ibid., 314.

366   "I must tell you": David Cecil quoted in Don W. King, *Hunting the Unicorn: A Critical Biography of Ruth Pitter* (Kent, Ohio: Kent State University Press, 2008), 82.

366   "closely-worked, carved": L. P. Hartley, "Poet of Many Moods," quoted in *Ruth Pitter: Homage to a Poet*, with an introduction by David Cecil, ed. Arthur Russell, (Chester Springs, Penn.: Dufour Editions, 1969), 66.

366   "a poet of the full singing voice": John Wain, "Poet of Living Form," in Russell, *Ruth Pitter*, 122.

366   "deeply struck": David Cecil, letter to Ruth Pitter, quoted in King, *Hunting the Unicorn*, 103.

366   "excited me more": Ruth Pitter, letter to David Cecil, July 13, 1942, in King, *Letters of Ruth Pitter*, 98.

366   "There were air raids at night": BBC interview with Stephen Black, June 24, 1955, quoted in King, *Hunting the Unicorn*, 118.

366   "driven to it": Palmer Papers, National Library of Australia, MS 1174. Quoted in Don W. King, "The Anatomy of a Friendship: The Correspondence of Ruth Pitter and C. S. Lewis, 1946–1962," *Mythlore* 24, no. 1 (Summer 2003), 2.

367   "My visit to you": Ruth Pitter, letter to C. S. Lewis, July 17, 1946, in King, *The Letters of Ruth Pitter*, 128.

367   "I was prepared for the more definitely mystical": Lewis, *Collected Letters*, vol. 2, 720.

367   "I know (or think)": Ibid., 724.

367   "greatly relieved . . . I often lust": Ibid., 735.

367   "The important thing": Ibid., 735.

368   "kindness and liking": Ibid., 881.

368   "Did he ever": Ruth Pitter, quoted in ibid., 882.

368   "in place, nationality, language": C. S. Lewis and Dom Giovanni Calabria, *The Latin Letters of C. S. Lewis*, trans. and ed. Martin Moynihan (South Bend: St. Augustine's Press, 1998), 83.

368 "a problem of the greatest importance . . . those things which still, by God's grace": Ibid., 29–33.

368 "never in the least": Ibid., 69.

369 "I actually wept": Tolkien, interview with Denys Gueroult in the BBC Oxford studio on January 20, 1965, broadcast in edited form on December 16, 1970, on the BBC Radio 4 program *Now Read On*.

369 "happy to announce": Tolkien, *Letters*, 116.

369 "this university business," Ibid., 131.

369 "to complete a number . . . which are said to be poisoning": Scull and Hammond, *J.R.R. Tolkien Companion and Guide: Chronology*, 345.

370 "curious shabby, happy-go-lucky": Ibid., 432.

370 "*Uton herian holbytlas* . . . I congratulate you": Lewis, *Collected Letters*, vol. 2, 990–91.

370 "was apparently not bored": Tolkien, *Letters*, 39.

370 "stoutly and with apparent sincerity": Canon Norman Power, "Recollections," *The J.R.R. Tolkien Centenary Conference 1992* [souvenir guide] (Oxford: Tolkien Society and Mythopoeic Society, 1992), 9–10. The leprechaun shoe incident is also described, with quotations drawn from an account by Power published in *Amon Hen* 28 (August 1977), in Scull and Hammond, *J.R.R. Tolkien Companion and Guide: Chronology*, 789–90.

371 "beyond even the expectations": Tolkien, *Letters*, 133.

371 "Dined with J at College": W. H. Lewis, *Brothers and Friends*, 230.

372 the idiosyncratic appeal: M. M. Mahood, review of *Arthurian Torso* in *Modern Language Review* 45, no. 2 (April 1950): 238–39.

372 "will . . . discredit the memory": John E. Housman, review of *Arthurian Torso* in *The Review of English Studies*, New Series, 1, no. 1 (January 1950): 84–85.

372 "be only the starting point": Lewis, *Collected Letters*, vol. 2, 886.

372 "among the two or three most valuable": Lewis, preface, *Essays Presented to Charles Williams*, vii.

373 "I know no more pleasant sound": Tolkien, *Letters*, 129.

373 shocked by the resurgent Christianity: See Haffenden, *William Empson: Against the Christians*.

374 "I've read your poem . . . I have been glad to see": Letter, T. S. Eliot to Owen Barfield, June 1, 1948, Barfield Archives, Bodleian Special Collections, Dep. c. 1055, #7.

374 "mark an advance in self criticism . . . a Copernican revolution": Lewis, *Collected Letters*, vol. 2, 889.

374 "has caused me more shame . . . Did I ever mention": Ibid., 929.

374 "I was under very heavy pressure . . . staved off": Owen Barfield, in *Owen Barfield: Man and Meaning, Transcript of the Award-winning Documentary Video*, ed. G. B. Tennyson (Encino, Calif.: OwenArts, 1995), 9.

375 "I must now write . . . a complex of responsibilities": Owen Barfield, *This Ever Diverse Pair* (London: Victor Gollanz, 1950; Edinburgh: Floris Classics, 1985), 13–15.

375 "a rather extraordinary sort of chap . . . a period of intellectual intercourse": Ibid., 60–61.

375 "just writes to his publisher": Ibid., 63.

376 "like Alice": Ibid., 52.

376 "The moment of pain": Ibid., 54.

376 "I'm going to kill you": Ibid., 112.

376 "the very profession itself . . . we Burgeons need always remain *sleeping* partners": Ibid., 114–15.

377 "enchanted . . . most anxious to meet the author": Barfield Archives, Bodleian Special Collections, Dep. c. 1055.

377 "I am humbled": Lewis, *Collected Letters*, vol. 2, 945.

377 "I have two lists of names": Ibid., 948.

378 "your prose works are": Letter, Ruth Pitter to Owen Barfield, October 11, 1949, in Barfield Archives, Bodleian Special Collections, Dep. c. 1055.

378 "a high and sharp philosophic comedy": C. S. Lewis, "Life's Partners," *Time and Tide* 31 (March 25, 1950): 286.

378 "the impression": Barfield, introduction to Gibb, *Light on C. S. Lewis*, xiv.

378 "*voulu*": Ibid., xi.

378 "a certain ill-concealed glee": Alan Watts, *Behold the Spirit: A Study in the Necessity of Mystical Religion* (New York: Pantheon Books, 1947; new ed., 1971), 186.

378 "became something like an obsession . . . *laudator temporis acti* [praiser of times past]": Barfield, *Owen Barfield on C. S. Lewis*, 18–23.

379 "on the wrong track altogether . . . a common bit": Ibid., 20.

379 "it is a particularly unfavorable season . . . fine though the poem is": George Rostrevor Hamilton, unpublished letter, April 16, 1950, Barfield Archives, Bodleian Special Collections, Dep. c. 1055.

16. "MAKING UP IS A VERY MYSTERIOUS THING"

380 "My house is unquiet": Lewis, letter to Father Calabria, in Lewis and Calabria, *Latin Letters of C. S. Lewis*, 51.

380 "stifling tyranny . . . Every day": Warren Lewis, "Memoir of C. S. Lewis," 21–22.

381 "How long, oh Lord . . . spirits-insomnia-drugs": W. H. Lewis, *Brothers and Friends*, 225.

381 "found the line 'dead' . . . a serious illness": Ibid., 226.

381 "out of control": Lewis, *Collected Letters*, vol. 2, 953.

381 "as long as [Warnie] is a dipsomaniac": Ibid., 957.

381 "wh. is not really a paradox": Ibid., 951.

382 "a man writing a story": C. S. Lewis, "It All Began with a Picture . . . ," *On Stories*, 53.

382 "Don't the ordinary": Lewis, *Collected Letters*, vol. 2, 802.

383 "This book is about four children": Quoted in Green and Hooper, *C. S. Lewis: A Biography*, 303.

383 "I have tried one": Lewis, *Collected Letters*, vol. 2, 802.

383 *The Lion, the Witch, and the Wardrobe: A Story for Children* (London: Geoffrey Bles, 1950). In later editions, the subtitle was dropped.

383 an Umbrian town: Green and Hooper, *C. S. Lewis: A Biography*, 306. Paul Ford notes several references to Narnia in Livy, Tacitus, Pliny the Elder, and Pliny the Younger; all sources Lewis might have encountered; Paul F. Ford, *Companion to Narnia*, rev. and exp. ed. (New York: HarperCollins, 2005), 316–17.

383 "a Faun carrying an umbrella . . . I don't know": Lewis, "It All Began with a Picture . . . ," 54.

384 the American poet and literary scholar Chad Walsh . . . "in the tradition of E. Nesbit": Chad Walsh, *The Literary Legacy of C. S. Lewis* (New York and London: Harcourt Brace Jovanovich, 1979), 129; *Chad Walsh Reviews C. S. Lewis* (Altadena, Calif.: Mythopoeic Press, 1998), 16; and Chad Walsh, *C. S. Lewis: Apostle to the Skeptics* (New York: Macmillan, 1949), 9–10.

384 "very good indeed": Green and Hooper, *C. S. Lewis: A Biography*, 307.

384 *Nymphs and Their Ways* was the title of one of the books in the Faun's cottage. Green and Hooper, *C. S. Lewis: A Biography*, 307.

384 literary malpractice: See extract from a 1955 letter of Tolkien's to Hugh Brogan, in Tolkien, *Letters*, 224.

386 "The Aunt and Amabel": Douglas A. Anderson has included this Nesbit story in his collection, *Tales Before Narnia: The Roots of Modern Fantasy and Science Fiction* (New York: Del Rey, 2008), 7–15.

386 "I don't know where the Lion came from": Lewis, "It All Began with a Picture . . . ," 53.

386 "in a very large . . . met all these knights and ladies": C. S. Lewis, *Studies in Medieval and Renaissance Literature* (Cambridge, UK: Cambridge University Press, 1966), 148.

387 "Logic!": C. S. Lewis, *The Lion, the Witch, and the Wardrobe* (New York: Harper Trophy, 2002), 52.

388 "son of the great . . . deeper magic": Ibid., 86, 171.

388 "'Myself,' said the voice": C. S. Lewis, *The Horse and His Boy* (New York: Harper Trophy, 1954), 176.

389 "supposal": Letter to James E. Higgins, December 2, 1962; published by Higgins as "A Letter from C. S. Lewis," *The Horn Book* 42 (October 1966): 533–34.

389 "If I spoke to him": C. S. Lewis, *The Magician's Nephew* (New York: Harper Trophy, 1983), 203.

390 "I thought I saw how stories": "Sometimes Fairy Stories May Say Best What's to Be Said," *The New York Times Book Review*, November 18, 1956. Reprinted in Lewis, *On Stories*, 47.

390 "which goes on forever": C. S. Lewis, *The Last Battle* (New York: Harper Trophy, 1994), 228.

391 "Where sky and water meet": C. S. Lewis, *The Voyage of the* Dawn Treader (New York: Harper Trophy, 1994), 22.

391 Christian educators: See, for example, John Warwick Montgomery, "The Chronicles of Narnia and the Adolescent Reader," *Religious Education* 54, no. 5 (September 1, 1959): 418–28.

391 "greatest addition . . . evangelizes through the imagination": Charles A. Brady, "Finding God in Narnia," *America* 96 (October 27, 1956): 103–105. Brady began writing about Lewis for *America* in 1944: "Introduction to Lewis" (May 27, 1944) and "C. S. Lewis II" (June 10, 1944). "You are the first of my critics so far who has really read and understood *all* my books," Lewis told him at that time, and he was especially grateful for Brady's treatment of Narnia. Lewis, *Collected Letters*, vol. 2, 629.

391 "Oxford Circle": Brady names Lewis, Williams, Tolkien, and Dorothy L. Sayers as members of the "Oxford Circle." Charles A. Brady, "Unicorns at Oxford," *Books on Trial* 15 (October 1956): 59–60.

391 "I don't like to hear of that 'bad patch'": Letter, Walter de la Mare to Owen Barfield, June 14, 1950, Barfield Papers, Bodleian Library, Dep. c. 1055.

391 "Between you and me": Letter, Walter de la Mare to Owen Barfield, November 16, 1949, Barfield Papers, Bodleian Library, Dep. c. 1055.

392 "you must be incurring . . . Dip and spare not": Lewis, *Collected Letters*, vol. 3, 31.

392 "It is . . . within my knowledge": Owen Barfield, "The Light of the World," supplement to *Anthroposophical Movement* 31, no. 2 (February 1954): 1–10, www.owen barfield.org/the-light-of-the-world/ [accessed August 11, 2014].

392–93 "an appreciable number of married women . . . get some mutual friend": Owen Barfield letter, July 6, 1951, Barfield Papers, Bodleian Library, Dep. c. 1055.

393 "Mrs. B has apparently": Lewis, *All My Road Before Me*, 439.

393 Susan Josephine Grant Watson: Details about Barfield's relationships with Josephine Grant Watson and Marguerite Lundgren are drawn from Blaxland–de Lange, *Owen Barfield*.

394 "Her mobility was exceptional": Annelies Davidson, "Eurhythmy and the English Language" in Rudolf Steiner, *Eurhythmy as Visible Speech*, trans. Alan Stott, Coralee Schmandt, and Maren Stott, with an introduction and a companion consisting of a forecast, notes and essays to the lectures, appendices on English Eurhythmy, and an overview (Weobley, UK: Anastasi, 2005), 367.

394 "the apotheosis": Marjorie Raffé, Cecil Harwood, and Marguerite Lundgren, *Eurythmy and the Impulse of Dance* ([London]: Rudolf Steiner Press, 1974), 3.

394 "whereas the experience of movement": Ibid., 13.

394 "one of the channels": Ibid., 27.

395 "Oh the mails": Lewis, *Collected Letters*, vol. 2, 1014.

395 "men . . . are only apes": Joy Davidman, "The Longest Way Round," in *These Found the Way: Thirteen Converts to Protestant Christianity*, ed. David Wesley Soper (Philadelphia: Westminster Press, 1951), 16.

395 "a powerful, well-written novel": John Cournos, "Geese in the Forum and Other New Works of Fiction," *The New York Times* (July 14, 1940): 72.

396 "what neglected": Davidman, "Longest Way Round," 22.

396 "All my defenses . . . God had always been there": Ibid., 23.

396 "moral responsibility . . . Not Shakespeare": Ibid., 24–25.

396 "an enduring impression . . . bursts of blasphemy": reviews of *Weeping Bay* by Granville Hicks, "Four New Novels of Interest," *The New York Times* (March 5, 1950): 211; *Catholic World*, June 1950; *Library Journal*, February 1, 1950.

396 "neither of us had ever heard of her": W. H. Lewis, *Brothers and Friends*, 244.

397 "no commitment": Milton Waldman, quoted in Tolkien, *Letters*, 134.

397 "I certainly shall try to extricate . . . I should": Ibid., 135.

398 "I am, I fear, a most unsatisfactory person . . . if you decline": Ibid., 135–37.

398 "'ONOMASTICAL-OUTING' . . . the whole Saga": Ibid., 138.

398 "I profoundly hope": Ibid., 139.

398 "if this is not workable": Rayner Unwin's comments enclosed by Stanley Unwin in a letter to Tolkien, quoted in ibid., 140.

399 "bitterly disappointed": Stanley Unwin letter to Tolkien, quoted in Scull and Hammond, *J.R.R. Tolkien Companion and Guide: Chronology*, 361.

399 "it is difficult": Extract from Tolkien's letter to Milton Waldman, Tolkien, *Letters*, 143.

399 "It is . . . only too likely": Tolkien, *Letters,* 160.

399 Rayner Unwin . . . still believed: Ibid., 443, note.

399–400 "behaved badly . . . Can anything be done": Ibid., 162–63.

400 "a great (though not flawless) work . . . larger number of people": Ibid., 164–65.

400 Tolkien "chose an area": Sayer, "Recollections of J.R.R. Tolkien," 23.

400 "*If* you believe": Rayner Unwin, *George Allen & Unwin: A Remembrancer* (Ludlow: Merlin Unwin, 1999), 99.

400–401 "inward chuckle . . . God bless you": Lewis, *Collected Letters,* vol. 3, 249–50.

401 "to know how soon": W. H. Lewis, *Brothers and Friends,* 233.

401 "it will be an enormous liberation . . . I hardly know how I feel": Lewis, *Collected Letters,* vol. 3, 28–29.

401 "grievous . . . *now* a house less horrible": Ibid., 37.

401 "We cd. read the whole *Aeneid*": Ibid., 39.

401 "Minto died": Ibid., 90.

402 "the rape of J's life . . . crushing misfortune": W. H. Lewis, *Brothers and Friends,* 236–37.

402 "Slav and Balkan": Ibid., 239.

402 "knaves . . . fools": Lewis, *Collected Letters,* vol. 3, 147.

403 "Just got a letter . . . Lord, he knocked my props out": Joy Davidman, *Out of My Bone: The Letters of Joy Davidman,* ed. Don W. King (Grand Rapids, Mich: Wm. B. Eerdmans, 2009), 116.

403 "as a result of something [Bill] did": Davidman, *Out of My Bone,* 141.

403 "she was in love with you": William Gresham to C. S. Lewis, quoted in ibid., 312.

403–404 "of medium height . . . Mind you": Sayer, *Jack: A Life of C. S. Lewis,* 352–53.

404 "completely 'circumvented' . . . asked for one week": Lewis, *Collected Letters,* vol. 3, 268.

404 "many merry days": W. H. Lewis, *Brothers and Friends,* 244.

404 "intensely feminine": Warren Lewis, "Memoir of C. S. Lewis," 43.

404 "there was nothing feminine": Chad Walsh, quoted in Lyle W. Dorsett, *And God Came In: The Extraordinary Story of Joy Davidman, Her Life and Marriage to C. S. Lewis* (Peabody, Mass.: Hendrickson, 2009), 68.

404 "we treated her": Sayer, *Jack: A Life of C. S. Lewis,* 353.

404 "a blessed release . . . Lewis strongly advised me": Davidman, *Out of My Bone,* 140.

404 "Davy's quite eager": Ibid., 141–42.

405 "Bill greeted me . . . 'Have you ever known me'": Ibid., 140–41.

17. THE LONG-EXPECTED SEQUEL

406 "This charming house has become uninhabitable": Tolkien, *Letters,* 165.

406 "endless labour": Ibid., 167.

406 "the 'infernal combustion' engine": Ibid., 77.

406 "billowing cloud": Ibid., 165.

406 "almost a world wide mental disease": Ibid., 88.

408 "enlarge the scene": J.R.R. Tolkien, "Sir Gawain and the Green Knight," *Monsters and the Critics,* 83.

408 "the original metre": Ibid., 74.

408 "a different metre is a different mode": T. S. Eliot, "What Dante Means to Me," in *To Criticize the Critic and Other Writings* (New York: Farrar, Straus and Giroux, 1965), 129.

409 "constructions that are . . . an idiom that is": Roger Sale, "Wonderful to Relate," *The Times Literary Supplement* 3861 (March 12, 1976): 289.

409 "style and diction": Scull and Hammond, *J.R.R. Tolkien Companion and Guide: Reader's Guide*, 932.

410 "linguistic shock . . . dislike exaggeration": J.R.R. Tolkien, travel diary (*Giornale d'Italia*), quoted in Scull and Hammond, *J.R.R. Tolkien Companion and Guide: Chronology*, 465. Tolkien Papers, Bodleian Library. All excerpts from the travel diary come from Scull and Hammond, *J.R.R. Tolkien Companion and Guide: Chronology*, 463–74, and *Reader's Guide*, vol. 2, 434–36.

410 "I remain in love": Tolkien, *Letters*, 223.

410 "elvishly lovely": Tolkien, travel diary, quoted in Scull and Hammond, *J.R.R. Tolkien Companion and Guide: Chronology*, 466.

411 "an exile . . . the cursed disease": Ibid., 464.

411 "tremendous babel of bells . . . the great choir": Ibid., 469–72.

411 "it is much paler . . . ochre, brick-red": Ibid., 464–70.

411–12 "much moved . . . it has nothing": Ibid., 466.

412 "impossible to disentangle": Ibid., 466.

412 "*The Lord of the Rings* is of course a fundamentally religious and Catholic work": Tolkien, *Letters*, 172.

412 "This book is like lightning . . . here are beauties": Lewis, "The Gods Return to Earth," *Time and Tide* (August 14, 1954): 1082.

413 "works like a coral insect": Lewis, *Collected Letters*, vol. 3, 1579.

413 Victorians likened missionaries to coral insects: See Michelle Elleray, "Little Builders: Coral Insects, Missionary Culture, and the Victorian Child," *Victorian Literature and Culture* 39, no. 1 (March 2011): 223–38.

413 "I met a lot of things": Tolkien, letter to W. H. Auden (June 7, 1955), *Letters*, 216.

413 "Make return of ring a motive . . . not very dangerous": Tolkien, *Return of the Shadow*, 41–42.

413 "at once native and alien": Tolkien's words in a letter to the novelist and poet Naomi Mitchison (sister of the biologist J.B.S. Haldane, the sometime nemesis of Lewis) on December 8, 1955, Tolkien, *Letters*, 229.

413 "detestable": Draft letter to "Mr. Rang" (Gunnar Urang, who later published *Shadows of Heaven: Religion and Fantasy in the Writing of C.S. Lewis, Charles Williams, and J.R.R. Tolkien*), dated by Tolkien August 1967, in *Letters*, 380.

414 Istari ("wise ones"): Tolkien explained their origins in a 1954 addendum, "The Istari," included by Christopher Tolkien in J.R.R. Tolkien, *Unfinished Tales of Númenor and Middle-earth*, ed. Christopher Tolkien (Boston: Houghton Mifflin, 1980), 371–84, and in drafts for an early 1956 letter to Michael Straight, editor of *The New Republic* (see Tolkien, *Letters*, 237).

414 "his joy, and his swift wrath": Tolkien, *Unfinished Tales of Númenor and Middle-earth*, 390–91.

415 Sam's real name . . . Shire place-names: See the detailed account of languages and nomenclature in *The Lord of the Rings*, Appendix F, "The Languages and Peoples of the Third Age." Tolkien also discusses nomenclature in his draft letter to Gun-

nar Urang (Tolkien, *Letters*, 379–87). Worried that foreign language editions of *The Lord of the Rings* would overlook such nuances, Tolkien eventually produced a document on "Nomenclature of *The Lord of the Rings*," specifying which names should be kept as is, and which were intended to have an intelligible meaning that should be conveyed by translation (for "Bracegirdle," Tolkien suggests *Gürtelspanner* in German). For a critical edition of this document, see Wayne G. Hammond and Christina Scull, *The Lord of the Rings: A Reader's Companion* (Boston and New York: Houghton Mifflin, 2005), 750–82.

415 the *Ancrene Wisse*, a sanctuary for Anglo-Saxon: J.R.R. Tolkien, "Ancrene Wisse and Hali Meiðhad," *Essays and Studies by Members of the English Association* 14 (1929): 106. See Shippey, *Road to Middle-earth*, 41, and Tolkien's 1965 letter to Dick Plotz, Tolkien, *Letters*, 360.

415 "an unobtrusive but very ancient people": Tolkien, *Lord of the Rings*, bk. 1, prologue, 1–2.

415 "more or less a Warwickshire village": Letter to Allen & Unwin, December 12, 1955, Tolkien, *Letters*, 230.

415 "in spite of all its obvious absurdities": C. S. Lewis, *That Hideous Strength*, 86.

415 "It would be a grievous blow": Tolkien, *Lord of the Rings*, bk. 1, chap. 2, 49.

416 "eleventy-first": The formation "eleventy" echoes the Old English *hund endleofantig*.

416 leaving Frodo to distribute the gifts: See Tolkien, *Letters*, 290–91, on Hobbit gift-giving.

416 "does not grow": Tolkien, *Lord of the Rings*, bk. 1, chap. 2, 47.

417 "des Ringes Herr": Richard Wagner, *Der Ring des Nibelungen: Das Rheingold*, scene 4, Alberich's curse.

417 "What a pity": Tolkien, *Lord of the Rings*, bk. 1, chap. 2, 59.

417 "the privates and my batmen": "My 'Samwise' is indeed (as you note) largely a reflexion of the English soldier—grafted on the village-boys of early days, the memory of the privates and my batmen that I knew in the 1914 War, and recognized as so far superior to myself." Letter to James Henry Cotton Minchin (April 16, 1956), currently in private ownership: a scanned image of this letter is reproduced as Lot Number 226 on the Sotheby's website, where it is listed as having sold for $31,250 on June 11, 2013: http://www.sothebys.com/en/auctions/ecatalogue/2013/books-manuscripts-n09066/lot.226.html (accessed August 22, 2014). A portion of Tolkien's draft of this letter—but not this passage—appears in Tolkien, *Letters*, 247–48. Minchin was a major in the service of the Cameronians and Royal Flying Corps who fought in World War I; he edited *The Legion Book* (1929), featuring wartime writing and illustrations by Rudyard Kipling, Stanley Spencer, and others. Humphrey Carpenter quotes this passage as "My 'Sam Gamgee' is indeed a reflexion of the English soldier, of the privates and batmen I knew in the 1914 war, and recognised as so far superior to myself." Carpenter, *Tolkien*, 81.

418 "from deadly peril": Tolkien, *Lord of the Rings*, bk. 1, chap. 5, 104.

418 sailing without coordinates: Tom Shippey quotes a letter he received from Tolkien in 1970 in which Tolkien stresses the difference between *The Lord of the Rings* as it took shape in the composition and the appearance of design in the finished product. Shippey, *Road to Middle-earth*, preface to the rev. and exp. ed., xviii.

418 "that Frodo has to be dug out": Shippey, *Road to Middle-earth*, 104.

419 "the Fall of Man": Tolkien, *Letters*, 387.

419 "order of Grace": Ibid., 172.

420 undermines the hero paradigm: See W. H. Auden, "The Hero Is a Hobbit," *The New York Times Book Review*, October 31, 1954; and Verlyn Flieger, "Frodo and Aragorn: The Concept of the Hero," in *Understanding* The Lord of the Rings: *The Best of Tolkien Criticism*, ed. Rose A. Zimbardo and Neil D. Isaacs (New York: Houghton Mifflin, 2004), 122–45.

420 "'I do not choose now'": Tolkien, *The Lord of the Rings*, book 6, chapter 3, 945.

420 "I do not think . . . motives and disposition": Tolkien, *Letters*, 326–27. From drafts of a letter to Eileen Elgar, who resided in the Hotel Miramar, where Tolkien and Edith stayed in Bournemouth. She was deaf, and Tolkien communicated with her mainly by letters. He began composing the letter in September 1963; a significantly altered final version was postmarked October 3, 1963, according to Scull and Hammond, *J.R.R. Tolkien Companion and Guide: Chronology*, 608.

420 "But I cannot do": Tolkien, *Sauron Defeated*, 38.

420 "All my choices have proved ill": Frodo speaking to Sam in *The Lord of the Rings*, bk. 4, chap. 1, 604; here Frodo, at the beginning of book 4, echoes Aragorn ("all that I do goes amiss") at the beginning of book 3 (*The Lord of the Rings*, bk. 3, chap. 1, 413). See also Aragorn in book 3, chapter 2, 426.

421 *ofermod*: Tolkien's interpretation of *ofermod* in the poem "The Battle of Maldon" is contested by Tom Shippey, among other scholars of Old English. See Richard C. West, "Túrin's *Ofermod*: An Old English Theme in the Development of the Story of Túrin" in *Tolkien's Legendarium: Essays on* The History of Middle-earth, ed. Verlyn Flieger and Carl F. Hostetter (Westport, Conn., and London: Greenwood Press, 2000), 233–45.

421 "I will diminish": Tolkien, *Lord of the Rings*, bk 2, chap. 7, 366.

421 "good news": C. S. Lewis, "The Gods Return to Earth," *Time and Tide* (August 14, 1954): 1082.

422 "All this stuff": Tolkien, *Letters*, 145.

422 "Our Lady": Ibid., 172.

422 "a great deal better": Letter to Rayner Unwin, September 9, 1954, in ibid., 184.

422 more harm than good: See Lewis, *Collected Letters*, vol. 3, 385.

422 "I should not have wished other": Tolkien, *Letters*, 184.

422 "If Ariosto rivalled it": C. S. Lewis, dust-jacket endorsement, *Fellowship of the Ring*.

423 "On the jacket Ariosto . . . whimsical drivel": J. W. Lambert, "New Fiction," *The Sunday Times* (London) 6851 (August 8, 1954): 3.

423 "sound prose" . . . anti-Soviet allegory: Alfred Leo Duggan, "Heroic Endeavour," *The Times Literary Supplement* 2743 (August 27, 1954): 541.

423 the allegory didn't gel: Alfred Leo Duggan, "The Saga of Middle Earth" (review of *The Return of the King*), *The Times Literary Supplement* 2804 (November 25, 1955): 704; Alfred Leo Duggan, "Middle Earth Verse" (review of *The Adventures of Tom Bombadil*, discussed in relation to *The Lord of the Rings*), *The Times Literary Supplement* 3169 (November 23, 1962): 892.

423 "a bewildering amalgam": Peter Green, "Outward Bound by Air to an Inappropriate Ending," *The Daily Telegraph and Morning Post* (August 27, 1954).

423–24 "I must say that I was unfortunate": Tolkien, *Letters*, 184.

424 "buffoonery . . . it seems almost as though he has added something": A. E. Cherryman, "Myth-maker," *Truth* (August 6, 1954): 988.

424 "alternating between": Edwin Muir, "Strange Epic," *The Observer* (August 22, 1954); "A Boy's World," *The Observer* (November 27, 1955).

424 "no fiction I have read": Auden, "Hero Is a Hobbit," 37.

424 "the suspense of waiting": W. H. Auden, "A World Imaginary, but Real," *Encounter* (November 1954): 59–62.

424 "some critics seem determined": Tolkien, *Letters*, 244.

424 "rarely remember a book": W. H. Auden, "At the End of the Quest, Victory," *The New York Times Book Review* (January 22, 1956): 226. Tolkien, *Letters*, 239.

425 "Oo, Those Awful Orcs! . . . certain people": Edmund Wilson, "Oo, Those Awful Orcs!" *The Nation* (April 14, 1956): 312–14. Reprinted with some changes in Edmund Wilson, *The Bit Between My Teeth: A Literary Chronicle of 1950–1965* (New York: Farrar, Straus and Giroux, 1965), 327–32.

425 "There was a time": Philip Toynbee, "Dissension Among the Judges," *The Observer* (August 8, 1961).

426 "The only criticism that annoyed": Letter to Houghton Mifflin, Tolkien, *Letters*, 220.

426 "I think the book quite unsuitable": Tolkien, *Letters*, 228.

426 "both J and I warned him": W. H. Lewis, *Brothers and Friends*, 235.

426 "My brother and I": Lewis, *Collected Letters*, vol. 3, 54.

427 "extremely well-written": Orville Prescott, "Books of the Times," *The New York Times* (March 17, 1954): 29.

427 "conscientious scholar": Albert Guerard, "At the Top Was the King," *The New York Times Book Review* (August 15, 1954): 10.

427 "The O HELL": Lewis, *Collected Letters*, vol. 2, 221–22.

428 "Platonism, Douglas, Lyndsay": From a progress report from Lewis, conveyed by Frank Percy Wilson to the Delegates of Oxford University Press, quoted by Walter Hooper in Lewis, *Collected Letters*, vol. 2, 235–36.

428 "ploughing through back numbers": Lewis, *Collected Letters*, vol. 3, 44–45.

428 "Joy, joy, my task is done": Letter of November 28, 1952, quoted in Hooper, *C. S. Lewis: A Complete Guide*, 480.

428 "Mr. Lewis, now as always": John Wain, "Pleasure, Controversy, Scholarship," *The Spectator* 193, no. 6588 (October 1, 1954): 403.

428 "dear and delectable": Ruth Pitter, journal entry quoted in King, *Letters of Ruth Pitter*, 292.

428 "The merits of this book": Dame Helen Gardner, "†Clive Staples Lewis, 1898–1963," in *Proceedings of the British Academy* 51 (1966): 426.

429 "the Jewish fierceness": C. S. Lewis, foreword to Joy Davidman, *Smoke on the Mountain* (Philadelphia: Westminster Press, 1954), 9.

429 "perhaps Miss Pitter's": Theresa Furse, "The Mortal Lot," *The Times Literary Supplement* 2690 (August 21, 1953): 537.

429 "Bright Angel!": Lewis, *Collected Letters*, vol. 3, 327.

430 "Welcome to what": Ibid., 389.

430 did not hit it off: Things did not improve after Lewis and Joy were married. Pitter's biographer, Don King, has found indications in a document among Pitter's restricted papers in the Bodleian Library that Pitter came to the conclusion (though

possibly only in retrospect) that Davidman "used her illness . . . to manipulate Lewis into marrying her and caring for her two sons." King, *Hunting the Unicorn*, 306, note 7. Further evidence of Pitter's resentment may be found in the oral history interview conducted by Lyle W. Dorsett for the Marion E. Wade Center, July 23, 1985.

430 "if he were not a confirmed bachelor . . . 'I've burnt my boats'": Sayer, *Jack: A Life of C. S. Lewis*, 348.

430 "The one miss": Lewis, *Collected Letters*, vol. 3, 635.

430 "Jack should have married": King, *Hunting the Unicorn*, 197

430 "if he was mistrustful": King, *Letters of Ruth Pitter*, 418.

431 "fortunately, the 'second string' declined": Helen Gardner, "†Clive Staples Lewis," 427–28.

432 "fixed up a kind of farewell . . . a pretty big disappointment": Blaxland–de Lange, *Owen Barfield*, 38–39.

432 "a literary oddity . . . at times": *The Penguin Book of Contemporary Verse*, selected with an introduction and notes by Kenneth Allott (Harmondsworth: Penguin Books, 1950), 71–72.

433 "I can see no reason . . . a subject worth attention": F. R. Leavis, *Common Pursuit*, 250–53.

434 "in many ways . . . as a substitute": Robert Conquest, "The Art of the Enemy," in *Essays in Criticism* 7 (1957): 42–55.

434 "absorbing after we have got": T. S. Eliot, "The Significance of Charles Williams," *The Listener* (December 19, 1946): 894.

434 a laudatory booklet: John Heath-Stubbs, *Charles Williams* (London: Longmans, Green, 1955), 7.

18. THE DIALECTIC OF DESIRE

436 "There may be times": Owen Barfield, *Saving the Appearances: A Study in Idolatry* (New York: Harcourt, Brace & World, 1957), 11.

437 "Somehow," Barfield recalled, "around that [phrase]": Quoted in *Owen Barfield: Man and Meaning*, video transcript prepared and edited by G. B. Tennyson with the assistance of George Michos (Encino, Calif.: OwenArts, 1985), 9.

437 "When I 'hear a thrush singing'": Barfield, *Saving the Appearances*, 20.

438 "It can do no harm . . . we should then have to write": Ibid., 37.

438 "goodness of heart": Ibid., 161.

439 "full (of course) of sap . . . V. good": Lewis, *Collected Letters*, vol. 3, 724–30.

439 "stunner": Ibid., 853.

439 "very high opinion": Barfield Papers, Bodleian Library, Dep. c. 1056, letter from T. S. Eliot to Barfield, March 25, 1960.

439 "highly": Letter, Owen Barfield to Valerie Eliot, April 23, 1976, Barfield Papers, Bodleian Library, Dep. c. 1055.

439 "I am feeling as flat": Tolkien, *Letters*, 217.

440 "[My] chief biographical fact": Ibid., 257.

440 "*feathery* . . . Why must I": Ibid., 305–307.

441 "a bit uncompromising . . . not attracted by": Rayner Unwin, letter to Tolkien, December 31, 1957, quoted in in Scull and Hammond, *J.R.R. Tolkien Companion and Guide: Chronology*, 518.

441 "orc-cults": Tolkien, *Letters*, 419. See J.R.R. Tolkien, "The New Shadow," in J.R.R. Tolkien, *The Peoples of Middle Earth* (*The History of Middle-earth*, vol. 12), ed. Christopher Tolkien (Boston and New York: Houghton Mifflin, 1996), 409–18.

441 "sinister and depressing . . . not worth doing": Tolkien, *Letters*, 344.

442 "sometimes the less specific complaints . . . As his retirement": Rayner Unwin, *George Allen & Unwin: A Remembrancer*, 116–17.

442 "the glint of money": Tolkien, *Letters*, 257.

442 "Why does Z": Ibid., 274.

442 "On Sept. 24 I was involved": Early English Text Society Archive, quoted in Scull and Hammond, *J.R.R. Tolkien Companion and Guide: Chronology*, 533.

443 "a massive metal 'model' ": Tolkien, *Letters*, 261.

443 "maggot-soup . . . remarkable": Ibid., 265. "Maggot-soup" meant nothing more alarming than mushroom soup, à la Farmer Maggot. A copy of the menu, signed by Tolkien, is listed under auction at Christie's, Sale 5138, Lot 365: www.christies.com/lotfinder/books-manuscripts/81lolkien-john-ronald-reuel-a-hobbit-dinne-4930908-details.aspx?from=searchresults&intObjectID=4930908&sid=6cdfcb56-ba08-4431-92c8-889100840e00 (accessed August 20, 2014).

443 "great delight . . . a legitimate satisfaction": Tolkien, *Letters*, 264.

444 "difficult collaborator": Anthony Kenny, *A Path from Rome: An Autobiography* (London: Sidgwick & Jackson, 1985), 117.

444 "Yesterday I went up to Cambridge": Davidman, *Out of My Bone*, 226.

445 "greatly exaggerated . . . continuity-in-mutability": C. S. Lewis, "*De Descriptione Temporum*," in Lewis, *Selected Literary Essays*, 2.

445 "somewhere between us and the": Ibid., 7.

445 "not the slightest agreement": Ibid., 9.

445–46 "trump card . . . the very milestones": Ibid., 10–11.

446 "I myself belong . . . There are not going to be": Ibid., 13–14.

446 "it was brilliant": Davidman, *Out of My Bone*, 228.

446 "mere episodes": Herbert Butterfield, *The Origins of Modern Science, 1300–1800* (London: G. Bell, 1949), vii.

447 "as clever as they make 'em": E. M. Forster, "Some Books" (February 3, 1943), in *The BBC Talks of E. M. Forster 1929–1960: A Selected Edition*, ed. Mary Lago, Linda K. Hughes, and Elizabeth MacLeod Walls (Columbia: University of Missouri Press, 2008), 223.

447 "obscurantism": E. M. Forster, "A Letter," *Twentieth Century* 157 (February 1955): 99–100; reprinted as a leaflet *I Assert that there is an Alternative in Humanism* (London: Ethical Union, 1955).

447 "the silliest of the lot": Lewis, *Collected Letters*, vol. 3, 578.

447 "high-minded old twaddlers": Ibid., 589.

447 against the humanist idolatry of culture: C. S. Lewis, "Lilies That Fester," *Twentieth Century* 157 (April 1955), reprinted in *The World's Last Night and Other Essays* (New York: Harcourt, Brace, 1960), 31–49.

447 shy and insecure . . . a comfortable daily round: See reminiscence by Richard W. Ladborough, "In Cambridge," in Como, *C. S. Lewis at the Breakfast Table*, 98–104.

448 "wild idea of Leavis . . . Is it just possible": C. S. Lewis Papers, Bodleian Library, MS Eng. Let. C. 220/4. Cited in Green and Hooper, *C. S. Lewis: A Biography*, 289.

448 "hearing Paxford . . . it is not Cambridge": W. H. Lewis, *Brothers and Friends*, 244.

449 "A complete flop": Charles Wrong, "A Chance Meeting," in Como, *C. S. Lewis at the Breakfast Table*, 109.

449 "far and away the best . . . my one big failure": Letter to Anne Scott, Lewis, *Collected Letters*, vol. 3, 1181; this echoes Lewis's words in an earlier letter to Herbert Palmer, *Collected Letters*, vol. 3, 891, and Audrey Sutherland, *Collected Letters*, vol. 3, 1148.

449 "worked at it": C. S. Lewis, introduction to the first British edition of *Till We Have Faces*, quoted in Hooper, *C. S. Lewis: A Complete Guide*, 243.

449 "kicked a few ideas around": Joy Gresham to William Gresham, quoted in Hooper, *C. S. Lewis: A Complete Guide*, 247.

449 "when they are preparing": C. S. Lewis, *Till We Have Faces: A Myth Retold* (San Diego: Harcourt, Brace, 1984), 97.

449 "every nice, affectionate": Lewis, *Collected Letters*, vol. 3, 590.

450 "I know now": Lewis, *Till We Have Faces*, 308.

450 "Most reviewers": Hooper, *C. S. Lewis: A Complete Guide*, 262.

450 "mumbo-jumbo": T. H. White, *Time and Tide* 37 (October 13, 1956): 1227–28.

450 libel risk: Lewis, *Collected Letters*, vol. 3, 581.

450 "partly in answer": Lewis, preface to *Surprised by Joy*, vii.

450 "long corridors": Lewis, *Surprised by Joy*, 10.

451 "'Do *you* like that?'": Ibid., 130.

451 "as fascinating": Ibid., 200.

451 "the most dejected": Ibid., 228–29.

451 "latter stages": Dorothy L. Sayers, "Christianity Regained," *Time and Tide* 36 (October 1, 1955): 1263.

451 "In a sense": Lewis, *Surprised by Joy*, 17.

451 "God moves, indeed": Norman Cornthwaite Nicholson, "Joy and Conversion," *The Times Literary Supplement* 2797 (October 7, 1955): 583.

451 "The limpidity of these waters": Sayers, "Christianity Regained," 1264.

452 "shimmering in the heat": Davidman, *Out of My Bone*, 258.

452 "smelled marriage": Eva Walsh, quoted in Dorsett, *And God Came In*, 128.

452 "it was now obvious": W. H. Lewis, *Brothers and Friends*, 245.

453 "Joy, whose intentions . . . the gap between the end": Ibid., 245.

453 "How did I get into this theology racket": Davidman, *Out of My Bone*, 278.

454 "place of unearthly beauty": Lewis, *Collected Letters*, vol. 3, 781.

454 "a v. fine, wild country . . . a 'St. Luke's summer'": Ibid., 797.

455 "I have got something really hellish . . . The X-rays showed": Davidman, *Out of My Bone*, 297.

455 "I never have loved her more": W. H. Lewis, *Brothers and Friends*, 245.

455 "physical agony": Davidman, *Out of My Bone*, 300.

455 "I am trying very hard": Ibid., 306.

455 "a notable act of charity . . . I found it heartrending": W. H. Lewis, *Brothers and Friends*, 246.

456 "a power which . . . Yes, in my legs": Coghill, "Approach to English," 63.

456 "gives me a wonderfully youthful figure": Lewis, *Collected Letters*, vol. 3, 875.

456 "a spiritualist picture": Ibid., 967.

456 "life-giving generosity": Coghill, "Approach to English," 63.

456 "One dreams of a Charles Williams substitution!": Lewis, *Collected Letters*, vol. 3, 901.

456 "hardly any hope": Ibid., 866.

456 "has improved": Ibid., 884.

456 "the improvement in my wife's condition": Ibid., 894.

456 "almost miraculous": Ibid., 903.

457 "by supposing Charles's theory": W. H. Lewis, *Brothers and Friends*, 232.

457 "My heart is breaking": Lewis, *Collected Letters*, vol. 3, 862.

457 "wd. be surprised": Ibid., 837.

457 "we are often . . . something which began in Agape": Ibid., 884.

457 "naturally I shall want": Quoted in Dorsett, *And God Came In*, 147.

457 "remember you as a man . . . If you do not relent": Lewis, *Collected Letters*, vol. 3, 843–45.

458 "the center of his life": Ladborough, "In Cambridge," 103.

458 "for the unlearned": C. S. Lewis, *Reflections on the Psalms* (New York: Harcourt, Brace, 1958), 1.

458 "Christians cry to God": Ibid., 12.

458 "that typically Jewish prison": Ibid., 17.

458 "are indebted": Ibid., 28.

458 "Father of Lights . . . good work": Ibid., 110.

459 "a little more technical equipment . . . only the most tenuous": Joseph Bourke, *Blackfriars* 40 (September 1959): 389–91.

459 "bring in nearly . . . Cartwheel": C. S. Lewis Papers, Bodleian Library, MS Eng. Let. C. 220/4, fol. 28, quoted in Green and Hooper, *C. S. Lewis: A Biography*, 387.

459 "Today I want to discuss": Joy Davidman, letter to Chad and Eva Walsh, *Out of My Bone*, 341.

459 "If people are already unlovable": Lewis, *The Four Loves*, 41.

460 "hard day's walking": Ibid., 72.

460 "Love Himself": Ibid., 128.

460 "vague and fluid . . . a novelist's insights": Martin D'Arcy, "These Things Called Love," *The New York Times Book Review* (July 31, 1960): 4.

461 "more like resurrection": Lewis, *Collected Letters*, vol. 3, 1000.

461 "drunk with blue mountains": Ibid., 967.

461 "like being recaptured by the giant": Ibid., vol. 3, 1101.

461 "Joy was often in pain": Green and Hooper, *C. S. Lewis: A Biography*, 396.

461 "in a *nunc dimittis* frame of mind": Lewis, *Collected Letters*, vol. 3, 1153.

461 "made an Amazon": Ibid.

461 "Don't get me a posh coffin": W. H. Lewis, *Brothers and Friends*, 250.

462 "I shall survive, unembittered . . . it does often strike me as preposterous": Owen Barfield letter, December 29, 1957, Barfield Papers, Bodleian Library, Dep. c. 1055.

463 "exist by virtue": Owen Barfield, *What Coleridge Thought* (Middletown, Conn.: Wesleyan University Press, 1971), 36.

463 "the subjectivity of the individual mind": Owen Barfield, quoted in Sugerman, *Evolution of Consciousness: Studies in Polarity*, 18.

463 "basis of his whole way": Barfield, quoted in ibid., 17.

463 "round box": Owen Barfield, *Worlds Apart: A Dialogue of the 1960's* (Middletown, Conn.: Wesleyan University Press, 1971), 210.

464 "so exciting . . . Your language sometimes disgruntles": Lewis, *Collected Letters*, vol. 3, 1328.

464 "recently deceased . . . a fascinating link": Thomas J. Altizer, review of *Worlds Apart*, *Journal of Bible and Religion* 32, no. 4 (October 1964): 384–85.

464 "metaphor, symbol, language, and problems of communication": Penciled note by Barfield recounting "Origin of U.S Connection," dated August 30, 1963, Barfield Papers, Bodleian Library, Dep. c. 1054.

464 "like starting a new life": Blaxland–de Lange, *Owen Barfield*, 39.

465 "now about 34 years behind . . . wide view": Tolkien, "Valedictory Address to the University of Oxford," 224.

465 "the foundation": Ibid., 225.

465 "the B.Litt. sausage-machine . . . the degeneration": Ibid., 226–27.

465 "the *duguð*": Ibid., 240.

465 "vigorous . . . crotchety": "Tolkien's Farewell," *Oxford Mail* (June 6, 1969): 4.

466 "in many ways a melancholy": Tolkien, *Letters*, 300.

466 "I am in fact utterly stuck": Ibid., 301.

466 "ponderous silliness": Ibid., 302.

466 "Forgive my chattiness": Tolkien Papers, Bodleian Library, quoted in Scull and Hammond, *J.R.R. Tolkien Companion and Guide: Chronology*, 574.

466 "a very pretty book": Quoted in Scull and Hammond, *J.R.R. Tolkien Companion and Guide: Chronology*, 599.

466 "I do not think . . . of course no dragon": Quoted in ibid., 595, 596.

466 "ingenious . . . hurrying rhythm": Alfred Duggan, "Middle Earth Verse," *The Times Literary Supplement* 3169 (November 23, 1962): 892.

467 "something close to genius": Anthony Thwaite, "Hobbitry," *The Listener* 1756 (November 22, 1962): 881.

467 "sagging faith . . . men's hearts": Tolkien, *Letters*, 336–37.

468 "Faith is an act of will . . . demented megalomaniac": Ibid., 337–38.

468 "fell in love . . . the greatest reform": Ibid., 338–40.

469 "plausible English pseudonym": Quoted in Lewis, *Collected Letters*, vol. 3, 1201.

469 "not written with publication": Hooper, *C. S Lewis: A Complete Guide*, 196.

469 "a defence . . . describe a *state*": C. S. Lewis, *A Grief Observed* (New York: Harper-One, 2009), 71.

469 "there are a lot of things": Lewis, *Collected Letters*, vol. 3, 1174.

470 "For those few years": Lewis, *Grief Observed*, 19–20.

470 "appall": Ibid., 29.

470 "the most precious gift": Ibid., 30.

470 "She is, like God": Ibid., 36.

470 "Cosmic Sadist": Ibid., 43.

470 "an instantaneous, unanswerable impression": Ibid., 57.

470 "Turned to God": Ibid., 73.

470–71 "Him as the giver": Ibid., 74.

471 "Not my idea of God": Ibid., 79.

471 "strange, firm magnetism . . . Religion—reassurance": Sylva Norman, "Argument with Sorrow," *The Times Literary Supplement* 3115 (November 10, 1961): 803.

471 "easy tone . . . continually interesting": William Empson, "Professor Lewis on Linguistics," *The Times Literary Supplement* 3057 (September 30, 1960): 627.

471 "unintelligible": Lewis, *Collected Letters*, vol. 3, 1202.

471 "as a substitute": C. S. Lewis, "Undergraduate Criticism," *Broadsheet* (Cambridge) 8, no. 17 (March 9, 1960): [1,] quoted by Walter Hooper in Lewis, *Collected Letters*, vol. 3, 1230. Discussed in an editorial, "Professor C. S. Lewis and the English Faculty," ibid., no. 22 (October 1960): 6–17.

472 "Pecksniffian disingenuousness": *Delta: The Cambridge Literary Magazine* 22 (October 1960): 6–17.

472 "Do not misunderstand": Lewis, letter to the editor, *Delta: The Cambridge Literary Magazine* 23 (February 1961): 4–7, reprinted in Lewis, *Collected Letters*, vol. 3, 1230–35.

472 "shrinking a little": Frank Kermode, "Against Vigilants," *New Statesman* 62, 1599 (November 3, 1961): 658–59. Kermode, who had also incurred the wrath of *Scrutiny*, was impressed by the artful way in which Lewis suggests, without naming names, the particular school of critics he has in mind; moreover, Kermode says, "there is no specific mention of that dreadful Vigilant arrogance which corrupts pleasure and judgment, and which is now available in paperback . . ."

472 "Tell me the date": C. S. Lewis, *An Experiment in Criticism* (Cambridge, UK: Cambridge University Press, 1961, 2004), 105.

472 "No poem will give": Ibid., 94.

472 "permits, invites": Ibid., 104.

473 "an enlargement of our being . . . In reading great literature": Ibid., 137–41.

473 "The saner and greater": I. A. Richards, *Coleridge on Imagination* (London: Kegan Paul, Trench, Trübner, 1934; Bloomington, Ind.: Indiana University Press, 1960), 171.

474 "not to 'think about'": F. R. Leavis, "Literary Criticism and Philosophy," *The Common Pursuit*, 213.

474 "Professor Lewis's own credo": Reginald P. C. Mutter, "The Function of Criticism," *The Times Literary Supplement* 3114 (November 3, 1961): 790.

474 "The actual history of Eng. Lit.": Lewis, *Collected Letters*, vol. 3, 1371.

474 "a perfectly sincere, disinterested, fearless, ruthless fanatic": Ibid., 1372.

475 "C. S. Lewis is dead": Leavis's remark was recorded by D. Keith Mano, quoted in James E. Person, Jr., "The Legacy of C. S. Lewis," *Modern Age* (Summer 1991): 409.

475 "whether we were his pupils": Helen Gardner, review of *The Discarded Image*, *The Listener* 1842 (July 16, 1964): 97.

475 "(a.) Having educated Betjeman": Lewis, *Collected Letters*, vol. 3, 1251.

475 "I never liked Eliot's poetry": Green and Hooper, *C. S. Lewis: A Biography*, 390.

476 "It was a quiet morning": Donald Swann, *Swann's Way: A Life in Song*, quoted in Green and Hooper, *C. S. Lewis: A Biography*, 403.

476 "During the year . . . I drank from": W. H. Lewis, *Brothers and Friends*, 252–53.

477 "a dipsomaniac retired major": Lewis, *Collected Letters*, vol. 3, 1312.

477 "I wear a catheter": Ibid., 1382.

477 If Lewis had taken a leave: See W. H. Lewis, *Brothers and Friends*, 272.

477 "But oh Arthur": Lewis, *Collected Letters*, vol. 3, 1456.

478 "By early October": W. H. Lewis, "Memoir of C. S. Lewis," 45.

478 John F. Kennedy: Kennedy died first, being shot at 12:30 Central Time (USA) and declared dead at 1:00 p.m.; Huxley died at 5:20 Pacific Time (having received two one-hundred milligram injections of LSD during his last hours, administered by

his wife, Laura Huxley); Lewis, as noted, died at about 5:30 p.m. Greenwich Mean Time in Oxford.

19. INKLINGS FIRST AND LAST

479 "time of close communion . . . So far I have felt": Tolkien, *Letters*, 341.

479 "My life continues": W. H. Lewis, *Brothers and Friends*, 254.

479 "SPB": Warnie's curious sobriquet for his brother. The letters stand for Small-piggiebotham (Warnie was the Archpiggiebotham), nicknames ultimately derived from their childhood nurse, Lizzie Endicott. A humorous "Pigiebotian" philosophy evolved between the two brothers, devoted to studied appreciation of inactivity. See Lewis's letter to Warnie, August 2, 1928 (Lewis, *Collected Letters*, vol. 1, 776).

479 "I forget quite important": W. H. Lewis, *Brothers and Friends*, 255.

479 "the absolutely unforgettable": Owen Barfield, "C. S. Lewis," *Owen Barfield on C. S. Lewis*, 3.

480 "You came to him": Owen Barfield, "Moira," *Owen Barfield on C. S. Lewis*, 163.

480 "I find the prospect exciting . . . 2 lectures a week": Letter, Owen Barfield to Philip Mairet, March 28, 1964, Barfield Papers, Bodleian Library, Dep. c. 1074.

480 "rather jumped at": Blaxland–de Lange, *Owen Barfield*, 40.

480 "spoke of Jack . . . flew from Los Angeles": Ibid., 307.

480 "you go at it": Lewis, *Surprised by Joy*, 200.

481 United States poet laureate: From 1937 to 1986, encompassing Nemerov's first term of service, the official title of the post was "Consultant in Poetry to the Library of Congress"; from 1986 to the present day, including Nemerov's second term of service, the title has been "Poet Laureate Consultant in Poetry to the Library of Congress."

481 "ambassador at the court": Donna L. Potts, *Howard Nemerov and Objective Idealism: The Influence of Owen Barfield* (Columbia: University of Missouri Press, 1994), 1.

481 "a strong affinity": Letter, Owen Barfield to Professor Coburn, February 16, 1963, Barfield Papers, Bodleian Library, Dep. c. 1054.

481 "had a muddled life": Barfield, *What Coleridge Thought*, 5.

482 "even my unsatisfactory children . . . I like the work": Blaxland–de Lange, *Owen Barfield*, 305.

482 "an interpenetration": Coleridge, *Biographia Literaria*, chap. 18, quoted in Owen Barfield, *Speaker's Meaning* (Middletown, Conn.: Wesleyan University Press, 1967), 82.

482 "plot": Barfield, *Speaker's Meaning*, 117.

483 "non-spatial relationships": Owen Barfield, *Unancestral Voice* (Middletown, Conn.: Wesleyan University Press, 1965), 143.

483 "stimulating and not infrequently": Ivor Thomas, "Hello Meggid," *The Times Literary Supplement* 3306 (July 8, 1965): 583.

483 "The events and troubles . . . I am at last recovering": Tolkien, letter to Rayner Unwin, May 28, 1964, quoted in Scull and Hammond, *J.R.R. Tolkien Companion and Guide: Chronology*, 618.

483 "I feel his loss": Quoted in Martin Bentham, "Literary Greats Exposed as Gossips and Snipes," *Sunday Telegraph*, February 7, 1999, and then in Scull and Hammond, *J.R.R. Tolkien Companion and Guide: Chronology*, 615.

483 "He was a great man": Tolkien, *Letters*, 341.

484 "a Catholic could not": Quoted in Christie's, *20th-Century Books and Manuscripts*, November 16, 2001, 22, and in Scull and Hammond, *J.R.R. Tolkien Companion and Guide: Chronology*, 612.

484 "And once again": C. S. Lewis, *Letters to Malcolm: Chiefly on Prayer* (New York: Harcourt, Brace & World, 1964), 124.

484 "I personally found": Tolkien, *Letters*, 352.

484 "about prayer": Quoted in A. N. Wilson, *C. S. Lewis*, xvii.

484 "ponderous silliness": Tolkien, *Letters*, 302.

485 "crops up regularly": Quoted in Scull and Hammond, *J.R.R. Tolkien Companion and Guide: Reader's Guide*, 1044.

485 "a remarkable creature . . . till people more aware": Tolkien, *Letters*, 353.

485 "my admiration for": Ibid., 356.

486 "confused": Ibid., 359.

487 "frequently fired verbal": Clyde S. Kilby, *Tolkien & The Silmarillion* (Wheaton, Ill.: Harold Shaw Publishers, 1976), 36.

487 "on a lawn": J.R.R. Tolkien, *Smith of Wootton Major* (London: George Allen & Unwin, 1967; New York: Ballantine Books, 1969), 31–33.

487 "a good tale": Robert Phelps, "For Young Readers," *The New York Times Book Review* (February 4, 1968): 76.

487 "Tolkien needs": Naomi Mitchison, "Why Not Grown-Ups Too?" *Glasgow Herald* (November 25, 1967): 9.

488 Some saw in the hero: For Smith as Anodos, see Mathew Dickerson, "Smith of Wootton Major (Character)," in Drout, *J.R.R. Tolkien Encyclopedia*, 619–20.

488 "an old man's": Tolkien, *Letters*, 389.

488 "periphery": Charles Moorman, *The Precincts of Felicity* (Gainesville: University of Florida Press, 1966), 101.

488 "in days to come": Moorman, *Precincts of Felicity*, 138.

488 "silly . . . frankly absurd": W. H. Lewis, *Brothers and Friends*, 268.

489 "died at the same instant . . . But little did I realize": Ibid., 269.

489 "Hell-hole": Ibid., 255.

490 "busybody . . . withering discourse": Ibid., 256–57. See discussion by Walter Hooper, introduction, *Letters of C. S. Lewis*, 12–17. Hooper's revised and enlarged edition of this book, published in 1988, included more complete versions of the letters Warnie had excerpted.

490 "on my death bed": Ibid., 277.

490 "that nice type": Ibid., 261.

490 "It is rather queer": Letter, Owen Barfield to R. J. Reilly, April 17, 1969, Barfield Papers, Bodleian Library, Dep. c. 1056.

490 "Red Indians . . . not unpleasingly": Quoted in Blaxland–de Lange, *Owen Barfield*, 309.

491 "his researches": G. B. Tennyson, "Barfield and the Rebirth of Meaning," *The Southern Review*, vol. 5, no. 1 (January 1, 1969): 42.

491 "I always felt . . . Towards the end": Letter, Nevill Coghill to Owen Barfield, July 1, 1965, Barfield Papers, Bodleian Library, Dep. c. 1056.

491 "I am so glad . . . since the *Times*": Letter, Colin Hardie to Owen Barfield, November 6, 1979, Barfield Papers, Bodleian Library, Dep. c. 1058. The *Times* had suspended

publication because of a labor dispute in November 1978. It resumed regular publication a week or so after Hardie wrote his letter.

492 "I heard from": Letter, Cecil Harwood to Owen Barfield, April 1972, Barfield Papers, Bodleian Library, Dep. c. 1057.

492 "that I wasn't": Blaxland–de Lange, *Owen Barfield*, 31.

492 "She is not well . . . What a life": Letter, Owen Barfield to Craig Miller, October 31,
1970, Barfield Papers, Bodleian Library, Dep. c. 1074.

492–93 "Contemplating in all . . . Where logical opposites": Barfield, *What Coleridge
Thought*, 35–36.

493 "a full-fledged theory": Ibid., 55

493 "*Yearning* . . . the whole": Ibid., 136–37.

493 "Like Hegel": Ibid., 177.

494 "orderly and lucid": Anthony C. Yu, *Journal of the American Academy of Religion*
42, no. 3 (September 1974): 579.

494 "quite indispensable": G. A. Cevasco, *Studies in Romanticism* 11, no. 2 (Spring
1972): 158.

494 "admirable grasp . . . minds of such dissimilar": John Colmer, *Modern Language
Review* 68, no. 4 (October 1973): 894–95.

495 "I think that receiving": Royal Society of Literature, Report, 1966–1967, 39,
quoted in Scull and Hammond, *J.R.R. Tolkien Companion and Guide: Chronology*, 703.

495 "in a world . . . And after all that has happened": Tolkien, letter of February 8,
1967, to Charlotte and Denis Plimmer commenting on a draft of their interview
with him for *The Daily Telegraph Magazine*, in Tolkien, *Letters*, 378.

495 "found none of them": Tolkien, *Letters*, 372.

496 leg would be amputated: Walter Hooper to the authors, personal interview, July 15,
2006.

496 "a ship or ark": Tolkien, *Letters*, 405.

496 "chaotic and illegible": Christopher Tolkien, "Late Writings," in Tolkien, *Peoples of
Middle-earth*, 294.

496 "'Stories' still sprout": Tolkien, *Letters*, 404.

496 "made his way": Clyde Kilby, "Woodland Prisoner," 13 in Kilby Files, 3–8, Wade
Collection, Wheaton College, Wheaton, Illinois, quoted in Drout, *J.R.R. Tolkien
Encyclopedia*, 89.

496 "things they design": Tolkien, *Letters*, 399.

497 "I am utterly bereaved": Ibid., 415.

497 "she was my": Sotheby's *English Literature and English History*, London, December
6–7, 1984, lot 273, quoted in Scull and Hammond, *J.R.R. Tolkien Companion and
Guide: Chronology*, 758. The Sotheby's catalogue has "raven" as "river"; we, following Scull and Hammond, have given "raven" as the likely correct transcription.

498 "before very long": "Tolkien Seeks the Quiet Life in Oxford," *Oxford Mail*
(March 22, 1972): 10.

498 "as the Road": *Oxford University Gazette*, CII, no. 3511 (June 8, 1972): 1079, quoted
in Lewis, *Collected Letters*, vol. 3, 1681.

498 "terrible words seen": Tolkien, *Letters*, 422.

498 "Peace to her ashes": W. H. Lewis, *Brothers and Friends*, 300.

499 "I have been assailed": Sotheby's *English Literature, History, Private Press & Children's Books*, London, December 12, 2002, 239, quoted in Scull and Hammond, *J.R.R. Tolkien Companion and Guide: Chronology*, 772.

499 "lost confidence . . . sits cold and unable": Tolkien, *Letters*, 431.

500 "the Meggid . . . entirely justified": Saul Bellow, *Letters*, ed. Benjamin Taylor (New York: Viking, 2010), 327–35.

500 "of course there's no guarantee": Letter, Owen Barfield to Friedrich Hiebel, October 25, 1975, Barfield Papers, Bodleian Library, Dep. c. 1057.

500 "a certain daily stability": Bellow, *Letters*, 334.

500 "I couldn't get up": Blaxland–de Lange, *Owen Barfield*, 54.

501 "I can't easily accept": Bellow, *Letters*, 369.

501 "damage . . . a peashooter": Blaxland–de Lange, *Owen Barfield*, 60.

501 "four or five years . . . I will have made": Bellow, *Letters*, 371–72.

501 "excruciating . . . a deep": Owen Barfield, "East, West, and Saul Bellow," *Towards* (Spring 1983): 26–28.

501 "perhaps your understanding . . . hard, militant and angry": Bellow, *Letters*, 399–400.

502 Crown Princess Michiko: See Letter, Raymond P. Tripp, Jr., to Owen Barfield, December 5, 1975, Barfield Papers, Bodleian Library, Dep. c. 1057.

503 unpublished: Both books were published after Barfield's death: Owen Barfield, *Night Operation* ([San Rafael]: Barfield Press, 2009), and Owen Barfield, *Eager Spring* ([U.K.: Barfield Press, 2009).

503 "North America has shown": Owen Barfield, "Information for my Literary Executors, April, 1985," Barfield Papers, Bodleian Library, Dep. c. 1255.

504 to declare her love: See Barfield Archives, especially Box 1058, Bodleian Library.

504 "I just can't imagine . . . I am a bit": Blaxland–de Lange, *Owen Barfield*, 294–95.

504 "once-born . . . see God not": William James, *The Varieties of Religious Experience*, quoted in Gerard Irvine, "David's Religion," in *David Cecil: A Portrait by His Friends*, ed. Hannah Cranborne (Stanbridge, UK: Dovecote Press 1991), 181.

505 "I'm so tired . . . I know what you're sad about": Personal interview with Walter Hooper, July 15, 2006.

EPILOGUE: THE RECOVERED IMAGE

507 "one fine evening": "Is There an Oxford 'School' of Writing? A Discussion Between Rachel Trickett and David Cecil," *The Twentieth Century (formerly the Nineteenth Century & After)* 157, no. 940 (June 1955): 570.

507–508 "there *is* something . . . savour of grace and gracious piety": Ibid., 561–65. See also James Patrick, *The Magdalen Metaphysicals: Idealism and Orthodoxy at Oxford 1901–1945* (Macon, Ga.: Mercer University Press, 1985).

508 more likely to be Christian: See C. S. Lewis, letter to Sister Penelope, Lewis, *Collected Letters*, vol. 2, 701.

508 "Sooner or later": C. S. Lewis, "The Decline of Religion," *The Cherwell* 26 (November 29, 1946): 8–10, reprinted in Lewis, *God in the Dock*. About the signs of a Christian revival at Oxford, Lewis observed, "No one would deny that Christianity is now 'on the map' among the younger intelligentsia as it was not,

say, in 1920. Only freshmen now talk as if the anti-Christian position were self-evident."

508 path of real conversion: Lewis himself was, in Walter Hooper's eyes, "the most thoroughly *converted* man I ever met." Walter Hooper, preface to Lewis, *God in the Dock*, 12.

508 essay in *Books on Trial*: Brady, "Unicorns at Oxford," 59–60.

508 "Lor' bless you": Lewis, *Collected Letters*, vol. 3, 824.

509 "I don't think Tolkien influenced me": Letter to Francis Anderson, Lewis, *Collected Letters*, vol. 3, 1458.

509 "short Xtian Dictionary": Letter to Dorothy L. Sayers, Lewis, *Collected Letters*, vol. 2, 721.

509 "a book of animal stories": Lewis, *Essays Presented to Charles Williams*, xii. See Diana Pavlac Glyer's valuable study *The Company They Keep* (Kent, Ohio: Kent State University Press, 2007) for more on the question of mutual influence.

510 "it has been my nightmare": Germaine Greer, in *W: The Waterstone's Magazine* (Winter/Spring 1997), quoted by Tom Shippey in his foreword to *J.R.R. Tolkien: Author of the Century*, xxii.

511 "I am in fact a *Hobbit*": Tolkien, *Letters*, 288.

511 "O great glory": Tolkien, *Lord of the Rings*, 954.

511 "All my choices have proved ill": Ibid., 604.

BIBLIOGRAPHY

The bibliography provided here includes the editions we consulted in preparing this book. It ranges beyond a "works cited" list, highlighting English-language books of general interest for Inklings studies, but it is not intended to be comprehensive. For more extensive bibliographies and publication histories, we recommend the following resources:

Brazier, Paul. *C. S. Lewis: An Annotated Bibliography and Resource.* Eugene, Ore.: Pickwick Publications, 2012.

Christopher, Joe R., and Joan K. Ostling. *C. S. Lewis: An Annotated Checklist of Writings About Him and His Works.* Kent, Ohio: Kent State University Press, 1974.

Drout, Michael D. C., ed. *J.R.R. Tolkien Encyclopedia: Scholarship and Critical Assessment.* New York: Routledge, 2007.

Glenn, Lois. *Charles W. S. Williams: A Checklist.* Serif Series 33. Kent, Ohio: Kent State University Press, 1975.

Hammond, Wayne G., with the assistance of Douglas A. Anderson. *J.R.R. Tolkien: A Descriptive Bibliography.* New Castle, Del.; Winchester: Oak Knoll Books; St. Paul's Bibliographies, 2013.

Hooper, Walter. *C. S. Lewis: A Complete Guide to His Life and Works.* San Francisco: HarperSanFrancisco, 1996. The definitive resource. Walter Hooper is the editor of some thirty books by Lewis, including the major collections of Lewis's letters. Formerly Lewis's literary executor and literary trustee for the Owen Barfield Estate, he is currently a literary advisor to the Lewis Estate.

Lee, Stuart D., ed. *A Companion to J.R.R. Tolkien.* Malden, Mass.: Wiley-Blackwell, 2014.

Lowenberg, Susan. *C. S. Lewis: A Reference Guide, 1972–1988.* Reference Guide to Literature Series. Toronto: Maxwell Macmillan International, 1993.

MacSwain, Robert, and Michael Ward, eds. *The Cambridge Companion to C. S. Lewis.* Cambridge Companions to Religion. Cambridge, UK, and New York: Cambridge University Press, 2010.

Matthew, H.C.G., and Brian Harrison, eds. *Oxford Dictionary of National Biography: In Association with the British Academy: From the Earliest Times to the Year 2000*. Oxford and New York: Oxford University Press, 2004.

Ruud, Jay. *Critical Companion to J.R.R. Tolkien: A Literary Reference to His Life and Work*. Facts on File Library of World Literature. New York: Facts on File, 2011.

Scull, Christina, and Wayne G. Hammond. *The J.R.R. Tolkien Companion & Guide: Chronology*. Boston and New York: Houghton Mifflin Company, 2006. Christina Scull and Wayne G. Hammond are research librarians and Tolkien scholars whose collaborative works are essential.

Scull, Christina, and Wayne G. Hammond. *The J.R.R. Tolkien Companion & Guide: Reader's Guide*. Boston and New York: Houghton Mifflin, 2006.

Tolkien, Christopher, ed. *The History of Middle-earth*. Published by George Allen & Unwin (London) and Houghton Mifflin (Boston) in twelve volumes (1983–1996) and an index (2002). Christopher Tolkien is the compiler, editor, and custodian of his father's literary legacy. In *The History of Middle-earth*, he reconstructs his father's mythology from a vast body of manuscript material and notes, elucidates the process by which *The Lord of the Rings* was composed, and provides a commentary that is at once historical, biographical, and bibliographical.

In addition, there are valuable bibliographies maintained online by societies devoted to our authors. For links to relevant web resources, the best place to begin is the website of the Marion E. Wade Center: www.wheaton.edu/wadecenter/Authors. The Wade Center—at once archive, library, and museum—houses the major research collection of manuscripts, publications, and other materials by and about Owen Barfield, G. K. Chesterton, C. S. Lewis, George MacDonald, Dorothy L. Sayers, J.R.R. Tolkien, and Charles Williams. The best bibliographic resource for Owen Barfield is maintained by the Owen Barfield Society at http://barfieldsociety.org/Bibliography.htm, with further information available at the website of the Owen Barfield Literary Estate: www.owenbarfield.org/.

For reasons of space, articles and essays cited in our notes have not been listed individually in the bibliography; but we consider the following journals indispensable for Inklings studies:

Christian History (issues devoted to Lewis, Tolkien, and the seven British authors collected and studied at the Wade Center)
Inklings: Jahrbuch für Literatur und Ästhetik (journal of the Inklings Gesellschaft)
The Journal of Inkling Studies
Mythlore (journal of the Mythopoeic Society)
Sehnsucht: The C. S. Lewis Journal
VII [SEVEN]: An Anglo-American Literary Review (annual journal published by the Marion E. Wade Center)
Tolkien Studies: An Annual Scholarly Review
Towards (Anthroposophical/Barfield journal, no longer published)
The Year's Work in English Studies

—and two journals of Elvish Linguistics: *Parma Eldalamberon* and *Vinyar Tengwar* (published by the Elvish Linguistic Fellowship).

There are many other journals and newsletters published by societies—in many lands and languages—devoted to the Inklings individually or together. Links to the major societies may be found on the "Authors" page of the Marion E. Wade Center: www.wheaton.edu/wadecenter/Authors.

In addition to the major mainstream publishers of Inklings books, there are specialty publishers—among them Mythopoeic Press, Walking Tree Publishers, the Barfield Press (UK), the Apocryphile Press, and Lindisfarne Press—whose lists include significant works by and about the Inklings.

The major archival collections are housed at the Marion E. Wade Center, Wheaton College, Wheaton, Illinois; the Bodleian Library, Oxford; and the J.R.R. Tolkien Collection at Marquette University, Milwaukee, Wisconsin.

OWEN BARFIELD: MAJOR WORKS

Barfield, Owen. *A Barfield Reader: Selections from the Writings of Owen Barfield*. Edited by G. B. Tennyson. Hanover: University Press of New England / Wesleyan University Press, 1999.

———. *A Barfield Sampler: Poetry and Fiction*. Edited by Jeanne Clayton Hunter and Thomas Kranidas. Albany: State University of New York Press, 1993.

———. *Eager Spring*. [UK]: Barfield Press, 2009.

———. *History in English Words*. London: Methuen, 1926.

———. *History, Guilt, and Habit*. Middletown, Conn.: Wesleyan University Press, 1981.

———. *Night Operation*. [San Rafael]: Barfield Press, 2009.

———. *Orpheus: A Poetic Drama*. Edited by John C. Ulreich, Jr. West Stockbridge, Mass.: Lindisfarne Press, 1983.

———. *Owen Barfield and the Origin of Language*. Spring Valley, N.Y.: St. George Publications, 1979.

———. *Owen Barfield on C. S. Lewis*. Edited by G. B. Tennyson. Middletown, Conn.: Wesleyan University Press, 1989.

———. *Poetic Diction: A Study in Meaning*. 2nd ed. Middletown, Conn.: Wesleyan University Press, 1973.

———. *The Rediscovery of Meaning, and Other Essays*. Middletown, Conn.: Wesleyan University Press, 1977.

———. *Romanticism Comes of Age*. 1st ed. London: Anthroposophical Publishing Company, 1944.

———. *Romanticism Comes of Age*. Middletown, Conn.: Wesleyan University Press, 1967.

———. *The Rose on the Ash-Heap*. Oxford: Barfield Press, 2009.

———. *Saving the Appearances: A Study in Idolatry*. New York: Harcourt, Brace & World, 1957.

———. *The Silver Trumpet*. Longmont, Colo.: Bookmakers Guild, 1986.

———. *Speaker's Meaning*. 1st ed. Middletown, Conn.: Wesleyan University Press, 1967.

———. *This Ever Diverse Pair*. Edinburgh: Floris Classics, 1985.

———. *Unancestral Voice*. Middletown, Conn.: Wesleyan University Press, 1965.

———. *What Coleridge Thought*. Middletown, Conn.: Wesleyan University Press, 1971.

————. *Worlds Apart: A Dialogue of the 1960's*. Middletown, Conn.: Wesleyan University Press, 1971.

Barfield, Owen, and C. S. Lewis. *Mark vs. Tristram: Correspondence Between C. S. Lewis & Owen Barfield*. Edited by Walter Hooper. [Oxford]: Oxford University C. S. Lewis Society, 1990.

Barfield, Owen, and Rudolf Steiner. *Calendar of the Soul: The Year Participated*. Forest Row, UK: Sophia Books, 2006.

————. *The Case for Anthroposophy: Being Extracts from Von Seelenrätseln=Riddles of the Soul*. Oxford: Barfield Press, 2010.

C. S. LEWIS: MAJOR WORKS

Calabria, Don Giovanni, and C. S. Lewis. *The Latin Letters of C. S. Lewis*. Edited by Martin Moynihan. South Bend, Ind.: St. Augustine's Press, 1998.

————. *Una Gioia Insolita: Lettere Tra Un Prete Cattolico E Un Laico Anglicano*. Edited by Luciano Squizzato. Translated by Patrizia Morelli. Milano: Jaca Books, 1995.

Lewis, C. S. *The Abolition of Man*. San Francisco: HarperSanFrancisco, 2001.

————. *The Allegory of Love: A Study in Medieval Tradition*. London: Geoffrey Cumberlege, Oxford University Press, 1936.

————. *All My Road Before Me: The Diary of C. S. Lewis, 1922–1927*. Edited by Walter Hooper. San Diego: Harcourt, 1991.

————. *Beyond Personality: The Christian Idea of God*. London: Geoffrey Bles, Centenary Press, 1946.

————. *Boxen: The Imaginary World of the Young C. S. Lewis*. Edited by Walter Hooper. 1st American ed. San Diego: Harcourt Brace Jovanovich, 1985.

————. *Broadcast Talks: Reprinted with Some Alterations from Two Series of Broadcast Talks (Right and Wrong: A Clue to the Meaning of the Universe and What Christians Believe) Given in 1941 and 1942*. London: Geoffrey Bles, Centenary Press, 1942.

————. *C. S. Lewis: Essay Collection and Other Short Pieces*. Edited by Lesley Walmsley. London: HarperCollins, 2000.

————. *C. S. Lewis Letters to Children*. Edited by Lyle W. Dorsett and Marjorie Lamp Mead. New York: Macmillan, 1985.

————. *C. S. Lewis's Lost Aeneid: Arms and the Exile*. Edited by A. T. Reyes. New Haven: Yale University Press, 2011.

————. *Christian Reflections*. Reprint ed. Grand Rapids, Mich.: Wm. B. Eerdmans, 1967.

————. *The Collected Letters of C. S. Lewis*. Vol. 1: *Family Letters 1905–1931*. Edited by Walter Hooper. New York: HarperCollins, 2004.

————. *The Collected Letters of C. S. Lewis*. Vol. 2: *Books, Broadcasts, and the War 1931–1949*. Edited by Walter Hooper. New York: HarperCollins, 2004.

————. *The Collected Letters of C. S. Lewis*. Vol. 3: *Narnia, Cambridge, and Joy, 1950–1963*. Edited by Walter Hooper. New York: HarperCollins, 2007.

————. *The Dark Tower, and Other Stories*. Edited by Walter Hooper. San Diego: Harcourt, Brace & Company, 1977.

————. *The Discarded Image: An Introduction to Medieval and Renaissance Literature*. Canto ed. Cambridge, UK: Cambridge University Press, 1994.

————. *English Literature in the Sixteenth Century Excluding Drama: The Completion of the Clark Lectures, Trinity College, Cambridge, 1944.* 1st edition. *Oxford History of English Literature*, edited by F. P. Wilson and Bonamy Dobree. Oxford: Clarendon Press, 1954.

————, ed. *Essays Presented to Charles Williams*. London: Geoffrey Cumberlege, Oxford University Press, 1947.

————. *An Experiment in Criticism.* Cambridge, UK: Cambridge University Press, 2004.

————. *The Four Loves.* New York: Harcourt, 1960.

————. *God in the Dock: Essays on Theology and Ethics.* Edited by Walter Hooper. Grand Rapids, Mich.: Wm. B. Eerdmans, 1970.

————. *The Great Divorce: A Dream.* San Francisco: HarperSanFrancisco, 2001.

————. *A Grief Observed.* New York: HarperOne, 2009.

————. *The Horse and His Boy.* New York: Harper Trophy, 1954.

————. *Image and Imagination: Essays and Reviews.* Edited by Walter Hooper. Cambridge, UK, and New York: Cambridge University Press, 2013.

————. *The Last Battle.* New York: Harper Trophy, 1994.

————. *Letters of C. S. Lewis, Edited and with a Memoir by W. H. Lewis.* Edited by W. H. Lewis and Walter Hooper. Rev. and enl. ed. San Diego: Harcourt, 1988.

————. *The Letters of C. S. Lewis to Arthur Greeves (1914–1963).* Edited by Walter Hooper. New York: Collier Books, 1986.

————. *Letters to an American Lady.* Edited by Clyde S. Kilby. Grand Rapids, Mich.: Wm. B. Eerdmans, 1967.

————. *Letters to Malcolm: Chiefly on Prayer.* 1st American ed. New York: Harcourt, Brace & World, 1964.

————. *The Lion, the Witch, and the Wardrobe.* New York: HarperTrophy, 2002.

————. *The Lion, the Witch, and the Wardrobe: A Story for Children.* London: Geoffrey Bles, 1950.

————. *The Magician's Nephew.* New York: Harper Trophy, 1983.

————. *Mere Christianity.* A Revised and Amplified Edition, with a New Introduction, of the Three Books *Broadcast Talks, Christian Behaviour, and Beyond Personality.* New York: HarperCollins, 2001.

————. *Miracles: A Preliminary Study.* 1st ed. London: Geoffrey Bles, Centenary Press, 1947.

————. *Miracles: A Preliminary Study.* Rev. ed. San Francisco: HarperSanFrancisco, 2001.

————. *Narrative Poems.* Edited by Walter Hooper. San Diego: Harcourt, 1969.

————. *Of Other Worlds: Essays and Stories.* Edited by Walter Hooper. New York: Harcourt Brace Jovanovich, 1975.

————. *On Stories, and Other Essays on Literature.* Edited by Walter Hooper. New York: Harcourt, Brace, 1982.

————. *Out of the Silent Planet.* New York: Scribner, 2003.

————. *Perelandra: A Novel.* Reprint ed. New York: Scribner, 1944.

————. *The Pilgrim's Regress: An Allegorical Apology for Christianity, Reason, and Romanticism.* 3rd ed. London: HarperCollins, 1977.

————. *Poems.* Edited by Walter Hooper. London: Geoffrey Bles, 1964.

————. *A Preface to Paradise Lost*. London: Oxford University Press, 1942.

————. *Present Concerns*. Edited by Walter Hooper. San Diego: Harcourt, 1987.

————. *Prince Caspian: The Return to Narnia*. London: Geoffrey Bles, 1951.

————. *Prince Caspian: The Return to Narnia*. New York: HarperCollins, 1994.

————. *The Problem of Pain*. San Francisco: HarperSanFrancisco, 2001.

————. *Reflections on the Psalms*. New York: Harcourt, Brace, 1958.

————. *Rehabilitations and Other Essays*. London: Oxford University Press, 1939.

————. *The Screwtape Letters: With Screwtape Proposes a Toast*. New York: Harper-Collins, 2009.

————. *Selected Literary Essays*. Edited by Walter Hooper. Cambridge, UK: Cambridge University Press, 1969.

————. *The Silver Chair*. New York: Scholastic, 1987.

————. *Spenser's Images of Life*. Edited by Alastair Fowler. Reprint ed. Cambridge, UK: Cambridge University Press, 1967.

————. *Spirits in Bondage: A Cycle of Lyrics*. Edited by Walter Hooper. San Diego: Harcourt, Brace, 1984.

————. *Studies in Medieval and Renaissance Literature*. Edited by Walter Hooper. Canto ed. Cambridge, UK: Cambridge University Press, 1966.

————. *Studies in Words*. 2nd ed. Cambridge, UK: Cambridge University Press, 1967.

————. *Surprised by Joy: The Shape of My Early Life*. New York: Harcourt, 1955.

————. *That Hideous Strength: A Modern Fairy-Tale for Grown-Ups*. New York: Scribner, 2003.

————. *Till We Have Faces: A Myth Retold*. San Diego: Harcourt, Brace, 1984.

————. *Transposition, and Other Addresses*. London: Geoffrey Bles, 1949.

————. *The Voyage of the Dawn Treader*. New York: Harper Trophy, 1994.

————. *The Weight of Glory and Other Addresses*. Edited by Walter Hooper. Rev. and exp. ed. New York: Collier Books / Macmillan, 1980.

————. *The World's Last Night, and Other Essays*. New York: Harcourt, Brace, 1960.

Tillyard, E.M.W, and C. S Lewis. *The Personal Heresy: A Controversy*. London and New York: Oxford University Press, 1939.

Williams, Charles, and C. S. Lewis. *Arthurian Torso: Containing the Posthumous Fragment of the "Figure of Arthur" by Charles Williams and a Commentary on the Arthurian Poems of Charles Williams, by C. S. Lewis*. London and New York: Oxford University Press, 1952.

J.R.R. TOLKIEN: MAJOR WORKS

Tolkien, J.R.R. *The Adventures of Tom Bombadil, and Other Verses from The Red Book, with Illustrations by Pauline Baynes*. London: George Allen & Unwin, 1962.

————. *Ancrene Wisse: The English Text of the Ancrene Riwle*. Edited from Ms. Corpus Christi College, Cambridge 402. London: Published for the Early English Text Society by Oxford University Press, 1962.

————. *The Annotated Hobbit*. Rev. and exp. ed. annotated by Douglas A. Anderson. Boston: Houghton Mifflin, 2002.

————. *The Art of the Hobbit*. Edited by Wayne G. Hammond and Christina Scull. London: HarperCollins, 2011.

————. *Beowulf and the Critics*. Edited by Michael D. C. Drout. 2nd ed., rev. Tempe: Arizona Center for Medieval and Renaissance Studies, 2011.

————. *Beowulf: A Translation and Commentary: Together with Sellic Spell*. Edited by Christopher Tolkien, 2014.

————. *Bilbo's Last Song: At the Grey Havens*. Boston: Houghton Mifflin, 1990.

————. *The Book of Lost Tales*, Part One. Edited by Christopher Tolkien. The History of Middle-earth. Vol. 1. Boston: Houghton Mifflin, 1984.

————. *The Book of Lost Tales*, Part Two. Edited by Christopher Tolkien. The History of Middle-earth. Vol. 2. London: HarperCollins, 1991.

————. *The English Text of the Ancrene Riwle*. London: Oxford University Press, 1962.

————. *The Fall of Arthur*. Edited by Christopher Tolkien. London: Harper Collins, 2013.

————. *Finn and Hengest: The Fragment and the Episode*. London: Harper Collins, 2006.

————. *The Hobbit, or, There and Back Again*. Boston and New York: Houghton Mifflin, 1997.

————. *The Hobbit: Or, There and Back Again*. 50th-anniversary ed. Boston: Houghton Mifflin, 1987.

————. *The Lays of Beleriand*. Edited by Christopher Tolkien. The History of Middle-earth. Vol. 3. London and Boston: George Allen & Unwin, 1985.

————. *The Legend of Sigurd and Gudrún*. Edited by Christopher Tolkien. London: HarperCollins, 2009.

————. *Letters from Father Christmas*. Edited by Baillie Tolkien. Rev. ed. Boston: Houghton Mifflin, 1999.

————. *The Letters of J.R.R. Tolkien*. Edited by Humphrey Carpenter and Christopher Tolkien. Boston: Houghton Mifflin, 1995.

————. *The Lord of the Rings*. 50th-anniversary 1-vol. ed. London and Boston: Harper-Collins; Houghton Mifflin, 2005.

————. *The Lost Road and Other Writings: Language and Legend Before "The Lord of the Rings."* Edited by Christopher Tolkien. The History of Middle-earth. Vol. 5. London: HarperCollins, 1991.

————. *A Middle English Vocabulary*. Oxford: Clarendon Press, 1922.

————. *The Monsters and the Critics: And Other Essays*. Edited by Christopher Tolkien. London: George Allen & Unwin, 1983.

————. *Morgoth's Ring: The Later Silmarillion*. Part One: *The Legends of Aman*. Edited by Christopher Tolkien. The History of Middle-earth. Vol. 10. Boston: Houghton Mifflin, 1993.

————. *Mr. Bliss*. Boston: Houghton Mifflin, 1983.

————. *Narn I Chîn Húrin: The Tale of the Children of Húrin*. Edited by Christopher Tolkien. Boston: Houghton Mifflin, 2007.

————. *The Old English Exodus*. Edited by Joan Turville-Petre. Oxford: Oxford University Press, 1981.

————. *The Peoples of Middle-earth*. Edited by Christopher Tolkien. The History of Middle-earth. Vol. 12. Boston: Houghton Mifflin, 1996.

————. *Pictures by J.R.R. Tolkien, with a Foreword and Notes by Christopher Tolkien*. Edited by Christopher Tolkien. Boston: Houghton Mifflin, 1979.

————. *Poems and Stories*. Boston: Houghton Mifflin, 1994.

———. *The Return of the Shadow: The History of The Lord of the Rings*, Part One. Edited by Christopher Tolkien. The History of Middle-earth. Vol. 6. London: HarperCollins, 1993.

———. *Roverandom.* Edited by Christina Scull and Wayne G. Hammond. Boston: Houghton Mifflin, 1998.

———. *Sauron Defeated: The End of the Third Age (The History of the Lord of the Rings, Part Four); The Notion Club Papers; and The Drowning Of Anadûnê.* Edited by Christopher Tolkien. The History of Middle-earth. Vol. 9. London: HarperCollins, 1992.

———. *The Shaping of Middle-earth: The Quenta, the Ambarkanta, and the Annals, Together with the Earliest "Silmarillion" and the First Map.* Edited by Christopher Tolkien. The History of Middle-earth. Vol. 4. Boston: Houghton Mifflin, 1986.

———. *The Silmarillion.* Edited by Christopher Tolkien. London and Boston: George Allen & Unwin, 1977.

———. *Sir Gawain and the Green Knight; Pearl; and Sir Orfeo.* London: George Allen & Unwin, 1975.

———. *Smith of Wootton Major; Farmer Giles of Ham.* New York: Ballantine Books, 1969.

———. *Smith of Wootton Major.* Exp. ed. Edited by Verlyn Flieger. London: HarperCollins, 2005.

———. *Tolkien on Fairy-Stories.* Edited by Verlyn Flieger and Douglas A. Anderson. London: HarperCollins, 2008.

———. *The Tolkien Reader.* New York: Ballantine Books, 2001.

———. *The Treason of Isengard: The History of The Lord of the Rings*, Part Two. Edited by Christopher Tolkien. The History of Middle-earth. Vol. 7. London: Unwin Hyman, 1989.

———. *Tree and Leaf.* London: George Allen and Unwin, 1964.

———. *Tree and Leaf: Including the Poem Mythopoeia; The Homecoming of Beorhtnoth, Beorhthelm's Son.* London: HarperCollins, 2001.

———. *Unfinished Tales of Númenor and Middle-earth.* Edited by Christopher Tolkien. Boston: Houghton Mifflin, 1980.

———. *The War of the Jewels: The Later Silmarillion.* Part Two: *The Legends of Beleriand.* Edited by Christopher Tolkien. The History of Middle-earth. Vol. 11. Boston: Houghton Mifflin, 1994.

———. *The War of the Ring: The History of the Lord of the Rings*, Part Three. Edited by Christopher Tolkien. The History of Middle-earth. Vol. 8. London: George Allen & Unwin, 1991.

Tolkien, J.R.R., and E. V. Gordon, eds. *Sir Gawain and the Green Knight.* Oxford: Clarendon Press, 1925.

Tolkien, J.R.R., E. V. Gordon, and others. *Songs for the Philologists.* Privately printed in the Department of English, University College, London, 1936.

CHARLES WILLIAMS: MAJOR WORKS

Williams, Charles. *All Hallows' Eve.* New York: The Noonday Press / Farrar, Straus and Giroux, 1971.

———. *Bacon.* New York: Harper, 1933.

————. *Charles Williams*. Woodbridge, UK: Boydell Press, 1991.

————. *Charles Williams: Essential Writings in Spirituality and Theology*. Edited by Charles C. Hefling. Cambridge, Mass.: Cowley Publications, 1993.

————. *Collected Plays*. London and New York: Oxford University Press, 1963.

————. *Descent into Hell*. New ed. London: Faber & Faber, 1949.

————. *The Descent of the Dove: A Short History of the Holy Spirit in the Church*. London: Longmans, Green, 1939.

————. *The Descent of the Dove: A History of the Holy Spirit in the Church*, with an introduction by W. H. Auden. New York: Meridian Books, 1956.

————. *The Detective Fiction Reviews of Charles Williams, 1930–1935*. Edited by Jared Lobdell. Jefferson, N.C.: McFarland, 2003.

————. *The English Poetic Mind*. Oxford: Clarendon Press, 1932.

————. *The Figure of Beatrice: A Study in Dante*. London: Faber & Faber, 1943.

————. *The Forgiveness of Sins*. London: Geoffrey Bles, 1942.

————. *The Greater Trumps*. New York: Farrar, Straus and Cudahy, 1950.

————. *He Came Down from Heaven: With Which Is Reprinted The Forgiveness of Sins*. Berkeley, Calif.: Apocryphile Press, 2005.

————. *The House of the Octopus*. London: Edinburgh House Press, 1945.

————. *The Image of the City and Other Essays*. Edited by Anne Ridler. London: Oxford University Press, 1958.

————. *James I*. London: A. Barker, 1934.

————. *Letters to Lalage: The Letters of Charles Williams to Lois Lang-Sims*. Kent, Ohio: Kent State University Press, 1989.

————. *Many Dimensions*. Grand Rapids, Mich.: Wm. B. Eerdmans, 1965.

————. *The Masques of Amen House: Together with Amen House Poems and with Selections from the Music for the Masques by Hubert J. Foss*. Edited by David Bratman. Altadena, Calif.: Mythopoeic Press, 2000.

————. *A Myth of Shakespeare*. London: H. Milford, Oxford University Press, 1928.

————, ed. *The New Book of English Verse*. London: Victor Gollancz, 1935.

————. *Outlines of Romantic Theology; with Which Is Reprinted, Religion and Love in Dante: The Theology of Romantic Love*. Edited by Alice Mary Hadfield. Grand Rapids, Mich.: Wm. B. Eerdmans, 1990.

————. *The Place of the Lion*. London: Faber & Faber, 1952.

————. *Poems of Conformity*. London: Oxford University Press, 1917.

————. *Poetry at Present*. Oxford: Clarendon Press, 1930.

————. *Queen Elizabeth I*. London: Duckworth, 1953.

————. *Reason and Beauty in the Poetic Mind*. Oxford: Clarendon Press, 1933.

————. *The Region of the Summer Stars*. London and New York: Oxford University Press, 1969.

————. *Rochester*. London: A. Barker, 1935.

————. *Seed of Adam: And Other Plays*. London and New York: Oxford University Press, 1954.

————. *Selected Writings*. Edited by Anne Ridler. London: Oxford University Press, 1961.

————. *Shadows of Ecstasy*. New York: Pellegrini & Cudahy, 1950.

————. *The Silver Stair*. London: Herbert & Daniel, 1912.

————. *Taliessin Through Logres: And The Region of the Summer Stars.* London: Oxford University Press, 1954.

————. *Thomas Cranmer of Canterbury.* London: H. Milford, Oxford University Press, 1936.

————. *To Michal from Serge: Letters from Charles Williams to His Wife, Florence, 1939–1945.* Edited by Roma A. King. Kent, Ohio: Kent State University Press, 2002.

————. *War in Heaven.* New York: Pellegrini & Cudahy, 1949.

————. *Witchcraft.* Meridian Books, 1959.

Williams, Charles, and C. S. Lewis. *Arthurian Torso: Containing the Posthumous Fragment of the "Figure of Arthur" by Charles Williams and a Commentary on the Arthurian Poems of Charles Williams, by C. S. Lewis.* London and New York: Oxford University Press, 1952.

OWEN BARFIELD: WORKS ABOUT

Adey, Lionel. *C. S. Lewis' "Great War" with Owen Barfield.* Wigton, UK: Ink Books, 2002.

Blaxland–de Lange, Simon. *Owen Barfield: Romanticism Come of Age, a Biography.* Forest Row, UK: Temple Lodge, 2006.

Diener, Astrid. *The Role of Imagination in Culture and Society: Owen Barfield's Early Work.* Glienicke, Berlin: Galda+Wilch, 2002.

Hammond, Wayne G. *C. S. Lewis–Owen Barfield: A Souvenir Book for the Centenary Celebration Held at Wheaton, Illinois, July 15–20, 1998.* Altadena, Calif.: Mythopoeic Society, 1998.

Potts, Donna L. *Howard Nemerov and Objective Idealism: The Influence of Owen Barfield.* Columbia: University of Missouri Press, 1994.

Sugerman, Shirley. *Evolution of Consciousness: Studies in Polarity.* Middletown, Conn.: Wesleyan University Press, 1976.

Tennyson, G. B., and David Lavery. *Owen Barfield: Man and Meaning.* Encino, Calif.: OwenArts, 1995.

Tennyson, G. B. *Owen Barfield: Man and Meaning, Transcript of the Award-Winning Documentary Video.* Encino, Calif.: OwenArts, 1995.

C. S. LEWIS: WORKS ABOUT

Adey, Lionel. *C. S. Lewis, Writer, Dreamer, and Mentor.* Grand Rapids, Mich.: Wm. B. Eerdmans, 1998.

————. *C. S. Lewis' "Great War" with Owen Barfield.* Wigton, UK: Ink Books, 2002.

Armstrong, Chris. *Medieval Wisdom: An Exploration with C. S. Lewis.* Grand Rapids, Mich.: Baker Academic, forthcoming.

Baggett, David J., Gary R. Habermas, Jerry L. Walls, and Thomas V. Morris, eds. *C. S. Lewis as Philosopher: Truth, Goodness and Beauty.* 1st ed. Downers Grove, Ill.: IVP Academic, 2008.

Barfield, Owen. *Owen Barfield on C. S. Lewis.* Edited by G. B. Tennyson. Middletown, Conn.: Wesleyan University Press, 1989.

Barkman, Adam. *C. S. Lewis & Philosophy as a Way of Life: A Comprehensive Historical Examination of His Philosophical Thought.* Wayne, Pa.: Zossima Press, 2009.

Bassham, Gregory, and Jerry L. Walls, eds. *The Chronicles of Narnia and Philosophy: The Lion, the Witch, and the Worldview.* Popular Culture and Philosophy. Vol. 15. Chicago: Open Court, 2005.

Beversluis, John. *C. S. Lewis and the Search for Rational Religion.* Grand Rapids, Mich.: Wm. B. Eerdmans, 1985.

Bloom, Harold, ed. *C. S. Lewis.* New York: Chelsea House, 2006.

———, ed. *C. S. Lewis's The Chronicles of Narnia.* New York: Chelsea House, 2006.

Boyd, Ian, ed. *The Chesterton Review: C. S. Lewis Special Issue.* Saskatoon, Sask.: Chesterton Review, 1991.

Brazier, Paul. *C. S. Lewis: An Annotated Bibliography and Resource.* Eugene, Ore.: Pickwick Publications, 2012.

———. *C. S. Lewis—on the Christ of a Religious Economy: I. Creation and Sub-Creation.* Eugene, Ore.: Pickwick Publications, 2013.

Carpenter, Humphrey. *The Inklings: C. S. Lewis, J.R.R. Tolkien, Charles Williams and Their Friends.* London: HarperCollins, 1997.

Christopher, Joe R. *C. S. Lewis.* Boston: Twayne, 1987.

Christopher, Joe R., and Joan K. Ostling. *C. S. Lewis: An Annotated Checklist of Writings About Him and His Works.* Kent, Ohio: Kent State University Press, 1974.

Como, James T., ed. *C. S. Lewis at the Breakfast Table, and Other Reminiscences.* New ed. San Diego: Harcourt Brace Jovanovich, 1992.

Derrick, Christopher. *C. S. Lewis and the Church of Rome: A Study in Proto-Ecumenism.* San Francisco: Ignatius Press, 1981.

Downing, David C. *Planets in Peril: A Critical Study of C. S. Lewis's Ransom Trilogy.* Amherst: University of Massachusetts Press, 1992.

Duriez, Colin. *C. S. Lewis: A Biography of Friendship.* Oxford: Lion Hudson, 2013.

———. *The C. S. Lewis Chronicles: The Indispensable Biography of the Creator of Narnia, Full of Little-Known Facts, Events and Miscellany.* New York: BlueBridge, 2005.

———. *Tolkien and C. S. Lewis: The Gift of Friendship.* Mahwah, N.J.: HiddenSpring, 2003.

Edwards, Bruce L., ed. *C. S. Lewis: Life, Works, and Legacy.* 4 vols. Westport, Conn.: Praeger, 2007.

———, ed. *The Taste of the Pineapple: Essays on C. S. Lewis as Reader, Critic, and Imaginative Writer.* Bowling Green, Ohio: Bowling Green State University Popular Press, 1988.

Ford, Paul F. *Companion to Narnia: A Complete Guide to the Magical World of C. S. Lewis's The Chronicles of Narnia.* Rev. and exp. ed. New York: HarperCollins, 2005.

Gibb, Jocelyn, ed. *Light on C. S. Lewis.* New York and London: Harcourt Brace Jovanovich, 1965.

Gilbert, Douglas R., and Clyde S. Kilby. *C. S. Lewis: Images of His World.* Grand Rapids, Mich.: Wm. B. Eerdmans, 2005.

Gilchrist, K. J. *A Morning After War: C. S. Lewis & WW I.* New York: Peter Lang, 2005.

Graham, David, ed. *We Remember C. S. Lewis: Essays and Memoirs.* Nashville, Tenn.: Broadman & Holman Publishers, 2001.

Green, Roger Lancelyn, and Walter Hooper. *C. S. Lewis: A Biography.* Fully rev. and exp. ed. London: HarperCollins, 2002.

Gresham, Douglas H. *Lenten Lands.* New York: Macmillan, 1988.

Hannay, Margaret P. *C. S. Lewis.* New York: Ungar, 1981.

Hardy, Elizabeth Baird. *Milton, Spenser and The Chronicles of Narnia: Literary Sources for the C. S. Lewis Novels.* Jefferson, N.C.: McFarland, 2007.

Harwood, Laurence. *C. S. Lewis, My Godfather: Letters, Photos, and Recollections.* Downers Grove, Ill.: IVP Press, 2007.

Hooper, Walter. *C. S. Lewis: A Complete Guide to His Life and Works.* San Francisco: HarperSanFrancisco, 1996.

——. *Past Watchful Dragons: The Narnian Chronicles of C. S. Lewis.* New York: Collier Books, 1979.

——. *Through Joy and Beyond: A Pictorial Biography of C. S. Lewis.* New York: Collier Books, 1982.

Howard, Thomas. *The Achievement of C. S. Lewis.* Wheaton, Ill: Harold Shaw, 1980.

Jacobs, Alan. *The Narnian: The Life and Imagination of C. S. Lewis.* New York: HarperSanFrancisco, 2005.

Keefe, Carolyn, and Thomas Howard. *C. S. Lewis: Speaker & Teacher.* Grand Rapids, Mich.: Zondervan, 1980.

King, Don W. *C. S. Lewis, Poet: The Legacy of His Poetic Impulse.* Rev. and exp. ed. Kent, Ohio: The Kent State University Press, 2001.

Kort, Wesley A. *C. S. Lewis Then and Now.* Oxford and New York: Oxford University Press, 2001.

Lawlor, John. *C. S. Lewis: Memories and Reflections.* Dallas, Tex.: Spence, 1998.

Lobdell, Jared. *The Scientifiction Novels of C. S. Lewis: Space and Time in the Ransom Stories.* Jefferson, N.C.: McFarland, 2004.

Lowenberg, Susan. *C. S. Lewis: A Reference Guide, 1972–1988.* Toronto: Maxwell Macmillan International, 1993.

MacSwain, Robert, and Michael Ward, eds. *The Cambridge Companion to C. S. Lewis.* Cambridge, UK, and New York: Cambridge University Press, 2010.

Manlove, C. N. *The Chronicles of Narnia: The Patterning of a Fantastic World.* New York: Twayne, 1993.

McGrath, Alister E. *C. S. Lewis—A Life: Eccentric Genius, Reluctant Prophet.* Carol Stream, Ill.: Tyndale House, 2013.

——. *The Intellectual World of C. S. Lewis.* Chichester, UK: Wiley-Blackwell, 2014.

McLaughlin, Sara Park. *A Word Index to the Poetry of C. S. Lewis.* West Cornwall, Conn.: Locust Hill Press, 1988.

Moorman, Charles. *The Precincts of Felicity: The Augustinian City of the Oxford Christians.* Gainesville: University of Florida Press, 1966.

Myers, Doris T. *Bareface: A Guide to C. S. Lewis's Last Novel.* Columbia: University of Missouri Press, 2004.

——. *C. S. Lewis in Context.* Kent, Ohio: Kent State University Press, 1994.

Pearce, Joseph. *C. S. Lewis and the Catholic Church.* San Francisco: Ignatius Press, 2003.

Phillips, Justin. *C. S. Lewis in a Time of War: The World War II Broadcasts That Riveted a Nation and Became the Classic Mere Christianity.* San Francisco: HarperSanFrancisco, 2002.

Poe, Harry Lee, and Rebecca Whitten Poe, eds. *C. S. Lewis Remembered: Collected Reflections of Students, Friends & Colleagues.* Grand Rapids, Mich.: Zondervan, 2006.

Reppert, Victor. *C. S. Lewis's Dangerous Idea: In Defense of the Argument from Reason.* Downers Grove, Ill.: IVP Academic, 2003.

Sayer, George. *Jack: A Life of C. S. Lewis.* 2nd ed. Wheaton, Ill.: Crossway Books, 1994.

Sayers, Dorothy L., ed. *Essays Presented to Charles Williams.* Freeport, N.Y.: Books for Libraries Press, 1972.

Schakel, Peter J. *Imagination and the Arts in C. S. Lewis: Journeying to Narnia and Other Worlds.* Columbia: University of Missouri Press, 2002.

———, ed. *The Longing for a Form: Essays on the Fiction of C. S. Lewis.* Kent, Ohio: Kent State University Press, 1977.

———. *The Way into Narnia: A Reader's Guide.* Grand Rapids, Mich.: Wm. B. Eerdmans, 2005.

Schofield, Stephen, ed. *In Search of C. S. Lewis.* South Plainfield, N.J.: Bridge Publishing, 1983.

Schwartz, Sanford. *C. S. Lewis on the Final Frontier: Science and the Supernatural in the Space Trilogy.* Oxford and New York: Oxford University Press, 2009.

Walsh, Chad. *C. S. Lewis: Apostle to the Skeptics.* New York: Macmillan, 1949.

———. *Chad Walsh Reviews C. S. Lewis.* Altadena, Calif.: Mythopoeic Press, 1998.

———. *The Literary Legacy of C. S. Lewis.* New York and London: Harcourt Brace Jovanovich, 1979.

Ward, Michael. *Planet Narnia: The Seven Heavens in the Imagination of C. S. Lewis.* New York: Oxford University Press, 2008.

Williams, Rowan. *The Lion's World: A Journey into the Heart of Narnia.* New York: Oxford University Press, 2012.

Wilson, A. N. *C. S. Lewis: A Biography.* 1st American ed. New York and London: W. W. Norton, 1990.

Wolfe, Judith, and Brendan N. Wolfe, eds. *C. S. Lewis and the Church: Essays in Honour of Walter Hooper.* London and New York: T & T Clark, 2012.

———. *C.S. Lewis's Perelandra: Reshaping the Image of the Cosmos.* Kent, Ohio: Kent State University Press, 2013.

J.R.R. TOLKIEN: WORKS ABOUT

Allan, Jim, ed. *An Introduction to Elvish.* Glenfinnan, UK: Bran's Head Books, 1978.

Atherton, Mark. *There and Back Again: J.R.R. Tolkien and the Origins of the Hobbit.* London and New York: I. B. Tauris, 2012.

Bailey, Derek. *J.R.R.T.: A Study of John Ronald Reuel Tolkien, 1892–1973.* London: Visual Corporation, 1992.

Bassham, Gregory, and Bronson, Eric. *The Lord of the Rings and Philosophy: One Book to Rule Them All.* Chicago: Open Court, 2003.

Birzer, Bradley J. *J.R.R. Tolkien's Sanctifying Myth: Understanding Middle-earth.* Wilmington, Del.: ISI Books, 2002.

Bloom, Harold. *J.R.R. Tolkien.* Philadelphia: Chelsea House, 2000.

———. *J.R.R. Tolkien's The Lord of the Rings.* Philadelphia: Chelsea House, 2000.

Boyd, Ian, and Stratford Caldecott, eds. *A Hidden Presence: The Catholic Imagination of J.R.R. Tolkien.* South Orange, N.J.: Chesterton Press, 2003.

Caldecott, Stratford. *The Power of the Ring: The Spiritual Vision Behind* The Hobbit *and* The Lord of the Rings. New York: Crossroad, 2012.

Caldecott, Stratford, and Thomas Honegger, eds. *Tolkien's The Lord of the Rings: Sources of Inspiration*. Zurich: Walking Tree Publishers, 2008.

Cantor, Norman F. *Inventing the Middle Ages: The Lives, Works, and Ideas of the Great Medievalists of the Twentieth Century*. New York: William Morrow, 1991.

Carpenter, Humphrey. *Tolkien: The Authorized Biography*. Boston: Houghton Mifflin, 1977.

Chance, Jane. *Tolkien and the Invention of Myth: A Reader*. Lexington: University Press of Kentucky, 2004.

———, ed. *Tolkien the Medievalist*. London and New York: Routledge, 2003.

———. *Tolkien's Art: A Mythology for England*. New York: St. Martin's Press, 1979.

Chance, Jane, and Alfred K Siewers, eds. *Tolkien's Modern Middle Ages*. New York: Palgrave Macmillan, 2005.

Clark, George, and Daniel Timmons. *J.R.R. Tolkien and His Literary Resonances: Views of Middle-earth*. Westport, Conn.: Praeger, 2000.

Croft, Janet Brennan, ed. *Tolkien on Film: Essays on Peter Jackson's The Lord of the Rings*. Altadena, Calif.: Mythopoeic Press, 2004.

———. *Tolkien and Shakespeare: Essays on Shared Themes and Languages*. Jefferson, N.C.: McFarland, 2007.

———. *War and the Works of J.R.R. Tolkien*. Westport, Conn.: Praeger, 2004.

Curry, Patrick. *Defending Middle-earth: Tolkien, Myth and Modernity*. New York: St. Martin's Press, 1997.

Drout, Michael D. C., ed. *J.R.R. Tolkien Encyclopedia: Scholarship and Critical Assessment*. New York: Routledge, 2007.

Ferré, Vincent, ed. *Dictionnaire Tolkien*. Paris: CNRS Éditions, 2012.

Fimi, Dimitra. *Tolkien, Race, and Cultural History: From Fairies to Hobbits*. New York: Palgrave Macmillan, 2009.

Fisher, Jason. *Tolkien and the Study of His Sources: Critical Essays*. Jefferson, N.C.: McFarland, 2012.

Flieger, Verlyn. *A Question of Time: J.R.R. Tolkien's Road to Faërie*. Kent, Ohio: Kent State University Press, 1997.

———. *Green Suns and Faërie: Essays on Tolkien*. Kent, Ohio: Kent State University Press, 2012.

———. *Interrupted Music: The Making of Tolkien's Mythology*. Kent, Ohio: Kent State University Press, 2005.

———. *Splintered Light: Logos and Language in Tolkien's World*. Kent, Ohio: Kent State University Press, 2002.

Flieger, Verlyn, and Carl F. Hostetter. *Tolkien's Legendarium: Essays on the History of Middle-earth*. Westport, Conn., and London: Greenwood Press, 2000.

Garth, John. *Tolkien and the Great War: The Threshold of Middle-earth*. Boston: Houghton Mifflin, 2003.

Gilliver, Peter, Jeremy Marshall, and E.S.C. Weiner. *The Ring of Words: Tolkien and the Oxford English Dictionary*. Oxford and New York: Oxford University Press, 2006.

Hammond, Wayne G., with the assistance of Douglas A. Anderson. *J.R.R. Tolkien: A Descriptive Bibliography*. New Castle, Del.: Oak Knoll Press, 2013.

Hammond, Wayne G., and Christina Scull. *The Art of The Hobbit by J.R.R. Tolkien*. London: HarperCollins, 2011.

———. *J.R.R. Tolkien: Artist & Illustrator*. Boston and New York: Houghton Mifflin, 1995.

———. *The Lord of the Rings: A Reader's Companion*. Boston and New York: Houghton Mifflin, 2005.

———, eds. *The Lord of the Rings, 1954–2004: Scholarship in Honor of Richard E. Blackwelder*. Milwaukee, Wis.: Marquette University Press, 2006.

Houghton, John Wm., Janet Brennan Croft, Nancy Martsch, John D. Rateliff, and Robin Anne Reid, eds. *Tolkien in the New Century: Essays in Honor of Tom Shippey*. Jefferson, N.C.: McFarland, 2014.

Isaacs, Neil David, and Rose A. Zimbardo. *Tolkien, New Critical Perspectives*. Lexington: University Press of Kentucky, 1981.

Johnson, Judith Anne. *J.R.R. Tolkien: Six Decades of Criticism*. Westport, Conn.: Greenwood Press, 1986.

———. *J.R.R. Tolkien: Six Decades of Criticism*. Westport, Conn.: Greenwood Press, 1986.

Kane, Douglas Charles. *Arda Reconstructed: The Creation of the Published Silmarillion*. Bethlehem, Penn.: Lehigh University Press, 2011.

Kilby, Clyde S. *Tolkien & The Silmarillion*. Wheaton, Ill.: Harold Shaw, 1976.

Kocher, Paul H. *Master of Middle-earth: The Fiction of J.R.R. Tolkien*. Boston: Houghton Mifflin, 1972.

Lee, Stuart D., ed. *A Companion to J. R. R. Tolkien*. Malden, Mass.: John Wiley & Sons, 2014.

———. *The Keys of Middle-earth: Discovering Medieval Literature Through the Fiction of J.R.R. Tolkien*. Basingstoke, UK: Palgrave Macmillan, 2005.

Lobdell, Jared, ed. *A Tolkien Compass*. 2nd ed. Chicago: Open Court, 2003.

Milbank, Alison. *Chesterton and Tolkien as Theologians: The Fantasy of the Real*. London and New York: T & T Clark, 2007.

Moseley, Charles. *J.R.R. Tolkien*. Plymouth, UK: Northcote House, in association with the British Council, 1997.

Noel, Ruth S. *The Languages of Tolkien's Middle-earth*. Boston: Houghton Mifflin, 1980.

Pearce, Joseph, ed. *Tolkien—a Celebration: Collected Writings on a Literary Legacy*. San Francisco: Ignatius Press, 2001.

Priestman, Judith. *J.R.R. Tolkien: Life and Legend. An Exhibition to Commemorate the Centenary of the Birth of J.R.R. Tolkien (1892–1973)*. Oxford: Bodleian Library, 1992.

Rateliff, John D. *The History of the Hobbit*. Part Two: *Return to Bag-End*. Boston: Houghton Mifflin, 2007.

Reynolds, Patricia, and Glen GoodKnight, eds. *Proceedings of the J.R.R. Tolkien Centenary Conference, 1992: Proceedings of the Conference Held at Keble College, Oxford, England, 17th–24th August 1992 to Celebrate the Centenary of the Birth of Professor J.R.R. Tolkien, Incorporating the 23rd Mythopoeic Conference (Mythcon XXIII) and Oxonmoot 1992*. Milton Keynes: Tolkien Society; Altadena, Calif.: Mythopoeic Press, 1995.

Rosebury, Brian. *Tolkien: A Cultural Phenomenon*. Basingstoke, UK: Palgrave Macmillan, 2003.

Ruud, Jay. *Critical Companion to J.R.R. Tolkien: A Literary Reference to His Life and Work*. New York: Facts on File, 2011.

Salu, Mary, and Robert T. Farrell, eds. *J.R.R. Tolkien, Scholar and Storyteller: Essays in Memoriam*. Ithaca and London: Cornell University Press, 1979.

Sassoon, Siegfried. *Memoirs of an Infantry Officer*. London: Faber & Faber, 1930.

Scull, Christina, and Wayne G. Hammond. *The J.R.R. Tolkien Companion and Guide: Chronology.* Boston and New York: Houghton Mifflin, 2006.

———. *The J.R.R. Tolkien Companion and Guide: Reader's Guide.* Boston and New York: Houghton Mifflin, 2006.

Shippey, T. A. *Roots and Branches: Selected Papers on Tolkien.* [Zurich]: Walking Tree, 2007.

Shippey, Tom. *J.R.R. Tolkien: Author of the Century.* Boston: Houghton Mifflin, 2000.

———. *The Road to Middle-earth: How J.R.R. Tolkien Created a New Mythology.* Rev. and exp. ed. Boston and New York: Houghton Mifflin, 2003.

Solopova, Elizabeth. *Languages, Myths and History: An Introduction to the Linguistic and Literary Background of J.R.R. Tolkien's Fiction.* [S.I.]: North Landing Books, 2009.

Tolkien, J.R.R., Marquette University, Patrick and Beatrice Haggerty Museum of Art, Marquette University, S.J. Library John P. Raynor, and Department of Special Collections and University Archives. *The Invented Worlds of J.R.R. Tolkien: Drawings and Original Manuscripts from the Marquette University Collection, October 21, 2004–January 30, 2005, Patrick and Beatrice Haggerty Museum of Art, Marquette University, Milwaukee, Wisconsin.* Milwaukee: The Museum, 2004.

Tolkien, John, and Priscilla Tolkien. *The Tolkien Family Album.* Boston: Houghton Mifflin, 1992.

Turner, Allan. *The Silmarillion: Thirty Years On.* Edited by Allan Turner. [Zurich]: Walking Tree, 2007.

Unwin, Rayner. *The Making of The Lord of the Rings.* Oxford: Willem A. Meeuws, 1992.

Wells, Sarah, ed. *The Ring Goes Ever On: Proceedings of the Tolkien 2005 Conference—Celebrating 50 Years of the Lord of the Rings.* 2 vols. Coventry, UK: Tolkien Society, 2008.

West, Richard C. *Tolkien Criticism: An Annotated Checklist.* Kent, Ohio: Kent State University Press, 1970.

———. *Tolkien Criticism: An Annotated Checklist.* Rev. ed. Kent, Ohio: Kent State University Press, 1981.

Wilson, Edmund. *The Bit Between My Teeth: A Literary Chronicle of 1950–1965.* New York: Farrar, Straus and Giroux, 1965.

Wood, Ralph C. *The Gospel According to Tolkien: Visions of the Kingdom in Middle-earth.* Louisville, Ky.: Westminster John Knox Press, 2003.

Zettersten, Arne. *J.R.R. Tolkien's Double Worlds and Creative Process: Language and Life.* New York: Palgrave Macmillan, 2011.

Zimbardo, Rose A., and Neil David Isaacs, eds. *Understanding The Lord of the Rings: The Best of Tolkien Criticism.* New York: Houghton Mifflin, 2004.

CHARLES WILLIAMS: WORKS ABOUT

Ashenden, Gavin. *Charles Williams: Alchemy and Integration.* Kent, Ohio: Kent State University Press, 2008.

Bray, Suzanne, and Richard Sturch, eds. *Charles Williams and His Contemporaries.* Newcastle upon Tyne, UK: Cambridge Scholars, 2009.

Glenn, Lois. *Charles W. S. Williams: A Checklist.* Kent, Ohio: Kent State University Press, 1975.

Hadfield, Alice Mary. *Charles Williams: An Exploration of His Life and Work*. New York: Oxford University Press, 1983.

———. *An Introduction to Charles Williams*. London: Robert Hale, 1959.

Heath-Stubbs, John. *Charles Williams*. London: Longmans, Green, 1955.

Howard, Thomas. *The Novels of Charles Williams*. New York: Oxford University Press, 1983.

Moorman, Charles. *Arthurian Triptych: Mythic Materials in Charles Williams, C. S. Lewis, and T. S. Eliot*. New York: Russell & Russell, 1973.

Shideler, Mary McDermott. *The Theology of Romantic Love: A Study of the Writings of Charles Williams*. New York: Harper, 1962.

Williams, Charles. *Charles Williams*. Woodbridge, UK, and Rochester, N.Y.: Boydell Press, 1991.

OTHER WORKS BY, ABOUT, AND RELATED TO THE INKLINGS

Allitt, Patrick. *Catholic Converts: British and American Intellectuals Turn to Rome*. Ithaca, N.Y.: Cornell University Press, n.d.

Allott, Kenneth, ed. *The Penguin Book of Contemporary Verse*. Harmondsworth: Penguin Books, 1950.

Anderson, Douglas A. *Tales Before Narnia: The Roots of Modern Fantasy and Science Fiction*. New York: Del Rey, 2008.

———. *Tales Before Tolkien: The Roots of Modern Fantasy*. New York: Del Rey, 2003.

Anglo-Catholic Congress. *Report of the Anglo-Catholic Congress. Subject: The Holy Eucharist. London, July, 1927*. Milwaukee, Wis.: Morehouse Publishing, 1927.

Annan, Noel. *The Dons: Mentors, Eccentrics, and Geniuses*. Chicago: University of Chicago Press, 1999.

———. *Our Age: English Intellectuals between the World Wars—a Group Portrait*. New York: Random House, 1990.

Anscombe, G.E.M. *The Collected Philosophical Papers of G.E.M. Anscombe*. Vol. 2: *Metaphysics and Philosophy of Mind*. Oxford: Blackwell, 1981.

Arnold, Matthew. *Essays, Letters, and Reviews*. Edited by Fraser Neiman. Cambridge, Mass.: Harvard University Press, 1960.

Atlas, James. *Bellow: A Biography*. New York: Random House, 2000.

Auden, W. H. *The Dyer's Hand and Other Essays*. London: Faber & Faber, 1963.

Beerbohm, Max. *The Works of Max Beerbohm*. Edited by John Lane. London: John Lane, The Bodley Head, 1921.

Bellow, Saul. *Saul Bellow: Letters*. Edited by Benjamin Taylor. New York: Viking, 2010.

Bellows, Henry Adams, ed. *The Poetic Edda*. Princeton, N.J.: Princeton University Press, 1936.

Bennett, J.A.W. *Chaucer at Oxford and at Cambridge*. Oxford: Clarendon Press, 1974.

———. *Early Middle English Verse and Prose*. Oxford: Clarendon Press, 1966.

———. *The Humane Medievalist: An Inaugural Lecture*. London and New York: Cambridge University Press, 1965.

———. *Middle English Literature*. Oxford History of English Literature, vol. 1, pt. 2. Oxford: Oxford University Press, 1986.

Bentley, Eric. *The Importance of Scrutiny; Selections from Scrutiny: A Quarterly Review, 1932–1948*. New York: New York University Press, 1964.

Bergonzi, Bernard. *Exploding English: Criticism, Theory, Culture.* Oxford: Oxford University Press, 1990.

Betjeman, John. *Collected Poems.* New York: Farrar, Straus and Giroux, 2006.

Bosanquet, Bernard. *Some Suggestions in Ethics.* London: Macmillan, 1918.

Brabazon, James. *Dorothy L. Sayers: A Biography.* New York: Scribner, 1981.

Burckhardt, Jacob. *Die Cultur der Renaissance in Italien: Ein Versuch.* Vienna: E. A. Seemann, 1885.

Butterfield, Herbert. *The Origins of Modern Science, 1300–1800.* London: G. Bell, 1949.

Carey, John. *The Unexpected Professor: An Oxford Life in Books.* London: Faber & Faber, 2014.

Carpenter, Humphrey. *The Inklings: C. S. Lewis, J.R.R. Tolkien, Charles Williams and Their Friends.* London: HarperCollins, 1997.

———. *Secret Gardens: A Study of the Golden Age of Children's Literature.* Boston: Houghton Mifflin, 1985.

Cecil, David. *The English Poets.* London: Collins, 1947.

———. *The Fine Art of Reading: And Other Literary Studies.* Indianapolis: Bobbs-Merrill, 1957.

———. *Lord M.; Or, The Later Life of Lord Melbourne.* London: Constable, 1954.

———. *Max: A Biography.* London: Constable, 1964.

———. *Melbourne.* Indianapolis: Bobbs-Merrill, 1954.

———. *The Stricken Deer; Or, The Life of Cowper.* London: Constable, 1930.

———. *Walter de la Mare.* English Association (Great Britain) Presidential Address 1973. London and New York: Oxford University Press, 1973.

Chaucer, Geoffrey. *The Canterbury Tales.* Translated by Nevill Coghill. Illustrated ed. London: Cresset Press, 1992.

Chesterton, G. K. *Alarms and Discursions.* New York: Dodd, Mead, 1911.

———. *The Defendant.* New York: Dodd, Mead, 1902.

———. *The Everlasting Man.* New York: Dodd, Mead, 1925.

———. *Orthodoxy.* London: John Lane, The Bodley Head, 1908.

Childs, Donald J. *T. S. Eliot: Mystic, Son, and Lover.* New York: St. Martin's Press, 1997.

Churchill, Randolph S., and Martin Gilbert. *Winston S. Churchill.* Vol. 6: *Finest Hour, 1939–1941.* London: Heinemann, 1983.

Churchill, Winston. *Into Battle: Speeches by the Right Hon. Winston S. Churchill.* London: Cassell, 1941.

Clutton-Brock, Arthur. *The Ultimate Belief.* New York: E. P. Dutton, 1916.

Coghill, Nevill. *The Collected Papers of Nevill Coghill, Shakespearian & Medievalist.* Edited by Douglas Gray. Sussex, UK: Harvester Press, 1988.

———. *Langland: Piers Plowman.* London: Published for the British Council by Longmans, Green, 1964.

Cole, G.D.H., and T. W. Earp, eds. *Oxford Poetry.* Oxford: Blackwell, 1915.

Cott, Jonathan. *Pipers at the Gates of Dawn: The Wisdom of Children's Literature.* New York: Random House, 1983.

Cranborne, Hannah, ed. *David Cecil: A Portrait by His Friends.* Wimborne, UK: Dovecote Press, 1990.

Dante Alighieri. *The Comedy of Dante Alighieri: The Florentine.* Harmondsworth, UK: Penguin Books, 1949.

Davidman, Joy. *Anya*. New York: Macmillan, 1940.

———. *Letter to a Comrade*. Edited by Stephen Vincent Benét. New Haven: Yale University Press, 1938.

———. *Out of My Bone: The Letters of Joy Davidman*. Edited by Don W. King. Grand Rapids, Mich., and Cambridge, UK: Wm. B. Eerdmans, 2009.

———. *Smoke on the Mountain: An Interpretation of the Ten Commandments*. Philadelphia: Westminster Press, 1954.

———. *Weeping Bay*. New York: Macmillan, 1950.

Davis, Norman, and C. L. Wrenn. *English and Medieval Studies: Presented to J.R.R. Tolkien on the Occasion of His Seventieth Birthday*. London: George Allen & Unwin, 1962.

Denham, Michael Aislable. *The Denham Tracts*. Publications of the Folk-Lore Society 35. London: D. Nutt, 1895.

Dorsett, Lyle W. *And God Came In: The Extraordinary Story of Joy Davidman: Her Life and Marriage to C. S. Lewis*. Peabody, Mass.: Hendrickson Publishers, 2009.

Dougill, John. *Oxford in English Literature: The Making, and Undoing, of "the English Athens."* Ann Arbor: University of Michigan Press, 1998.

Duriez, Colin. *The Inklings Handbook*. St. Louis, Mo.: Chalice Press, 2001.

———. *Tolkien and C.S. Lewis: The Gift of Friendship*. Mahwah, N.J.: HiddenSpring, 2003.

Dyson, H.V.D. *Augustans and Romantics, 1689–1830*. London: Cresset Press, 1950.

Edel, Leon. *Bloomsbury: A House of Lions*. Philadelphia: Lippincott, 1979.

Eliot, Charles. *A Finnish Grammar*. Oxford: Clarendon Press, 1890.

Eliot, T. S. *To Criticize the Critic, and Other Writings*. New York: Farrar, Straus and Giroux, 1965.

Ellis, David. *Memoirs of a Leavisite: The Decline and Fall of Cambridge English*. Liverpool: Liverpool University Press, 2013.

Empson, William. *Argufying: Essays on Literature and Culture*. Edited by John Haffenden. Iowa City: University of Iowa Press, 1987.

———. *Essays on Renaissance Literature*. Vol. 2: *The Drama*. Edited by John Haffenden. Cambridge, UK, and New York: Cambridge University Press, 1994.

———. *Selected Letters of William Empson*. Edited by John Haffenden. Oxford: Oxford University Press, 2006.

———. *William Empson: Essays on Renaissance Literature*. Vol. 1: *Donne and the New Philosophy*. Edited by John Haffenden. Cambridge, UK, and New York: Cambridge University Press, 1993.

Epstein, Joseph, ed. *Masters: Portraits of Great Teachers*. New York: Basic Books, 1981.

Evans, G. R. *The University of Oxford: A New History*. London and New York: I. B. Tauris, 2010.

Forster, E. M. *The BBC Talks of E. M. Forster, 1929–1960*. A selected edition. Edited by Mary Lago, Linda K. Hughes, and Elizabeth MacLeod Walls. Columbia: University of Missouri Press, 2008.

Fox, Adam. *Poetry for Pleasure: An Inaugural Lecture Delivered Before the University of Oxford by Adam Fox, Professor of Poetry*. Oxford: Clarendon Press, 1938.

Fox, Adam, and Plato. *Plato for Pleasure*. Rev. ed. London: John Murray, 1962.

Fredrick, Candice, and Sam McBride. *Women Among the Inklings: Gender, C. S. Lewis, J.R.R. Tolkien, and Charles Williams*. Westport, Conn.: Greenwood Press, 2001.

Fussell, Paul. *The Great War and Modern Memory*. New York: Oxford University Press, 1975.

Gadili, Mario. *San Giovanni Calabria: Biografia Ufficiale*. Cinisello Balsamo (Milano): San Paolo, 1999.

Gale Research Company. *John Wain. Contemporary Authors: Something About the Author*. Detroit, Mich.: Gale Research, 1986.

Gilbert, R. A. *A. E. Waite: Magician of Many Parts*. Wellingborough, UK: Crucible, 1987.

———. *The Golden Dawn Companion: A Guide to the History, Structure, and Workings of the Hermetic Order of the Golden Dawn*. Wellingborough, UK: Aquarian, 1986.

Glyer, Diana Pavlac. *The Company They Keep: C. S. Lewis and J.R.R. Tolkien as Writers in Community*. Kent, Ohio: Kent State University Press, 2007.

Gollancz, Victor. *My Dear Timothy: An Autobiographical Letter to His Grandson*. New York: Simon and Schuster, 1953.

Gordon, George Stuart. *The Letters of George S. Gordon, 1902–1942*. London and New York: Oxford University Press, 1945.

Gordon, Mary C. Biggar. *The Life of George S. Gordon 1881–1942*. London: Oxford University Press, 1945.

Graves, Robert. *Fairies and Fusiliers*. New York: Alfred A. Knopf, 1918.

Griffiths, Bede. *The Golden String: An Autobiography*. London: Harvill Press, 1954.

Haffenden, John. *William Empson*. Vol. 1: *Among the Mandarins*. Oxford: Oxford University Press, 2005.

———. *William Empson*. Vol. 2: *Against the Christians*. Oxford: Oxford University Press, 2006.

Hardie, Colin. *The Georgics: A Transitional Poem*. Exeter, UK: University of Exeter, 1980.

Harrison, Brian Howard, ed. *The History of the University of Oxford*. Vol. 8: *The Twentieth Century*. Oxford: Clarendon Press, 1994.

Harwood, Cecil. *The Voice of Cecil Harwood: A Miscellany*. Edited by Owen Barfield. London: Rudolf Steiner Press, 1979.

Hay, Ian [pseudonym for John Hay Beith]. *The Lighter Side of School Life*. Edinburgh: Ballantyne Press, 1914.

Hillegas, Mark R. *Shadows of Imagination: The Fantasies of C. S. Lewis, J.R.R. Tolkien, and Charles Williams*. Carbondale: Southern Illinois University Press, 1969.

Hillier, Bevis. *Young Betjeman*. London: John Murray, 1988.

Hitler, Adolf. *Hitler: Speeches and Proclamations, 1932–1945: The Chronicle of a Dictatorship*. Vol. 3: *The Years 1939 to 1940*. Edited by Max Domarus. Wauconda, Ill.: Bolchazy-Carducci, 1997.

Hynes, Samuel. *A War Imagined: The First World War and English Culture*. New York: Atheneum, 1991.

Isherwood, Christopher. *Lions and Shadows: An Education in the Twenties*. London: L. & Virginia Woolf at the Hogarth Press, 1938.

Joyce, James. *Selected Letters of James Joyce*. Edited by Richard Ellman. Reprint ed. 1992. London: Faber & Faber, 1975.

Kelly, Richard J., ed. *The Blickling Homilies*. London: Continuum, 2010.

Kenny, Anthony. *A Path from Rome: An Autobiography*. London: Sidgwick & Jackson, 1985.

Ker, I. T. *Catholic Revival in English Literature, 1845–1961: Newman, Hopkins, Belloc, Chesterton, Greene, Waugh*. Notre Dame, Ind.: University of Notre Dame Press, 2003.

King, Don W. *Hunting the Unicorn: A Critical Biography of Ruth Pitter*. Kent, Ohio: Kent State University Press, 2008.

Kirby, W. F., ed. *Kalevala: The Land of Heroes*. Translated from the original Finnish. Vol. 1. London: J. M. Dent, 1907.

Larsen, Timothy. *Crisis of Doubt: Honest Faith in Nineteenth-Century England*. Oxford and New York: Oxford University Press, 2006.

Lawlor, John, ed. *Patterns of Love and Courtesy: Essays in Memory of C. S. Lewis*. Evanston, Ill.: Northwestern University Press, 1966.

Lawlor, John, and W. H Auden, eds. *To Nevill Coghill from Friends*. London: Faber & Faber, 1966.

Leavis, F. R. *The Common Pursuit*. London: Chatto & Windus, 1952.

———. *Revaluation: Tradition and Development in English Poetry*. Chicago: I. R. Dee, 1998.

———, ed. *A Selection from Scrutiny*. 2 vols. Cambridge, UK: Cambridge University Press, 1968.

———, ed. *Scrutiny: A Quarterly Review*. Vol. 20: *Retrospect and Index*. Cambridge, UK: Cambridge University Press, 2008.

Leavis, Q. D. *Fiction and the Reading Public*. London: Chatto & Windus, 1932.

Lejeune, Anthony, ed. *Time and Tide Anthology*. London: André Deutsch, 1956.

Lewis, W. H. *Assault on Olympus: The Rise of the House of Gramont Between 1604 and 1678*. London: André Deutsch, 1958.

———. *Brothers and Friends: The Diaries of Major Warren Hamilton Lewis*. Edited by Clyde S. Kilby and Marjorie Lamp Mead. San Francisco: Harper & Row, 1982.

———. *Levantine Adventurer: The Travels and Missions of the Chevalier d'Arvieux, 1653–1697*. New York: Harcourt, Brace & World, 1963.

———. *Louis XIV: An Informal Portrait*. New York: Harcourt, Brace, 1959.

———. *The Scandalous Regent: A Life of Philippe, Duc d'Orléans, 1674–1723, and of His Family*. New York: Harcourt, Brace & World, 1961.

———. *The Splendid Century: Life in the France of Louis XIV*. New York: Doubleday, 1953.

———. *The Sunset of the Splendid Century: The Life and Times of Louis Auguste de Bourbon, Duc Du Maine, 1670–1736*. London: Eyre & Spottiswoode, 1955.

Lings, Martin. *Muhammad: His Life Based on the Earliest Sources*. New York: Inner Traditions International, 1983.

Mabbott, J. D. *Oxford Memories*. Oxford: Thornton's of Oxford, 1986.

MacDonald, George. *The Complete Fairy Tales of George MacDonald*. New York: Schocken Books, 1977.

———. *George MacDonald: An Anthology*. Edited by C. S. Lewis. New York: Macmillan, 1947.

———. *The Golden Key*. 2nd ed. New York: Farrar, Straus and Giroux, 1976.

———. *Lilith: A Romance*. New York: Dodd, Mead, 1895.

———. *Phantastes: A Faerie Romance for Men and Women*. Boston: Loring, 1850.

———. *The Princess and Curdie*. Harmondsworth, Middlesex: Puffin Books, 1966.

———. *The Princess and the Goblin*. New York: William Morrow, 1986.

Madeleva, M. *My First Seventy Years*. New York: Macmillan, 1959.

Mandell, Gail Porter. *Madeleva: A Biography*. Albany: State University of New York Press, 1997.

Mathew, Gervase. *Byzantine Aesthetics*. New York: Viking Press, 1964.

Matthew, H.C.G., and Brian Harrison, eds. *Oxford Dictionary of National Biography: In Association with the British Academy: From the Earliest Times to the Year 2000*. Oxford and New York: Oxford University Press, 2004.

Milton, John. *The English Poems of John Milton*. Introduction by Charles Williams. Edited by H. C. Beeching. London: Oxford University Press, 1940.

Moorman, Charles. *The Precincts of Felicity: The Augustinian City of the Oxford Christians*. Gainesville: University of Florida Press, 1966.

Morris, Jan. *Oxford*. Rev. ed. Oxford and New York: Oxford University Press, 1987.

———, ed. *The Oxford Book of Oxford*. Oxford and New York: Oxford University Press, 2002.

Nesbit, E. *Five Children and It*. London: E. Benn, 1957.

Nott, Kathleen. *The Emperor's Clothes*. Bloomington: Indiana University Press, 1958.

Orwell, George. *The Collected Essays, Journalism, and Letters of George Orwell*. Edited by Sonia Orwell and Ian Angus. Boston: David R. Godine, 2000.

Osborne, Charles. *W. H. Auden: The Life of a Poet*. New York: Harcourt Brace Jovanovich, 1979.

Palmer, D. J. *The Rise of English Studies*. London: Oxford University Press, 1965.

Patrick, James. *The Magdalen Metaphysicals: Idealism and Orthodoxy at Oxford, 1901–1945*. Macon, Ga.: Mercer University Press, 1985.

Phillips, J. B. *Ring of Truth: A Translator's Testimony*. New York: Macmillan, 1957.

Pitter, Ruth. *The Letters of Ruth Pitter: Silent Music*. Edited by Don W. King. Newark: University of Delaware Press, 2014.

Plantinga, Alvin. *Warrant and Proper Function*. New York: Oxford University Press, 1993.

Poe, Harry Lee, with photography by James Ray Veneman. *The Inklings of Oxford: C. S. Lewis, J.R.R. Tolkien, and Their Friends*. Grand Rapids, Mich: Zondervan, 2009.

Pope, Alexander. *Poetry and Prose: With Essays by Johnson, Coleridge, Hazlitt &c, with an Introduction and Notes by H.V.D. Dyson*. Edited by H.V.D. Dyson. Oxford: Clarendon Press, 1933.

Raffé, Marjorie, Cecil Harwood, and Marguerite Lundgren. *Eurythmy and the Impulse of Dance*. London: Rudolf Steiner Press, 1974.

Ransome, Arthur. *Signalling from Mars: The Letters of Arthur Ransome*. Edited by Hugh Brogan. London: Jonathan Cape, 1997.

Reilly, R. J. *Romantic Religion: A Study of Owen Barfield, C. S. Lewis, Charles Williams and J.R.R. Tolkien*. Great Barrington, Mass.: Lindisfarne Books, 2007.

Reynolds, Barbara. *Dorothy L. Sayers: Her Life and Soul*. 1st American ed. New York: St. Martin's Press, 1993.

———. *The Passionate Intellect: Dorothy L. Sayers' Encounter with Dante*. Kent, Ohio: The Kent State University Press, 1989.

Richards, I. A. *Coleridge on Imagination*. Bloomington: Indiana University Press, 1960.

———. *Practical Criticism: A Study of Literary Judgment*. New York: Harcourt, Brace, 1929.

———. *Principles of Literary Criticism*. London and New York: Routledge, 2001.

Robson, W. W. *Critical Essays*. London: Routledge & Kegan Paul, 1966.

Rowse, A. L. *Oxford in the History of England*. New York: Putnam, 1975.

Russell, Arthur, ed. *Ruth Pitter: Homage to a Poet*. Introduction by David Cecil. Chester Springs, Penn.: Dufour Ed., 1969.

Russo, John Paul. *I. A. Richards: His Life and Work*. Baltimore: Johns Hopkins University Press, 1989.

Sassoon, Siegfried. *Memoirs of an Infantry Officer*. London: Faber & Faber, 1930.

Sayers, Dorothy L. *Further Papers on Dante*. New York: Harper, 1957.

———. *Introductory Papers on Dante*. London: Methuen, 1954.

———. *The Letters of Dorothy L. Sayers, 1899–1936: The Making of a Detective Novelist*. 1st American ed. New York: St. Martin's Press, 1996.

———. *The Letters of Dorothy L. Sayers, 1937–1943: From Novelist to Playwright*. 1st American ed. New York: St. Martin's Press, 1998.

———. *The Letters of Dorothy L. Sayers, 1944–1950: A Noble Daring*. Cambridge, UK: Dorothy L. Sayers Society, 1998.

———. *The Letters of Dorothy L. Sayers, 1951–1957: In the Midst of Life*. Cambridge, UK: Dorothy L. Sayers Society, 2000.

———. *The Mind of the Maker*. Bridgeheads. London: Methuen, 1941.

———. *The Poetry of Search and the Poetry of Statement, and Other Posthumous Essays on Literature, Religion, and Other Language*. London: Victor Gollancz, 1963.

———. *The Zeal of Thy House*. London: Victor Gollancz, 1937.

Schiller, F.C.S. *Mind! A Unique Review of Ancient and Modern Philosophy Edited by A. Troglodyte*. London: Williams and Norgate, 1901.

Soper, David Wesley. *Exploring the Christian World Mind*. London: Vision Press, 1964.

———. *These Found the Way: Thirteen Converts to Protestant Christianity*. Philadelphia: Westminster Press, 1951.

Steiner, Rudolf. *Eurythmy as Visible Speech: Fifteen Lectures Given in Dornach, Switzerland 24th June to 12th July, 1924 with Other Lectures*. Translated by Alan Stott, Coralee Schmandt, and Maren Stott. Weobley, UK: Anastasi, 2005.

Sutcliffe, Peter H. *The Oxford University Press: An Informal History*. Oxford: Clarendon Press, 1978.

Sweet, Henry, and Charles Tallut Onions. *Sweet's Anglo-Saxon Reader in Prose and Verse*. Oxford: Clarendon Press, 1954.

Tames, Richard. *A Traveller's History of Oxford*. New York and Northampton, Mass.: Interlink Books, 2003.

Tillyard, E.M.W. *The Elizabethan World Picture*. London: Chatto & Windus, 1943.

Tolkien, Christopher. *The History of Middle-earth Index*. The History of Middle-earth. Vol. 13. London: HarperCollins, 2010.

———, ed. *The Saga of King Heidrek the Wise*. London and New York: Nelson, 1960.

Treglown, Jeremy. *Romancing: The Life and Work of Henry Green*. 1st American ed. New York: Random House, 2000.

Turville-Petre, Gabriel, and Christopher Tolkien, eds. *Hervarar Saga Ok Heiðreks*. London: Viking Society for Northern Research, University College, 1956.

Tuve, Rosemond. *Allegorical Imagery: Some Mediaeval Books and Their Posterity*. Princeton, N.J.: Princeton University Press, 1966.

Unwin, Rayner. *George Allen & Unwin: A Remembrancer*. Ludlow, U.K.: Merlin Unwin Books, 1999.

Urang, Gunnar. *Shadows of Heaven: Religion and Fantasy in the Writing of C. S. Lewis, Charles Williams, and J.R.R. Tolkien*. Philadelphia: Pilgrim Press, 1971.

Wain, John. *Hurry on Down*. London: Secker and Warburg, 1953.

———. *Preliminary Essays*. New York: St. Martin's Press, 1957.

————. *Sprightly Running: Part of an Autobiography.* New York: St. Martin's Press, 1962.

Waley, Arthur. *The Way and Its Power: A Study of the Tao Tê Ching and Its Place in Chinese Thought.* London: Allen & Unwin, 1934.

Watkin, E. I. *Roman Catholicism in England, from the Reformation to 1950.* London and New York: Oxford University Press, 1957.

Watson, George. *British Literature Since 1945.* New York: St. Martin's Press, 1991.

————. *Never Ones for Theory?: England and the War of Ideas.* Cambridge, UK: Lutterworth Press, 2000.

Watts, Alan. *Behold the Spirit: A Study in the Necessity of Mystical Religion.* New ed. New York: Pantheon Books, 1971.

Wayne, Jenifer. *The Purple Dress: Growing Up in the Thirties.* London: Victor Gollancz, 1979.

Whistler, Theresa. *Imagination of the Heart: The Life of Walter de La Mare.* London: Duckworth, 1993.

Wilson, A. N. *Betjeman: A Life.* New York: Farrar, Straus and Giroux, 2006.

Winter, J. M. *The Great War and the British People.* 2nd ed. Basingstoke, UK: Palgrave Macmillan, 2003.

Woolf, Virginia. *Mr. Bennett and Mrs. Brown.* London: L. and Virginia Woolf, 1924.

Wrenn, C. L. *The English Language.* London: Methuen, 1963.

Wrenn, C. L., and W. F. Bolton, eds. *Beowulf: With the Finnesburg Fragment.* 3rd rev. ed. New York: St. Martin's Press, 1973.

Wright, Elizabeth Mary. *The Life of Joseph Wright.* London: Oxford University Press, 1931.

Wyrall, Everard. *History of the Somerset Light Infantry 1914–1919.* London: Methuen, 1927.

ACKNOWLEDGMENTS

We are grateful first of all to Paul Elie for his generous encouragement, beginning when he acquired *The Fellowship* for Farrar, Straus and Giroux and continuing without break after he left for Georgetown University's Berkley Center. Happily, Paul entrusted us to Alexander Star at FSG, who steered *The Fellowship* safely to its conclusion; we are full of admiration for Alex's penetrating and learned insight into all aspects of our project. Our thanks go also to editorial assistant Laird Gallagher, copy editor Frieda Duggan, production editor Chris Peterson, senior vice president Jeff Seroy, president and publisher Jonathan Galassi, and everyone else at FSG.

A special thank-you is extended to Owen Barfield, whose letters and phone calls in the 1980s to a young writer (Philip Zaleski) helped inspire this book. We owe a great debt to Owen A. Barfield (grandson, and trustee of the Owen Barfield literary estate), Léonie and Stratford Caldecott, Kate Farrell, Alastair Fowler, Walter Hooper, Lois Lang-Sims, and Fr. Robert Murray, S.J., for generously sharing their firsthand knowledge of our subjects. We thank the Bodleian Library in Oxford for the privilege of reading unpublished Inklings material, including the recently catalogued Barfield Papers. For the same privilege, we thank associate director Marjorie Lamp Mead, archivist Laura Schmidt, and former archivist Heidi Truty at the Marion E. Wade Center at Wheaton College in Illinois. We were deeply honored to receive the Wade Center's award of the Clyde S. Kilby Research Grant for 2014.

For help in locating photographs and for permission to use them, we especially wish to thank the Tolkien scholar John Garth and Alison Wheatley, archivist of the Schools of King Edward VI in Birmingham (for identifying and sharing the rare photo of Tolkien with the KES cadet corps), Sister Jean Frances, C.S.M.V. (for Sister Penelope), Adrian Rance-McGregor and Kathryn Spink (for the young Bede Griffiths), Owen A. Barfield, Douglas Gilbert, Martin Macgregor, Harry Lee Poe, and Laura Schmidt at the Wade Center. We thank our wonderful agents, Kimberly Witherspoon and David Forrer of InkWell Management, for years of friendship, guidance, and support, and Frederick T. Courtright and the Permissions Company for skillfully handling a very complicated set of permissions issues. We thank Smith College for generous sabbatical research time and funding; and the acquisitions, circulation, interlibrary loan, and reference staff at Neilson Library, Smith College, for their kind attention and selfless assistance. We thank our student assistants for their enthusiasm for all things Inkling, medieval, and Romantic: Kiersten Acker, Liz Casler, Emma De Lisle, Gwen Gethner, Megan Kearney, Natalie Sargent, and Alexandra Zaleski; Janet Brennan Croft, Craig Davis, Robert Easting, Alan Jacobs, Fr. Ian Ker, William Oram, Kimberley Patton, Fr. Gregory Phillips, O.S.B., the late G. B. Tennyson, John F. Thornton, and Ptolemy Tompkins for encouragement and advice; Kriston Rucker and Anne Larlarb for love and cheer; John Zaleski for translation help; Andy and John Zaleski for filling our lives with joy, wisdom, love, and exuberance; and the Caldecott family for true fellowship in Oxford and beyond.

We are especially grateful to the scholars cited in our notes and bibliography, who have devoted their lives to conserving, editing, and interpreting the literary legacy of Tolkien, Lewis, Barfield, Williams, and their associates, and to all those, named and unnamed, whose contributions to the growing field of Inklings studies would, if listed in full, swamp the book.

ÍNDEX

PERMISSIONS ACKNOWLEDGMENTS

Grateful acknowledgment is made for permission to reprint the following material:

Owen Barfield: Excerpts from the introduction to *Romanticism Comes of Age*; excerpt from "Moira" from *Owen Barfield on C. S. Lewis*, edited by G. B. Tennyson. Both reprinted by permission of Wesleyan University Press. Excerpt from "Air Castles" from *Punch* (February 14, 1917); excerpts from "C.S.L.: Biographica Theologica"; Owen Barfield Papers, Marion E. Wade Center OB/MS-6. English translation by John Zaleski. Excerpt from a letter (July 6, 1951), Owen Barfield Archives, Bodleian Special Collections, Dep. C1055. Excerpt from a letter (December 29, 1957), Owen Barfield Archives, Bodleian Special Collections, Dep. C1055. Excerpt from "Origin of U.S. Connection" (August 30, 1963), Owen Barfield Archives, Bodleian Special Collections, Dep. C1054. Excerpts from a letter to Philip Mairet (March 28, 1964), Owen Barfield Archives, Bodleian Special Collections, Dep. C1074. Excerpt from a letter to Professor Colburn (February 16, 1963), Owen Barfield Archives, Bodleian Special Collections, Dep. C1054. Excerpt from a letter to R. J. Reilly (April 17, 1969), Barfield Papers, Bodleian Library, Dep. C1056. Excerpt from a letter to Craig Miller (March 28, 1964), Owen Barfield Papers, Bodleian Special Collections, Dep. C1074. Excerpt from "Information for My Literary Executors" (April 1985), Barfield Papers, Bodleian Library, Dep. C1255. Excerpts from an interview with Walter Hooper (July 15, 2006). All reprinted with the permission of the Owen Barfield Estate.

Owen Barfield and C. S. Lewis: Excerpts from "Poema de XVI Animalibus arcem Noam intrantibus" (January 1929), Owen Barfield Papers, Bodleian Library, Dep. C1104, folio 3. In Latin, with English translation by Carol Zaleski. Excerpt from "Abecedarium Philosophicum" from *The Oxford Magazine* 52 (November 30, 1933): 298. Extracts by C. S. Lewis copyright © C. S. Lewis Pte., Ltd. Both reprinted with the permission of the Owen Barfield Estate and C. S. Lewis Pte., Ltd.

John Betjeman: Excerpt from "A Hike on the Downs" from *Continual Dew: A Little Book of Bourgeois Verse*, copyright 1937 by John Betjeman. Reprinted by permission of Farrar, Straus and Giroux, LLC, and Hodder Headline, plc.

Simon Blaxland–de Lange: Excerpts from *Owen Barfield: Romanticism Come of Age, a Biography*, copyright © 2006 by Simon Blaxland–de Lange. Reprinted with the permission of Temple Lodge Publishing Ltd.

David Cecil: Excerpts from a letter to Ruth Pitter, from Don W. King, *Hunting the Unicorn: A Critical Biography of Ruth Pitter*, copyright © 2008 by the Kent State University Press. Reprinted with the permission of the publishers.

Neville Coghill: Excerpt from "The Approach to English" from *Light on C. S. Lewis*, edited by Jocelyn Gibb, copyright © 1965 by Geoffrey Bles Ltd., renewed © 1993 by Elizabeth Gibb. Reprinted by permission of HarperCollins Publishers, Ltd., and Houghton Mifflin Harcourt Publishing Company. All rights reserved.

Joy Davidman: Excerpts from *Out of My Bone: The Letters of Joy Davidman*, edited by Don W. King, copyright © 2009. Reprinted with the permission of Wm. B. Eerdmans Publishing Company.

Walter de la Mare: Excerpts from letters to Owen Barfield (June 14, 1950, and November 16, 1949), Barfield Papers, Bodleian Library, Dep. C1055. Used by permission of the Literary Trustees of Walter de la Mare and the Society of Authors as their representative.

Roger Lancelyn Green: Excerpt from diary, from Roger Lancelyn Green and Walter Hooper, *C. S. Lewis: A Biography, Fully Revised and Expanded Edition*, copyright © 1974 by Roger Lancelyn Green, as Executor of the Estate of Roger Lancelyn Green and Walter Hooper, copyright © C. S. Lewis Pte., Ltd. Reprinted by permission of Scirard Lancelyn Green, the C. S. Lewis Co., Ltd., Houghton Mifflin Harcourt Publishing Company and HarperCollins Publishers, Ltd. All rights reserved.

Alice Mary Hadfield: Excerpts from *Charles Williams: An Exploration of His Life and Work*, copyright © 1983 by Alice Mary Hadfield. Reprinted by permission of Oxford University Press, Ltd., www.oup.com.

Albert Lewis: Excerpts from letters to C. S. Lewis and Warren Lewis, and diary entries, from "The Lewis Family Papers or Memoirs of the Lewis Family (1850–1930)." Unpublished typescript edited by Warren Hamilton Lewis in 11 volumes, 1933–1935. © C. S. Lewis Pte., Ltd. All reprinted with the permission of the Marion E. Wade Center, Wheaton College, Wheaton, Il., and the C. S. Lewis Co., Ltd.

C. S. Lewis: Excerpts from preface, "On Stories," and "It All Began with a Picture" from *Essays Presented to Charles Williams*; reprinted by permission of Oxford University Press, Ltd., www.oup.com. Excerpts from letters and diary excerpts; excerpts from *The Collected Letters of C. S. Lewis, Volume 1: Family Letters 1905–1931*, edited by Walter Hooper, from *The Collected Letters of C. S. Lewis, Volume 2: Books, Broadcasts, and the War 1931–1949*, edited by Walter Hooper, and from *The Collected Letters of C. S. Lewis, Volume 3: Narnia, Cambridge, and Joy 1950–1963*, edited by Walter Hooper; excerpts from "My Life during the Exmas Holadays of 1907" from "The Lewis Family Papers or Memoirs of the Lewis Family (1850–1930)," III: 88–92; unpublished typescript edited by Warren Hamilton Lewis in 11 volumes, 1933–1935; excerpt from unsigned review of J.R.R. Tolkien, *The Hobbit*, from *The Times* (London) 47810 (October 8, 1937); excerpt from dust cover for J.R.R. Tolkien, *The Fellowship of the Ring*; five-line verse

A NOTE ABOUT THE AUTHORS

Philip Zaleski and Carol Zaleski are the coauthors of *Prayer: A History* and editors of *The Book of Heaven*. Philip Zaleski is the author of *The Recollected Heart*, coauthor of *Gifts of the Spirit*, and editor of the Best Spiritual Writing and Best American Spiritual Writing series, and Carol Zaleski is a professor of world religions at Smith College and the author of *Otherworld Journeys* and *The Life of the World to Come*.